# TREE HUNTING

A constant explorer of cities and the irrepressible, boisterous nature they support, PAUL WOOD is the author of several books, including *London is a Forest* and *London's Street Trees*. He has been fascinated by trees ever since he noticed a beech seedling unfurling in his back garden as a child. He lives in London under the canopy of a pair of Victorian plane trees.

# TREE HUNTING

1,000 Trees to Find in Britain and Ireland's Towns and Cities

# PAUL WOOD

PARTICULAR BOOKS

Vernon Wood, 1933–2023
A proud Glaswegian

> I must frankly own, that if I had known, beforehand, that this book would have cost me the labour which it has, I should never have been courageous enough to commence it.

Isabella Beeton, *Mrs. Beeton's Book of Household Management*, 1861

# CONTENTS

INTRODUCTION 1
INDIVIDUAL TREE NAMES 7
GLOSSARY 9

SCOTLAND'S HIGHLANDS & ISLANDS 14
EASTERN SCOTLAND 38
SOUTHERN SCOTLAND 62
NORTH OF ENGLAND 80
NORTH WEST ENGLAND 94
YORKSHIRE 126
EAST MIDLANDS 154
WEST MIDLANDS 178
EAST OF ENGLAND 206
LONDON 236
SOUTH EAST ENGLAND 268
SOUTHERN ENGLAND 296
SOUTH WEST ENGLAND 326
DEVON & CORNWALL 356
SOUTH & WEST WALES 382
MID & NORTH WALES 410
NORTHERN IRELAND 424
REPUBLIC OF IRELAND 446

SELECT BIBLIOGRAPHY 481
INDEX 485
ACKNOWLEDGEMENTS 506

# Map of the United Kingdom and Ireland

**Regions and cities shown:**

- **NORTHERN IRELAND** — Belfast ⊙ — 99-132
- 887-925
- **REPUBLIC OF IRELAND** — Dublin ⊙, Cork ○ — 926-1000
- **NORTH ENGLAND** — Newcastle upon Tyne ○ — 133-158
- **YORKSHIRE** — York ○, Leeds ○, Hull ○, Sheffield ⊙ — 228-288
- **NORTH WEST ENGLAND** — Liverpool ⊙, Manchester ⊙, Chester ○ — 159-227
- **EAST MIDLANDS** — Nottingham ○, Leicester ○ — 289-340
- **EAST of ENGLAND** — Norwich ⊙, Cambridge ○ — 407-474
- **WEST MIDLANDS** — Birmingham ⊙, Coventry ○ — 341-406
- **NORTH & MID WALES** — 862-886
- **SOUTH & WEST WALES** — Cardiff ⊙, Swansea ○ — 806-861
- **SOUTH WEST ENGLAND** — Bristol ⊙, Bath ⊙ — 683-752
- **DEVON & CORNWALL** — Exeter ○, Torbay ○, Plymouth ⊙, Penzance ○ — 753-805
- **SOUTHERN ENGLAND** — Oxford ○, Reading ⊙, Southampton — 618-682
- **LONDON** — 475-558
- **SOUTH EAST ENGLAND** — Brighton & Hove ⊙ — 559-617

**Seas and channels:** Irish Sea, St George's Channel, Bristol Channel, Celtic Sea

# INTRODUCTION

ANYONE WHO HAS ventured through a few of Britain and Ireland's cities, towns and villages will agree that they each have their own character. But what is it that makes a place distinct? Geography and climate; people and customs; monuments and architecture? Yes, of course – all of those are particular to a place. But I believe there is an undersung, yet equally important detail distinguishing these places: trees.

Much of our urban environment today is, with some notable exceptions, the legacy of architects working in the nineteenth century or later. We celebrate their creations, praising and affording legal safeguards to buildings that have survived for many decades or centuries, or which have gained important cultural associations. Yet seldom do we do the same for our trees. We tend not to recognise that, as our towns and cities mature, so do the monumental living beings that define them – and that, like buildings, these trees need our protection.

Our urban trees are quietly becoming ever more striking as the years pass by, shaping and being shaped by the places they grow in. Some soar to unbelievable heights, while others boast enormous girth, their roots having tapped underground springs; some appear to be defying the passage of time, growing only infinitesimally despite being hundreds or even thousands of years old; others are cheerfully eating postboxes, or becoming smooth with the clambering of children over their branches.

These individuals are often valued by the people who live alongside them, and many of us know that trees play a vital role in mitigating the environmental crises we face today – that they can alleviate air pollution, warming temperatures, even the epidemic of mental ill health. And yet, time and time again, our trees are threatened for the most spurious of reasons (the construction of another car park, perhaps).

Our passionate response to trees' destruction shows how deeply we know it is wrong: to lose them feels heart-wrenching – outrageous, even – as though we were losing parts of ourselves. Perhaps the most infamous example occurred in 2023, when the veteran tree at the Sycamore Gap in Hadrian's Wall was chainsawed by vandals. There was a national outpouring of grief, and the story made international headlines.

Many of us are attuned to the vulnerabilities of trees, and many of us share an innate urge to protect them. But how can we do this? Where do we start? The answer is simple: by knowing them. By celebrating them, by identifying them and by naming them, we can start to establish trees as an essential part of the fabric of our towns and cities. We have the power to recognize them as valuable individual beings, not replaceable decorations or, worse, obstacles to ever-denser urban development.

Appreciating trees in this way is akin to entering a parallel – a more-than-human – universe. Once you start noticing trees, your experience of the places they grow changes; you become as aware of them as of the architecture around you. Suddenly, the trees make you think, and feel, differently about the built environment. It is endlessly rewarding: you can discover the same tree, on the same street, in the same park or urban woodland again and again, getting to know it in different weather, different seasons, even at different times of day.

Here are what I believe to be the 1,000 most marvellous individual trees growing in Britain and Ireland today. You can discover them by roadsides, bus stops, churches, temples, supermarkets and more, scattered throughout the villages, towns and cities that most of us live, work and dream in. I hope you can start by finding those closest to where you live, and thereby look afresh at your hometown. Even better, if you find yourself further afield – in, say, Perth, or Nottingham, or Saundersfoot, or Tralee – seeking out interesting, eye-catching or storied trees, then you will have discovered the endlessly rewarding pursuit of tree hunting.

WE ARE NOT, I should admit, the first tree hunters. Between 1900 and 1913, the botanists Henry Elwes and Augustine Henry toured the estates of Britain and Ireland cataloguing the most notable trees planted in their grounds. It resulted in seven lavish volumes: *The Trees of Great Britain and Ireland*, a magnificent work that describes all the tree species then growing in these islands, and chronicles their finest specimens.

An account of the greatest 1,000 individual trees of Britain and Ireland in the twenty-first century looks very different. The trees that people know and cherish are not limited to those in aristocratic estates or historic parklands. Today, great trees are – I would like to argue – the wonders that we walk, cycle and drive by every day, regardless of whether they have been acknowledged as such by historic catalogues and gazetteers. This book is devoted to these urban individuals, whether they are as famous as the MAJOR OAK (294), the ALLERTON OAK (210) or the BIRNAM OAK (32), or more intimate and obscure gems like the PONTCANNA PLANE (826), the BIRMINGHAM DWARF (367) and the SUPERVALU HORSE CHESTNUT (926), which are nonetheless equally worthy of our admiration.

The trees in this book are all accessible by foot and are, with very few exceptions, free to visit. I have selected them using a range of criteria: does it have an interesting story to tell? Does it offer a new perspective on the place where it grows? Is it a rare species? Is it a particularly old, large, strange-looking, lovely or well-positioned tree? Has it been previously recorded, and have other people noticed it?

In answering these questions, I have brought together a motley crew: ancient and modern trees; relics of previous landscapes; stalwarts of Georgian squares, Victorian cemeteries and Edwardian parks; trees on postwar estates and university campuses; and twenty-first-century trees planted to revitalise our city streets. There are trees that survived the Blitz like POOR SUSAN'S PLANE (557) close to St Paul's in London, or the BLUECOAT PLANE (227) in Liverpool; trees serving as monuments to historic events that shaped whole countries, such as the HEZLETT CHESTNUT* (887) near Coleraine; and trees that have become memorials to significant individuals, like the TURING ASH (171) in Manchester, or the MOSELEY BOG OAK (376) in Birmingham. Through trees like these, we have a living link to the past; with them, we can trace our shared history. Others might simply be astonishing for their sheer physical presence, their incredible age, captivating beauty or great rarity.

ONE THOUSAND TREES is a significant number, but even so I could have included many more. It has been a difficult process whittling it down. I have tried to balance the competing claims of geographic area and population, and, since my focus is urban trees, the distribution corresponds loosely to where people live. Areas with fewer people have fewer tree entries, while London has more. Inevitably, some cities are particularly rich in trees, and where a single city has more than twenty trees of note, I have dubbed it a Tree City. Each of these is a major arboreal centre whose cultural and historical legacies are connected to the urban forest that grows there.

Of course, some trees have been so integral to a city they are named for them, such as the London plane and the Manchester poplar, as well as less-known species and cultivars like the Corstorphine plane, named for a suburb of Edinburgh, or the Bristol whitebeam. Other trees originated in our towns and cities: the Camperdown elm is from Dundee, Fennessey's oak from Waterford and Lucombe oaks came to light in Exeter. Some urban trees are the only known examples of their type: the last Blandford elms are in Edinburgh, and there is a lone Lombarts' elm in Brighton.

While this book is focused on Britain and Ireland, the story of our trees is also deeply international: migrants have been arriving on these shores for centuries. Mulberries, sweet chestnuts and figs came to us in antiquity, and have been followed by hundreds more species from Asia, Africa, the Americas and Australasia. Still they keep coming – trees that have already become landmarks, like the OLDEST DAWN REDWOOD (448), only arrived in 1947. Though the countryside is home to many important oaks, beeches and ash trees, our towns and cities are hotbeds of arboreal diversity. This is where you will find trees that reflect us all: like the human inhabitants of Britain and Ireland, they have come from all corners of the world, and they are all ages, shapes and sizes. Even our ideas of how we plant and manage trees in towns and cities have come from overseas. Street trees as we know them today were first planted in Paris, and ornamental landscapes like Greenwich Park were influenced by André Le Nôtre, who laid out Versailles in the seventeenth century.

OVER THE LAST four years, I have travelled tens of thousands of miles across the length and breadth of Britain and Ireland to see and record the trees you will find here. It has been an epic and rewarding journey, during which I have encountered towns and cities I thought I knew well in a completely new way.

Before setting off on a tree hunt, I would research an itinerary of likely places and trees to visit. I was aided by an array of online resources, especially the *Tree Register of Britain and Ireland* and the *Ancient Tree Inventory*, and a growing collection of independently published books about the trees of specific localities, the titles of which can be found in the bibliography. I was often fortunate to make contact with local experts who were happy to show me around their city, or who provided me with tip-offs for trees I should see. Through their generosity, I was able to discover such delights as NEWBIGGIN'S ANCIENT ASH (138) in Newcastle and the CLIMBERS' LIME (119) in Glasgow.

Despite my research, preparation and best intentions, there were inevitably trees that I simply stumbled across, mostly by driving past them, and I am sure that I will not have been the first to recognise these landmarks. On countless occasions I arrived at a place to discover a tree that I had researched was no longer there. When I arrived in Beauly to see Scotland's oldest wych elm, I found I was years too late; all that was left was a skeletal stump. Frequently, though, where one great tree grows, another is waiting in the wings. At Beauly, the incredible CONSOLATION SYCAMORE (13) is thriving just metres from the remains of the elm.

I set out with the objective of recording 1,000 distinct individual trees, but I soon encountered exceptions. The DOORS OF DURIN YEWS (684) at Stow-on-the-Wold are two trees that intertwine over a church door; they are so inseparable, I have regarded them (and a few similar composites) as single entries. Where two or more trees grow together in a distinctive group, I have featured the benchmark, like the MEIKLEOUR FIRST TREE (37), a constituent of the incredible 300-metre-long beech hedge in Perthshire. Occasionally, it has been impossible to choose between a pair, so, like the TRINITY TWINS (943 & 944) in Dublin, there are two trees to see.

I should also admit to my own biases: there are certain species that I am more drawn to than others. I am sure other dendrophiles have their own proclivities, some overt, some unconscious, and maybe readers of this book will ascertain what mine are. I feel duty bound to say that, as a city dweller, I am particularly attuned to the majesty of planes, even though I am afflicted by the minute hairs they shed in May, which cause me to weep and splutter for a fortnight. I love beeches and cedars of Lebanon too: these were the first two species I was awed by as a child. When I was a teenager, I was influenced by a view, fashionable in the 1980s and 90s, that non-native sycamores should be given short shrift because they overwhelmed our own flora and supported few codependent species. I now realise this is not true, and have come to admire the great maple. If you are lucky enough to visit some of the astonishing sycamores I highlight, particularly those in Scotland, I am sure that, even if you harbour doubts about this species, you will be won over too. The list of tree species I admire could go on for some time, so I will just mention one other that I came to adore while researching this book: the exquisite paperbark maple, a bewitching small tree that seems to thrive virtually everywhere.

With billions of trees in Britain and Ireland, there are bound to be individuals worthy of inclusion that do not feature. I regret that there are a few places like Stornoway, Aberystwyth, Enniskillen or Guildford that I was unable to visit, or had only the briefest time in, and I am sure there are remarkable trees just waiting to be recognised; I welcome any tips about others worth hunting. I am sure, too, that from the moment of publication, this book will be out of date: there will inevitably be trees recorded here that will have succumbed to one catastrophe or another. The effects of the climate crisis will no doubt impact many trees, and some will be lost to the increasingly intense stresses they now face. I am hopeful, though, that in a century's time, many of the trees in this book will still be standing.

Happy tree hunting!

# INDIVIDUAL TREE NAMES

EVERY TREE IN THIS book has a unique individual name, such as THE FORTINGALL YEW* (28), or the TORTWORTH CHESTNUT* (692). Some of the names I have recorded have been in use for decades or even centuries, while others are more recent: VERNON OAK* (276) in Sheffield was named for Vernon Road, the street it grows on, during the protests of the 2010s against tree-felling there. Some names refer to the place where the tree grows. BARNEY* (496) can be found in the well-to-do Southwest London enclave of Barnes, for instance. Others reflect a particular physical attribute, like THE NOBBLY TREE* (890) or BIG BELLY* (728). Sometimes trees remember people, like EPPIE CALLUM'S OAK* (44), or, occasionally, like the FATAL OAK* (770), a historical event, whether sad or celebratory. These names can change: a fine old tree known as THE GREAT OAK* (406) in Herefordshire was first recorded as the Eardisley Oak two centuries ago. THE ARBOUR OAK* (311) in Nottingham is an astonishing old tree named many years ago, but, when I visited, I met a fellow tree hunter paying their respects who was nonplussed when I voiced the name I had heard. She told me she had known it since her childhood simply as Big Tree.

You will notice some trees have asterisks after their names. These are those with pre-existing names. But many of the trees I have included in these pages did not have a popular name, however (or, if they did, I was not aware of it). So it is with these precedents in mind that I set about giving names to the trees. Those I have dreamed up should be regarded as provisional. I invite you to take them as a starting point: maybe, when you visit, a tree will suggest something more appropriate, something that reflects its location, its appearance or its history. I would love to hear your names for the trees in this book, and for those I have not yet become acquainted with.

Incidentally, THE BIG TREE* (4) grows in Kirkwall, a long way from Nottingham; I think it is important every tree has a unique name.

# GLOSSARY

ANCIENT TREES
Very old trees that are often collapsing and are approaching the end of their lives are termed 'ancient'. They could be many hundreds or even thousands of years old, and will host often rare insect and fungal life forms that specialise in the habitats ancient trees offer. Most ancient trees are oaks or yews, but ancient ashes, field maples, sweet chestnuts, beeches, hawthorns and sycamores might also be encountered.

ARBORETUM
A botanical garden dedicated to the study and cultivation of trees.

ARBORICULTURIST
A person who maintains trees, sometimes known as an arborist or urban forester.

ARCHAEOPHYTE
A term used to describe a plant that arrived in Britain or Ireland in prehistory. Sweet chestnuts and strawberry trees are two archaeophyte species.

BOLE
The bulging bottom of a tree's trunk, specifically the segment from the ground up to the first branches.

CATKINS
Flowing, flowering stalks named for their resemblance to a cat's tail. The word is borrowed from the Dutch *katteken*, meaning 'kitten'. Hornbeams, alders and birches produce prominent catkins.

CHAMPION TREES
Some of the trees in this book have been certified by the *Tree Register of Britain and Ireland* as champions. They are trees

that are the tallest or stoutest of their species throughout Britain or Ireland, or within one of the constituent countries or even counties.

**CONIFER** — A tree that produces its seeds inside cones, like pines, cedars and firs. Most conifers are also **evergreen**.

**COPPICING** — The practice of regularly cutting trees back to the ground to promote a regular supply of new growth. Like **pollarding**, coppicing is an ancient and sustainable method for managing trees for wood production. Coppicing is the activity, while a coppice may describe a small woodland or even an individual tree. Regularly coppiced trees can live for many centuries.

**CULTIVAR** — A tree that has been selected by humans for desirable traits. For instance, *Ulmus glabra 'Horizontalis'* is a wych elm cultivar prized for its low, spreading 'tabletop' crown. To maintain these desirable features, cultivars are reproduced clonally, and so budding gardeners or urban foresters wishing to plant them can do so via **cuttings** or **grafts**. If left to reproduce naturally, their offspring will usually revert to their species' typical form. Cultivar names are appended to the species name; for instance, the copper beech is *Fagus sylvatica 'Purpurea'*, while the great white cherry is *Prunus serrulata 'Tai Haku'*.

**CUTTING** — A small part of a plant – perhaps a young branch shoot – that is cut from the main body and planted elsewhere. If the cutting takes root and survives, it will be genetically identical to its parent plant and will show the same traits.

**DECIDUOUS** — Trees which shed their leaves or needles annually.

**DIOECIOUS** — A species with separate male and female plants – a dioecious tree will only ever have male or female flowers, and requires pollination by the other to reproduce.

**EVERGREEN** — Trees that retain their leaves or needles throughout the year, even in winter, when **deciduous** trees shed theirs.

| | |
|---|---|
| FAMILY | The taxonomic term for a group of **genera** (the plural of **genus**). The beech family – the *fagaceae* – for instance, comprises eight genera, including beech (*Fagus*), chestnut (*Castanea*) and oak (*Quercus*), all of which produce nutritious woody fruits. |
| FASTIGIATE | When a tree's branches grow upright and closely packed together, running near-parallel to the trunk to create towering, often pointed crowns. |
| GENUS | A group of related species. In taxonomy, a genus is one level below a **family** in the hierarchy of classifications and one step above a **species**. *Quercus*, for example, is the genus representing oak species, and includes the three most common oaks in the British Isles – the pedunculate oak (*Quercus robur*), whose acorns grow on stalks; sessile oak (*Quercus petraea*), whose acorns do not grow on stalks; and the evergreen holm oak (*Quercus ilex*). Incidentally, if it's not acorn season, you can tell pedunculate and sessile oak trees apart by paying close attention to their leaves where these characteristics are reversed: pedunculate oak leaves have no stalks (or petioles), while sessile oak leaves have long stalks. |
| GRAFTING | The process of joining the limb of one tree, known as the scion, to the planted trunk and roots of another, known as the stock. Over time, the scion and stock fuse together to make a new, single plant. A distinct mark at the point where the original graft occurred is often quite noticeable. |
| HYBRID | When two different species cross-pollinate, the offspring their seeds produce, often with features intermediate between the parents, are known as hybrids. For instance, common limes are a hybrid between small-leaved (*Tilia cordata*) and large-leaved (*Tilia platyphyllos*) lime species. Hybridity is denoted in a species' botanical name by the '×' symbol, so the common lime is *Tilia × europaea*. |
| LAYERING | The process, which can occur naturally or at the encouragement of horticulturalists, whereby a tree grows branches that droop |

| | |
|---|---|
| | so heavily that they touch the ground, sprouting roots of their own. Over time, the layering branches become trunks in their own right and can even separate from the parent tree. |
| MAIDEN | A tree that has never been pollarded. A term particularly applied to oaks, a maiden tree will have a distinct leading trunk that does not split into multiple branches above a short bole. |
| MONOECIOUS | A species with universally bisexual, or 'perfect', flowers, such as a cherry, or with both male and female flowers on the same plant, like an oak. |
| NATIVE | A term used to describe trees that have been growing in Britain or Ireland since the end of the last ice age, when the islands were connected by a land bridge to the continent. Their native credentials are attested by the appearance of their preserved pollen in post-glacial lake deposits – the pollen record. |
| NON-NATIVE | Species that arrived after sea levels rose, causing Britain and Ireland to become islands. Some non-native species arrived in prehistory (these are called **archaeophytes**), while others arrived much more recently, such as dawn redwoods in 1947. |
| NURSERY | A garden that propagates plants from seeds, grafts or cuttings, typically for commercial purposes. The horticulturalists who work in nurseries are known as nurserymen and nurserywomen. |
| PINNATE | Pinnate leaves have feather-, frond- or lobe-like leaflets on either side of the central stalk, or petiole – imagine an ash or a walnut. |
| POLLARDING | Historically, pollarding was a kind of pruning that removed the upper branches of a tree above the bole to promote new, dense branch growth. The resulting tree is known as a pollard. Pollards don't climb to the same heights as their siblings which have been left to grow naturally, but they can live far longer. Today, pollarding often refers to the frequent pruning street trees undergo, especially London planes or common limes. |

| | |
|---|---|
| SPECIES & SUBSPECIES | Occasionally, a tree might have characteristics that distinguish it from others to which it is closely related, without making it distinct enough to be a species in its own right. The wild black poplar, *Populus nigra ssp. betulifolia*, is an example of a subspecies, in this case of *Populus nigra*, the black poplar. |
| SPECIMEN TREE | A tree used as a focal point in a formal park or garden. |
| STREET TREES | Trees that have been planted on pavements and are often managed by councils. |
| PLANT TAXONOMY | The botanical discipline of naming, identifying and classifying plants in a hierarchical system. Taxonomic labels in botany include **cultivar, variety, species, genus** and **family**. |
| URBAN FOREST | All the trees and shrubs, public and private, that grow in a single town or city. |
| VARIETY | A tree that deviates from the norm for its species, expressing its own traits, yet which is not so genetically distinct as to be a new species or subspecies. |
| VETERAN TREES | Trees that are old for their species are often called veterans. They may exhibit some of the characteristics of **ancient trees**, like hollows, fallen limbs, great girth or height, but are not so old that they should be classed as ancient. I have used the term to describe individual trees that are clearly old, and are among the older examples of their species in Britain or Ireland. These might include planes, holm oaks, horse chestnuts or limes, as well as species that are also represented by ancient examples. |

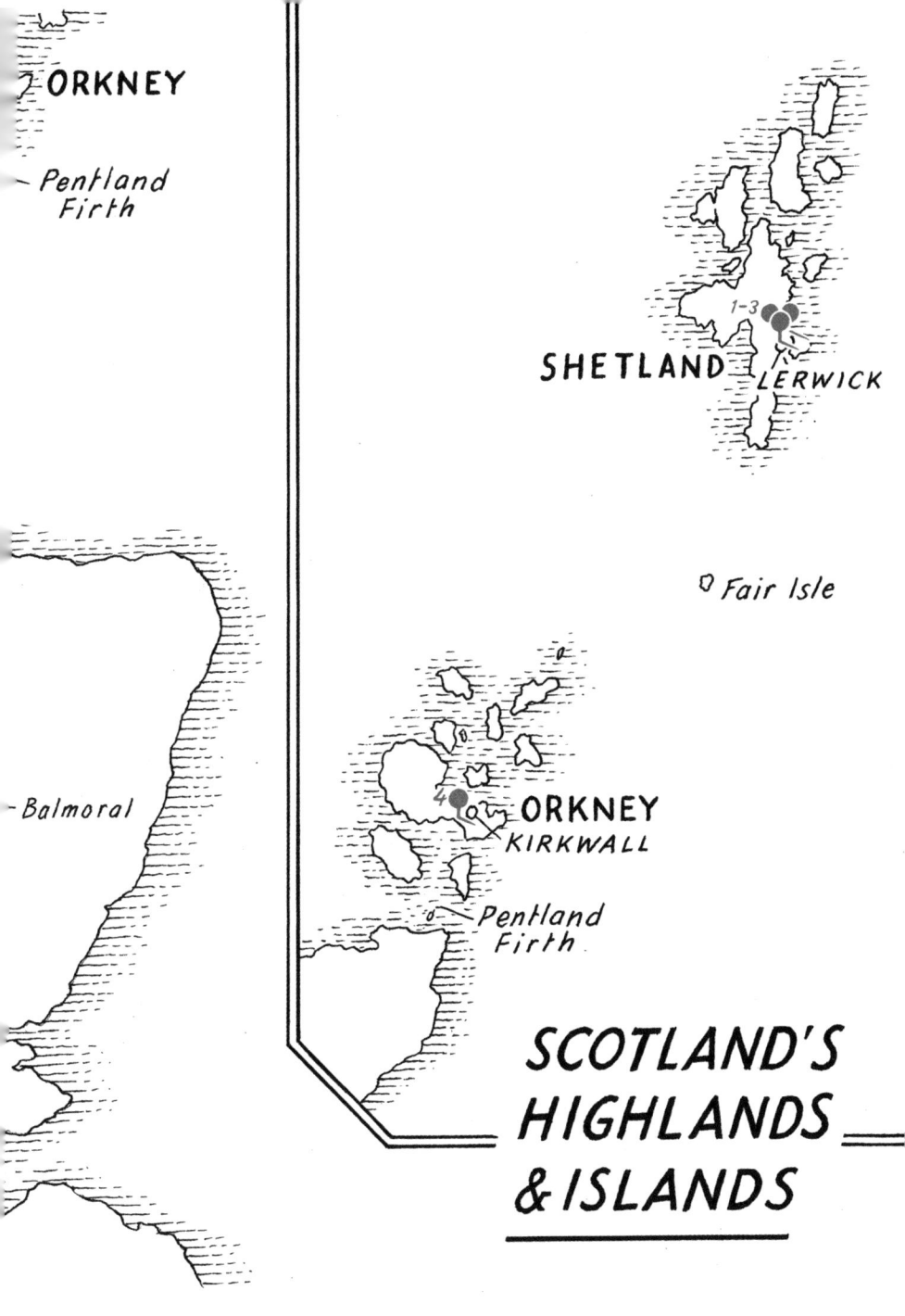

## SCOTLAND'S HIGHLANDS & ISLANDS

*Shetland*
*Orkney*
*Eilean Siar*
*Highland*
*Argyll & Bute*
*Stirling*
*Perth & Kinross*

SIGNATURE SPECIES:
*Sycamore*

Newcomers to more-or-less treeless Orkney may be as surprised as I was to discover **THE BIG TREE (4)**, a captivating landmark sycamore in the centre of Kirkwall. It is a tree held in high regard by Orcadians. When I first saw it around a decade ago, I could understand why: it is both beautiful and peculiar – it seems miraculous that a veteran town-centre tree has survived for so long, so far north.

I had The Big Tree in mind when I started researching this book. I felt sure there must be trees to see even further north, and promptly made the epic journey from London to Shetland. I was delighted to discover many more sycamores growing there, as well as an elm or two and, most remarkably, the youthful **CHESTNUT FOAL (2)**, a horse chestnut growing close to the walls of Fort Charlotte in Lerwick. It is partly because Shetland was one of the first places I visited, and partly to lend a geographic logic, that this book's first entries start in this northern extremity of the British and Irish archipelago.

Below the Northern Isles, Scotland's Highlands are a region of mountain, moor and conifer plantation; a beautiful but tough landscape shaped by weather, highland clearances, intense livestock grazing and modern forestry. But they are punctuated with sheltered glens, fertile river valleys and protected sea lochs, as well as settlements that teem with fascinating trees. From Lerwick, Shetland's only town, to the mainland cities of Inverness, Perth and Stirling, dozens of remarkable individuals can be tracked down.

It will come as no surprise that there are exceptional conifers to be found up here, like the **PARENT LARCH (29)** at Dunkeld or the **BREACH PINE (16)** at Inverness, but the species that thrives in all Scottish climates, from salty coasts to exposed hillsides, is the familiar sycamore. Indeed, the sycamore – or Celtic Maple – does so well in Scotland that some of the most astonishing trees to be found anywhere in Britain or Ireland are the sycamores of the north. From the stunted **ZETLAND SYCAMORE (1)** to the magnificent specimens at Birnam, Blair Drummond and Beauly, it is ubiquitous, and has a good claim to being Scotland's tree.

Of course, the title of 'Scotland's tree' has already literally been taken by the Scots pine. Pines were the dominant trees of the Caledonian Forest that once stretched from Loch Lomond in the south to Loch Broom in the north west, and to Deeside in the east. Today, a few remnants of this most alluring woodland habitat can be found in remote gullies and mountainsides, where it offers shelter to red squirrels, pine martens and capercaillie. But in the easily accessible town of Aviemore, it is possible to get a taste of this landscape without needing to trek for miles. Between the Spey and the Cairngorms large tracts of forest remain, and a veteran, perfectly shaped tree – the **CAIRNGORM BEACH PINE (23)** – can be admired on the sandy shores of Loch Morlich.

For all the sycamores and conifers, the trees of northern Scotland are also diverse, and many are a long way from home. The beloved horse chestnut, a species originating from the Balkans, is frequent throughout the region, while sweet chestnuts, another southern-European species, have been growing happily north of Inverness for hundreds of years. On the west coast, the Atlantic ensures winters are wild but mild, and the **PLOCKTON PALM (12)** (actually not a palm, but an unrelated cabbage tree from New Zealand) offers proof of the Gulf Stream's potency.

Still, over the last two centuries, Scotland's uplands have increasingly been carpeted with commercial conifer plantations, and two species – Sitka spruce and Douglas fir – have come to define these. They are both North American, and both were introduced by David Douglas, a native of the village of Scone on the outskirts of Perth. The Sitka spruce arrived in 1831, while the Douglas fir landed five years earlier in 1826. For good or ill, Douglas's influence has been enormous, and fine specimens of both these trees can be examined at Scone. **EXHIBIT 'A' (40)** is a young Sitka spruce, while in the grounds of historic Scone Palace, the enormous **PACIFIC PIONEER (39)**, raised from the first shipment of seed to arrive in Scotland, can be appreciated.

THE BIG TREE* (4)

1. **ZETLAND SYCAMORE**
   *Sycamore / Acer pseudoplatanus*
   Burgh Road,
   Lerwick ZE1 0LB
   60.153851, -1.1528770

   Hardly taller than a Shetland pony, a broad and stocky sycamore has sheltered for decades against a wall in a tiny parcel of urban woodland behind Lerwick's Montfield Health Centre. It is the first tree you encounter on the footpath off Burgh Road, the benchmark in an astonishing group of squat, wide-spreading specimens, embodying the hardiness of this species in the face of a cool, blustery climate: they are growing out rather than up. ///accusing.mascot.throat

2. **CHESTNUT FOAL**
   *Horse chestnut Aesculus hippocastanum*
   Charlotte Street,
   Lerwick ZE1 0JL
   60.154983, -1.1446410

   Growing close against the stone fortifications of eighteenth-century Fort Charlotte, what is surely the northernmost horse chestnut is a young tree in a protected location. It has every chance of growing into a significant tree – by Shetland standards. Further south, horse chestnuts will flower in May, but this far north, visit at midsummer to catch its glorious white flower panicles, or candles. ///crackles.splint.focal

3. **BANK LANE ELM**
   *Wych elm / Ulmus glabra*
   Bank Lane, off
   Commercial Street,
   Lerwick ZE1 0DL
   60.153231, -1.1440990

   Low-growing sycamores line a steep lane off stony Commercial Street, their canopies interweaving to create a tunnel offering leafy solace from the elements, which can be temperamental at this high latitude. Halfway along, the maple monoculture is interrupted by the startling asymmetric leaves of a wych elm, perhaps Britain's most northerly individual. ///darts.quite.stags

4. **THE BIG TREE***
   *Sycamore / Acer pseudoplatanus*
   Albert Street,
   Kirkwall KW15 1HJ
   58.982522, -2.9595630

   Fertile but windswept Orkney's most celebrated tree is an elderly, hollow sycamore that stands proudly, aided by an internal steel prop, opposite the Bank of Scotland in the middle of Albert Street. Latitude, weather and its town-centre position have conspired to ensure The Big Tree has remained relatively small, despite its popular name. ///throwaway.solar.debater

5. **VILLAGE HALL CHERRY**
   *'Kanzan' Japanese cherry / Prunus serrulata 'Kanzan'*
   Ullapool Village Hall,
   4 Market Street,
   Ullapool IV26 2XE
   57.897653, -5.1596380

   Thomas Telford's eighteenth-century planned settlement of Ullapool is well stocked with street trees, a sight that may surprise visitors arriving by ferry from Stornoway, or those who have travelled across the denuded highlands. On Market Street, almost all the trees are white-flowering cherries, but come in May to see the exception – a shocking-pink *'Kanzan'* breaks the conformity opposite the village hall. ///squeezed.interviewer.exporters

6. **OLD CHURCH SYCAMORE**
Sycamore / *Acer pseudoplatanus*
Old Edderton Church,
Tain IV19 1JU
57.828900, -4.1579330

Distinguished by a dense, domed canopy and a flared bole typical of maturing sycamores, this veteran tree stands to the east of picturesque Edderton Old Church. The church, a mile or more from the village, overlooks the Dornoch Firth and was built in 1734. We can assume this impressive sycamore was planted then too. ///squirted.weds.autumn

7. **SOLID BEECH**
Copper beech / *Fagus sylvatica 'Purpurea'*
Cathedral Square,
Fortrose IV10 8TB
57.581029, -4.1313580

Mirroring the red sandstone of the cathedral ruins, a row of weather-beaten copper beeches line the kirkyard's northern perimeter. Further south, trees of this species can become giant purple pom-poms; up here, though, the canopy is more gaunt, striking a jazzy contrast between silver bark and purple leaves. The stocky, twisted westernmost tree is the biggest and the best of the bunch. ///flickers.devours.dove

8. **DINGWALL WEEPING ASH**
Weeping ash / *Fraxinus excelsior 'Pendula'*
Joe Yates Court,
Dingwall IV15 9HP
57.594478, -4.4275110

One of the most impressive weeping ash trees in Scotland is marooned on a patch of lawn between a car park and the backs of the High Street shops at Dingwall. It has a fine shape and is in excellent condition, its cascading branches thick with leaves in summer, something that cannot be said for many of its clonal siblings, which are often among the first to show symptoms of ash dieback. ///deprives.tend.breathy

9. **1550 SWEET CHESTNUT***
Sweet chestnut
*Castanea sativa*
Castle Leod,
Strathpeffer IV14 9AA
57.598628, -4.5328350
*Paid entry; check opening times and dates.*

Despite its name, this magnificent tree was actually planted three years later in 1553 by John Mackenzie, chief of his clan, to mark a visit by Mary Guise, the mother of Mary Queen of Scots who was soon to become queen regent. This is the most northerly sweet chestnut, and is in fine shape as it approaches its quincentenary. There are few trees this old that can trace their lineage with such certainty. ///trendy.washable.hers

10. **PAVILLION REDWOOD**
Giant redwood
*Sequoiadendron giganteum*
The Square,
Strathpeffer IV14 9DW
57.587282, -4.5379180

Trees do well in the genteel spa town of Strathpeffer, having been nurtured for centuries by the sulphurous springs that once drew Victorian tourists. At the resort's heart, the timber Strathpeffer Pavilion is overshadowed by an array of towering conifers, the most magnificent of which is the first of two giant redwoods, a strapping tree standing 30 metres high with an impressive, spongy-barked bole. ///drifter.proofread.commuting

SOLID BEECH (7)

11. **CHIMNEY SWEEP'S PUZZLE**
*Monkey puzzle*
*Araucaria araucana*
Bosville Terrace,
Portree IV51 9DG
57.412988, -6.1900010

Like the Northern Isles, settlements on Hebridean islands are surprisingly bosky. In the sheltered town of Portree on Skye, growing in the car park of a B&B overlooking the spiky Cuillin Hills, a mature monkey puzzle commands attention. Its tiny canopy perches precariously on top of 15 metres or more of rough-barked trunk, marked with distinct contours where branches, discarded as its height increased, once grew. It looks rather like a giant chimney brush. ///nibbles.preheated.textiles

12. **PLOCKTON PALM**
*Cabbage palm*
*Cordyline australis*
The Plockton Hotel,
41 Harbour Street,
Plockton IV52 8TN
57.338441, -5.6511350

Unexpected New Zealand cabbage palms give sheltered Plockton a holiday vibe. A particularly well-branched example is in the beachside garden of the Plockton Hotel. Frosts are rare on the west coast, so plants that would freeze further east are able to thrive in the Atlantic-tempered climate if they are protected from the worst winter storms. ///pads.nail.fetching

13. **CONSOLATION SYCAMORE**
*Sycamore / Acer*
*pseudoplatanus*
Beauly Priory,
Beauly IV4 7DY
57.484490, -4.4586090

Beyond Beauly Priory's kirkyard gates – and the bleached remains of a once monumental wych elm that succumbed to Dutch elm disease in 2018 – one of Scotland's most impressive sycamores can be seen standing close to the priory ruins. Unlike the priory, it stands resolute: a giant in height and girth, it is in rude health, its irregular form conveying the centuries it has grown in this bucolic spot overlooking the broad, fertile floodplain of the Beauly River. ///retrain.alleyway.flukes

14 & 15. **ST STEPHEN'S TWINS** → Despite originating from southern Europe, golden-flowered laburnums thrive in these islands, and it seems the further north you go, the more magnificent they become. At Inverness, the climate must be perfect. A stout pair glisten in June in the storied graveyard of Old High St Stephen's Church, the site of bloody Culloden reprisals. They have a commanding position overlooking the Ness.

**ST STEPHEN'S TWINS** *Voss's laburnum / Laburnum × watereri 'Vossii'* Old High St Stephen's Church, Church Street, Inverness IV1 1EY 57.479800, -4.2292470 ///trades.shorts.chest

| | | |
|---|---|---|
| 16. | **BREACH PINE**  *Austrian pine / Pinus nigra var. nigra*  Inverness Castle,  Inverness IV2 3EG  57.476189, -4.2261580 | Perched on a low hill, Inverness Castle dominates the city's skyline; it is a discordant but undeniably romantic mashup of Victorian red-sandstone towers, walls and turrets. The buildings are framed by trees, and most noticeable among them is a deep green, multi-trunked Austrian pine that has grown taller than the battlements, offering rather too easy access for would-be attackers. ///dame.drama.brass |
| 17. | **THREE GRACES SYCAMORE**  *Sycamore / Acer pseudoplatanus*  Ness Bank,  Inverness IV2 4SA  57.475164, -4.2262080 | Many fine trees line the banks of the Ness, but the biggest, and maybe the oldest, is this graceful sycamore with a distinctive twisted trunk. It is a landmark at the junction of Castle Road and Ness Bank, and across the road is the Three Graces statue, which once adorned the rooftop of a city-centre department store. ///bonds.puns.apply |

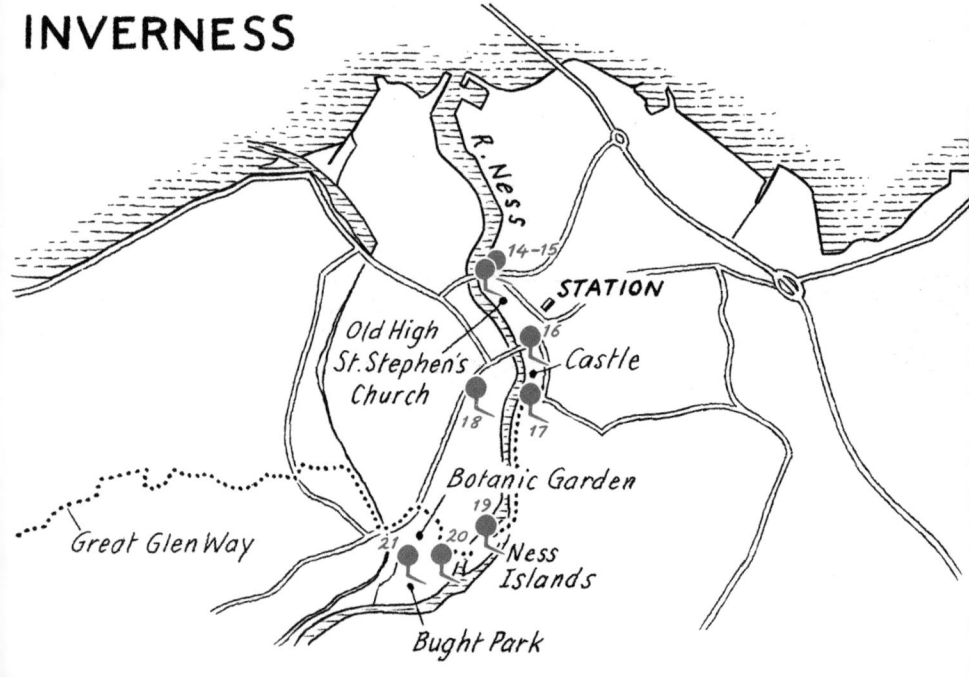

### 18. URBAN LARCH
*European larch*
*Larix decidua*
Bishops Road,
Inverness IV3 5SB
57.472469, -4.2329770

It's a surprise to find a larch, normally a forestry staple, in such an urban setting, but this mature tree proves how well suited these deciduous conifers are to life in town. It's the most prominent tree among a small copse of Inverness's urban forest, which is otherwise composed mostly of broadleaf trees. It has taken on the species' characteristic solid, spreading form with a jaunty angular canopy. ///stamp.list.visa

### 19. NESS ISLAND FIR
*Douglas fir*
*Pseudotsuga menziesii*
Ness Islands, Great Glen Way, Inverness IV2 4RT
57.463333, -4.2315730

Upstream from Inverness city centre, the well-conifered Ness Islands are landmarks in the River Ness. Cross from either riverbank on one of the elegant iron suspension bridges to admire the city's finest Douglas fir. It is a towering tree, one of a group on the larger northern island, next to the short inter-island bridge. Look out for Douglas fir cones: papery 'mouse's tails' poke out of each scale. ///surely.space.brave

### 20. GRAND BUGHT REDWOOD
*Giant redwood*
*Sequoiadendron giganteum*
Inverness Leisure, Bught Lane, Inverness IV3 5SS
57.463279, -4.2388940

Now an extensive area of leisure facilities, Bught Park was once the grounds of a stately home that survived until the 1960s. Despite the house disappearing to development, many old trees from its former grounds continue to prosper, and an impressive giant redwood opposite the swimming pool gives a sense of the grandeur that once must have been. ///dreams.create.join

### 21. PORCELAIN BIRCH
*Himalayan birch*
*Betula utilis var. jacquemontii*
Inverness Botanic Gardens, Bught Lane, Inverness IV3 5SS
57.462740, -4.2407490
*Check opening times.*

Not many cities the size of Inverness can boast botanic gardens, and, while small, these are an unforeseen delight, replete with glasshouses and a café. They are a recent innovation, and consequently the trees here are young. So it seems appropriate that the Garden's most memorable is a hard-to-miss young upstart: a dazzlingly white-barked *jacquemontii* variety of Himalayan birch. ///eating.quench.motor

### 22. TRIPLE-TRUNKED BIRCH
*Silver birch*
*Betula pendula*
Craigellachie National Nature Reserve, Aviemore PH22 1PR
57.186759, -3.8384860

Craigellachie National Nature Reserve, separated from Aviemore's other attractions by the elevated A9, shrouds the hills above town with thousands of elegant-but-tough silver birches. Just before wee Loch Puladdern, a three-trunked specimen forces the path to curve round it, enabling close inspection of its pelt of lichen. Craigellachie is one of Scotland's largest and most important birchwoods. ///thin.spillage.chilling

23. **CAIRNGORM BEACH PINE** → Aviemore visitors should explore Glenmore Forest, which stretches from the edge of town to the Cairngorm tree line. Among the plantations, remnants of rare Caledonian forest are preserved: a gorgeous open woodland of heather, birch, juniper and pine that once covered much of the Highlands. On the unexpected beach at Loch Morlich, a perfect veteran Scots pine cuts an almost Mediterranean silhouette against golden sand.

**CAIRNGORM BEACH PINE** *Scots pine / Pinus sylvestris* Glenmore, Aviemore PH22 1QU
57.166626, -3.7009500 ///envisage.bunch.goals

24. **TOBERMORY TILLEUL**
*Common lime*
*Tilia × europaea*
Breadalbane Street,
Tobermory,
Isle of Mull PA75 6PE
56.623127, -6.0713970

There's more to charming Tobermory than its brightly painted quayside buildings. Explore the grid of streets above the harbour to discover a squat lime pollard on Breadalbane Street. Holding court outside the Breadalbane Street Studio and Gallery, it is the largest of several lime trees on this street. Its closely clipped form is reminiscent of trees in formal French gardens, lending a continental air to the Hebrides. ///tracking.graph.burn

25. **RANNOCH ROWAN**
*Rowan / Sorbus aucuparia*
A82, Bridge of Orchy
PA36 4AD
56.580948, -4.753941

Perched on a rock by the side of the main road through Rannoch Moor and Glencoe, the Rannoch Rowan acts as a landmark for folk traversing this dramatic, and otherwise treeless, country north of Tyndrum. The tree is remarkable for sustaining itself on what appears to be bare rock, which has lifted it above the reach of browsing sheep and deer. Its scarlet berries are a particularly pleasing sight for both humans and birds in the autumn. ///motivator.washroom.speeches

26. **INVERARAY'S FYNE CHERRY**
*Double-flowered wild cherry*
*Prunus avium 'Plena'*
Front Street East,
Inveraray PA32 8UZ
56.231687, -5.0729770

A welcome milestone for those arriving in Inveraray from Glasgow and the south, this brave cherry tree opposite the Visitor Centre is a delight in late April when its cheery white flowers appear. The rest of the year, it's noteworthy both for its beautiful location overlooking Loch Fyne, and for the luxurious moss and lichen covering its trunk and branches like the softest of green jumpers. ///supper.given.lifeguard

27. **ROBERTSON OAK**\*
*Sessile oak*
*Quercus petraea*
Perth Road,
Pitlochry PH16 5LY
56.697836, -3.7227870

Follow your nose to the Robertson Oak, an old tree which ignominiously now finds itself next to Pitlochry's sewage works. Its name remembers George Robertson of Faskally, a Jacobite rebel who, fleeing south after defeat at Culloden, found the tree's canopy – presumably considerable in 1746 – the ideal place to hide from pursuing government troops. He evaded capture and made his escape to France. ///unhappy.plausible.argue

28. **THE FORTINGALL YEW**\*
*Yew / Taxus baccata*
Kirkton Cottages,
Fortingall,
Aberfeldy PH15 2LL
56.598251, -4.0509560

The Fortingall Yew is a truly ancient tree, possibly the oldest in Britain or Ireland. Preserved behind a stone wall as remnant shards of a single trunk that rotted away centuries ago, it is impossible to date accurately, but its lifespan can be measured in millennia. Visitors may retreat to the nearby Fortingall Hotel to ponder its great age and the veracity of a legend that an infant Pontius Pilate played beneath it. ///pulps.large.spearing

29. **PARENT LARCH**\*
*European larch*
*Larix decidua*
Riverside,
Dunkeld PH8 0AG
56.565289, -3.5911920

Planted by the Duke of Atholl in 1737 from Tyrolean seed, this was the first larch to grow in these islands and, remarkably, it thrives to this day (the Duke planted four more which weren't so lucky). It is impressive: a conifer with a distinctive asymmetric character closer to a broadleaf tree, something you could mistake it for during needle-less winter months. It grows on the footpath behind the Cathedral. ///gains.leafing.exclusive

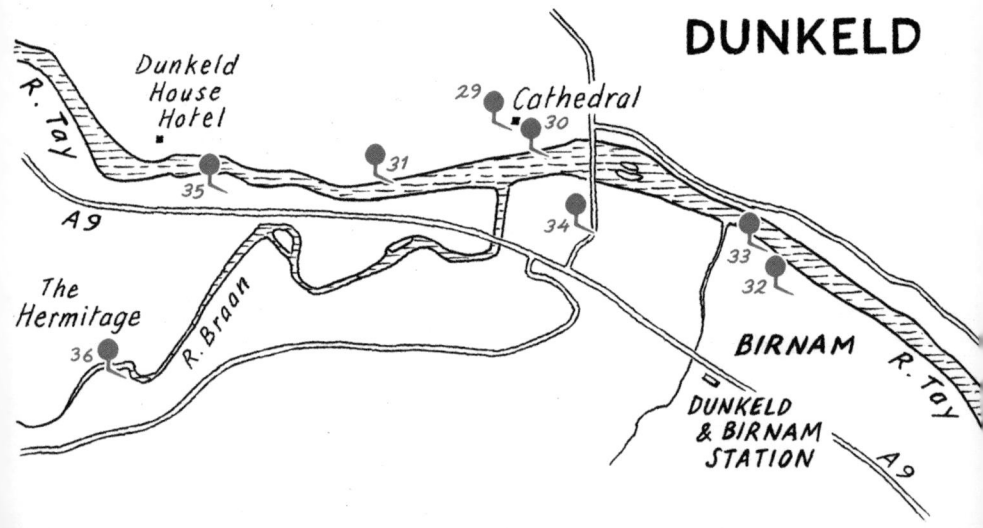

30. **CATHEDRAL CHRISTMAS TREE**
*Caucasian fir*
*Abies nordmanniana*
Dunkeld Cathedral,
Cathedral Street,
Dunkeld PH8 0AW
56.564589, -3.5901640

Caucasian or Nordman firs are the UK's most popular Christmas tree species, but large, mature examples of these attractive trees are rare. One of the finest, along with a range of other unusual conifers, can be admired in the grounds stretching down to the river in front of Dunkeld Cathedral. It stands on the western side and can be distinguished by its telltale blunt needles. ///parading.planting.luggage

31. **THE DUNKELD LARCH**
*Dunkeld larch*
*Larix × marschlinsii*
Riverside,
Dunkeld PH8 0AG
56.563645, -3.5987320

Many commercial plantations grow the hybrid Dunkeld larch, a tree that exhibits all the benefits of hybridity: vigorous growth, good health and high-quality timber. It is a cross between the European and Japanese species, which first occurred at Dunkeld where the two species grow close together. A fine example can be spotted growing along the path beyond the cathedral leading to Dunkeld House Hotel. ///trips.meanwhile.promoting

32. **BIRNAM OAK***
*Sessile oak*
*Quercus petraea*
Dunkeld PH8 0BL
56.561274, -3.5754750

Birnam, the southern Tayside extension of Dunkeld, is home to two of Scotland's most celebrated trees, one of which is the Birnam Oak. This tree has the great honour of being the sole survivor of the medieval Birnam Wood made famous by Shakespeare in *Macbeth*. Find it close to the riverbank, propped up by a series of wooden poles alongside a lavish interpretation panel explaining its glorious history. ///january.doctor.birdcage

33. **BIRNAM SYCAMORE***
*Sycamore / Acer pseudoplatanus*
Dunkeld PH8 0BL
56.561435, -3.5761600

Just metres from the BIRNAM OAK (32), grows the vast and vigorous Birnam Sycamore. Though it is altogether more sublime than its historic neighbour, being a sycamore it has not been accorded the status the oak enjoys. A small interpretation board offers defamatory claims that the tree is less than 300 years old (unlikely) and that it is 'non-native'. ///surcharge.vine.tiles

34. **BIRNAM WALNUT**
*Walnut / Juglans regia*
A923, Dunkeld PH8 0AF
56.562055, -3.5852180
*In a private garden, but visible from the street.*

Look out for the distinctive, aromatic leaves of a rather grand-looking walnut tree next to the zebra crossing on the A923 as you approach Dunkeld Bridge. It has a distinctive kink to its trunk, and a branch socket ideal for an owl. It sits behind a front garden fence, but, while notionally private, it is a significant landmark and much of its copious canopy shades the highway. ///retina.crescendo.securing

BIRNAM OAK* (32)
BIRNAM SYCAMORE* (33)

**35. NIEL GOW'S TREE***
*Sessile oak*
*Quercus petraea*
Dunkeld PH8 0HX
56.563295, -3.6075450

You can take in another centuries-old tayside oak while sitting on an odd, hair-clip shaped bench placed beneath its branches. Growing just beyond the River Braan's confluence with the Tay, this massive, rugged individual is said to have been the tree under which Niel Gow, the celebrated eighteenth-century fiddler, would sit to compose his popular and enduring tunes, played in Scottish pubs to this day. ///patching.hires.buckling

**36. APPRENTICE FIR**
*Douglas fir*
*Pseudotsuga menziesii*
Old Military Road,
Dunkeld PH8 0JR
56.557474, -3.6139590

The Hermitage, just off the A9, is a thrilling landscape of boulders, waterfalls and towering trees. Follow the River Braan, and where it curves, Britain's tallest tree, a 63-metre Douglas fir, once grew. It fell during a 2017 storm, but dozens more Hermitage firs vie for the title. Its most promising apprentice grows close to the river. ///though.recline.overgrown

**37. MEIKLEOUR FIRST TREE**
Beech / *Fagus sylvatica*
Meikleour PH2 6FB
56.530199, -3.3647540

The soaring Meikleour Beech Hedge – the longest hedge in Britain – was planted to mark the Jacobite uprising of 1745. It is best approached from the south, where, 100 metres after the A93 crosses the River Isla, the Meikleour First Tree marks the start of this awe-inspiring living wall. This is the preamble, and the road soon curves to reveal the full splendour of the hedge, 300 metres long. ///shepherds.bubbles.total

**38. THIS IS NOT JUST A WALNUT**
Walnut / *Juglans regia*
Highland Gateway,
Ruthvenfield Road,
Perth PH1 3EE
56.419995, -3.468262

The out-of-town Highland Gateway Retail Park on the northern edge of Perth does not sound like a likely home for an interesting tree, but opposite Marks & Spencer, you can find Scotland's most magnificent walnut. It is a huge, old multi-stemmed individual that would once have been a landmark on the old high road. Crush a leaf to experience its wonderful fragrance. ///advancing.defected.dislodge

**39. PACIFIC PIONEER**
*Douglas fir*
*Pseudotsuga menziesii*
Scone Palace,
Perth PH2 6BD
56.422879, -3.4343530
*Paid entry.*

David Douglas, a native of Scone and famous early-nineteenth-century plant collector, is memorialised in the common English name for *Pseudotsuga menziesii*. He was the first to bring seeds of the species to Europe in 1826. In the pinetum at Scone Palace, a towering veteran with a low-arching branch resembling a woody mammoth's trunk was grown from that pioneering seed. ///slips.blackbird.compiled

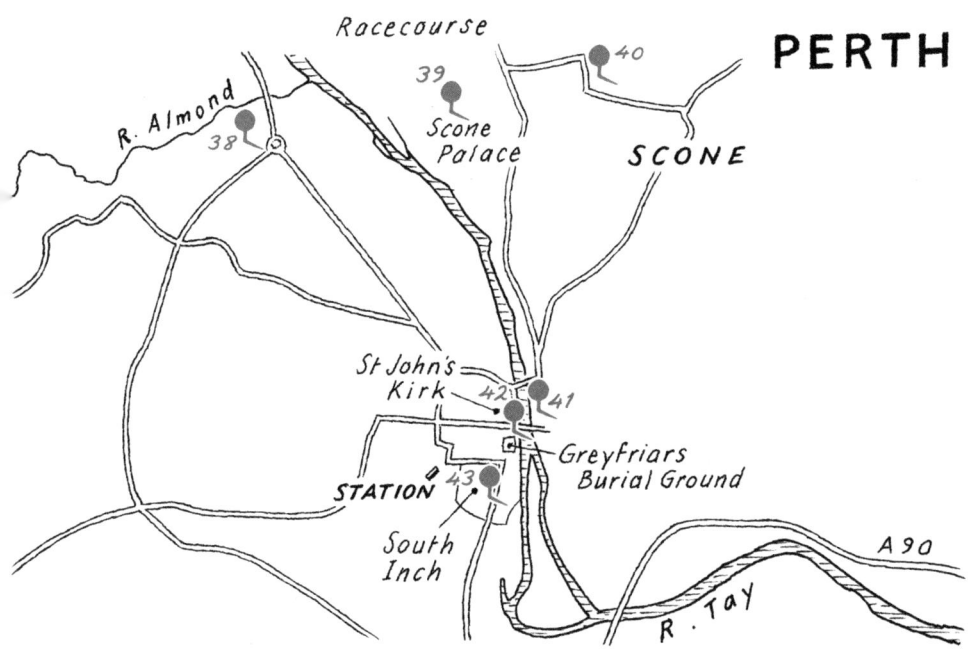

40. **EXHIBIT 'A'**
    *Sitka spruce*
    *Picea sitchensis*
    Woollcombe Square,
    Scone, Perth PH2 6PN
    56.425574, -3.4139590

A rapidly growing Sitka spruce flanked by veteran oaks on the edge of Woollcombe Square is an opportunity to see one of Scotland's most important forestry trees planted as a specimen. There are thousands, if not millions, of taller and older Sitka spruces all over the highlands, but this one is a homage to Scone lad David Douglas who brought this Pacific North West species into European cultivation. ///shifts.purchaser.appear

41. **TAYBANK WILLOW**
    *White willow / Salix alba*
    Norrie-Miller Walk,
    Riverside, Perth PH2 7TR
    56.395389, -3.4238550

Between the bridges on Tay Street is the best place to admire the trees on the eastern bank of the River Tay, which flows urbanely through Perth. Among them, the wonderful silver-canopied Taybank Willow leans out, billowing romantically over the river from Norrie-Miller Walk. ///areas.social.lines

SCOTLAND'S HIGHLANDS & ISLANDS   33

42. **GREYFRIARS MAPLE** → Close to St John's Kirk, where the Scottish Reformation was born in 1559, lies secluded Greyfriars Burial Ground, the site of a Franciscan friary destroyed in that upheaval. Now a small, green plot surrounded by buildings and a car park, it conceals three of the most magnificent Cappadocian maples in Scotland. Pre-eminent among them is a wonderfully thick-trunked individual, standing proudly in the middle of the space.

**GREYFRIARS MAPLE** *Cappadocian maple / Acer cappadocicum* Greyfriars Burial Ground, Canal Street, Perth PH2 8PJ 56.393394, -3.4271690 *Limited opening times.* ///behave.survey.fled

43. **PURPLE PRETENDER**
*Copper beech*
*Fagus sylvatica*
*'Purpurea'*
Edinburgh Road,
Perth PH2 8AN
56.389109, -3.4299950

Perthshire is known as Big Tree Country for the wealth of giants that reside in its aristocratic estates, but grand trees are not limited to these country piles; the city of Perth is well endowed with large, mature trees, too. Its centre is bounded by North and South Inch, two parks of ancient foundation. Tree-lined Edinburgh Road bisects South Inch, where a memorable purple-leaved copper beech soars effortlessly over the otherwise green-canopied avenue. ///horn.deflection.dairy

44. **EPPIE CALLUM'S OAK**\*
*Pedunculate oak*
*Quercus robur*
Turretbank Road,
Crieff PH7 4LN, UK
56.377816, -3.8532410
*In a private garden, but visible from the street.*

Busy Crieff lies on a cattle drover's route from the Highlands to markets further south. It is no surprise that a large oak here has become a landmark: legend has it that folk hero Rob Roy used it as a hiding place from the English. Its notability has been aided by its location outside an inn whose landlady in times past was named Eppie Callum. The inn is long gone, but the magnificent 400-year-old tree remains, now residing in a suburban garden. ///clear.beanbag.stealthier

45. **BICYCLE TREE**\*
*Sycamore / Acer pseudoplatanus*
Brig o' Turk Tearoom,
Brig o'Turk,
Callander FK17 8HT
56.230662, -4.3654690

Brig o' Turk's tree of note is a sycamore that once stood by a blacksmith's shop. A century or more of steady growth next to a long-forgotten pile of scrap metal has obliged it to almost completely consume a bicycle frame. Just the handlebars and a wheel fork protrude from the tree's now substantial trunk, on the edge of a woodland 200 metres beyond the tearoom on Glen Finglas Road. ///thickened.zoom.meal

46. **POKER TREE***
*Sessile oak*
*Quercus petraea*
Bailie Nicol Jarvie Court,
Lochard Road,
Aberfoyle FK8 3SZ
56.178647, -4.3853920

The Poker Tree is not large, but several centuries have endowed it with great presence. Its name refers to Sir Walter Scott's *Rob Roy*, in which the Bailie, Nicol Jarvie, fights a clansman at a nearby inn, setting fire to his kilt with a red-hot poker. In a case of life imitating art, a poker was hung in the tree at some point during the region's nineteenth-century tourism boom. ///generated.loaders.credited

47. **RETIRING SYCAMORE**
*Sycamore / Acer pseudoplatanus*
Kincardine-in-Menteith Church, Blair Drummond FK9 4UX
56.165225, -4.0641940

Undoubtedly predating its sombre Victorian kirk, the Retiring Sycamore is one of the finest but least known of Scotland's great sycamores. It is the first in a well-spaced row of trees marking the edge of kirk land before an overgrown dip into the field below. Several huge limbs curve low down from the massive trunk, suggesting it has been open-growing and protected for several centuries by generations of guardians from the reach of grazing animals. ///tidy.grudging.decreased

48. **SERPENT TREE**
*Père David's maple*
*Acer davidii*
University of Stirling,
Stirling FK9 4LA
56.144203, -3.9207560

Visit the University of Stirling to admire the striking, snake-skin-like bark of a Père David's maple in the raised bed outside the Logie Lecture Theatre and opposite the main reception. This decidedly un-maple-like maple is a small tree with barely lobed leaves, but in the autumn, winged samaras – or 'helicopter seeds' – will prove its *Acer* credentials. ///payer.clipboard.refrained

49. **WALLACE'S OAK**
*Pedunculate oak*
*Quercus robur*
Airthrey Castle,
Hermitage Road,
Stirling FK9 4LA
56.146548, -3.9136900

Among the youthful specimens of a recently planted arboretum at Airthrey Castle on the University of Stirling's campus, several veteran oaks show it to be a location where trees will do well. One giant individual stands out for its bulk and fine silhouette. It is doubly splendid when viewed from the south with the Wallace Monument, commemorating the Scots hero, in the distance beyond. ///culminate.education.parts

50. **STIRLING SYCAMORE**
*Sycamore / Acer pseudoplatanus*
Beechwood Park,
Stirling FK7 9AA
56.105043, -3.9432760

Despite its name, Beechwood Park is noteworthy not for its beech trees, but rather a fine eighteenth-century sycamore, the most perfectly shaped in an old row that marks the park's boundary with Stirling High School. It has a strong, flared bole and a broad canopy, and could one day reach the mammoth proportions of trees like the **RETIRING SYCAMORE (47)**. ///branded.super.oldest

WALLACE'S OAK (49)

## EASTERN SCOTLAND

*Aberdeenshire*
*Moray*
*Clackmannanshire*
*Falkirk*
*West Lothian*
*Midlothian*
*City of Edinburgh*
*East Lothian*
*Fife*
*Dundee City*
*Angus*
*Aberdeen City*

**TREE CITY:**
*Edinburgh*

**SIGNATURE SPECIES:**
*Camperdown elm*

Scotland's largest cities, bar Glasgow, are concentrated on the east coast, and they are all thickly treed. The climate on this side of Scotland is drier than in the west, and temperatures on summer days can soar into the high twenties. But winters are harsh, and trees in this region must be able to cope with icy conditions – in Aberdeen, average winter temperatures barely reach 3°C. It's clear that some species are at their northern limits up here. London planes, for instance, can be seen in Edinburgh and Dundee – the **DEBATABLE PLANE (63)** is perhaps the most northerly – but not in Aberdeen.

It will come as no surprise that Scotland's capital city, Edinburgh (like its biggest, Glasgow), has exceptional trees, but there are others not far behind. The granite city, Aberdeen, has been planting trees for a long time, and was noted in the nineteenth century for its pioneering work in this regard. Along with St Andrews, it was in the vanguard of Scottish street-tree planting during the 1860s. Not to be outdone, Dundee has several vintage trees right in its city centre, like the **ROSEANGLE PLANE (67)**.

Beech trees, despite being a species native to southern England, do well throughout Scotland, and many soaring examples can be seen up here. But it is this region's elms that really stand out. In the nineteenth century there was an elm revolution: horticulturalists developed and distributed myriad types, each with specific features affecting, for instance, leaf size or colour, branch trajectory, or eventual size. Several wych elm cultivars from this period originated, and can still be found, in eastern Scotland. Some, like the Blandford elm, are now very rare, but two – the tabletop and Camperdown elms, can still be encountered across the region, although Dutch elm disease continues to take its toll.

These remarkable east-coast elms are a legacy of the early civic planting era, when the species was favoured as a reliable, sturdy tree, impervious to cool summers and salt-laden air from the North Sea. That is, until Dutch elm disease arrived. Sadly, many elms, particularly in Aberdeen, have been lost to the disease. Surviving Aberdonians like

SCOTLAND 40

the **SPLIT THE WINDS TREE (54)** and the **MITHER KIRK ELM (56)** should therefore be dearly cherished. Edinburgh has the richest elm collection – indeed it is one of the finest anywhere in the world – and includes great rarities like the **UMBRELLA ELM (96)** on Bruntsfield Links and the **SCARCE SUPERBA (78)** in Leith.

Of the east-coast cities, Dundee is perhaps the greatest surprise. Scotland's fourth city is often overlooked by prospective visitors, but it is a verdant delight that has even given the world a tree originating from within its city limits – the Camperdown elm. Discovered by chance in the city's Camperdown Park, scions of this instantly recognisable, dramatically weeping tree have travelled the world. In order to propagate Camperdown elms (along with many other ornamental trees), a cutting from a parent tree, the 'scion', with all the genes that have caused the peculiar downward habit of the Camperdown's branches, must be grafted onto the upward-growing trunk, or 'stock', of a regular wych elm, allowing its pendulous cupola to be lifted off the ground. Tens of thousands of grafts have been taken from the original or from a scion, ensuring the continued survival of a charismatic dynasty.

Happily, the original parent tree, **THE CAMPERDOWN ELM (62)**, which is now approaching 200 years old, can still be tracked down in Camperdown Park. Its diminutive dome can be difficult to find in its retirement among the woods, but it is, in my opinion, well worth the effort. An easier spot is the **HOWFF WRAITH (64)**, one of the Camperdown's splendid offspring, which can be found growing in the old-established Howff graveyard – close to the DC Thomson building, home of the *Beano*, another of Dundee's great exports.

51. **KEITH CHESTNUT**
*Horse chestnut*
Aesculus hippocastanum
Bridge Street,
Keith AB55 5HJ
57.538392, -2.9485690

The A96 is enlivened at Keith by a very fine horse chestnut that marks the town's commercial centre. Your eye will be drawn to its copious canopy, an interesting green bulb offering a visual respite on the otherwise uniformly straight road. It even shades its own mini-piazza on the corner of Bridge Street. /// smelter.broadens.fruity

52. **AULD ALLIANCE SYCAMORE**
*Sycamore / Acer pseudoplatanus*
Seaton Park, Don Street,
Old Aberdeen,
Aberdeen AB24 1XS
57.170831, -2.1009810

Handsome Seaton Park hosts many fine trees. The most memorable is a hulking 250-year-old sycamore that casts substantial shade on the grassed area to the east of the charismatic Cathedral Walk. This tree is thought to be a daughter of saplings planted in the fifteenth century to mark the renewal of the Auld Alliance between Scotland and France in their many wars against England. /// shorts.sculpture.hurray

53. **CRUICKSHANK ROBLE**
*Roble / Nothofagus obliqua*
Cruickshank Botanic
Garden, St Machar Drive,
Aberdeen AB24 3UU
57.16854, -2.105162
*Check opening times.*

Cruickshank Botanic Garden is a small oasis in Old Aberdeen packed with delightful trees that will enthral any tree hunter. Among the dozens of noteworthy specimens in the arboretum, the giant roble, a species of southern beech from Patagonia, stands out. Three thick trunks split at the base of this unusual tree, each propelling a portion of its voluminous crown to more than 20 metres. /// shower.shrimp.rival

54. **SPLIT THE WINDS TREE**
*Wych elm / Ulmus glabra*
Split the Winds Church,
Powis Place,
Aberdeen, AB25 3TT
57.157651, -2.109512

A buttressed trunk and great arching limbs, each with many decades of moss accumulation, ensure this grand old wych elm is an Aberdeen landmark. This status is aided by its prominent position by the church at Split the Winds, the junction with George Street. It is one of the largest and probably oldest urban trees of its type – only Sheffield's **NUMBER ONE ELM (287)** comes close. /// filed.appear.hours

55. **BON ACCORD SYCAMORE**
*Sycamore / Acer pseudoplatanus*
Union Terrace Gardens,
Union Terrace,
Aberdeen AB10 1NJ
57.147572, -2.104042

While it does not compete with some of Scotland's exceptional veteran sycamores for age or size, the tree that stands at the northern end of Union Terrace Gardens, near the Bon Accord planting display, is nevertheless an outstanding city landmark. High branches are covered in a thick coat of leaves from May to October, and a kink in its tall, slender trunk ensures you will notice this tree in the depths of winter too. /// across.crew.dive

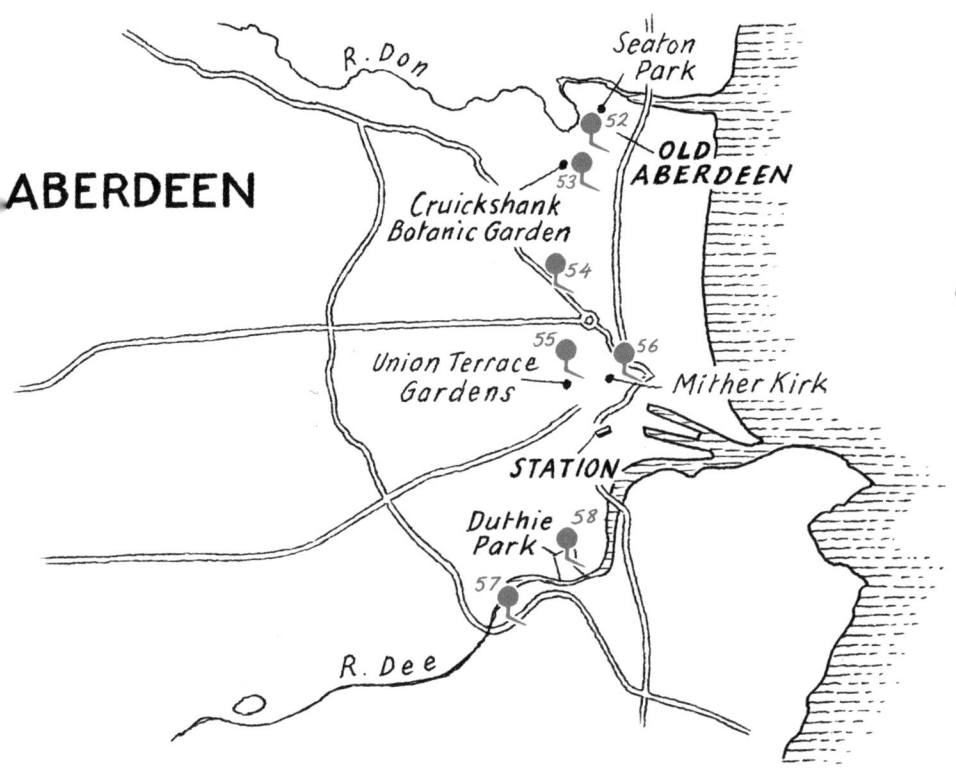

**56. MITHER KIRK ELM**
*Tabletop wych elm / Ulmus glabra 'Horizontalis'*
St Nicholas Kirkyard,
Union Street,
Aberdeen AB10 1JL
57.146925, -2.0991700

The old kirkyard of St Nicholas on Union Street, Aberdeen's main drag, offers a retreat into a quieter, greener world. Several elms are scattered among the crumbling stone memorials, but sadly most have succumbed to disease. The exception is a singular tabletop wych elm that spreads over Correction Wynd on the kirkyard's eastern side. ///vest.shed.fortunate

**57. GREAT SOUTHERN BEECH**
*Copper beech / Fagus sylvatica 'Purpurea'*
Great Southern Road,
Bridge of Dee,
Aberdeen AB12 5XA
57.122830, -2.1162840

Silver-grey beech bark is reminiscent of Aberdeen's granite cityscape. Like the buildings, it glistens in the sun, and is austere on less balmy days. It is appropriate, then, that the Great Southern Road, one of the main arteries into the city, has been planted with copper beeches. A particularly fine tree starts the avenue outside the Harvester, beside the Bridge of Dee roundabout. ///menu.backup.rides

**58. DUTHIE BEECH**
*Beech / Fagus sylvatica*
Duthie Park,
Polmuir Road,
Aberdeen AB11 7TH
57.129272, -2.1023020

Hardy beech trees thrive in north east Scotland, and the Duthie Beech has taken so kindly to the formal surroundings of Duthie Park that it has developed ten metres or more of smooth, unbranched trunk. Perhaps it once had to jostle for light within a group, but now it stands in splendid isolation towering over the boating pond. /// combining.kicks.placed

**59. EDZELL GRANNY PINE**
*Scots pine / Pinus sylvestris*
High Street, Edzell,
Brechin DD9 7TF
56.80556, -2.653886

In January 2023, a storm ripped through Edzell, flattening most of the trees in the plantation on the village's southern edge. Of the few survivors, an old Scots pine stands next to the golf club. Its thick trunk soon becomes a mass of twisting, orange-barked branches – hinting that it is no regimented plantation tree. In the nearby Cairngorms, similar solitary trees are known as granny pines. This one could soon be surrounded by a throng of grandchildren. /// overheard.bounty.ranged

**60. THE DIBBLE TREE***
*Cricket bat willow*
*Salix alba 'Caerulea'*
Ferrier Street,
Carnoustie DD7 7HT
56.500229, -2.7135910

At over 200 years old, The Dibble Tree is older than the coastal town of Carnoustie itself. It grew from a planting stick, or 'dibble', left in the ground in 1797. Now, it is firmly on the Carnoustie sightseeing circuit, with an interpretation board and a local theatre named after it. But, for tree hunters, it is most remarkable for being a willow, a genus that rarely lives a century, let alone two. /// stored.producers.websites

**61. BURRY MAN TREE**
*Monkey puzzle*
*Araucaria araucana*
Camperdown Park,
Dundee DD2 4TD
56.484759, -3.0416910

Once you've passed the splendid preamble of oaks and sycamores lining the drive, Camperdown Park's most eye-catching tree is surely the exceptional monkey puzzle on the lawn close to the house. It is a great Burry Man of a tree, with an extravagant pelt of pendulous, spiny tentacles covering the entire trunk from the ground up. /// mess.talked.heartened

**62. THE CAMPERDOWN ELM***
*Camperdown elm*
*Ulmus glabra 'Camperdownii'*
Camperdown Park,
Dundee DD2 4TD
56.482441, -3.042033

Tucked away near the wildlife centre in Camperdown Park, a fabulously contorted cascading dome of an elm can be found. Around 1835, this individual was discovered growing in nearby woods and was transplanted here. Every other Camperdown elm is a scion of this little tree. Being the original, this one has not been grafted onto a standard wych elm, so it remains a small, old and distinguished parent. /// sports.taxed.sideboard

DUTHIE BEECH (58)

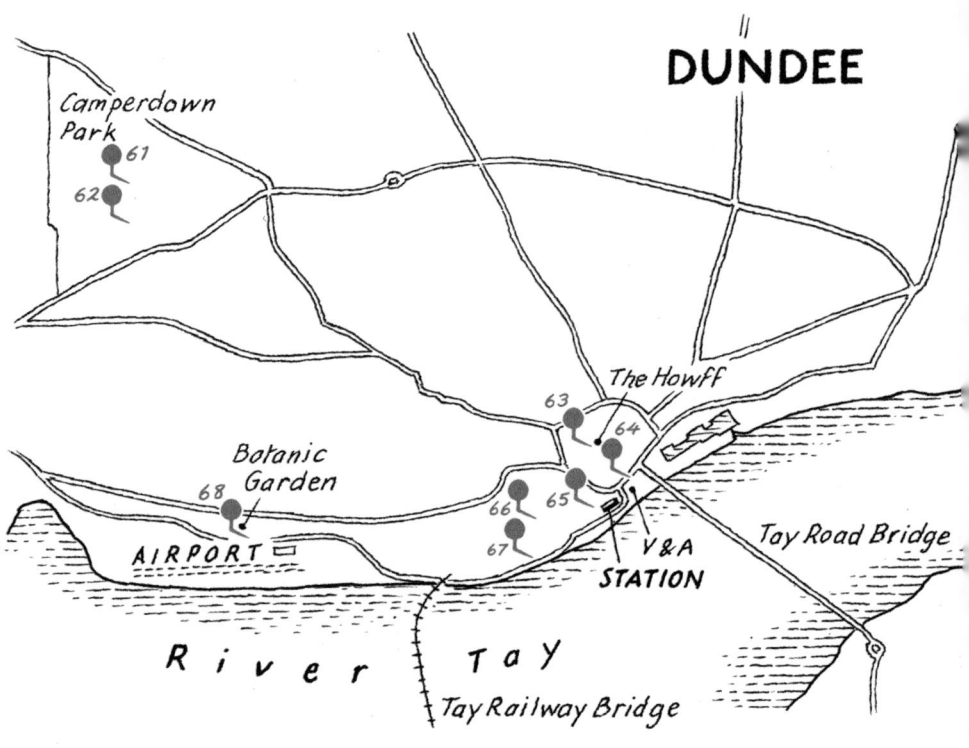

63. **DEBATABLE PLANE**
    *London plane*
    *Platanus* × *hispanica*
    Bernard King Library,
    West Bell Street,
    Dundee DD1 1HG
    56.462524, -2.9767240

The modern library of Abertay University looks out on a much older neighbour, a gnarly old plane. Get close to examine twin trunks growing around a hollow base, and to admire what may be the most northerly plane in Scotland. It is about the same vintage as the ROSEANGLE PLANE **(67)**, and it is worth comparing the two: the leaves of this tree are incised, but those of the Roseangle tree are more so; that tree is certainly an oriental plane, but could this possibly be one too? ///cares.future.loads

64. **HOWFF WRAITH**
    *Camperdown elm*
    *Ulmus glabra*
    *'Camperdownii'*
    The Howff, Meadowside,
    Dundee DD1 1AA
    56.461258, -2.9728719

Eerie Howff graveyard, a Grade A listed site dating back to 1564, is resplendent with the supernatural silhouettes of its elms. Most are tabletop elms, but at the southern end, the finest is a scion of THE CAMPERDOWN ELM **(62)**, but this one has been grafted at human head height onto a standard wych elm. Get under the canopy to examine the extreme contortions of its branches, most spectacular in winter. ///class.insist.oldest

SCOTLAND 46

### 65. NETHERGATE ELM
*Tabletop wych elm / Ulmus glabra 'Horizontalis'*
St Andrew's RC Cathedral, Nethergate, Dundee DD1 4EA
56.457619, -2.9748980

St Andrew's Cathedral is an unassuming Victorian affair, made remarkable by a fabulous tabletop wych elm, a frequent occupant of kirkyards, growing in a postage stamp of ground to the left of its front door. Sometimes known as a weeping elm, *'Horizontalis'* elms originate from Perth. Their silhouette brings to mind a cedar of Lebanon. /// dearest.copy.engineers

### 66. TREE OF LIBERTY*
*Ash / Fraxinus excelsior*
Duncan of Jordanstone College of Art and Design, Perth Road, Dundee DD1 4HT
56.456757, -2.9836800
*Located next to the steps between the Crawford and Matthew Buildings.*

This young ash is the latest iteration of the Tree of Liberty, a tree 'borrowed' from a nearby garden in 1793 and transplanted to the town centre in an act of solidarity with French revolutionaries by rebellious Dundonians. Dundee's Provost was forced to walk around it shouting 'Liberty and equality forever!' Soon after, however, he stealthily had the tree moved back to its original position – its repatriation took place 'in the quiet of a Sabbath morning', when the agitators were sleeping. /// severe.kettles.kebab

### 67. ROSEANGLE PLANE
*Oriental plane Platanus orientalis*
Roseangle, Dundee DD1 4LR
56.455220, -2.9835820
*In a private garden, but visible from the street.*

In the sheltered south-facing garden next to the Roseangle Gallery grows a mature oriental plane that was probably planted at the same time as the handsome Victorian villa behind it was built. It is quite a size, with a broad canopy shading the street. It may be the most northerly of its type in Britain, suggesting the species might make a fine tree, given similar conditions, even further north. /// january.stag.unlimited

### 68. BOTANICAL BEE-BEE
*Bee-bee tree Tetradium daniellii*
Dundee Botanic Garden, Riverside Drive, Dundee DD2 1QH
56.455490, -3.0230040
*Paid entry.*

Dundee's Botanic Garden, just across the road from the airport, is an arboreal treasure house. Established in 1970, it houses a significant collection of maturing trees, many beautiful, and some very rare. Among the rarities is an Asian bee-bee tree, one of the largest in Scotland, which can be admired from the café. Look out for masses of pollinators buzzing around its flowers in May. /// scavenger.debating.army

### 69. BALMERINO CHESTNUT*
*Sweet chestnut Castanea sativa*
Balmerino Abbey, Balmerino Village, Newport-on-Tay DD6 8SB
56.409969, -3.0409110

Fife's oldest tree is an arresting sweet chestnut. Twisted branches, some dead, flail from two main trunks that branch close to the ground. It is secured behind a fence in the grounds of ruined Balmerino Abbey, a few miles down the road from Newport-on-Tay. Studies by the National Trust for Scotland conclude it is about 450 years old. /// mural.coasted.contexts

HOWFF WRAITH (64)
ROSEANGLE PLANE (67)

70. **FIFE'S OLDEST YEW**
*Yew / Taxus baccata*
St Athernase Kirk, School
Hill, Leuchars KY16 0HB
56.381697, -2.8834550

Romanesque St Athernase Kirk, in the Fife town of Leuchars, is one of Scotland's oldest and loveliest. In its kirkyard grow several low and neatly canopied yews. Most are relatively young, but the stoutest has an impressive girth, suggesting it has been here for many centuries, although it is still a youngster compared to the ancient FORTINGALL YEW* **(28)**, 60 miles to the west in Perthshire. /// bibs.sober.officials

71. **QUEEN MARY'S THORN***
*Hawthorn*
*Crataegus monogyna*
St Mary's College,
South Street,
St Andrews KY16 9JP
56.338953, -2.7944660

Visit St Andrews in May to see the reclining, multi-limbed Queen Mary's Thorn in flower. It grows in the quad of St Mary's College, and is believed to have been planted by Mary Queen of Scots in the 1560s. Hawthorns are known for their long lives, but this one is truly ancient, relying on numerous supports to keep it from entirely collapsing. /// metals.brick.firepower

72. **ST MARY'S OAK***
*Holm oak / Quercus ilex*
St Mary's College,
South Street,
St Andrews KY16 9JP
56.339087, -2.7941730

Close to QUEEN MARY'S THORN **(71)**, grows the comparatively young, but much larger, St Mary's Oak. It is a broad-canopied evergreen holm oak, which is claimed to have been planted around 1740 (an early date for this species). Holm oaks originate from southern Europe and are rare in Scotland, but judging by this, one of the most northerly trees, they can thrive up here. /// kickbacks.oxidation.spooned

73. **THE KING TREE***
*Sweet chestnut*
*Castanea sativa*
Chestnut Crescent,
Dunipace,
Denny FK6 6LF
56.026129, -3.9195360

Despite its great age of around 450 years, The King Tree is in relatively sound condition, and may yet survive another century or more in this unlikely spot, close to the kerb on Chestnut Crescent, in the shadow of the M80. It stands in what was once the grounds of Herbertshire Castle and is now an interwar housing estate. Come in the autumn to seek out a prickly chestnut. /// truckload.clauses.delays

74. **FORTH BRIDGE YEW**
*Yew / Taxus baccata*
Hawes Inn,
Newhalls Road, South
Queensferry EH30 9TA
55.990338, -3.3843320

The iconic Forth Rail Bridge, one of three mighty bridges each built in a different century to span the Firth of Forth, soars above the finest yew tree in West Lothian, which nestles in the garden of the Hawes Inn. The inn dates from 1638, and the yew is probably the same age. Its shade is a fine place to admire the view and to ponder the various river crossings the tree has witnessed over the last four centuries. /// learn.finders.named

SCOTLAND

THE KING TREE* (73)

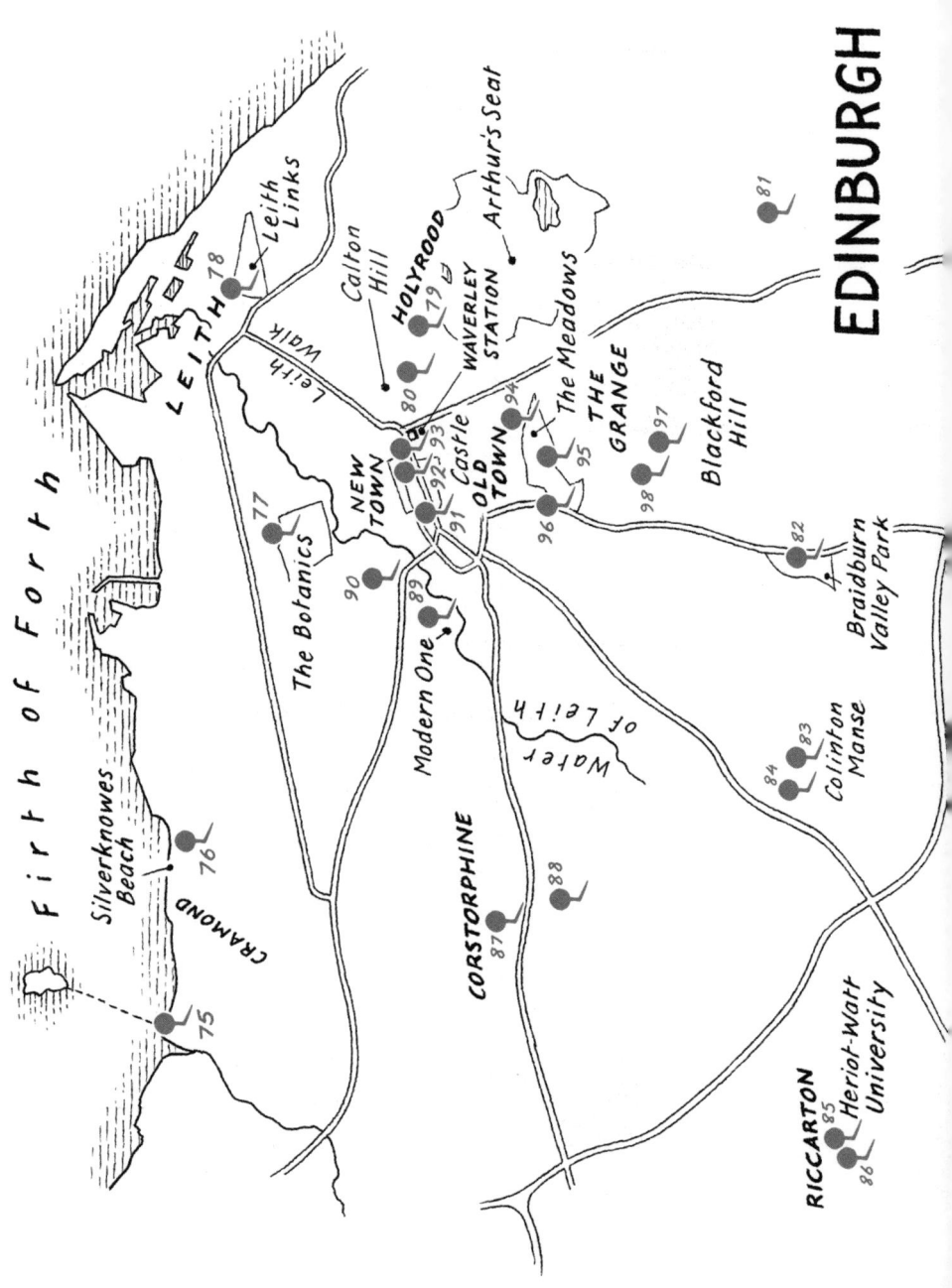

# TREE CITY: EDINBURGH
## SIGNATURE SPECIES: *Corstorphine plane*

Head up to the summit of Blackford Hill in the south of Edinburgh, and you'll be met with fantastic views across the city to the Firth of Forth. Stretching from the airport in the west to Musselburgh in the east, the city will appear before you as a tract of woodland within which low-rise buildings nestle, with the castle, cathedral spires and the great volcanic slab of Arthur's Seat rising above the canopy. Immediately below lies The Grange, one of Edinburgh's leafiest suburbs, where the wealth of the city's trees is particularly apparent.

Edinburgh is a city known for its elms, a significant and diverse collection of which have so far outwitted Dutch elm disease, due in no small part to the vigilance of the City Council. The **ROYAL ELM (79)** is the rarest; it is a Wentworth elm, a type represented by just two specimens anywhere in the world, both in Edinburgh. Despite quietly growing next to the Palace of Holyroodhouse for more than a century, they were only positively identified in 2016. I wonder what else is yet to be discovered lurking in the verdant Scottish capital?

Of course, no visit to Edinburgh is complete without taking in the Royal Botanic Garden's world class tree collection. Dozens of champion trees are here – that is, trees with the greatest height or girth for their species. But I was particularly drawn to a relatively small specimen: the **PALM HOUSE PAPERBARK (77)**, an exceptional example of an attractive east-Asian maple species, with peeling, copper-coloured bark, that presides over a lawn near the famous palm houses.

Over two-and-a-half centuries, beautiful Edinburgh has come to understand the importance of trees in defining and ennobling a place. When the New Town was developed, green spaces like Queen Street Gardens, now thickly forested with mature trees, were key to attracting the emerging Georgian middle classes. This set the tone for the later landscapes of Princes Street Gardens, the Botanics and residential areas like Craiglockhart, which all contribute to a bosky city. The council has worked hard to plant and maintain large trees over generations, and many rare specimens, installed in collaboration with the Botanics, await discovery throughout the city.

Trees from all across the globe can be admired here, and in return Edinburgh has given the world Corstorphine planes, a sycamore cultivar that originated centuries ago at Corstorphine Castle. It is unrelated to the London plane, despite its 'plane' moniker, but in decades past Scots applied this name to the sycamore maple, probably because of the two species' similarly shaped leaves. It is a tree to look out for in the early spring, when it produces stunning golden leaves quite unlike those of a regular sycamore, which appear later and are, by comparison, an unremarkable green. Dozens of Corstorphine planes are planted across Edinburgh and beyond. You can pay homage to this legacy by visiting **CORSTORPHINE'S PLANE (88)** in the kirkyard of that west Edinburgh suburb.

PALM HOUSE PAPERBARK (77)

75. **ROMAN LIME**
*Common lime*
*Tilia × europaea*
Cramond Kirk, Cramond
Glebe Road, Cramond,
Edinburgh EH4 6NS
55.978237, -3.2993100

Trees do well in Cramond's fertile soils, close to the River Almond as it feeds into the North Sea on Edinburgh's western edge. Behind a charming fifteenth-century kirk, growing on what was once the perimeter wall of a Roman fort, a giant Victorian common lime, the loftier and more strident of a pair, commands your attention as it towers effortlessly above the church tower. /// drive.open.eagle

76. **SUBLIME PINE**
*Scots pine*
*Pinus sylvestris*
Silverknowes Beach,
Marine Drive,
Edinburgh EH4 5EP
55.979692, -3.2674820

The Sublime Pine is a lonesome tree, surrounded by tarmac while its pals are grouped together on the nearby grass. Its crooked form is particularly romantic when seen from the landward side, looking out over the Firth of Forth with Inchkeith in the distance. Edinburgh's most picturesque tree is worthy of Caspar David Friedrich. /// weds.elaborate.crib

77. **PALM HOUSE PAPERBARK**
*Paperbark maple*
*Acer griseum*
Royal Botanic Garden,
Arboretum Place,
Edinburgh EH3 5NY
55.966810, -3.2088880
*Check entry times.*

To select a representative tree from the Botanics is difficult. As well as being one of the finest arboretums in the world, stuffed to the gills with remarkable trees, it is one of Edinburgh's most cherished green spaces and is freely accessible to all. This beautiful tree in front of the nineteenth-century palm houses is guaranteed to catch your attention: a small but perfectly formed paperbark maple with rufous, cinnamon-coloured bark. ///pitch.lease.pest

78. **SCARCE SUPERBA**
*Blandford elm*
*Ulmus glabra 'Superba'*
Links Gardens, Leith,
Edinburgh EH6 7EB
55.969343, -3.1651480

There are fewer than ten known Blandford elms in the world, and three are in Edinburgh. The benchmark tree is on the Hermitage Place side of Leith Links, opposite the Culane House hotel. Superb, extra-large leaves (for an elm) characterise this very rare wych elm cultivar, a plant developed in a nursery in the Dorset town of Blandford Forum during the 1840s. /// motion.bits.duke

79. **ROYAL ELM**
*Wentworth elm*
*Ulmus × hollandica 'Wentworthii Pendula'*
Palace of Holyroodhouse,
Canongate,
Edinburgh EH8 8DX
55.952094, -3.1705920
*Paid entry.*

Two Wentworth elms have survived in the garden of Holyroodhouse since 1909, but were only 'discovered' in 2016. They are the last known trees of this gently weeping variety in the world, but you have to buy a ticket – or, if you are lucky, get invited to a garden party – to see them. The taller and more splendid tree stands proudly on the lawn to the south of the palace. /// silks.calls.cones

## 80. HIDDEN TULIP TREE
*Tulip tree*
*Liriodendron tulipifera*
Dunbar's Close Garden,
Canongate,
Edinburgh EH8 8BW
55.951959, -3.1787810

Dunbar's Close Garden is a little gem, accessible through a discreet alley next to the seventeenth-century Canongate Kirk. It was formally laid out in the 1970s, and is notable for a leaning, low-branching tulip tree, a species easy to identify by its squared-off leaves, but one rarely encountered in Scotland. It is the centrepiece of the knot garden, surrounded by a quartet of more workaday whitebeams. /// builds.system.waddled

## 81. REMINDER REDWOODS
*Giant redwood*
*Sequoiadendron giganteum*
Greenpark,
Edinburgh EH17 7TA
55.914551, -3.1471560

It feels like a small victory for common sense when old trees grow among new housing. A single green skyscraper, actually a pair of towering giant redwoods, are miraculous survivors of a previous landscape, having managed to find their place among the low-rise apartment blocks of the modern Greenpark development off Gilmerton Road. /// rope.sang.jokes

## 82. BRAIDBURN ROW TREE
*Wheatley elm*
*Ulmus minor 'Sarniensis'*
Comiston Road,
Edinburgh EH10 6HD
55.912961, -3.2137460

For those arriving in Edinburgh by road from the Borders in the south, the first Wheatley elm in the Braidburn Row is a familiar natural landmark. It is superbly tall and regular, with an almost coniferous silhouette soaring above a bus stop on Comiston Road. The row of trees forms the boundary of Braidburn Valley Park and is the finest line of these stately trees anywhere in Britain or Ireland. /// stacks.minute.ruler

## 83. SIXPENNY TREE*
*Small-leaved lime*
*Tilia cordata*
Colinton Road,
Edinburgh EH13 0LB
55.908487, -3.2519970

Where Redford Road joins Colinton Road, a lone lime stands on a traffic island. It is a young tree, the latest iteration of the historic Sixpenny Tree. It was either the centrepiece around which people danced holding a sixpence or, more likely, where factory workers employed in mills on the nearby Water of Leith paid their dues of sixpence to the Paper Makers' Union. /// clubs.shack.extend

## 84. ROBERT LOUIS STEVENSON'S YEW
*Yew / Taxus baccata*
Colinton Parish Church, Dell Road,
Edinburgh EH13 0JR
55.908891, -3.2555570

*Below the yew – it is still there –*
*Our phantom voices haunt the air . . .*

So wrote Robert Louis Stevenson in 1887 about the garden of his childhood home at Colinton Manse. The same yew, a fluted, 400-year-old elder statesman, now competes for space with the Swing Café, from where it is possible to view the tree, complete with child's swing attached. /// cakes.latter.elder

**85. HANDSOME MAGYAR**
*Hungarian oak*
*Quercus frainetto*
Heriot-Watt University,
Riccarton Campus,
Edinburgh EH14 4AS
55.909376, -3.3199340

Hungarian oaks do well in Scotland, as the tree next to Heriot-Watt's main entrance attests. It is a strapping, straight-trunked tree with a typically dense, egg-shaped crown. Although Hungarian oaks are close in appearance to our two native oak species, their leaves are distinctly larger and their overall stature is more powerful. /// rapid.memory.length

**86. RICCARTON CEDAR** → All that remains of Riccarton House are the trees that once surrounded it. When Heriot-Watt University took over the estate, many trees were retained and now form a green oasis in the middle of campus. There are dozens of veterans and rarities here, and I was particularly drawn to the double-trunked western red cedar with its chestnut-brown bark worn smooth by decades of climbing and carousing.

**RICCARTON CEDAR**
*Western red cedar*
*Thuja plicata*
Heriot-Watt University,
Riccarton Campus,
Edinburgh EH14 4AS
55.908676, -3.3231570
/// boot.gates.lazy

87. **BLACKSMITH'S TREE**\*
*Copper beech / Fagus sylvatica 'Purpurea'*
St John's Road,
Corstorphine,
Edinburgh EH12 7UU
55.943146, -3.2865850

'The future influences the present just as much as the past,' declares a plaque next to the Blacksmith's Tree. It is a quote from Friedrich Nietzsche and an appropriate comment about the young tree, an early-2000s replacement for a vast copper beech that once shaded a blacksmith's shop here. It reminds us of the past, while its youthful potential makes us wonder what it will become in centuries hence. /// closes.pest.dangerously

88. **CORSTORPHINE'S PLANE**
*Corstorphine plane Acer pseudoplatanus 'Corstorphinense'*
Corstorphine Old Kirk,
Corstorphine High Street,
Edinburgh EH12 7ST
55.941098, -3.2822010

The original Corstorphine plane was blown over in 1998. It was thought to be 400 years old, a survivor from the grounds of Corstorphine Castle, demolished in 1797. It is in fact a maple – a sycamore cultivar distinguished by an early-spring flush of cheering golden leaves. The Victorians loved them, and, with admirable foresight, planted a fine specimen to mark the entrance to Corstorphine Old Kirk. /// merit.fresh.factor

89. **MODERN ART CHESTNUT**
*Sweet chestnut Castanea sativa*
National Gallery of Modern Art, Belford Road,
Edinburgh EH4 3DR
55.951205, -3.2273360

Visit Modern One at the National Gallery of Modern Art to see Edinburgh's finest sweet chestnut tree. It is a stately individual that can be found within a group of younger colleagues, all sycamores. The definite spiral to its trunk, a typical feature of the species, is an indicator that it may be a contemporary of the 200-year-old neoclassical building – a tree of the old guard. /// chew.chew.views

90. **COMELY BANK PLANE**
*London plane Platanus × hispanica*
Comely Bank Road,
Edinburgh EH4 1HG
55.959425, -3.2158320

The Comely Bank Plane is the most elegant tree in a row of sixteen lining Comely Bank Road. The seventh from the Stockbridge end, it leans out over the road before arching back towards the light. This row would have been planted at the beginning of the twentieth century when the street was developed, and represents Edinburgh's best plane avenue, a rare sight in this northerly city. /// oldest.towers.will

91. **THE CONTORTIONIST**
*Camperdown elm / Ulmus glabra 'Camperdownii'*
The Parish Church of St Cuthbert, Lothian Road,
Edinburgh EH1 2EP
55.949480, -3.2046480

Elms come in all shapes and sizes, and St Cuthberts is home to one of the weirdest, in the form of a Camperdown elm, a wych elm cultivar from Dundee. Witness the extreme architecture of its canopy from the path sloping down into Princes Street Gardens: tight whorls held aloft on two boughs branching from the head-height graft point. /// misty.tone.goat

MODERN ART CHESTNUT (89)

## 92. RAMSAY TREE
*Wheatley elm / Ulmus minor 'Sarniensis'*
Princes Street,
Edinburgh EH2 2ER
55.951717, -3.1975190

Five towering Wheatley elms line Princes Street west of the Mound, the first shading a statue of Enlightenment poet Allan Ramsay. Wheatley elms were once a mainstay of British towns and cities, but disease has decimated their number, so the Ramsay Tree and its neighbours represent an invaluable part of our urban heritage; they lend distinction to Edinburgh's most important street, making it stand out from plane-lined streets in other cities. /// tapes.horns.skills

## 93. WAVERLEY ASH →→ 
Weeping ash trees were much favoured by Victorians, who frequently planted them as centrepieces in civic schemes, a job the tree in East Princes Street Gardens still performs with poise. It is a distinctive cultivar of the common European ash, and is thus susceptible to ash dieback. We must treasure this landmark tree, surrounded by many of Edinburgh's stone landmarks, while we can.

**WAVERLEY ASH**
*Weeping ash / Fraxinus excelsior 'Pendula'*
East Princes Street Gardens,
Edinburgh EH2 2EJ
55.951555, -3.1944850
/// tribes.truly.drip

### 94. JAWBONE WALK CHERRY
*'Kanzan' Japanese cherry*
*Prunus serrulata*
*'Kanzan'*
The Pavilion Café,
Melville Drive,
Edinburgh EH9 1JZ
55.940775, -3.1944850

The gaudy, pink blossom of The Meadows' much-admired *'Kanzan'* cherry trees indicate that spring has (finally) arrived. The blossom-lined walks act as a magnet for Edinburghers in late April. The marvellously named Jawbone Walk traverses north to south ending at the Pavilion Café, a good place to admire a particularly stout-trunked tree at the intersection of Jawbone and Coronation Walks. /// energetic.event.makes

### 95. MEADOWS APOGEE
*Wheatley elm / Ulmus minor 'Sarniensis'*
Meadow Place,
Edinburgh EH9 1JZ
55.940182, -3.1943880

The Wheatley elm is a tree that defines Edinburgh, and while many are found in avenues, like the BRAIDBURN ROW TREE (82) or the RAMSAY TREE (92), they also make exceptional specimen trees. You can see an outstanding individual with a full crown tapering to a fine pinnacle just beyond The Meadows on the corner of Melville Drive and Meadow Place, at the edge of Marchmont. /// decks.haven.spray

### 96. UMBRELLA ELM
*Spaeth's field elm*
*Ulmus minor*
*'Umbraculifera Gracilis'*
Alvanley Terrace,
Edinburgh EH9 1DU
55.937594, -3.2032510

Only three individuals of Spaeth's field elm are known: one is in the Botanics, one is in Ohio, and the third is here on Brunstfield Links. In the past, there was a programme of planting specimens of rare elm species around the city, and some have flourished into maturity. The cultivar name *'Umbraculifera Gracilis'* suggests a shade-giving tree with narrow leaves. That's about right. /// rope.bright.neck

### 97. VE DAY CEDAR
*Blue Atlas cedar / Cedrus atlantica 'Glauca'*
Newbattle Terrace,
Edinburgh EH10 4SF
55.929428, -3.1957370
*Access may be restricted during redevelopment.*

The Astley Ainslie Hospital opened in 1923 in the grounds of a grand villa in The Grange. The inherited arboretum surrounding the hospital proved to be a tonic for recuperating patients. The site is being redeveloped, so we must hope its astonishing trees will continue to prosper. The blue-grey foliaged Atlas cedar, planted on the first anniversary of VE Day in 1946, is one of many focal points. /// guides.decide.hurray

### 98. CHANDELIER PINE
*Bhutan pine*
*Pinus wallichiana*
Newbattle Terrace,
Edinburgh EH10 4SF
55.930156, -3.1989640

Soon after entering the grounds of Astley Ainslie at Grange Loan, past gatehouses and wrought iron gates, the road sweeps round to the original villa and an imposing, multi-trunked Bhutan pine. These are not usually long-lived trees, but this one is conspicuously aged, though it shows no sign of decrepitude, and seems to be thriving. /// ripe.slap.rewarding

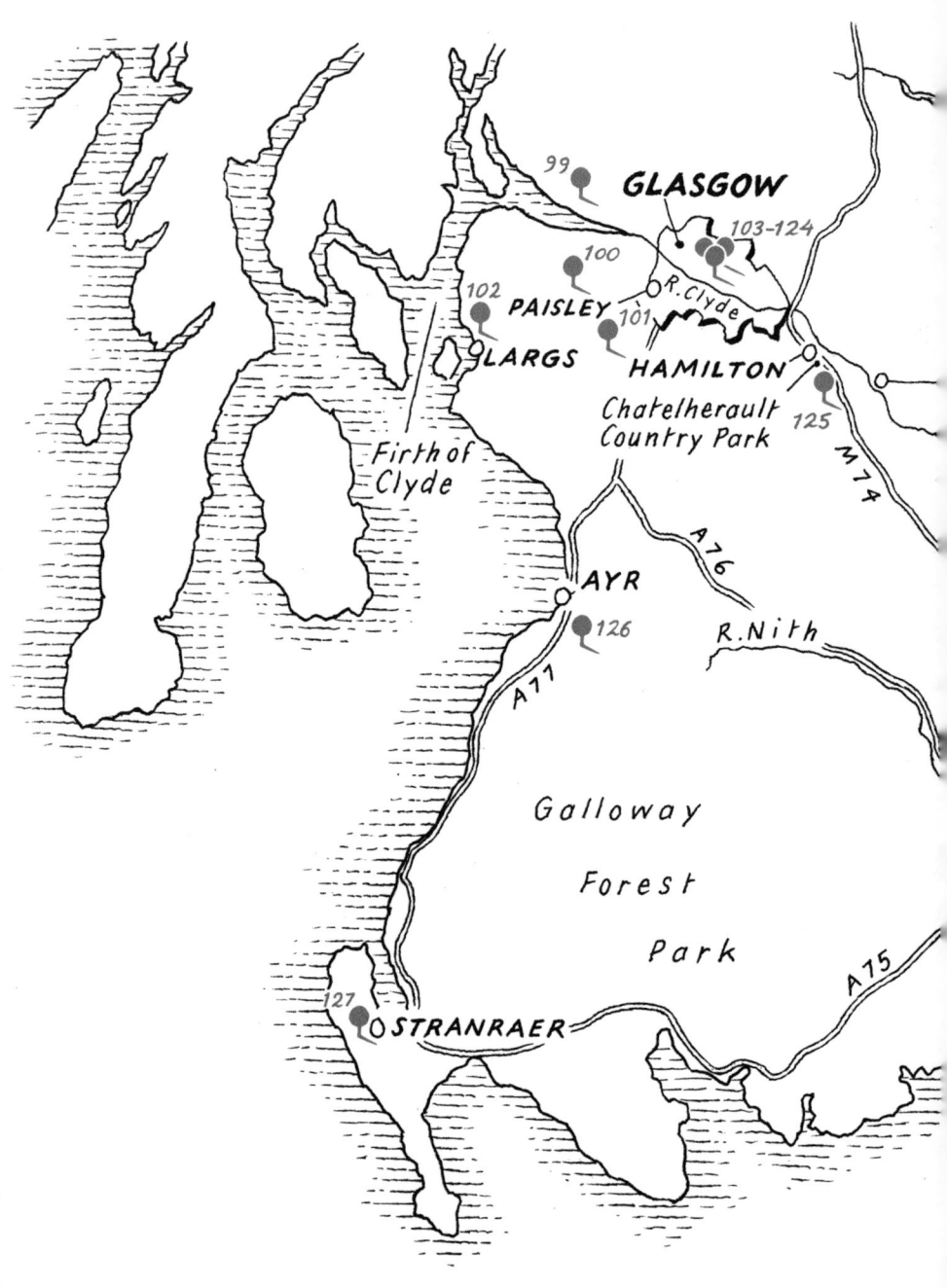

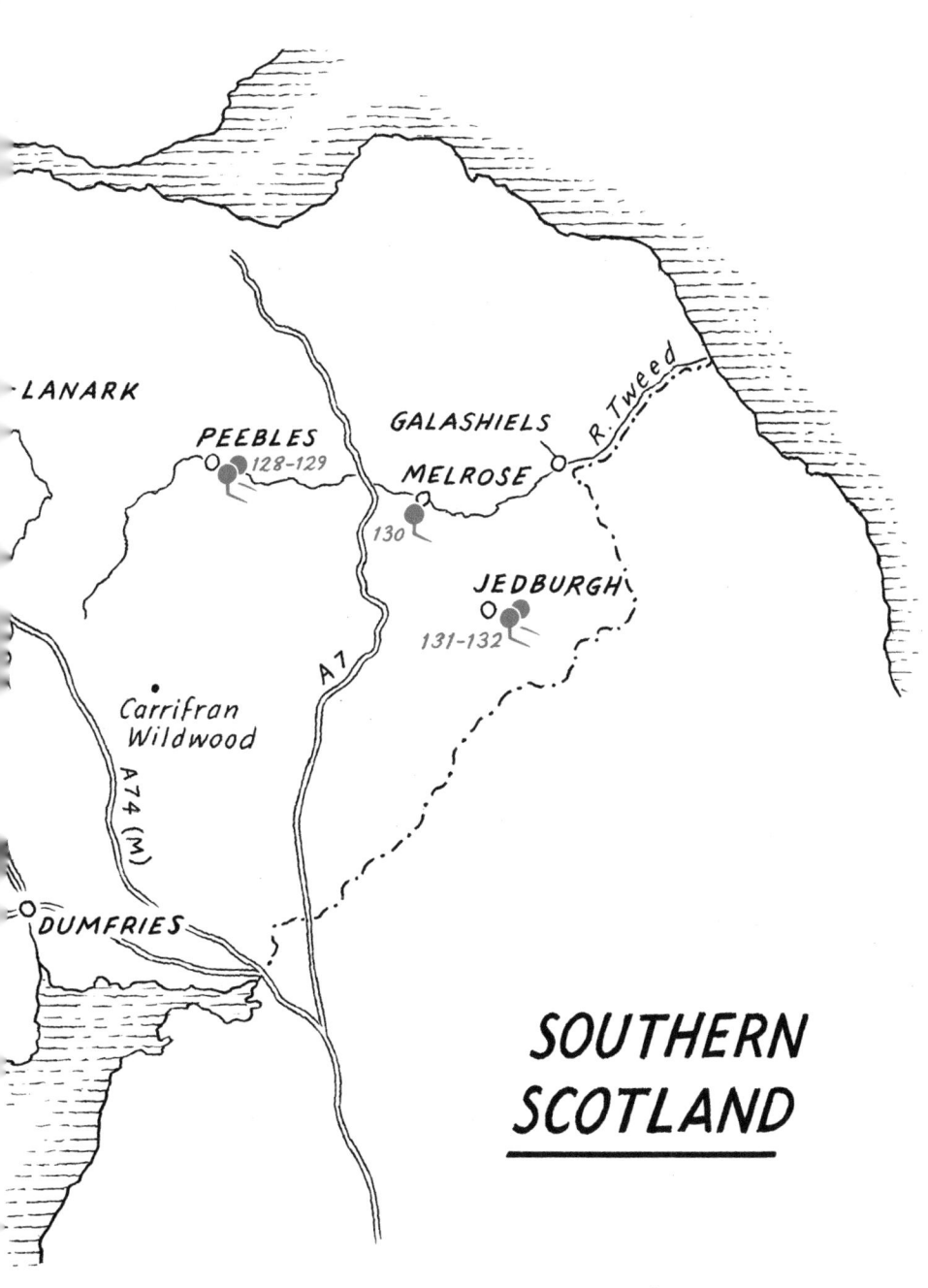

## SOUTHERN SCOTLAND

*East and West Dunbartonshire*
*Glasgow City*
*Renfrewshire*
*East Renfrewshire*
*Ayrshire*
*Dumfries & Galloway*
*Scottish Borders*
*North and South Lanarkshire*

TREE CITY:
*Glasgow*

SIGNATURE SPECIES:
*Sessile oak*

As you travel south beyond Glasgow, the relatively unpopulated and – compared to the Highlands – little-visited southern uplands begin. To the east, they are broken up by the river systems of the Nith, the Tweed and the Clyde, while rolling Ayrshire lies to the south west. Towns and villages like Ayr, Peebles and Jedburgh are spread right across this area: places steeped in the rich cultural, agricultural and industrial history of Scotland, and full of treasures for the tree hunter.

Unlike the more populous east coast, a single city – Scotland's largest – dominates this region. And, unlike its eastern counterparts, Glasgow has a distinct urban forest where elms are rare. Instead, ash and sycamore abound: the **ELDER ASH (116)** is a fine example of the former, while the **FIRE EXIT SYCAMORE (120)** shows just how successfully trees and architecture can interact. It is a constituent of the woods that grow only a metre or so from the plate glass of the Burrell Collection in the Pollok Estate: so close that the woodland appears as an installation, almost invited into the gallery space.

Towns like Hamilton, Johnstone and Dumbarton are now considered part of the Greater Glasgow area but, in each, fascinating historic trees remind us that these are distinct settlements that evolved on their own over the centuries before Glasgow became an industrial behemoth. Take Dumbarton, once the capital of the ancient Kingdom of Strathclyde: its former Strathleven estate has become an industrial estate, but Strathleven House remains intact, along with some of its gardens. Here, the centuries old **SENIOR FIELD MAPLE (99)** survives – remarkable both for being an unusual species in Scotland, and for having all the stoutness and irregular form of a very old tree. But the jewel in southern Scotland's crown must be the **CADZOW OAK\* (125)** and its companions in the Clyde Valley's Chatelherault Country Park. While sessile oaks are more common in this region and across Scotland, these oaks are pedunculate, the type more often associated with drier southern English regions. They are said to have been planted in 1314, and are in stately decline with all the rich deadwood, hollow cavities and associated biodiversity (like specialist sulphur tubic moths, and *Dictenidia bimaculata* – a dramatic cranefly known as the twin-mark comb-horn) that very old trees accumulate.

In Elderslie, a suburb of Johnstone, the **WALLACE YEW*** **(101)** marks the family estate where Scots hero William Wallace, who fought the forces of the English King Edward I in the First War of Scottish Independence, was born in 1270. Debate rages as to whether this now rather battered yew tree was here at Wallace's birth. But, not far away, a tree that almost certainly was alive 800 years ago can be seen. The **CRAIGENDS YEW*** **(100)** is remarkable for its vast size, attained by centuries of boughs arching downwards, and eventually layering: taking root in the soil where they touch down, causing new clonal offspring to spread around the original tree. Further afield, on the Ayrshire coast, the **KELBURN LARCH*** **(102)** near Largs, another great spreading tree, is an irresistible curiosity, while, at Alloway, one of Scotland's admirable old sycamores grows close to the ruins of the Auld Kirk and has a good claim, through age and location, to featuring as one of the Groaning Trees in Rabbie Burns's epic 'Tam o' Shanter'.

In these more southerly latitudes, old oaks become ascendant, replacing the monumental sycamores further north. The lovely town of Jedburgh is famed for the **CAPON TREE*** **(132)**, an ancient, twisted sessile oak, a surviving constituent of the once extensive Jedforest. Its survival may have been aided by its isolated position on a sliver of land between the road and the Jed Water. Jedburgh's interest doesn't stop at the Capon Tree, however: the **JETHEART PEAR (131)** is a reminder of former times when the town was famed for its pear orchards. Many different varieties were grown, some sweet dessert fruit that we would be familiar with today, while others were tough old wardens, a term used for cooking-pears that, before potatoes, were an important staple, particularly valued as they would keep through the winter.

99. **SENIOR FIELD MAPLE** → Until 2004, Scotland's fattest pedunculate oak, the Bruce Tree – so called because a local legend claims it was planted by Robert the Bruce 600 years ago – grew in the grounds of Strathleven House on the edge of an industrial estate. It was set on fire by vandals, but out of its shadow a fabulously lumpy, long-overlooked field maple emerged, quite possibly Scotland's oldest, and it is now the area's most senior tree.

**SENIOR FIELD MAPLE** *Field maple / Acer campestre*
Strathleven House, Vale of Leven Industrial Estate, Dumbarton G82 3PD
55.969289, -4.570337  ///equipment.spider.handfuls

100. **CRAIGENDS YEW***
*Yew / Taxus baccata*
Gryfebank Crescent,
Houston,
Johnstone PA6 7NY
55.862616, -4.526264

One of the most awe-inspiring yews to be seen anywhere grows in the middle of a late-twentieth-century housing estate next to the river Gryfe. Unlike the ancient **FORTINGALL YEW*** **(28)** or the younger, upright **FORTH BRIDGE YEW** **(74)**, the Craigends Yew is remarkable for how, over centuries, branches have collapsed and regrown where they touch the soil, enabling this tree to boast a circumference of 100 metres. ///bottled.solutions.repay

101. **WALLACE YEW***
*Yew / Taxus baccata*
Main Road, Elderslie,
Johnstone PA5 9EN
55.835341, -4.488586

The Wallace Yew grows in what was once the family estate of William Wallace. You'll find the tree in a sorry state – damaged by storms and diminutive in stature – but, now well cared for, there are signs that she is beginning to revive. Yews are dioecious (meaning each individual is either male or female) and, this being a female, you may notice red fruits, a popular snack for blackbirds. ///stages.begins.wooden

102. **KELBURN LARCH***
*Weeping larch*
*Larix decidua 'Pendula'*
Kelburn Estate, Fairlie,
Largs KA29 0BE
55.770604, -4.844673

The famous larch at Kelburn is a worthy detour from the attractions of nearby seaside resort, Largs. It is a prodigiously unkempt tree that, in less than 200 years, has flopped its way across a large area of the lawn near Kelburn Castle. Compared to regular larches, which can reach great heights, like the **PARENT LARCH*** **(29)** at Dunkeld, the unusual undulatory form of this one is incredible. ///immune.stunning.surcharge

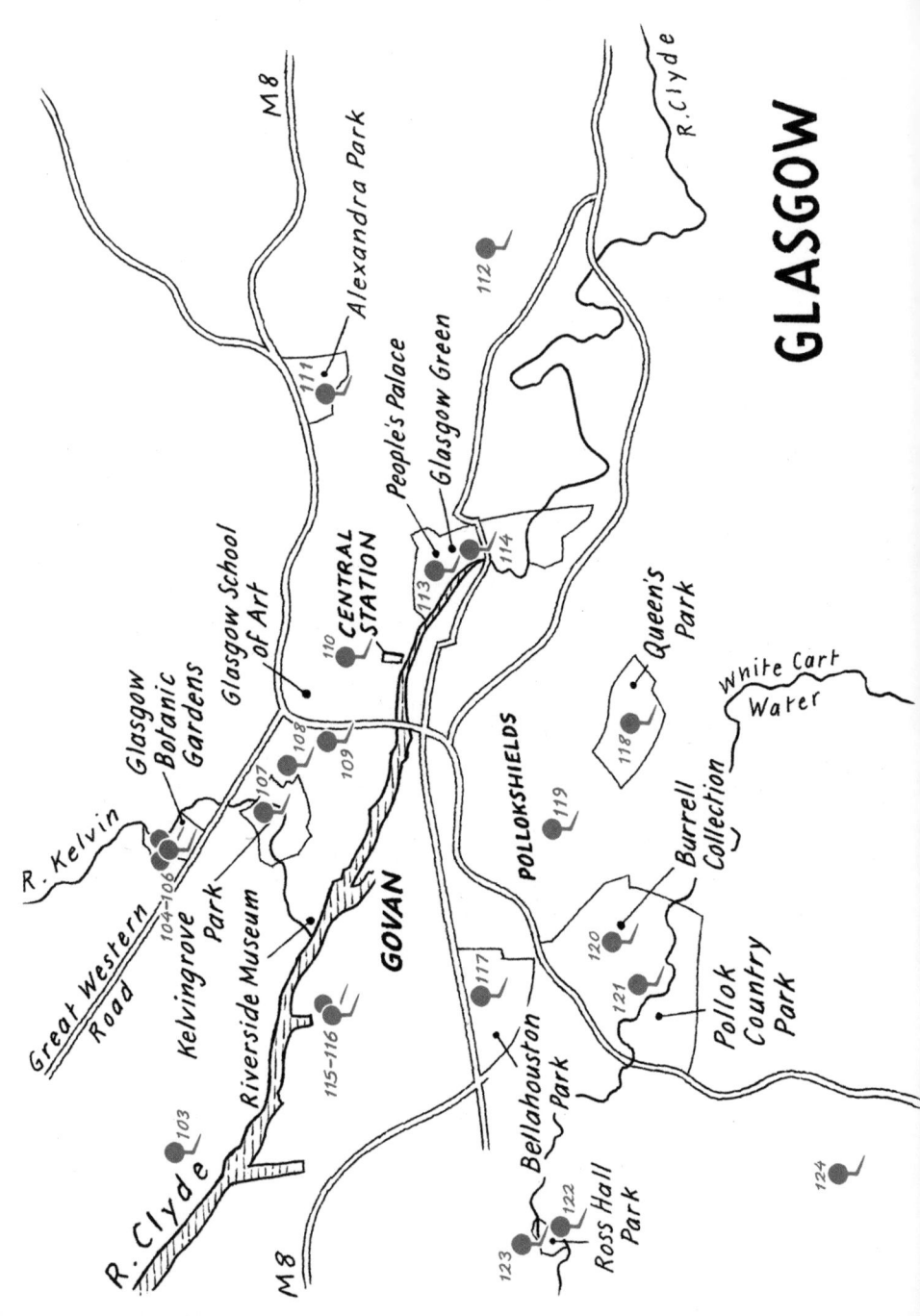

# TREE CITY: GLASGOW
## SIGNATURE SPECIES: *Hungarian oak*

On 20 April 1918, months before the end of the First World War, a Hungarian oak was planted in Kelvingrove Park in the presence of suffragist groups from across Scotland to mark the (limited) enfranchisement of women. Today, the **SUFFRAGE OAK\* (107)** is Glasgow's best-known tree, one that aptly represents Glasgow, a city that takes pride in championing progressive causes but does not hide its tangled past.

Along with internationally important cultural institutions and world-class architecture, a long history of political struggle, industrial might, great wealth and shocking poverty combine to give Scotland's biggest city its unique character. Its many trees form part of this story too. Glasgow is popularly known as the 'dear green place', a creative translation of the Gaelic *Glaschu*; its mild, damp climate – it is the rainiest city in Britain – ensures it is verdant.

As a result, trees flourish here. Glasgow's oldest tree is probably the **DARNLEY PLANE\* (124)**, although it is unlikely to be quite as old as the 500 years some claim for it. Another significant old tree is the **PRELAPSARIAN CHESTNUT (118)**, which predates Joseph Paxton's mid-nineteenth-century landscaping of Queen's Park, one of Glasgow's earliest urban green spaces. Like other great industrial cities, dozens of parks were laid out and opened to the public as the city expanded in the nineteenth and early-twentieth centuries. These places now boast some of Glasgow's greatest trees. One of the city's parks, Glasgow Green, is far older however: it has existed in one form or another since the Middle Ages, and, while no trees survive from that time, there are certainly many specimens that will reward the tree hunter.

Sycamores, along with ash and lime, have been the mainstays of historic urban tree-planting here, and fine examples of these species can be seen throughout the city. In the twentieth century, the city council planted a lot of hardy Swedish whitebeams which have likewise fared well. More recently, the palette has expanded, and the **GEORGE SQUARE MAPLE (110)** is typical of the more diverse planting carried out over the last thirty years.

While the working people of Glasgow have been shaded for many decades by relatively common species, the great and the good have enjoyed a more rarefied canopy. Trees that once grew in the grounds of their grand estates may now be enjoyed by all. Ross Hall Park, formerly an estate belonging to the Earls of Glasgow on the city's Southside, has a fine collection within a lushly intimate setting, while the huge Pollok Country Park, an estate gifted to the city by the Maxwell shipping-magnate family, boasts tracts of woodland, as well as the most northerly Lucombe oak featured in these pages.

But a highlight of Glasgow's tree diversity is the historic Botanic Gardens on the Great Western Road. Here dozens of rare, often mature trees can be found, epitomised by the **KIBBLE PALACE CHAMPION (106)**, the finest example I have encountered of a very unusual castor oil tree.

### 103. MIGHTY SWEDE
*Swedish whitebeam*
*Sorbus intermedia*
Queen Victoria Court,
Queen Victoria Drive,
Glasgow G14 9AX
55.879919, -4.351063
*In a private garden, but visible from the street.*

Glasgow's municipal tree-planters of decades past favoured the Swedish whitebeam. There are hundreds of these attractive trees around the city, mostly now mature. They are neat trees and relatively small, but seem to grow larger and live longer in the north. The Mighty Swede hanging over Queen Victoria Drive is one such tree – a giant among Swedish whitebeams, with the girth of a beech. ///waving.took.tummy

### 104. HA'PENNY ALDER
*Japanese alder*
*Alnus japonica*
Botanic Gardens
Arboretum, Kirklee
Road, Glasgow G12 0SS
55.88318, -4.289333

Upstream from the Botanic Gardens, just beyond the Ha'penny Bridge, you can explore its annex: the informal, less visited Arboretum. On the grassy bank sloping down to the River Kelvin are dozens of unusual trees. The most elegant of them is the Japanese alder, a tree rarely encountered, but one which ought to be. The multi-stemmed Ha'penny Alder stands out with graceful form and delicate leaves. ///couches.light.card

### 105. CACTUS MAPLE
*Oregon maple*
*Acer macrophyllum*
Wyndham Street,
Glasgow G12 0SS
55.882937, -4.291017

There should be more Oregon maples in Glasgow. Hanging over Wyndham Street in the furthest reaches of the Arboretum, a stately tree shows this species to be both magnificent and ideally suited to growing in the rainy west of Scotland. Enthusiastic tree hunters be warned: one reason they may be uncommon is that the minute hairs on the helicopter seeds can be very irritating if handled. ///serve.acute.popped

### 106. KIBBLE PALACE CHAMPION
*Castor oil tree*
*Kalopanax septemlobus*
Botanic Gardens,
Great Western Road,
Glasgow G12 0UE
55.878652, -4.288563

Castor oil trees are rare, and not, in fact, the source of castor oil; the glossy leaves of this tree only resemble those of *Ricinus communis*, the true castor oil plant. The Kibble Palace Champion is a splendid curiosity. It has a trunk with venous grooves and ornamental leaves, and is a uniquely impressive example of its kind. Its splendour is enhanced by its position next to one of Glasgow's architectural gems. ///risks.digits.impact

### 107. SUFFRAGE OAK*
*Hungarian oak*
*Quercus frainetto*
Kelvin Way,
Glasgow G12 8LX
55.87151, -4.285491

The Suffrage Oak, planted in 1918 to mark the introduction of women's suffrage, was voted Scotland's Tree of the Year in 2015 by Scots of all genders. Despite growing in sheltered Kelvingrove Park, it was damaged in a 2017 storm; it is slowly recovering. You may be surprised to spot its large, wide leaves: it is a Hungarian rather than a native oak. ///await.guess.shine

KIBBLE PALACE CHAMPION (106)

GEORGE SQUARE MAPLE (110)

### 108. STAR OF THE CIRCUS
*Turkey oak / Quercus cerris*
Park Circus,
Glasgow G3 6BE
55.869246, -4.279147

Park Circus is in the heart of Glasgow's West End, and at its centre an oval private 'square' provides a green centrepiece. It has been planted with an array of trees in recent years, and on the south side a Turkey oak – with shaggy acorns and less rounded leaves than other oaks – hangs over the fence. In years to come this tree will likely become the Circus's dominant feature. ///panels.mute.divide

### 109. CHARING CROSS CHANCER
*Tulip tree*
*Liriodendron tulipifera*
Charing Cross,
Glasgow G3 7UJ
55.866955, -4.271602

Tulip trees are rare in Scotland, and when they have been planted, like the HIDDEN TULIP TREE (80) in Edinburgh or the pair outside the Kelvingrove Museum, they tend to be specimen trees planted to make a statement. It is a surprise then, to find a brave individual has been planted in a rather more inauspicious spot: at the base of the Charing Cross footbridge, within earshot of the M8. ///bunk.gifted.report

### 110. GEORGE SQUARE MAPLE
*Norway maple*
*Acer platanoides*
George Square,
Glasgow G2 1DU
55.861349, -4.249495

From Turkish hazels on Sauchiehall Street to Scots pines outside City of Glasgow College, interesting new trees are being planted across the city, introducing more diversity to the ash, sycamore and limes of decades past. Norway maples were installed in George Square in the early 2000s and one tree, closest to the City Chambers on the north side, is the poster child of a revitalised urban forest. ///lakes.translated.same

### 111. SARACEN ASH
*Manna ash*
*Fraxinus ornus*
Alexandra Park,
Glasgow G31 3LJ
55.864691, -4.208886

In the formal gardens near the entrance of Alexandra Park is the Saracen Fountain, an ornate black-and-gold cast-iron affair. The fountain is surrounded by a neat array of trees, including one of the most northerly manna ash trees I have found in these islands. It is a slow-growing species with a floss of creamy flowers in May and, happily, is more resistant to ash dieback than other ashes. ///stress.belong.chain

### 112. WINTER GARDENS OAK
*Hungarian oak*
*Quercus frainetto*
Tollcross Park, Wellshot Road, Glasgow G32 7AX
55.847442, -4.180868

If you have tracked down the storm-battered SUFFRAGE OAK* (107), Tollcross Park is worth a visit too, to see an established and undamaged Hungarian oak at its very best. It is a large, shapely dome growing opposite the park's Winter Gardens, beyond the formal rose beds. It is certainly the most striking tree here, as well as the largest. ///often.string.kept

### 113. PEOPLE'S PLANE
*London plane*
*Platanus × hispanica*
People's Palace,
Templeton Street,
Glasgow G40 1AT
55.851943, -4.237385

While harsher conditions mean London planes don't attain the great heights of those further south, they can become impressive trees. This is borne out by the tree growing by the People's Palace on Glasgow Green, one of the chunkiest and most memorable of Scottish planes. The palace was opened in 1898, but given the city's cool, growth-slowing summers, the tree may have been here before the palace. ///fever.hello.steep

### 114. CLYDESIDE WILLOW
*White willow / Salix alba*
Glasgow Green,
Glasgow G40 1HB
55.846822, -4.23676

The venerable Clydeside Willow has a distinct twist to its deeply fissured trunk, and is the most strident of several old white willows dotted along the banks of the Clyde at Glasgow Green. It has not been pollarded – a traditional willow-neatening regime – for decades, allowing thick branches to rise from its bole above head height. ///nuns.sands.flesh

### 115. SHIPYARD SYCAMORE
*Purple-leaved sycamore*
*Acer pseudoplatanus*
*'Spaethii'*
Elder Park, Govan Road,
Glasgow G51 4AA
55.861268, -4.327254

The last major shipyard on the Clyde, across the road from Elder Park, is a meagre reminder of Govan's vanishing maritime past. Those who lived and worked in this industrial heartland must have cherished Elder Park, opened in 1884 by philanthropist Isabella Elder in memory of her engineer husband, John. His statue stands near the park's finest purple-leaved sycamore, an upstanding example of a type that abounds here. ///branded.items.plus

### 116. ELDER ASH
*Ash / Fraxinus excelsior*
Elder Park, Govan Road,
Glasgow G51 4AA
55.862373, -4.323169

Ash trees are a key constituent of Glasgow's urban forest. Large individuals can be seen right across the city, so the looming threat of ash dieback weighs heavily in the dear green place. In Elder Park, a prominent tree – the park's biggest and maybe oldest – the Elder Ash, is an apt monument to the entire marvellous species. ///delay.cherry.vote

### 117. BELLAHOUSTON ALGERIAN
*Mirbeck's oak*
*Quercus canariensis*
Bellahouston Park,
Dumbreck Road,
Glasgow G41 5BW
55.845313, -4.317834

At the highest point of Bellahouston Park, a tangle of trees grows amidst the ruins of past edifices. The original Bellahouston House once stood here, as did Tait's Tower, the centrepiece of the 1938 Empire Exhibition. Of the trees, several unusual specimens lurk, including a Mirbeck's or Algerian oak, one of the most northerly examples, overlooking Mosspark to the south. Look out for its bright, glossy leaves. ///alert.funny.breed

118. **PRELAPSARIAN CHESTNUT**
*Sweet chestnut*
*Castanea sativa*
Queen's Park, Langside Road, Glasgow G42 9TZ
55.829223, -4.266585

Glasgow's history stretches back to its sixth-century founding by Saint Mungo, but few trees remain that have witnessed pre-industrial times, before the city's nineteenth-century expansion. One rare survivor of these more innocent days can be found on the southern edge of Queen's Park, in the shape of a wizened old sweet chestnut that predates the development of Glasgow's first Victorian park. ///repair.brass.town

119. **CLIMBERS' LIME** → Maxwell Park's near-recumbent silver pendent lime is a climbing tree par excellence, which has entertained generations of kids from Pollokshields and beyond. Many years ago it must have been partially uprooted, and in this precarious state it has remained, but it has managed to strengthen its connection with the ground, and happily copes with dozens of young climbers with, so far, no props to support it.

**CLIMBERS' LIME**
*Silver pendent lime*
*Tilia tomentosa*
*'Petiolaris'*
Maxwell Park, Terregles Avenue, Glasgow G41 4DQ
55.83836, -4.287846
///roofs.photo.divide

RAINFOREST MAPLE (123)

120. **FIRE EXIT SYCAMORE**
*Sycamore / Acer pseudoplatanus*
Burrell Collection,
2060 Pollokshaws Road,
Glasgow G43 1AT
55.831272, -4.307916

The modernist architecture of the Burrell Collection, set deep within the Pollok Estate, is surrounded on two sides by woods which press right up against the plate glass, distracting tree-enamoured visitors from the world-class exhibits within. From the fire exit midway along the museum's northern perimeter, the stoutest sycamore in the woods stands out. ///pints.tinsel.doll

121. **POLLOK OAK**
*Lucombe Oak Quercus × crenata 'Lucombeana'*
Pollok House Gardens,
Pollok House,
Glasgow G43 1AT
55.827337, -4.315404

At one time, the Pollok estate was famed for the superlative beech tree that grew on a mound in the gardens to the south east of Pollok House. The mound is still there, though the tree is not. But, below the mound, in a far less exposed position, a fabulous cork-barked Lucombe oak is a welcome surprise. It is a vast semi-evergreen tree, and one of the most northerly examples of its kind. ///wooden.spices.pinks

122. **GROTTO BEECH**
*Weeping beech Fagus sylvatica 'Pendula'*
Ross Hall Park,
Crookston Road,
Glasgow G52 3NW
55.838225, -4.36349

Formerly the gardens of neighbouring Ross Hall House, which is now a hospital, Ross Hall Park is a hidden oasis. In its magical rock garden and grotto, a fabulous weeping beech can be found. It is a tree that demands to be experienced by getting under its great mantle of extraordinary twisted branches, where you may startle blackbirds and robins who have had the same idea. ///trendy.bigger.shower

123. **RAINFOREST MAPLE**
*Japanese maple Acer palmatum*
Ross Hall Park,
Crookston Road,
Glasgow G52 3NW
55.838521, -4.364403

On a summer day in Glasgow, the lush, damp depths of Ross Hall Park can feel like a tropical rainforest. There are fern- and moss-fringed pools, and dozens of unusual trees planted more than a century ago. One of the most striking of the now mature plants is the magnificent Japanese maple close to the edge of the park near the hospital. Come in the spring to catch the first flush of its delicate leaves. ///under.paints.closer

124. **DARNLEY PLANE***
*Sycamore / Acer pseudoplatanus*
Kennishead Road,
Glasgow G53 7PJ
55.80777, -4.347566

The Darnley Plane is named for the Darnley family, whose members included Henry Stuart, Lord Darnley, second husband to Mary Queen of Scots. Legend says that Mary nursed Darnley under this very tree in the 1560s. While it is perhaps unlikely the tree has survived half a millennium, it is certainly several centuries old, and gorgeous for it. ///finger.strut.moment

### 125. CADZOW OAK*
*Pedunculate oak*
*Quercus robur*
Chatelherault
Country Park,
Hamilton ML3 7UE
55.758234, -4.019203

Hamilton's urban sprawl has been halted by the grounds of Chatelherault Country Park, which contains the ancient Cadzow oaks, dozens of trees planted after the Battle of Bannockburn in 1314. Follow the signs to find them: the first tree on the footpath is startling, but the hollow, splayed-out individual just beyond is jaw-dropping: it is humbling being in the presence of a 700-year-old tree. ///riders.guard.gross

### 126. GROANING TREE
*Sycamore / Acer pseudoplatanus*
Alloway, Ayr KA7 4PQ
55.427838, -4.637567

Alloway Auld Kirk features as a haunted landmark, which is lit up by lightning in Robert Burns' epic poem 'Tam o' Shanter':

> *When, glimmering thro' the groaning trees*
> *Kirk-Alloway seem'd in a bleeze.*

Maybe one of the groaning trees was the standout old sycamore growing on the southern edge, close to the ruined kirk. It could well have been here in Burns's time. ///fetch.bags.rust

### 127. WELCOME TO SCOTLAND ELM
*Golden wych elm*
*Ulmus glabra 'Lutescens'*
Agnew Park,
Agnew Crescent,
Stranraer DG9 7JZ
54.906924, -5.0348

One of the first landmarks you notice arriving by ferry into Stranraer is the Welcome to Scotland Elm, a rare wych elm cultivar with conspicuous yellow leaves that continue to glow through the summer and early autumn. This elm is a low-domed tree among a row of whitebeams on Agnew Crescent, overlooking Loch Ryan. ///shatters.flukes.tastings

### 128. TWEED PLANE
*Corstorphine plane*
*Acer pseudoplatanus 'Corstorphinense'*
Tweed Green,
Peebles EH45 8AP
55.650995, -3.188193

Charming Peebles has always attracted refugees from Edinburgh, and that applies to trees as well as people. A very old Corstorphine plane – bigger and older than any in Edinburgh – grows out of the pavement on Tweed Green. It is so fat that double yellow lines curve to accommodate it in what is a particularly awkward spot. ///conquests.submitted.amplifier

### 129. PRECOCIOUS OAK
*Sessile oak*
*Quercus petraea*
Victoria Park,
Kingsmeadows Road,
Peebles EH45 9AS
55.648488, -3.187954

Prominent among the trees of Victoria Park on the south bank of the Tweed is a magnificent memorial oak. A metal plaque tells us it was planted by Lady Hay to mark the coronation of George V in 1911. You may be surprised by its youthfulness: the Precocious Oak is a virile sessile oak (look out for leaves with stalks) that many would assume to be decades, or even a century, older. ///cross.inches.expecting

### 130. CHEERING FIR
*Douglas fir*
*Pseudotsuga menziesii*
Weirhill Place,
Melrose TD6 9SE
55.59976, -2.726733
*In a private garden, but visible from the street.*

Melrose is famed for rugby, and for a town of just 2,500 inhabitants, its sporting success is a source of great pride. Unsurprisingly, the black and yellow Greenyards stadium is a prominent feature of the town. Nearby, in a garden on the corner of High Cross Avenue and Weirhill Place, Melrose's most prominent arboreal landmark grows: an exuberant and sprouty Douglas fir. ///elder.commended.saved

### 131. JETHART PEAR
*Pear / Pyrus communis ssp. sativa*
Queen Mary's House,
Queen Street,
Jedburgh TD8 6EN
55.478587, -2.552012

Jedburgh was once famed for its pears, which were sold as far afield as London. The town was surrounded by orchards that produced many different varieties: the term Jethart was used to describe any pear from Jedburgh. The orchards are long gone, but a historic pear tree does still thrive in the grounds of Queen Mary's House in the centre of town. ///formation.blast.maker

### 132. CAPON TREE* ⇸
It's a fifteen-minute schlepp out of town, along a pavement by the busy A68, to the incredible Capon Tree. This 1,000-year-old sessile oak rests close to the Jed Water in a fenced enclosure. Gravity has prevailed, and the tree now sprawls in a tangle of slow decay – but its great limbs, cleaved off centuries ago, still burst forth each spring.

**CAPON TREE***
*Sessile oak / Quercus petraea*
A68, Jedburgh TD8 6NY
55.462309, -2.553677
///stones.hours.precluded

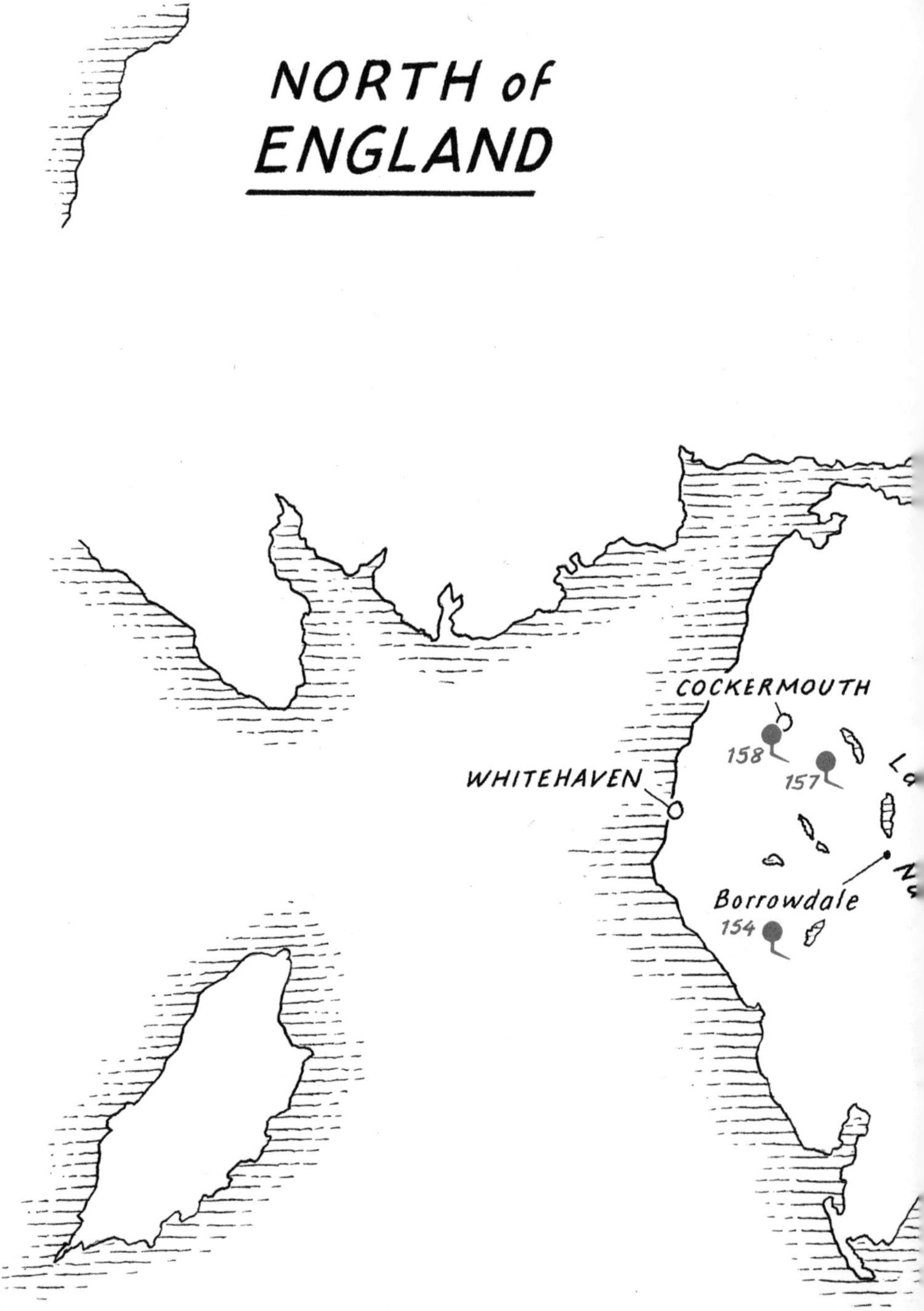

# NORTH of ENGLAND

COCKERMOUTH
158
157
WHITEHAVEN
Borrowdale
154

## NORTH OF ENGLAND

*Northumberland*
*Cumbria*
*Teesside*
*County Durham*
*Tyne & Wear*

The north of England is home to relatively few people, but scattered across this region, in the towns and villages that nestle close to the expanses of the Lake District, the North Pennines and the Northumberland National Park, arboreal treasures await the intrepid tree hunter.

The proximity of the Gulf Stream makes conditions close to the Irish Sea coast so temperate that the most northerly cork oak (that I know of) is able to thrive. In the tiny village of Gosforth, an uncommonly upright 200-year-old tree, the **GOSFORTH SHOWSTOPPER (154)**, can be found in the churchyard near a unique Viking cross. Close to Penrith, another special oak grows within earshot of the M6. **THE REBEL TREE\* (156)** was likely planted in 1745, and serves as a poignant reminder of the last armed struggle between English and Scottish forces. And if you're in Cumbria, be sure to explore Kendal Green, where the **APOLLO REDWOOD (152)** is of particular note: it is, I think, the most perfect giant redwood in England. Almost within touching distance, the **SOYUZ CYPRESS (153)** – an impressive Nootka cypress, a species frequently overshadowed by more glamorous trees – also reaches for the stars. If you find yourself tree hunting in the Lakes, you might also make a pilgrimage to the extraordinary, 1,000-year-old **PRIDE OF LORTON VALE\* (157)**. It grows only a few miles from remote Borrowdale, where 'Worthier still of note' – according to William Wordsworth's 1803 poem 'Yew-Trees' – are the remaining three of the poem's 'Fraternal Four' yews, but these are hardly as accessible.

At Carlisle, the Romantic trees give way to the peculiar, as **BEER BELLY (134)**, England's most northerly baobab plane – a lovable, dumpy form of London plane – staggers into view. It is a most urban tree, growing in front of a pub, one that thousands must see daily as they travel up and down the busy London Road.

But this region's most renowned tree is one that is no longer with us. The memory of the landmark tree at Sycamore Gap on Hadrian's Wall will live on in the public consciousness for decades to come, and no doubt a

**SIGNATURE SPECIES:**
*Pear*

replacement will soon be growing in this most cinematic location. But there are other trees of great age and interest up here. The temperate Irish Sea is a distant memory on the chilly Northumbrian side of the region, where the **REIVER TREE (133)**, an aged sycamore – considerably older than the Sycamore Gap tree – grows in a tiny hamlet on the edge of the Northumberland National Park. Not only is this one of England's most marginally urban trees, its semi-wild situation and its weather-beaten form are reminiscent of the great Scottish sycamores.

As sycamores become ever more magnificent the further north you head, so, too, do walnuts. There are two old trees on either side of the Pennine watershed, the **HAYTON VICTOR (135)** in Cumbria, and another on Tyneside. Both have distinct presence and rugged good looks, but the Geordie **FORAGERS' WONDER (145)** is remarkable for growing just 2 miles from the centre of Newcastle – a city once famed for its polluting nineteenth-century heavy industry. Newcastle's trees trace the city's long history, underscored by the **TOON WALL PLANE (143)**, which grows in the churchyard of twelfth-century St Andrew's, and **NEWBIGGIN'S ANCIENT ASH (138)**, a rare example of a very old pollarded ash tree on the western edge of the city.

Tree hunters will also note the preponderance of pears in the north east. Like the **JETHEART PEAR (131)** just over the border in Jedburgh, the old trees here hint at the former importance of fruit (and nut) trees as sources of food. The **KEPIER PEAR (149)** in Durham is clearly an orchard remnant; it even grows at the end of Orchard Road. The **ECCLESIASTICAL PEAR (136)** at Hexham Abbey is a puzzling, twisted old heap of tree, but one that reminds us that monasteries would frequently have extensive agricultural lands to help sustain the monks who resided there. But the ace in the pack must be the **PREGNANT PEAR (141)**, a magnificent old character growing in Newcastle. It is approaching 200 years old and is still going strong, though its fruits are small and hard, suggesting it was originally planted for its abundant spring blossom.

**133. REIVER TREE**
*Sycamore / Acer pseudoplatanus*
St Mary the Virgin,
Holystone,
Morpeth NE65 7AJ
55.317796, -2.072739

The tiny village of Holystone on the edge of the Northumberland National Park consists of a few houses, a stone chapel and the mysterious Lady's Well. But Holystone is also noteworthy for its magnificent sycamore. It is perhaps 300 years old, oozing over the rocky landscape, and forms the corner of two walls defining the churchyard. ///haunt.biggest.paddocks

**134. BEER BELLY**
*Baobab London plane Platanus × hispanica 'Baobab'*
St Nicholas Arms,
47 London Road,
Carlisle CA1 2LE
54.888031, -2.924705

Baobab planes are so called because of their dramatically swollen trunks, which resemble the massive trunks of Madagascan baobab trees. They are short, fat cultivars of the London plane and are immediately distinguishable from their lofty siblings. It is astonishing to find one outside a pub on such a busy road in Carlisle: they are frequently found near churches, and usually much further south. ///cards.lists.race

**135. HAYTON VICTOR**
*Walnut / Juglans regia*
Fenton Gate, Hayton,
Carlisle CA8 9HR
54.912046, -2.7692763

There are two Haytons in Cumbria, but only one has a walnut. The Hayton between Carlisle and Brampton is the one you should head for to see a remarkable Cumbrian tree, rivalling Newcastle's FORAGERS' WONDER (145) for age and character. The Hayton tree, a hollow veteran, has survived threats from the local authority to remove it, and those who valiantly campaigned to save it have been vindicated by its continuing to thrive. ///falters.guises.obstruct

136. **ECCLESIASTICAL PEAR** → This intriguing pear grows against the southern wall of Hexham Abbey in what was once the cloister garth. It is an old, spidery tree consisting of twisting limbs that spread from a prone trunk – its form suggests it must have suffered some catastrophe many years ago.

ECCLESIASTICAL PEAR *Pear / Pyrus communis ssp. sativa* Hexham Abbey, Beaumont Street, Hexham NE46 3NB 54.971391, -2.103039 ///withdraws.engage.remodels

### 137. BELTINGHAM YEW*
*Yew / Taxus baccata*
St Cuthbert's Church,
Beltingham,
Hexham NE47 7BZ
54.969747, -2.330303

The oldest tree in the north east can be found behind St Cuthbert's church in the village of Beltingham. It could be as much as 1,000 years old, the oldest of three that grow here. Iron bands, now widely out of favour because of their restrictive tendencies, encircle the tree's twisted trunk in an attempt to hold it together. They attest to the regard in which the tree has been held for generations. ///pack.premises.rewrites

### 138. NEWBIGGIN'S ANCIENT ASH
*Ash / Fraxinus excelsior*
Newbiggin Lane,
Newcastle upon Tyne
NE5 4HX
55.007587, -1.688793

It is hard to compete with yews for age, but Newbiggin's Ancient Ash might not be far behind the BELTINGHAM YEW* (137). It is a quietly spectacular tree that has been here, marking the highway, for centuries. Ash trees are not generally long-lived, but this one clearly has an extensive history of pollarding, a practice that has enabled it to reach a truly impressive age. ///host.shark.chins

### 139. REMEMBRANCE BEECH
*Beech / Fagus sylvatica*
Park Villas,
Wallsend NE28 7NW
54.995297, -1.532107

The Remembrance Beech is another old pollard, the most striking of several growing here due to its heft (no doubt achieved over centuries) and twisted form. It grows on a strip of land off leafy North Road, and is likely to have once belonged to nearby Wallsend Hall whose lands have gradually been encroached on over the last century and a half. ///prime.asleep.digits

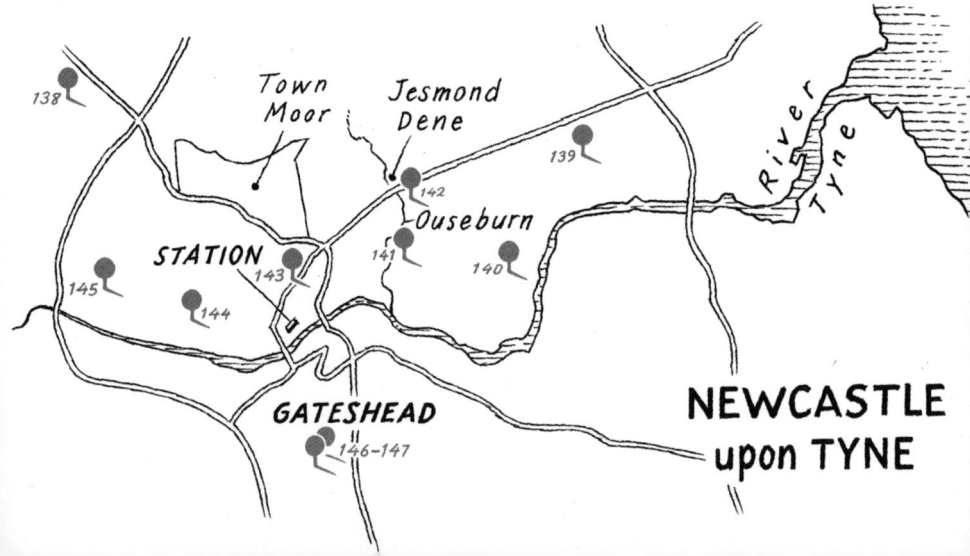

### 140. WALKER ASH
*Ash / Fraxinus excelsior*
Walker Church, Duncan Street, Newcastle upon Tyne NE6 3BS
54.973386, -1.546435

Ash trees are one of the commonest trees throughout Britain and Ireland, and in the north of England they are ubiquitous enough to have become defining features of land- and cityscapes. Several individual ashes perform this role particularly well in Newcastle: one of the most striking is the Walker Ash, an old, multi-stemmed tree that now finds itself in a car park outside Walker parish church. ///fields.enable.letter

### 141. PREGNANT PEAR
*Pear / Pyrus communis ssp. sativa*
Heaton Park, Heaton Park View, Newcastle upon Tyne NE6 5BF
54.983789, -1.584672

At 180 years old or more, Heaton Park's pear is one of its oldest and most striking trees. It must have already been growing when the council adopted the park in the 1880s. For a fruit tree it is huge, similar in stature to the KEPIER PEAR (149), and appears to be in fine fettle despite a holly sapling growing out of a split in its trunk, 2 metres up. ///limes.mercy.lively

### 142. SHOE TREE*
*Sycamore*
*Acer pseudoplatanus*
Armstrong Park, Burlington Gardens, Newcastle upon Tyne NE6 5QJ
54.985163, -1.586692

Close to Armstrong Park's Jesmond Lane entrance, a clearing opens up in front of the Shoe Tree, a mature sycamore famously adorned with hundreds of pairs of shoes, which have been mysteriously appearing since the 1970s. A clue to solving the enigma lies in its proximity to Jesmond, one of Newcastle's most lively suburbs thanks to its large student population. Keep an eye out for shoeless nighttime revellers.///yoga.piano.spring

### 143. TOON WALL PLANE
*London plane*
*Platanus × hispanica*
St Andrews Church, Newgate Street, Newcastle upon Tyne NE1 5SS
54.973655, -1.618964

The distribution of London planes thins out the further north you travel, but they still make for handsome trees as the lively cluster in St Andrews churchyard confirm. One tree, a burry individual closest to the remains of the medieval town wall, is particularly photogenic. The church, Newcastle's oldest, had significant work done in 1726 and 1866; the latter is a likely planting date. ///racing.debit.skirt

### 144. TYNE VALLEY VIEWPOINT
*Turner's oak*
*Quercus × turneri*
St John's Cemetery, Elswick, Newcastle upon Tyne NE4 8HT
54.968022, -1.649497

Urban cemetery construction had its heyday in the 1800s, as newly industrialised cities expanded and purpose-built rest gardens became necessary, and fashionable. They often shelter interesting trees planted among their gothic memorials. St John's has a rare semi-evergreen Turner's oak growing near the Elswick Road entrance. Contemplate the views up and down the Tyne valley from here. ///pest.agent.both

145. **FORAGERS' WONDER** → One of the most impressive walnuts in Britain or Ireland grows in an unlikely spot, surrounded by housing in Newcastle's West End. It is a survivor from the grounds of Benwell Hall, a Georgian country house demolished in 1980. The tree is contorted with age, but is otherwise in good condition and continues to produce a healthy crop of walnuts, attracting squirrels from far and wide.

**FORAGERS' WONDER** *Walnut / Juglans regia* Benwell Hall, Benwell Hall Drive, Newcastle upon Tyne NE15 7PJ 54.975488, -1.676273 ///gown.rises.likes

146. **SALTWELL MULBERRY**
*Black mulberry*
*Morus nigra*
Saltwell Park, East Park Road, Low Fell,
Gateshead NE9 5AX
54.942688, -1.603299

Saltwell Park in Gateshead is undoubtedly Tyneside's loveliest. At its heart is Saltwell Towers, an elaborate gothic pile originally built for William Wailes, a Victorian stained-glass magnate. To the east of the building, an area of lawn protected by battlements and a row of lime trees leads to a charismatic old mulberry, the most northerly specimen in this book. ///ropes.career.usual

147. **KEMP'S FERN-LEAF BEECH**
*Fern-leaved beech*
*Fagus sylvatica*
*'Asplenifolia'*
Saltwell Park, East Park Road, Low Fell,
Gateshead NE9 5AX
54.942553, -1.605175

Kemp's Fern-leaf Beech is a real statement piece: the finest of several large specimen trees growing on the lawn between Saltwell Towers and its well-clipped maze. It vies for attention with a monkey puzzle, but holds its own with a low dome of delicate incised leaves. It was planted by Edward Kemp, Saltwell's designer and a keen specifier of the 'Asplenifolia' cultivar, which appear in many of the landscapes he designed (including the **FLAYBRICK FERN-LEAVED BEECH (205)**). ///patch.custom.king

148. **MACKEM TROPHY**
*Swedish whitebeam*
*Sorbus intermedia*
Mowbray Park, Burdon Road, Sunderland
SR1 1QB
54.901426, -1.38046

Football derbies between Newcastle and Sunderland are the most conspicuous expression of the deep-rooted rivalry between Geordies and Mackems, but they are by no means the only outlet for intercity competitiveness. Wearsiders can pride themselves on the trees that grow in spruce Mowbray Park, chief among which is a magnificent Swedish whitebeam growing on a bank towards the park's southern end. ///keeps.enable.orders

GARDENER'S SECRET (151)

### 149. KEPIER PEAR
*Pear / Pyrus communis ssp. sativa*
Orchard Drive,
Durham DH1 1LA
54.78311, -1.563061

Residential Durham finishes abruptly at the end of Orchard Drive on the right bank of the Wear, where, appropriately enough, an old orchard begins. It is connected to the ruined Kepier Hospital, whose remnants are incorporated into the farm beyond the orchard. One tree, an upstanding old pear, stands out among this landscape of veteran fruit trees in an advanced state of decay. ///oval.single.prompting

### 150. SCALY KEYAKI
*Japanese zelkova
Zelkova serrata*
Botanic Garden, South Road, Durham DH1 3DF
54.760659, -1.575874
*Paid entry.*

Durham University's current Botanic Garden is only recently established, having opened in 1970. It is a surprising place, and, despite being just 10 hectares, it is easy to get lost among its glades and slopes. There are dozens of significant trees here, and the lovely Japanese zelkova or keyaki is one of the most impressive anywhere. Take a moment to admire its delicately scaly bark – something that improves with age. ///supporter.cheer.salads

### 151. GARDENER'S SECRET
*Giant redwood
Sequoiadendron giganteum*
South Park,
Darlington DL1 5TD
54.515214, -1.561014

Like mythical giants, layering giant redwoods are very rarely encountered, but in Darlington, magically, there are two. They grow next to one another, not far from the Parkside entrance to South Park. The cause of this magnificent mutation, which causes multiple trunks to grow in a grove, each clearly attached to the others, is a secret still kept by the Victorian gardeners who planted them. ///trying.mount.pint

### 152. APOLLO REDWOOD
*Giant redwood
Sequoiadendron giganteum*
Kendal Green,
Kendal LA9 5PN
54.334964, -2.753819

Few settings do giant redwoods justice like Kendal Green does. A single tree dominates the expanse of lawn as it slopes up from Green Road. As well as being perfectly positioned to showcase its scale, the Apollo Redwood's impeccably regular and rocket-like silhouette appears ready to launch the tree into the stratosphere. ///processes.smokers.fairy

### 153. SOYUZ CYPRESS
*Nootka cypress
Callitropsis nootkatensis*
Kendal Green,
Kendal LA9 5PN
54.335341, -2.75419

Tree hunters admiring the peerless APOLLO REDWOOD (152) will notice, no doubt, another conifer heading for the stars 100 metres beyond. While its canopy is less abundant, the Soyuz Cypress is certainly competing with the redwood for height. A North American like its neighbour, it is worth inspecting because it is the only Nootka cypress in this volume, included as an enormous specimen of the species ///toasted.teams.fussy

### 154. GOSFORTH SHOWSTOPPER
*Cork oak / Quercus suber*
Wasdale Road, Gosforth,
Seascale CA20 1AZ
54.419348, -3.43078

Cumbria's Gosforth is not to be confused with its Geordie namesake, an inner-city suburb of Newcastle. This Gosforth is a rural village on the western edge of the Lake District, where the churchyard of St Mary's is remarkable for its old cork oak, Europe's most northerly, a lovely tree planted in 1833 and now protected by an iron fence. ///slider.retailing.bucks

### 155. LAKELAND MOUNTAIN PINE
*Mountain pine*
*Pinus mugo ssp. uncinata*
St Patrick's, Patterdale,
Penrith CA11 0NL
54.536856, -2.939404

Another Lake District church with a compelling tree to hunt is St Patrick's at Patterdale. The churchyard is next to the A592 as it curves round at the southern end of Ullswater, and, at the edge furthest from the road, a large mountain pine can be found. They are often seen as dwarf rockery trees, but the strapping Lakeland Mountain Pine – a giant for the species – is no ornamental conifer. ///reapply.beginning.riverside

### 156. THE REBEL TREE*
*Pedunculate oak*
*Quercus robur*
Jacobite Gardens, Clifton,
Penrith CA10 2FG
54.629757, -2.718377

The Rebel Tree marks the spot where, according to legend, fifteen Jacobite soldiers were buried following the Clifton Moor Skirmish in 1745, the last battle of the Jacobite rising fought on English soil. The tree, now surrounded by the detached commuter homes of Jacobite Gardens, is a tangible memorial to the rebellion, which was quelled by the British government the following year. ///passport.increases.showrooms

### 157. PRIDE OF LORTON VALE*
*Yew / Taxus baccata*
Yew Tree Hall, High
Lorton, Cockermouth
CA13 9UJ
54.617467, -3.300396
*On private land, but visible from the road.*

In 1803, the old yew at Lorton was immortalised in the opening line of William Wordworth's 'Yew-Trees':

> *There is a Yew-tree, pride of Lorton Vale*
> *Which to this day stands single, in the midst*
> *Of its own darkness, as it stood of yore*

It can still be seen growing behind Yew Tree Hall from the bridge over the Whit Beck. ///brotherly.slower.calls

### 158. COCKERMOUTH KNOBBLY ASH
*Ash / Fraxinus excelsior*
Derwentside Gardens,
Cockermouth CA13 0JF
54.665126, -3.3658264

On the banks of the River Derwent, in Cockermouth's Memorial Park, grows a fabulous twisted veteran ash that may have been pollarded in the past, so it could be very old indeed. It is a much-loved local landmark that survived a fire in 2021, which, according to the fire service, was started by a tea light falling into the tree's hollow trunk. ///lamenting.hazy.poppy

THE REBEL TREE* (156)

# NORTH WEST ENGLAND

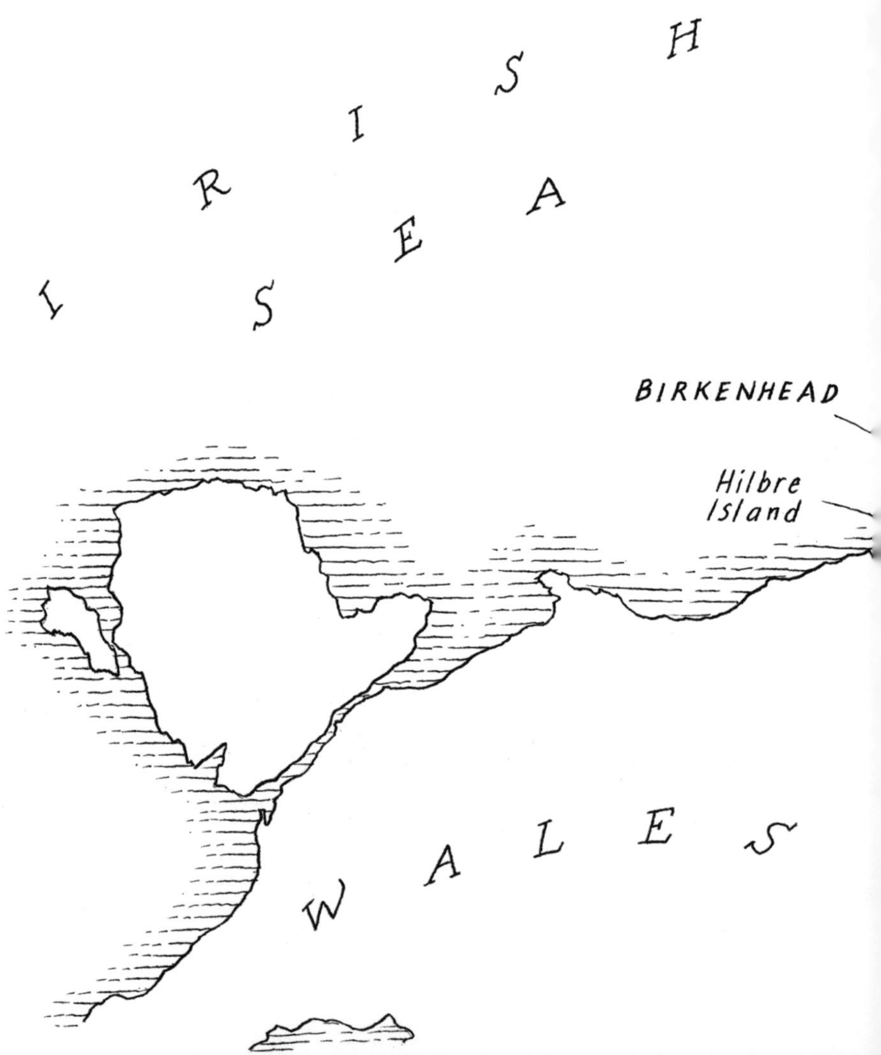

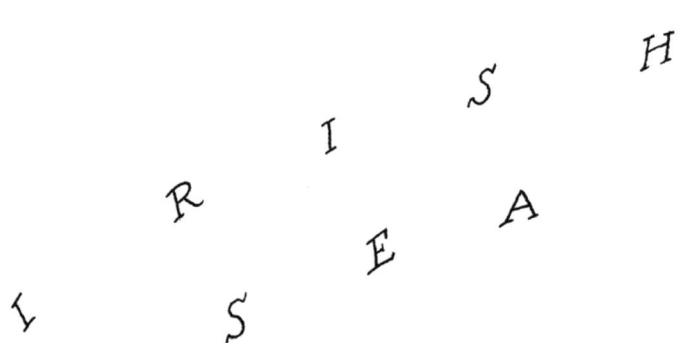

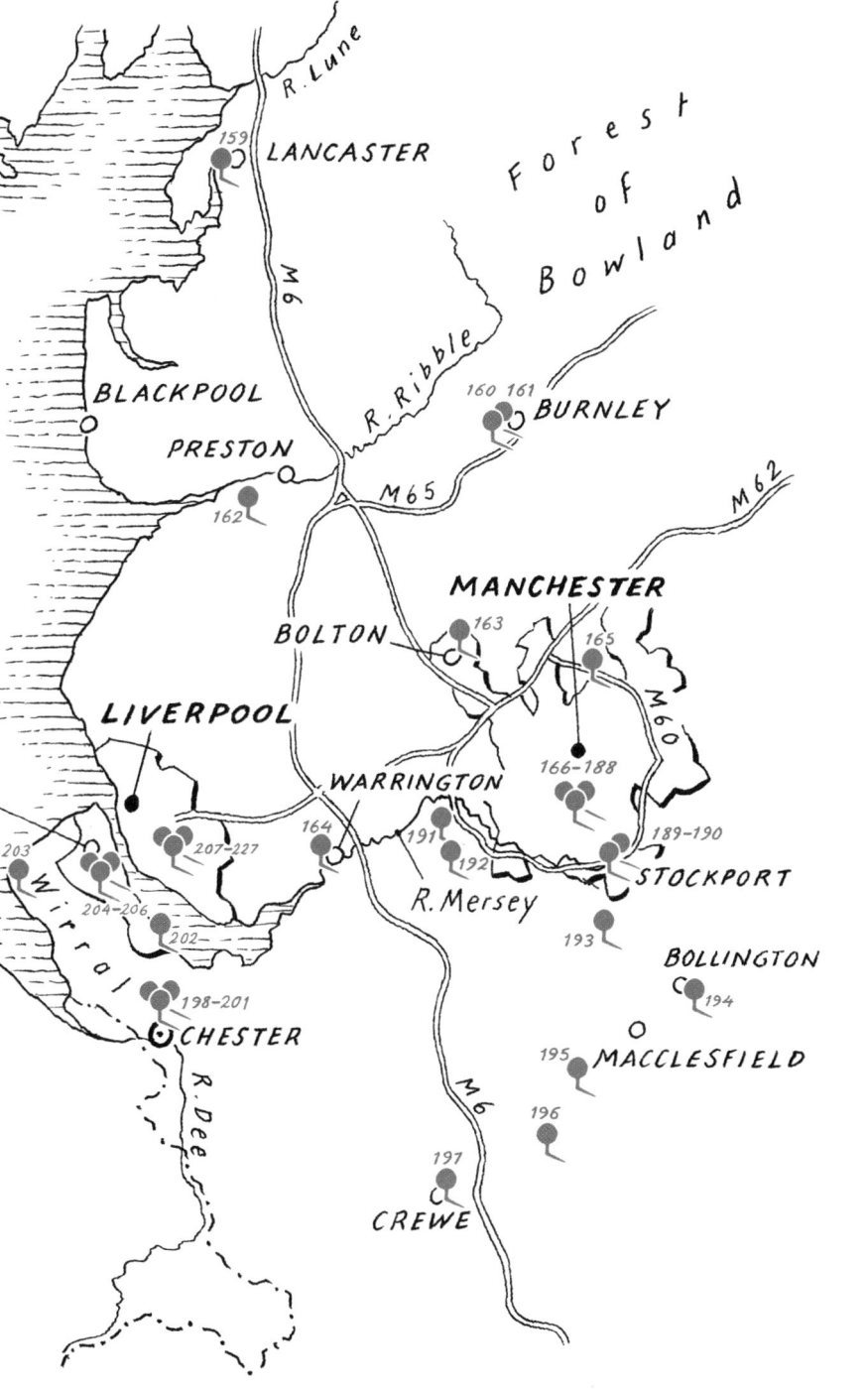

## NORTH WEST ENGLAND

*Lancashire*
*Merseyside*
*Cheshire*
*Greater Manchester*

**TREE CITIES:**
*Manchester*
*Liverpool*

**SIGNATURE SPECIES:**
*Beech*

From the eighteenth century, the north west of England rose to prominence as the engine of the Industrial Revolution. Its proximity to Atlantic ports and navigable rivers and canals, along with readily available coal, a large workforce and new technologies, made Lancashire an ideal place to mill imported, slave-grown cotton. By the nineteenth century, Liverpool was the world's most advanced port, while Manchester – nicknamed Cottonopolis – was the world's most industrialised city. Rampant, unregulated development during this period meant that great wealth came hand-in-hand with unimaginable deprivation. As the century matured, however, campaigns to alleviate the poor living conditions of the working class led to the development of some of the world's earliest municipal parks: places that would, in contrast to Royal Parks or private estates, be open to all members of society. In these new green spaces, everyone could escape the stifling squalor and pollution to mingle, enjoy public events, participate in sporting activities and simply enjoy 'the countryside in the city'.

As I walked round Alexandra Park in Manchester, I was struck not only by the impressive trees, and at least one marvellous oddity in the shape of the **FAIRYTALE BEECH (177)**, but by the sense of calm and wonder such a green oasis must have brought during the height of industrialisation. It would have been a resort for both the well-heeled residents of Whalley Range and the industrial poor of Moss Side, a place that is as much a part of Manchester's history as the belching factories of the past.

Many of the most magnificent municipal parks of the nineteenth century are located in the north west. The string of green spaces encircling Liverpool's city centre are particularly noteworthy, and many of them are the creations of important Victorian landscape designers. Perhaps the most influential of these was Joseph Paxton. Paxton's glittering career started in the employ of the Duke of Devonshire at Chatsworth in Derbyshire, and he is best known for designing the Crystal Palace in London. However, it is his park designs that have endured. The first was

Liverpool's Prince's Park (where the diminutive `NAMELESS PLANE (220)` may date to the park's opening in 1843), while his masterpiece must be Birkenhead Park, which opened in 1847. It is a vast, bosky landscape with many memorable features, including `PAXTON'S PERFECT PARK TREE (204)`, and was famously the inspiration for New York's Central Park.

Paxton's apprentices likewise left their mark with greater élan in the north west than anywhere else. Edward Kemp is of special interest to us, as he had an evident taste for particular trees. He was the first superintendent of Paxton's Birkenhead Park, and would go on to design the town's Flaybrick Cemetery, where many unusual trees vie for your attention; among them, the `FLAYBRICK FERN-LEAVED BEECH (205)` stands out – the most finely shaped of several of these superbly elegant trees growing here. Kemp is also responsible for the presence of several Mirbeck's oaks, a tree seldom planted today. In Crewe, the impressive `RAILWAY OAK (197)` in Queen's Park is one of these, as is `REFEREE (207)` in Liverpool's Stanley Park, a landscape he laid out in 1870. But perhaps his most impressive design is Grosvenor Park in Chester, home to the striking `ROCKET BEECH (200)`. While this is not a tree that dates back to Kemp's day, it may be regarded both as an homage to a man who loved beeches, and as a worthy representative of the diversity of beech trees growing in this region. From much-loved, regular individuals like `CROMWELL'S BEECH* (184)` in Wythenshawe to graceful, unusual cultivars (that is, a type with a particular cultivated attribute, like purple leaves), the north west is home to some of the most impressive beeches anywhere in these islands.

LADS AND GIRLS ELM (163)

**159. CASTLE ELM**
*Wych elm / Ulmus glabra*
Priory Vicarage, Priory
Close, Lancaster LA1 1YZ
54.050385, -2.806069

Up on the high ground overlooking the River Lune, adding extra splendour to the buildings, are handsome Lancaster's finest trees, the most significant of which is a surviving wych elm, a tree that dominates the scene between Priory Church and the substantial medieval castle. ///line.crate.limes

**160. TOWNELEY CEDAR**
*Cedar of Lebanon*
*Cedrus libani*
Towneley Park, Holmes
Street, Burnley BB11 3RQ
53.774135, -2.220906

Towneley Hall and its extensive park were opened to the public in 1902, having been bought by the council the previous year. Close to the house, now Burnley's handsome museum and art gallery, an old cedar of Lebanon grows. It is one of the finest examples in the north of England. ///ending.activism.public

**161. BURNLEY'S OLDEST OAK**
*Sessile oak / Quercus petraea*
Towneley Park,
Holmes Street,
Burnley BB11 3RQ
53.771736, -2.221591

Burnley's Oldest Oak grows in a field 100 metres through the woods to the south of the Hall. It is a magnificent sessile oak with an enormous 10-metre girth, suggesting it is more than 400 years old. Its gnarled structure can be especially appreciated in the leafless winter months. ///apply.rinse.moment

**162. BOOTHS' BAOBAB**
*Baobab London plane*
*Platanus × hispanica*
*'Baobab'*
Booths, Liverpool
Road, Longton,
Preston PR4 5NB
53.727294, -2.784304

North-west grocery chain Booths is renowned for high-quality produce, and at the Longton branch these standards extend to the superb *'Baobab'* London plane by the entrance. Only the TESCO GIANT REDWOOD (751) at Shepton Mallet or THIS IS NOT JUST A WALNUT (38) at Perth come close in the supermarket-tree stakes. Booths opened in Longton on the site of a former mansion: a clue to this tree's origins. ///dinner.refers.salt

**163. LADS AND GIRLS ELM**
*Field elm*
*Ulmus minor var. minor*
Spa Road,
Bolton BL1 4AG
53.57863, -2.435526

Next to Bolton Lads and Girls Club, one of the UK's oldest and largest youth clubs, a historic tree grows. It is a rare surviving field elm that has toughed out the Dutch elm disease pandemic. Find it towering over the corner of Spa Road and White Lion Brow. ///villa.proof.cotton

**164. PRE-THEATRE ELM**
*Tabletop elm / Ulmus glabra 'Horizontalis'*
Parr Hall, Palmyra
Square South,
Warrington WA1 1BL
53.387573, -2.5972

Warrington's cultural quarter is centred around the Victorian rectangle of Palmyra Square and the Parr Hall concert venue. Thousands of concert-goers must have noticed the tabletop elm on the edge of the square. Worth hunting in April when the canopy is covered with green fruits. Look closely to see a small seed surrounded by a papery disc. ///herb.advice.finishing

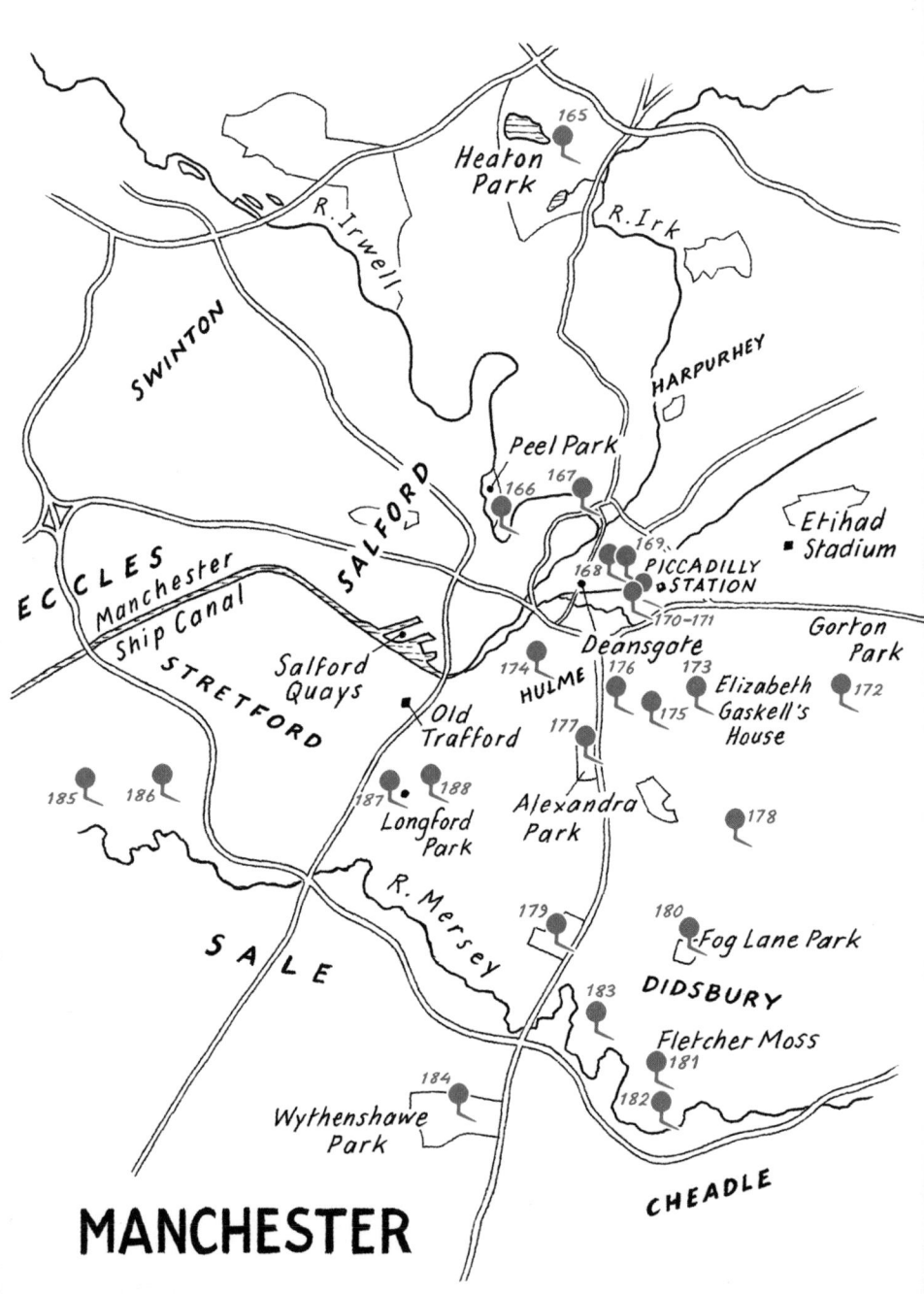

# TREE CITY: MANCHESTER
**SIGNATURE SPECIES:** *Foxglove tree*

While London has its planes, Manchester has its poplars. From the late-nineteenth to the early-twentieth century, tens of thousands of pollution-hardy Manchester poplars were planted across the conurbation, from Salford to Stockport and from Oldham to Hale. Most of the planting was done by temporarily jobless industrial workers during lean economic times, a way for local authorities to provide some paid employment while improving a notoriously polluted environment. The trees coped well with industrial grime, but they are sadly now extremely rare, the majority having succumbed to a fungal infection in the early 2000s.

Manchester poplars are a male clone of the native wild black poplar – each tree was propagated from cuttings, which can all be traced back to a single plant. Poplars are dioecious: each individual is either male (with red, pollen-dispersing catkins) or female (green catkins), and, in this case, the original was male. Because Manchester poplars are all genetically identical, they are equally susceptible to pathogens, which can have devastating consequences on a large clonal population. There are still many fine poplars in Manchester, like the **HOPPY POPLAR (176)**, but these are mostly hybrid black poplars which don't have the gnarly, unkempt character of the wild black poplar. One or two true black poplars do remain, though. One is the **GORTON SURVIVOR (172)**, a splendid old boy in the city's south east; another stunted one grows close to **MRS GASKELL'S MULBERRY (173)**.

The city has moved on from poplars in recent years, and the heart of Manchester has been boldly planted with unusual trees typified by the **BLUE FOX (168)**, one of many dramatic foxglove trees scattered across the revamped city centre. Their scented, blue flower spikes have stopped many Mancunians in their tracks when they bloom in May. This species could be thought of as twenty-first-century Manchester's signature tree. Not far away, the **VIMTO REDWOOD (170)** is another recent arrival, adding character to the modern city while complementing the magnificent mature trees that have been here for decades.

Many of Manchester's notable trees have connections to the city's rich cultural life. The **CEMETRY OAK (179)**, for instance, grows in the sprawling Southern Cemetery, made famous by The Smiths song 'Cemetry Gates'. But it is arguably L. S. Lowry's paintings of industrial Manchester and Salford that have given the world its distinct view of the 'shock city' of the industrial age. In his sketchbooks and paintings, alongside his visions of belching factories and endless terraced housing, Lowry turns again and again to a greener, more arboreal subject: the oasis of Salford's Peel Park, one of the very first Victorian parks. Lowry studied at the Salford Technical Institute overlooking it; he would have known the giant poplar (a hybrid) that is today the biggest tree in the park, featured here in his honour as **LOWRY'S TREE (166)**.

BLUE FOX (168)

**165. HEATON HYBRID**
*Hybrid buckeye*
*Aesculus × hybrida*
Heaton Hall, Heaton Park, Prestwich, Manchester M25 2SW
53.536586, -2.254013

Manchester's most visited park contains dozens of fine trees, including a great rarity in the shape of a hybrid buckeye. It is something of a landmark too: a smallish, twin-trunked tree close to Heaton Hall. Buckeyes are related to the horse chestnuts, but they come from North America. Their shiny brown chestnuts are reminiscent of the deep, glossy brown of a deer's eyes. ///tricks.scam.cubes

**166. LOWRY'S TREE**
*Hybrid black poplar*
*Populus × canadensis*
Peel Park, The Crescent, Salford M5 4WU
53.486807, -2.271309

L. S. Lowry was enrolled in evening courses at the Salford Technical Institute overlooking Peel Park, the subject of many of his lesser-known paintings and drawings. It is home to several trees dating from the park's opening that he certainly would have known. The most eye-catching is a poplar just south of the Brotherton statue, which you might be able to glimpse in Lowry's 1944 painting *Peel Park*. ///fits.cape.others

**167. EFFLUENT FIG**
*Fig / Ficus carica*
Blackfriars Street, Salford M3 5AL
53.484004, -2.247939

Several urban waterways – the Don in Sheffield, or the Avon in Bristol – have incongruous fig trees growing on their banks. The River Irwell is another, where a huge tree clings to the sheer wall on the Salford bank next to Blackfriars Street Bridge. It is likely that its seed was carried here in human waste, a significant constituent of the river's water in decades past. ///shift.bags.jump

**168. BLUE FOX**
*Foxglove tree*
*Paulownia tomentosa*
St Peter's Square, Manchester M2 3AA
53.478399, -2.243365

Central Manchester has been spruced up in recent decades, and nowhere is this more evident than in St Peter's Square. It is rapidly growing into a European-style piazza shaded by unusual trees, including dozens of blue-flowering foxglove trees. The finest is between the tram platform and the Town Hall Extension. Visit in May to see – and smell – the head-turning blue-mauve flowers. ///unwanted.cliff.shark

**169. PRESERVATION PLANE**
*London plane*
*Platanus × hispanica*
Bloom Street, Manchester M1 3ED
53.479045, -2.235394

Just to the north of Manchester's Victorian Crown Court building, thirty-one London planes enclose three sides of a square car park facing Aytoun Street. In 2021, the glorious specimen on the corner of Bloom Street and Aytoun Street was the first to be given a tree-preservation order by Manchester City Council, part of a long-running battle to save this landmark row from impending development. ///movie.stole.years

**170. VIMTO REDWOOD**
*Dawn redwood*
*Metasequoia*
*glyptostroboides*
Granby Row,
Sackville Street,
Manchester M1 3WE
53.47538, -2.234307

Vimto, a once-popular fizzy drink created in Manchester in 1908, was manufactured in premises on Granby Row. Giant painted models of a Vimto bottle and its key ingredients commemorate them in what is now known as Vimto Park. Just beyond the sculpture, a burgeoning dawn redwood may take its place as the centre of attention in years to come, as the drink fades into obscurity. ///prom.cowboy.spicy

171. **TURING ASH** → Alan Turing was many things: a brilliant computer scientist, a gay man facing unbearable discrimination, a national hero. His statue was erected in 2001 in Sackville Gardens, close to Canal Street and Manchester's Gay Village. It is shaded by a tall, well-proportioned ash tree that was probably planted around 1900 when the Gardens were first laid out.

**TURING ASH**
*Ash / Fraxinus excelsior*
Sackville Gardens,
Sackville Street,
Manchester M1 3WA
53.476674, -2.236119
///sculpture.ruled.craft

### 172. GORTON SURVIVOR
*Manchester poplar*
*Populus nigra ssp.*
*betulifolia 'Manchester'*
Annie Lees Park,
Mount Road, Gorton,
Manchester M18 7BQ
53.458535, -2.181227

A very rare surviving Manchester poplar grows close to the Mount Road entrance to Annie Lees Park. It appears somewhat unloved, but its significance is considerable. Manchester poplars – all clones of a single native black poplar – once grew in huge numbers, but disease killed them off in the early 2000s. This tree is one of just a handful of Manchester's defining species growing today. ///bond.flat.blues

### 173. MRS GASKELL'S MULBERRY
*Black mulberry*
*Morus nigra*
Swinton Grove Park,
Swinton Grove,
Manchester M13 0EU
53.463495, -2.220267

Across the road from Elizabeth Gaskell's house, and now museum, lies Swinton Grove Park, a plot of land which she no doubt knew when she lived here in the mid-1800s. On the eastern perimeter between Plymouth Grove and the enclosed sports pitch grows an elderly and characterful, but easy to overlook, mulberry. I'm convinced Gaskell must have once picked the delicious fruit of this tree. ///gravy.faster.aura

### 174. VIGILANT REDWOOD
*Dawn redwood*
*Metasequoia*
*glyptostroboides*
Old Birley Street, Hulme,
Manchester M15 5GL
53.46406, -2.247939

Once in the grounds of a school, the Vigilant Redwood, a deciduous dawn redwood, soars in a parcel of land saved from development in the 1990s. It turns a vibrant auburn colour before its needles drop in autumn in this otherwise discreet corner that has remained undeveloped. We must hope that, when the inevitable occurs, this much-loved landmark tree is saved from the chainsaw once more. ///locate.shave.rams

### 175. EXHIBITION ASH
*Ash / Fraxinus excelsior*
Whitworth Art Gallery,
Oxford Road,
Manchester M15 6ER
53.459802, -2.229959

The Whitworth's café extends from the main building out into the park, an elongated glass box at first floor level, enabling patrons to commune with the mature trees left in situ when it was built. They are ash trees, the most notable of which is just a metre from the building. A sign warns visitors against climbing on the sculpture next to it. Presumably climbing on the trees is okay. ///limbs.activism.choice

### 176. HOPPY POPLAR
*'Serotina' hybrid black poplar*
*Populus × canadensis*
*'Serotina'*
Moss Lane East,
Manchester M14 4ND
53.45867, -2.243139

For many people, Heineken's giant brewery on Princess Parkway is Moss Side's defining landmark. However, I would instead plump for the billowing poplar on Moss Lane East, opposite the brewery's southern edge. It is a *'Serotina'* cultivar of the hybrid black poplar: a huge tree, and one that is rarely planted today. ///clock.probe.phones

### 177. FAIRYTALE BEECH
*Weeping beech*
*Fagus sylvatica 'Pendula'*
Alexandra Park,
Russell Street,
Manchester M16 7JL
53.452957, -2.24726

Charming Chorlton Lodge welcomes visitors to historic Alexandra Park. A piece of Victorian fairytale gothic straight out of *Hansel and Gretel*, it was originally built to house a lucky park official; today it houses offices. Its fantasy effect is heightened by the peculiar weeping beech that has been planted next to it. Still young, it will be an ever-lovelier landmark in years to come. ///ready.exam.engage

### 178. STURDY GUM
*Small-leaved gum*
*Eucalyptus parvula*
Whitworth Lane,
Fallowfield,
Manchester M14 6ZQ
53.444736, -2.215421

In an unregarded corner of the University of Manchester's Fallowfield campus, a stout small-leaved gum grows between the Limes Building and a halls of residence on Whitworth Lane. Small-leaved gums are rare, but are far handsomer than other more common eucalypts, which can often appear gaunt and leggy. It is pleasantly surprising to see such a good example, especially this far north. ///wiring.stole.insert

### 179. CEMETRY OAK
*Pedunculate oak*
*Quercus robur*
Southern Cemetery,
Barlow Moor Road,
Manchester M21 7GL
53.429024, -2.254552

The vast, Victorian Southern Cemetery inspired Morrisey to write 'Cemetry Gates', B-side to The Smiths' 1986 single 'Ask'. It's a great place to wander abjectly among collapsing memorials and huge trees. Avenues of different species run north to south; perhaps the plane avenue is the most impressive, but the tree to admire is a single oak planted on what might once have been a grave close to Nell Lane. ///modest.cover.doll

### 180. FOGGY LIME
*Silver lime / Tilia tomentosa*
Fog Lane Park,
Fog Lane, Parkville Road,
Manchester M20 4UP
53.4249, -2.221218

The biggest and most striking silver limes are often the gently weeping *'Petiolaris'* variety, a popular Victorian statement tree, but in Fog Lane Park the enormous silver limes on the northern perimeter are the regular species. These tend to be relatively small trees, but this individual is an enormous, eye-catching dome on the edge of the park. ///with.bigger.margin

### 181. YE OLDE COCK TREE
*Tree of heaven*
*Ailanthus altissima*
Wilmslow Road,
Didsbury,
Manchester M20 2RN
53.410832, -2.230524

Pollution-tolerant trees of heaven were once recommended for planting in the 'smokier districts' of industrial cities including Manchester. Posh Didsbury village, which could hardly be described as one of the smokier districts, nevertheless has a fabulous example of this vigorous species. With several metres of clear trunk, it grows from the pavement on Wilmslow Road opposite Ye Olde Cock Inn. ///hill.wallet.undulation

**182. THE BRONTOSAURUS**
*Weeping giant redwood Sequoiadendron giganteum 'Pendula'*
Fletcher Moss Park, Stenner Lane, Didsbury, Manchester M20 2RQ
53.409053, -2.2298

Fletcher Moss Park is a remarkable place, not least because Emily Watson and Eliza Phillips helped to co-found the RSPB here at The Croft in 1891. But it is the substantial rockery, stretching out below The Croft, that will be of most interest to tree hunters. Rearing out of this subtropical glade like a giant, shaggy, green herbivore is a weeping giant redwood – a rare and singular perch, ideal for a spirited robin. ///dizzy.slice.sweep

**183. MARIE LOUISE'S CHESTNUT** ⇸ A series of family tragedies led to the creation of Marie Louise Gardens in 1903, a place of remembrance for a wealthy heiress, who named the gardens after her daughter. The gardens were planted with dozens of unusual trees, and many are still here, including a towering tulip tree – increasingly uncommon the further north you get – but the huge, spiralling sweet chestnut on the northern edge is the most memorable.

**MARIE LOUISE'S CHESTNUT**
*Sweet chestnut / Castanea sativa*
Marie Louise Gardens, Holme Road, Manchester M20 2UP
53.418648, -2.243003
///pounds.junior.hope

**184. CROMWELL'S BEECH**\*
*Beech / Fagus sylvatica*
Wythenshawe Park,
Wythenshawe Road,
Manchester M23 0AB
53.405765, -2.278253

A Victorian statue of Oliver Cromwell was moved to Wythenshawe Park in 1967, and has, presumably, given this magnificent beech its name. The tree has been here longer than the statue, though, and is likely Georgian. Towering over ancient Wythenshawe Hall, it has been attracting pilgrims for years, many of whom have carved their names – arborglyphs – into its bark. ///herb.shave.bronze

**185. SEVEN SISTERS**\*
*Copper beech / Fagus sylvatica 'Purpurea'*
Flixton House,
Flixton Road,
Manchester M41 5GJ
53.445356, -2.382948

The story goes that seven saplings grew together to form the Seven Sisters, a landmark tree in the formal garden next to Flixton House. Bundle planting, the practice of grouping saplings together, was sometimes used to provide plentiful fodder for livestock, but here it was perhaps employed to rapidly grow a single large tree, which today has developed flamboyant fluting. ///outermost.manly.held

**186. LEFTOVER OAK**
*Sessile oak / Quercus petraea*
Crofts Bank Road,
Urmston,
Manchester M41 0TQ
53.449911, -2.353329

Glimpses of a leafier past can occasionally be detected in our towns and cities, where old trees are left among more recent developments. In Manchester, the Leftover Oak appears to be one of these, the only oak in a row of limes and horse chestnuts. It is a wonderful, shapely tree, spreading over Crofts Bank Road almost as far as Sainsburys. ///even.equal.fills

**187. LONGFORD RED OAK**
*Red oak / Quercus rubra*
Longford Park,
Edge Lane, Stretford,
Manchester M32 8PX
53.445922, -2.292912

Despite the name, in these islands the leaves of North American red oaks tend to drift into the brown spectrum come autumn, but they are nevertheless very handsome trees. The individual in Longford Park is among the finest anywhere, dating back to at least 1857 when the park was laid out. It shows signs of fungal infection, so admire it while you can. ///deeply.part.bolts

**188. RYEBANK COLLECTIVE**
*Aspen / Populus tremula*
Ryebank Fields,
Chorlton-cum-Hardy,
Manchester M21 9WW
53.448914, -2.285666

Rewilded before the term was invented, Ryebanks Fields has variously hosted a brickworks, landfill and sports fields. This last use ceased in 1996, and the fields have been left to nature ever since. Manchester Metropolitan University owns the land, and has caused local consternation by threatening to sell it for development. So go now to experience the susurrating leaves of the remarkable clonal aspen grove in the north-east corner before it is too late, and the leaves fall silent. ///verse.listed.tribes

CROMWELL'S BEECH* (184)

189. **OVERBEARER**
*London plane*
*Platanus × hispanica*
Great Underbank,
Stockport SK1 1NE
53.410535, -2.159225

Stockport town centre is a concrete clearing in Greater Manchester's urban forest, so its few trees stand out. One landmark is the grand old London plane on Pickford's Brow, a path from High Bank Side to Great Underbank. The tree grows next to a protruding rock and towers over a younger plane planted rather too close. Surely another spot could have been found for the diminutive successor? ///visual.sends.over

190. **PINCH BELLY WINGNUT** ⇢ Vernon Park was popularly known as Pinch Belly Park when it opened in 1857. Local unemployed mill workers were hired to create it, and 'pinch belly' refers to their hunger. Many features have been added over the years, including the 1930s rockery, next to which grows a lovely wingnut – originally from the Hyrcanian forest around the southern Caspian sea. Still relatively young, it will be a magnificent tree in future decades; admire its large, pinnate leaves and dangling winged nuts.

**PINCH BELLY WINGNUT**
*Caucasian wingnut*
*Pterocarya fraxinifolia*
Vernon Park, Turncroft Lane, Stockport SK1 4AR
53.413662, -2.139364
///slide.judge.sticky

### 191. PRIDE OF TIMPERLEY
*Yoshino cherry*
*Prunus × yedoensis*
De Quincey Park, De
Quincey Road, Timperley,
Altrincham WA14 5PJ
53.407238 , -2.3499058

Late March is when the cherry trees in De Quincey Park reach peak blossom. This bijou green space sits calmly next to the busy Manchester Road, but unknown to the thousands of passing motorists, one of the finest yoshino cherries anywhere can be found within. It is a short, spreading tree with a very stout bole holding aloft a canopy that puts out masses of elegant white flowers. ///give.prove.glove

### 192. ALTRINCHAM PUZZLE
*Fern-leaved beech / Fagus sylvatica 'Asplenifolia'*
John Leigh Park,
Altrincham WA14 4UF
53.392397, -2.355841

The Altrincham Puzzle is a particularly elegant fern-leaved beech, a peculiar type with indented leaves, which give it a delicate countenance but which can confuse admirers accustomed to the simple leaf shape of a regular beech. You can find it to the east of the circular ornamental flower bed towards the entrance. ///closet.bonus.puns

### 193. BESTY'S OAK
*Pedunculate oak*
*Quercus robur*
Hall Moss Lane, Bramhall,
Stockport SK7 1RD
53.348763, -2.17636

When legendary Manchester United winger George Best died in 2005, the well-proportioned oak tree on the corner of Blossoms and Hall Moss Lanes became a makeshift shrine to the technical and theatrical footballing genius. Beyond the tree, the low, modernist house surrounded by a high hedge is the home he built when he played for United during the 1960s and 70s. ///composers.groom.online

### 194. WHITE NANCY'S HANDKERCHIEF TREE
*Handkerchief tree*
*Davidia involucrata*
Higher Lane,
Bollington SK10 5AR
53.288581, -2.096568

In a woodland garden on the edge of Bollington, below the enigmatic White Nancy – a white, beehive-like structure on top of Kerridge Hill, built to commemorate the victory at Waterloo – unexpected trees are tucked away. A footpath leads between Higher Lane and Redway Lane, where a large, ghostly handkerchief tree unfurls its huge white bracts for those in the know. ///teeth.magic.curvy

### 195. PALLADIAN MAPLE
*Sycamore / Acer pseudoplatanus*
School Lane, Henbury,
Macclesfield SK11 9PH
53.254568, -2.187838

By the side of a country lane grows the Palladian Maple, the north west's largest, and maybe oldest, sycamore. School Lane, south of Henbury, skirts the perimeter of Henbury Park, an old country estate that houses a pastiche Palladian temple from the 1980s, a perfectly postmodern confection. The tree is the real deal, however: a massive, unmissable sight that marks the entrance to the estate. ///megawatt.twit.organs

196. **ASTBURY FRAGMENT**
Yew / *Taxus baccata*
Peel Lane, Astbury,
Congleton CW12 4RQ
53.150941, -2.230965

Astbury's parish church of St Mary's is a very old and celebrated building, accommodating an even older yew in its churchyard. The tree – a sinewy lattice with a remarkably full canopy – grows next to a path that curves around it. Careful visitors are able to pass between the precariously leaning fragment of trunk and the substantial props that have arrested the tree's collapse. ///force.laptop.waving

197. **RAILWAY OAK**
Mirbeck's oak
*Quercus canariensis*
Queen's Park, Victoria
Avenue, Crewe CW2 7SJ
53.097227, -2.466572

Queen's Park in Crewe is a grand Victorian venture, designed as an oval by railway engineer and local hero Francis Webb, with evident help from the great nineteenth-century landscape architect Edward Kemp. Many of its original features remain, including trees approaching 150 years of age. The most magnificent of these is the tall, densely canopied Mirbeck's oak in the relative isolation of the playground. ///asking.shall.quarrel

198. **MURAGE SYCAMORE**
Sycamore / *Acer pseudoplatanus*
Dean's Field, Rufus
Court, Chester CH1 2JW
53.194009, -2.891896

Chester's ancient city walls run for roughly 2 miles and have been extended, altered and repaired over millennia, their upkeep financed through murage, a medieval tax levied on the townspeople for this purpose. Trees grew up beside the walls as their defensive functions waned: the oldest are near the cathedral, including the 200-year-old Murage Sycamore, a strapping individual in the corner before the car park. ///vanish.strut.salads

199. **CINNAMON MAPLE**
Paperbark maple
*Acer griseum*
St Werburgh Street,
Chester CH1 2DY
53.191556, -2.889646

Chester cathedral's distinctive red sandstone exterior is mirrored in the colour of its paperbark maple. It is a small but perfectly formed tree, with equally distinctive peeling cinnamon bark. This individual competes with Edinburgh's **PALM HOUSE PAPERBARK (77)** for the crown of loveliest of its type. Enjoy it in the rain when the bark's colour and texture are gloriously accentuated. ///rapid.blame.shakes

200. **ROCKET BEECH**
'Dawyck' beech
*Fagus sylvatica* 'Dawyck'
Grosvenor Park,
Grosvenor Park Road,
Chester CH1 1QQ
53.190802, -2.880962

Another of Edward Kemp's memorable public gardens, Grosvenor Park was opened in 1867, but, unlike the others we have seen, this one hosts a pleasing *Dawyck*. Fastigiate *Dawyck* beeches have a purposeful, upright habit, and the Rocket Beech is one of the best. Robust and tall, it is nonetheless too young to have been planted by the great man himself. ///album.critic.fake

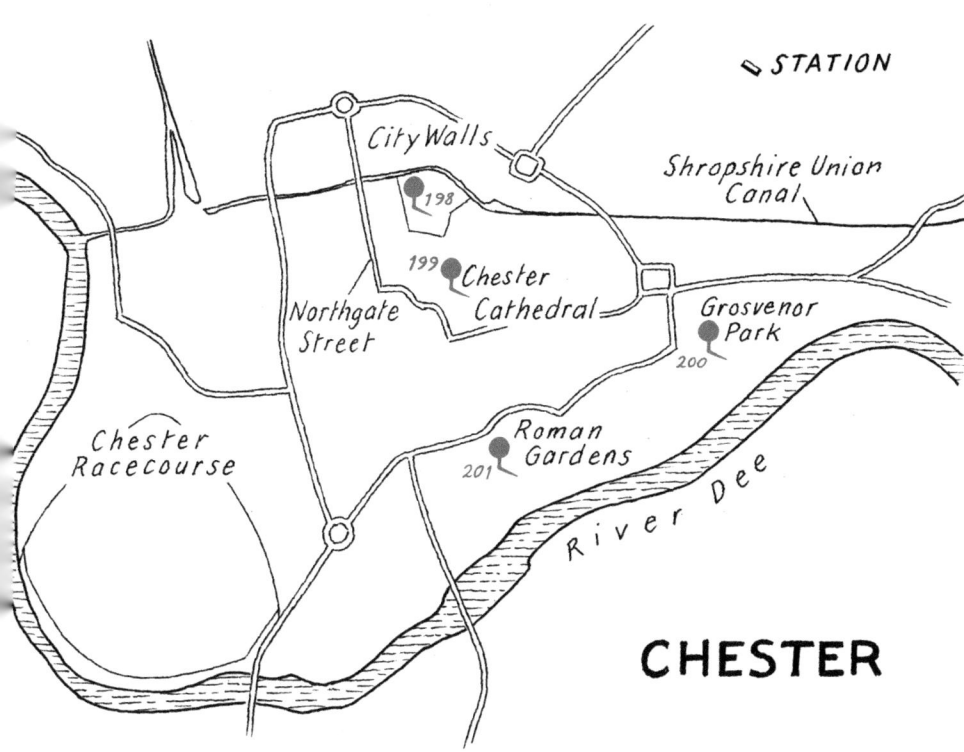

### 201. ROMAN GARDENS MULBERRY
*White mulberry*
*Morus alba*
Roman Gardens, Pepper Street, Chester CH1 1DQ
53.188187, -2.887531

Chester was founded as Deva Victrix, an important Roman military base. Legionnaires stationed here came from all corners of the Roman world, and brought now-familiar plants with them. While they certainly introduced black mulberries, the related, but much rarer, white mulberry – like the spreading, glossy-leaved Roman Gardens Mulberry – didn't arrive on these shores until the sixteenth century. ///circle.spout.hung

### 202. WARD OF EASTHAM
*Yew / Taxus baccata*
St Mary's Church, Stanley Lane, Eastham, Birkenhead CH62 0AG
53.313214, -2.961155

Perhaps 1,500 years old, the Ward of Eastham is a youngster compared to Cheshire's other ancient tree, the ASTBURY FRAGMENT (196), but what is remarkable about this one is its recorded history. It first appears in 1152, when Eastham changed hands and the villagers, passionate conservationists even 900 years ago, entreated the new owners 'to have a care of ye olde yew'. ///exhaled.lifestyle.initiates

**203. PESTO PINE** ⇢ Invigorating West Kirby has a very surprising tree. A V-shaped stone pine, the source of edible pine nuts, is one of England's most northerly. It frames a view of Hilbre Island from the top of Grange Road where it curves round to descend into town. This famous pine once grew in the garden of Abbey Manor, but the road cut through in the 1920s, beaching the tree on the pavement, where it thrives to this day.

**PESTO PINE** Stone pine / *Pinus pinea* Grange Road, West Kirby, CH48 4ET
53.3731, -3.172655 ///thrashed.comment.templates

**204. PAXTON'S PERFECT PARK TREE**
*Pedunculate oak*
*Quercus robur*
Park Drive,
Birkenhead CH41 8AU
53.391912, -3.045309

Several parks vie for the title of Britain's oldest public park (a label complicated by definitions and dates), but Birkenhead Park, opened in 1847, has a very strong claim. It is certainly one of the finest public parks anywhere, and even inspired New York's Central Park. Laid out by Joseph Paxton of Crystal Palace fame, it is now a mature tree-filled landscape. A pedunculate oak, likely an original, has attained a superb shape on Cannon Hill. ///finishing.switch.clear

**205. FLAYBRICK FERN-LEAVED BEECH**
*Fern-leaved beech / Fagus sylvatica 'Asplenifolia'*
Flaybrick Memorial Gardens, Tollemache Road, Birkenhead CH41 0DG
53.396601, -3.063676

Flaybrick Cemetery, last resting place of Birkenhead's great and good, is another of the town's historic landscapes harking back to more prosperous days. It has dozens of interesting trees, including three fulsome fern-leaved beeches, the finest of which is just inside the main gate on the left. The trees were planted in 1864 by Flaybrick's landscape architect, the renowned Edward Kemp. ///dock.vivid.being

**206. SET PIECE ELM**
*Tabletop elm / Ulmus glabra 'Horizontalis'*
Hamilton Square,
Birkenhead CH41 6DQ
53.392963, -3.015721

The contrast between classical Hamilton Square and its less salubrious surroundings is stark. Designed by Edinburgh architect James Gillespie Graham in 1825, it is one of the finest late-Georgian squares in England. The buildings enclose well-kept public gardens where the sculpted form of the Set Piece Elm in the south-east corner adds a fine detail to an architectural masterpiece. ///intend.garage.nest

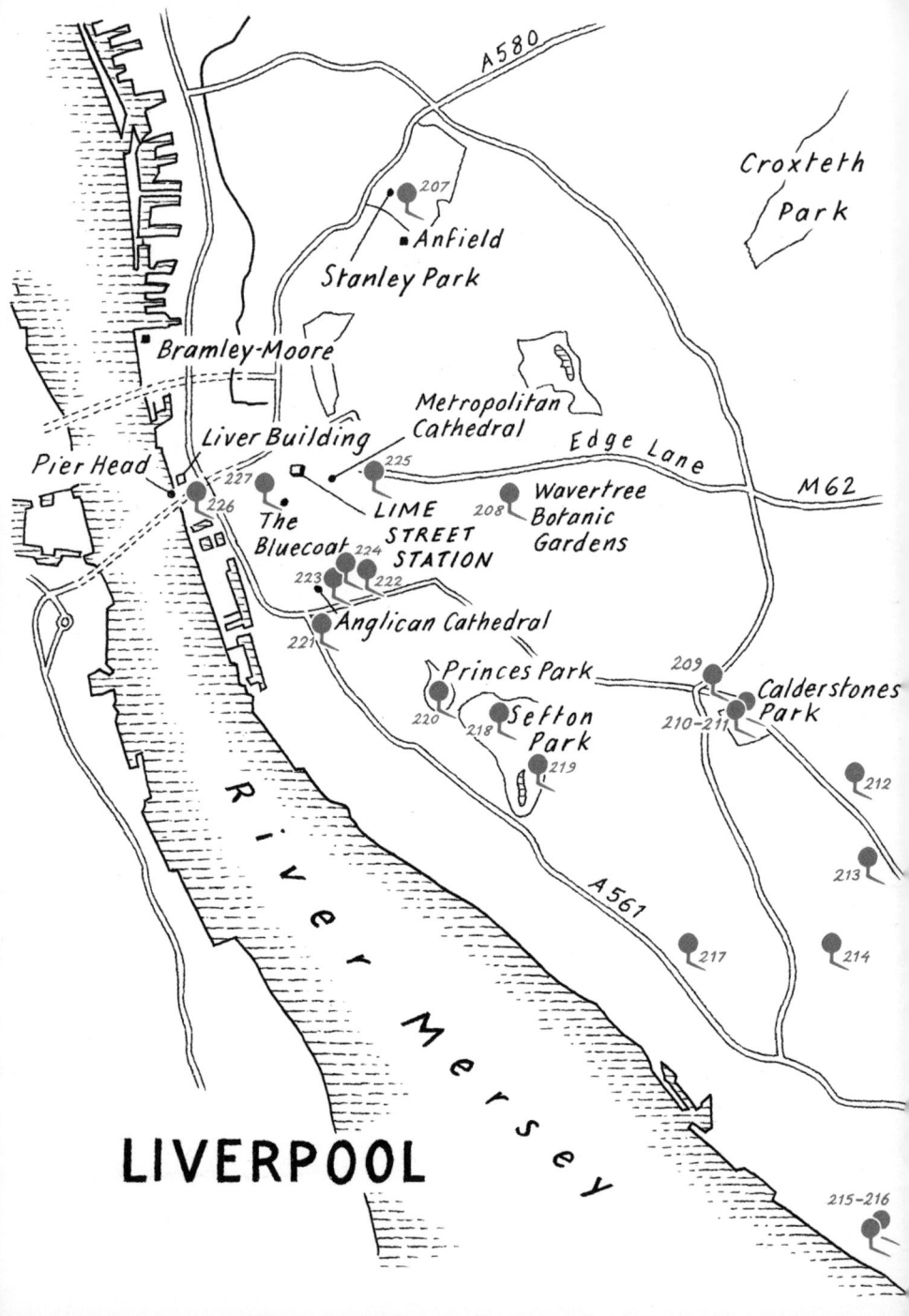

# TREE CITY: LIVERPOOL
### SIGNATURE SPECIES: *Dawn redwood*

Anyone who knows Liverpool will appreciate how densely green this city is. It is filled with historic parks and verdant boulevards designed to impress, like beech-lined Mather Avenue or plane-lined Brodie Avenue.

Whether resident or passer-by, all tree hunters visiting Liverpool should make a special effort to pay their respects to the astonishing **ALLERTON OAK*** **(210)**, an ancient tree thought to be in the region of 1,000 years old, older than the city itself. No other city can boast a tree of such antiquity so close to its city centre.

It can be found in a quiet corner of Calderstones Park, once home to Charles McIver, co-founder of Cunard, whose family bequeathed the park, and the oak, to the city in 1902. Oak trees can live for a very long time, and their final years, or the senescent stage of their lives, can last for centuries. The Allerton Oak is typical of ancient trees: it is in a state of gradual collapse and its limbs are now propped up behind railings. It will be home to a large, diverse array of other life, which find shelter in its hollows and sustenance in its mouldering carcass. When I visited I was lucky enough to catch sight of a tree creeper stealthily seeking out insects hiding in its cavities.

Calderstones Park is just one in Liverpool's superb collection of historic parks, ten of which have been listed by the Register for Historic Parks and Gardens, a number second only to London. Together they make Liverpool a true Tree City, and they link (or separate) its landmarks – like Stanley Park, which sits between the iconic football grounds of Anfield and Goodison Park, and is home to **REFEREE (207)**, an unusual Mirbeck's oak. But Liverpool's finest park of all must be Sefton Park. It is the largest and most enchanting green space in the city, home to the elegant Palm House and the **SEFTON GIANT (218)**, a particularly gargantuan London plane, among dozens of other mature and impressive trees.

The city's historic green spaces continue at Wavertree, where the botanic garden, now a little-visited park rather than a scientific establishment, was founded in the early nineteenth century. Here you can discover the **SERVICE TREE OF WAVERTREE (208)**, a particularly good example of *Sorbus latifolia*. Given that they readily reproduce from bird-attracting berries, this is likely a descendent of the originals.

Then there are Liverpool's garden squares, like Falkner Square to the east of the city centre, which dates back to the 1830s and boasts a wealth of mature London planes. Among them, the **FALKNER FLAILING PLANE (222)** stands out: it is a particularly unkempt tree, suggesting it may have been planted before the others around it.

But Liverpool continues to reinvent itself arboreally, and as the twenty-first century matures, so will newer trees like the **PIER HEAD DAWN REDWOOD (226)**, an example of a species planted abundantly around the city's most iconic buildings. In the future, they may define this city as much as the Mersey skyline.

### 207. REFEREE
*Mirbeck's oak*
*Quercus canariensis*
Stanley Park, Priory Road,
Liverpool L4 0TQ
53.433067, -2.960892

When it comes to football, Stanley Park is currently a neutral space, separating Everton and Liverpool football clubs, whose stadiums border it. However, once Everton vacate Goodison Park for their swanky new dockside home Bramley-Moore, the lovely, leaning Mirbeck's oak close to the park's Anfield Road entrance might incline towards Liverpool FC's Anfield stadium, its near neighbour. ///sugars.bride.send

### 208. SERVICE TREE OF WAVERTREE
*Service tree of Fontainebleau*
*Sorbus latifolia*
Wavertree Botanic Gardens, Edge Lane,
Liverpool L7 9PL
53.406924, -2.941029

In 1836, Wavertree Botanic Gardens opened to private subscribers, but it was another decade before the public were allowed in to admire the grounds too. Today it is a quiet, rather wild public park; rows of overgrown beds are the only remaining suggestion of an ordered scientific past. On the eastern side, a large service tree of Fontainebleau – the stoutest of a group – marks a good point from which to ponder the forgotten history of this landscape. ///keen.store.paints

### 209. GREEN LANE ASH
*Single-leaved ash*
*Fraxinus excelsior 'Diversifolia'*
Green Lane,
Liverpool L18 6HD
53.386414, -2.901805

Grand tree-lined avenues run right across Liverpool, and the aptly named Green Lane is typical in its showcasing of a particular species, here the single-leaved ash. Where ash trees usually have pinnate leaves, this one has a single, larger leaf, which will confuse many tree hunters. Standing at the corner of Menlove Avenue, this tree is a classic. ///loads.rich.poppy

### 210. ALLERTON OAK*
*Hybrid oak*
*Quercus × rosacea*
Calderstones Park,
Calderstones Road,
Liverpool L18 3JB
53.382587, -2.892802

Among Liverpool's arboreal treasures, the Allerton Oak is the jewel in the crown. Visitors are frequently amazed to find such an impressive tree surviving in a quiet corner of a city park. It is reputedly 1,000 years old and unsurprisingly is now in a state of collapse. A fence protects it and reclining limbs are propped up. Like Nottingham's ARBOUR OAK* (311), it is a hybrid of sessile and pedunculate parentage. ///vibrates.transmitted.bumpy

### 211. JAPANESE GARDEN MAPLE
*Purple-leaved Japanese maple / Acer palmatum 'Atropurpurea'*
Calderstones Park,
Calderstones Road,
Liverpool L18 3JB
53.381967, -2.894567

Calderstones Park's Japanese Garden was only created in 1969, but in that time it has become a timeless secret garden, close to the old mansion. Appropriately enough, the tree that stands out in this lush glade is the purple-leaved Japanese maple, a tree of remarkable dimensions for one that is so young, barely fifty years old. ///trap.throw.beside

**212. STRAWBERRY FIELDS LIME**
*Common lime*
*Tilia × europaea*
Strawberry Field,
Beaconsfield Road,
Liverpool L25 6EJ
53.380323, -2.883664

Tall, old trees can make a big impression, especially on children. Could the towering lime growing just inside the famous gates of Strawberry Field have made a particular impact on a young John Lennon? The Beatles' 1967 hit 'Strawberry Fields Forever' recalls a place of solace, and even features Lennon's esoteric musing that no one, he thinks, is in his tree. ///extra.trail.critic

**213. GIANT HAYSTACK TREE** → Allerton Tower is long gone, but its charming gardens remain. There are many trees that date back to the estate's nineteenth-century foundation, including a memorable false acacia, but the tree that lodged itself in my mind is the superb monkey puzzle. Some monkey puzzles take on the silhouette of a chimney brush, but this one has an opulent, spiny carapace that covers four-fifths of its height.

**GIANT HAYSTACK TREE**
*Monkey puzzle*
*Araucaria araucana*
Allerton Tower Park,
Woolton Road,
Liverpool L25 7UL
53.370027, -2.879542
///lease.arrow.cheer

**214. WOOLTON WINGNUT**
*Caucasian wingnut*
*Pterocarya fraxinifolia*
Woolton Road,
Liverpool L25 7UW
53.363424, -2.883971

An avenue of Caucasian wingnuts would be spectacular: they are statuesque, broad-spreading trees with dense canopies, but their propensity for suckering (sprouting saplings from their roots) may cause headaches for urban foresters. It seems the idea was mooted in Liverpool, and a weirdly twisted tree, part of a trial started on Woolton Road at the junction with Springwood Avenue, will make you smile. ///discrepancy.tubes.kings

**215. ADAM AND EVE***
**& 216.** *Yew / Taxus baccata*
Speke Hall, The Walk,
Speke, Liverpool L24 1XD
53.33685, -2.874209
*Paid entry.*

Liverpudlians have been visiting Speke Hall ever since the City Council, and then the National Trust, became its custodians. One of the very best Tudor manor houses, it is remarkable for its exterior and interior architecture. But, for tree hunters, its chief attractions are Adam and Eve, a pair of old yews in the central courtyard. Adam, a male tree, is curiously much larger than Eve, a female. ///simply.pest.reset

**217. FRIENDLY PLANE**
*London plane*
*Platanus × hispanica*
Brodie Avenue,
Liverpool L19 7NE
53.36302, -2.901098

Mather Avenue undoubtedly offers an impressive route into town, but the city's finest is the less-celebrated Brodie Avenue. London planes and limes are planted four deep – one on each pavement and two in the central reservation – to create a magnificent processionary way. It is best appreciated where Long Lane ends and the first plane seems to offer a generous arm to gently shade those waiting at the bus stop. ///vision.poetic.lived

**218. SEFTON GIANT** → On the perimeter of Sefton Park, near where Aigburth Drive becomes Croxteth Drive, a gargantuan plane tree thrives. The park dates from 1872, so it's unlikely the tree is older, but it is huge, and could easily be mistaken for a 200-year-old veteran. Perhaps, like the ABBEY GREEN PLANE (721) in Bath, the roots of the Sefton Park Giant have found an underground spring.

**SEFTON GIANT** *London plane / Platanus × hispanica* Sefton Park, Aigburth Drive, Liverpool L17 4JG 53.38539, -2.945146 ///wishes.player.flat

### 219. PAMEEN'S ASH
*Raywood ash*
*Fraxinus angustifolia*
*'Raywood'*
Sefton Park, Aigburth
Drive, Liverpool L17 4JG
53.380727, -2.93741

'You'll Never Walk Alone' announces a brass plaque screwed into a Sefton Park tree trunk, a memorial for someone called Pameen. It could take decades for the tree to consume it, or the authorities might remove it sooner. But it is unsurprising that this beautiful Raywood ash was the chosen trunk. In the summer its foliage is supremely elegant, and in autumn it turns spectacularly scarlet, purple and orange. ///values.duty.family

### 220. NAMELESS PLANE
*Oriental plane*
*Platanus orientalis*
Princes Park, Devonshire
Road, Liverpool L8 3TZ
53.386549, -2.953153

Princes Park was laid out by Joseph Paxton in 1842, and its design was hugely influential. Follow the path round the western side of the lake to find a diminutive twin-forked oriental plane, almost certainly an original planting, a long-forgotten and nameless cultivar very occasionally found in old parks by eagle-eyed tree hunters. ///speak.clubs.brief

### 221. NIGHTINGALE BLACK POPLAR
*Manchester poplar*
*Populus nigra ssp.*
*betulifolia 'Manchester'*
The Nightingale Lodge,
Princes Road,
Liverpool L8 1TG
53.396009, -2.967042
*In private grounds, but visible from the street.*

Could a Manchester poplar have drifted down the Mersey, or lost its way on the A57 and ended up in neighbouring Liverpool? Despite the rivalry between these great cities of the North West, they are inextricably linked by geography, trade, ideas, canals, football – and trees. The rare native black poplar that hangs over the Florence Nightingale monument is, like the GORTON SURVIVOR (172) in Manchester, an excellent example of this clone. Very few of these enigmatic trees remain in England and Wales. ///guides.manliness.pump

### 222. FALKNER FLAILING PLANE
*London plane*
*Platanus × hispanica*
Falkner Square,
Liverpool L8 7NZ
53.398353, -2.963468

Liverpool's Georgian Quarter is less famous than its counterparts in Edinburgh and Dublin, yet it is one of the most coherent and best preserved of any large city. Within Falkner Square Gardens, on the western side, the giant Falkner Flailing Plane stands out with its serious tilt and mass of flailing branches, the oldest of its companions. ///cans.plots.influencing

### 223. ST BRIDE'S OAK
*Turner's oak*
*Quercus × turneri*
St Bride's, Percy Street,
Liverpool L8 7LT
53.397167, -2.968761

Neoclassical St Bride's has a curious oak growing in its churchyard. The dense canopy hanging over Huskisson Street belongs to a Turner's oak, a hybrid between pedunculate and holm oaks. Further south, some of these hybrids can keep their leaves right through the winter, but on Merseyside the leaves have usually fallen by early December. ///player.belly.bunch

FALKNER FLAILING PLANE (222)

**224. HEAVENLY TREE**
*Tree of heaven*
*Ailanthus altissima*
Catholic Chaplaincy,
Catharine Street,
Liverpool L8 7NL
53.399054, -2.968852
*In private grounds, but visible from the street.*

Peer through the railings, past the grand classical columns and even grander mature plane trees into the murky depths of the little romanesque garden of the Catholic Chaplaincy on Catharine Street to admire the Heavenly Tree. Its powerful trunk shows this to be one of the best examples of a tree of heaven in the north west, surely planted by a pious gardener many decades ago. ///punchy.entertainer.play

**225. METROPOLITAN PLANE**
*London plane*
*Platanus × hispanica*
Brownlow Hill,
Liverpool L69 3GH
53.406007, -2.967992

You can best appreciate the Metropolitan Plane from the steps of Liverpool Metropolitan Cathedral. It is not as spectacular as others in the city, but its position and natural resilience on this otherwise treeless stretch of road – the only natural thing in view surrounded by harsh concrete, glass and steel – is a relief, and imbues it with great authority. ///poet.fact.once

**226. PIER HEAD DAWN REDWOOD**
*Dawn redwood*
*Metasequoia glyptostroboides*
Pier Head,
Liverpool L3 1AH
53.405873, -2.994413

Liverpool's Three Graces are the three iconic buildings that line the waterfront at Pier Head. In recent years the Royal Liver, the Cunard and the Port of Liverpool have been joined by avenues of dawn redwoods which will, in only a decade or two, bring even more grandeur. On the central reservation opposite Water Street, the second tree to the south east is sturdy and symmetrical. My bet is on this one to be a landmark of the future. ///excuse.frozen.safely

227. **BLUECOAT PLANE** → At 300 years, Bluecoat Chambers is one of the oldest buildings in Liverpool, housing the first arts centre in the UK. The Chambers are flanked by four London planes, all survivors of the 1941 Blitz that caused extensive damage to the building. The one behind a fence to the right of the entrance extends an arm invitingly into town – but, taken as a group, the trees become symbols of Liverpool's resilience.

**BLUECOAT PLANE** *London plane / Platanus × hispanica* The Bluecoat, School Lane, Liverpool L1 3BX 53.404471, -2.983781 ///names.amber.dice

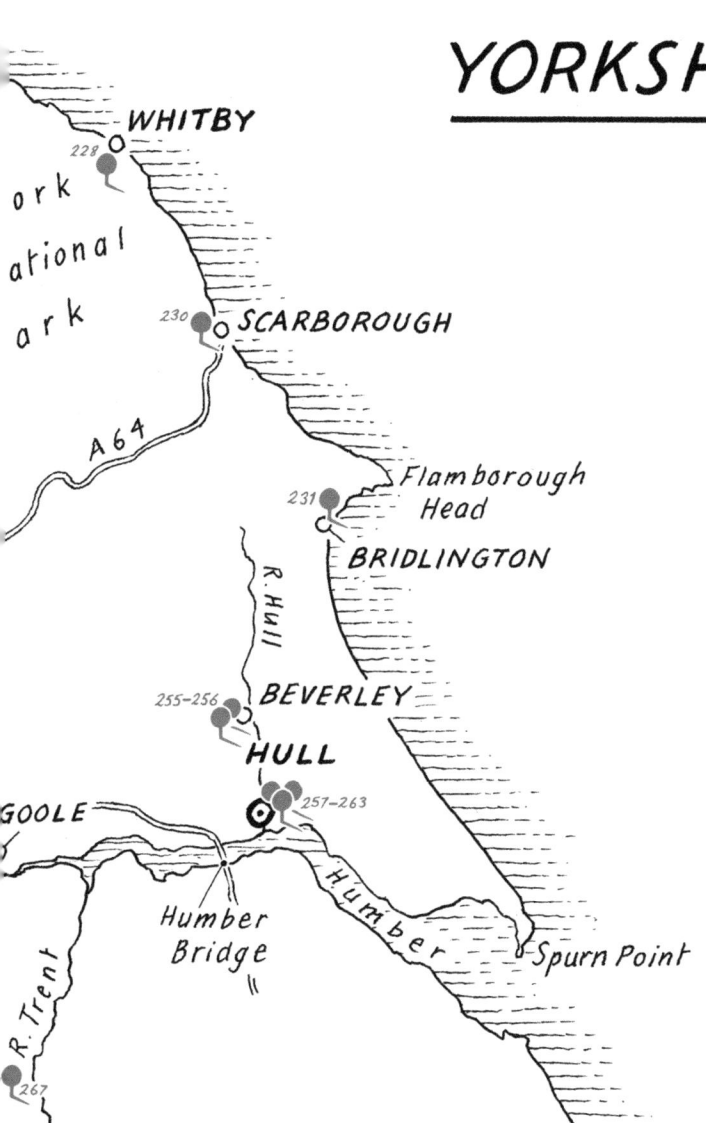

## YORKSHIRE

*North Yorkshire*
*West Yorkshire*
*South Yorkshire*
*East Riding*

Yorkshire is a region of contrasts. The great industrial towns and cities of West and South Yorkshire – Leeds, Halifax, Bradford, Sheffield and Rotherham for instance – give way to the wilds of the Peak District, the Yorkshire Dales and the North York Moors. Of Yorkshire's major settlements, the industrial port city of Hull is the outlier: the terminus of transport routes, it is a place on the way to nowhere, but one I particularly recommend you visit for its superlative trees. It has one of the mightiest oriental plane trees in England in the shape of the **TALON TREE (257)**, and **LARKIN'S LIME (260)** is surely the best small-leaved lime in any British or Irish city.

Yorkshire's coastal towns also have much to see. Bridlington, Scarborough and Whitby all have trees worth hunting, while scattered among the wilder and more agricultural parts, centres like Ilkley, Harrogate, Northallerton and Beverley show a more genteel side to the region. These are green and pleasant towns with trees to match. Ilkley, for instance, just 12 miles from the centre of Bradford, is still bordered to its north by ancient woodland, and the **STUBHAM OAK (232)** – a 500-year-old remnant of more extensive woods – can be seen in a front garden on Curly Hill. In Beverley, an elephantine sycamore, the **YORKSHIRE BEST (255)** is a tree high on anyone's bucket list, while the spa town of Harrogate is of particular note for the huge **HARROGATE GIANT (236)**, the most conspicuous of several surviving elms in the town. It is a majestic and rare true Dutch elm, a type distinct from another elm, the Huntingdon, also represented by fine Yorkshire specimens like the **LAKESIDE ELM (258)** in Hull and the **HEARTWOOD ELM (279)** in Sheffield. Either of these species could be regarded as the signature tree of the region, but due to its greater frequency, I have awarded that accolade to the Huntingdon elm.

But it is Sheffield, this region's Tree City, that a student of urban tree history should visit – in order to see the sites made notorious by the protests against tree-felling that took place there, but also to visit the delightful Botanical Gardens.

**TREE CITY:**
*Sheffield*

**SIGNATURE SPECIES:**
*Huntingdon elm*

Both Sheffield and York are noteworthy for botanic gardens that were opened in the early nineteenth century as places where those who could afford it came to admire and study botanical curiosities that were pouring into Europe. Differing from the municipal parks and former private gardens seen in Bradford and Leeds respectively, the Museum Gardens in York and Sheffield Botanic Gardens, both dating from the 1830s, contain fabulous examples of rare tree species. Many are types that are hardly ever planted these days, and some are among the oldest of their kind. The **PHILOSOPHER'S ASH (238)** in York is a rare narrow-leaved ash, while a Corstorphine plane, **SHEFFIELD'S WITNESS (283)**, is one of the best of its type.

Yorkshire has many settlements, that, like those of the north west, became industrial powerhouses during the nineteenth century. As these towns and cities grew rapidly, their expanding boundaries occasionally extended around existing aristocratic parks. Landowners, faced with their country idylls being encroached upon by industry, pollution and the great unwashed, frequently sold up to developers, but occasionally their landscapes remained intact. In 1872, Leeds Corporation acquired Roundhay Park, formerly a vast private estate on its north-western edge, and after the First World War The Hollies was gifted to the city. There can be few other urban parks quite like The Hollies: it is a magical woodland garden stuffed with unusual plants including many rare trees. The **MIDDLE-EARTH WALNUT (247)** is one of the most unusual and a relatively easy one to find in this wild acreage. Visitors will soon understand how it would have inspired J. R. R. Tolkien, who is said to have been a frequent visitor when he was a young lecturer at the University of Leeds.

SPLASH TREE (229)

228. **JET TREE**
*Monkey puzzle*
*Araucaria araucana*
Pannett Park,
Whitby YO21 1RE
54.485541, -0.620105

Jet, a black gemstone used in Victorian jewellery, comes from Whitby. It is formed from the trunks of a prehistoric ancestor of the monkey puzzle, compressed over millions of years. As such, monkey puzzles are of great importance to the town and, while the Jet Tree may not be the most spectacular, its location in hilltop Pannett Park is a great prompt to drink in the view while wondering how the Jurassic landscape may once have appeared all those aeons ago. ///taster.wiggling.drones

229. **SPLASH TREE**
*Variegated sycamore*
*Acer pseudoplatanus*
*'Leopoldii'*
All Saints Parish Church,
High Street,
Northallerton DL7 8DJ
54.342564, -1.43706

This Northallerton sycamore makes a splash, growing on the triangle of green to the north of the town's parish church. Its variegation is dramatic: great dollops of yellow appear to have been tossed onto its leaves, making this a bright, especially eye-catching tree in summer. While variegated sycamores are not particularly uncommon in Yorkshire, this is one of the best. ///woke.staple.intestine

230. **WORKHOUSE ELM**
*Tabletop elm / Ulmus*
*glabra 'Horizontalis'*
Dean Road,
Scarborough YO12 7SP
54.284754, -0.40541900

A curious tabletop wych elm was planted outside Scarborough's workhouse in 1859, according to a plaque recently installed beside it. It spent many years languishing in a car park, its fortunes keenly followed by many in Scarborough and beyond, before sympathetic redevelopment ensured its survival in a raised bed. ///bumps.feeds.spaces

231. **BRIDLINGTON SPIRE**
*Wheatley elm*
*Ulmus minor 'Sarniensis'*
Stepney Gardens,
Bridlington YO16 7AN
54.095286, -0.20918400

You know you've arrived in Brid when the shapely Wheatley elm on the kerbside next to Stepney Gardens comes into view. This tree has so far avoided Dutch elm disease, as well as the rigours of its urban setting. The rocket-shaped tree, oblivious to the traffic turning off the Scarborough Road, strains towards the heavens, ready to take off. ///apples.caged.asset

232. **STUBHAM OAK**[*]
*Pedunculate oak*
*Quercus robur*
Curly Hill,
Ilkley LS29 0AY
53.933498, -1.8254810
*In a private garden, but*
*visible from the street.*

The woods through which Curly Hill climbs are remnants of Stubham Forest, which once covered much of the northern side of Wharfedale around Ilkley. At Middleton Avenue, the western end of Curly Hill is lined with spacious detached houses set among the trees. One front garden proudly hosts the Stubham Oak, a remnant of the forest, half a millennium old. ///hops.ramble.installs

**233. WHARFE POPLAR**
*Wild black poplar*
*Populus nigra ssp.*
*betulifolia*
East Holme Fields,
Ilkley LS29 0BZ
53.928943, -1.8204900

Cross the Wharfe on Ilkley's New Bridge, and downstream a tree-fringed river beach can be seen. The largest trees lining the riverbank are rare native black poplars, growing here in their natural habitat of shifting river sands. A particularly rugged tree stands out, and a riverside path allows the inquisitive to get a close look at its deeply fissured bark. ///rollover.plots.hampers

**234. OLICANA ASH**
*Ash / Fraxinus excelsior*
Church Street,
Ilkley LS29 9DS
53.926922, -1.8241990

While the Romans definitely reached Ilkley, debate rages as to whether the town is the Olicana mentioned by Ptolemy in his *Geographia*. Regardless, there was certainly a Roman fort here, the footprint of which can be admired next to All Saints parish church and a magnificent ash tree. Ashes are frequently encountered in these parts, and this tree shows just what presence they have in maturity. ///gadgets.stitching.loom

**235. VALLEY WALNUT**
*Manchurian walnut*
*Juglans mandshurica*
Valley Gardens,
Valley Drive,
Harrogate HG1 2SZ
53.992359, -1.550261

Manchurian walnuts are rare but very attractive trees that warrant more frequent planting. The Valley Gardens specimen is testament to how well they can do. It is a broad tree, growing on the lawn below the Sun Colonnade pergola. The Manchurian species can be distinguished from other walnuts by its large, frond-like pinnate leaves. Like other walnuts, the leaves are richly aromatic when crushed. ///myself.farm.reduce

236. **HARROGATE GIANT** → There are several significant elms in Yorkshire, and this one competes with Sheffield's **NUMBER ONE ELM (287)** for height and grandeur. The Sheffield tree is a wych elm, while this is a far rarer true Dutch elm. It is an enormous landmark, stark in winter and verdant in summer, its scale emphasised by the quaint stone buildings it towers above on the grass verge next to the busy Skipton Road.

**HARROGATE GIANT** *True Dutch elm / Ulmus × hollandica 'Belgica'*
Devonshire Place, Harrogate HG1 4AA 53.997291, -1.528351///gift.woke.mutual

**237. SPA TAI HAKU**
*Great white cherry*
*Prunus 'Tai Haku'*
Valley Gardens,
Valley Drive,
Harrogate HG1 2SZ
53.988532, -1.555808

Harrogate's Valley Gardens is home to such an exceptional tree collection that two trees are included here, and dozens more fascinating specimens await discovery. Beyond the mini-golf course, the upper reaches of the park become wilder, but a low, spreading *'Tai Haku'* cherry tree, readily identifiable in April by its large white flowers and bronze leaves, is a civilizing influence. It is the finest in Yorkshire – there must be something in the water. ///popped.terms.rots

**238. PHILOSOPHER'S ASH**
*Caucasian*
*narrow-leaved ash*
*Fraxinus angustifolia*
Museum Gardens,
Museum Street,
York YO1 7FR
53.96115, -1.087436

In the 1830s, the Yorkshire Philosophical Society built York Castle Museum and laid out the Museum Gardens as a botanical garden. While the gardens have since become a less-manicured public park, they still contain several trees that date back to their more esoteric heyday. Of these, the splendid narrow-leaved ash with its elegant foliage is an outstanding tree, and represents a species rarely seen in Yorkshire. ///type.hips.many

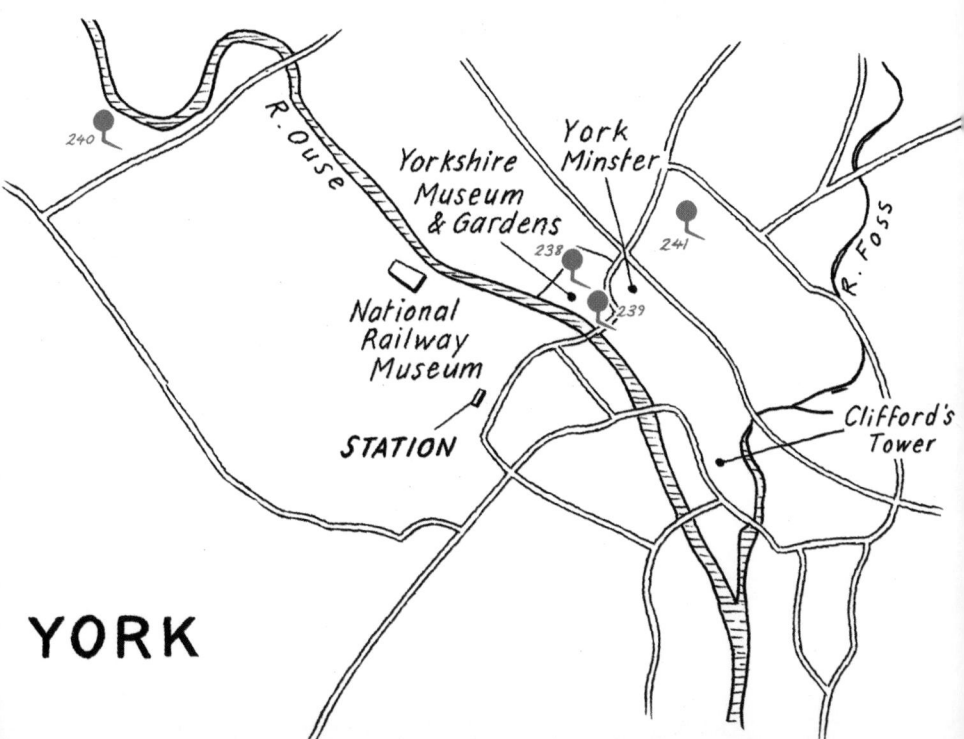

# YORK

**239. PADDLING PLANE**
*London plane*
*Platanus × hispanica*
Lendal Bridge, Bishophill,
York, England, YO1 7DP,
United Kingdom
53.960476, -1.086886

Next to the Star Inn, a magnificent London plane soars above Lendal Bridge, despite growing from ground several metres beneath it. Like other planes close to water – the Ouse is within easy reach of adventurous roots – its age is difficult to determine. It looks old, perhaps pre-dating the Museum Gardens, but having a ready water supply could mean it is younger, like the mammoth ABBEY GREEN PLANE (721) in Bath. ///moved.snaps.crop

**240. WATERWORKS CATALPA**
*Southern catalpa*
*Catalpa bignonioides*
Water Works, Landing
Lane, York YO26 4RH
53.965435, -1.113059
*Visible from the street.*

Close to a bend in the Ouse, on a road few will have ventured along, York's waterworks can be found. It is a small industrial complex surrounded by a high fence. Just inside the main gate an unlikely sight awaits the intrepid. A large, mature southern catalpa softens the entrance. It has a distinct golden hue to its leaves, and is startling when in flower during early July. ///penny.trees.jabs

**241. FINEST BEECH**
*Beech / Fagus sylvatica*
Minster Yard,
York YO1 7JJ
53.963279, -1.081706

For a tree to get noticed in the vicinity of York Minster it needs to be impressive. North of the chapter house there is a tree that fits the bill. The Finest Beech is one of the most awe-inspiring beech trees in England. It appears to be in its prime: tall and straight with a full canopy that dangles around its substantial trunk. ///work.office.ruby

**242. COLOSSAL BIRCH**
*Paper birch*
*Betula papyrifera*
Cedar Glade,
Dunnington
YO19 5QZ
53.961931, -0.98136700

Birches all tend to have white bark and small leaves, which make it difficult to distinguish one species from another. Many urban examples are silver birch or the rapidly increasing Himalayan birch. But at Dunnington, North American paper birches, a type with papery, horizontally peeling bark, have been planted. A trio of enormous specimens grow on a corner of the ironically named Cedar Glade, one of which is officially the UK's fattest. ///jogging.spurted.barmaid

**243. LONELY TREE**
*Wheatley elm*
*Ulmus minor 'Sarniensis'*
Ring Road, Moortown,
Leeds LS17 6BJ
53.847415, -1.5433360

Countless motorists will have been cheered by the unmistakable outline of a neatly pyramidal Wheatley elm growing by the Leeds Ring Road at Moortown. Perhaps there were once more trees alongside it, since decimated by Dutch elm disease; this rare surviving landmark is quietly spectacular, and deserves greater recognition. ///pillow.flops.toxic

**244. ROUNDHAY GEM**
*Whitebeam / Sorbus aria*
Roundhay Park, Princes
Avenue, Leeds LS8 2EP
53.838791, -1.5029960

Roundhay Park, Leeds's great green lung, is very popular, very large (in Britain and Ireland only Sutton, Richmond and Phoenix Parks are larger urban parks), and very bosky. Many of its most interesting trees grow in a grove between Princes Avenue and The Mansion. Despite the park's superb rarities, the most memorable tree is a humble whitebeam that has grown huge in the clement conditions here. ///hooks.daisy.half

**245. LAKESIDE**
**& 246. CAFÉ GUARDS**
*London plane*
*Platanus × hispanica*
The Lakeside Café,
Roundhay Park,
Leeds LS8 2JL
53.834964, -1.49673

Familiar to generations of Loiners, a pair of sentry-like London planes stand guard either side of the bridge leading to the Lakeside Café, an essential stop on days out to Roundhay Park. Judging by their immense size and copious canopies, they may have been planted when the park was landscaped in the 1870s. With the café entrance straight ahead, the right-hand tree is maybe the more magnificent of the two. ///loose.patrol.slower

**247. MIDDLE-EARTH WALNUT**
*Japanese walnut*
*Juglans mandshurica var.*
*sachalinensis*
The Hollies, Weetwood
Lane, Leeds LS16 5PA
53.836042, -1.5813890

Urban distractions are left behind at The Hollies, an enchanting woodland garden straddling the Meanwood Beck. J. R. R. Tolkien began his academic career in Leeds, and some speculate that The Hollies provided inspiration for the woods of Middle-earth. It is well stocked with interesting and unusual trees – look out for a rare Japanese walnut with exuberantly downy foliage in the formal garden near the car park. Oh, and avoid disturbing the goblins. ///offer.club.letter

**248. BUNGALOW TREE**
*Yew / Taxus baccata*
Meanwood Park, Green
Road, Leeds LS6 4LT
53.831433, -1.5748580

Meanwood Park's yew is not ancient, but it is a fantastic climbing tree ideally suited for beginners or the risk averse. It is considerably broader than it is high; it can be no taller than a bungalow. Get under the canopy to appreciate its impressive, aged branches which have entertained many generations of children. ///much.being.adding

**249. SLANTED THORN**
*Hawthorn*
*Crataegus monogyna*
Queen Square,
Leeds LS2 8AJ
53.803673, -1.5455270

Georgian Queen Square is part of the Leeds Beckett University campus. The gardens, laid out in 1822, are much favoured by students, surely drawn here on warm May days to admire the flowering of the lovely old hawthorns that dot the perimeter. The most charismatic tree is a twisted, leaning specimen on the northern side in front of the pedimented terrace. ///safe.vent.unity

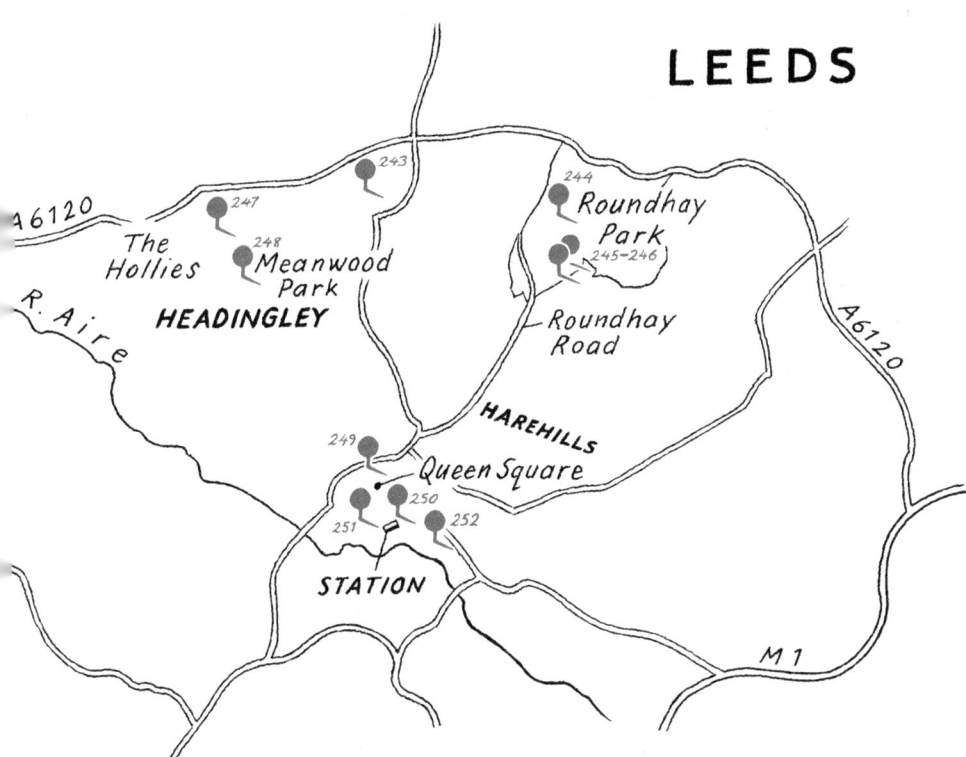

### 250. HEADROW BASTARD SERVICE TREE
*Bastard service tree*
*Sorbus × thuringiaca*
The Headrow,
Leeds LS1 8EQ
53.799766, -1.5470350

Charmingly named bastard service trees have been staples of urban planting for decades. They are neither large nor particularly long-lived, but they are tough and attractive, with creamy blossom in spring and orange berries in the autumn. This solitary individual on Leeds's Headrow shows how a tree can become a landmark and a natural beacon in a streetscape otherwise dominated by stone, glass and steel. ///really.smooth.raft

### 251. OLD WYCH
*Wych elm / Ulmus glabra*
Park Square North,
Leeds LS1 2NP
53.799119, -1.5511920

Park Square is an elegant, peaceful enclave in the city centre. It is now a public park with mostly young trees, but in the north-east corner close to the railings is a fine wych elm. While it is not as old as the square, its size shows that it is clearly older than the other trees here. Its trunk forks not far from the ground. ///labels.spare.jabs

**252. PENNY POCKET CHERRY**
*Double-flowered wild cherry / Prunus avium 'Plena'*
Penny Pocket Park, Kirkgate, Leeds LS2 7DJ
53.795804, -1.5344710

Separated from the Minster Church by busy Kirkgate, and then split in two by the elevated railway, Penny Pocket Park was once the graveyard for Leeds Parish Church. The gravestones were laid flat as the churchyard became a park, but in the eastern corner an impressively fat cherry with a spiralling trunk is flexing its roots, doing its best to re-erect the old stones, or perhaps the skeletons that lie beneath . . . ///tree.plenty.vows

**253. HUMBLE BEECH**
*Variegated beech Fagus sylvatica 'Albovariegata'*
Lister Park, Bradford BD9 4NS
53.813807, -1.7734600

Handsome Lister Park is well endowed with interesting trees, but the most notable is a curious variegated beech. Other beech cultivars – copper beech, for instance – are common, whereas this one is most definitely not. It may not be as striking as its purple-leaved sibling, but up close its cream-edged leaves make this an intriguing tree nonetheless. Find it on the west side of the lake. ///zones.media.fund

**254. FROZEN GIANT**
*Silver pendent lime Tilia tomentosa 'Petiolaris'*
Peel Park, Cliffe Road, Bradford BD3 0LT
53.808740, -1.7432610

Silver pendent limes appear as great shaggy domes cloaking self-conscious giants. Peel Park has several close to its statue of two-time prime minister Sir Robert Peel, one of which appears frozen, as if caught stepping gingerly down the slope. The park is one of England's oldest: its founding was secured in 1850, the year of Peel's death, and it opened in 1853, a likely planting date for the tree. ///caring.plug.deeper

**255. YORKSHIRE BEST** → Yorkshire's largest sycamore is a prodigious tree. It appears to have stood outside the former Sessions House since it was built in 1814, possibly longer. During that time, it must have been a lone specimen tree, its branches allowed free rein to extend horizontally. Now it is a great dome, with some branches almost reaching New Walk's grass verge.

**YORKSHIRE BEST** *Sycamore / Acer pseudoplatanus* The Sessions House, New Walk, Beverley HU17 7AE 53.847793, -0.44047300 ///property.writing.gracing

**256. GOOD NEIGHBOUR**
*Deodar cedar*
*Cedrus deodara*
The Cedar Grove,
Beverley HU17 7EP
53.852752, -0.44852300
*In a private garden, but visible from the street.*

The Cedar Grove in Beverley is appropriately named. An optimistic mid-twentieth-century development of detached housing is laid out among a pre-existing avenue of deodar cedars. Several houses have giant trees sprouting from manicured lawns. Many have magnificent, unbranched trunks, but the most arresting is a multi-stemmed individual near the junction with The Ridings. ///symphony.competent.contained

**257. TALON TREE**
*Oriental plane / Platanus orientalis 'Digitata'*
The Lawns, Cottingham,
Hull HU16 5SE
53.785212, -0.42440200
*Access may be restricted during redevelopment.*

The Talon Tree is an impressive tree growing at a former University of Hull halls of residence. When I visited, the site was pending redevelopment, but the tree, one of the tallest oriental planes in England, can be seen near the entrance road off Harland Way, a vantage point from which this *'Digitata'* cultivar's deeply incised claw-like leaves can be clearly discerned. ///golf.locals.master

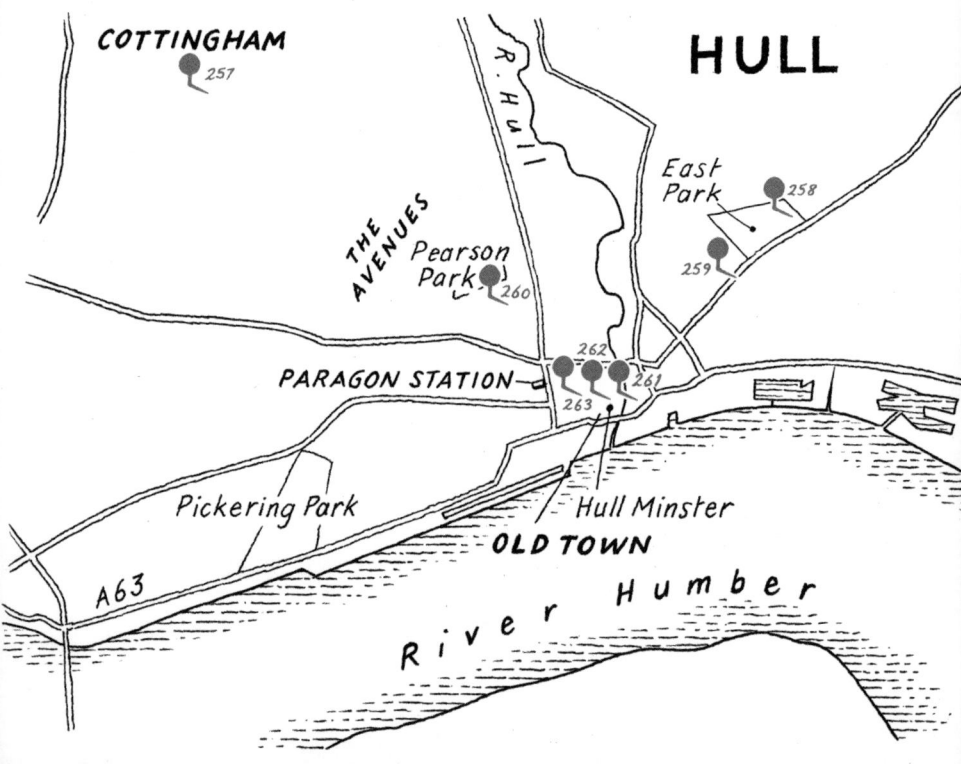

### 258. LAKESIDE ELM
*Huntingdon Elm*
*Ulmus × hollandica*
*'Vegeta'*
East Park, Holderness
Road, Hull HU8 8JU
53.766750, -0.29451900

Opened in 1887, East Park is Hull's largest. It contains many fine trees, including lots of good Turkey oaks, but the finest is the mature Huntingdon elm towards the south-east end of the lake that may well be contemporary with the park's foundation. Look out for asymmetric leaves, lobed on one side where the leaf meets its stalk, a feature common to all elms. ///atomic.snack.office

### 259. KNOTTED ACACIA
*False acacia*
*Robinia pseudoacacia*
Acacia Drive, Garden
Village, Hull HU8 8PB
53.759878, -0.30930500

Acacia Drive is a small, mid-twentieth-century estate on the edge of leafy Garden Village, beyond the northern edge of well-forested Holderness House. It is set among a canopy of fine old false acacias, a tree that has often lent its name to suburban streets. One tree – predating the estate by many decades, a rough, gnarly old thing – shows how this species can develop great character. ///shrimp.could.ends

### 260. LARKIN'S LIME
*Small-leaved lime*
*Tilia cordata*
Pearson Park,
Hull HU5 2GT
53.758395, -0.35229600

For many years, Hull's famous adopted son, Philip Larkin, lived in a flat overlooking Pearson Park, inspiring his poetry collection *High Windows*, which includes 'The Trees'. In the south-east corner, next to the tennis courts, the 8-hectare park's finest tree can be seen: a staggeringly huge and probably very old small-leaved lime. Inspirational. ///inner.lanes.field

### 261. WILBERFORCE MULBERRY
*Black mulberry*
*Morus nigra*
Wilberforce House,
23–25 High Street,
Hull HU1 1NQ
53.744273, -0.330074

Kingston upon Hull's Old High Street, once its commercial centre, runs parallel to the River Hull and is lined with several historic buildings. Among them is Wilberforce House, birthplace of the famous Hullensian and abolitionist William Wilberforce. The house was built in 1656, and, from the front garden, a bountiful mulberry tree hangs over the street. Despite its timeless appearance, it was planted as recently as the 1950s – it is a delight. ///raves.device.lobby

### 262. PURIFYING PLANE
*London plane*
*Platanus × hispanica*
St Mary's Lowgate,
Lowgate, Hull HU1 1EJ
53.743680, -0.33239900

With its tower jutting out into Lowgate, fifteenth-century St Mary's is an obvious landmark. It's not just the gothic architecture that catches the eye, though: the small churchyard to the south is home to central Hull's oldest trees. Three London planes have been soaking up pollution here for well over a century. The most impressive is a splendid tree with a low-branching trunk. ///boxer.judges.given

PHONE BOX WILLOW (263)

### 263. PHONE BOX WILLOW
*Weeping willow*
*Salix × sepulcralis*
*'Chrysocoma'*
Paragon Street,
Hull HU1 3ND
53.744057, -0.34060400

Hull suffered badly during the Second World War and, as shopping streets were renewed during its reconstruction, the city centre drifted west. Paragon Street is typical of the new Hull, and sports maturing weeping willows, a tree not normally associated with city streets. The Phone Box Willow with its curving trunk, next to one of Hull's signature cream telephone boxes, is particularly memorable. ///candy.shuts.safely

### 264. PUNCHBOWL ALDER
*Italian alder*
*Alnus cordata*
Punchbowl Inn,
Field Side, Thorne,
Doncaster DN8 4BE
53.614314, -0.96917000

Italian alders can grow straight and tall, and reach great heights in no time. But the tree in the Punchbowl Inn's car park is old and not especially tall – it does, however, have a characterful lean and a robustness which in winter could cause it to be mistaken for an old willow or even an oak. In February its disguise is cast off and its identity is revealed when striking golden catkins cover its branches. ///inviting.reclaimed.glitz

### 265. TASSEL TREE
*Caucasian wingnut*
*Pterocarya fraxinifolia*
Regent Square,
Doncaster DN1 2DS
53.522060, -1.1263830

Rather than stuccoed regency terraces, Doncaster's Regent Square comprises largely Victorian buildings that surround the central garden. On the western side a burgeoning Caucasian wingnut grows head and shoulders above the other trees planted here. In high summer it is a great shade-giver, and long dangling nut clusters mean it is hard to miss. ///fears.hurls.audit

### 266. SPROTBROUGH SPECIMEN
*Sycamore*
*Acer pseudoplatanus*
Methodist Church,
Park Drive, Sprotbrough,
Doncaster DN5 7LA
53.513300, -1.1823310

Not quite on the scale of the huge old YORKSHIRE BEST (255), Sprotbrough's tree is nevertheless impressive. It has great arching limbs, giving it an open shape and suggesting that perhaps it spent its early years as a specimen tree in long-gone Sprotbrough Park. Today it grows somewhat incongruously on the lawn of the twentieth-century Methodist church, a reminder of a past landscape. ///cheat.influence.fitter

### 267. WEDDING TREE
*Turkey oak / Quercus cerris*
Bawtry Hall, Pemberton Grove, Bawtry,
Doncaster DN10 6SD
53.428835, -1.0238450
*On private land, but visible from the street.*

Turkey oaks, which have less rounded leaves than our native oaks and hairy rather than bobbly acorn cups, can become very big trees, growing far faster and often far larger than the common pedunculate and sessile species. This individual is enormous, one of the largest in Yorkshire. It grows on the lawn behind Bawtry Hall, a wedding venue, and can be seen from Pemberton Grove. ///simply.masks.slacker

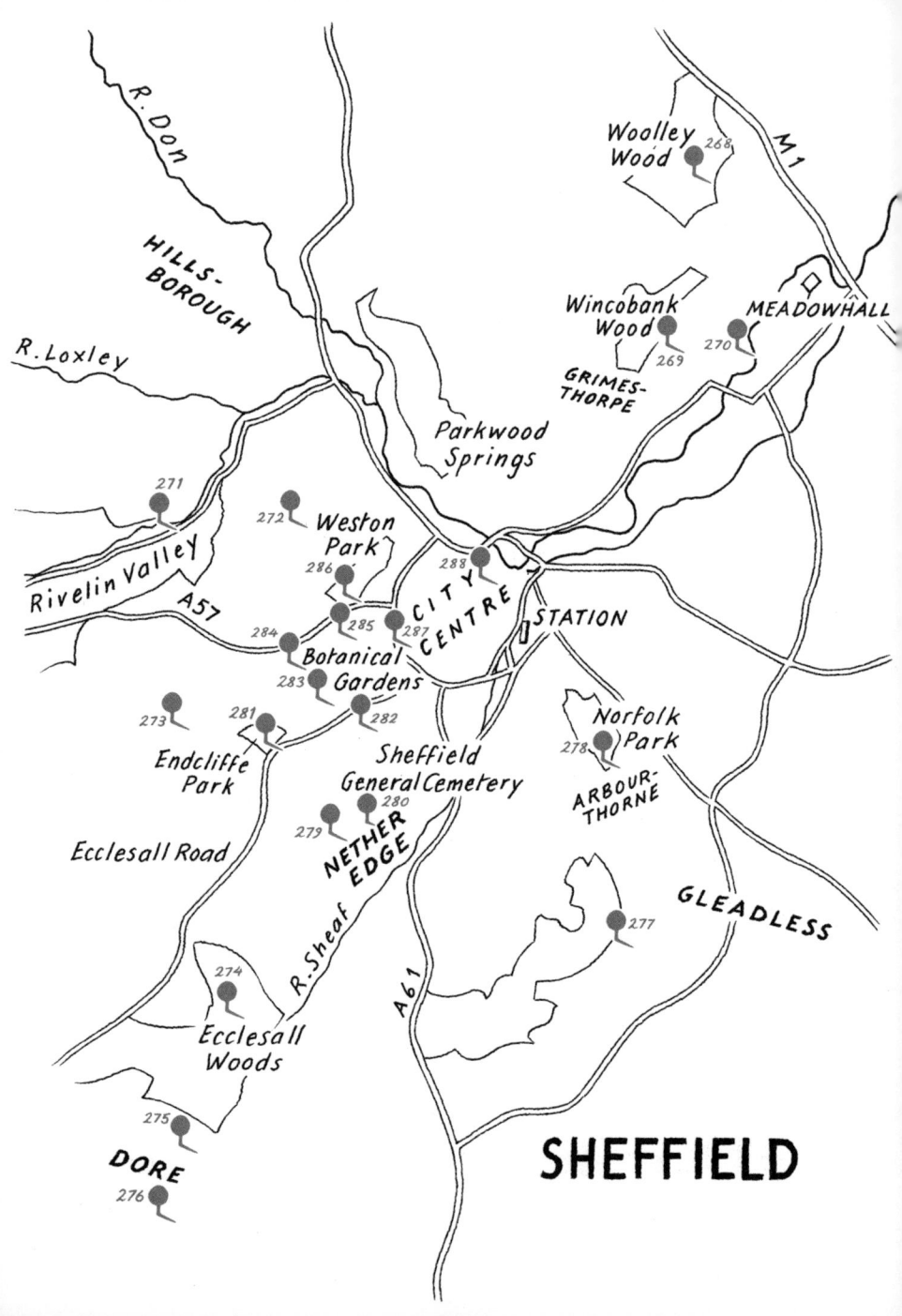

# TREE CITY: SHEFFIELD
## SIGNATURE SPECIES: *Fig*

Sheffielders describe their undulating city as the biggest village in the world. If you walk up Norfolk Park's avenue of limes to the **NORFOLK TURKEY (278)** and look down on the city, this notion starts to make sense. Sheffield is set among several small valleys, its districts separated by its hilly geography.

The influence of Sheffield's great industrial heritage on the shape and sprawl of the city is revealed from the **WINCOBANK OAK STOOL (269)** on the steep slopes of Wincobank Hill, the site of an iron-age fort. From here, much of the remaining heavy industry can be seen, as the Don valley broadens and the river flows past the gleaming post-industrial Meadowhall shopping mall. Somewhere below is the **DON FIG (270)**. Fig trees have a near-mythical status in Sheffield lore; they could justly be described as the city's signature tree. Their presence dates to a time when the water was warmer (and more polluted) due to industry's use of rivers for cooling and power generation.

Near the city's western edge, the **WOOD COLLIER'S TREE (274)** in ancient Ecclesall Woods marks the grave of George Yardley, a man who worked the woods as a charcoal burner in the eighteenth century. But Ecclesall Woods are not unique, and visitors are often surprised by how well-wooded Sheffield is: there are many woodlands snaking along its river valleys. They owe their survival to the city's industrial awakening: Sheffield relied on local charcoal to fire its cutler's furnaces before the arrival of cheap and plentiful coal.

The city boomed as the cutlery and steel industries grew, and, starting in the early nineteenth century, grand civic projects, including the General Cemetery and the Botanical Gardens, were initiated. Both these institutions are home to old trees planted more than 150 years ago, as well as more recent and unusual trees. The **CURATOR'S STRAWBERRY TREE (284)** in the Botanical Gardens is a species that may not have been able to thrive this far north just a few decades ago, but, in today's warming climate, such tender plants appear more frequently.

In the twenty-first century, Sheffield's tree story has been defined by protest. Between 2015 and 2019, the City Council and its contractor decided to 'rationalise' the city's urban forest. It quickly became clear that, in reality, roughly half the city's street trees would be felled. In the face of whole streets of mature limes, planes, sycamores and horse chestnuts being felled, people started to organise. Condemned trees had yellow ribbons tied around them, individual trees became focal points, and news of Sheffield's tree massacre went far beyond the city.

In 2018, the council changed course, but the experience of Sheffield is a cautionary tale for other towns and cities. On one hand, it highlighted the financial pressure councils are under to reduce costs – something that removing mature, expensive-to-maintain street trees can achieve – but it also shows how deeply we care about our city trees, and how much they need our help to survive.

WINCOBANK OAK STOOL (269)

**268. WOOLLEY MAMMOTH**
*Hornbeam*
*Carpinus betulus*
Woolley Wood, Ecclesfield Road, Sheffield S9 1NW
53.425439, -1.4233020

Though only 100 metres from the M1, Woolley Wood is a sanctuary. It is an ancient woodland, carpeted with bluebells in spring, and remarkable for its hornbeams, a species that could be mistaken for beech were it not for their decidedly muscular trunks. As a woodland constituent, hornbeam is associated with the south east of England, but the mighty tree on the upper path of the wood suggests they have been doing well in Yorkshire for a long time. ///fancy.cycles.plant

**269. WINCOBANK OAK STOOL**
*Pedunculate oak*
*Quercus robur*
Jenkin Road, Sheffield S5 6AR
53.413608, -1.4339710

Steep Wincobank Hill offers excellent views over industrial and post-industrial Sheffield. Once an iron-age hill fort, then woodland, it was an important source of charcoal for the city's metal industries. This past is evidenced in the massive oak coppice stools – the low stumps to where branches are cut back – the largest is on the perimeter path. ///notion.mops.stale

**270. DON FIG**
*Fig / Ficus carica*
Weedon Street Bridge, Sheffield S9 1BS
53.409727, -1.4221180

Sheffield's industries relied on five rivers variously providing water for cooling, power and transport. Approaching vast Meadowhall on the eastern outskirts, they coalesce into the Don. Here, bushy fig trees grow along its banks. They are an industrial legacy: fig seed, carried downriver in sewage, suited the microclimate of industry-warmed waters. A nice big one can be seen at Weedon Street Bridge. ///accent.curvy.keys

**271. RIVELIN ASH**
*Ash / Fraxinus excelsior*
Rivelin Valley Road, Sheffield S6 5FE
53.390753, -1.523276

Walking along the Rivelin Valley is like visiting an abandoned settlement that nature has been allowed to reclaim. The valley was once filled with quarries, dams and mills, whose ruins now peek through the alders, ashes and sycamores. A haunting steel sculpture of a chair stands where once there was a weir: appreciate the Rivelin Ash from here as it leans dramatically over the river. ///brain.broom.ended

**272. VICTORIOUS PLANE**
*London plane*
*Platanus × hispanica*
Western Road, Sheffield S10 1LF
53.388139, -1.5064020

'The trees in Western Road and Gillott Street were planted in grateful appreciation of the part taken by former pupils of this school in the Great War.' So a plaque on the wall of Westways School reads. The plaque, and a condemned London plane at the corner of Northfield Road, were rallying points in the battle for Sheffield's trees. The tree survives. ///trades.life.harp

**273. CUTLER'S OAK**
*Pedunculate oak*
*Quercus robur*
Graham Road,
Sheffield S10 3GQ
53.370297, -1.5190480

On the corner of Graham Road and Riverdale Road, in the upmarket Ranmoor area of Sheffield, a majestic lone oak stands on the pavement. It must have been left to grow when the big Victorian houses were built, many of which became homes for Sheffield industrialists involved in producing steel or cutlery. Perhaps it was left as a reminder of how their industry had originally been fuelled. ///voting.gets.host

**274. WOOD COLLIER'S TREE**
*Sweet chestnut*
*Castanea sativa*
Ecclesall Woods Visitor Centre, Sheffield
S11 9NW
53.339438, -1.5152070

Deep in ancient Ecclesall Woods, a solitary eighteenth-century gravestone to George Yardley, marked by a sweet chestnut, can be found between Abbey Lane and Whirlowdale Road. Yardley made charcoal from the woodlands that abound in Sheffield. They were a vital source of fuel for nascent metal industries, so were sustainably managed and therefore protected, providing a wonderful legacy for today's city dwellers. ///patch.script.runner

**275. SHEFFIELD'S LOVELIEST CHERRY**
*Yoshino cherry*
*Prunus × yedoensis*
Abbeydale Park Rise,
Sheffield S17 3PD
53.324480, -1.5248060

Sheffield's finest cherry-tree avenue is Abbeydale Park Rise, a suburban hillside on the edge of the city lined with white-flowering Japanese yoshinos. They have been here for decades, something their bottle-shaped boles reveal in pronounced necks, where yoshino scions were grafted to faster-growing wild cherry stock. The tree with the most outstanding trunk is on the eastern side, a third of the way up. ///beside.strike.tips

**276. VERNON OAK\***
*Pedunculate oak*
*Quercus robur*
Vernon Road,
Sheffield S17 3QE
53.321407, -1.5270630

As Sheffield expanded in the nineteenth century, housing was carved out of the Derbyshire Dales. Vernon Oak is all that remains of that rural landscape. When he was targeted for removal in the 2010s, outraged locals were galvanised, and, thanks partly to his own Twitter account, news of Vernon's (avoided) fate reached a global audience. ///mirror.crab.bland

**277. GLEADLESS OAK**
*Sessile oak*
*Quercus petraea*
Blackstock Road,
Sheffield S14 1LD
53.351512, -1.4476460

Gleadless Valley was nowt but fields and woods until the mid-twentieth century when the utopian Gleadless Valley Estate was built. Modernist buildings were placed sympathetically within the hilly landscape; many of the original trees were retained. The most charismatic is a solitary, perfectly shaped oak, perhaps once a boundary marker, on a grassy bank between Spotswood and Blackstock Roads. ///scar.cones.rush

278. **NORFOLK TURKEY**
 *Turkey oak*
 *Quercus cerris*
 Norfolk Park, Granville
 Road, Sheffield S2 2RP
 53.367225, -1.4479170

Norfolk Park, a classic, rounded former deer park in an elevated position above the city, offers excellent views of Sheffield's undulating geography and extensive greenery. One of the best vantage points is on the southern edge near the café, under the shade of the leaning Norfolk Turkey. You can best appreciate it from the Granville Road entrance, at the end of the grand lime avenue. ///frames.return.films

279. **HEARTWOOD ELM** ↠ The Heartwood Elm surrounded by Sheffielders is the defining image of the protests against plans to fell thousands of trees across the city. A rare Huntingdon elm, it supports a colony of white-letter hairstreak butterflies. At the Sheffield Street Tree Festival in 2018, a choir premiered Robert Macfarlane's poem 'Heartwood' under the tree.

**HEARTWOOD ELM**
*Huntingdon elm*
*Ulmus × hollandica*
*'Vegeta'*
Chelsea Road,
Sheffield S11 9BP
53.357630, -1.4950060
///faded.extra.hunt

**280. TRAFFIC STOPPER**
*Common lime*
*Tilia × europaea*
Ryle Road,
Sheffield S7 1LP
53.360945, -1.4877300

Street trees are usually planted in the pavement, but on Ryle Road the term has been taken literally, and a thriving common lime tree grows in the middle of the street at its junction with Montgomery Road. It has become an unusual and much loved landmark. No doubt it is cursed by motorists in a hurry or those with a predilection for acceleration, but it appears unscathed despite its precarious position. ///bucket.diary.lions

**281. BAD HAIR TREE***
*Weeping beech*
*Fagus sylvatica 'Pendula'*
Endcliffe Park, Ecclesall Road, Sheffield S11 8TF
53.367629, -1.5030050

Just inside Endcliffe Park grows one of Sheffield's most cherished natural landmarks. A peculiarly horizontal weeping beech has stood here for many human generations, slowly growing out and down. To some, its shape resembles undulating dales, but Sheffield legend Jarvis Cocker, who nominated it as his favourite tree in the city, described it as looking like 'bad hair'. ///drives.stress.bend

**282. GENERAL PLANE**
*Oriental plane*
*Platanus orientalis*
Sheffield General Cemetery,
Sheffield S11 8FW
53.369704, -1.4862840

Close to the chapel, just inside the Cemetery Road entrance, a crooked old oriental plane is the General Cemetery's most notable tree. There are hundreds if not thousands of London planes in Sheffield, but far fewer oriental planes – identifiable by their deeply incised leaves – so it is worth comparing this tree with the GRANDE PLANE **(285)**. Both may be connected to renowned garden designer Robert Marnock. ///supply.beard.verse

**283. SHEFFIELD'S WITNESS** → The Botanical Gardens opened in 1836 in the genteel outer suburbs of the expanding city, and have watched over Sheffield's fortunes ever since. Over the years, many trees here have silently borne witness to cycles of decline and prosperity, including some old Victorians like the Corstorphine plane growing close to the Clarkehouse Road entrance. Visit in late March to see its dazzling canopy unfurl.

**SHEFFIELD'S WITNESS** *Corstorphine plane / Acer pseudoplatanus 'Corstorphinense'*
Sheffield Botanical Gardens, Clarkehouse Road, Sheffield S10 2LN
53.372992, -1.4979440 ///waddle.invite.stays

GRANDE PLANE (285)

**284. CURATOR'S STRAWBERRY TREE**
*Strawberry tree*
*Arbutus unedo*
Sheffield Botanical Gardens, Clarkehouse Road, Sheffield S10 2LN
53.373289, -1.4978990

Another popular Botanical Gardens tree is the luxuriant strawberry tree, one of the most northerly I know, pressed against the wall just to the left of the entrance. An evergreen, it is eye-catching all year round. Situated next to the Curator's House, now the café, its simultaneous flowers and edible red fruit can be admired from the suntrap terrace on a fine October day. ///losses.loss.jeeps

**285. GRANDE PLANE**
*Oriental plane*
*Platanus orientalis*
Western Bank, Sheffield S10 2TJ
53.381051, -1.4921960

Next to Starbucks, a capacious canopy extends over busy Western Bank opposite Weston Park Museum. It is a landmark for many and belongs to an old oriental plane tree that has likely been here for at least 150 years. Robert Marnock laid out Weston Park in 1873, having previously designed the Botanical Gardens and Sheffield General Cemetery, where another oriental plane is worth visiting. ///closed.hatch.flags

**286. MUSEUM MAPLE**
*Cappadocian maple*
*Acer cappadocicum*
Weston Park Museum, Western Bank, Sheffield S10 2TP
53.381617, -1.491879

The southern wing of Weston Park Museum, a monumental classical stone building, is softened by a perfectly shaped Cappadocian maple growing on its lawn. It is relatively young, perhaps planted after this part of the building was completed in the 1930s, but despite its youth it is certainly the most eye-catching tree in Weston Park. ///taking.allows.royal

**287. NUMBER ONE ELM**
*Wych elm / Ulmus glabra*
Wilkinson Street, Sheffield S10 2GB
53.379299, -1.4843690

A massive wych elm, surely one of the largest anywhere, dominates a corner of Upper Hanover Street, Sheffield's inner ring road. It grows in the front garden of a handsome early-nineteenth-century house, now solicitors' offices, on Wilkinson Street. It competes with the steeple of nearby St Andrew's church for height, but admire it first and foremost for its perfectly rounded crown. ///help.itself.buzz

**288. GOTH PLANE**
*London plane*
*Platanus x hispanica*
East Parade, Sheffield S1 2ET
53.383261, -1.468716

In a sliver of greenery on the gloomy eastern side of Sheffield's spiky medieval cathedral, a burly old London plane grows. It is a wonderful tree with thick, flailing branches and a scaly, rugged trunk that has encroached on the flagstones leading to a statue of the Scottish-born Victorian worthy James Montgomery. Clearly, hanging out in the churchyard is doing wonders for it. ///with.elaborate.inspector

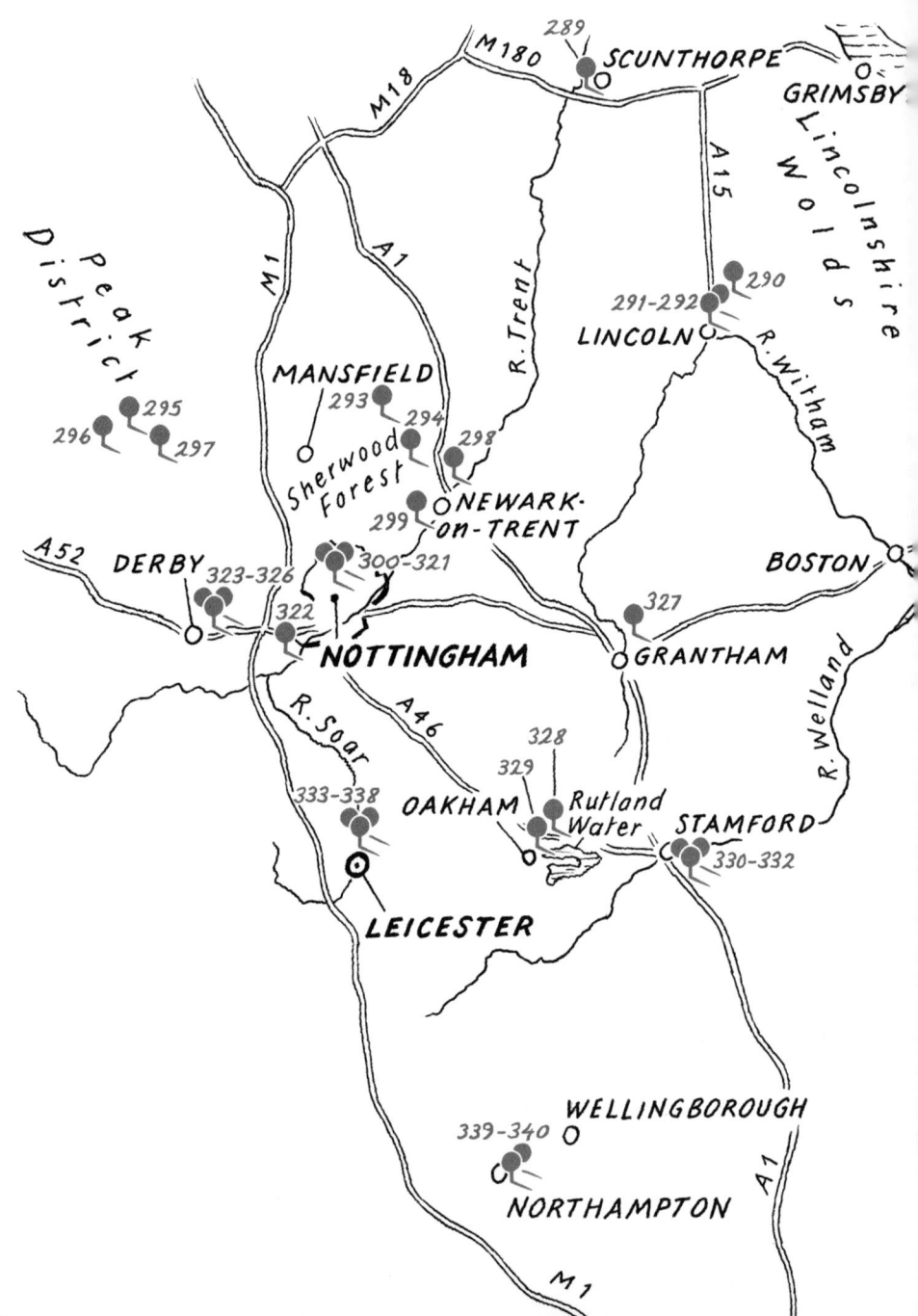

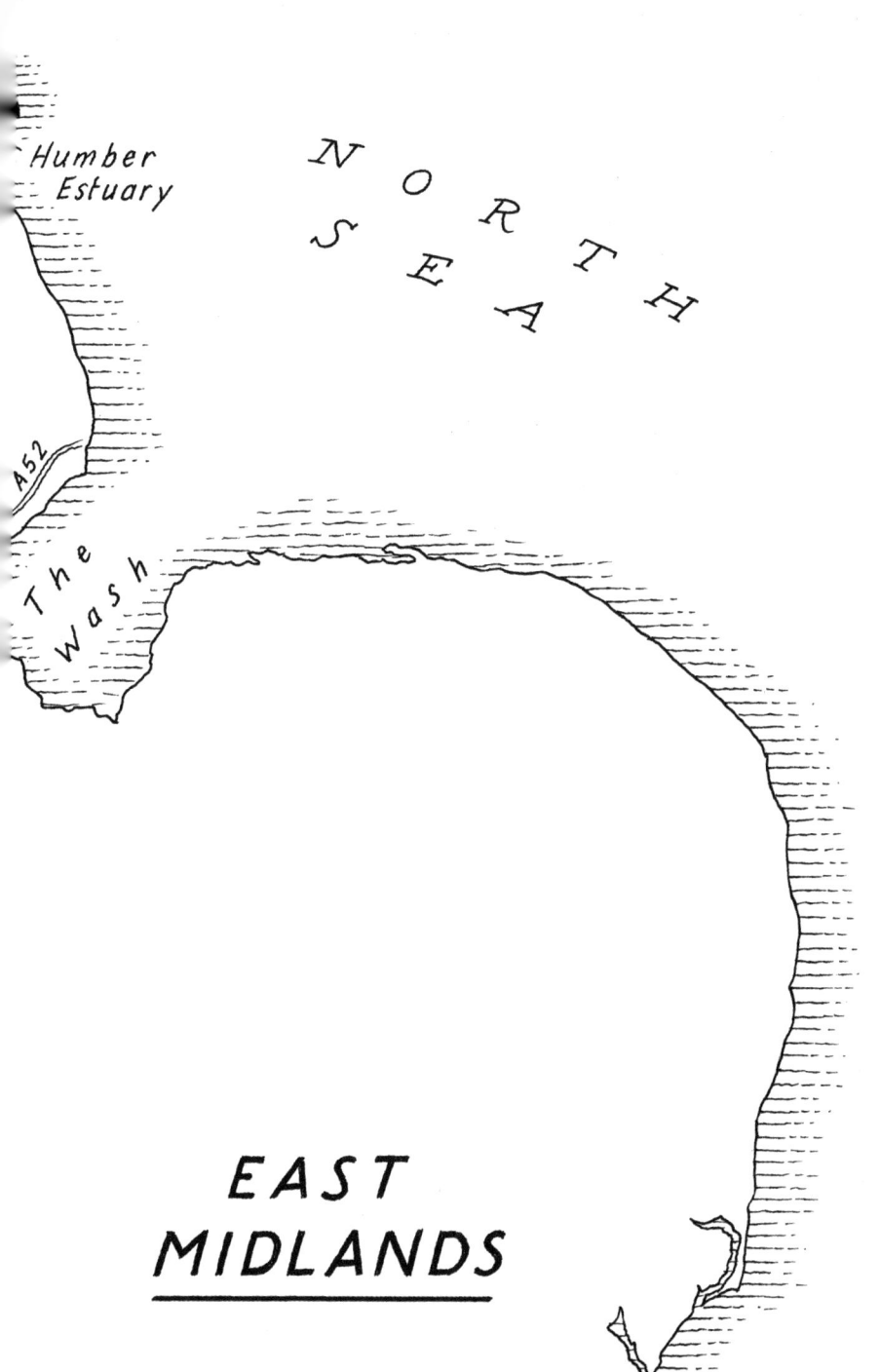

## EAST MIDLANDS

*Lincolnshire*
*Nottinghamshire*
*Derbyshire*
*Leicestershire*
*Northamptonshire*
*Rutland*

Beyond the urban centres of Nottingham, Leicester and Derby, and the eastern edge of the Peak District in Derbyshire, the East Midlands is a flat and largely agricultural region drained by the River Trent and its tributaries. It is a land rich in aristocratic estates, especially around the area of Nottinghamshire known as the Dukeries, and in centuries past it was richly wooded – Sherwood Forest once stretched to the edge of Nottingham. This is the heart of England, and it is home to many fine examples of that most English of trees, the pedunculate oak. One of the country's most famous individuals, **MAJOR OAK\* (294)** grows on the edge of the village of Edwinstowe, just 7 miles from Mansfield.

But there are two oak species that are native to these islands, and their territories overlap: where the pedunculate oak grows, you may find sessile oaks not far away. To add to our confusion, these two species hybridise frequently and their progeny can display characteristics of both parents: **THE ARBOUR OAK\* (311)** in Nottingham is a hybrid oak.

Besides its plentiful oaks, the other detail sure to tempt tree hunters in this region is the abundance of arboretums. If the north west of England is home to some of the best and oldest public parks in Britain, and Yorkshire is notable for its early botanic gardens, then the East Midlands should be highlighted for its public arboretums at Derby, Nottingham and Lincoln. Another great gift of the nineteenth century, arboretums were part public park and part botanical collection, more thickly planted with trees than other parks.

The first of these pioneering arboretums opened in Derby in 1840, to a design by famous horticulturalist and landscape designer John Claudius Loudon. It was a triumph, enabling the public to wonder at exotic new trees pouring in from all corners of the world and thrilling new cultivars being developed by nurseries across Europe. As we are engrossed by an Attenborough wildlife documentary today, Loudon's vision was for nineteenth-century arboretum visitors to enjoy grandstand views of such marvellous curiosities as catalpas from the southern United States, a narrow-leaved ash from the Caucasus, or a curious

**TREE CITY:**
*Nottingham*

**SIGNATURE SPECIES:**
*Pedunculate oak*

medlar-thorn created by hybridising a medlar with a hawthorn. Many of these still stand, including the gorgeous **SEEN-IT-ALL HAZEL (326)**, which is today one of the very oldest examples of its species in Britain or Ireland. Twelve years later, Nottingham opened its own arboretum. It has been replanted over the years, so fewer of the original trees survive, but some excellent specimens can still be found there. Many of the mature beech trees around its perimeter are original, as is the lakeside **ANTEDILUVIAN ALDER (307)**, a cultivar of our native alder with perplexing oak-like leaves. It is a great head-scratcher: a beautiful and rare tree, but one which seems un-showy, unhurriedly coming into its own in maturity, something impatient humans have struggled to reconcile. Since its nineteenth-century heyday this alder cultivar has been largely forgotten, with few specimens planted over the past 150 years; we would do well to bring it back into cultivation.

The third great East Midland arboretum is in Lincoln. It opened in 1872 to a design by Edward Milner. Many old trees survive here, including the **PRODIGIOUS PEAR (291)**, which, because it grows among a cluster of other trees, you will need to look hard for – unless of course you visit during spring to catch its dazzling white blossom. The same cannot be said for this arboretum's most conspicuous tree: the enormous **FRAGRANT GIANT (292)**, a vast small-leaved lime tree that billows over the lovely cast-iron bandstand.

As we move south, and the climate becomes more clement, tree diversity becomes noticeably greater. Leicester, for example, is home to a diverse half dozen remarkable trees. My favourite might be **LEICESTER'S PRIDE OF INDIA (333)**, an arboreal celebration of the city's South Asian culture. But it is to Leicester's eastern suburbs that any tree hunter wanting to see the genuinely extraordinary should head. Here you will find **MISTAKEN IDENTITY (335)**, a towering giant redwood, one of more than a dozen that line the regular suburban street of Pine Tree Avenue. The name is partially correct – one point for the conifer connection – but, considering the longevity and eventual stature of giant redwoods compared with pines, lamentably understated.

**289. SCUNTHORPE OLIVE**
*Russian olive*
*Elaeagnus angustifolia*
Kingsway, Scunthorpe
DN15 7ER
53.58995, -0.682138

Kingsway Gardens is a scrappy park forming a wedge between the Doncaster Road and Kingsway. Where the roads converge, the thin edge of the wedge is defined by a reclining, silver-leaved Russian olive. It is broader than it is tall, and gives this junction the incongruous air of some ancient Mediterranean olive grove. This tree has probably only been here for a few decades, and is unrelated to the true olive. ///post.keeps.truth

**290. WELTON WALNUT**
*Walnut / Juglans regia*
Vicarage Lane, Welton,
Lincoln LN2 3HZ
53.303916, -0.484403

A giant arboreal landmark can be seen in the centre of Welton, a picturesque village six miles north of Lincoln. On the grassy expanse in front of The Park, a development of low-rise housing, the enormous Welton Walnut has been in residence for many years. From a low bole, massive limbs arch upwards, while below the surface, its roots may stretch to the clear waters of nearby Welton Beck. ///gratuity.weeds.composer

**291. PRODIGIOUS PEAR**
*Pear / Pyrus*
*communis ssp. sativa*
The Arboretum,
Lindum Terrace,
Lincoln LN2 5RT
53.232064, -0.525158

In high summer, the giant old pear tree in Lincoln Arboretum could be mistaken for a beech. Its leaves are deep green and its developing fruit can resemble ripening nuts. The cracked bark, however, confirms this is no beech. It produces small, hard, unpalatable fruits, so the best time to visit is in early spring when white blossom covers the canopy. ///piano.miss.stiff

292. **FRAGRANT GIANT** → Like the **PRODIGIOUS PEAR (291)**, the huge small-leaved lime that dominates Lincoln Arboretum's southern glade is an original, dating back to its opening in 1872. Small-leaved limes flower in June, and, although their blooms are subtle, the heady scent they produce is exquisite: the sweet aroma of early summer. Tree hunters should visit in the early evening when the perfume is at its most sublime.

**FRAGRANT GIANT** *Small-leaved lime / Tilia cordata* The Arboretum, Lindum Terrace, Lincoln LN2 5RT 53.230959, -0.526554 ///meals.fairly.native

**293. 1,296TH LIME**
*Common Lime*
*Tilia × europaea*
Limetree Avenue,
Clumber Park,
Worksop S80 3BQ
53.255646, -1.077539

Limetree Avenue runs for 2 miles through Clumber Park in the Dukeries to the south of Worksop. It is the longest tree-lined avenue in Europe, and a double avenue to boot, comprising two parallel rows of trees on each side of the road. At the south-west corner, the first (or last) of the 1,296 trees can be admired. It is one of the oldest, as many have been replaced over the years. ///sweeper.vouch.static

294. **MAJOR OAK*** → Major Oak, one of the most famous trees in England, has grown in Sherwood Forest for hundreds of years, maybe even a millennium. What is left of the forest, which once stretched to the edge of Nottingham, now surrounds the village of Edwinstowe. A forest trail to this incredible tree can be followed from the visitor centre, not far from the cringingly Robin Hood-themed fun park.

**MAJOR OAK***
*Pedunculate oak*
*Quercus robur*
Edwinstowe,
Mansfield NG21 9PF
53.204547, -1.072602
///catchers.hampers.feels

**295. DARLEY DALE YEW***
*Yew / Taxus baccata*
St Helen's Church,
Church Road, Darley
Dale DE4 2GG
53.16323, -1.602369

One of the very fattest yews in England sits squarely by the porch of St Helen's in Darley Dale. It is a tremendous tree, and a sign attached to its enclosing fence claims it could be 2,000 years old. Unlike other very old yews, such as the MUCH MARCLE HOLLOW YEW* **(404)** or the WHITE'S YEW **(661)**, this tree has not yet developed a visible hollow, suggesting it has several millennia to go. ///spectacle.directors.crawler

**296. PEAK CONKER**
*Horse chestnut*
*Aesculus hippocastanum*
Main Street, Winster,
Matlock DE4 2DJ
53.141777, -1.641159
*On private land, but visible from the street.*

Winster is a picture-postcard village on the edge of the Peak District, lined with handsome stone buildings. Next to the finest, a Georgian town house set back from Main Street, a stone bus shelter is shaded by the village's landmark horse chestnut. Being 250 metres up in the dales, it flowers a week or two later than horse chestnuts at lower elevations. ///evening.matter.universal

**297. CLEFT REDWOOD**
*Coastal redwood*
*Sequoia sempervirens*
Knowleston Gardens,
Knowleston Place,
Matlock DE4 3BU
53.134716, -1.551128

Coastal redwoods, the tallest trees in the world, are very unusual among conifers for their ability to develop new shoots if they are cut back. The tree in Knowleston Gardens next to Bentley Brook appears to have experienced some calamity when young and now grows from two thick trunks. In this sheltered location, with ample water, this tree could well become a leviathan. ///rebounds.renovated.beaks

**298. FRIAR'S DELIGHT**
*Oriental plane*
*Platanus orientalis*
Friary Gardens, Friary
Road, Newark NG24 1LE
53.078226, -0.803889

The Friar's Delight is one of the biggest oriental planes in England. The small park in which it resides was a short-lived friary in the 1500s, but, while this tree is old, it is certainly not that old. There is some debate as to when the species, a native of Greece and western Asia, arrived in these islands. What we do know is that it was first described in William Turner's 1548 volume *The Names of Herbes.* ///employer.voltages.venue

**299. THE BRAMLEY APPLE***
*Bramley apple*
*Malus domestica*
*'Bramley's Seedling'*
75 Church Street,
Southwell NG25 0HG
53.07642, -0.94813
*Can be seen on annual open day*

An annual open day is held at 75 Church Street, Southwell, where the original Bramley apple tree, raised from a pip by a child, Mary Ann Brailsford, in 1809, can be seen. Years later, the house and tree came into the ownership of one Matthew Bramley. Realising the apple's worth, he gave cuttings to a nurseryman whom he permitted to commercialise the variety, on the proviso it bore Bramley's name. ///quieter.worms.unsettled

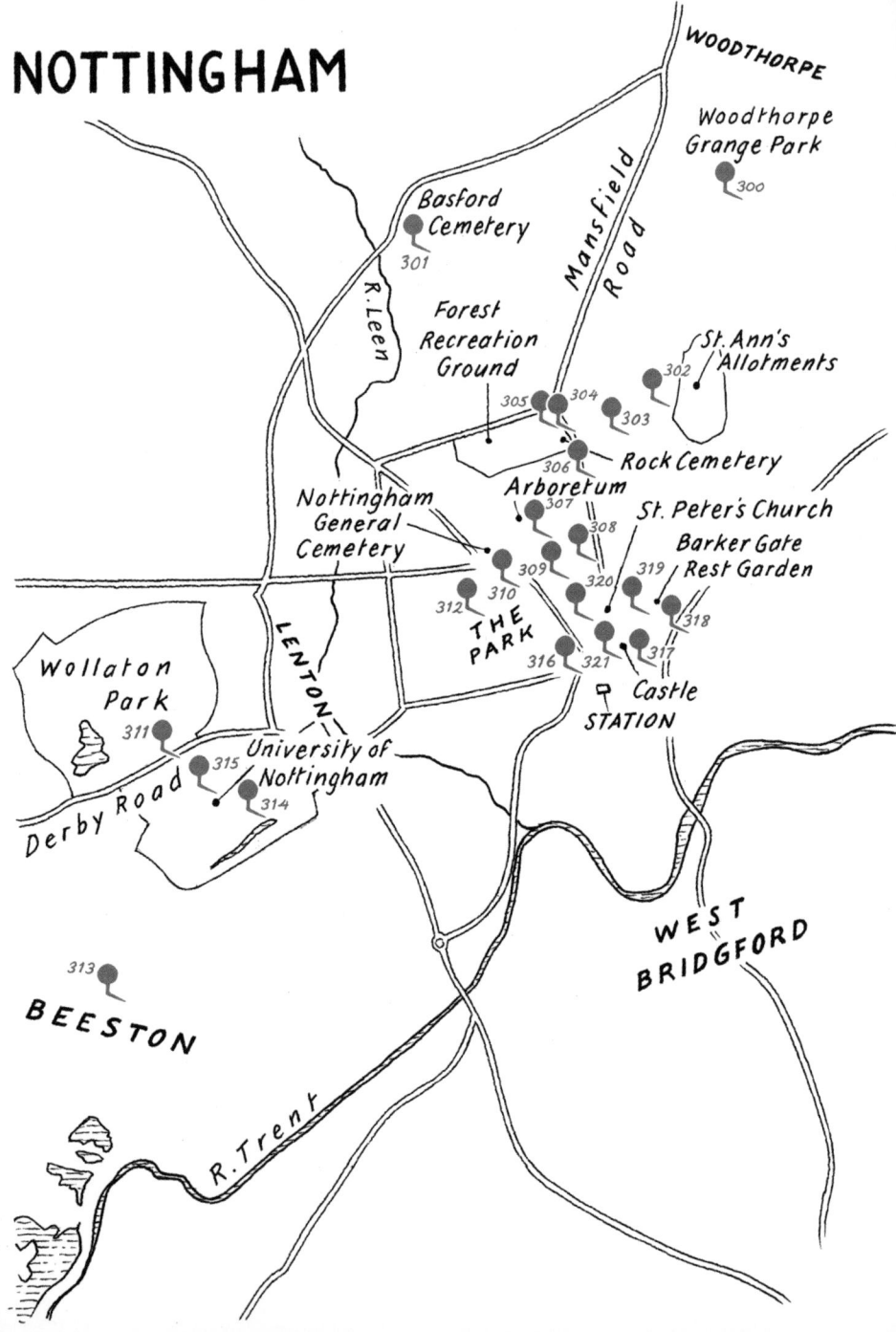

## TREE CITY: NOTTINGHAM
### SIGNATURE SPECIES: *Yellow catalpa*

'Nottingham is one of the most pleasant and beautiful towns in England.' So declared Daniel Defoe on his tour of Great Britain in the early 1700s. At that time the city was renowned for its gardens and its proximity to Sherwood Forest, which then defined the northern edge of the town. By the middle of the nineteenth century, this bucolic vision was a distant memory. Nottingham's population had grown steadily but its boundaries remained unchanged, constrained by the commons and landed estates that surrounded it. By 1832, it had become home to 52,000 people, a teeming mass of humanity who lived in an area of less than 400 hectares – about twice the size of Wollaton Park.

In the same year, unsanitary conditions led to a cholera epidemic resulting in hundreds of deaths. Many burials took place in what is now the peaceful Barker Gate Rest Garden, a tiny parcel of land shaded by the **CHOLERA PLANE (318)**, a tree that may well date to this time. This helped promote the cause of city expansion, and in 1845 the Nottingham Enclosure (sometimes 'Inclosure') Act was passed and the transformation of the city began. While Nottingham's enclosures were contentious, as they resulted in country people losing their rights to use the land, the city gained 52 hectares of recreation ground – more than any other city subject to an enclosure act – and the slums were swept away. Very soon after the act was passed, the **INCLOSURE OAK\*(305)** was planted in the new Forest Recreation Ground, which was carved out from the southern limits of Sherwood Forest as a resort for the townspeople to engage in healthful leisure and sporting activities.

As Nottingham grew rapidly in the nineteenth century, it – like almost all other British cities – enveloped formerly rural landscapes and aristocratic country estates. The best preserved of these is Wollaton Park where the city's oldest and most magnificent tree, **THE ARBOUR OAK\* (311)**, can be found; this is one of the finest examples anywhere of a hybrid between the native pedunculate and sessile oak species. Elsewhere, the grounds of Lenton Hall now house the University Park campus and the remnants of an early university arboretum, where the **NOTTINGHAM MEDLAR (314)** can be sought out among a copse of interesting trees. Below Nottingham Castle, the Park Estate was constructed on the castle's former deer park. This grand but idiosyncratic residential estate – it is still lit by gas lamps and double blue lines indicate where parking is not permitted – is home to the **PARK PLANE (312)**, Nottingham's finest, and likely tallest, street tree.

Nottingham has made great strides in increasing and diversifying its urban forest in recent decades, and evidence of these efforts can be seen throughout the city. The **SURPRISE BUCKEYE (308)**, a rare Ohio Buckeye outside Nottingham Trent University's Arkwright Building, is a good example of this trend, but more remarkable is the **HOCKLEY CATALPA (319)**, a yellow-flowering tree in Nottingham's hippest neighbourhood.

**300. FEATHER-DUSTER BEECH**
*Fern-leaved beech / Fagus sylvatica 'Asplenifolia'*
Woodthorpe Grange Park,
Woodthorpe Drive,
Nottingham NG5 4HA
52.98449, -1.132191

Woodthorpe Grange Park became a public park when the council bought it in the 1920s from various local bigwigs. There are lots of interesting trees, mostly near the Victorian mansion house. To the south, a fern-leaved beech with the demeanour of a feathery pom-pom, takes pride of place in a small formal garden. ///lifted.lance.stay

**301. MOURNING BEECH**
*Weeping beech*
*Fagus sylvatica 'Pendula'*
Basford Cemetery,
Nottingham Road,
Nottingham NG6 0HY
52.980204, -1.171976

Nottingham has plenty of old cemeteries endowed with interesting trees. Basford Cemetery, a gently mouldering Victorian affair, has three weeping beeches. One in the south west, between the cemetery chapels and the lodge, has the best shape, its low canopy resembling a relief model of a mountain range. The trees add a touch of gothic mournfulness, but are rather younger than most of the graves. ///intend.wipe.pushed

**302. NOTTS HOSPICE SPECIAL**
*Copper beech / Fagus sylvatica 'Purpurea'*
Nottinghamshire Hospice,
384 Woodborough Road,
Nottingham NG3 4JF
52.970232, -1.140614

Legend has it that the spectacular copper beech at the Nottinghamshire Hospice is 275 years old, a great, if rather improbable, age for a beech. It is easy to see why it is thought to be so old – its thick, twisted trunk has evolved dramatically over many years. Could it have been here for a century before the hospice, housed in the former home of Victorian cigarette magnate John Player? ///share.stared.couches

**303. CORPORATION OAK\***
*Turkey oak*
*Quercus cerris*
Corporation Oaks,
Nottingham NG3 5DP
52.966513, -1.145094

Corporation Oaks is a short section of Nottingham's memorable Walks where over one hundred oak trees grow. The trees were planted by members of the town council when the Walks opened in 1851, and their names were sanctified by cast-iron plaques at the foot of each tree. To welcome you, the first tree on the right, a Turkey oak, stands next to the Corporation Oaks name sign. ///breed.meals.inches

**304. FOREST MAPLE**
*Cappadocian maple*
*Acer cappadocicum*
Forest Recreation Ground, Mansfield Road,
Nottingham NG5 2BU
52.966297, -1.15392

A very fine mature Cappadocian maple with a prominent graft mark grows close to the *INCLOSURE OAK\** **(305)**. It is a less celebrated but nevertheless striking tree in the garden of the Lodge, now a cake shop, at the Forest Recreation Ground's Mansfield Road entrance. Influential landscape designer Joseph Paxton advised on the layout and planting. Could he have specified the Forest Maple in 1854? ///cargo.laser.river

305. **INCLOSURE OAK**\*
*Pedunculate oak*
*Quercus robur*
Forest Recreation
Ground, Mansfield Road,
Nottingham NG5 2BU
52.966378, -1.154503

A cast-iron plaque at the foot of the Inclosure Oak says it grew from an acorn taken from Windsor Great Park and was planted in 1845. This was the year in which the former common land – the southernmost extent of Sherwood Forest – was gifted to the people of Nottingham by way of the Inclosure Act, which allowed the city's planned expansion. A surprisingly small tree for eighteen decades' growth. ///animal.giant.urban

306. **ROCK CHERRY** → The Rock, or Church, Cemetery, is a dramatic landscape, in places resembling a quarry, with catacombs and burial enclosures carved out of the soft bare rock. An excavated amphitheatre has created a sheltered environment where a Tibetan cherry takes centre stage. It is a particularly large tree for this species, one grown for its dramatically metallic brown bark rather than spring flowers or autumnal fruit.

**ROCK CHERRY**
*Tibetan cherry*
*Prunus serrula*
Rock Cemetery,
Forest Road East,
Nottingham NG1 4HT
52.965139, -1.153651
///calm.fails.middle

TREE CITY: NOTTINGHAM  165

307. **ANTEDILUVIAN ALDER** → Opened in 1852, the Arboretum is Nottingham's oldest park, and was, naturally, the first place I visited when I arrived in the city. There are a handful of trees dating back to its foundation, including the 'Laciniata' alder cultivar close to the Waverley Street entrance. It is large and old, both uncommon traits in an urban alder, and its unusual incised leaves can bamboozle even the most confident tree hunter.

**ANTEDILUVIAN ALDER** *Oak-leaf alder / Alnus glutinosa 'Laciniata'* Nottingham Arboretum, Waverley Street, Nottingham NG7 4HF 52.959991, -1.157415 ///cages.keen.fishery

308. **SURPRISE BUCKEYE**
*Ohio buckeye*
*Aesculus glabra*
Arkwright Building,
Shakespeare Street,
Nottingham NG1 4FQ
52.957754, -1.152412

Nottingham Trent University is the new kid in town, university-wise, and has carved out its campus around several landmark properties in the city centre. One of the finest is the gothic Arkwright Building on Shakespeare Street, where a young Ohio buckeye can be found. They are unusual trees that look like regular horse chestnuts most of the year, but visit in May to see yellow flowers. ///groom.apron.stiff

309. **NTU J. C. TEAS**
*Hybrid catalpa*
*Catalpa × erubescens*
*'J. C. Teas'*
Chaucer Building,
Chaucer Street,
Nottingham NG1 5LP
52.957457, -1.155232

Another tree originating from the American Midwest illuminates a nondescript late-twentieth-century Nottingham Trent University building on Chaucer Street. A particularly tall and an occasionally spectacular catalpa grows on the grass slope, and in July it can flower abundantly with loose bunches of horse chestnut-like white blossom. It is a hybrid catalpa, known as *'J. C. Teas'* after the Indiana nursery in which it was first propagated. ///random.horns.cargo

310. **GENERAL ASH**
*Weeping ash / Fraxinus*
*excelsior 'Pendula'*
General Cemetery,
Alfreton Road,
Nottingham NG1 5GP
52.956676, -1.161677

General Ash is steadily consuming a Victorian gravestone in the General Cemetery. The tree has been at it for many years, but it will be many more before the memorial is entirely swallowed. It is a humorous sight, tempered by the inscription to John Smith Thorpe who died aged just forty in 1871, while his four sons all died before they were ten. ///answer.custom.cargo

311. **THE ARBOUR OAK**⁎⇢ The Arbour Oak is a 550-year-old tree at the peak of its powers. It grows some distance from Wollaton Hall, an Elizabethan house which it predates by at least a century. Find it on Arbour Hill close to the Beeston Lodge entrance on the southern edge of Wollaton Park. Today it is surrounded by woodland, but great, spreading limbs suggest that at one time it was not so hemmed in.

**THE ARBOUR OAK**⁎ *Hybrid oak / Quercus × rosacea* Beeston Lodge, Derby Road Nottingham NG7 1AB 52.953792, -1.165346 ///policy.sheep.invest

312. **PARK PLANE**
*London plane*
*Platanus × hispanica*
Tattershall Drive,
Nottingham NG7 1AB
52.943254, -1.203835

A towering nineteenth-century London plane grows on Tattershall Drive near the corner with Newcastle Drive in The Park, Nottingham's leafiest and most upmarket neighbourhood situated on what was once Nottingham Castle's deer park. Its separateness is reinforced by the gas street lighting and road markings painted in blue. ///successes.custom.ballots

313. **BEESTON BEECH**
*Copper beech / Fagus sylvatica 'Purpurea'*
Tesco Petrol Station,
Middle Street, Beeston,
Nottingham NG9 2AR
52.92641, -1.210996

Beeston has been revamped since the trams arrived, after some delays, in 2015. Despite all the disruptive work, the Beeston Beech, a grand copper beech, was left in situ. It is both a benign presence for motorists filling up at the petrol station it now shades, and a lovely landmark for those arriving in Beeston by tram. ///cliff.stack.card

314. **NOTTINGHAM MEDLAR**
*Medlar / Mespilus germanica 'Nottingham'*
Old Botanic Garden,
Arboretum Walk,
University Park,
Nottingham NG7 2QL
52.939265, -1.193766

An old, well-maintained medlar (come in early autumn to catch the fruit, which you need to blett, or let almost rot, before eating) grows on the University of Nottingham's extensive University Park campus. It is a remnant of the Old Botanic Garden, a small area once used for teaching students of botany. Today there is a diverse woodland of unusual trees including the Nottingham Medlar, a cultivar that was presumably first grown in the city. ///herbs.paper.charge

**315. HAYSTACK TREE**
*Weeping hornbeam*
*Carpinus betulus 'Pendula'*
The Downs,
University of Nottingham,
Lenton Hall Drive,
Nottingham NG7 2BF
52.940155, -1.198554

The Downs is a tree-fringed area of sloping grassland on the northern side of the University Park campus. An alluring tree appearing as a green dome on the high ground demands close inspection: the seasoned tree hunter will realise it is a rare weeping hornbeam. Unlike dramatic weeping beeches, weeping hornbeams are more subtle; the Haystack Tree's branches meet the ground in such a way as to give it the impression of a neat, leafy haystack. ///venues.dress.drama

316. **BOULEVARD PLANE** → Nottingham's boulevards form three sides of a square around the city centre. Part of the grand Victorian urban plan following the Nottingham Enclosure Act, they are still resplendent with nineteenth-century London planes. One of the most impressive is just off Castle Boulevard, next to the phone box on Peverill Drive, with the bare rock of the cliff below the castle as its backdrop.

**BOULEVARD PLANE**
*London plane*
*Platanus × hispanica*
Peverill Drive,
Nottingham NG7 1FE
52.948698, -1.153621
///wicked.canny.villa

### 317. CLIFF FIG
*Fig / Ficus carica*
Cliff Road,
Nottingham NG1 1GT
52.950558, -1.143372

Take the steps to the side of Nottingham Contemporary from High Pavement down to Cliff Road, then turn left until a gap in the derelict buildings reveals a huge and sprawling fig tree clinging precariously to the bare rock. While it does not grow on a riverbank, this part of the city has always been heavily populated. Perhaps Salford's EFFLUENT FIG (167) offers a clue to the tree's origins? ///risks.habit.zips

### 318. CHOLERA PLANE
*London plane*
*Platanus × hispanica*
Barker Gate Rest Garden,
Barker Gate,
Nottingham NG1 1JU
52.95293, -1.141895

Barker Gate Rest Garden is a peaceful pocket park dominated by a stately old London plane. It was originally a burial ground, one of the few plots set aside for this purpose in pre-Enclosure Act Nottingham, and in 1832, when a notorious cholera epidemic killed hundreds, many of the victims were buried here. It's possible the plane tree was planted around this time, perhaps as a memorial. ///mini.boost.payer

### 319. HOCKLEY CATALPA
*Yellow catalpa*
*Catalpa ovata*
Carlton Street,
Nottingham NG1 1NL
52.953603, -1.144938

Clearly a Nottingham urban forester had a thing for unusual yellow-flowering trees. Complementing the SURPRISE BUCKEYE (308) on Shakespeare Street, another rare tree with buttery blooms can be seen on Carlton Street in Hockley. It is a yellow catalpa. Like the buckeye, it's a youthful specimen but is from Asia rather than the American Midwest. ///storm.camera.print

### 320. M&S PLANE
*London plane*
*Platanus × hispanica*
Albert Street,
Nottingham NG1 7DA
52.952121, -1.148519

Between Marks & Spencer and St Peter's Church, an old London plane tree, one of several adding character to this part of Nottingham city centre, is singled out by a semicircular bench around its trunk. The bench is recent but the tree has stood here for generations. It is knobblier, though shorter, than the PARK PLANE (312). Many shoppers must have admired it, and even felt moved to caress its knotted bole. ///vine.fired.took

### 321. ST PETER'S PRIVET
*Chinese tree privet*
*Ligustrum lucidum*
St Peter's Church,
St Peter's Gate,
Nottingham NG1 2NW
52.952175, -1.148161

Sit on the bench beneath the M&S PLANE (320) to admire the exotic triple-trunked St Peter's Privet growing in the churchyard. It is an unusual evergreen tree that can sometimes be seen thriving in the mild south east, but it is rare elsewhere. Its presence in Nottingham signifies how conditions in the Midlands have begun to favour tender plants that would struggle further north. ///mercy.they.brains

### 322. EREWASH PHAROS
*Bolle's poplar*
*Populus alba*
*'Pyramidalis'*
Milner Road,
Long Eaton NG10 1LB
52.897329, -1.275416

The Erewash Pharos can be seen for miles around; it is a soaring tree growing next to a lock on the towpath of the Erewash Canal in the Derbyshire town of Long Eaton. It can be admired from the iron footbridge crossing the canal between Milner Road and West Park, where its silvery, toothed leaves and dimpled bark will distinguish it from other tall poplars with fissured bark and triangular leaves growing nearby. ///quiet.sentences.lasted

### 323. DARLEY PARK DEN TREE
*Weeping one-leaved ash*
*Fraxinus excelsior*
*'Diversifolia Pendula'*
Darley Park, Darley
Abbey, Derby DE22 1EJ
52.940074, -1.478137

Generations of Derby children have adored the Darley Park Den Tree, a low dome whose branches sweep down to the lawn enclosing a space impenetrable to adults, which doubles as a prime natural climbing frame. It is also a very unusual tree, a rare weeping ash cultivar, whose single rather than compound leaves distinguish it from other ashes. ///marble.arrive.roses

### 324. BLUSHING TREE
*Purple Norway maple*
*Acer platanoides*
*'Schwedleri'*
Darley Park, Darley
Abbey, Derby DE22 1EJ
52.939777, -1.479167

In recent decades, Norway maple cultivars with very dark purple leaves have appeared around Britain and Ireland, but the tree on the path into Darley Park from the car park is an older *'Schwedleri'* variety, with far less brutal colouring. Its leaves open red in spring before fading back to green as the summer progresses. Even if it didn't have such distinctive leaf colour, this is a magnificent example of a Norway maple. ///above.marble.moving

### 325. LOUDON'S BLACK WALNUT
*Black walnut/Juglans nigra*
Derby Arboretum,
Arboretum Square,
Rose Hill Street,
Derby DE23 8FR
52.912368, -1.472796

Derby Arboretum is important. It was designed by John Claudius Loudon, originator of the Gardenesque style and arguably the most influential nineteenth-century landscape designer. Opened in 1840, it is also one of England's oldest public parks. Several trees from this period survive, including a black walnut growing on one of the ridges close to the Lodge. This is the Arboretum's most impressive tree. ///gifted.season.slap

### 326. SEEN-IT-ALL HAZEL
*Turkish hazel*
*Corylus colurna*
Derby Arboretum,
Arboretum Square,
Rose Hill Street,
Derby DE23 8FR
52.912826, -1.473467

Like LOUDON'S BLACK WALNUT (325), the Seen-It-All Hazel is another original from 1840. Turkish hazels have been much planted as street trees in recent decades, as, unlike the unruly multi-stemmed hazel of coppice woodlands and hedgerows, they become large but neat pyramidal trees. Old trees of this species are very rare indeed – this one, a great curiosity, now requires propping up in its dotage. ///baked.rise.tester

SEEN-IT-ALL HAZEL (326)

### 327. THE GRANTHAM OAK*
*Pedunculate oak*
*Quercus robur*
Belton Lane,
Grantham NG31 9PR
52.924119, -0.62905

The Grantham Oak is a much celebrated tree, as the fence surrounding it, the bunting draped from its hefty trunk and a nearby interpretation panel attest. It may be over 500 years old, and was once a pollard, perhaps marking a field boundary. While the field gave way to urban expansion decades ago, the row of houses on Belton Lane nonetheless curves deferentially around it. ///reboot.arose.rated

### 328. BLACK BULL ELM
*Huntingdon elm / Ulmus × hollandica 'Vegeta'*
Teigh Road,
Market Overton,
Oakham LE15 7PW
52.738748, -0.687478

Elm lovers will want to make a beeline for the Black Bull in Market Overton, from where it is possible to admire, and raise a glass to, a fine pair of old Huntingdon elms. They stand proudly side-by-side at the T-junction where Main Street meets Teigh Road. Both are splendid, but the tree closest to the pub is by some distance the larger and is altogether the more impressive of the two. ///excavated.monitors.unwanted

### 329. RUTLAND MAPLE
*Norway maple*
*Acer platanoides*
Vicarage Road,
Oakham LE15 6EG
52.670561, -0.722496

Oakham must once have been noteworthy for its oaks. Today it is still a leafy place, but it is a mighty Norway maple that impresses. Norway maples are a staple of many towns, with thousands planted in the last fifty years. It is unusual to see an old tree, however, and one the size of the Rutland Maple is particularly rare. ///harmlessly.walkway.pounds

### 330. TIMELESS PLANE
*London plane*
*Platanus × hispanica*
Water Street,
Stamford PE9 2NW
52.650213, -0.475857

Omnipresent cars are one of the few reminders of the here and now in Stamford, a remarkably well-preserved English town otherwise barely tarnished by modern developments. Several distinctive trees grace the town, the largest being a massive London plane on Water Street. It grows in this species' favourite position: on the banks of a river, in this case the slow-flowing Welland dotted with water lilies. ///status.woof.panel

### 331. ST GEORGE'S WHITEBEAM
*Whitebeam / Sorbus aria*
St George's Church,
St George's Square,
Stamford PE9 2BN
52.651614, -0.476124

Achingly pretty St George's Square is set off by the whitebeam growing from the churchyard at the western end. It is a perfectly proportioned tree for the diminutive Grade I-listed church and square – not too large, with a cottage-garden feel to it. Whitebeams are at their best as their downy white leaves unfurl in spring, reminding me of luxurious candelabra-like magnolia blooms. ///slug.clear.detail

**332. COALITION TREE**
*Dawn redwood*
*Metasequoia*
*glyptostroboides*
Town Meadows, Bath Row, Stamford PE9 2QU
52.650213, -0.4795

In 2024 the TIMELESS PLANE (330) was Stamford's largest tree, but, in a few decades, there is every chance that distinction may pass to this young dawn redwood growing in the Town Meadows. It is a large, twin-trunked individual with a plaque which is sadly difficult to read, but which mentions a 'Twin Town'. Perhaps the tree is in fact two planted close together, which, as they've grown over the years, have melded in an act of civic fraternity? ///hammer.fire.frozen

**333. LEICESTER'S PRIDE OF INDIA**
*Golden rain tree*
*Koelreuteria paniculata*
Abbey Park, Abbey Park Road, Leicester LE4 5AQ
52.648596, -1.137815

A nod to Leicester's status as home to one of the largest South Asian populations in England, a splendid pride of India, or golden rain tree, stands out in Abbey Park near the ruins. Despite their name, pride of India trees originate from China and Korea. Visit in high summer to see masses of yellow flowers, the eponymous golden rain. ///wake.castle.heat

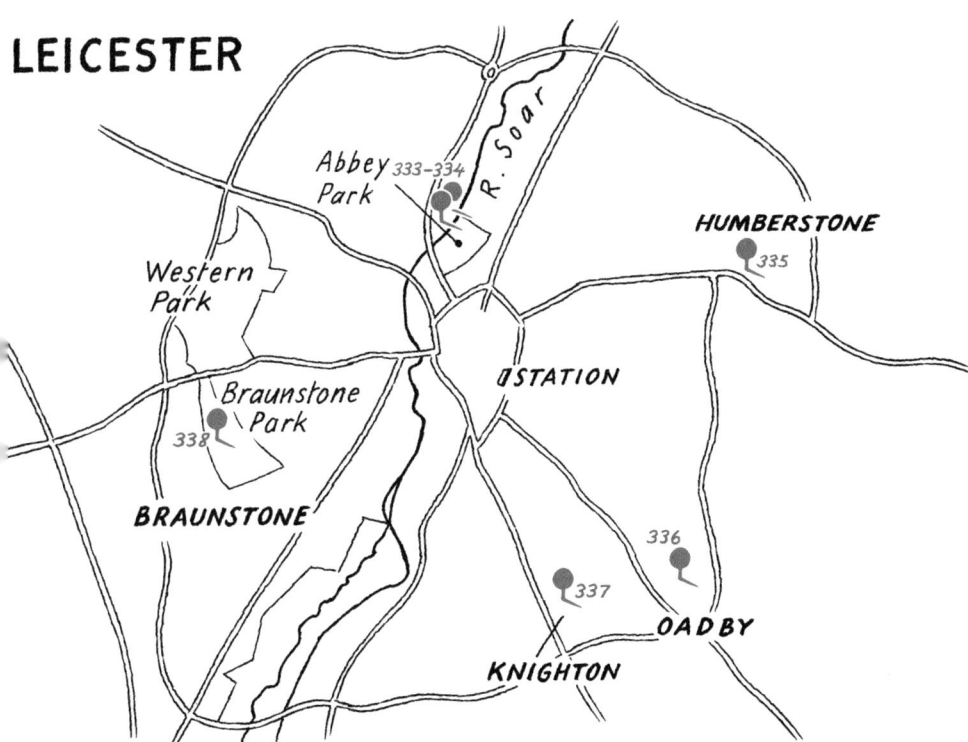

**334. LUSCIOUS-LOCKED GINKGO**
*Ginkgo*
*Ginkgo biloba*
Cavendish House, Abbey Park, Abbey Park Road, Leicester LE4 5AQ
52.649054, -1.138704

In Abbey Park, close to the sixteenth-century ruin of Cavendish House, the Luscious-Locked Ginkgo grows, an historic sight in itself. It is at least a century old and multi-stemmed, possibly a bundle-planting of two or more saplings growing together. Ginkgos' distinctive leaves have earned the species another popular name – the maidenhair tree, an obscure reference to the maidenhair fern, itself thought to resemble the sumptuous locks of a fair maiden. ///tuck.trend.horns

**335. MISTAKEN IDENTITY** → Whoever named Pine Tree Avenue needs to go back to tree school. The giant trees that line this suburban Leicester street are conifers, but these are no mere pines. Incredibly, they are giant redwoods, the finest of which is outside number 15. Once they lined the driveway up to Humberstone Hall, a country house demolished in 1926 to make way for Leicester's expansion. At least the trees survived.

**MISTAKEN IDENTITY**
*Giant redwood*
*Sequoiadendron giganteum*
Pine Tree Avenue, Leicester LE5 1AJ
52.64334, -1.081934
///couch.still.fight

### 336. GLITTERBALL WILLOW
*Silver willow*
*Salix alba var. sericea*
University Botanic
Garden, Glebe Road,
Oadby, Leicester
LE2 2LD
52.608385, -1.091529

The university's delightful botanic garden is a popular resort for Leicesterians, created by combining four separate gardens belonging to large Edwardian houses. As a result, several distinct gardens coalesce into a succession of different spaces. There are dozens of memorable trees too, the most dazzling of which is the shimmering silver willow, a variety of white willow with pristine white leaves. ///glaze.fuel.driven

### 337. ATTENBOROUGH HORSE CHESTNUT
*Horse chestnut*
*Aesculus hippocastanum*
Attenborough
Arboretum, Carisbrooke
Road, Leicester LE2 3TQ
52.608061, -1.115383

Semi-wild Attenborough Arboretum, opened by Sir David Attenborough in 1997 to showcase British native trees, was once farmland at the village of Knighton, but is now entirely surrounded by the city of Leicester. At its heart, a handsome old tree can be glimpsed through the scrub and saplings. Ironically, this, the oldest tree on site, the Attenborough Horse Chestnut, is a species from the Balkans. ///trim.giant.took

### 338. REGENCY CEDAR
*Cedar of Lebanon*
*Cedrus libani*
Braunstone Park,
Gooding Avenue,
Leicester LE3 1JS
52.624879, -1.177083

Braunstone House and its grounds were enveloped by the growing city in the early twentieth century; the council acquired the estate and turned it into Braunstone Park. In the gardens, a picturesque cedar of Lebanon with unusual glaucous foliage takes pride of place. It was probably planted not long after the house was built. ///spots.occupy.horn

### 339. GARRICK'S MULBERRY
*Black mulberry*
*Morus nigra*
Abington Park,
Park Avenue South,
Northampton NN3 3AB
52.246591, -0.866081

A tree with a known planting date is always interesting, and helps us estimate the age of others of its species. In 1778 the celebrated actor David Garrick planted a cutting of SHAKESPEARE'S MULBERRY (394) on the lawn of Abington Park in Northampton as a mark of his friendship with its resident, Anne Thursby. The tree still thrives, although now it is entirely recumbent, and is best visited in winter to appreciate its twisted, meandering form. ///loudly.help.film

### 340. DELAPRÉ TULIP TREE
*Tulip tree*
*Liriodendron tulipifera*
Delapré Abbey,
London Road,
Northampton NN4 8AW
52.224545, -0.88828

Just beyond the south-east corner of Delapré Abbey, a tree hunter's paradise begins. Lots of magnificent characters vie for attention, but the tallest in a group of three is the best: a giant tulip tree with a huge, swollen base. It is flanked by an enormous western red cedar and a very large Ohio buckeye. Visit in May to catch it in flower. ///sheet.spaces.charge

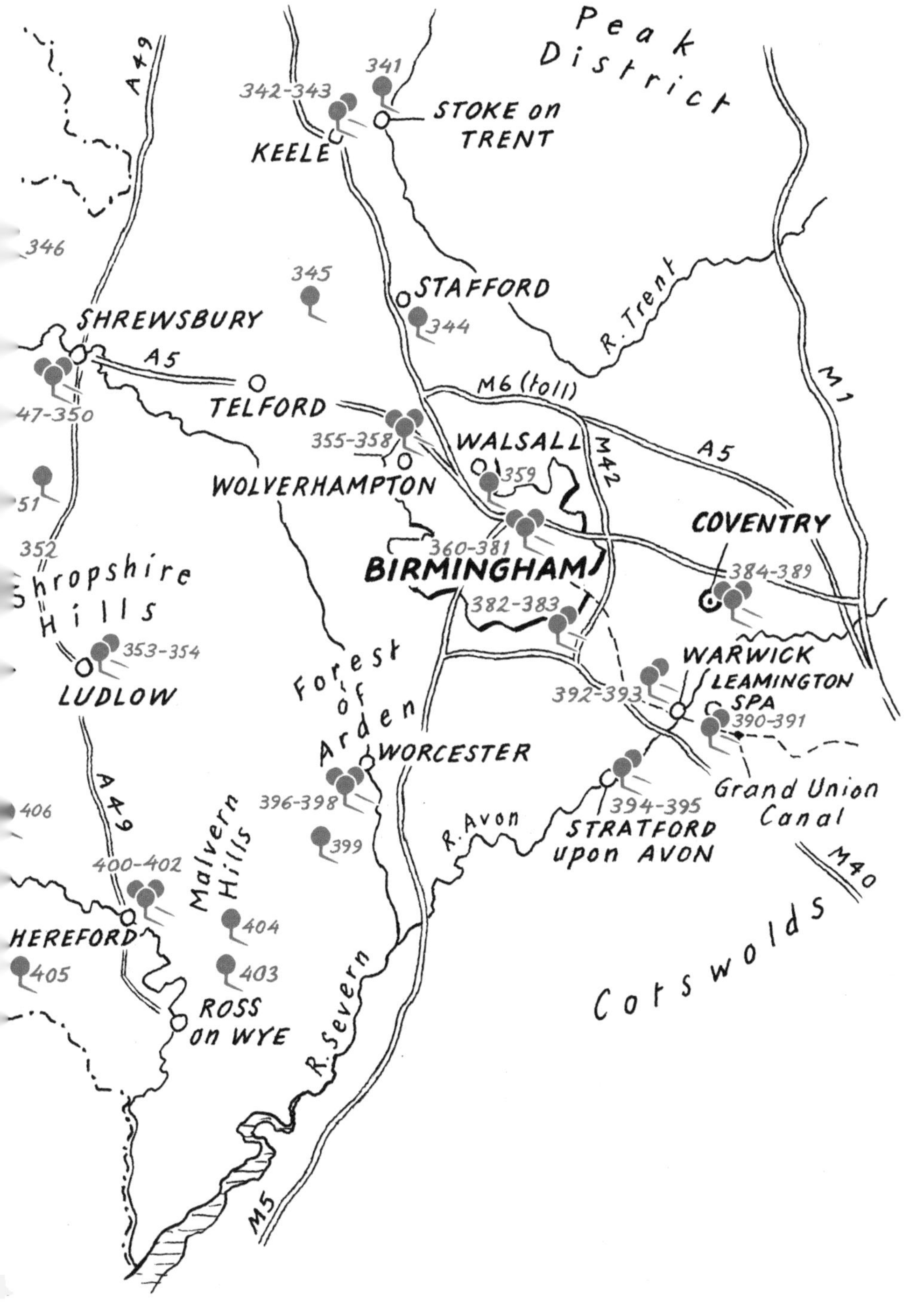

# Map

**Peak District**

341 — Stoke on Trent
342-343 — Keele
345
344 — Stafford
346
Shrewsbury
A5
347-350
Telford
351
355-358 — Wolverhampton
352
Shropshire Hills
Walsall
359
M6 (toll)
M42
A5
Coventry
360-381 — Birmingham
384-389
382-383
353-354 — Ludlow
Forest of Arden
Warwick / Leamington Spa
392-393
390-391
Grand Union Canal
Worcester
396-398
399
R. Avon
394-395 — Stratford upon Avon
M40
406
400-402
Malvern Hills
404
Hereford
405
403
Ross on Wye
R. Severn
Cotswolds
M5

## WEST MIDLANDS

Staffordshire
Shropshire
Herefordshire
Worcestershire
Warwickshire
West Midlands

**TREE CITY:**
*Birmingham*

**SIGNATURE SPECIES:**
*Black mulberry*

Our Victorian forebears left a great civic legacy in the green spaces that still grace our cityscapes. They are defining features of our towns and cities and, as they have mellowed into mature landscapes, they have become some of the most fruitful places to discover noteworthy trees. I have already highlighted the arboreal treasures that can be seen in the municipal parks of the north west, the arboretums of the East Midlands and the botanic gardens of Yorkshire and eastern Scotland. But there is another type of commonly encountered urban landscape also worthy of your attention: the nineteenth-century cemetery. Dozens of trees that feature in this book are located in these spaces, often designated as 'rest gardens', a term that emphasises their green and bosky quietude. While the West Midlands boasts many parks, arboretums and botanic gardens – like Burslem Park in Stoke-on-Trent, home of **MAWSON'S EXTRAORDINARY CHERRY (341)**; the historic Birmingham Botanical Gardens, where the **BIRMINGHAM DWARF (367)** stands; and Walsall Arboretum with the **WALSALL RAZZO (359)** – it is the region's cemeteries that are particularly enticing.

As our cities rapidly burgeoned in the nineteenth century, the parish churchyards where people had been buried for generations became overcrowded – or worse. Following outbreaks of cholera and other deadly, highly transmissible diseases, it was decided that dedicated cemeteries were required, and throughout the century they opened in virtually every urban district. In south Birmingham, this region's Tree City, Brandwood End Cemetery is a good, late-Victorian example dating from 1899. Despite being a relative youngster, its crossed rows of giant redwoods, best appreciated under the **BRANDWOOD BEACON (379)**, have become a sight many tree hunters will want to see. To some, these landscapes may seem melancholic, but they were intended as peaceful havens for the living just as much as for the dead. One of the most spectacular anywhere is the London Road Cemetery in Coventry. It was laid out on a hilly site to a design by Joseph Paxton in 1847, and has many trees typical of this time. There are dozens of old conifers, spectacular copper beeches, Lucombe-type hybrid Spanish oaks and a towering silver pendent lime, but the most memorable tree is the **CEMETERY ASH (388)**. It is an elegant *'Lentiscifolia'* cultivar of narrow-leaved ash, one of at least two here, a species that is able to thrive in the more southerly latitudes of the Midlands. The Victorians appreciated this tree far more than twentieth-century tree planters, and they have rarely been planted since the 1800s, so this specimen, along with the handful of others elsewhere, should be regarded as particularly historic.

Merridale Cemetery in Wolverhampton is another mid-nineteenth-century affair, opened in 1850, but the tree to admire here is one that is quite probably even older. A magnificent hornbeam, the **MERRIDALE MONUMENT (357)**, once perhaps a shapely hedgerow tree, seems to have been left in situ by the cemetery developer. Today it is a living reminder of the passage of time, a witness to events we can only imagine.

Arboreal relics of the distant past can be seen in the most unlikely places. As they become ever more aged, their wonder only increases. The West Midlands has plenty of such relics, like the ancient **LODE LANE CHESTNUT (383)** growing at a busy Solihull road junction; **THE GREAT OAK\* (406)**, a landmark in the Herefordshire village of Eardisley, which has been celebrated for centuries; or the more recent **GREYFRIARS SPANISH OAK (387)**, one of a row of old trees in Coventry that are all that remain of a pre-Second World War feature of this radically rebuilt city.

### 341. MAWSON'S EXTRAORDINARY CHERRY
*'Albi-plena' Japanese cherry / Prunus serrulata 'Albi-Plena'*
Burslem Park, Moorland Road, Burslem,
Stoke-on-Trent ST6 1EB
53.048849, -2.188307

Delightful Burslem Park opened in 1894 following a scheme by T. H. Mawson, the designer of Bellevue Gardens in Newport. In Burslem, a strikingly strange tree grows next to the bowling green. It is a beautiful *'Albi-Plena'* cherry, which distinguishes itself with long branches from which stubby twigs grow, giving it a weird, almost prehistoric look. In April it is fleetingly covered in white flowers, presumably once sought out by herbivorous dinosaurs. ///fortunate.cheat.invite

### 342. TAWNEY YOSHINO →
Keele University is home to the National Cherry Collection. Hundreds of ornamental trees are dotted across this large campus, which almost feels like a small town. Dozens are very beautiful cherry trees, many of which are rare varieties hardly ever seen even in suburban gardens or town parks. One of the most exquisite is a Japanese weeping yoshino outside the Tawney Building.

**TAWNEY YOSHINO**
*Weeping yoshino cherry*
*Prunus × yedoensis 'Ivensii'*
Keele University, Keele,
Newcastle under Lyme
ST5 5BG
53.002897, -2.272941
///reduce.danger.count

**343. CHANCELLOR'S BRIDE**
*'The Bride' Fuji cherry*
*Prunus incisa 'The Bride'*
Keele University, Keele,
Newcastle under Lyme
ST5 5BG
53.003598, -2.272358

Another of Keele's loveliest cherries is *'The Bride'*, a recent cultivar of Japanese Fuji cherry selected by a Belgian nursery. The Keele tree is one of the first to be planted in the UK. Seek it out near the Chancellor's Building in March to catch its superabundant pristine white blossoms, each developing a central red spot as their season matures. ///tested.tulip.bolts

**344. STAFFORD PUZZLE OAK**
*Pedunculate oak*
*Quercus robur*
St Mary's Castle Church,
Newport Road,
Stafford ST16 1DJ
52.796531, -2.140458

Like many old churches, St Mary's Castle Church has an ancient tree growing in its churchyard. But, unlike most, this one is an oak. The church stands on the edge of Stafford below the castle, a fortification much altered over the centuries but with its original Norman foundations intact. The tree is clearly very old, and looks out of place, posing the question of how it came to grow here. ///birds.riots.appear

**345. NEWPORT CONTRARIAN**
*Winter-flowering cherry*
*Prunus × subhirtella*
*'Autumnalis'*
St Nicholas, High Street,
Newport TF10 7AY
52.769526, -2.3793

St Nicholas's church is the focal point of Newport, but visit between December and March and it may be the tree against the church's south front that causes heads to turn. It is a winter-flowering cherry, one of the biggest anywhere. It flowers shyly yet continuously throughout the winter months, and will occasionally be covered in cheering white flowers – an unexpected joy of this species. ///november.pounding.motoring

**346. COVETED YEW**
*Dovaston's yew / Taxus*
*baccata 'Dovastoniana'*
Dovaston Close,
Twyford Cross, West
Felton SY11 4EQ
52.826447, -2.971427

In the past, rather than being reared in nurseries, cultivars were often selected from wild plants with unusual characteristics, and if one were deemed interesting, it could become hot property, with gardeners all over the world demanding their own. This is what happened with the now-rare Dovaston's yew. The original, 'discovered' in 1777, still grows in what is now the garden of a West Felton housing development. ///panoramic.sporting.pounding

**347. DARWIN OAK**
*Pedunculate oak*
*Quercus robur*
Shelton Rough,
Shrewsbury SY3 8BH
52.718615, -2.792535

For five and a half centuries, the powerful and voluminous Darwin Oak has been towering over Shelton Rough close to Charles Darwin's birthplace on The Mount in Shrewsbury. The veteran tree, along with its dependent community of plants and animals, now lies in the path of the proposed North West Relief Road – an environmentally catastrophic development if it is given the green light. ///helpful.doubt.develops

**348. PRIDE OF SHREWSBURY**
*London plane*
*Platanus × hispanica*
St Mary's Lane,
Shrewsbury SY1 1ED
52.708347, -2.751625

At the top of Pride Hill, turn right into Church Street to admire Shrewsbury's tallest tree. A pair of strapping London planes grow in the churchyard of St Mary's. The narrowness of the medieval streets accentuates their height, and it is impossible to get far enough away to judge accurately which is the highest, but the corner tree won my heart by dint of its splendid location. ///secure.clock.bunch

**349. SEVERN BANK POPLAR**
*Wild black poplar*
*Populus nigra ssp.*
*betulifolia*
Abbey Gardens,
Shrewsbury SY2 6AA
52.707161, -2.747354

Several landmarks stand out when crossing the English Bridge from west to east. Straight ahead is the bulk of Shrewsbury Abbey's tower, to the right is the spire of the United Reformed Church, while to the left is the billowing splendour of a giant black poplar. It has an unruly silhouette and typical clumpy foliage, and grows here in its perfect setting on the banks of the Severn. ///times.pill.grid

**350. ABBEY TREE OF HEAVEN**
*Tree of heaven*
*Ailanthus altissima*
Abbey Foregate,
Shrewsbury SY2 6BQ
52.707134, -2.741395

There appears to be a sweet spot for trees of heaven, starting around Shropshire and stretching north up to Lancashire. In this zone, they seem to thrive but do not yet show the troubling invasive tendencies they exhibit further south. Shrewsbury's Abbey Tree of Heaven is a particularly fine example, growing happily on busy Abbey Foregate not far from Shrewsbury Abbey. ///violin.echo.smoke

**351. OLD MAN OF THE WOODS\***
*Sweet chestnut*
*Castanea sativa*
Rectory Wood,
Church Street, Church
Stretton SY6 6DQ
52.539982, -2.810793

Follow the path around the northern edge of Rectory Woods in order to approach the Old Man of the Woods from below. A fat old sweet chestnut leans over the path, which splits around it, and it is from this angle that the Old Man's jolly face – a burr on the side of the trunk – can be seen grinning out at passers-by. ///backtrack.tutorial.baked

**352. ARBOR TREE\***
*Wild black poplar*
*Populus nigra ssp.*
*betulifolia*
School Bank,
Aston on Clun SY7 8ES
52.4301965, -2.8946626

Oak Apple Day, a traditional celebration to mark the Restoration of 1660, is observed in Aston on Clun on the last Sunday of May. The village festivities centre around the Arbor Tree, which is dressed with flags that remain on the tree until they are replaced the following year. The current Arbor Tree is a rapidly growing scion taken from the original 300-year-old black poplar, which succumbed to a storm in 1995. ///doghouse.trip.probe

SEVERN BANK POPLAR (349)

### 353. LOVELIEST HORNBEAM
*Hornbeam*
*Carpinus betulus*
St Laurence, College Street, Ludlow SY8 1AN
52.368383, -2.719346

In 1951, John Betjeman famously described Ludlow as the 'loveliest town in England'. It is a town of few trees, but in recent decades, a hornbeam has been planted in St Laurence's churchyard. It is already of exceptional shape, broad, symmetrical and a little unkempt, and will be Ludlow's loveliest tree as its size increases in years to come. ///nerve.pokes.face

### 354. CAR PARK COPPER BEECH
*Copper beech / Fagus sylvatica 'Purpurea'*
Castle Street Car Park, Ludlow SY8 1AT
52.367871, -2.721067

Set back from Ludlow's marketplace on Castle Street is a particularly large and handsome Georgian town house. In summer, the purple canopy of a huge copper beech watches over it. The tree is a giant that grows in what was once a back garden, now largely incorporated into the car park. Today, those visiting the public toilets or queuing for a parking ticket get the best view of it. ///thin.majors.grownup

### 355. RICKETY OAK
*Pedunculate oak*
*Quercus robur*
Tettenhall Green, Wergs Road, Tettenhall, Wolverhampton WV6 9AY
52.599949, -2.169132

Residents of Tettenhall describe it as a village, but expanding Wolverhampton has now entirely consumed it. However, hints at its more bucolic past still survive. One of the most prominent is Upper Green, with its hollow oak tree by the paddling pool. This poignant tree has survived for several centuries but has suffered from vandals breaking branches and setting fires in its hollow. Fortunately, a protective fence now surrounds it. ///cheer.rods.care

### 356. ROCK YEW
*Yew/ Taxus baccata*
St Michael and All Angels, Church Road, Tettenhall, Wolverhampton WV6 9AJ
52.600703, -2.162025

St Michael's churchyard nestles under a sandstone escarpment, and contains three veteran yew trees. The tree nearest the church is the largest and boasts a charismatic hollow. It is remarkable it has survived for so long in Wolverhampton – humans have such a propensity to adorn, deface and damage trees that very old urban trees are rare. ///putty.wooden.bunk

### 357. MERRIDALE MONUMENT
*Hornbeam*
*Carpinus betulus*
Merridale Cemetery, Jeffcock Road, Wolverhampton WV3 7AA
52.579978, -2.150448

Like many Victorian cemeteries, Merridale has some captivating trees. The finest is a very old hornbeam near the Jeffcock Road entrance. The cemetery opened in 1850, but the tree appears to be rather older. Mature trees like this were often retained in newly constructed nineteenth-century cemeteries and parks, a practice we should ensure continues in the space-hungry twenty-first century. ///opens.coins.palace

**358. MIDLAND MADRONE**
*Pacific madrone*
*Arbutus menziesii*
West Park, Park Road
West, Wolverhampton
WV1 4PH
52.588845, -2.13937

Tree hunters will love West Park, one of England's finest. Although it underwent a major restoration in the 1990s, it has been lovingly maintained since and retains many original late-Victorian features. Nineteenth-century trees rub shoulders with newer arrivals, including many rarities. A particularly striking addition is the Pacific madrone with amber bark that shelters under a giant redwood near the tea rooms. ///photos.simply.splash

**359. WALSALL RAZZO** → The Victorians believed that accessible arboretums would 'improve' the society they served: through exposure to trees from all over the world, people would be educated and entertained. Today, Walsall Arboretum is primarily a park rather than a specialist tree collection, but it does have dozens of impressive trees focused around the Walsall Razzo, an Italian rocket of a tree blasting off by the Hoar Brook.

**WALSALL RAZZO**
*Lombardy poplar / Populus nigra 'Plantierensis'*
Broadway North,
Walsall WS1 2QB
52.590246, -1.969638
///pint.rank.sadly

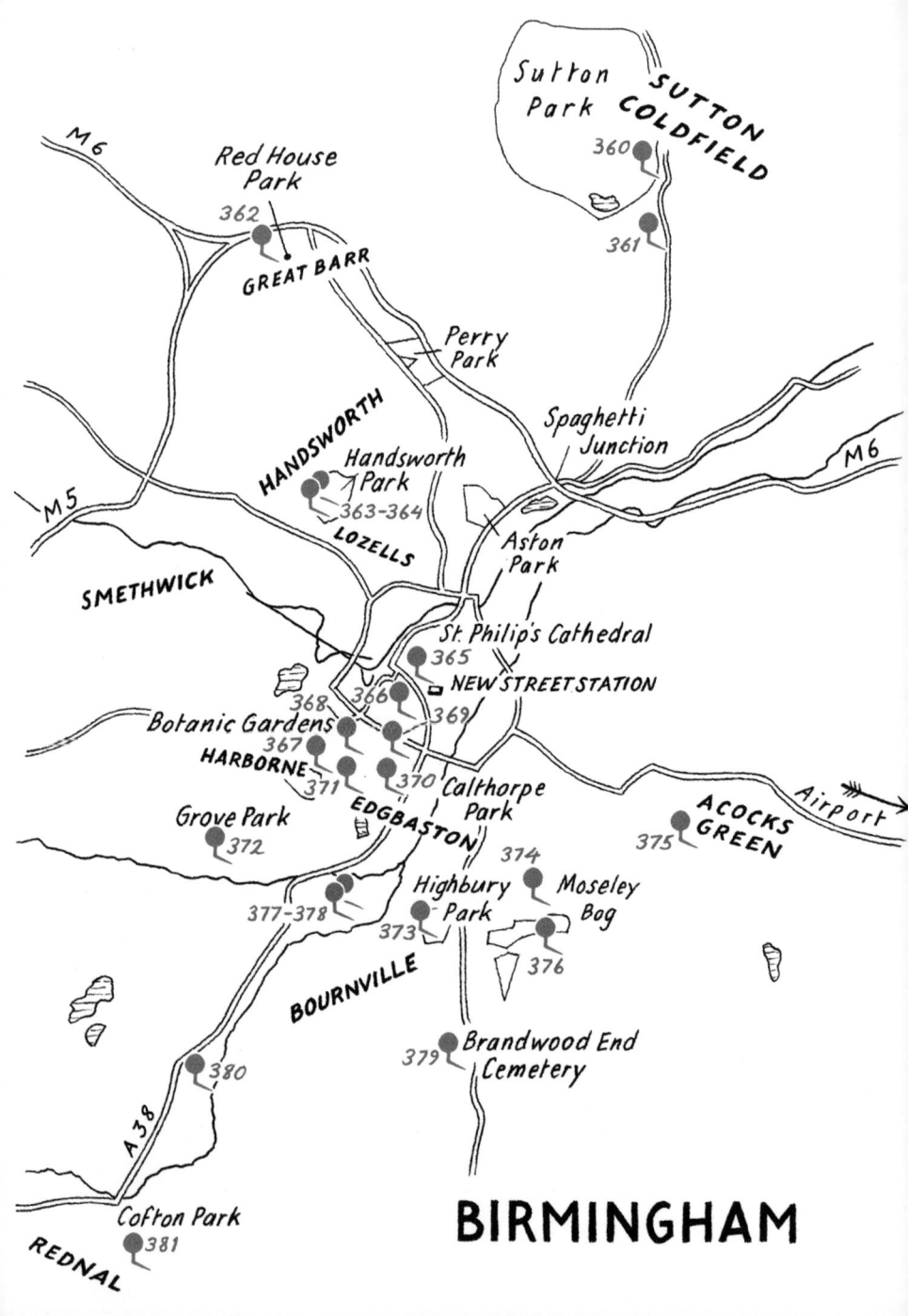

# TREE CITY: BIRMINGHAM
## SIGNATURE SPECIES: *Atlas cedar*

Of all the fantastic beings portrayed in the works of J. R. R. Tolkien, the tree-like Ents from *The Lord of the Rings* are among the most memorable. There have been many visualisations of the 'shepherds of the trees', with each illustrator imagining their Ents differently. But the tree that has the best claim to being Tolkien's inspiration is an old oak growing in Birmingham.

Tolkien grew up in the city, and many aspects of it are said to have inspired his later works. The Lickey Hills resemble the Shire, while Moseley Bog suggests Mirkwood – and it is within the damp, dark depths of this unlikely nature reserve, just three miles from the centre of Birmingham, that the **MOSELEY BOG OAK\* (376)** grows. The tree has been sculpted by time and humans – it appears to have been pollarded in the distant past – and has taken on an aged, animated appearance that makes an intense impression on those who encounter it today. Surely this is the original Ent.

Still, this is not the only great old oak worth hunting in Birmingham – try the **JOCKEY ROAD OUTRIDER (361)** in Sutton Coldfield or, even more intriguingly, the **ACOCKS GHOST (375)**, a tree of such significance that the developers of now-suburban Arden Road left it untouched, where it grows today in its own traffic island.

Despite the city's many old oaks, it is cedars that define Birmingham. There are dozens of these most aristocratic trees in the city's parks, or even, like the **CROSSROADS CEDAR (374)**, at busy road junctions. The most significant trees are associated with major figures whose influence on the city is still celebrated. **CHAMBERLAIN'S CEDAR (373)**, a fine Atlas cedar at Highbury Park, grows in the grounds of what was once the home of former Birmingham mayor Joseph Chamberlain, who is credited with important improvements to the city, while **ATTWOOD'S CEDAR (372)**, a perfectly shaped cedar of Lebanon at Grove Park, remembers the early-nineteenth-century champion of Birmingham and other new industrial cities, the politician and reformer Sir Thomas Attwood.

Unsurprisingly, many of Birmingham's most exciting trees can be found in its historic Botanical Gardens. These represent John Claudius Loudon's first major landscape project and remain little changed from his 1829 design.

Of all Birmingham's neighbourhoods, perhaps Handsworth is most known beyond the city limits. B21 was described by its most famous son, Benjamin Zephaniah, as the 'Jamaican Capital of Europe', and Victorian Handsworth Park is at the heart of the community. While Handsworth has changed since Zephaniah's childhood and the notorious riots of the 1980s, some things have remained rooted to the same spot for well over a century. The gargantuan **COLOSSAL POPLAR (364)**, is likely to be an original planting from the 1880s, along with the **POET'S TREE (363)**, a rare surviving elm. After Zephaniah died in 2023, his family asked that people plant flowers and trees around Birmingham to remember him. Perhaps the Poet's Tree is one that remembers Benjamin.

### 360. BULGING OAK
*Pedunculate oak*
*Quercus robur*
Sutton Park, Park Road,
Sutton Coldfield,
Birmingham B74 2YT
52.562702, -1.838858

Sutton Park was granted by Henry VIII to the townspeople of Sutton Coldfield, who have cared for it ever since. While no trees from that time remain, the park has retained its ancient character and is today a vast expanse of heath and woodland. Not far from the visitor centre, a mature oak with a strangely swollen base is the park's most curious tree. ///toned.labels.chair

### 361. JOCKEY ROAD OUTRIDER
*Pedunculate oak*
*Quercus robur*
Jockey Road,
Sutton Coldfield,
Birmingham B73 5PN
52.550951, -1.838192

The lone oak on Jockey Road in Sutton Coldfield appears to predate the early-twentieth-century houses that now surround it. The street is only two blocks from Sutton Park, and was once surrounded by fields, so the tree, it seems, must be a remnant of a former landscape. As the only tree on this long street, it elevates Jockey Road from rather ordinary to very interesting. ///flag.chimp.likes

### 362. RED HOUSE MULBERRY
*Black mulberry*
*Morus nigra*
Red House Park,
Hill Lane,
Birmingham B43 6NA
52.548202, -1.940784

The Red House is just that: a solid, red brick Victorian house constructed in 1841. Next to it grows a lovely old mulberry, gently collapsing behind protective railings. It is held together by an old iron brace, a type of arboricultural device that fell out of use decades ago, so this and the particular stoutness of its trunk suggest it could well have been here before the house was built. ///proper.verge.kick

### 363. POET'S TREE
*Field elm*
*Ulmus minor var. minor*
Handsworth Park,
Hinstock Road,
Birmingham B20 2EU
52.511387, -1.926662

Like most British and Irish cities, Birmingham boasted many impressive elms before Dutch elm disease arrived, so it is heartening to discover a surviving field elm in Handsworth Park, possibly an original planting. It is a tall, gaunt tree with a typical elm silhouette, growing on the west side of the cricket pitch near Hinstock Road. I think of it as a peaky memorial to the great Handsworth poet, Benjamin Zephaniah. ///apron.front.dices

### 364. COLOSSAL POPLAR
*Wild black poplar*
*Populus nigra ssp. betulifolia*
Handsworth Park,
Hinstock Road,
Birmingham B20 2EU
52.510255, -1.926751

Growing north of the bandstand at the east end of the lake, the Colossal Poplar is the most conspicuous tree in the park, and may even be Birmingham's largest. It is an enormous wild black poplar, with a huge billowing canopy standing head and shoulders above any of the other trees here. It is popular with the city's growing and luminosuly green parakeet population, too. ///memo.driven.buzz

BULGING OAK (360)

PRODI'S ALDER (366)

**365. ST PHILIP'S ELM**
*Tabletop elm*
*Ulmus glabra*
*'Horizontalis'*
St Philip's Cathedral,
Colmore Row,
Birmingham B3 2QB
52.481525, -1.899199

St Philip's, a 300-year-old church surrounded by gardens, is arguably the loveliest and greenest spot in central Birmingham. The handsome early-Georgian building is complemented by an intriguing tabletop elm, likely a Victorian addition. Thousands of people who have waited for a bus on Colmore Row must have admired and wondered about this unusual tree with its striking horizontal branches. ///mobile.cliff.paint

**366. PRODI'S ALDER**
*Italian alder*
*Alnus cordata*
St Thomas's Peace
Garden, Granville Street,
Birmingham B1 1RY
52.473413, -1.906062

The 1998 G8 Summit was held in Birmingham, and the world leaders in attendance symbolically planted trees in St Thomas's Peace Garden. Several have not survived, but, a quarter of a century after its planting, the Italian alder planted by Romano Prodi is rocketing away. Jacques Chirac's beech is catching up – but Bill Clinton's giant redwood will probably be the eventual winner. ///brave.tells.elbow

**367. BIRMINGHAM DWARF**
*'Jacqueline Hillier' elm*
*Ulmus 'Jacqueline Hillier'*
Birmingham Botanical
Gardens, Westbourne
Road, Birmingham
B15 3TR
52.467483, -1.930415
*Paid entry.*

Birmingham Botanical Gardens is of immense importance, as it was John Claudius Loudon's very first significant project, predating his work at Derby Arboretum by a decade. Several large original trees remain, but the most interesting specimen is more subtle: a *'Jacqueline Hillier'* elm, a rare dwarf variety. It was first discovered just a mile or two down the road, growing in a Selly Park garden in 1966. ///trips.purely.insert

**368. ST GEORGE'S CHESTNUT**
*Sweet chestnut*
*Castanea sativa*
St George's Church,
Westbourne Crescent,
Birmingham B15 3DQ
52.467349, -1.922179

When the industrial revolution arrived in Birmingham, the Calthorpe Estate, which was (and still is) the major landowner in Edgbaston, forbade the building of factories and warehouses on its grounds. This has, therefore, always been a leafy part of the city, and you can find plenty of old trees in its streets. One of the oldest is the contorted sweet chestnut opposite St George's. ///worked.slug.plug

**369. WHEELEYS' ORIENTAL PLANE**
*Oriental plane*
*Platanus orientalis*
Wheeleys Road,
Birmingham B15 2LJ
52.465327, -1.914386

The twisted old plane tree outside Wheeleys Road Co-op is an oriental rather than a London plane, a species rarely seen in Birmingham. It now grows awkwardly next to a copper beech in a raised bed by the car park entrance. Another oriental plane leans over the fence from a garden across the road. Could they be related? ///puzzle.looked.table

### 370. ASPIRATIONAL PLANE
*London plane*
*Platanus × hispanica*
Gough Road,
Birmingham B15 2JG
52.464384, -1.910445

Gough Road was laid out in the mid-1800s as an upmarket residential street. Part of the appeal, then and now, are the trees that line its northern side. They are London planes, over 150 years old and probably the oldest street trees in Birmingham. The splendid kerb-busting tree outside number 117 offers a good vantage point from which to appreciate the whole avenue. ///warns.tribal.rots

### 371. HALLS-OF-RESIDENCE CEDAR
*Atlas cedar / Cedrus atlantica 'Glauca'*
The Vale, Church Road,
Birmingham B15 3SR
52.462551, -1.922755

Students living in the Vale have one of England's most impressive university landscapes on their doorstep. The extensive grounds slope down to the University of Birmingham campus and are dotted with many fine trees planted back when these were the grounds of Wydrington, an Edgbaston mansion. Between the halls on Church Road, examples of three cedar species can be seen, the most impressive being an Atlas cedar with fine glaucous foliage. ///exact.decks.seated

### 372. ATTWOOD'S CEDAR
*Cedar of Lebanon*
*Cedrus libani*
Grove Park,
Harborne Park Road,
Birmingham B17 0BJ
52.4508, -1.955878

Of all the cedars in Birmingham, this one is the best looking. With its signature horizontal branches arranged symmetrically, it is an unusually well-shaped cedar of Lebanon in Grove Park at Harborne, once the grounds of the Grove, a grand Georgian house. The tree may have been planted by a former resident, parliamentarian Sir Thomas Attwood. ///patrol.damp.vision

### 373. CHAMBERLAIN'S CEDAR
*Atlas cedar / Cedrus atlantica 'Glauca'*
Highbury Park,
Yew Tree Road,
Birmingham B13 8QG
52.441502, -1.900809

Highbury Park was the home of Birmingham grandee Joseph Chamberlain, father of Prime Minister Neville Chamberlain. Close to his gothic pile, Highbury Hall, another of Birmingham's magnificent cedars can be seen. It is a blue-grey foliaged *'Glauca'* Atlas cedar, and it competes with ATTWOOD'S CEDAR (372) to be Birmingham's best. It is not as elegant, but it does have the fattest trunk of any in Brum. ///period.path.summer

### 374. CROSSROADS CEDAR
*Cedar of Lebanon*
*Cedrus libani*
Wake Green Road,
Birmingham B13 9PU
52.443119, -1.871174

Cedars abound in Birmingham and, as if to underscore this fact, a landmark cedar of Lebanon has stood for decades, perhaps even centuries, at the crossroads of Yardley Wood and Wake Green Roads. How many people have used this tree as a milestone on their journeys to home, work, school or nearby Moseley Bog? ///tapes.rift.mild

**375. ACOCKS GHOST**
*Pedunculate oak*
*Quercus robur*
Arden Road,
Birmingham B27 6AH
52.450908, -1.826942

Like the JOCKEY ROAD OUTRIDER (361), the Acocks Ghost is a haunting reminder of a former landscape. Maybe the Forest of Arden, remembered in the street name, once reached here. Standing proudly as the landmark centrepiece of a tree-lined street, it is a veteran, at least a couple of centuries old, and has been pollarded in recent years. ///studio.wide.manliness

376. **MOSELEY BOG OAK*** ⇻ Moseley Bog is actually a dark, damp wood with several ponds and the Coldbath Brook running through it. Its claim to fame is its association with J. R. R. Tolkien, who grew up nearby and used landscapes in and around Birmingham as inspiration for his novels. Moseley Bog is said to have been the model for Mirkwood in *The Hobbit*, and the fabulous Moseley Bog Oak could be the original Ent.

**MOSELEY BOG OAK***
*Pedunculate oak*
*Quercus robur*
Yardley Wood Road, Moseley,
Birmingham B13 9JX
52.437352, -1.866131
///deal.jaws.woods

BRANDWOOD BEACON (379)

**377. SELLY BEECH**
*Beech / Fagus sylvatica*
Selly Manor Museum,
Maple Road, Bournville,
Birmingham B30 2AE
52.43091, -1.934337

The patrician Cadbury family moved their chocolate-manufacturing business to what became Bournville in the 1870s, and set about designing their model workers' village around it. In 1907, George Cadbury bought Selly Manor and moved it lock, stock and barrel to the position it now occupies. It is dominated by a magnificent beech that is younger than Selly Manor, but which would nevertheless have been here before the building was transported to this spot. ///pocket.under.lamp

**378. FRIENDS CEDAR**
*Fastigiate Atlas cedar*
*Cedrus atlantica*
*'Fastigiata'*
Linden Road,
Birmingham B30 1JT
52.430398, -1.936195

The neatest tree in the neat garden village of Bourneville is a very unusual *'Fastigiata'* cultivar of the North African Atlas cedar. It can be seen in front of the Friends Meeting House, an essential institution for the Quaker Cadburys. Compared with the other more dishevelled Atlas cedars you will see in Birmingham, this one has a compact, sugar-loaf shaped crown. ///opens.ruby.label

**379. BRANDWOOD BEACON**
*Giant redwood*
*Sequoiadendron giganteum*
Brandwood End Cemetery,
Woodthorpe Road,
Birmingham B14 5AE
52.41606, -1.896982

No fewer than forty-four giant redwoods were planted in Brandwood End Cemetery in 1898. From the war memorial in the centre, they form an avenue to the north east and south west of the stone cross. The first tree on the north-east branch is a great place to admire them all – like its companions, it has thick, reddish-brown bark that is warm and spongy to the touch. ///losses.rider.theme

**380. ST LAURENCE'S YEW**\*
*Yew / Taxus baccata*
St Laurence's Church,
Northfield, Church Road,
Birmingham B31 2LX
52.411802, -1.96463

St Laurence's Church is best approached from the south. Look up Church Hill to its substantial buttressed walls, overhung by the dark canopy of St Laurence's Yew. Steps under the tree's canopy lead into the churchyard from where this very old tree can be examined. It is Birmingham's oldest tree, probably planted when the church was built in the twelfth century. ///farmer.form.cowboy

**381. SHIRE CHESTNUT**
*Sweet chestnut*
*Castanea sativa*
Cofton Park,
Northfield, Rednal,
Birmingham B45 8UN
52.387923, -1.996664

Generations of Brummies have enjoyed a day out in the Lickey Hills to the south of the city. Before arriving at the Lickey Hills Country Park, Cofton Park on Lickey Road is worth exploring. It is a semi-wild former estate with many memorable trees. Chief among them is a sweet chestnut in its prime, growing between Lickey Road and Lowhill Lane. It is a towering tree with dramatically spiralling bark. ///modern.heavy.unions

### 382. COPSHOP DEODAR
*Deodar cedar*
*Cedrus deodara*
Solihull Police Station,
Homer Road,
Solihull B91 3QL
52.411748, -1.780687

Homer Road is a street with many fine trees but rather fewer fine buildings. It is the preserve of office buildings, car parks and Solihull's police station, a forlorn 1970s slab made interesting by the impressive deodar cedar that grows next to it. In the right location, deodars can become tall trees with a pyramidal canopy of gently weeping branches. This is clearly the right location. ///proper.scam.encounter

### 383. LODE LANE CHESTNUT
*Sweet chestnut*
*Castanea sativa*
Seven Star Road,
Solihull B91 2BN
52.420777, -1.776606

Solihull Bypass is travelled by thousands of scurrying motorists every day, many of whom must notice the massive sweet chestnut marking the junction with Lode Lane, a much older thoroughfare from a pre-combustion engine era. The tree has several elephantine limbs that branch close to the ground, causing it to sprawl over a patch of green. Its substantial, aged form is best appreciated in the winter. ///asleep.idea.with

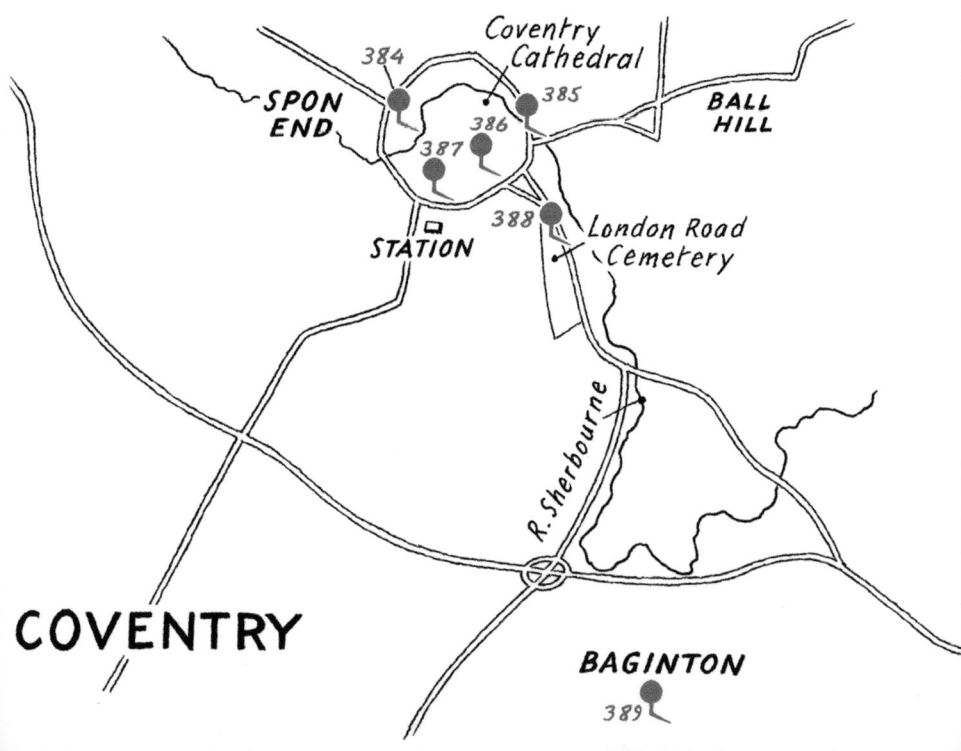

### 384. FALL FROM GRACE
*Black mulberry*
*Morus nigra*
Croft Road,
Coventry CV1 3AZ
52.408056, -1.517564

A very old and flailing mulberry, which must have once grown in the garden of one of medieval Spon Street's ancient houses, now finds itself unloved in a corner of a car park. Its situation is humiliating for a tree that is as much a part of Coventry's rich history as any of the city's buildings. ///trials.tree.last

### 385. RINGWAY TREE
*Tree of heaven*
*Ailanthus altissima*
Grove Street,
Coventry CV1 5PH
52.407436, -1.502364

'Ghost Town', The Specials' greatest hit, conjures up an urban dystopia which might have been inspired by the band's hometown. Take, for instance, the bleak car park beyond the Coventry University buildings on Grove Street, under the thundering Ringway: this truly is a landscape that chimes with the song's gritty lyrics. But even here, between two elevated lanes of traffic, a tree of heaven holds its own among the noise, pollution and concrete. ///dress.intro.feels

### 386. SALTS' GOLDEN CATALPA
*Golden catalpa / Catalpa bignonioides 'Aurea'*
Salts Tobacconists,
New Union Street,
Coventry CV1 2HN
52.404956, -1.508727

On the corner of Little Park Street and New Union Street, a tree was planted when the row of mid-century shops including Salts Tobacconists was built in the postwar reconstruction of Coventry. That tree, a golden catalpa, has grown a wonderful broad canopy that has remained low-rise like the buildings it complements. Visit in late spring to catch its golden leaves at their peak. ///slime.relay.joined

### 387. GREYFRIARS SPANISH OAK
*Spanish oak*
*Quercus × crenata*
Warwick Road,
Coventry CV1 1EE
52.404875, -1.51372

Despite the destruction of the Second World War and Coventry's subsequent redevelopment, glimpses of the past have remained intact, and on Greyfriars Green a row of hybrid Spanish oaks mark some former boundary or thoroughfare. Next to the statue of one-time Lord Mayor of London and Coventry benefactor Sir Thomas White on Warwick Road, a memorable tree branches a metre from the ground, forming a broad, leafy crucible. ///rift.pinch.hung

### 388. CEMETERY ASH
*Narrow-leaved ash*
*Fraxinus angustifolia var 'Lentiscifolia'*
London Road Cemetery,
London Road,
Coventry CV1 2JT
52.400455, -1.500022

Several old ash trees grow in the London Road Cemetery. The most pleasing of the bunch is towards the middle of the northern section of this landscape, designed by Joseph Paxton in 1847. Like the GREYFRIARS SPANISH OAK (387), it has a very apparent graft mark a metre from its base where two, then three large trunks splay apart. ///deputy.salt.vine

### 389. THE BAGINTON OAK*
*Pedunculate oak*
*Quercus robur*
Baginton,
Coventry CV8 3AT
52.367925, -1.492121

An oak marks the ancient junction where Church Road forks off from the Coventry Road at Baginton. The tree is four or five centuries old, and has been pollarded in the past. A pub nearby is called The Oak, and across the road new houses have been built on Oak Close. It is clearly an inspirational tree, with great local significance – and it is certainly worth a stop if you are nearby. ///member.search.punch

### 390. GINGER PEEL
*Paperbark maple*
*Acer griseum*
Jephson Gardens,
Newbold Terrace,
Leamington Spa
CV32 4AA
52.287961, -1.531426

Jephson Gardens is a well-loved feature of Leamington Spa. It is a long-established park, although much has been added since it first opened as Newbold Gardens in 1836. Many fine trees have been planted, but one stands out: the auburn paperbark maple near the glasshouse is a lovely, mature example of this most sriking of Asian species. Notice its compound leaves (made up of three leaflets), an unusual feature for a maple. ///toward.hidden.ankle

### 391. OAG OAK
*Spanish oak*
*Quercus × crenata*
Old Art Gallery,
Avenue Road,
Leamington Spa
CV31 3NN
52.285913, -1.536491

Leamington Spa's fascinating hybrid Spanish oak stands on the pavement where a footpath leads to the side of the Old Art Gallery and Library building. It is an upright tree, and rather more evergreen than the more often encountered *'Lucombe'* cultivar of the same species. It shows a distinct, swollen graft line about a metre from the base, with corky bark above the mark, and fissured bark below. ///send.these.each

### 392. ST NICHOLAS' KEYAKI →
Japanese zelkova or keyaki trees are handsome but, like their splendid cousin the Caucasian zelkova, they are surprisingly rare. It is fantastic to see one in its prime next to the Avon in Warwick's St Nicholas' Park. At a mere fifty years or so, this tree is relatively young – in Japan one individual is thought to be 1,000 years old – but it is mature enough to display a regular, widely domed canopy and beautiful mottled bark.

**ST NICHOLAS' KEYAKI** *Japanese zelkova / Zelkova serrata*
St Nicholas' Park, Warwick CV34 4QY  52.280145, -1.578687 ///flesh.unfair.could

**393. GOTHIC CATALPA**
*Western catalpa*
*Catalpa speciosa*
St Mary's, Old Square,
Warwick CV34 4RA
52.282247, -1.587275

Warwick has an unusual western catalpa languishing in St Mary's churchyard. It is broad and spreading, although hemmed in by the surrounding trees and buildings. Ivy grows round its trunk, giving a decidedly gothic air, and twisted limbs suggest it is an old tree. Western catalpas are similar to the more common southern catalpas, but *Catalpa speciosa* grows larger and has narrower leaves. ///pine.thin.asserts

**394. SHAKESPEARE'S MULBERRY***
*Black mulberry*
*Morus nigra*
5 Chapel Lane, Stratford-upon-Avon CV37 6ER
52.190909, -1.706199
*Paid entry, but can be seen from the street.*

Stratford-upon-Avon is dotted with old mulberries, but the best known is Shakespeare's Mulberry, which grows in New Place Garden on Chapel Lane – once Shakespeare's home. This is not the sixteenth-century original, however; it is a scion of that tree planted sometime after 1750, when the then owner of New Place, fed up with pilgrims wanting to pay their respects to the Bard's tree, cut it down. ///rock.oiled.they

**395. HOLY TRINITY CORKSCREW PINE**
*Stone pine / Pinus pinea*
Holy Trinity, Old Town,
Stratford-upon-Avon
CV37 6BG
52.186489, -1.707783

Stratford's Holy Trinity church is the last resting place of the Bard, and is therefore a must-see on any self-respecting Shakespeare tourist's itinerary. And, for tree hunters, an unusual sight awaits – next to the church porch grows an old stone pine. It appears to have been heavily pruned in its youth only to grow back with an impossible-looking corkscrew spiralling in its trunk. ///action.copies.shakes

**396. CATHEDRAL TRIPLET**
*London plane*
*Platanus × hispanica*
Cathedral, 8 College Yard,
Worcester WR1 2LA
52.189265, -2.220763

Compared to other English cathedrals, Worcester's has a relatively small close, but it does still boast three terrific London planes. In order to fit them in, they were planted within a couple of metres of each other, and over the decades – perhaps twenty – they have each taken on a distinct lean in different directions. The one nearest the war memorial is the most energetic. ///fries.pure.second

**397. CRIPPLEGATE WARDEN**
*Black Worcester pear*
*Pyrus 'Black Worcester'*
Cripplegate Park, 45 Tybridge Street,
Worcester WR2 5BA
52.190559, -2.227187

Cripplegate Park was opened in 1932 by the then Prince of Wales, who would briefly become King Edward VIII. He planted the Cripplegate Warden to mark the occasion and it is still going strong. Black Worcesters have large, dark, awkward-looking fruit that are a traditional cooking pear, or warden. Visit in the autumn to see the fantastic fruits. ///share.worth.remain

### 398. NEEDLE'S NEIGHBOUR
*Dawn redwood*
*Metasequoia*
*glyptostroboides*
St Andrew's, Deansway,
Worcester WR1 2ES
52.19099, -2.222567

The Glover's Needle is an almost impossibly tall and slender church spire, and a prominent Worcester landmark. It is all that remains of St Andrew's church, demolished in the 1940s to make way for a widened road and an ornamental garden in which a dawn redwood grows. In less than seventy years it has reached the top of the tower – in another seventy it could reach the tip of the spire. ///grab.lunch.pool

### 399. PRIORY PINE
*Monterey pine*
*Pinus radiata*
Great Malvern Priory,
Church Street, Great
Malvern WR14 2AY
52.111161, 2.328218

Great Malvern Priory is one of England's finest parish churches, with peerless medieval stained glass, misericords and tiles. It has a fine retinue of trees in its churchyard too. It is particularly rich in conifers, including deodar cedars and a giant redwood, but the tree that is most worthy of admiration is an exuberant Monterey pine just beyond the holm oak. ///gladiators.eating.wanted

### 400. EVIL TWIN
*Cedar of Lebanon*
*Cedrus libani*
Drybridge House,
St Martin's Street,
Hereford HR2 7SG
52.05079, -2.718487

Anyone crossing the historic Wye Bridge will notice the unmistakable chimney-sweep's-brush silhouette of a mature cedar of Lebanon beyond a run of attractive brick buildings. Get closer to see that two trees were planted rather too close together many years ago. One has suffered the indignity of having branches removed in order to accommodate its more thrusting sibling. ///drive.flag.every

### 401. BISHOP'S MEADOW TULIP TREE
*Tulip tree*
*Liriodendron tulipifera*
Bishop's Meadow,
Hereford HR2 7RB
52.050871, -2.712873

A bronze plaque explaining how the Bishop's Meadow was gifted to the city of Hereford stands at the foot of Victoria Bridge, just behind the enormous Bishop's Meadow Tulip Tree. The tallest tree in the area, it stands apart from its companions, its green leaves contrasting with the purple of the neighbouring copper beeches. This riverside location is clearly to its liking. ///fixed.clips.mash

### 402. WYE WAY SILVER LIME
*Silver pendent lime*
*Tilia tomentosa*
*'Petiolaris'*
Wye Way,
Hereford HR1 2NP
52.050574, -2.711162

Across the river and downstream from the BISHOP'S MEADOW TULIP TREE (401), another giant stands tall. It is a silver pendent lime, whose distinctively uneven canopy towers magisterially over the other trees around it. The tree was likely planted in the mid-1800s, making it just a few decades younger than the former Hereford General Hospital, the Georgian building behind it. ///throw.coast.bind

**403.  LINTON MIRACLE** → Just off the M50, near Ross-on-Wye, the little village of Linton clusters round St Mary's Church where you can find one of England's oldest yew trees. There are a pair of old prodigies here, but the elder is obvious. Its enormous hollow trunk resembles a fennel bulb, and there is another, younger trunk growing within it. Sadly, the tree was set on fire in 1998, but it is slowly recovering.

**LINTON MIRACLE** *Yew / Taxus baccata* St Mary's Church, Linton, Herefordshire HR9 7RX 51.925655, -2.49565 ///reflect.fuzz.splice

**404. MUCH MARCLE HOLLOW YEW***
*Yew / Taxus baccata*
St Bartholomew, Church Lane, Much Marcle
HR8 2LY
51.991928, -2.500897

The Much Marcle Hollow Yew, like the **LINTON MIRACLE (403)**, is another very old tree with an immense trunk. It is hollow, and a wooden bench placed within the trunk itself invites visitors to experience this living cavern. It has been celebrated for centuries, and a scaffold of iron pillars and connecting planks surrounds the tree in an attempt to lift the canopy and aid inspection. ///access.desk.sprains

**405. BAOBAB POPLAR**
*Wild black poplar*
*Populus nigra ssp. betulifolia*
The Dog, Ewyas Harold
HR2 0EU
51.953037, -2.893079

Opposite the Dog Inn at Ewyas Harold, a burry and swollen black poplar can be admired. It is not on the scale of trees across the border, like the **CAWR WYSG (883)**, as its constrained position on the road next to the Dulas Brook has meant that regular pollarding has been necessary to keep it under control – but this does mean the tree could be very old indeed, much older than it first appears. ///snored.agents.reverted

**406. THE GREAT OAK***
*Pedunculate oak*
*Quercus robur*
Great Oak, Eardisley
HR3 6PP
52.140726, -3.024679

The hamlet of Eardisley is renowned for The Great Oak. John Claudius Loudon described it as 'a fine old tree' in his 1844 work *Arboretum et Fruticetum*, at which time it was known as the Eardisley Oak. It would be recognisable to Loudon today, so I wonder at what point its new name was adopted, officially bestowing greatness. ///protrude.proven.create

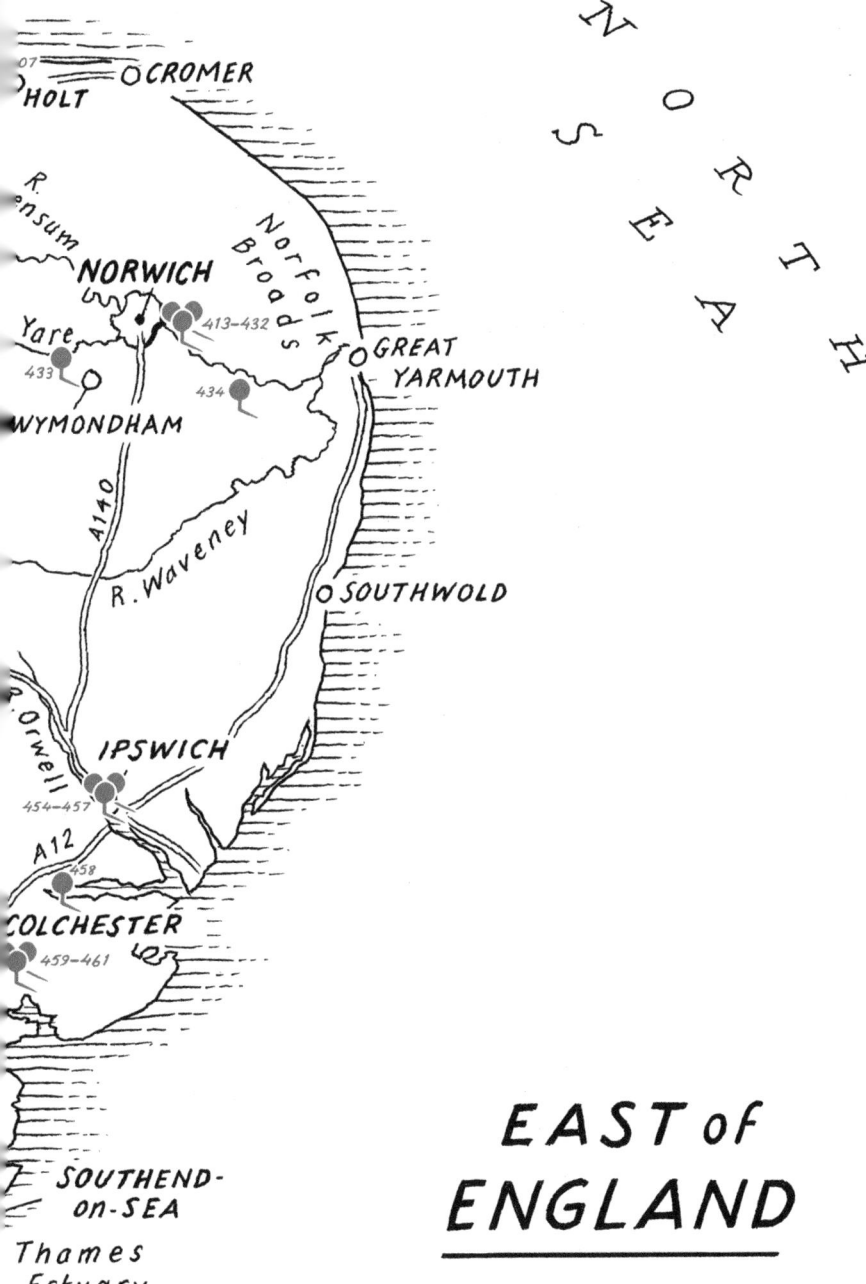

# EAST OF ENGLAND

*Norfolk*
*Cambridgeshire*
*Bedfordshire*
*Hertfordshire*
*Essex*
*Suffolk*

Icy winds often blast in from Scandinavia across the flatlands of eastern England, so trees here must be tough to survive. Oaks do well, and dozens of battle-scarred characters – many of which have survived for centuries – can be seen throughout the region, from north Norfolk to the commuter belt of Essex and Hertfordshire. On the exposed Breckland of Norfolk and Suffolk even tougher trees can be seen, including wind-breaking pine rows twisted into unbelievable shapes, like the **LOOP-THE-LOOP PINE (436)** on the edge of Thetford. At the same time, rainfall is relatively low, and, in Cambridge, some of England's hottest summer temperatures have been recorded. It is a region of climate contrasts, and the trees here are correspondingly dramatic.

They are also surprising. While researching this book, I often arrived with a good idea of the places I would visit and the trees I wanted to see, but it was sometimes the trees I simply stumbled across that were the most interesting. So it was when I was travelling through the agricultural expanses of Norfolk on my way to Norwich and my car broke down. Waiting in a layby for the AA to arrive, I made my way to the only feature on the long, straight highway: a wizened old tree that had caught my attention growing by the side of this mercifully quiet road. There was a rusty old fence surrounding it, with a sign emblazoned with 'Ketts Oak 1549'. It turned out to have quite a story. **KETT'S OAK* (433)** remembers Robert Kett, the leader of a 16,000-strong rebellion of 1549, demanding the end of the enclosure of commons, which the landless rural population relied on to graze their animals. The rebels marched on Norwich, and though they took the city, repelling counter attacks for some weeks, they were eventually defeated by government forces, who showed no mercy. Kett was executed at Norwich castle in December 1549, and Kett's Oak is said to be where nine other rebels were hanged.

Throughout these islands, there are many trees that have names. Some are well known, like **MAJOR OAK (294)** in Nottinghamshire, but often, like Kett's Oak, they are known only to those who live near them. These are names

**TREE CITY:**
*Norwich*

**SIGNATURE SPECIES:**
*False acacia*

that have been circulating for as long as anyone can remember. As a tree ages, the memory of the person or event it is named for recedes into the mists of time, and it often becomes the last link to historic events. If it were not for the tree, that slice of history may otherwise have been forgotten. Named trees are living history.

Some named trees may have acquired their monikers more recently. **OLD KNOBBLEY (458)** is an oak growing close to the Essex village of Mistley. Its name is very appropriate: a decrepit giant growing in the sheltered woods on the edge of the village, it is far larger and older even than Kett's Oak. Meeting Old Knobbley caused me to reflect on how short our human lives are, to marvel at what this great living thing must have experienced in its very long life, and wonder just how it had collected all the burrs, lumps and pockmarks that give it its name.

Many more trees do not have popular names at all, and so, as elsewhere in these pages, I have taken the liberty of giving them one. Those, like the **FAT CHESTNUT (455)**, a sweet chestnut in Ipswich, the **ST JOHN'S REMNANT MULBERRY (461)** in Colchester, or the **DOWNHAM FIELD MAPLE (465)**, are examples of very old trees that lots of people will have noticed, and may even have given names, though, to my knowledge, they haven't been recorded. I do not claim to have a monopoly on naming trees, and many of the names in this book are whimsical and should be regarded as a starting point; I welcome alternative suggestions. In Bury St Edmunds, dozens of interesting trees can be seen in Abbey Gardens, a fascinating collection of historic sites, including an early-nineteenth-century botanic garden alongside the Abbey ruins. I was spoilt for choice, and, while I was admiring an old black poplar, a passer-by drew my attention to a splendid tree, one they had admired for decades but could not identify. Not only was I able to solve the mystery of its botanical identity – it is a rare oak-leaf alder – we jointly agreed that it should be known as the **CONUNDRUM TREE (450)**.

WITCH'S BROOM (412)

**407. MARKET PLACE MULBERRY**
*Black mulberry*
*Morus nigra*
Market Place,
Holt NR25 6BD
52.905927, 1.090866

Holt's town-centre bus stop, a fanciful structure complete with pitched roof and mini clock tower, is dignified by an unruly mulberry rambling over its pantiles. It grows in the garden of Gresham's School behind, and from Church Street a gap in the hedge allows curious morusophiles to admire the gnarled and leaning trunk of an elderly specimen. ///radio.mural.brochure

**408. TUESDAY PLANE**
*London plane*
*Platanus × hispanica*
Tuesday Market Place,
King Street,
King's Lynn PE30 1EZ
52.755916, 0.393694

Tuesday Market Place is one of England's great historic townscapes, but, like much of King's Lynn, it was constructed in the unenlightened days before trees were considered an integral part of urban design. So it is heartening that an unapologetic London plane has snuck in on Ferry Street, where it spills into the vast piazza. ///land.update.offers

**409. CATHEDRAL TREE**
*False acacia*
*Robinia pseudoacacia*
Peterborough Cathedral,
Peterborough PE1 1XS
52.572971, -0.238663

False acacias often develop great character as they age, but they rarely become giant trees. A few become tall and sprouty, and very occasionally they grow tall and straight. The superb tree in Peterborough's Cathedral Close has somehow managed this, with two trunks splitting at the base. ///dads.cove.player

**410. TEE TREE**
*Scots pine / Pinus sylvestris*
Swaffham Road,
Gooderstone, PE37 8AW
52.601323, 0.632218

Pine rows characterise the Breckland landscape of south west Norfolk and north west Suffolk. Look out for the twisted, T-shaped Scots Pine on the pine-lined Swaffham Road, opposite the entrance to a forest ride. ///bootleg.whimpered.book

**411. COCKLEY CONKER**
*Horse chestnut*
*Aesculus hippocastanum*
Swaffham Road, Cockley
Cley, Norfolk PE37 8AL
52.605986, 0.645722

Girdled by an octagonal wooden bench, the Cockley Conker is relatively small but a perfectly shaped horse chestnut tree. It grows on a grassy triangle at the centre of this picturesque village. After a sit on the bench, cross the busy Swaffham Road to the intriguingly named Twenty Churchwardens pub to admire both bench and tree. ///stupidly.issuer.gliders

**412. WITCH'S BROOM**
*Caucasian zelkova 'James Gordon'/ Zelkova carpinifolia*
St Andrew, off Hillside,
North Pickenham
PE37 8JZ
52.628355, 0.754642

On the northern edge of St Andrew's churchyard, a Caucasian zelkova cuts a distinctive witch's-broom silhouette, something that is particularly apparent in winter. It is a large tree with a mass of branches sweeping upward from a short bole. Caucasian zelkovas are rare, so it is a surprise to encounter one in a quiet Norfolk village. ///punctual.finishers.kingpin

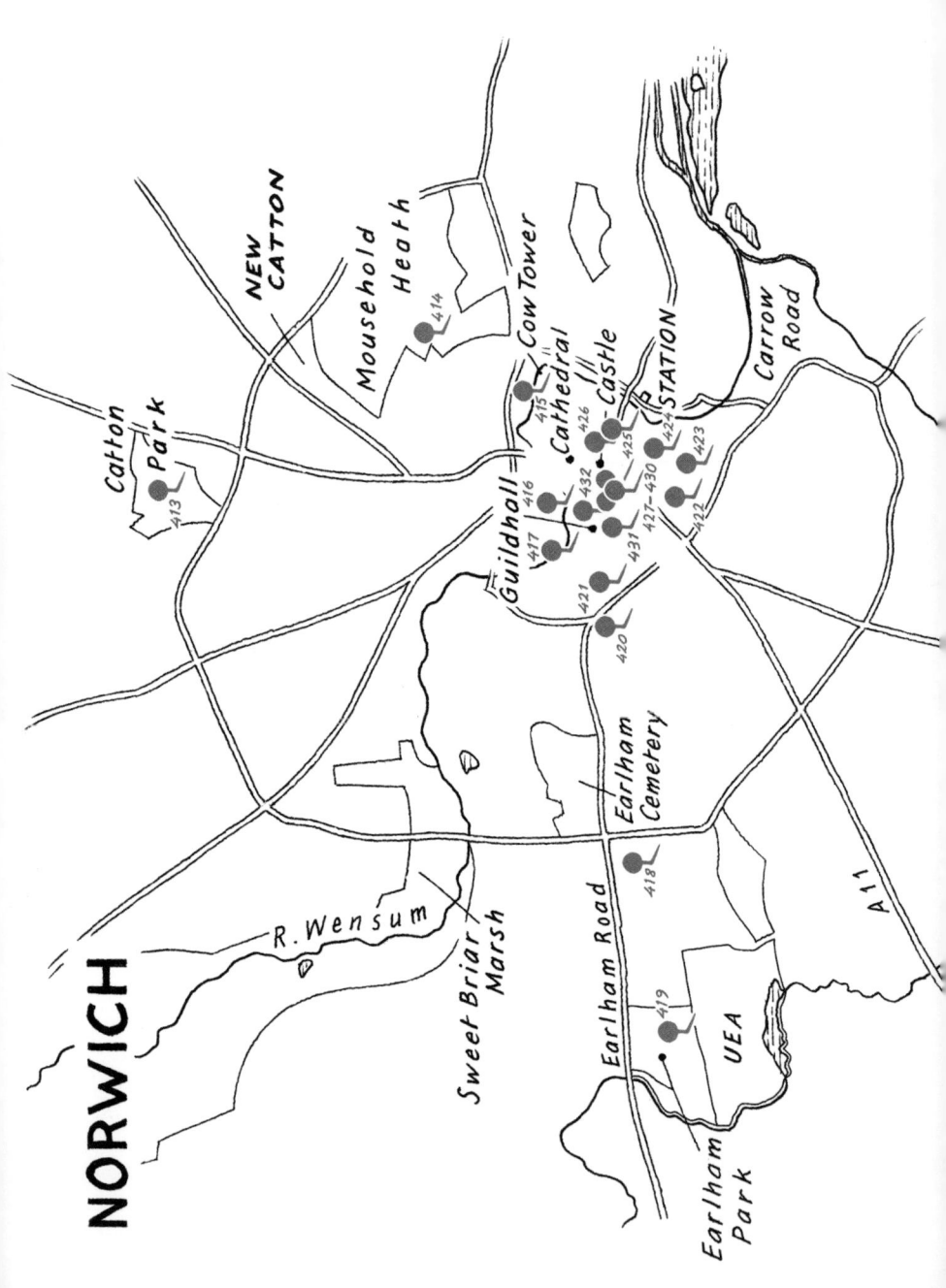

# TREE CITY: NORWICH
**SIGNATURE SPECIES:** *Tree of heaven*

From the Middle Ages to the beginning of the eighteenth century, Norwich was the second-largest city in Britain and Ireland, its size and wealth founded on trade with continental Europe. At its peak, the city boasted fifty-eight parishes, from which thirty-one medieval churches survive today. Many were lost centuries ago, while two were destroyed during the Norwich Blitz of 1942. One of these, St Michael at Thorn, has been redeveloped along with its tiny parish, save for the **THORN LANE LOCUST (423)**, a spiny old false acacia which grows on a street corner close to where the church once stood.

Norwich has consistently and thoughtfully planted interesting trees right up to the present, making tree hunting in the city a delight. Many noteworthy trees grow close to fascinating old churches, and so will lead you to discover other aspects of the city's rich history. None of these ecclesiastical trees is of great antiquity, but thought has been given to their selection. The **CHURCHYARD JEWEL (424)**, a suitably biblical Judas tree, grows in the churchyard of St Peter Parmentergate. Meanwhile, two of the finest churchyard trees are trees of heaven: the **OVER THE WATER TREE OF HEAVEN (416)** at St Clement is eye-catching, while its sibling, the **HUNGATE TREE OF HEAVEN (429)**, is a leviathan in the miniscule garden of St Peter Hungate.

Among the city's older trees are those remembering two well known Norvicians: **REPTON'S OAK (413)**, which frames the view of Norwich Cathedral, memorialises Humphry Repton, the famous eighteenth-century English landscape designer, while **ELIZABETH FRY'S OAK (419)** recalls the great prison reformer who was born in 1780 and brought up in the city.

By the nineteenth century Norwich's significance had waned, although it continued to slowly expand. By 1856 its population warranted the opening of Earlham Road Cemetery where dozens of unusual trees can be found. One of these was a beloved weeping beech that I intended to include here, until it was claimed in 2022 by a fungal infection – a reminder that tree life, like human life, is finite.

Norwich is also remarkable for the frequency of mature oriental planes around the city. Elsewhere, this species tends to be found in the relatively rarefied surroundings of parks and gardens, but here they have been planted on streets. Right in the heart of the city, the elegant **GUILDHALL PLANE (432)** seems to proclaim Norwich's determination to differentiate itself, albeit rather subtly, from other cities who took their plane-planting cues from the capital.

Elsewhere, true service trees appear less well suited to urban locations: the **CLOISTER SERVICE TREE (426)** and its colleagues are struggling in a car park. However, it is noteworthy that these rare and lovely trees have been planted at all; perhaps the authorities might be persuaded to provide more care for a group that is almost unique.

COW TOWER POPLAR (415)

**413. REPTON'S OAK**
*Pedunculate oak*
*Quercus robur*
Catton Park, Oak Lane,
Norwich NR6 7DB
52.658568, 1.294932

Catton Park may look ancient, and the old oaks dotted around appear to support this. However, it is not as old as it appears. This is in fact the first landscape designed by Humphry Repton, in around 1788. Repton removed several trees to enable a view of Norwich Cathedral's spire from Catton Hall, but left the most stately oak, which frames the vista to this day. ///flight.aware.human

**414. SPREADING OAK**
*Turner's oak*
*Quercus × turneri*
Gurney Road, Mousehold
Heath NR1 4HW
52.641615, 1.314121

Mousehold Heath is a large tract of woodland not far from Norwich city centre, but in the 1800s it was treeless heathland. The woods grew up as the city expanded and grazing ceased. On Gurney Road, outside the Mousehold Diner, an unusual semi-evergreen Turner's oak grows, its low, spreading branches suggesting it may have once grown in a much more open space. ///shine.stove.woof

**415. COW TOWER POPLAR**
*Wild black poplar*
*Populus nigra ssp. betulifolia*
Cow Tower,
Cotman Fields,
Norwich NR1 4AA
52.634204, 1.307281

On the bank of the River Wensum, downstream from the cathedral and just before the fourteenth-century Cow Tower, a giant black poplar stands out. It grows within a row of mature horse chestnuts, which it dwarfs. Those strolling along the Riverside Walk will notice the deeply fissured bark of a trunk whose prodigious girth must be three or four times that of its neighbours. ///danger.adopt.chefs

**416. OVER THE WATER TREE OF HEAVEN**
*Tree of heaven*
*Ailanthus altissima*
St Clement, St Clements Alley, Norwich NR3 1LJ
52.633341, 1.296353

Not quite in the same league as the HUNGATE TREE OF HEAVEN (**429**) when it comes to girth, the tree in St Clement's churchyard is nevertheless a splendid specimen, whose lofty canopy dominates Colegate. Trees of heaven are notoriously short-lived – seventy is a good age – but succession is in hand in the shape of a rare Amur cork tree growing in its shadow. ///simple.rocky.prone

**417. COSLANY MONGOL**
*Mongolian lime*
*Tilia mongolica*
Coslany Street,
Norwich NR3 3DT
52.632641, 1.2912

Mongolian limes' small, toothed leaves are distinctive and unusual for a lime species. While their compact form makes them an excellent species for street-tree planting, they have only become popular in recent years, so I was astonished to find a veritable giant growing happily across the road from St Michael Coslany, a Grade I-listed church resplendent with intricate flushwork, a site it must have called home for decades. ///fallen.ports.sheets

418. **BUS STOP BENCHMARK** ⇾ Earlham Road is one of the very best plane-lined streets in the country. It is a row rather than an avenue, with dozens of trees lining the southern side of the street, out to the University. They are old, and have been lovingly managed so each tree branches at the same height to form a large domed canopy. A tree growing near the Henderson Road bus stop is the yardstick.

**BUS STOP BENCHMARK** *London plane / Platanus × hispanica* Earlham Road, Norwich NR4 7HL 52.629326, 1.25784 ///fears.lung.fortunate

419. **ELIZABETH FRY'S OAK**
*Pedunculate oak*
*Quercus robur*
Earlham Park,
Norwich NR4 7TQ
52.623342, 1.239272

The great early-nineteenth-century prison reformer Elizabeth Fry grew up in Earlham Hall, now part of the University of East Anglia. Earlham Park, surrounding the hall, is known by many as an outdoor concert venue, but it retains its original parkland feel and several gorgeous old oaks Fry would have known still grow here. The most spectacular is towards the south-east corner. ///fight.lofts.famous

420. **GRAPES STRAWBERRY TREE**
*Strawberry tree*
*Arbutus unedo*
Grapes Hill,
Norwich NR2 2RA
52.628921, 1.28507

In autumn, patrons of the Temple Bar pub can pluck crimson fruits from an old strawberry tree hanging over the garden from Grapes Hill. Several old buildings were lost in the twentieth century, when Grapes Hill was remodelled to construct the ring road. Perhaps the tree, which now stands bravely next to the thundering traffic, was saved from a long-lost garden. ///early.payer.habit

421. **CHAPELFIELD PRINCESS**
*Foxglove tree*
*Paulownia tomentosa*
Chapelfield Gardens,
Norwich NR2 1TN
52.627439, 1.287735

Chapelfield Gardens is a sliver of a Victorian park containing several fine oriental planes that rival those of the Guildhall. But it is the princess, or foxglove, tree that draws the crowds in May. This is a relatively young tree, planted towards the end of the last century. In May it is covered in blue foxglove-shaped flower spikes and a heady scent fills the air. ///index.grew.marked

### 422. TIMBER HILL ELM
*'Sapporo Autumn Gold'  
elm / Ulmus 'Sapporo Autumn Gold'*  
St John the Baptist,  
Timber Hill,  
Norwich NR1 3LA  
52.626226, 1.29582

Pedestrians walking up Timber Hill, one of Norwich's oldest thoroughfares, will be enchanted by the distinctive canopy of the elm tree growing in St John the Baptist's churchyard. It is an example of *'Sapporo Autumn Gold'*, a Dutch elm disease-resistant cultivar occasionally planted in the 1970s and 80s. This enormous individual strikes a great contrast with the more conservative Victorian limes also growing here. ///drops.forks.drag

### 423. THORN LANE LOCUST
*False acacia  
Robinia pseudoacacia*  
Thorn Lane,  
Norwich NR1 1QU  
52.625229, 1.298396

Climb up Thorn Lane in order to admire a thorny old false acacia, or black locust, on the corner of Paradise Place. The parish church of St Michael at Thorn, destroyed in the Norwich Blitz, once stood where there is now a car park, and the neat postwar housing surrounding it was once an area of densely populated medieval closes. Could the tree have been a boundary-marker for a lost parish? ///chin.feels.them

### 424. CHURCHYARD JEWEL
*Judas tree  
Cercis siliquastrum*  
St Peter Parmentergate,  
King Street,  
Norwich NR1 1PG  
52.627062, 1.299596

On the climb up to Norwich Castle, just inside the entrance to St Peter Parmentergate's churchyard on King Street, you can admire a remarkably tall, straight-trunked judas tree (an apt species for the location). The spot it inhabits in the shadow of the church may have induced its upward trajectory. Its magenta flowers appear in May, and considerably brighten up this otherwise gloomy churchyard. ///lines.bucks.scar

### 425. OLD FAITHFUL
*Horse chestnut  
Aesculus hippocastanum*  
James Stuart Garden,  
Recorder Road,  
Norwich NR1 1NR  
52.630242, 1.302483

Horse chestnuts are cherished by many, perhaps because of their associations with childhood conker collecting. Individual trees are often notable for their fine shape or landmark position, but very occasionally one stands out for its sheer size and presence. These are the characteristics of the giant Old Faithful in James Stuart Garden. ///tidy.remove.risen

### 426. CLOISTER SERVICE TREE
*True service tree  
Sorbus domestica*  
The Close,  
Norwich NR1 4DH  
52.631104, 1.301417

True service trees are rare, and might be mistaken for a rowan, but given time they will grow into far larger, longer-lived trees, which bear distinct apple- or pear-shaped fruits. The surprise of finding several in the car park next to the cathedral cloister is tempered by that same fact: that they are growing in a car park and are not in the finest condition. The first tree on the left is the best, but could do with some love. ///logic.bucks.hurry

**427. TOMBLAND PLANE**
*London plane*
*Platanus × hispanica*
Tombland,
Norwich NR3 1HE
52.630943, 1.298619

Tombland, an evocative name, was once the site of a market. The road that now runs through the old square, defined by a diagonal lime avenue, effectively cuts it in two. In the north west, tucked behind the limes, a fat London plane grows out of the old cobbles. It has great presence and hints at a time when the traffic was slower. ///sweat.maple.serves

428. **PATAGONIAN SKYSCRAPER** →→ There can be no more elegant roble – or Patagonian oak – growing in these islands than the supremely tall and slender specimen in the little churchyard of St Michael at Plea. The tree soars above its surrounding buildings and the neighbouring sweetgum, itself an impressive tree. Together they make an unlikely yet complementary pairing of a North and South American.

**PATAGONIAN SKYSCRAPER**
*Roble*
*Nothofagus obliqua*
St Michael at Plea,
Redwell Street,
Norwich NR2 4SN
52.630404, 1.297197
///swear.debate.bids

TREE CITY: NORWICH

**429. HUNGATE TREE OF HEAVEN**
*Tree of heaven*
*Ailanthus altissima*
St Peter Hungate,
Princes Street,
Norwich NR3 1AE
52.630997, 1.296797

At the junction of Elm Hill and Princes Street, next to the charming flint church of St Peter Hungate, the city's finest tree of heaven is an even more arresting landmark. It is a huge tree with a thick, rippling trunk growing for several unbranched metres before its canopy starts to spread up and out. Its presence is made more impressive by the narrow lanes and close buildings that surround it. ///sketch.future.counts

**430. INSTAPLANE**
*London plane*
*Platanus × hispanica*
Elm Hill, Norwich
NR3 1HN
52.631455, 1.296842

In a city with dozens of picturesque streets, Elm Hill is surely Norwich's most Instagrammable. Midway along this ancient cobbled thoroughfare, the junction with Waggon and Horses Lane forms a timeless little square. The towering London plane that shades the cast-iron water pump completes the scene, its place-making effect enhanced by the bench built around it. #Instaplane ///simply.bats.ideal

**431. GATEKEEPER**
*Silver maple*
*Acer saccharinum*
Pottergate,
Norwich NR2 1DS
52.629784, 1.292888

A silver maple marks an opening in the narrow lanes at the start of Pottergate, opposite the church of St John the Baptist. Close by, a blue plaque to Anthony de Solempne, Norwich's first printer – a refugee from the Netherlands whose output included by-laws for the city corporation – adorns a brick wall. The North American tree and the plaque to a Dutchman are reminders that the wealth of this city was built on trade and the exchange of ideas. ///coast.joke.skirt

**432. GUILDHALL PLANE** → The 1930s City Hall dominates the western edge of Norwich Market, but for hundreds of years before it was built, the fifteenth-century Guildhall to the north would have been the principal building. The Victorians added a clock in 1850 and built the southern porch in 1861, and around this time the fluted oriental planes on Guildhall Hill would have been planted. Stand under the northern tree to admire the Guildhall's facade.

**GUILDHALL PLANE** *Oriental plane / Platanus orientalis*
Guildhall Hill, Norwich NR2 1JS 52.629002, 1.292977 ///green.them.calls

**433. KETT'S OAK**\*
*Pedunculate oak*
*Quercus robur*
B322, Hethersett
NR9 3DJ
52.587686, 1.155673

The B322 between Hethersett and Wymondham is a typically straight Norfolk road distinguished by an eye-catching oak growing next to the eastbound carriageway, just after a lay-by. It is an old tree held together by iron braces and surrounded by railings on which there is a notice, 'Kett's Oak 1549', which commemorates the tanner Robert Kett, who led a revolt against local land enclosures, a crime for which he was subsequently executed. ///safest.recruiter.couches

**434. JUBILEE OAK**\*
*Pedunculate oak*
*Quercus robur*
Norwich Road,
Chedgrave NR14 6ND
52.539578, 1.480918

Next to Chedgrave's village green the forthright Jubilee Oak grows. It was planted to mark Queen Victoria's Golden Jubilee on 21 June 1887 and, when compared with Nottingham's **INCLOSURE OAK**\* **(305)** of 1845, it demonstrates how, in different locations, oaks can grow at varying rates: despite being four decades younger, the Jubilee Oak is considerably larger. Perhaps its proximity to a reliable water source – the village pond, since filled in and grassed over – got it off to a good start. ///hiding.warbler.trifling

**435. WORKHOUSE WALNUT**
*Walnut / Juglans regia*
St Barnabas Close,
Thetford IP24 3EW
52.405711, 0.746399

Tree hunters arriving at Thetford from the south on Bury Road will be struck by the ample canopy billowing beyond a flint wall, just before the houses start on the right-hand side of the road. It belongs to a huge old walnut tree growing on a patch of land, the former grounds of Thetford Workhouse, just off St Barnabas Close. ///triangle.aliens.stick

436. **LOOP-THE-LOOP PINE** → Thirty minutes walk from Thetford town centre, the Loop-the-Loop Pine lurks in a woodland on the edge of Barnhamcross Common. This astonishing natural sculpture is not shaped like a regular conifer; indeed, it is hard to imagine how it acquired its loop-the-loop trunk. It's thought the pines, which thrive on Breckland's sandy soils, may have been pruned as hedges when they were young.

**LOOP-THE-LOOP PINE** *Scots pine / Pinus sylvestris* Barnhamcross Common,
Bury Road, Thetford IP24 3EB 52.400024, 0.734955 ///fractions.when.dude

**437. BISHOP'S PLANE***
*London plane*
*Platanus × hispanica*
Chapter House, The
College, Ely CB7 4DL
52.398245, 0.261422
*On private property, but
visible from the street and
by prior arrangement.*

**438. RAMBLING JUDAS**
*Judas tree*
*Cercis siliquastrum*
St Mary, Church Street,
Buckden, Saint Neots
PE19 5TL
52.294294, -0.252844

**439. BUCKDEN RETIREE**
*London plane*
*Platanus × hispanica*
Buckden Towers, High
Street, Buckden, Saint
Neots PE19 5TA
52.2961, -0.25108

**440. MODEL MAPLE**
*Silver maple*
*Acer saccharinum*
De Parys Avenue,
Bedford MK40 2TU
52.144742, -0.467146

**441. PUBLIC-PRIVATE
PARTNERSHIP PLANE**
*Oriental plane*
*Platanus orientalis*
Kimbolton Road,
Bedford MK40 2NX
52.142559, -0.460157

Ely's giant old London plane is one of the very largest, quite possibly the most famous and, together with the BUCKDEN RETIREE **(439)** and BARNEY* **(496)** in London, it is certainly one of the oldest of its species. Apparently, a young tree was gifted to the Bishop Peter Gunning, who planted it in the grounds of his newly revamped palace, now the King's School, around 1674. ///park.heckler.expecting

Buckden once straddled the Great North Road between St Neots and Huntingdon, but today, bypassed by the A1, it is a sleepy village, rather cut off from the world. It has two significant ecclesiastical buildings, though, remnants of a more bustling past. In the churchyard of the prominent parish church, a marvellous elderly judas tree grows tall against the wall of Buckden Towers next door. ///pothole.chilled.haystack

Buckden Towers was once the Bishop of Lincoln's fortified palace, and is home to two of the very oldest London planes in Britain or Ireland. The Bishop is said to have planted the now-gargantuan trees in the 1660s. Ironically, the more prominent of the pair, while at least 200 years old, is a replacement. The very, very old tree – resembling BARNEY* **(496)** – is tucked away in the north-east corner. ///moment.mountain.bulky

The junction of De Parys Avenue and Park Avenue is marked by a magnificent silver maple, the first in a splendid series. North American silver maples are a species badly served by heavy pollarding, but here, with plenty of room to attain their potential, sensitive management has helped produce admirable forms – a lesson to gardeners and tree officers elsewhere. This avenue is one of the best anywhere. ///space.matter.levels

A superb oriental plane towers over Kimbolton Road opposite the hospital on the corner of Pemberley Lane. Its ownership is unclear – does it belong to the house whose front garden it shades, or does it reside in the street? Its trunk is ivy-clad, suggesting it has been untended for some time, a fate no doubt exacerbated by this ambiguity. ///slides.stands.work

PUBLIC-PRIVATE PARTNERSHIP PLANE (441)

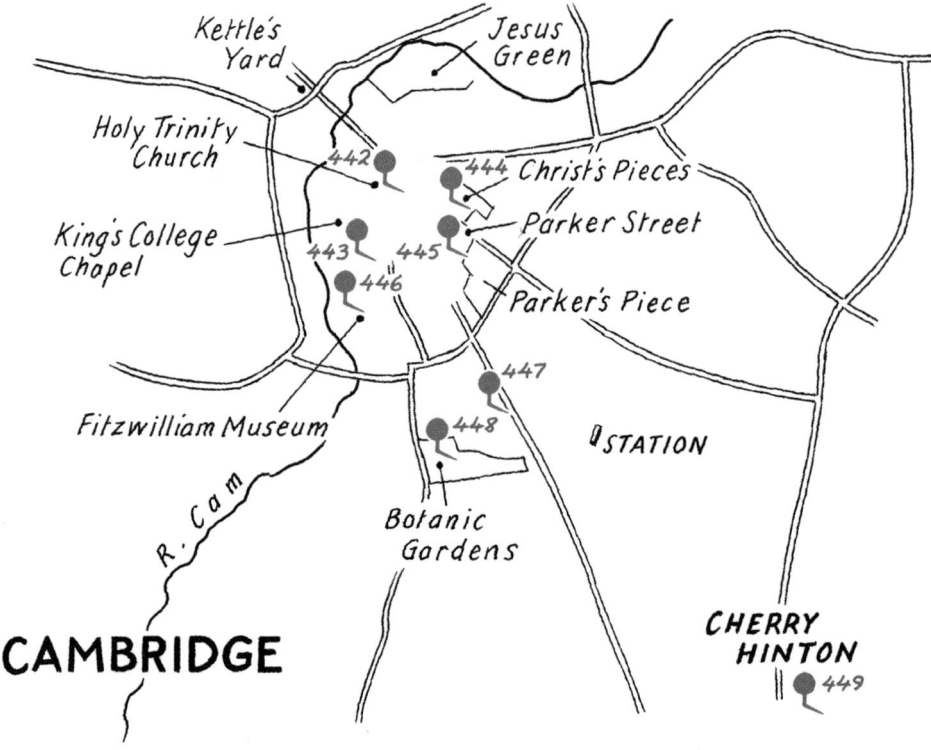

**442. SHAPESHIFTER**
*False acacia*
Robinia pseudoacacia
Holy Trinity,
Market Street,
Cambridge CB2 3NZ
52.206029, 0.120446

Tucked into a square between the western end of the nave and the north transept of Holy Trinity, a fine black locust, or false acacia, dominates the corner of Market Street and Sydney Street. It is a particularly tall, straight-growing tree, which is transformed during the leafless months, when a ball of mistletoe is revealed in the highest branches. ///nodded.sweep.zebra

**443. KING'S CONKER**
*Horse chestnut*
Aesculus hippocastanum
King's College Chapel,
King's Parade,
Cambridge CB2 1ST
52.205032, 0.117366

Like the CATHEDRAL CONKER (758) at Exeter, the King's Conker helps to define the most photographed corner of Cambridge. The horse chestnut tree seems to bubble up from the lawn at the eastern end of King's College Chapel. It is best viewed from King's Parade where visitors can particularly enjoy its flower candles in May, and in winter its perpendicular structure and dramatic, ground-sweeping lower branches can be seen in all its glory. ///wallet.cheer.showed

**444. CHRIST'S CONKER**
*Horse chestnut*
*Aesculus hippocastanum*
Christ's Pieces,
Emmanuel Road,
Cambridge CB1 1JW
52.206568, 0.124318

Christ's Pieces, central Cambridge's most thickly treed park, is home to the city's other great horse chestnut, a distinctly different character to the KING'S CONKER (443). Whereas that tree is tall with branches reaching the ground, Christ's Conker is broad and spreading with a high canopy. Find it growing close to a wall separating the park from Milton's Walk and Christ's College Fellows' Garden beyond. ///buns.courier.verge

**445. TENTACLE TREE**
*Oriental plane*
*Platanus orientalis*
Parker Street,
Cambridge CB1 1JW
52.204843, 0.125154

Cambridge has dozens of noteworthy trees hidden away in college quads and gardens, most of them rarely seen except by those who study or work in the university grounds. Occasionally, however, you can glimpse something remarkable from the street, and this is the case for those waiting for a bus on Parker Street where an octopus-like oriental plane flails over the wall from the Fellows' Garden at Emmanuel College. ///worked.oiled.rated

**446. PUNTER'S ASH**
*Ash / Fraxinus excelsior*
Granta Place,
Cambridge CB2 1RS
52.201151, 0.116134

Granta Place runs parallel to the River Cam for 100 metres or so, passing The Mill pub and a punting station where a memorable urban ash tree grows. It has a gnarled and flared base, the result, perhaps, of decades of punters tying up their vessels to the trunk. It thrives here next to the river, its feet in the water, as a landmark for generations of students. ///speeds.lonely.undulation

**447. CORONATION STREET AWNING**
*Japanese pagoda tree*
*Styphnolobium japonicum*
Coronation Street,
Cambridge CB2 1HJ
52.197054, 0.127486

Coronation Street is a narrow lane off Hills Road, opposite the brick tower of St Paul's Church. About 100 metres down the lane, a looming canopy acts as a green awning over the full width of the street, providing welcome shelter on hot summer days. It belongs to a pleasing, fizzing Japanese pagoda tree growing on the lawn between two mid-century apartment blocks typical of this part of town. ///gifted.linked.exit

**448. OLDEST DAWN REDWOOD**
*Dawn redwood*
*Metasequoia glyptostroboides*
Cambridge Botanic Gardens, Brookside,
Cambridge CB2 1JE
52.193631, 0.124098

The first dawn redwood to be planted in Britain or Ireland is a highlight of Cambridge Botanic Gardens. It was grown from seed supplied by Boston's Arnold Arboretum in 1949, and has reached dizzying heights in less than a century. It grows close to the Trumpington Road gate, and can be seen from the street, next to a slightly shorter (but twice as old) giant redwood for comparison. ///online.manliness.among

**449. CHERRY CINNAMON** → On the corner of Mowbray Road and Glebe Road in Cambridge's Cherry Hinton neighbourhood, a very impressive cinnamon arbutus, or hybrid strawberry tree, grows in a front garden. Just in front of it, a bright red pillar box draws attention to its dramatic oxblood-coloured bark. It is an unusual tree, its hybrid vigour causing it to grow larger than a regular strawberry tree, one of its parent species.

**CHERRY CINNAMON** *Hybrid strawberry tree / Arbutus × andrachnoides*
Mowbray Road, Cambridge CB1 8TH 52.182878, 0.150893
*In a private garden, but visible from the street.* ///limit.showed.rising

**450. CONUNDRUM TREE**
*Oak-leaf alder*
*Alnus glutinosa*
*'Laciniata'*
Abbey Gardens,
Angel Hill, Bury
St Edmunds IP33 1LS
52.245378, 0.719963

Selecting a superlative tree from Bury St Edmunds' thrilling Abbey Gardens is difficult, but, when I was appreciating a fine old poplar shading the River Lark, a passer-by told me how much they admired another, nearby tree, though they had no idea what it was. It turned out to be something special: a rare, and confusing, oak-leaf alder, one of the finest anywhere, and a worthy exemplar of one of the best municipal tree collections in England. ///burst.outhouse.bearable

**451. ANACONDA TREE**
*Père David's maple*
*Acer davidii*
Abbey Gardens,
Angel Hill, Bury
St Edmunds IP33 1LS
52.244381, 0.71853

Abbey Gardens has a long history, both as the churchyard for St Edmund's Abbey, whose ruins lie to the east of the present cathedral, and as an early botanic garden and a nursery for medicinal herbs. Over the years, the gardens have morphed into a public park. Along with the **CONUNDRUM TREE (450)**, this colossal Père David's maple, held together with ropes, is worth seeking out near the ruins. ///star.conspire.twinkling

**452. HARDWICK CEDAR**
*Cedar of Lebanon*
*Cedrus libani*
Broadland Road, Bury
St Edmunds IP33 2TG
52.227563, 0.718001

Home Farm Lane once marked the edge of Hardwick Heath and the Hardwick Estate. To the east were tree-dotted fields, now covered by a 1970s housing estate. Generous open spaces were left between the houses, and one between Croft Rise and Broadland Road is graced by a particularly fine cedar of Lebanon, a one-time mainstay of country estates, suggesting these must have once been very aristocratic fields. ///pills.direct.dares

ARRIVISTE REDWOOD (456)

### 453. HOME FARM OAK
*Pedunculate oak*
*Quercus robur*
Home Farm Lane, Bury
St Edmunds IP33 2QL
52.226647, 0.713068
*In a private garden, but visible from the street.*

Large detached houses stand among pollards from Hardwick Heath, which once covered a much larger area than the current cedar-scape of municipal Hardwick Heath Park. The estate was auctioned off in the 1920s and its extensive grounds put to new uses. In one corner, many old oaks have survived, adding character to the houses. The most impressive is at the end of Home Farm Lane. ///liberated.theory.victory

### 454. REID MOIR OAK*
*Pedunculate oak*
*Quercus robur*
Westwood Avenue,
Ipswich IP1 4EQ
52.067392, 1.142697

The Reid Moir Oak is here today thanks to the efforts of a concerned citizen, James Reid Moir, who campaigned to save it from the path of a proposed new road in 1935. Many Ipswichians were appalled that the tree might be felled, and, under mounting pressure, the road was diverted and the dashing 450-year-old oak was saved. ///hike.brings.bottom

### 455. FAT CHESTNUT
*Sweet chestnut*
*Castanea sativa*
Christchurch Park, Bolton
Lane, Ipswich IP4 2BX
52.062487, 1.159145

On the eastern side of ancient Christchurch Park, just north of Ipswich town centre, the park's fattest and possibly oldest tree can be found. It is an aged sweet chestnut, the largest of several, and may be even older than Tudor Christchurch Mansion. Several limbs, which appear to be dripping with wood, branch at head height, suggesting the tree was pollarded in the distant past. ///tiger.jeeps.factories

### 456. ARRIVISTE REDWOOD
*Giant redwood*
*Sequoiadendron giganteum*
St Margaret's Church,
Bolton Lane,
Ipswich IP4 2BT
52.059495, 1.158443

St Margaret's church once dominated the corner of Bolton Lane and Soane Street. Today, the handsome fifteenth-century church plays second fiddle to a Victorian giant redwood growing in its churchyard. Giant redwood seedlings were first germinated in Britain in 1854 and have been soaring skywards ever since. In this sleepy corner of Ipswich it might be regarded as something of an arriviste. ///neck.tested.surely

### 457. ST CLEMENT'S LIME
*Silver pendent lime*
*Tilia tomentosa*
*'Petiolaris'*
St Clement Church, Fore
Street, Ipswich IP4 1JZ
52.053781, 1.161908

One of Ipswich's loveliest trees is marooned between busy roads, hidden by a medieval church and shrouded by several other towering trees. But the determined tree hunter is rewarded by the sight of an enormous silver pendent lime growing in the churchyard of St Clement. It sits on the south side of the church. Come in June to catch its flowers and their olfactory pleasures. ///eager.sing.spoon

**458. OLD KNOBBLEY**\*
*Pedunculate oak*
*Quercus robur*
Mistley Village Hall,
Shrublands Road,
Mistley CO11 1HS
51.938079, 1.081475

Old Knobbley is a wonderful old codger: an almost collapsed oak clinging to life deep in the woods on the southern edge of the Essex village of Mistley. Set off from the village hall down Shrublands Road and then turn left into the woods. You'll find him on the brow of a low hill surrounded by much younger, and less knobbly, trees gathered round to hear his words of wisdom. *///mercy.enclosing.bravery*

**459. NATURAL HISTORIAN**
*Copper beech / Fagus sylvatica 'Purpurea'*
Natural History Museum,
High Street,
Colchester CO1 1DN
51.889432, 0.90411

Like Norwich, Colchester was once one of England's largest towns, and a wealth of medieval churches, many now redundant, are reminders of its historical importance. All Saints has become the Natural History Museum, and in the former churchyard a magnificent copper beech dominates the corner of Queen Street and Culver Street East. It is surely one of the museum's best loved exhibits. *///blocks.report.dots*

**460. CASTLE BONSAI**
*Sycamore*
*Acer pseudoplatanus*
Colchester Castle,
Colchester CO1 1TJ
51.890403, 0.902887

The sycamore growing on top of Colchester Castle's south-east tower was planted by the mayor's daughter in 1815 to commemorate the defeat of Napoleon at Waterloo. As a result of its position and limited soil, it is rather smaller than other 200-year-old trees. It had to be removed in 1985 for wall repairs but it survived, and returned to its post in 1987, after a two-year sabbatical. *///scores.bottle.candle*

**461. ST JOHN'S REMNANT MULBERRY**
*Black mulberry*
*Morus nigra*
Londinium Road,
Colchester CO2 7NU
51.885255, 0.901446

Like one or two other very old mulberries, this ancient tree now finds itself languishing in a car park. But its lodgings were not always so lowly: this was once the Abbey of St John, and then a house destroyed in the 1648 Siege of Colchester. It grows on a low mound, partly protected by a fence, just beyond historic St John's Abbey Gate. *///solve.goats.hotels*

**462. BBC GINKGO**
*Ginkgo / Ginkgo biloba*
New London Road,
Chelmsford CM2 0GG
51.725676, 0.46240400

Across the road from BBC Essex, an old ivy-covered ginkgo forms part of the dividing hedge between some houses and a block of flats on the New London Road. It appears to have been here for considerably longer than the buildings on either side, a remnant of some nineteenth-century garden. If the ivy that obscures it were removed, the tree's full glory would be revealed. *///volunteered.sticks.froth*

**463. NONCONFORMIST OAK**
*Turner's oak*
*Quercus × turneri*
Nonconformist Cemetery,
New London Road,
Chelmsford CM2 0AW
51.727051, 0.46568

Chelmsford's nonconformist cemetery feels like the land that time forgot. It is little visited and rather overgrown, so, although it is small by Victorian cemetery standards, you can quite easily get lost. In the eastern corner, furthest from the only entrance on London Road, a huge Turner's oak grows. Judging by its dimensions, it must have been planted around the time the cemetery opened in 1846. ///slowly.much.yard

**464. LITTLE PARNDON OAK***
*Pedunculate oak*
*Quercus robur*
Hodings Road,
Harlow CM20 1RL
51.774755, 0.083922

An ancient pedunculate oak survives in the mid-twentieth-century town of Harlow, on the corner of Park Mead and Hodings Road. It is a stout tree, hundreds of years old, and a lapsed pollard (many years ago it would have had its branches regularly cut back), judging by its short trunk and tangle of tentacular limbs. The tree, a veteran of parkland, once grew in the parish of Little Parndon. ///money.salsa.rubble

**465. DOWNHAM FIELD MAPLE**
*Field maple / Acer campestre*
St Mary's Church,
Castledon Road,
Downham, Billericay
CM11 1LH
51.629838, 0.498371

The hamlet of Downham nestles in rural Essex between Wickford and Billericay, its old brick church surrounded by fields. In the churchyard, one of the oldest field maples in these islands can be found. Often regarded as a plant for hedgerows or woodland edges, this impressive 500-year-old tree shows that this overlooked species can give some old oaks a run for their money. ///sparkles.wizards.january

**466. WESTCLIFF OAK**
*Pedunculate oak*
*Quercus robur*
London Road, Westcliff,
Southend on Sea
SS0 9SU
51.545669, 0.678482

A veteran oak grows on a grass verge next to the busy London Road just outside Chalkwell Park. There are a couple of other old oaks here, but the Westcliff Oak is the tallest and fattest, and is between 300 and 400 years old. Despite its proximity to the traffic, it appears to be in rude and boisterous health, impervious to the noise and pollution. ///skills.grants.retire

**467. UNHOLY UNION**
*London plane and common lime / Platanus × hispanica + Tilia × europaea*
Chalkwell Park, Chalkwell Avenue, Westcliff,
Southend on Sea SS0 8NL
51.545238, 0.677484

Two of the most common urban tree species appear locked in embrace in Westcliff's Chalkwell Park. A London plane and a common lime were planted within inches of each other a century or more ago, and today they are touching to the point that the plane appears to be snogging the somewhat disinterested lime, which has sprouted branches to grow away from its pursuer. ///label.bunch.repair

**468. DITTON COURT PINE**
*Bhutan pine*
*Pinus wallichiana*
Ditton Court Road,
Westcliff,
Southend on Sea SS0 7HF
51.538662, 0.69170600

Southend has an enviable collection of street trees which contribute to making the city's urban forest particularly diverse and interesting. On Ditton Court Road in Westcliff, near the junction with Canewdon Road, a Bhutan pine with arching limbs holding distinctive, delicate needles grows in the verge between street and pavement – possibly the only example of this species planted as a street tree. ///sorry.dots.fire

**469. LEIGH LIBRARY LEBANON**
*Cedar of Lebanon*
*Cedrus libani*
Broadway West, Leigh on Sea,
Southend on Sea SS9 2DA
51.541545, 0.653724

Leigh on Sea's veteran cedar of Lebanon is said to have been planted in 1792, making it one of the oldest of its kind in Britain and Ireland. In order to accommodate the low-growing tree and the buildings with which it is entangled, compromises have been made: several branches have been removed over the years, while the buildings have been carefully positioned around the tree's giant bole. ///hurls.rarely.news

**470. ST STEPHEN'S CEDAR**
*Cedar of Lebanon*
*Cedrus libani*
St Stephen's Church,
Watling Street,
St Albans AL1 2PT
51.740904, -0.347549

In a letter to *The Times* in 1925, the Rev J. B. Booth boasted that the cedar of Lebanon growing in his vicarage garden had a girth of nearly 9.5 metres. A century later, the vicarage garden is no more; it has been reinvented as St Stephen's Play Area. But the magnificent cedar still stands, and its girth remains more or less the same. ///smiled.agree.reap

**471. CHAPTER HOUSE CEDAR**
*Cedar of Lebanon*
*Cedrus libani*
Waxhouse Gate, St Albans
AL1 1BT
51.750067, -0.341854

The Chapter House Cedar must, I am convinced, be the people of St Albans' favourite tree, and, like **ST STEPHEN'S CEDAR (470)**, it is another old cedar of Lebanon. It is not as huge as that tree, but its prime position next to the cathedral is eye-catching. The tree was planted on 25 March 1803 by the Dowager Countess Spencer, making it one of the older examples of its species. ///finely.sushi.joins

**472. WHEATHAMPSTEAD WINGNUT**
*Hybrid wingnut*
*Pterocarya × rehderiana*
St Helen's Church,
Church Street,
Wheathampstead
AL4 8AA
51.811786, -0.294961

The most unusual thing about the quiet Hertfordshire village of Wheathampstead is what grows in the churchyard of St Helen's. An unmissable hybrid wingnut, a huge and rare tree, hangs over the Church Street entrance. Could it have been noted – or even planted – by William Beach Thomas, a First World War correspondent and, later, renowned nature writer who was buried here in 1957? ///loaded.fault.leaned

### 473. GROTTO OAK

*Sessile oak / Quercus petraea*
Russellcroft Road,
Welwyn Garden City
AL8 6QN
51.802353, -0.209839

Little more than a hundred years ago, Welwyn Garden City's tree-lined boulevards were fields in rural Hertfordshire. It would have been in one of those fields, or perhaps on its edge, that the Grotto Oak stood for centuries. Now it survives in a patch of green close to the town centre, noticed by children who have dressed the tree and turned a hollow at its base into a fairy chamber. ///humans.drum.eagles

### 474. HANDSIDE CATALPA →

Utopian Welwyn was laid out so that every street would have a wide grass verge suitable for planting and nurturing large street trees. On the corner of Handside Lane and Russellcroft Road, a soaring hybrid catalpa has taken full advantage of these benign conditions and grown into a landmark. A slightly leaning and dramatically spiralling trunk supports a canopy that spreads high above the roofs of nearby houses.

**HANDSIDE CATALPA**
*Hybrid catalpa*
*Catalpa × erubescens*
*'J. C. Teas'*
Handside Lane,
Welwyn Garden
City AL8 6SH
51.802649, -0.212587
///candy.eating.liability

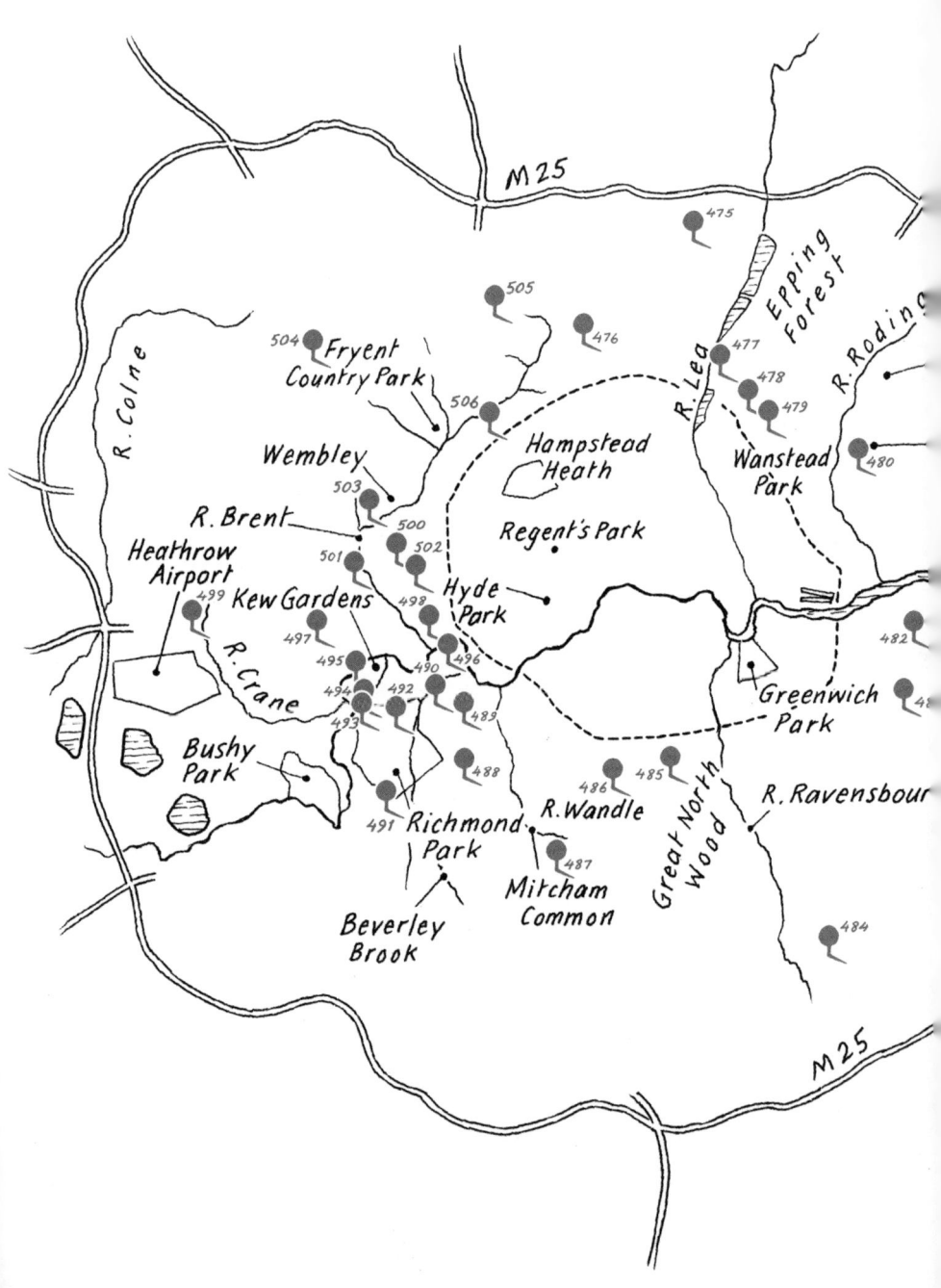

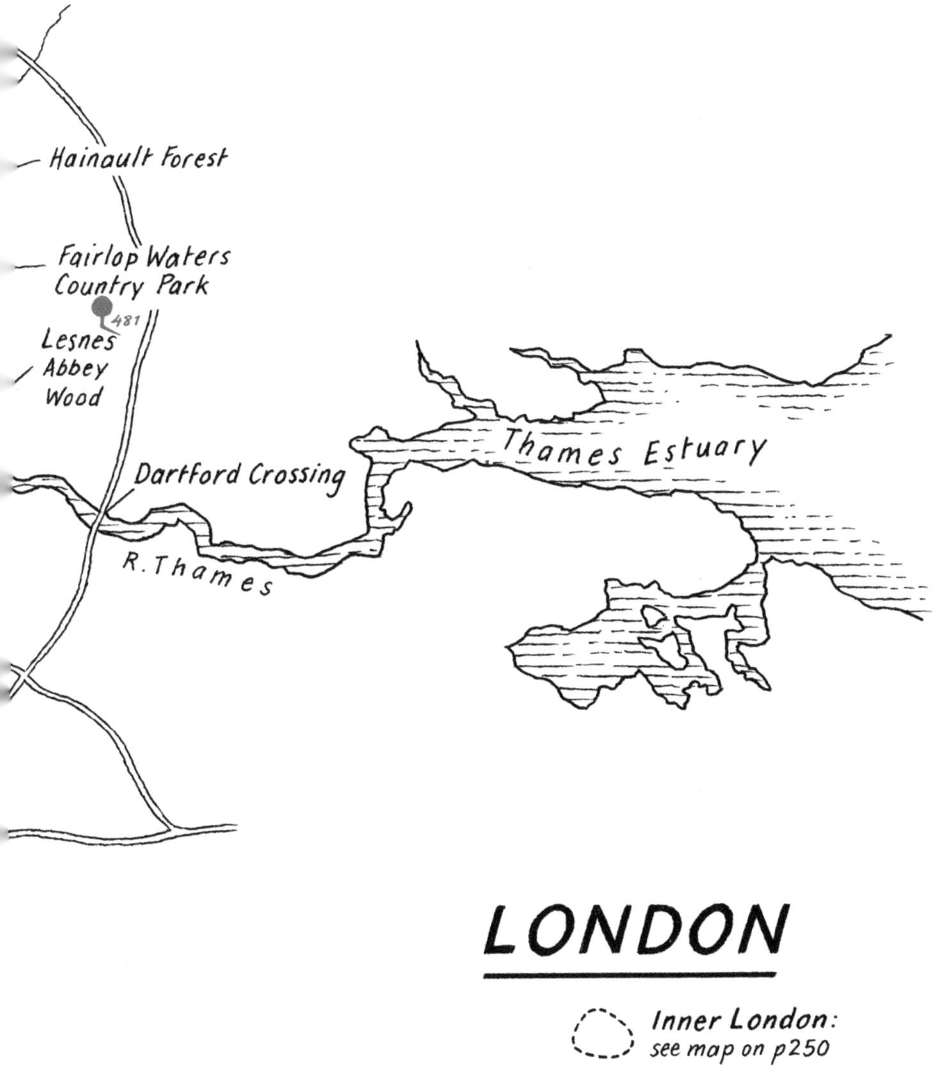

- Hainault Forest
- Fairlop Waters Country Park
- Lesnes Abbey Wood 481
- Dartford Crossing
- R. Thames
- Thames Estuary

# LONDON

Inner London: see map on p250

# LONDON

*Greater London*

England's vast, dense capital is bristling with trees. In fact, their canopy covers more than 20 per cent of the city – enough, technically, to call it a forest. Anywhere you go, you will be greeted by leafy individuals of all shapes and sizes. **BAZALGETTE'S PLANE (550)** near the Houses of Parliament is a good starting point for the tree hunter. It grows on land reclaimed from the Thames for Joseph Bazalgette's great engineering scheme of 1870 to deal with the scourge of pollution, a side effect of the city's rapid growth, and to build a grand riverside thoroughfare. The new Victoria Embankment was the first large-scale, tree-lined street in the city and was a great novelty, becoming the place to see and be seen – a promenade worthy of a powerful imperial capital.

The triumph of the Victoria Embankment kick-started a new urban tree-planting fashion across London. Where before trees might have grown in the city's garden squares and private gardens, now they were planted directly on the street; new avenues were modelled on those of great continental cities, especially Paris. The tree that became synonymous with these new thoroughfares was, of course, the hybrid plane, planted in such abundance in London it became known as the London plane. Fine examples like the **WINDRUSH PLANE (531)** in Brixton or the **FRIENDSHIP TREE (507)** in Wood Green date from the decades after the Victoria Embankment opened.

But planes had grown in London for many years before their nineteenth-century apogee. Old trees, predating the Victorian and Edwardian plantings, still survive: the **BERKELEY PLANE (554)** in Mayfair dates from 1789, while **POOR SUSAN'S PLANE (557)** in the City is likely even older. But the very oldest, and most spectacular, despite its out-of-the-way location, is **BARNEY* (496)**, a tree thought to date back to the late 1600s.

London planes are the quintessential urban tree, almost always human-planted and often growing in human settlements. They are a hybrid tree, their parent species hailing from different continents, introduced to one another

**SIGNATURE SPECIES:**
*London plane
(of course)*

through human travel and trade, reminding us that commercial, cultural and botanical exchange is burnt into London's DNA. Arboreally speaking, nowhere is this more apparent than at Kew, perhaps the greatest botanical gardens in the world, where the **KEW COLOSSUS (495)** is just one of hundreds of incredible trees growing there that could fill a whole volume.

London's great cosmopolitans don't stop with the worldly plane, however: the city is also home to some old and striking examples of the black mulberry, a species which has been spread by human migration since prehistory. The **LESNES ABBEY MULBERRY (482)** is worth seeking out, as is the **SENIOR MULBERRY (517)**, which has a good claim to being one of the royal specimens imported by James I as part of his failed bid to start a silk industry (he imported the wrong species: it is the white, not the black, mulberry that silkworms prefer).

Like other cities, London has trees – often oaks – that are remnants of a rural past, which now find themselves in the inner city, like the impressive **BRUCE CASTLE OAK\* (508)** in Tottenham or the **ELEPHANT TREE\* (501)** in Ealing, while very old trees like **THE MASTER\* (504)** or the **EDGE OF LONDON OAK (481)**, protected by the Green Belt, are on the perimeter of the twenty-first-century city.

Beyond these historic specimens, there is plenty more to see. In the twentieth and twenty-first centuries huge strides have been made to plant more trees throughout London, and these efforts have added great character to the modern city. Today, more diverse planting is possible than ever before, due in part to the warmer temperatures generated by the climate crisis, which are exacerbated by the urban heat island effect. This is obviously an ominous portent for the future, and is already changing tree life in the present. Still, the broadening palette of trees found in the capital will excite tree hunters: species that just a few decades ago might have been considered too tender now thrive. But the prize for London's most unlikely landmark tree must go to the **ROTHERHITHE SILKY OAK (523)**, a subtropical Australian that has, against the odds, been happily growing on the site of a former police station for more than twenty years.

GEORGE GREEN CHESTNUT* (479)

475. **FORTY HALL CEDAR**\*
*Cedar of Lebanon*
*Cedrus libani*
Forty Hall Estate, Forty
Hill, Enfield EN2 9HA
51.669402, -0.067654

Some claim the Forty Hall Cedar, planted by early horticulturalist Robert Uvedale, who died at Enfield in 1722, is the second oldest in the country. Until 2024, when it lost several limbs, it was also one of the most impressive. Despite this calamity, it is worthy of visiting for its historical significance and setting in front of Forty Hall. ///return.ruins.lend

476. **MINCHENDEN OAK**\*
*Sessile oak*
*Quercus petraea*
Minchenden Oak Garden,
Waterfall Road,
London N14 7JN
51.624286, -0.129102

One of London's oldest oaks is little known outside Southgate in North London, where it grows in a tiny park bearing its name next to Christ Church. To find this most retiring of aged oaks, enter the secret garden through a gate in a high brick wall. Once inside, you cannot miss it: a huge trunk is surmounted by several thick branches, the result of pollarding all those centuries ago. ///closet.lace.warns

477. **NORTH CIRCULAR CORK OAK**\*
*Cork oak / Quercus suber*
Cork Tree Retail Park,
Hall Lane,
London E4 8JA
51.61205, -0.031359

The Cork Tree Retail Park in Chingford was once the site of the Cork Manufacturing Company. Nothing is left of the works, but a cork oak, planted over a century ago, does survive in this most unlikely corner just off the thundering North Circular. Remarkably, the tree is thriving, showing how well adapted these Mediterranean trees are to life next to the fast lane. ///edgy.glue.engine

478. **WOOD STREET WITNESS**
*Horse chestnut*
*Aesculus hippocastanum*
78 Wood Street,
Walthamstow,
London E17 3HX
51.589222, -0.004405

The single-storey clapboard shop under the sprawling canopy of Walthamstow's landmark horse chestnut is a barometer of changing times. It was once a butcher's shop, but is now an organic health food store. The shop must be 200 years old, and perhaps its guardian tree is too. Visit in early May to catch its iconic flower candles, or, technically, panicles. ///hint.hill.focal

479. **GEORGE GREEN CHESTNUT**\*
*Sweet chestnut*
*Castanea sativa*
George Green, Wanstead,
London E11 2RN
51.57483, 0.028074

In the early 1990s, a 250-year-old sweet chestnut in Wanstead was at the centre of protests against the construction of the M11 link road. Despite a high-profile and well-supported campaign, the tree was felled to construct a cut-and-cover tunnel under George Green. The current George Green Chestnut, the largest in an unmissable group of three surviving chestnuts, gives an inkling of what arboreal riches were lost in the name of 'progress'. ///regime.happen.serves

**480. OUTFIELDER**
*Field maple*
*Acer campestre*
Valentines Park,
Cranbrook Road,
Ilford IG1 4TG
51.571542, 0.072689

Ilford's Valentines Park was put together from various parcels of land by improving Victorians, and its rough-and-ready joins can still be discerned. The ancient field maple on the edge of the cricket pitch is one such reminder. It could be 400 years old, and for much of its life would have been part of a boundary hedge, which accounts for its careworn appearance and twisted limbs. ///loose.muddy.part

**481. EDGE OF LONDON OAK**
*Pedunculate oak*
*Quercus robur*
Little Gaynes Lane,
Upminster RM14 2JR
51.548661, 0.245079

Little Gaynes Lane is on the very edge of London, bounded by fields on one side and the city on the other. An impressive oak – several hundred years old, with flared roots – resides here, in what would, for most of its life, have been rural Essex and is now a suburban street corner. ///ending.lands.acid

**482. LESNES ABBEY MULBERRY**
*Black mulberry*
*Morus nigra*
Lesnes Abbey,
Abbey Road,
Belvedere DA17 5DH
51.489314, 0.128747

An aged, recumbent mulberry grows in a fenced-off area next to the ruins of Lesnes Abbey. This is one of the most photogenic of London's many old mulberries. Because mulberries are often associated with monastic communities, its proximity to the thousand-year-old abbey ruins suggests it may just be the latest of generations of mulberry trees to have grown here. ///mime.spared.weds

**483. BEXLEY CHARTER OAK***
*Pedunculate oak*
*Quercus robur*
Danson Park,
Danson Road,
Bexleyheath DA15 9PW
51.454924, 0.118056

The London Borough of Bexley has a tiny oak on its coat of arms, a representation of the Bexley Charter Oak, a splendid tree in Danson Park. The tree is a 200-year-old landmark growing behind a fence on the lawn between the lake and Danson House. The charter that brought the modern-day borough's predecessor, the *Municipal Borough of Bexley*, into existence was signed under the canopy on the 30th September in 1935. ///hurry.using.taped

**484. DARWIN'S YEW***
*Yew / Taxus baccata*
St Mary's Church,
High Street, Downe,
Orpington BR6 7US
51.335772, 0.054339

Darwin's Yew vies with the TOTTERIDGE YEW* (505) for the title of London's Oldest Tree. It is certainly ancient – over 1,000 years old – and chances are only a very few centuries separate the two, a trifling period for this species. The tree resides in the churchyard of St Mary's at Downe, on the very edge of London, where Charles Darwin, the great naturalist and upsetter of Victorian religious orthodoxies, is buried. ///perky.wizard.swing

**485. SYDENHAM BOUNDARY OAK**
*Pedunculate oak*
*Quercus robur*
Lawrie Park Avenue,
London SE26 6HA
51.42455, -0.061678

Spreading in splendid isolation on a roundabout, the Sydenham Boundary Oak is just that: a boundary tree that still fulfils its original purpose. Today it marks the boundary between the London Boroughs of Lewisham and Bromley, but it has marked other borders before. For many decades it was where London and Kent met. While the tree is here, there will always be a boundary. ///media.divide.complains

**486. SKELETON STRAWBERRY TREE**
*Strawberry tree*
*Arbutus unedo*
Norwood Grove,
Crescent Way,
London SW16 3AL
51.419025, -0.113469

Like an ancient yew, the Skeleton Strawberry Tree appears as a group of separate trees, the result of recumbent branches layering themselves over a period of many years. Compared to the CRÈME DE LA CRÈME (539) in Highgate, an example of this species in its prime, the tree at Norwood Grove is a veteran in gradual decline. It is one of the oldest strawberry trees in England. ///begun.desire.swift

**487. CARSHALTON LEVIATHAN**
*London plane*
*Platanus × hispanica*
Sutton Ecology Centre,
Festival Walk,
Carshalton SM5 3NY
51.365311, -0.165522

Like the RICHMOND RIVERSIDE PLANE (493), the Carshalton Leviathan grows close to water, a necessary condition for the biggest London planes, with their deep and sprawling roots, to reach their full potential. It is comparatively difficult to appreciate the soaring height of this massive tree in its woodland location, but its great bole – 7 metres in diameter – is an indicator of its enormity. ///career.likes.shins

**488. CANNIZARO GUM**
*Broad-leaved kindling bark / Eucalyptus dalrympleana*
Cannizaro Park,
Westside Common,
London SW19 4UE
51.425655, -0.230292

Cannizaro Park is another reminder of south-west London's aristocratic past. For centuries it formed the grounds of a private estate, eventually coming into council ownership and opening as a park in 1948. Among a wonderful collection of rare plants, including many fine old trees, the most dramatic is a massive white-trunked broad-leaved kindling bark, a type of eucalyptus from Tasmania. ///palms.flies.gains

**489. PAVEMENT HOG**
*Sweet chestnut*
*Castanea sativa*
Heathview Gardens,
London SW15 3SZ
51.448887, -0.230897

The Pavement Hog is a remnant from Putney Heath, a landscape surrounding the houses of Heathview Gardens, which were built here about a hundred years ago. It must have been a striking sweet chestnut back then, and was left to grow in the pavement. Today, its swirling trunk takes up the whole width of the pavement. ///ships.grand.rises

**490. MODERNIST OAK**
*Lucombe oak*
*Quercus × crenata*
*'Lucombeana'*
Danebury Avenue,
Roehampton,
London SW15 4EQ
51.451366, -0.247036

Like Putney, much of Roehampton was redeveloped after the Second World War, and traces of a grander past can still be seen among the trees. Overlooking Richmond Park, the much-admired Alton Estate was built around existing parkland and boasts a superior treescape. The finest is the massive Lucombe oak, the larger of a pair growing near Bus Stop L on Danebury Avenue. ///award.theme.return

**491. GATEWAY OAK**
*Turner's oak*
*Quercus × turneri*
Queen's Road, Kingston upon Thames KT2 7SR
51.419726, -0.28602

Not far from the Kingston Gate into Richmond Park, a large Turner's oak hangs over the corner of Queen's Road and Liverpool Road. It has an enormous, dense canopy held up by a stocky trunk that leans out and branches low in order to keep its capacious headpiece aloft. The tree is outcompeting several others planted nearby, and partly conceals a neighbouring row of terraced houses. ///credit.rooms.shout

**492. ROYAL OAK\***
*Pedunculate oak*
*Quercus robur*
Richmond Park,
Star and Garter Hill,
Richmond TW10 5HS
51.444629, -0.283511

At around 600 years old, the Royal Oak is probably the oldest tree in Richmond Park, and is certainly the most picturesque. It is not tall, but what it lacks in stature, it makes up for with a splendid fat, hollow trunk that could accommodate a five-a-side football team. It is of such significance that it commands its own enclosure between Sidmouth Wood and Queen Elizabeth's Plantation. ///words.beast.degree

**493. RICHMOND RIVERSIDE PLANE**
*London plane*
*Platanus × hispanica*
The Towpath, Riverside,
Richmond TW10 6UJ
51.45646, -0.304712

London's plane trees keep on growing, and, as 350-year-old BARNEY\* (496) shows, most of the nineteenth-century population are mere adolescents. Several trees have reached the staggering height of 40 metres or more, and one whose vastness is easy to comprehend is the tree growing on the riverside path at Richmond. It is truly magnificent, casting its shade over the outdoor seating of a steakhouse. ///wedge.from.slams

**494. MAIDS OF HONOUR STONE PINE\***
*Stone pine*
*Pinus pinea*
Richmond Green,
Richmond TW9 1PA
51.461392, -0.30871

It was one of Anne Boleyn's ladies-in-waiting at Richmond Palace who first baked a delectable pastry now known as Maids of Honour. Though the cakes survive, little is left of the palace save for the gatehouse on the western edge of Richmond Green, next to which grows one of the oldest and broadest stone pines in Britain or Ireland. ///belly.grades.deflection

ROYAL OAK* (492)

BARNEY* (496)

### 495. KEW COLOSSUS
*Chestnut-leaved oak*
*Quercus castaneifolia*
Royal Botanic Gardens,
Kew, Kew Road,
Richmond TW9 3AB
51.480258, -0.294071
*Paid entry.*

Where should tree hunters start at Kew Gardens' world-class arboretum? I'm sure there are many opinions, but, for me, the tree to head for is the incredible chestnut-leaved oak near the water-lily house. It is stupendous: the biggest tree at Kew, and the biggest example of this rare oak anywhere in the world. Look out for saw-tooth-edged leaves that resemble those of a sweet chestnut. ///rips.frame.traps

### 496. BARNEY*
*London plane*
*Platanus × hispanica*
Barn Elms Playing Fields,
London SW13 9SA
51.474356, -0.231007

Barney is the oldest London plane in the city. It is said to have been planted in 1680, around the same time as the BUCKDEN RETIREE (439) and the BISHOP'S PLANE (437) in Ely, making it one of the very oldest in the country. It is hidden in woodland near Barn Elms playing fields and is tricky to locate, but when you do, it does not disappoint. ///items.hello.landed

### 497. OSTERLEY GOLDEN RAIN TREE
*Golden rain tree*
*Koelreuteria paniculata*
Great West Road,
Osterley,
Isleworth TW7 4PU
51.480959, -0.351806

Osterley tube station on the Piccadilly line is one of London's most admired 1930s modernist buildings, so the tree which accentuates it needs to be exceptional: with its gleaming yellow blooms in high summer, the Osterley Golden Rain Tree delivers. Despite growing in a challenging position next to the Great West Road, it is one of the very best examples of its kind in these islands. ///traded.music.reason

### 498. HOGARTH'S MULBERRY*
*Black mulberry*
*Morus nigra*
Hogarth's House,
Hogarth Lane, Great West Road, London W4 2QN
51.487023, -0.255262

Fortitude is required to navigate the A4 at Chiswick in order to see one of London's oldest mulberries at Hogarth's House. When the artist William Hogarth acquired his country house in 1749, the tree, now such a feature of the small garden, was already present. It might be 350 years old, only slightly younger than the SENIOR MULBERRY (517), and is a dazzling, hugely important natural monument. ///acute.humble.power

### 499. IMPERILLED CEDAR
*Cedar of Lebanon*
*Cedrus libani*
St Peter & St Paul's Church, St Peter's Way,
Harlington UB3 5AB
51.492656, -0.434187

One of the tallest and most majestic cedars of Lebanon in London grows in the churchyard of St Peter and St Paul at Harlington, sandwiched between Heathrow airport's perimeter and the M4. Its striking silhouette can be seen by anyone travelling along the motorway, but the future of this historic church and landmark tree is overshadowed by proposed expansion of the airport. ///insist.gone.renew

**500. OMG SWAMP CYPRESS**
*Swamp cypress*
*Taxodium distichum*
Julian Avenue,
London W3 9JF
51.513947, -0.272221

Julian Avenue is a nondescript Edwardian terrace in Acton where one of London's most astonishing trees grows: a rare veteran hemmed in on a narrow street. Like Ealing, Acton was once popular with wealthy London commuters, and, back then, the OMG Swamp Cypress likely grew in a spacious country-house garden. It now towers over the houses and irritates motorists by taking up half the road, but it thrills the tree hunter. ///adults.mason.camera

501. **ELEPHANT TREE*** ⇥ An Ealing urban myth recounts how a Victorian circus elephant dropped dead while trooping down Castlebar Road and was promptly buried, its grave marked by an oak on Carlton Road, which became known as the Elephant Tree. The tree, an obstacle in the middle of the street, is certainly in the right place, but it must be hundreds of years old, predating this legend.

**ELEPHANT TREE***
*Pedunculate oak*
*Quercus robur*
Carlton Road,
London W5 2DJ
51.516858, -0.309248
///custom.plants.linen

### 502. 1811 CEDAR
*Cedar of Lebanon*
*Cedrus libani*
Goldsmiths' Almshouses,
East Churchfield Road,
London W3 7LL
51.509446, -0.260254

The classical portico of the Goldsmiths' Almshouses bears the year 1811, providing a planting date for the lovely cedar of Lebanon that now fills the western half of the courtyard. It is a thoughtful tree: taking its lead from the architecture, it has barely grown taller than the building. Though perhaps the residents, whose natural light is limited, feel differently. ///claim.note.talent

### 503. WEMBLEY ELM*
*European white elm*
*Ulmus laevis*
Harrow Road,
Wembley HA9 6LL
51.553269, -0.285532

European white elms are rare but occasionally seen in unlikely places, none more so than the Wembley Elm which grows outside a pub just off the Harrow Road in the shadow of Wembley Stadium. It is an old tree, perhaps part of a field boundary once upon a time. Its current situation, witness to great streams of rowdy football fans, is a world away from the quiet life it will have known for most of its years. ///juror.person.fund

### 504. THE MASTER*
*Pedunculate oak*
*Quercus robur*
Bentley Priory Nature
Reserve, Embry Way,
Stanmore HA7 3AY
51.620378, -0.333181

Take the footpath at the end of Embry Way towards the lake to find The Master, an ancient oak in Bentley Priory Nature Reserve. It is a massive, very impressive individual, which could be 500 years old. You will be struck by the number of limbs that sprout exuberantly from its short but gargantuan trunk, the result of pollarding that last took place some 200 years ago or so. ///covers.bother.local

### 505. TOTTERIDGE YEW*
*Yew / Taxus baccata*
St Andrews Church,
Totteridge Village,
London N20 8PR
51.632371, -0.200534

The Totteridge Yew is North London's oldest tree. Like many other yews, it grows in a churchyard and is far older than its church. Find it just beyond St Andrews lychgate, and look closely under the canopy to marvel at its hollow and twisted limbs. It could be anything between 1,000 and 2,000 years old – a range so wide because old, hollow trees are extremely difficult to age. ///spine.less.gossip

### 506. RELATIVE GIANT
*Japanese maple*
*Acer palmatum*
Hendon Park, Queens
Road, London NW4 2TL
51.582242, -0.223443

The largest Japanese maple in Britain or Ireland can be found in Hendon Park. It's an impressive sight even though its position next to the tennis courts is admittedly rather modest. Way larger than the little potted maples of balconies and patios, this tree has been here since the park opened in 1903. In that time it has become an impressive giant. Relatively speaking. ///rubble.acting.escape

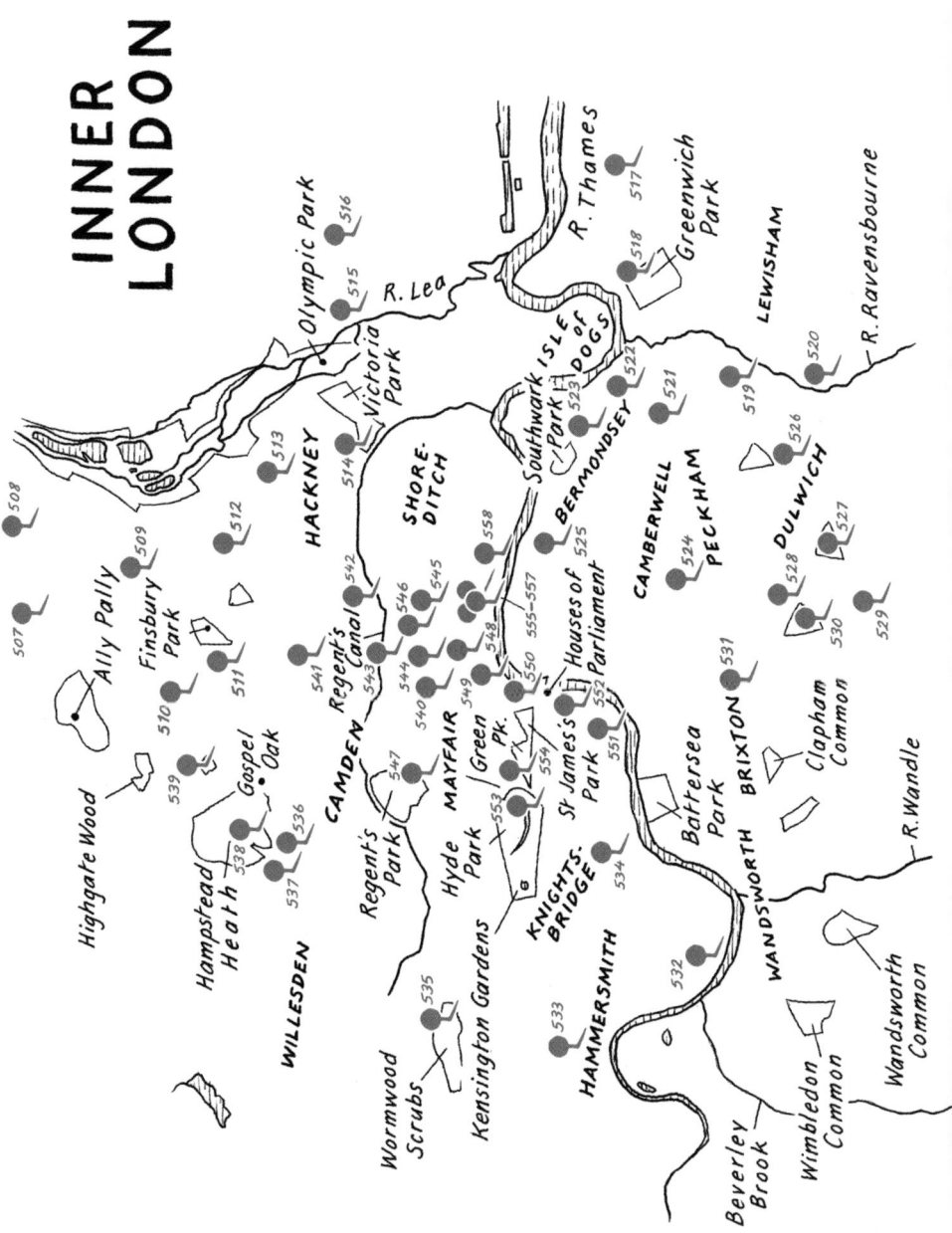

### 507. FRIENDSHIP TREE*
*London plane*
*Platanus × hispanica*
Morley Avenue, Noel
Park, London N22 6NG
51.596984, -0.103407

The Friendship Tree, a fine London plane, lies at the heart of Noel Park, a model estate in Wood Green. Over 2,000 homes were built here at the end of the nineteenth century, led by thoughtful and humane design principles. Planted in the middle of Morley Avenue, the Friendship Tree causes the houses, which everywhere else are built in straight rows, to curve round it. ///brand.grit.preoccupied

### 508. BRUCE CASTLE OAK*
*Sessile oak*
*Quercus petraea*
Bruce Castle Park,
Lordship Lane,
London N17 8NU
51.600326, -0.074805

Conventional wisdom suggests sessile oaks are associated with northern and western parts, while pedunculate oaks are the kings of rolling southern landscapes. This notion is challenged by several mighty trees dotted around London. In Tottenham, one of the city's oldest and most spectacular oaks, a propped-up tree in the centre of Bruce Castle Park, turns out to be a sessile oak on close inspection. ///angel.lend.path

### 509. ST ANN'S THORN
*Dotted thorn*
*Crataegus punctata*
St Ann's Hospital,
St Ann's Road,
London N15 3TH
51.580194, -0.09159
*Access may be restricted during redevelopment.*

St Ann's Hospital grounds are home to a rare tree in the shape of a dotted thorn – a handsome North American hawthorn with minutely speckled fruit. Looking like a tree transported from a savannah, it is old, wide and not very tall. It nestles against buildings that are set to be demolished as part of the site's redevelopment. Dozens of rare true service trees also grow in this secret arboretum. ///closed.third.handle

### 510. MUNICIPAL SYCAMORE
*Sycamore / Acer*
*pseudoplatanus*
Hornsey Town Hall,
The Broadway,
London N8 9JJ
51.578927, -0.123157

Sycamores love disturbed ground, and therefore do well in towns and cities, often to such an extent they have acquired a reputation for being a weed species. The example outside Hornsey Town Hall shows another side: it is a splendid tree, and a Crouch End landmark that is considerably older than the building. While large for south-east England, it is not a patch on great Scottish trees like the CONSOLATION SYCAMORE (13). ///oasis.junior.grin

### 511. SPIRAL ALMOND
*Almond / Prunus dulcis*
Charter Court,
Stroud Green Road,
London, N4 3SG
51.568874, -0.110497

The Spiral Almond flaunts the first blossom of the year in this corner of North London; in a mild winter, its big pink flowers can bloom spectacularly at the end of January. At other times of year, it's worth visiting for its bizarre trunk that corkscrews around on itself. How this came to pass is an intriguing mystery. ///sunset.hint.relax

512. **SPRAWLING HANDKERCHIEF TREE** → Tiny Kynaston Gardens, formerly the back gardens of buildings on Stoke Newington High Street, is distinguished by a low and spreading handkerchief tree that fits neatly into its constrained surroundings. Sprawling and unkempt, it is an entirely different character to London's other notable example, the **POSTMAN'S POCKET HANDKERCHIEF (556)** in the City. Visit in May for its dramatic blooms.

**SPRAWLING HANDKERCHIEF TREE** *Handkerchief tree / Davidia involucrata*
Kynaston Gardens, Kynaston Avenue, London N16 0PJ 51.560896, -0.07425 ///traded.brick.limbs

513. **LODDIGES SERVICE TREE**
*True service tree*
*Sorbus domestica*
Clapton Square,
London, E5 8HE
51.551544, -0.053698

For over a hundred years, the celebrated nursery of Loddiges occupied land where Hackney Town Hall now stands. Loddiges distributed hundreds of plant species, many of which were decidedly unusual. During the 1800s, these included true service trees. An elderly couple grows in Clapton Square. The one near the north-east gate is the loveliest: a large, stout tree, covered in creamy blossom in May and intriguing pear-shaped fruits come the autumn. ///nerve.memory.life

514. **VICTORIA PARK ASH**
*'Lentiscifolia' narrow-leaved ash*
*Fraxinus angustifolia*
*'Lentiscifolia'*
Victoria Park,
Sewardstone Road,
London E2 9JG
51.534969, -0.045374

The focal point of Victoria Park's western side is a narrow-leaved ash. It is a magnificent elder statesman with a vast canopy of great leafy dollops in summer. One of the finest examples of its kind anywhere, it looks as though it dates back to the park's opening in 1845. Narrow-leaved ash trees can be distinguished from the more familiar common ash by their daintier pinnate leaves. ///brass.sorters.total

515. **POST-INDUSTRIAL FIG**
*Fig / Ficus carica*
Greenway, Stratford High
Street, London E15 2FU
51.534322, -0.008086

Like many urban fig trees, the sprawling Post-Industrial Fig has been growing close to the Waterworks River, an old industrial waterway, for as long as anyone can remember. It has managed to cling on against the odds to a forgotten sliver of land – an impressive feat in rapidly developing Stratford, so close to the Olympic Park. ///obey.maker.saints

**516. FOTHERGILL'S MULBERRY**
*Black mulberry*
*Morus nigra*
West Ham Park, Upton Lane, London E7 9PU
51.538203, 0.02144

West Ham Park was originally a botanic garden created by eighteenth-century physician and botanist John Fothergill, before becoming a public park in 1874. Several interesting trees grow here, but the most spectacular is one of the best and most extravagantly sprawling mulberries in London, perhaps an original from Fothergill's garden. ///traps.flies.toxic

**517. SENIOR MULBERRY**
*Black mulberry*
*Morus nigra*
Charlton House, Charlton Road, London SE7 8RE
51.481201, 0.036361

Of all London's old mulberries, this is the oldest, and has the greatest claim to royal pedigree. It could well be one of the trees planted in the early 1600s as part of King James I's failed attempt to start an English silk industry. It now finds itself tucked away behind a fence near the car park of Charlton House, a stunning Jacobean mansion built for Henry, James's son, who died before he could move in. ///detail.round.bands

**518. PRIME MERIDIAN CHESTNUT**
*Sweet chestnut*
*Castanea sativa*
Greenwich Park, London SE10 8QY
51.476728, 0.007212

Greenwich Park is on tourist itineraries for its location on the prime meridian and the spectacular views it affords across the city from the observatory, but tree hunters will want to come here to experience over 300 sweet chestnut trees dating from the park's landscaping in 1660. My pick is a particularly stout tree, found against the fence of the Flower Garden in the park's south-east corner. ///placed.slowly.lift

**519. PINE TREE MULBERRY**
*Black mulberry*
*Morus nigra*
Pine Tree Way, London SE13 7GA
51.462686, -0.015917

On one hand, the developers of new housing just to the south of Lewisham town centre should be applauded. They protected the delightful mulberry that grows on a square of earth surrounded by a low wall on the corner of Elmira Street and Pine Tree Way, but on the other hand . . . Pine Tree Way? With no conifers in sight, it is a total mystery how this street got its name. ///react.snail.storm

**520. LADYWELL ELM\***
*European white elm*
*Ulmus laevis*
Ladywell Fields, London SE13 7HP
51.450639, -0.024468

The Ravensbourne, a Thames tributary, can still be seen flowing bucolically through south east London. On the river's right bank, as it progresses through the northern portion of Ladywell Fields, the billowing Ladywell Elm grows. Like the WEMBLEY ELM **(503)**, it is a wonderful and rare European white elm; however, a nearby interpretation panel has mislabeled it as a *'Klemmer'* or Flanders elm. ///harsh.super.poem

**521. PLATFORM 1 GIANT REDWOOD**
*Giant redwood*
*Sequoiadendron giganteum*
New Cross Gate Station,
New Cross Road,
London SE14 6AR
51.475596, -0.040172

Many thousands of people passing through New Cross Gate station must have noticed the giant redwood growing precariously on a narrow strip of edgeland next to Platform 1. Planted by a railway worker in the early 1980s where the engineers' tea hut once stood, the young whippersnapper has grown at a tremendous pace and already towers over everything around it. ///puzzle.silent.slave

522. **EVELYN'S MULBERRY** → John Evelyn, the seventeenth-century diarist and author, lived in Deptford, close to the dockyards. The last scrap of his celebrated garden survives as Sayes Court Park, where a contorted mulberry grows behind a fence. A plaque installed by the Russian Embassy insists it was planted by Peter the Great in 1698, but tests suggest it is rather younger.

**EVELYN'S MULBERRY**
*Black mulberry*
*Morus nigra*
Sayes Court Park, Grove Street, London SE8 3NA
51.484651, -0.030903
///basis.drip.legend

### 523. ROTHERHITHE SILKY OAK
*Silky oak*
*Grevillea robusta*
Lower Road,
London SE16 2XF
51.496052, -0.05178

How the Rotherhithe Silky Oak arrived outside what was once the local police station is a mystery. The received wisdom suggests this subtropical Australian species should not survive in dank London, but it's been doing very well here for many years. Following redevelopment, it now takes pride of place outside a new apartment block. ///minute.visa.tribe

### 524. CAMBERWELL TULIP
*Tulip tree*
*Liriodendron tulipifera*
Lucas Gardens,
Camberwell,
London SE5 8NX
51.473008, -0.082402

Tulip trees can become enormous in the right circumstances, and the Camberwell Tulip in Lucas Gardens will not fail to wow you. Compared to some, it is a relative youngster and hasn't yet developed the fat, burry trunk which is so often a feature of old trees of this species. Nevertheless, it has matured into one of the largest of its type in London and towers over this secret corner of Camberwell. ///honey.glitz.lofts

### 525. ADA SALTER'S TREE OF HEAVEN
*Tree of heaven*
*Ailanthus altissima*
Alfred Salter Playground,
Druid Street,
London SE1 2EZ
51.500957, -0.076678

Assertive trees of heaven are increasingly invasive in London, so their planting is effectively proscribed. As with all rules, though, there are exceptions, and a specimen planted in the last few decades remembers Bermondsey's tree-planting pioneer of the 1920s, Ada Salter, whose favourite tree was this species. Growing on a raised bed, it is ripe for inspection in the Alfred Salter Playground, named after her husband. ///actors.photos.beam

### 526. OAK OF HONOR*
*Pedunculate oak*
*Quercus robur*
One Tree Hill,
Honor Oak Park,
London SE23 3LE
51.451259, -0.05177

According to legend, Elizabeth I, while on her way to knight a courtier, stopped for lunch under the shade of the oak on One Tree Hill. Graced by such a visitor, the tree became known as the Oak of Honor – or should that be Sir Oak? One scurrilous account suggests Elizabeth was so tipsy after lunch she knighted the tree. Elizabeth's tree is no more, but the present tree, planted in 1905, is still impressive. ///legend.count.lovely

### 527. GIANT OF SOUTH LONDON
*Turkey oak*
*Quercus cerris*
College Road,
London SE21 7EB
51.44409, -0.081062

The Giant of South London grows on the south-western edge of Dulwich Park and is one of the city's most spectacular trees. It has attained a grand, symmetrical form befitting its size and age. There are many fine trees here, including old oaks harking back to a pre-1890 rural landscape, but this one is peerless, and, being the lone Turkey oak, differs from the others most noticeably by its bristly cupules, or acorn cups. ///shady.drips.wheels

**528. HERNE HILL HANAMI TREE**
*Yoshino cherry*
*Prunus × yedoensis*
Winterbrook Road,
London SE24 9HZ
51.45231, -0.098369

March is the time to visit Winterbrook Road near Herne Hill station. The whole street was planted with elegant yoshino cherries in the early 2000s, and now that the trees have reached generous proportions pilgrims come from far and wide for *hanami*, the fleeting display of blossoms. Stand under the tree where the road curves for the finest views; then look up and lose yourself in drifts of pinkish white blooms. ///sand.roof.radio

**529. MRS BEETON'S FIELD MAPLE**
*Field maple*
*Acer campestre*
West Norwood Cemetery, Norwood Road, London SE27 9JU
51.432177, -0.096032

West Norwood, opening in 1837, was the second of the Magnificent Seven garden cemeteries built around what was then the edge of London. Some trees from the previous landscape became features of the new cemetery: not far from the grave of Mrs Beeton, Victorian compiler of the *Book of Household Management*, a lone, stout-trunked and ivy-clad field maple survives, proud and lovely to behold. ///window.league.export

**530. BROCKWELL OAK***
*Pedunculate oak*
*Quercus robur*
Brockwell Park,
London SE24 0PA
51.448159, -0.106114

At anything up to 700 years old, the imposing Brockwell Oak is one of the largest and oldest oaks in London, dominating the grassy slope between the café and the Norwood Road entrance to Brockwell Park. You need to get up close and personal to best admire its massive trunk and comprehend the enormity of the tree. Its true scale is difficult to appreciate from a distance. ///wants.blitz.stove

**531. WINDRUSH PLANE**
*London plane*
*Platanus × hispanica*
Windrush Square,
Effra Road,
London SW2 1JQ
51.461015, -0.11532

Brixton Library, the Ritzy Cinema and the Black Cultural Archives cluster around Windrush Square, a paved piazza with the Windrush Plane at its centre. It is a Victorian London plane that has had room to grow with only light-touch human intervention. Consequently, it has formed a magnificent pyramidal crown, its spreading branches providing shade for the benches below. ///camps.trucks.foster

**532. OLDEST HOLM OAK**
*Holm oak*
*Quercus ilex*
Fulham Palace,
Bishop's Avenue,
London SW6 6EA
51.469559, -0.214722

Holm oaks are an established component of London's flora, but they have only been with us for 500 years. The species originates in southern Europe, and this multi-trunked individual, growing close to the walled garden in Fulham Palace, is thought to be the oldest in Britain or Ireland. It was likely planted by Bishop Grindal in the 1550s. ///stays.tamed.moves

**533. URBAN MYTH TREE**
*Baobab London plane*
*Platanus × hispanica*
*'Baobab'*
Ravenscourt Park,
Ravenscourt Avenue,
London, W6 0SL
51.496672, -0.238717

The Urban Myth Tree squats alone in the middle of Ravenscourt Park. In this position, it is easy to appreciate the bulk of its car-sized trunk and to wonder about its curious form. One apocryphal tale says it was hit by the Luftwaffe in the London Blitz, another that it suffers from a viral infection. But other trees, like MASTERS' MARVELLOUS PLANE (576) in Canterbury, confirm that this is just how it is supposed to grow. ///wage.jaws.eager

534. **KENSINGTON POSTBOX TREE** → On the corner of Drayton Gardens and Priory Walk, an Edwardian postbox is being consumed by a London plane. The tree is making good progress, but unlike the GREEDY TREE (838) in Cardiff, the postbox is still in use. Planes seem to have a propensity for consuming human-made objects, or perhaps we humans just put things too close to them, not realising how fast and large they grow.

**KENSINGTON POSTBOX TREE**
*London plane*
*Platanus × hispanica*
Priory Walk,
London SW10 9SP
51.488586, -0.181198
///surely.fries.tries

### 535. SCRUBS PUZZLE
*Single-leaved Caucasian Ash*
*Fraxinus angustifolia*
*'Monophylla'*
Little Wormwood Scrubs,
Dalgarno Gardens,
London W10 5LL
51.521925, -0.226955

The Scrubs Puzzle is an enigma left by a mischievous gardener for future generations to wonder at. A bulbous band a metre from the ground is a graft, revealing this tree to be a cultivar. However, its puzzling parentage is displayed in the confounding leaves. It is a single-leaved ash, but they are slender rather than broad; it is a variant of the narrow-leaved ash, rather than the common ash. ///petal.coffee.yappy

### 536. KEATS MULBERRY*
*Black mulberry*
*Morus nigra*
Keats House,
10 Keats Grove,
London NW3 2RR
51.555749, -0.167902

John Keats stayed at Wentworth House, now known as Keats House, between 1818 and 1820, and it was here that he wrote 'Ode to a Nightingale'. Apparently Keats's inspiration came while he was sitting under a plum tree in the garden. That tree does not survive, but it is entirely plausible he knew the mulberry, now a famous old sprawler, selected as one of seventy trees for the Queen's Green canopy in 2022. ///twin.pocket.drama

### 537. BARRICADE TREE
*London plane*
*Platanus × hispanica*
Christchurch Hill,
London NW3 1BX
51.558713, -0.174189

On Christchurch Hill in leafy Hampstead, one of the tallest and widest street trees in London can be admired. It is a London plane, perhaps more than 200 years old, so large that it entirely blocks the pavement. Planted on an incline, its great height is emphasised from below. Take in its full splendour from the Wells Tavern with a glass in hand. ///magic.music.uses

### 538. HOLLOW BEECH*
*Beech*
*Fagus sylvatica*
Hampstead Heath,
Vale of Health,
London NW3 1AU
51.563726, -0.172195

Hampstead Heath is one of London's wilder corners, and people right across town gravitate here to enjoy this swathe of countryside in the city. Alongside its hills, meadows and swimming ponds, the Heath sports pockets of dark woodlands where many old trees have survived. The most visited of these is the Hollow Beech, a remarkable tree near the Vale of Health, much loved by clambering kids of all ages. ///straw.custom.tribal

### 539. CRÈME DE LA CRÈME
*Strawberry tree*
*Arbutus unedo*
Lauderdale House,
Waterlow Park, Highgate
Hill, London N6 5HD
51.56909, -0.143319

A very old and luxuriant strawberry tree is a focal point of the formal gardens by Lauderdale House in Highgate's Waterlow Park. It has a broad canopy held up by multiple trunks, many worn smooth by tree-climbing children, that spread out in all directions ensuring it is far wider than it is tall. In October it will simultaneously flower and fruit – a beautiful sight. ///melt.pine.itself

### 540. BRUNSWICK SQUARE PLANE
*London plane*
*Platanus × hispanica*
Brunswick Square,
London WC1N 1AX
51.524243, -0.121857

London planes add grandeur to avenues and public spaces, and are usually managed over many years to ensure they pose no obstacle to traffic or pedestrians. But the tree in Brunswick Square has been left to its own devices. It is vast, perhaps dating back to the Square's construction over 200 years ago, and has branches that reach to the ground, enclosing a sanctuary within. ///kind.flap.rubble

### 541. MILLION POUND PLANE
*London plane*
*Platanus × hispanica*
St Mary Magdalene
Garden, Holloway Road,
London N7 8LT
51.547663, -0.108329

London's Tree Officers, the folk who look after public trees, have determined that a tree in St Mary Magdalene Garden is London's most valuable. It is a corpulent old London plane valued at £1 million, a sum that reflects the tree's age, size and the benefits it provides for the community. The tree can't be sold, but the money would be due if the tree were intentionally destroyed. ///apples.prone.spout

### 542. VALPARAISO REFUGEE
*Chilean wine palm*
*Jubaea chilensis*
Packington Square,
London N1 7FX
51.535535, -0.095842

The Valparaiso Refugee grows next to a children's playground in Islington. It was planted in 1906, but not in N1. It only arrived here in the twenty-first century, having been shipped from Valparaiso in Chile where it was under threat from developers. It is ironic that it undertook such a perilous journey to find a home in a new housing development in North London. ///public.diary.haven

### 543. GRIMALDI POPLAR
*Wild black poplar*
*Populus nigra ssp.*
*betulifolia*
Joseph Grimaldi Park,
Collier Street,
London N1 9JU
51.53152, -0.114356

Despite their wetland-loving reputation, majestic wild black poplars can be seen in several towns and cities. In London, the Grimaldi Poplar, an old tree hanging over Pentonville Road, has been heavily pollarded and so has not reached its great and fulsome potential, but it is nonetheless a remarkable survivor from a bygone age, and should one day be allowed to resume its expansion. ///fish.behind.ripe

### 544. LENIN'S MAPLE
*Montpellier maple*
*Acer monspessulanum*
Percy Circus,
London WC1X 9EE
51.529256, -0.114226

In 1905, Vladimir Lenin, then in exile, spent time in London at 16 Percy Circus. No doubt he would have admired the circle of plane trees on his doorstep, and perhaps he would have noted the rare maple at the centre. It is a fine example of a rarely planted Montpellier maple. ///posts.moving.blitz

LENIN'S MAPLE (544)

545. **TOP DECK DAZZLER** → Top-deck bus passengers travelling along Clerkenwell Road are offered a treat in July when the golden rain tree in the Charterhouse gardens bursts into flower. A bright yellow dome looms over the wall next to the bus stop near the junction with St John Street. The tree can also startle daydreaming passengers at other times of year: in April its leaves appear pink, and in winter intriguing seed 'lanterns' cling on.

**TOP DECK DAZZLER** *Golden rain tree / Koelreuteria paniculata*
Clerkenwell Road, London EC1M 5PX 51.522626, -0.100915 *Paid Entry.*
*Gardens open only occasionally, but tree visible from the street.* ///evenly.summer.almost

546. **TEACHING AID FIG**
*Fig / Ficus carica*
Amwell Street,
London EC1R 1UN
51.528258, -0.110107

While figs have a tendency to crop up in unexpected places, the Teaching Aid Fig appears to have been intentionally planted in front of the Clerkenwell Parochial Schools. It has probably been here since the schools opened in 1827, and may have been planted, in part, to help illustrate biblical stories. Since then, the tree has become sprawling and multi-branched, and is held aloft with assistance. ///pots.teams.shaky

547. **MARYLEBONE ELM***
*Huntingdon elm*
*Ulmus × hollandica*
*'Vegeta'*
Marylebone High Street,
London W1U 5JE
51.521898, -0.151687

One of London's most celebrated trees is a spectacular survivor. The Marylebone Elm is a monumental and rare Huntingdon elm growing on Marylebone High Street next to St Marylebone School. It survived the Dutch elm disease catastrophe of the 1970s to become a landmark – its great size emphasised by its position on one of the city's swankiest shopping streets. ///drain.bottle.lift

548. **LEGAL HIGH**
*Dawn redwood*
*Metasequoia*
*glyptostroboides*
Carey Street,
London WC2A 2JB
51.514998, -0.112838

The Seven Stars, one of London's oldest pubs, can be found on Carey Street behind the Royal Courts of Justice. It is a great location for contemplating the row of rocketing dawn redwoods that make this street so characterful. The easternmost tree is superb, and is one of a pair that bracket a much-photographed quartet of red phone boxes. ///outer.scars.salon

**549. WHITEHALL CLIMBER**
*Southern catalpa*
*Catalpa bignonioides*
Whitehall Gardens,
London, WC2N 5DG
51.506024, -0.123331

Two old southern catalpas, probably original plantings from 1870, are iconic features of Whitehall Gardens. Don't dwell for too long on the western tree, which is upright but ailing. The eastern tree, which is nearly horizontal and propped, is flourishing. Its heart-shaped leaves are luxurious in summer, and release a medicinal scent when crushed. Weary parents on family days out can look on as children make use of this appealing climbing frame. ///basket.mental.amber

**550. BAZALGETTE'S PLANE**
*Oriental plane*
*Platanus orientalis*
Victoria Embankment,
Horse Guards Avenue,
London SW1A 2JL
51.504595, -0.123374

Opened in 1870, Victoria Embankment was the first grand tree-lined street in London. It made a huge impression and led to the construction of many others in the capital and beyond. It was planted with planes, as it still is, but few originals survive. One that does is a solitary oriental plane on the corner of Horse Guards Avenue; it has more deeply indented leaves and smaller seed balls than its companion hybrid London planes. ///fake.inner.stones

**551. BILLY HUGHES'S WATTLE**
*Mimosa*
*Acacia dealbata*
Lupus Street,
London SW1V 3EB
51.488451, -0.137366

Mimosas, or silver wattle trees, originate in sunny Australia where they flower in the coolest months; but they thrive in London, too, with their yellow aromatic flowers, which appear in January some years, lighting up the winter gloom. In Pimlico the dashing mimosa on the corner of Lupus Street and Moreton Terrace remembers a fellow Australian: look out for a blue plaque to Billy Hughes, a former Australian Prime Minister, who was born at number 7. ///scrap.less.vouch

**552. TEN STOREY GINKGO** → St John's Gardens has a long history. It started life as the disconnected churchyard of St John's Smith Square, becoming a garden in the nineteenth century. The ginkgo on the north side dates from this period, making it one of the oldest in London, but what is truly impressive is its great height: it is the tallest I have seen, growing as high as the ten storey building next to it.

**TEN STOREY GINKGO** *Ginkgo / Ginkgo biloba* St John's Gardens, Horseferry Road, London SW1P 2AF 51.4943, -0.1284 ///glory.fakes.risks

**553. ROSE GARDEN ZELKOVA**
*Caucasian zelkova*
*Zelkova carpinifolia*
*'James Gordon'*
Hyde Park Rose Garden,
London SW1X 7NL
51.504245, -0.156152

In my opinion, the Rose Garden Zelkova is the most magnificent tree in any of central London's parks. A rare specimen tree growing in a prime position towering over Hyde Park Rose Garden, it has a lovely, fluted trunk and a dense bundle of branches flying into the sky. It is one of the finest Caucasian zelkovas in England, on a par with **PRINCESS VICTORIA'S ZELKOVA (717)** in Bath. ///waving.when.moral

**554. BERKELEY PLANE →** Nightingales no longer sing in Berkeley Square (if they ever did), but there are pigeon roosts aplenty on the magnificent London planes that shade this corner of Mayfair. The planes date from 1789, making them some of the oldest trees in central London. They are all remarkable, but one near the south-west corner with two low-growing limbs is the finest.

**BERKELEY PLANE**
*London plane*
*Platanus × hispanica*
Berkeley Square,
London W1J 6EE
51.509473, -0.14527
///policy.moons.cook

ENGLAND 266

### 555. ST PAUL'S SWEETGUM
*American sweetgum*
*Liquidambar styraciflua*
St Paul's Cathedral churchyard,
London EC4M 8AD
51.513624, -0.097793

Sweetgums have been frequently planted across London in recent years, and the biggest example in town is the tree on the southern side of St Paul's Cathedral. It is huge, competing with the giant old planes on the north side for height. But this tree is, perhaps surprisingly, a postwar planting, demonstrating the strapping presence even young individuals of this glamorous species can achieve. ///dine.forms.define

### 556. POSTMAN'S POCKET HANDKERCHIEF
*Handkerchief tree*
*Davidia involucrata*
Postman's Park, King Edward Street,
London EC1A 7BT
51.516696, -0.097836

A towering London plane marks the discreet King Edward Street entrance to pocket-sized Postman's Park, for those in the know. A large handkerchief tree grows in this hidden oasis, an amazing sight in May, when cloaked in its white 'handkerchiefs'. Today the park is frequented by City workers who appreciate its lush privacy, and by those seeking the curious Memorial to Heroic Self Sacrifice, which commemorates ordinary people who gave their lives to save another. ///type.lush.best

### 557. POOR SUSAN'S PLANE
*London plane*
*Platanus × hispanica*
Wood Street,
London EC2V 7WS
51.514432, -0.094801

Poor Susan's Plane has been a City landmark for centuries. It grows in what was once the tiny churchyard of St Peter Cheap on the corner of Wood Street, and soars over the low-rise shops of Cheapside.

> *At the corner of Wood-Street, when day-light appears*
> *There's a Thrush that sings loud, it has sung for three years.*

Could it be the perch of Wordsworth's thrush in 'The Reverie of Poor Susan'? ///shift.puzzle.legal

### 558. ST MAGNUS'S HEADACHE
*California bay*
*Umbellularia californica*
St Magnus the Martyr,
Lower Thames Street,
London EC3R 6DN
51.509473, -0.086433

Lower Thames Street can be a hellish place, a sunken canyon among the City's angular glass and concrete. Much-needed Baroque respite is provided by Christopher Wren's St Magnus the Martyr church and its greenery: a very unusual California bay, or headache tree, grows under the canopy of a soaring beech. An evergreen, the tree is most striking in winter when the beech is not in leaf. Crushing a leaf will reveal the origin of the 'headache' name, but take care – some may react more acutely than others. ///hotel.faster.luxury

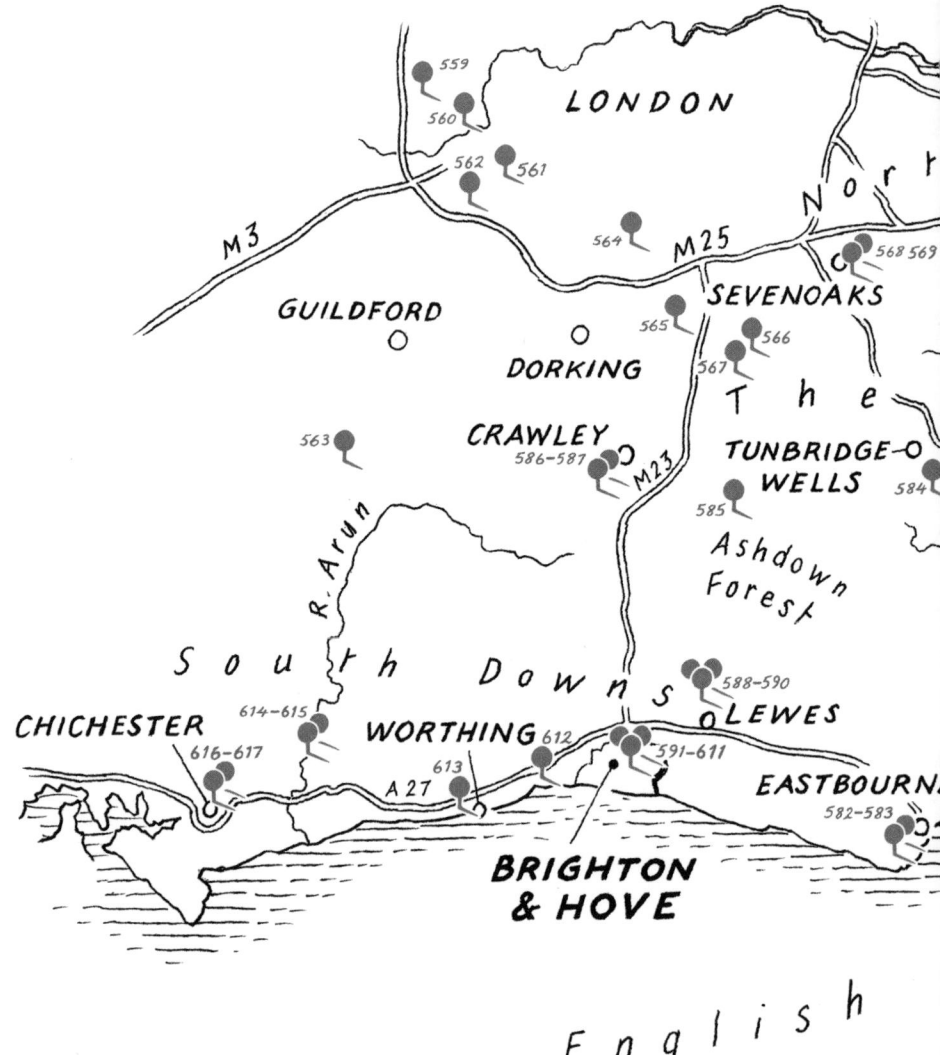

## SOUTH EAST ENGLAND

*Surrey*
*West Sussex*
*East Sussex*
*Kent*

TREE CITY:
*Brighton & Hove*

SIGNATURE SPECIES:
*Baobab London plane*

The south east of England has been at the forefront of exchange between Britain and the rest of Europe since sea levels rose at the end of the last ice age. Standing next to the **HELLFIRE CORNER ELM (580)**, a striking salt-tolerant tabletop elm close to the seafront at Dover, it is possible to appreciate just how connected we are. On a clear, calm day you can see the cliffs of France across the English Channel – it looks very close indeed.

It was from this coastline that the Romans began their conquest of Brittania, and it is thought many now-familiar plants arrived in their wake. These include mulberries, like the **SOUTHOVER MULBERRY (589)** in Lewes, and sweet chestnut trees, like the **SBS CHESTNUT (612)** at Shoreham. Another is the English elm – a distinct clone of the European field elm – that, despite its 'English' epithet, originates from Spain where it was used, as elsewhere in southern Europe, for training vines. The Romans may well have put it to the same use in southern England (where, today, viticulture is once again becoming more widely practised as the climate becomes more favourable). The English elm suckers freely (new shoots spring up from the tree's roots) and so they became a frequent constituent of hedges and were often boundary-marker trees. Dutch elm disease wiped out millions but, remarkably, thousands of elms of many different species and cultivars still grow in Brighton, this region's Tree City, including the **PRESTON TWIN\* (595)**, said to be the oldest surviving English elm.

A slightly younger, if more flamboyant, migrant from similarly warm climes is the **MEGA MAGNOLIA (590)** in Lewes. A huge old evergreen southern magnolia growing close to Southover Grange, it is approaching 200 years old and is a sight to behold. It is a glamourous species with large, glossy leaves and giant white blooms that pump out their heady scent from July, and it has remained popular with gardeners since it arrived from the southern United States in the early eighteenth century. The Lewes tree grows against a wall, a typical protective position for a plant that originates from latitudes far lower than our own. Occasionally, an old example of this species can be seen, like the **NONSUCH MAGNOLIA (564)** just beyond the southern edge of London, which has been left to grow in the open, showing what a fine specimen tree they can become.

But the signature tree of the south east must be the *'Baobab'* plane, that peculiar short, fat cultivar of the London plane, often developing a bole so corpulent it reminds many of an African baobab tree. They are infrequent in England, Wales and Ireland, and I know of none in Scotland, but the highest concentration of them is in Kent. A sign next to one in the grounds of Canterbury Cathedral says it was supplied by William Masters, a pious nineteenth-century Canterbury nurseryman in the 1820s, and it notes there are five in the city. Frequently found near churches, like the **KNOBBLIEST BAOBAB (574)** in Faversham, we now know there are actually seven of these trees in Canterbury, planted across the city in positions that describe a cross when plotted on a map. The finest and most accessible tree is **MASTERS' MARVELLOUS PLANE (576)** in Westgate Gardens. Others can be found in the Cathedral grounds, next to the ruins of Canterbury castle, in a garden on Beer Cart Lane, and in an office car park on the Old Dover Road. The last two, the foot of the cross, are in the churchyard at the former St Gregory's church.

CROUCH OAK* (562)

### 559. MIDDLESEX MULBERRY
*Black mulberry*
*Morus nigra*
Memorial Gardens,
Staines upon Thames
TW18 4EA
51.432366, -0.512353

I was surprised to discover an old mulberry in Staines. A fine old tree, collapsed with age, reclines in a town-centre park close to the Thames. The Memorial Gardens were opened in 1897, but the tree looks older; perhaps it was saved from a private garden or an orchard where it once grew before the park was developed. ///rail.nest.vocal

### 560. SUNBURY STINKER
*Ginkgo / Ginkgo biloba*
Kenton Avenue,
Sunbury on Thames
TW16 5AR
51.413419, -0.3911

Ginkgos are dioecious, meaning each plant is either male or female. Most ginkgos you encounter are male, but the old tree growing on Kenton Avenue in Sunbury is female. No doubt the residents of this street understand why females are rare. Their fruits, while containing an edible nut, emit an unforgettable stench when squashed – tree hunters be warned. The tree predates the twentieth-century houses and is a likely remnant of the Sunbury Court Estate. ///breath.slap.atom

### 561. HOMEBASE KŌWHAI
*Kōwhai / Sophora tetraptera*
Homebase, New Zealand
Avenue, Walton on
Thames KT12 1PL
51.383961, -0.418331

During the First World War, thousands of New Zealanders came to fight for the British Empire, and many wounded soldiers ended up in a special, purpose-built New Zealand hospital at Walton on Thames. The connection is remembered on New Zealand Avenue, where a yellow-flowering Kōwhai tree was planted by the New Zealand High Commission in 1970, in what is now the Homebase car park. ///timing.kicked.spark

### 562. CROUCH OAK*
*Pedunculate oak*
*Quercus robur*
Crouch Oak Lane,
Addlestone KT15 1TS
51.373504, -0.492552

The Crouch Oak is an ancient tree. One of the very oldest oaks anywhere – approaching 1,000 years old – it is a defining feature of the Surrey commuter town of Addlestone. There are streets, GP practices and even a pub named after it. The tree's fame has been helped by its conspicuousness: it grows on the busy Chertsey Road, on the edge of a housing estate. ///rates.human.master

### 563. CHIDDINGFOLD THORN*
*Hawthorn*
*Crataegus monogyna*
The Green, Chiddingfold,
Godalming GU8 4TX
51.110002, -0.628802

Growing on a raised bed on The Green, the Chiddingfold Thorn is a curious feature of this quaint Surrey village. Hawthorns have a tendency to lean, a characteristic they evince within a few years of planting, and this remarkable ancient individual is thought to have been leaning here for over 500 years. Look closely to appreciate the hollows and sinews of its centuries-old trunk. ///nurture.frock.flattery

**564. NONSUCH MAGNOLIA** → Originating from the southern United States, *Magnolia grandiflora* was considered tender by earlier generations of tree planters, and, as such, old individuals often hug aristocratic walls for the protection they offer from the worst of the weather. In the twenty-first-century climate, they are happy to grow in more open situations like the four in the formal gardens of Nonsuch Park. The most majestic of the quartet is the perfectly shaped tree in the south-east corner.

**NONSUCH MAGNOLIA** *Southern magnolia / Magnolia grandiflora*
Nonsuch Park, Cheam SM3 8AL 51.357226, -0.227569 ///banks.clues.rift

**565. RIPPLING BEECH**
*Beech / Fagus sylvatica*
Redstone Cemetery,
Philanthropic Road,
Redhill RH1 4DG
51.230689, -0.159457

More than one beech in this book might be described as elephantine for its great size and silvery-grey bark, but the tree in Redstone Cemetery would be more properly described as being Shar Pei-like. Its remarkable characteristic is bark that ripples as if it has a layer of blubber just below the surface, like those memorable canines. ///share.youth.tells

**566. CROWHURST YEW***
*Yew / Taxus baccata*
St George's Church,
Crowhurst Lane,
Crowhurst,
Lingfield RH7 6LR
51.209425, -0.010309

The Crowhurst Yew is said to be over 4,000 years old, although, like other yews of great age, of which there are dozens in this region, the precise number of thousands is largely down to guesswork. It was first recorded in 1630, and was mentioned by the diarist John Evelyn in 1664. A small wooden door attached to the trunk adds to its romantic appearance – a portal for the imagination. ///fans.giving.relax

**567. GAOL OAK**
*Pedunculate oak
Quercus robur*
Village Cage
and St Peter's Cross,
Plaistow Street,
Lingfield RH7 6AL
51.174604, -0.018875

Adding to the charm of this Surrey commuter village, the Gaol Oak is a 300-year-old hollow oak shading an historic cell where petty criminals were incarcerated until the late nineteenth century. The gaol, or Village Cage, and the adjoining medieval St Peter's Cross are a scheduled historic monument, but the fabulous old tree, surely of equal importance, has no official listing. ///lace.speeds.worm

LAMB-DRESSED-AS-MUTTON TREE (570)

### 568. VINE OAK
*Turkey oak*
*Quercus cerris*
The Vine,
Sevenoaks TN13 3SY
51.276291, 0.19461

The great hurricane of 1987 caused the demise of many trees across the south east of England, and the town of Sevenoaks was, infamously, reduced to Oneoak. That oak, a burgeoning Turkey oak showing no signs of storm damage, can be found on the perimeter of the historic Vine Cricket Ground, alongside six replacements. ///dwell.clown.luxury

### 569. KNOLE TREE
*Sycamore*
*Acer pseudoplatanus*
Knole House,
Sevenoaks TN15 0HT
51.266669, 0.204132
*National Trust property; the grounds are freely accessible.*

There aren't many sycamores in the south of England that have reached the age and size of the great veterans of Scotland and northern England, but, on the edge of Sevenoaks, an astonishing tree can be seen in front of Knole House. It is thought to have been planted around 1800, possibly earlier, and is very large, with its dense canopy held aloft by generous, spreading branches. ///large.state.prone

### 570. LAMB-DRESSED-AS-MUTTON TREE
*Southern catalpa*
*Catalpa bignonioides*
The Precinct,
Rochester ME1 1SN
51.38954, 0.503004

Southern catalpas have a habit of collapsing as they age, and the tree outside Rochester Cathedral has done it with aplomb. It split in two in 2015 and is now a mass of branches, well protected by an iron fence. A plaque claims it is 'over one hundred years old', surprisingly young for a tree that appears as if it was planted when the medieval cathedral was built. ///brings.barn.former

### 571. PLANEZILLA
*Baobab London plane*
*Platanus × hispanica*
*'Baobab'*
Turkey Mill,
Ashford Road,
Maidstone ME14 5PP
51.270874, 0.537552

Maidstone, like Canterbury, is well endowed with baobab London plane trees; indeed, it is home to Britain's fattest. The vast tree, resembling a giant petrified sea monster with tentacles rising from its bloated body, grows at Turkey Mill, a former paper mill and now a business park. Consigned to the car park, Planezilla grows in a walled enclosure close to the River Len. ///moth.ramp.alarm

### 572. PATH-BREAKING PLANE
*Baobab London plane*
*Platanus × hispanica*
*'Baobab'*
Medway Footpath,
Lockmeadow,
Maidstone ME16 8LW
51.268098, 0.518291

A theme emerges at Lockmeadow, where another Maidstone baobab London plane has been consigned to a plot near a car park. Connected to the Medway Footpath, it may once have been part of a riverside row. Several others grow along the path, but the finest is this burry giant that causes the path to swerve around it: no-one messes with the Path-Breaking Plane, or else. ///bright.hats.amused

**573. OLD YEW**\*
*Yew / Taxus baccata*
All Saints Church,
Ulcombe Hill, Ulcombe,
Maidstone ME17 1DN
51.217079, 0.642497

All Saints churchyard at Ulcombe is a special place, carpeted with primroses in spring and home to four ancient yews. Old Yew is the largest of the four and grows close to the tower of the fine twelfth-century church, not far from Young Yew, a slightly slimmer tree. Churchyard yews often predate their churches, the building having been constructed on a pre-existing site of pagan worship confirmed as a sacred space by its resident yews. ///otter.ordeals.puzzled

**574. KNOBBLIEST BAOBAB**
*Baobab London plane*
*Platanus × hispanica*
*'Baobab'*
St Mary of Charity
Church, Church Road,
Faversham ME13 8GZ
51.316448, 0.894604

Four baobab London planes form a row just beyond St Mary of Charity's southern churchyard wall. They now grow in the car park of newbuild housing, but were perhaps once connected to the church. The third tree from the road is the knobbliest and most commanding. Some authorities claim the *'Baobab'* cultivar is an oriental plane, but it holds its large seedballs in twos or threes, a feature of London planes. ///tinny.rarely.puzzles

**575. BATSMAN'S LIME**
*Common lime*
*Tilia × europaea*
St Lawrence Ground,
Old Dover Road,
Canterbury CT1 3NZ
51.267586, 1.092791

Since it opened in 1847, an old lime tree grew just within the boundary of the St Lawrence Ground, home of Kent County Cricket Club in Canterbury. Any batsman hitting the tree scored an automatic four, clearing it a six. In 2005 the tree blew over and a new one was planted. Sadly the replacement is just outside the boundary, but it is a reminder of a more idiosyncratic game. ///camps.boost.deaf

**576. MASTERS' MARVELLOUS PLANE** → A nineteenth-century Canterbury horticulturalist, William Masters, may have been the supplier of the strange 'Baobab' planes dotted around the south east of England (as well as some further afield, like BEER BELLY (134) in Carlisle). Canterbury has seven such trees and the finest grows in Westgate Gardens. Intriguingly, when the seven are mapped they form the shape of a cross within the city. Apparently Masters was a very religious man.

**MASTERS' MARVELLOUS PLANE** *Baobab London plane / Platanus × hispanica 'Baobab'*
Westgate Gardens, St Peter's Street, Canterbury CT1 2BQ 51.280792, 1.074349 ///cloth.meant.speech

**577. PLATANUS XL**
*London plane*
*Platanus × hispanica*
High Street, Wingham,
Canterbury CT3 1BX
51.27621, 1.215895

At the northern end of the pretty half-timbered village of Wingham, just beyond Petts Lane, a giant London plane towers over the bus stop and a development of bungalows. It is such a large tree that, in summer, a copper beech that might otherwise be regarded as significant is cast in the plane's shadow. ///calculate.pizzas.shares

**578. DOUR CEDAR** → I have known the Dour Cedar since my childhood and it is still one of the very largest and most impressive cedars of Lebanon I have ever encountered. It is a massive, multi-trunked tree, now protected by a fence, growing in an unrivalled position on the lawn at Kearsney Abbey with the river Dour flowing nearby. A great limb fell in 2023 but it remains magnificent. An inspirational tree.

**DOUR CEDAR**
*Cedar of Lebanon*
*Cedrus libani*
Kearsney Abbey Gardens,
Alkham Road,
Dover CT16 3DZ
51.147491, 1.270489
///appeal.claims.grant

**579. POOR YEW**
*Yew / Taxus baccata*
St Andrews Buckland,
Crabble Meadows,
Dover CT17 0TR
51.1376, 1.293236

In the mid-1800s, the church tower and the ancient yew tree at St Andrews were both badly damaged by lightning. If this were not enough, in 1880 the tree was moved 50 metres to accommodate a church extension. Remarkably, the tree is today in rude health, despite the indignities it has had to put up with; its only complaint is neglect. It is a heritage tree few towns can boast, and is worthy of greater care and perhaps a display board to tell its amazing story. ///lobby.term.formal

**580. HELLFIRE CORNER ELM**
*Tabletop elm / Ulmus glabra 'Horizontalis'*
Granville Gardens,
Camden Crescent,
Dover CT16 1LE
51.123423, 1.315743

Tiny Granville Gardens and its striking *'Horizontalis'* wych elm lie just beyond Dover's seafront, where once the equally striking mid-twentieth-century Dover Stage hotel stood. The hotel is long gone, but the elm has grown into a local landmark. It is at its fleeting best when the copious seeds appear in spring, quickly followed by asymmetric leaves, a typical elm feature. ///magazines.fever.modes

**581. PEACE GINKGO**
*Ginkgo / Ginkgo biloba*
Alexandra Park,
St Helen's Road,
Hastings TN34 2LQ
50.865661, 0.570321

Alexandra Park is a treasure trove of fine mature trees, many rare and exceptional. One of the easiest to appreciate is the stout old ginkgo close to the road near the Peace Garden. It may be part of the original planting scheme, and, unusually, it is a female, so adventurous tree hunters wanting to experience the vintage aroma of its fruits should come in the autumn. ///secret.short.ruler

**582. AN EASTBOURNE ELM**
*Wheatley elm / Ulmus minor 'Sarniensis'*
Carlisle Road,
Eastbourne BN21 4JR
50.762222, 0.280386

Like its coastal neighbour, Brighton, Eastbourne planted lots of elms in the past. Although they have not fared so well here, the streets around Carlisle Road are still lined with mature Wheatley elms, rare survivors of Dutch elm disease. One planted on the verge not far from the Towner Art Centre has an intriguing swollen root plate. ///dices.danger.baked

**583. SIGHT SCREEN ELM**
*Huntingdon elm / Ulmus × hollandica 'Vegeta'*
Blackwater Road,
Eastbourne BN21 4HD
50.763974, 0.27932
*On private land, but visible from the street.*

A row of trees screening cricketers on the lawns of Eastbourne College from the sun – and pedestrians on the pavement from sixes – is punctuated halfway along by a giant that dominates the streetscape. It is a Huntington elm, one of the tallest and noblest elm varieties, whose broad, open crowns add to their monumental presence and differ markedly from conical Wheatley elms. ///finely.cattle.tribal

**584. QUEEN ANNE'S OAK**
*Pedunculate oak*
*Quercus robur*
London Road,
Tunbridge Wells
TN1 1DN
51.129649, 0.259868

Across London Road from the Premier Inn, Tunbridge Wells Common begins. A path has been worn into the woodland and, not far along it, iron railings encircle the rather ungainly Queen Anne's Oak. It is a tree of historic interest, and a plaque tells us that it was planted to commemorate several visits to Tunbridge Wells by Princess Anne, later Queen Anne, around 1700. ///finely.traps.necks

**585. ALMSHOUSE BAOBAB**
*Baobab London plane*
*Platanus × hispanica*
*'Baobab'*
High Street, East
Grinstead RH19 3BX
51.124043, -0.004231

A strange plane grows on East Grinstead's High Street in front of the Sackville College almshouses. It is of the same lumbering, portly appearance as the baobab London planes at Canterbury, Faversham and Maidstone, marking a Sussex outlier of this otherwise Kentish cluster of fatties. The Almshouse Baobab could be younger than the trees in Kent, explaining its less beefy bole and more vigorous limbs, but one day its belly will catch up. ///income.spill.rally

**586. TILGATE HAWTHORN**
*Hawthorn*
*Crataegus monogyna*
Constable Road,
Crawley RH10 5LW
51.099059, -0.176181

Crawley's oldest resident grows by a row of garages on a cul-de-sac off Constable Road. It is a hollow, propped-up hawthorn that has survived here for more than two centuries. For most of its life it grew in aristocratic parkland, but for the last six decades it has been surrounded by a housing estate. It continues to thrive in more chastened environs. ///unions.lined.afford

**587. CREAM SODA TREE**
*Tulip tree*
*Liriodendron tulipifera*
Tilgate Park,
Tilgate Drive,
Crawley RH10 5PQ
51.095151, -0.178887

Tilgate Park is a tree hunter's paradise, containing dozens of old and unusual trees. The best is a giant tulip tree with an incredible burry trunk, growing just behind the inexplicably Wild West-themed restaurant close to the car park. Summer diners can enjoy the tree from the shaded patio beneath its canopy, and if you come in May, you should smell its lovely tulip-shaped flowers: pure American cream soda. ///reform.zebra.fails

**588. LEWES ELM**
*Exeter elm*
*Ulmus 'Exoniensis'*
Barber Court, St Pancras
Road, Lewes BN7 1JQ
50.870001, 0.001774

Confusingly, the Lewes Elm is an Exeter elm, an elm cultivar of uncertain parentage spawned in an Exeter nursery two centuries ago. This tree is a fraction of that age, perhaps as old as the mid-twentieth-century flats behind it. It is, however, a fine specimen of a rather unusual tree that can be distinguished by its crisply contorted leaves. ///influence.spearhead.blown

### 589. SOUTHOVER MULBERRY
*Black mulberry*
*Morus nigra*
Southover Grange Gardens, Southover Road, Lewes BN7 1TL
50.870647, 0.007714

Southover Grange was built in 1572 and came into public ownership just under 400 years later. Because their branches frequently collapse, it's always tricky to age a mulberry, but it's likely the fabulous tree in its gardens was planted a century or so after the Grange was built. It is therefore one of the oldest mulberries in England, and for generations it was a favourite climbing tree, an activity discouraged by a fence erected in recent years. ///respected.sway.couple

### 590. MEGA MAGNOLIA → As well as the old mulberry, Southover Grange Gardens is home to a lustrous southern magnolia growing against the south-facing wall of the Grange. It produces a succession of sparse but enormous waxy flowers from July to October; visit on a summer morning when their lemony scent seems to be at its pungent best.

**MEGA MAGNOLIA**
*Southern magnolia*
*Magnolia grandiflora*
Southover Grange Gardens, Southover Road, Lewes BN7 1TL
50.870728, 0.007372
///stance.chest.scooters

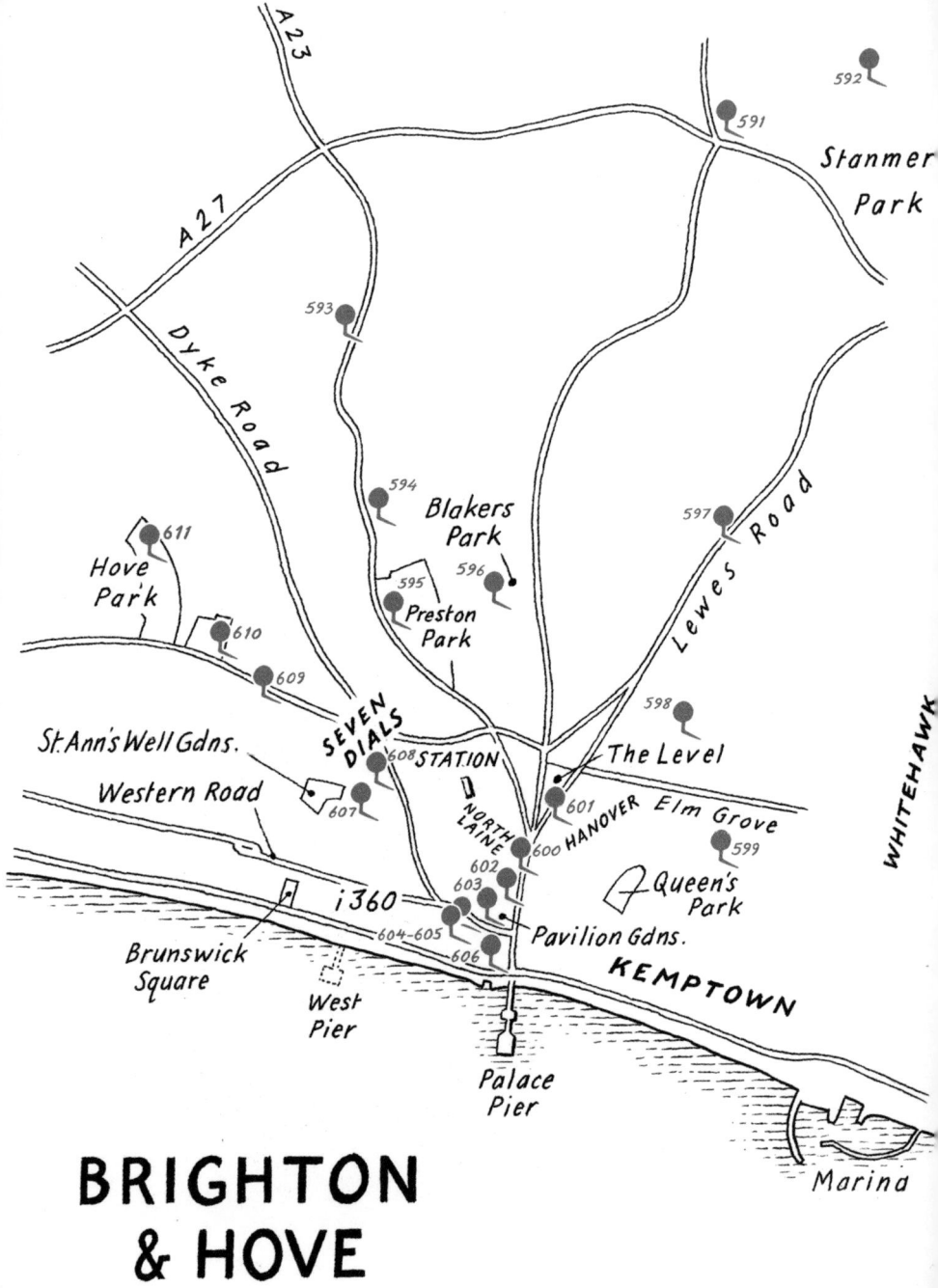

## TREE CITY: BRIGHTON & HOVE
### SIGNATURE SPECIES: *Wheatley elm*

In 1815, when the architect John Nash completed the fantastic mughal-gothic Royal Pavilion for the then Prince Regent, land was acquired to lay out gardens around it. Those gardens are now one of Brighton's most popular parks and boast many mature trees, including several elms which date back to its foundation just over two centuries ago. But there is one tree, the **LOVE LOCK ELM (603)**, which is even older than the garden, a likely remnant from the fields that preceded it. It proves that elms, the tree genus which defines Brighton and Hove, have been growing here for centuries.

Elms are well suited to salt-laden sea air, and have survived in Brighton as boundary trees and vestiges of old hedgerows (a role played by oaks elsewhere in southern England). The **GATEWAY ELM (600)** and the **SECOND OLDEST ELM (597)** are both veteran English elms that hark back to a more rural past. As Brighton grew in the nineteenth century, The Level, Brighton's oldest park, was revamped, and in 1844 tough Dutch elms were planted around its perimeter; many still survive, including the **LEVEL DUTCH ELM (601)**.

Today, Brighton and Hove is a ribbon-like city of over 200,000 people, teetering on the edge of the English Channel with the steep escarpment of the South Downs behind it. Alongside astute management by an enlightened city council, it is this unusual geography that has helped the city's elms escape the worst ravages of Dutch elm disease: the beetle that carries the deadly fungus is blocked by the high downs to the north and the impassable sea to the south.

As a result, Brighton and Hove is home to the 17,000-tree strong National Elm Collection. Among these are some superlative individuals – the famed **PRESTON TWIN\* (595)** (another former boundary tree) is thought to be the oldest English elm in the world; the **LONELIEST ELM IN THE WORLD (598)** is the only known Lombarts' elm anywhere; and the **BLAKERS PARK GIANT (596)** is certainly the fattest and, in my opinion, the most magnificent Wheatley elm on the planet. There are elms of different species and cultivars growing all over the city, thousands of which are mature street trees. They offer a tantalising vision of the sort of cityscape rich in elms that would once have been common across Europe.

It would be wrong, however, to think of Brighton and Hove as an elm monoculture. There are many other spectacular trees here too. Montpelier Crescent, a handsome Regency terrace curving around a semicircular garden, is home to the colossal **CRESCENT OAK (607)**. Like elms, evergreen holm oaks thrive in the salty air, and this is one of the finest anywhere.

With its abundant and varied urban forest, priceless estate of elms, and tree-sensitive council, this truly is a first-rate tree city. In the past, Brighton and Hove have investigated the potential of World Heritage status for its Regency seafront; if it were to revisit making a bid, its unique city-wide elmscape could be a deciding feature.

591. **STANMER BEECH** ⤳ Stanmer Park on the northern edge of Brighton is an early-Georgian landscape of woods and downland, and in the woods near Coldean Lane an avenue of old, steely-trunked beech trees can be admired. Well suited to the chalky conditions, they have taken on fantastic shapes. Look out for the tree with a dozen limbs lifting its canopy to great heights.

**STANMER BEECH** *Beech / Fagus sylvatica* Stanmer Park, Stanmer, Brighton BN1 9RE 50.870701, -0.117885 ///free.lived.shift

592. **BRIGHTON'S OLDEST TREE**
*Yew / Taxus baccata*
Stanmer Church, Stanmer, Brighton BN1 9PZ
50.870459, -0.101816

Brighton's oldest tree is only just inside the city boundary. It is, unsurprisingly perhaps, an ancient yew growing in an old churchyard. But the tree itself is a wonderful surprise: a hollow and twisted old thing first recorded in 1833 (although it is older than this) along with another younger example, also still thriving. Find it to the north of the church. ///sling.earth.badly

593. **WELCOME TO BRIGHTON TREE**
*Ginkgo / Ginkgo biloba*
Brangwyn Way, Brighton BN1 8XA
50.858169, -0.152927

Thousands of day trippers arriving by road will have driven past the shapely ginkgo at Patcham that signals the start of Brighton. Was it planted here, among the bland detached houses, to add a bit of (autumn) colour? Did an urban forester plant it with an eye for a future landmark? Or is it just happenstance that such an interesting tree was planted next to the A23, Brighton's busiest road? ///sooner.cycles.bunny

594. **ALL ABOUT THAT BASE**
*Tulip tree*
*Liriodendron tulipifera*
Cliveden Close, Brighton BN1 6UB
50.84782, -0.151944

A series of grand houses once lined the London Road north of Preston Park; few of them survive, but some garden remnants do. At Cliveden Close, beyond a Victorian gatehouse, an old, tall and sleek tulip tree grows in front of 1960s flats. As well as being Brighton's tallest tree of this species, its huge bulbous base makes it doubly interesting. ///gums.then.plants

**595. PRESTON TWIN***
*English elm*
*Ulmus minor 'Atinia'*
Preston Park, Preston
Road, Brighton BN1 6SD
50.841675, -0.150662

A pair of ancient English elms known as the Preston Twins used to grow in the north-western corner of Preston Park. Only one survives; the other fell victim to Dutch elm disease and was felled in 2019. The remaining tree, quite possibly the oldest elm in the world, is Brighton's most celebrated, reminding us of the rich elm landscape we have all but lost, and the need to protect what endures. ///that.brave.daring

**596. BLAKERS PARK GIANT**
*Wheatley elm*
*Ulmus minor 'Sarniensis'*
Blakers Park, Cleveland
Road, Brighton BN1 6FG
50.842483, -0.137585

Unbelievable. The Blakers Park Giant is a Wheatley elm of enormous proportions. Other trees of this species that come close are also in Brighton: there are several whoppers in Preston Park. But this monster, ascending over the coffee kiosk to the east of the clock tower, is an order of magnitude bigger. It is the plumpest, if not the tallest, in England. ///daisy.sends.trade

**597. SECOND OLDEST ELM**
*English elm*
*Ulmus minor 'Atinia'*
Cockcroft Building,
University of Brighton,
Lewes Road,
Brighton BN2 4GJ
50.845502, -0.117073

The second oldest elm in Brighton grows on Lewes Road, outside the University of Brighton. Despite its great age, it flies under the radar, hiding in plain sight on the side of the road. It has been cut back over the years, but boasts a gargantuan trunk with prodigious girth. It is an easily accessible tree, offering a chance to consider its asymmetric leaves, a feature all elms share. ///trout.text.book

**598. LONELIEST ELM IN THE WORLD**
*Lombarts' elm*
*Ulmus 'Lombartsii'*
Brighton and Preston
Cemetery, Hartington
Road, Brighton BN2 3PL
50.834209, -0.120235

There used to be two *'Lombartsii'* elms either side of the gothic gateway into Brighton and Preston Cemetery on Hartington Road. One was lost to Dutch elm disease, so the other is now the only Lombarts' elm left in the world. It is a Dutch cultivar from the early twentieth century, and despite its graceful, pendulous branches, it seems never to have been very popular. Cuttings should be taken to save it from extinction. ///impose.when.runner

**599. JACQUELINE ELM**
*'Jacqueline Hillier'*
elm / *Ulmus 'Jacqueline Hillier'*
Craven Road,
Brighton BN2 0FF
50.826286, -0.117081

Jacqueline Elm is rare and lovely, and quite unlike Brighton's other elms. It is a dwarf *'Jacqueline Hillier'* cultivar, and, while this is the largest of its kind in Britain or Ireland, that is hardly the point. What is more relevant is its elegance, and the fact it grows among social housing on chalk (a difficult substrate for many trees) rather than in the rarefied surroundings of a botanical garden. ///famed.since.spray

PRESTON TWIN* (595)

**600. GATEWAY ELM** →→ Planted in formal rows, the elms that line the southern and western edges of Victoria Gardens are approaching 200 years old, a demonstration of how these trees were used to beautify towns and cities. One in particular, regularly pruned so exuberant new growth is encouraged, on the curve of Marlborough Place, commands a spectacular position opposite the domed entrance to Pavilion Gardens. A great introduction to Brighton's elm heritage.

**GATEWAY ELM** *English elm / Ulmus minor 'Atinia'* Victoria Gardens, Marlborough Place, Brighton BN1 1WN 50.823941, -0.137018 ///shield.deflection.powder

**601. LEVEL DUTCH ELM**
*Dutch elm / Ulmus × hollandica 'Major'*
The Level, Union Road, Brighton BN1 4ZN
50.829277, -0.133944

The Level, Brighton's oldest park, was planted with elms in 1844. Many were lost to the hurricane of 1987, but eighty Dutch elms survived. One of the best is in the south-east corner standing next to the coffee kiosk. They are very similar to English elms, but can be distinguished by their leaves, which appear later in spring and drop earlier in autumn. ///winner.transmitted.brain

**602. PAVILION TABLETOP**
*Tabletop elm / Ulmus glabra 'Horizontalis'*
Royal Pavilion Gardens, New Road,
Brighton BN1 1UG
50.823024, -0.138341

Most elms – big, billowing trees with similar leaves – are difficult to tell apart, but there are some cultivars that, through selection and hybridisation by horticulturalists, have grown quite distinct. One of these, a striking *'Horizontalis'* elm with spreading, horizontal branches, grows in the Pavilion Gardens. It is a cultivar that clearly likes the seaside. ///newly.sector.mostly

**603. LOVE LOCK ELM**
*English elm*
*Ulmus minor 'Atinia'*
Royal Pavilion Gardens, New Road,
Brighton BN1 1UG
50.822647, -0.138683

The old English elm on the southern edge of the Royal Pavilion Gardens is a beautiful tree of great age. Held together with iron braces, it is a relic from a former landscape. The tree is hollow, and a grille covering the cavity has become a popular place for the romantically inclined to leave their increasingly numerous love locks. ///rust.linked.line

**604. JUST GOOD FRIENDS**
**& 605.** *Fig / Ficus carica*
Friends Meeting House,
Ship Street,
Brighton BN1 1AF
50.822, -0.141116

The Friends Meeting House on Ship Street comes as something of a relief in this busy part of Brighton otherwise populated with bars and boutiques. The Meeting House Garden offers a shady respite from the bustle, due in no small part to a pair of fig trees nestling against the wall. One grows from a single fat trunk, while its companion has two. ///await.tall.swaps

**606. DUTCH COURAGE ELM** → Elm growers around the world have been selectively breeding disease-resistant cultivars for decades, and new varieties often get tried out in Brighton, whose urban foresters are always keen to add to the National Collection. A type that has proved very successful is the neat 'Lobel' with upward sweeping branches, and on East Street, outside the Sussex Arms pub, one of the tallest examples yet grown can be seen.

**DUTCH COURAGE ELM**
*'Lobel' elm / Ulmus 'Lobel'*
The Sussex Arms,
East Street,
Brighton BN1 1HL
50.821246, -0.139067
///lance.stable.begun

ENGLAND 292

### 607. CRESCENT OAK
*Holm oak / Quercus ilex*
Montpelier Crescent,
Brighton BN1 3JF
50.829466, -0.148587

Montpelier Crescent, a stone's throw from the REGENCY SPLENDOUR **(608)**, is one of Brighton's stuccoed Regency terraces. It curves round semicircular gardens containing dozens of trees. The evergreen holm oaks define them, and one stands out. Masquerading as a copse of several trees towards the southern end, it is in fact one tree: a vast, multi-trunked dome with a giant dense canopy. ///costs.life.tennis

### 608. REGENCY SPLENDOUR
*Wheatley elm*
*Ulmus minor 'Sarniensis'*
Seven Dials,
Brighton BN1 3JL
50.830679, -0.147605

Wheatley elms have a handsome, consistent form, making them an ideal tree for cities where regularity is valued. Despite this uniformity, individuals achieve notoriety through age, like the BLAKERS PARK GIANT **(596)**, or through their position. The Regency Splendour has done just that. It is a landmark tree, so valued that it was saved from developers' chainsaws in 2013. What were they thinking? ///dame.fits.exact

### 609. HOVE'S ELM ACTUALLY
*Hoersholm elm / Ulmus minor 'Hoersholmensis'*
Old Shoreham Road,
Hove BN3 6GF
50.836635, -0.163654

Hoersholm elms are great, green balloon-shaped trees originating from Denmark. Fine examples grace public spaces in Copenhagen and other Scandinavian cities, but in these islands very few are known. The best one can actually be found in Hove, a street tree growing on the Old Shoreham Road opposite an impressive holm oak on the corner of Radinden Manor Road. ///butter.scuba.begin

### 610. SHIRLEY DRIVE ZENITH
*Wheatley elm / Ulmus minor 'Sarniensis'*
Shirley Drive,
Hove BN3 6NQ
50.839977, -0.165192

To appreciate the majesty of mature elms, Hove is the place to go. Shirley Drive is a wonderful avenue of uniform Wheatley elms. A fine specimen, typical of this most urban-friendly species, is the first in a row opposite Hove Recreation Ground looking towards the sea. If only all suburban streets were planted with such impressive trees. ///tree.heats.bells

### 611. INTERLOPER PLANE
*London plane*
*Platanus × hispanica*
Hove Park, Woodland Drive, Hove BN3 7RA
50.844936, -0.17485

Brighton and Hove's remarkable elmscape is occasionally punctuated by other trees. In Hove Park, a giant, spreading London plane partially shades the miniature railway in the northern section. Though ubiquitous in other English towns and cities, London planes are not frequently encountered in this corner of Sussex, so the Interloper Plane might be considered something of a rarity. ///chase.grabs.noises

**612. SBS CHESTNUT**
*Sweet chestnut*
*Castanea sativa*
Buckingham Park,
Shoreham-by-Sea
BN43 6BX
50.841648, -0.267286

All that is left of Buckingham House is its ornate classical facade among the mock-Georgian houses on Woodview. The house would once have looked out over its bucolic grounds, which has today become the extensive, tree-dotted parkland of Buckingham Park. Two chestnuts still grow towards the western edge; our tree is the larger of the pair, a perfect example of an ancient sweet chestnut with a dramatic hollow trunk. ///apparatus.landed.prune

**613. MIDSUMMER TREE***
*Pedunculate oak*
*Quercus robur*
Broadwater Street West,
Worthing BN14 9DJ
50.832377, -0.381126

At one time, the Midsummer Tree was an important Worthing landmark, but today it is a shadow of its former self. An old, hollow oak, much cut back and largely forgotten, grows near the junction of the A24 and A27. But it is still remarkable for the intriguing folk story attached to it, whose origins are lost to time: legend holds that skeletons rise up and dance around its trunk each year, from midsummer eve until sunrise on midsummer's day. ///darker.stuck.claims

**614. ADUR HYBRID**
*Hybrid strawberry tree*
*Arbutus × andrachnoides*
Jubilee Gardens,
Queen Street,
Arundel BN18 9NZ
50.853506, -0.552372

Arundel's Jubilee Gardens lie on either side of the River Adur, and the smaller southern garden at the foot of the bridge on Queen Street is home to a rare hybrid strawberry tree (apparently until recently an even bigger one once grew in the northern garden). Its striking cinnamon-coloured bark rewards a closer look in summer, when it peels to reveal new, bright green bark below. Look out for dainty white bell-shaped flowers, and its round, red strawberry-like fruit from late summer if the birds have left any for you to admire. ///life.survivor.cornering

**615. ALLOTMENT CEDAR**
*Cedar of Lebanon*
*Cedrus libani*
London Road Allotments,
London Road,
Arundel BN18 9BZ
50.855285, -0.556261
*On private land, but*
*visible from the street.*

Many allotments boast an apple tree or two, even a medlar or mulberry, but in Arundel, in the shadow of its majestic castle, things are grander. The London Road allotments, which are hidden from view behind a high flint wall, are shaded by an enormous cedar of Lebanon whose canopy stretches over most of the patch, as well as the London Road. It is particularly tall, its horizontal branches starting high up its trunk, which allows at least some sunlight to reach the vegetable plots below. ///pony.swims.surreal

**616. BISHOP'S ELM**
*'Lobel' elm*
*Ulmus 'Lobel'*
Bishop's Palace Garden,
Canon Lane,
Chichester PO19 1PX
50.835745, -0.783697

English cathedrals often have old or interesting trees associated with them, and Chichester is particularly well stocked. In its delightful Bishop's Palace Garden, one of the most striking trees is a relative youngster: a broom-like '*Lobel*' elm, which holds its own among a collection of superb, mostly older trees in this historic garden. ///grants.bonus.flags

**617. PALACE TULIP TREE** → Even larger than the upstart **BISHOP'S ELM (616)**, the Palace Tulip Tree is the pre-eminent tree of Chichester Cathedral. It shades the Bishop's Palace Garden's Pergola Walk from behind a wall bordering private grounds, meaning that tree hunters who would like to embrace this giant must content themselves with simply admiring and, on a hot day, taking advantage of its shady canopy.

**PALACE TULIP TREE**
*Tulip tree*
*Liriodendron tulipifera*
Bishop's Palace Garden,
Canon Lane,
Chichester PO19 1PX
50.835826, -0.782714
*In a private garden, but visible from a public place.*
///today.shot.lung

SOUTH EAST ENGLAND 295

# SOUTHERN ENGLAND

# SOUTHERN ENGLAND

*Buckinghamshire*
*Oxfordshire*
*Berkshire*
*Hampshire*
*Isle of Wight*

TREE CITY:
*Reading*

SIGNATURE SPECIES:
*Yew*

Trees are plentiful in this slice of England's mild southern counties. Ancient yews abound, in churchyards of course, but also in more unlikely places – like a pub garden. Many are so old they have disintegrated to a point where they cannot be accurately dated. The age of **WHITE'S YEW (661)** in Hampshire, which certainly predates the medieval church it now grows alongside, can only be estimated in millennia. It illustrates the importance of yew trees to humans throughout history (and prehistory). In the pre-Christian world, yews denoted sacred places, and this symbolism was co-opted by the new religion when it spread through Britain. Churches were built on these existing sites of worship, ensuring the yew tree's significance would alter, but endure.

Equally ancient and evocative are this region's many oaks. It was in Windsor's vast Great Park that the Ancient Tree Inventory began life as the Ancient Tree Hunt, such was the number and quality of great oaks preserved here. One very old tree on the edge of this fascinating landscape, the **ANCIENT TREE HUNT OAK\* (655)**, named in 1994, remembers this. But the urban centres of southern England have a wealth of trees, too: just look at cities like Reading (the featured Tree City in this chapter), Southampton and Winchester. I would, however, invite the tree hunter to begin their travels in Oxford, where the great harmonising effect trees have on town- and cityscapes is perhaps most perfectly expressed.

The great architectural historian Nikolaus Pevsner was smitten by Oxford's High Street, describing it as 'one of the world's great streets. It has everything. It is on a slight curve so the vistas always change.' Anyone experiencing this lovely street will be struck by what I have dubbed **PEVSNER'S SYCAMORE (626)**. It punctuates the informal array of buildings, drawing the eye and softening the whole ensemble with its natural, changing form. I am convinced the presence of this tree must have been an ingredient, whether consciously or unconsciously, in his evaluation of the High Street's glory.

As Oxford shows, buildings and trees do not merely live side-by-side, but are, at best, mutually enriching. Trees that might otherwise go unnoticed can become landmarks because of their position in the built environment, like the **PRINCIPAL'S HORSE CHESTNUT (623)**, which hangs over a wall from Jesus College to define Turl Street, or the **REMARKABLE REDWOOD (622)**, which is an exclamation mark to the high-gothic Museum of Natural History. This relationship is visible elsewhere, as on Castle Hill in Reading, where the **NEOCLASSICAL CEDAR (649)**, a towering cedar of Lebanon, not only catches the eye of anyone traversing this incline, but also draws attention to the delightful Georgian building that encloses it on three sides. And, like Oxford's High Street, Reading's Prospect Street in Caversham is made interesting by the beautiful **HEAVENLY PROSPECT (631)** growing in a pub car park where the street curves, enlivening an otherwise perfunctory thoroughfare.

The temperate climate of southern England enables trees to flourish, so it is unsurprising to find some impressive examples of unusual species here, a few of which are among the finest of their kind in Britain or Ireland. These rarities are noteworthy for their often-unlikely locations, as well as their unfamiliar, occasionally sublime qualities. Many are demonstrably well suited to the conditions they grow in, but remain mystifyingly infrequent. In Southampton, the **SHIRLEY HACKBERRY (672)** is the largest European hackberry, or nettle tree, in these islands. Not far away, the **PIGTAIL PINE (676)**, a beautiful Mexican weeping pine, is another gem – and, beyond these, Southampton's city centre is stuffed full of splendid, tree-rich Victorian parks. Also in Hampshire, the town of Lyndhurst is worth a detour from the New Forest that surrounds it, for the strapping and rather rare variegated tulip tree at the police station on the edge of town. The **POLICE STATION TULIP TREE (679)** is magnificent in May, when its leaves first appear. They glow a luminous acid yellow.

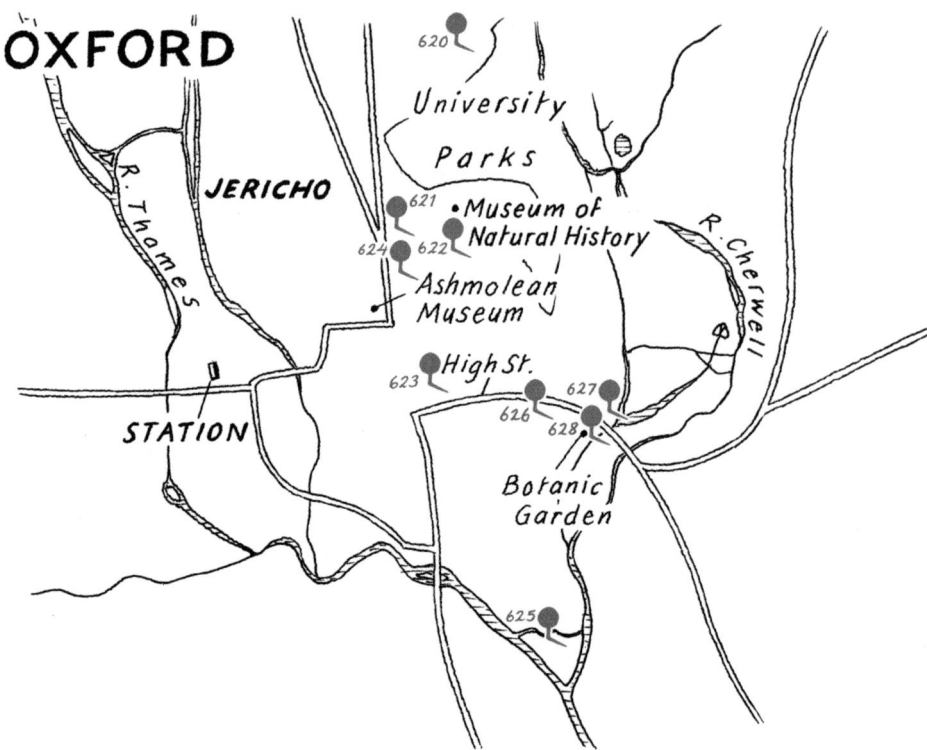

**618. ST MARY'S PLANE**
*Oriental plane*
*Platanus orientalis*
St Mary's Church, Horse
Fair, Banbury OX16 0AA
52.061732, -1.339276

Banbury's grand neoclassical church of St Mary's was rebuilt in 1790, a likely planting date for the half-dozen astonishing oriental planes that surround it. These six trees are one of the finest and perhaps oldest groups of the species in Britain or Ireland. Each has taken on a distinct individual character, but the twisting, snake-like tree nearest the portico has the most alluring form. ///pine.price.serves

**619. OU MULBERRY**
*Black mulberry*
*Morus nigra*
Walton Hall,
Open University,
Milton Keynes MK7 6AA
52.024674, -0.711203

Milton Keynes is renowned for the millions of trees planted since its establishment as a New Town in the 1960s. Most are only just reaching maturity, but there are some that are older than the city. The most wonderful of these is a veteran mulberry in the heart of the Open University campus. Although propped, it is remarkable for having a short but perpendicular bole that has so far defied gravity, something few old mulberries can boast. ///inform.slower.oldest

**620. DRAGON MAPLE**
*Trident maple*
*Acer buergerianum*
Norham End, Benson
Place, Oxford OX2 6SG
51.766481, -1.255775

Trident maples are rare in these islands. One of the largest and oldest examples is an attractive, sinewy tree with weeping branches, growing not in Oxford's Botanic Garden or a college quad, but by the entrance to a block of flats on the corner of Benson Place and Dragon Lane. ///bind.beam.forest

**621. ZIG-ZAG PLANE**
*'Spiralis' London plane*
*Platanus* × *hispanica*
*'Spiralis'*
St Giles', Oxford OX1 3LE
51.759258, -1.25961

On the corner of St Giles' and Keble Road is a London plane with its branches akimbo. There are many variations of London planes with memorable forms; this one, too, with its zig-zag branches, is distinct. Could it be a forgotten Victorian cultivar? If so, it needs a name. *'Spiralis'*, perhaps. ///crisis.cube.chill

**622. REMARKABLE REDWOOD**
*Giant redwood*
*Sequoiadendron giganteum*
Oxford University Museum of Natural History, Parks Road, Oxford OX1 3PW
51.758422, -1.256298

Giant redwoods have presence – they can turn the mundane into the remarkable and, when coupled with fine architecture, can become celebrated landmarks. That is what has happened at Oxford's Museum of Natural History, where a particularly tall, skinny tree takes pride of place on the lawn in front of this high Victorian masterpiece. ///waddled.cheek.stale

**623. PRINCIPAL'S HORSE CHESTNUT**
*Horse chestnut / Aesculus hippocastanum*
Jesus College, Turl Street, Oxford OX1 3DW
51.753787, -1.256429

The corner of Ship Street and Turl Street is dignified and, in summer, cooled by one of Oxford's most splendid horse chestnuts. The Principal's Horse Chestnut grows in the Principal's Garden of Jesus College but is very much a public tree, its abundant canopy magnified by the narrowness of the street and the closeness of the buildings. ///took.fence.scars

**624. POMFRET'S PASSION TREE**
*Horse chestnut / Aesculus hippocastanum*
Lamb and Flag Passage, Oxford OX1 3JS
51.757398, -1.259

Oxford's other notable horse chestnut can be found in Lamb and Flag Passage, next to a pub with many literary connections. It is a stout, leaning tree whose low canopy occupies the whole alley. In Dorothy L. Sayers's *Gaudy Night*, Mr Pomfret declares his undying love for Harriet 'in the shadow of the big horse-chestnut by the Lamb and Flag'. ///weep.aspect.daily

**625. TREE***
*Caucasian zelkova / Zelkova carpinifolia 'James Gordon'*
Christ Church Meadow Walk, Oxford OX1 4JF
51.744246, -1.249499

A Caucasian zelkova in Christ Church Meadows known simply as Tree is one of Oxford's most celebrated, and has won outlandish praise: 'Lost for words'; 'hiked from Suffolk to see Tree'; 'The rest of Oxford is skippable'. I urge you to see it for yourself and make up your own mind. ///cycles.commented.rides

### 626. PEVSNER'S SYCAMORE
*Sycamore / Acer pseudoplatanus*
High Street, Oxford
OX1 4AN
51.752843, -1.252027

Oxford's High Street has been eulogised by many – Nikolaus Pevsner went so far as to describe it as 'one of the world's great streets' in *The Buildings of England,* his comprehensive survey of Britain's architectural heritage. But its defining feature is not Magdalen Tower or the spire of St Mary's, it is surely the inspiring sycamore that grows from the Warden's Lodge of All Souls, marking the street's curve. ///report.clubs.energy

### 627. MAGDALEN PLANE*
*London plane*
*Platanus × hispanica*
Magdalen College,
Oxford OX1 4AU
51.752736, -1.246622
*Paid entry; combined ticket available for Botanic Garden and Magdalen College.*

A stone plaque next to the strapping Magdalen Plane tells us that it was planted in 1801, and goes on to say it is 'a scion of the hybrid plane first raised in the Botanic Garden in 1666'. This is a reference to an early-twentieth-century claim that London planes originate from Oxford, a creation myth amplified by the renowned Irish dendrophile Augustine Henry over a century ago but which is now debunked. But what a tree – clearly hybrid planes do well here. ///pits.coins.losses

### 628. OXFORD PAPERBARK
*Paperbark maple*
*Acer griseum*
Oxford Botanic Garden,
High Street,
Oxford OX1 4AU
51.751738, -1.247712

Formal beds between the High Street and the entrance to the Botanic Garden offer a taste of what lies within. Several interesting mature trees grow here, mostly to the south east, but in the western corner, furthest from the street in front of the Daubeny Building, a youthful paperbark maple holds its own. Its tawny bark is spectacular, especially in the otherwise gloomy leafless winter months. ///device.behind.power

### 629. CONVALESCENT YEW
*Yew / Taxus baccata*
All Saints Church, Lydalls Road, Didcot OX11 7EA
51.610891, -1.25102

Ancient churchyard yews tend to grow in picturesque, often sleepy village parishes; only occasionally are they found in towns or cities. Didcot is one of those exceptions. An old, hollow yew tree grows next to a sprightly young neighbour: the twelfth-century All Saints Church. The tree has been vandalised in the past but is slowly recovering. ///pretty.approvals.visitors

### 630. BULL YEW*
*Yew / Taxus baccata*
The Bull Inn,
Streatley RG8 9JJ
51.522491, -1.149432

Yews are usually associated with churchyards, but occasionally old trees can be found in other settings. The Bull Yew has chosen a more wayward path and grows in the garden of The Bull, a charming fifteenth-century inn at Streatley. To add a scandalous note, it is reputed to have a nun and a monk buried beneath it. ///spenders.nimbly.arranges

PEVSNER'S SYCAMORE (626)

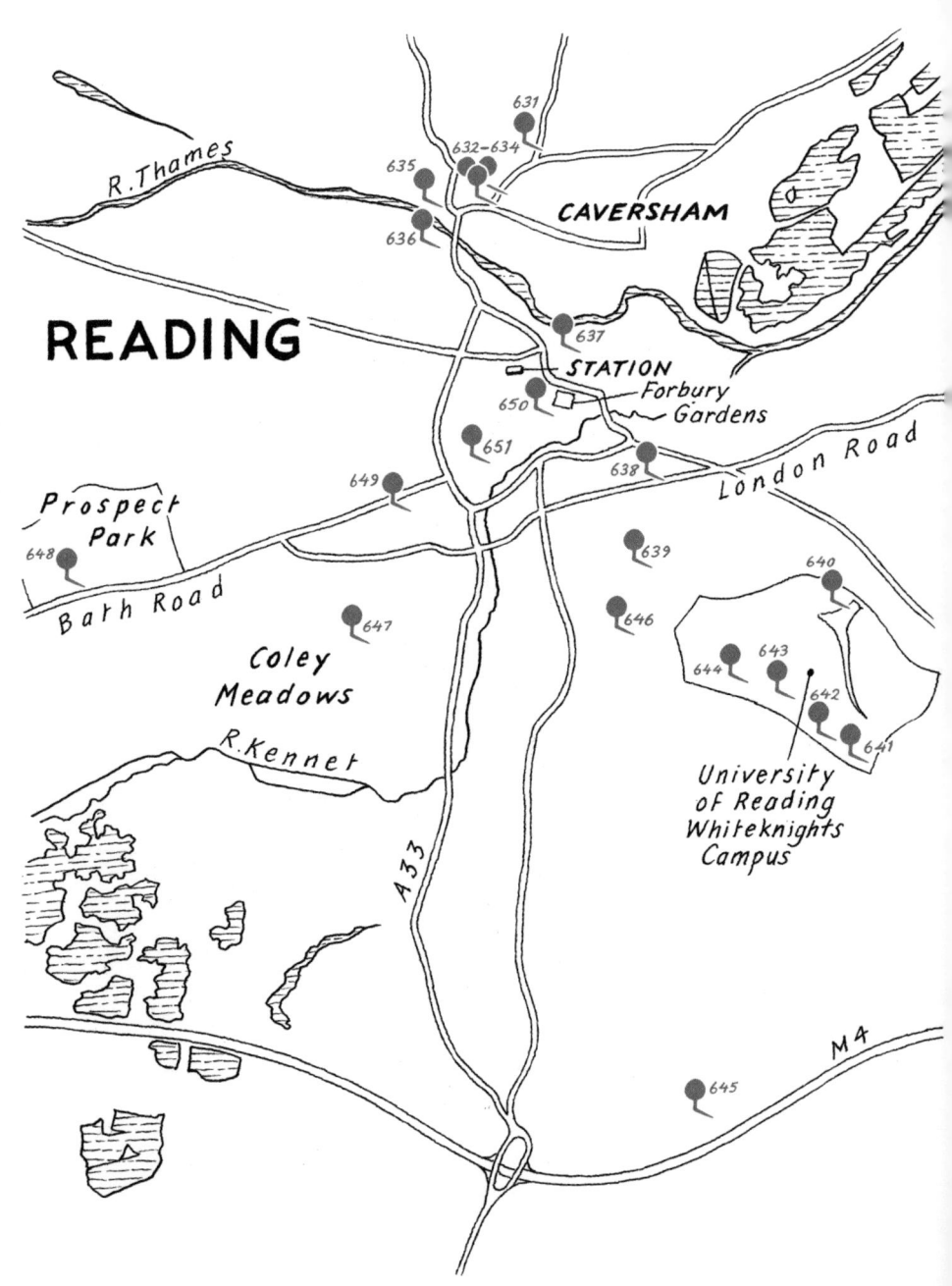

# TREE CITY: READING
**SIGNATURE SPECIES:** *Giant redwood*

Mention Reading and, for many, roundabouts, trading estates and the incarceration of Oscar Wilde spring to mind. Conveniently located at the confluence of the Thames and Kennet rivers, Berkshire's county town is a busy transport hub and bustling centre of retail parks, private housing estates and corporate campuses. But it also has important ecclesiastical, academic and aristocratic histories that have contributed to an ample arboreal legacy.

Reading's riparian geography helped make it an accessible religious centre in the 1100s, and a desirable location for aristocratic estates over the following centuries. Today, waterways and their undeveloped floodplains are still a significant feature of the city, breaking up the urban sprawl and driving wedges of green space right into the centre of town. The Kennet meanders through southern Reading, passing the spectacular **MOTHER WILLOW (647)**, a layering crack willow in Coley Meadows, and the nineteenth-century panopticon of the now-unoccupied Reading Gaol – itself a Victorian squatter on land once occupied by Reading Abbey, whose ruins lie just to the west. At Kings Meadow, where the Kennet meets the Thames, the **ODD ONE OUT (637)** grows, part of a row of impressive London planes.

Reading has always been a bridging point on the Thames, and, in 1911, the city itself crossed the river to absorb the settlement of Caversham on the north bank. Caversham retains its distinct character and hosts a significant number of fine trees, including the **CAVERSHAM SPRAWLER (635)** in Caversham Court Gardens. The gardens were laid out in 1660 beside the twelfth-century church of St Peters. It is difficult to accurately date yews, but this tree may be contemporary with the church, making it likely Reading's oldest tree.

Reading's historic ecclesiastical sites boast a number of unmissable old trees, but it was arguably the aristocratic estates that did the most for the city's treescape. Prospect Park owes the survival of its many veteran and ancient oaks to the Liebenrood family, who owned the land until 1902. Since the late-eighteenth century, they had maintained a landscaped Regency garden complete with ancient wood pasture.

But the jewel in Reading's crown is the former Whiteknights estate. In the twenty years George Spencer-Churchill, the Marquess of Blandford, called Whiteknights home, the Marquess indulged his interests in art, rare books and, above all, exotic plants, transforming his fiefdom in the process. These passions ultimately led to his bankruptcy in 1819, resulting in the division and sale of the estate which, by then, included one of the finest botanical collections in the land. By 1867, the estate had been split into six smaller mini-estates, where many of the rare and notable trees languished in the custody of their new owners until the land was acquired, unified and restored by the newly created university in 1947. Remarkably, many of the Marquess of Blandford's landscape features still survive on the campus today.

CAVERSHAM SCHOLAR (632)

**631. HEAVENLY PROSPECT**
*Tree of heaven*
*Ailanthus altissima*
Prospect Street,
Reading RG4 8JN
51.469316, -0.97048300

In late summer, the view up Prospect Street from the south is made spectacular by the glowing canopy of a tree of heaven laden with copious orange fruits. This glorious individual grows with several others on a strip of land between the pavement and a pub car park. Our tree has the rippling trunk typical of mature specimens. ///cure.basket.rainy

**632. CAVERSHAM SCHOLAR**
*Japanese pagoda tree*
*Styphnolobium japonicum*
Hemdean Road,
Caversham,
Reading RG4 8AU
51.467941, -0.974251

The Caversham Scholar is a truly magnificent Japanese pagoda, or scholar tree; there can be few that equal this specimen in such an urban setting. It dwarfs Caversham Library, a building emblazoned with the year 1907, providing a likely planting date for the tree. Visit in late August to see the canopy covered in small, aromatic white flowers, an increasingly common sight as temperatures rise. ///slap.master.vote

**633. COSTA OAK**
*Holm oak / Quercus ilex*
St Martins Precinct,
Church Street,
Caversham,
Reading RG4 8BA
51.467564, -0.974467

Reading has two clusters of significant trees. One is at the university's Whiteknights campus, and the other is in central Caversham where several notable trees can be seen within a few hundred metres of each other. Opposite the library and the magnificent CAVERSHAM SCHOLAR **(632)**, the massive, spreading evergreen canopy of a holm oak adds to the scene outside the Costa Coffee on Church Street. ///dive.delay.under

**634. LUCKY MAGNOLIA**
*Southern magnolia*
*Magnolia grandiflora*
Church Street, Caversham,
Reading RG4 8AU
51.467699, -0.97607
*In a private garden, but visible from the street.*

Those arriving in Caversham from across the river can admire a southern magnolia on the corner of Priory Avenue and Church Street. It grows in the tiny front garden of an old building which has recently been restored – recognition is due to the anonymous developer who protected this landmark tree during the redevelopment process. Reading tree hunters can rest easy once more. ///best.crowd.chain

**635. CAVERSHAM SPRAWLER**
*Yew / Taxus baccata*
Caversham Court Gardens, Church Road,
Reading RG4 7AD
51.467995, -0.981397

Caversham Court Gardens hosts several trees of note, but the best is the centuries-old yew. Seventeenth-century gardeners encouraged the tree to begin layering itself – branches have been trained to ground level and buried, before later re-emerging. Underground, roots have taken, and today the resulting plant system is akin to a mother tree surrounded by its offspring. ///gaps.frost.enjoy

636. **THAMESIDE SWAMP CYPRESS** → A fine old swamp cypress and its colleagues provide a distinctive landmark on the Thames path just west of the rowing club. The trees are no doubt admired by Reading Festival revellers each August bank holiday weekend, but only those who are in Reading in the autumn can appreciate the burnt-orange colour of the foliage, before the needles fall from this rare deciduous conifer.

**THAMESIDE SWAMP CYPRESS** *Swamp cypress / Taxodium distichum*
Reading Rowing Club, The Boathouse, Richfield Avenue, Reading RG1 8BD
51.466756, -0.980618 ///issued.trendy.vibes

637. **ODD ONE OUT**
*London plane*
*Platanus × hispanica*
King's Meadow Road,
Reading RG1 8BN
51.460395, -0.965935

Reading's finest row of London planes lines King's Meadow Road on the section leading down to the Thames. They appear to be of the *'Pyramidalis'* cultivar, characterised by large burry trunks – except the one nearest the river, which has much smoother bark and a clearer trunk. It really stands out. Perhaps this is from a different, earlier planting? ///super.engage.hooks

638. **OFFICE MULBERRY**
*Black mulberry*
*Morus nigra*
Eldon Road,
Reading RG1 4DJ
51.453442, -0.958528

Reading is endowed with several characterful mulberries whose innate desire to recline and sprawl makes them appear older than they are. The charming Office Mulberry, a tree that probably goes unnoticed by the multitude of white-collar workers who pass by every day, masquerades as a multi-centenarian, but is perhaps a mere 150 years old. It clings on precariously outside an unfashionable office block. ///herb.misty.puns

639. **MERL ASH**
*Velvet ash*
*Fraxinus velutina*
Museum of English Rural Life, Redlands Road,
Reading RG1 5EX
51.44886, -0.960778

As well as a unique set of old wooden farm wagons, the excellent Museum of English Rural Life has an interesting tree collection in its quiet gardens, where a rare North American velvet ash takes pride of place. Look, and feel, carefully: its leaves are more robust than a common European ash and are decidedly downy. ///nuns.dive.crib

BLANDFORD'S DEBATABLE OAK (641)

**640. WALK WILD SERVICE TREE**
*Wild service tree*
*Sorbus torminalis*
University of Reading,
Whiteknights Road,
Reading RG6 7BY
51.444575, -0.941264

The Walk Wild Service Tree is a large old tree growing next to the footpath on the north side of the Whiteknights campus lake. Its presence suggests the parkland here was previously ancient woodland which has, remarkably and happily, survived with little human intervention. This tree is pipped to being Berkshire's largest by an even bigger one in Windsor Great Park. ///songs.skips.fonts

**641. BLANDFORD'S DEBATABLE OAK**
*Cypress oak / Quercus robur 'Fastigiata'*
The Harris Garden,
Pepper Lane,
Reading RG6 5SH
51.436543, -0.938322

There is some debate as to whether this cypress oak (an oak cultivar which is so narrow when young it resembles an Italian cypress), planted around 1800 by the Marquess of Blandford, is the first ever tree of its type to be grown in Britain or Ireland. Younger trees are neat and perpendicular, but this specimen has spread somewhat, although its branches do head upwards. ///meals.duck.sparks

**642. WHITEKNIGHTS PEAR**
*Oleaster-leaved pear*
*Pyrus elaeagrifolia*
The Lord Zuckerman Research Centre,
Reading RG6 6LA
51.438053, -0.940918

One might be forgiven for not noticing it in summer, but at less leafy times the splendour of this rare pear becomes apparent. It is a twisted tree of indeterminate but very great age, hidden in a corner of the university campus between the Lord Zuckerman Research Centre and Philip Lyle Road. Visit in late April to catch it in flower. ///shirt.chops.amber

**643. UNIVERSITY MAPLE**
*Cretan maple*
*Acer sempervirens*
Whiteknights Campus,
University of Reading,
RG6 6UR
51.440209, -0.946629

One of the many prizes awaiting you at the University of Reading's Whiteknights campus is a relatively small Cretan maple. An intriguing species very rarely seen in northern Europe, it is noteworthy for its semi-evergreen habit of retaining leaves through the winter and shedding them just as new leaves and acid-green flowers appear in the spring, which is a sight well worth beholding. ///shack.stuff.about

**644. CHANCELLOR'S REDWOOD**
*Giant redwood*
*Sequoiadendron giganteum*
Chancellor's Way,
University of Reading,
Reading RG6 6DR
51.440694, -0.949918

There are dozens of great giant redwoods in Reading, gifts from the Victorians who might not have guessed what landmarks they would become. Perhaps the tallest tree in town is the redwood that stands in a commanding position at the edge of a sports field near the Chancellor's Building, just north of Chancellor's Way. In this instance, the tree's solitude emphasises its grandeur ///engage.flash.brave

### 645. CIRRUS OAK
*Pedunculate oak*
*Quercus robur*
Cirrus Drive,
Reading RG2 9FP
51.417489, -0.952124

A pair of veteran oaks greet visitors to a new housing estate on the edge of Reading, close to the M4. These aged pollards are relics of the former meteorological centre grounds, and long before that of a wood pasture landscape. The Cirrus Oak – the fatter tree with a fuller canopy – and its eastern companion preside over a manicured lawn opposite pastiche village housing typical of Thames Valley urban sprawl. ///fancy.purely.admiral

### 646. CINTRA CEDAR
*Deodar cedar*
*Cedrus deodara*
Cintra Avenue,
Reading RG2 7AU
51.4432, -0.95974

Sought-after Edwardian houses on the west side of Cintra Avenue have fine views of the monumental conifers separating them from newer housing to the east. There's a giant redwood in the avenue, but the dominant trees are deodars. A fabulous tree midway along, at the point where a side lane veers off the main road, branches enthusiastically. Take a look up close, then turn around and admire the whole ensemble: a memorable avenue and surely a sought-after address. ///limes.moon.harp

### 647. MOTHER WILLOW
*Crack willow / Salix fragilis*
The Brookmill, Coley Park, Reading RG1 6DD
51.440882, -0.987388

Coley Meadows has a layering tree of immense proportions. It is a crack willow, perhaps a century old, whose branches have split or 'cracked' off, and rooted themselves to form a circular copse 50 metres or so in diameter. Left to its own devices, this giant clone will eventually become several distinct trees surrounded by their offspring. ///purely.themes.hero

### 648. PROSPECT PARK CEDAR
*Cedar of Lebanon*
*Cedrus libani*
Prospect Park,
Liebenrood Road,
Reading RG30 2ND
51.449022, -1.011012

Prospect Park has a history dating back centuries. Once it was wood pasture, a landscape of scattered trees and open meadows maintained by grazing livestock. The veteran oaks that give such character to the park are from this time. But the standout tree is the much-loved cedar of Lebanon up on the hill close to the Mansion House. ///circle.souk.jeeps

### 649. NEOCLASSICAL CEDAR
*Cedar of Lebanon*
*Cedrus libani*
Castle Hill,
Reading RG1 7SY
51.451528, -0.98159
*On private property, but visible from the street.*

The Neoclassical Cedar is a landmark and a friendly presence for travellers on the busy Bath Road. It is thought to have been growing in its Georgian courtyard since 1776, which would be very early for this species, but just about plausible. Regardless of its age, this tree is a delight, soaring over a handsome building which could have been designed specially to accommodate it. ///dime.stir.burn

### 650. ST LAURENCE'S JUDAS TREE
*Judas tree*
*Cercis siliquastrum*
St Laurence's Churchyard,
Reading RG1 1DA
51.456622, -0.969129

The footpath from Forbury Gardens to Town Hall Square leads through St Laurence's churchyard where a particularly attractive Judas tree with a splay of low branches can be admired. The species originates from the eastern Mediterranean where it flowers profusely in April. In southern England it often flowers abundantly, but you will have to wait until May. ///during.middle.exists

### 651. SUPERANNUATED CATALPA ⇉ 
Reading's best-known tree has to be the old southern catalpa, now in its final years, growing in St Mary's churchyard facing the bus stops of St Mary's Butts. Generations of Readingites have witnessed this tree age and dramatically flower each July over the past century and a half. A replacement has been planted, so the spectacle will continue.

**SUPERANNUATED CATALPA**
*Southern catalpa*
*Catalpa bignonioides*
St Mary's Churchyard,
Chain Street,
Reading RG1 2HX
51.454331, -0.973931
///vibes.dock.valid

### 652. NOT THE ROYAL OAK
*Red oak / Quercus rubra*
Burchetts Green,
Maidenhead SL6 6QZ
51.525078, -0.791688

The Crown, a popular gastropub, is a well-known landmark in the hamlet of Burchetts Green. But many people must also notice the magisterial red oak that spreads over the crossroads of Burchetts Green Road and Hall Place Lane, opposite the pub. Despite its magnificence, it is regarded merely as a noticeboard by some, judging from the neighbourhood-watch signs improperly nailed to its trunk. ///dodging.thinkers.ribcage

### 653. IRON AGE OAK
*Pedunculate oak
Quercus robur*
Camp Road, Gerrards
Cross SL9 8SZ
51.581029, -0.564148

Bulstrode Camp is an iron-age hill fort hiding among the millionaire's mansions of Gerrards Cross. Hundreds of years ago the perimeter of the hill fort, a significant ditch, was planted with oak trees; about forty remain, gently declining, some with bricked up hollows, some mere fragments. One of the best is a tree near the southern entrance which still appears to have many years to go. ///launch.bump.sketch

### 654. WINDSOR WEEPING BEECH
*Weeping beech / Fagus sylvatica 'Pendula'*
St John the Baptist, High Street, Windsor SL4 1LT
51.481444, -0.606224

I'm sure I am not alone in having a soft spot for the melodramatic charms of weeping beeches. The tree that dangles over Windsor's High Street from St John the Baptist church is well known to locals and noticed by discerning visitors. When in leaf it appears like a comic ghost trying, unsuccessfully, to frighten passers-by; during the winter, you can see a conspicuous graft mark on its gravity-defying trunk through a tangle of bare branches. ///couch.shave.loaded

### 655. ANCIENT TREE HUNT OAK* →
Windsor Great Park is one of the best places to see ancient oak trees anywhere in the world. There are dozens of them, and hundreds more veterans. Back in 2004, the Ancient Tree Hunt, a citizen science project recording old and interesting trees, was launched here, and actress Prunella Scales stood in the great hollow of this glorious, propped-up old tree 100 metres beyond the Cranbourne Gate entrance.

ANCIENT TREE HUNT OAK* *Pedunculate oak / Quercus robur* Cranbourne Gate Car Park, Sheet Street Road, Windsor SL4 2BT 51.446542, -0.635665 ///pizza.passes.slide

**656. ANKERWYCKE YEW***
*Yew / Taxus baccata*
Wraysbury, Staines
TW19 5AD
51.444656, -0.556659

Close to Runnymede, where the Magna Carta was signed in 1215, and the nearby ruins of St Mary's Priory, where Henry VIII was said to have first met Anne Boleyn in the 1520s, stands the ancient and celebrated Ankerwycke Yew. Given its great age and impressive stature, it would already have been a significant tree at both these points in time. ///cave.army.remain

**657. CUL-DE-SAC CHESTNUT**
*Sweet chestnut*
*Castanea sativa*
Julius Hill, Warfield,
Bracknell RG42 3UN
51.421477, -0.725922

The Warfield Park Estate did not fare well in the face of Bracknell's expansion. But an area known as The Chestnuts did survive, and is a sanctuary for old, full-canopied sweet chestnuts, mercifully saved from the bulldozer. Obligingly, the grandest tree grows close to the path. A nearby interpretation panel suggests the trees were planted in 1795, but they appear even older. ///storm.patrol.voice

**658. FIRST WELLINGTONIA**
*Giant redwood*
*Sequoiadendron giganteum*
Wellingtonia Avenue,
Finchampstead,
Crowthorne RG45 6AE
51.366362, -0.82256

Wellingtonia Avenue is an uninterrupted, dead-straight, 600-metre stretch of home-counties suburbia lined with 112 Wellingtonia, or giant redwoods. Their canopies form a green canyon, their 30-metre-plus spires shielding the homes below from the traffic speeding between Crowthorne and Finchampstead. Anticipating your visit, the first tree now grows in a raised bed surrounded by a lawn, allowing you to get up close and personal. ///decreased.just.lock

**659. WAITROSE PLANE**
*Oriental plane*
*Platanus orientalis*
Rectory Road,
Wokingham RG40 1BB
51.411829, -0.835041

Well-to-do Wokingham's finest tree is best viewed, unsurprisingly perhaps, from Waitrose. A marvellous, twisting tree that is small for a plane, it is nevertheless a veteran thought to be in the region of 250 years old. It was probably an exotic status symbol planted in the garden of Montague House, a sixteenth-century building that backs on to the supermarket's car park. ///ritual.string.frame

**660. CHANTRY PLANE**
*London plane*
*Platanus × hispanica*
Market Place, High Street,
Andover SP10 1NT
51.207916, -1.479705

Perhaps the fine old London plane in Andover's Market Place was originally planted to offer shelter to market traders and their customers. Now it separates old Andover from new, in the shape of the Chantry Shopping Centre. It is still a much-loved feature of the town centre, and is distinguished by an encircling metal bench. ///going.rate.tune

WAITROSE PLANE (659)

HILLIER'S WALNUT (663)

**661. WHITE'S YEW**
*Yew / Taxus baccata*
All Saints, Church Road,
Upper Farringdon
GU34 3EG
51.113586, -0.984085

The great naturalist Gilbert White, known for the landmark 1789 publication *The Natural History of Selborne,* was curate at Farringdon for many years. He writes about the ancient yew at Selborne church, and the yew at Farringdon gets a mention too. The Selborne tree is no more, but the Farringdon one is a natural wonder. Split into several fragments, it is one of the very oldest in England. ///gradually.slide.risking

**662. ABBEY DOVE TREE**
*Handkerchief tree*
*Davidia involucrata*
College Street,
Winchester SO23 9NA
51.060923, -1.309239

Winchester has a great many interesting trees, and, right in the middle of town, Abbey Gardens is a good place to start. The most spectacular tree here is one of the best dove trees – or handkerchief trees – in Britain or Ireland. It is a mature example with a fine spreading form, proving that it has been well tended over the decades. ///sway.policy.waking

**663. HILLIER'S WALNUT**
*Cut-leaf walnut*
*Juglans regia 'Laciniata'*
Greenhill Close,
Winchester SO22 5DZ
51.06405, -1.331252

Sandwiched between HMP Winchester and the university's West Down campus, a twentieth-century housing estate occupies the former site of the famous Hillier plant nursery (the Sir Harold Hillier Gardens near Romsey are also part of this same legacy). Dozens of exceptional trees still grow around the estate, including the exquisite cut-leaf walnut on Greenhill Close. ///starch.families.lordship

**664. HOME NURSERY LIME**
*Oliver's lime / Tilia oliveri*
Nursery Gardens,
Winchester SO22 5DT
51.062891, -1.331295

Home Nursery Gardens, once part of the Hillier nursery, became a community garden when the housing on Nursery Gardens was completed in the late 1970s. It is a cluster of yet more rare trees, the loveliest of which is a graceful Oliver's lime, an unusual Chinese species similar to a silver lime. This one has a bench constructed part way around its trunk. ///than.gazes.seashell

**665. DEAN'S MAGNOLIA**
*Chinese evergreen magnolia*
*Magnolia delavayi*
The Close,
Winchester SO23 9LS
51.059737, -1.313187

Magnolias are more varied than you might expect: as well as the spectacular flowering shrubs of early spring, several evergreen species exist, which flower less copiously but for longer and later in the year. North American southern magnolias are the most common of these, but, against an old wall behind the Deanery in the grounds of Winchester Cathedral, the Dean's Magnolia, a rare Chinese evergreen, has grown to enormous proportions. ///quitter.joins.papers

**666. OLD LEANER**
*Yew / Taxus baccata*
St Thomas, Bidbury Lane,
Bedhampton,
Havant PO9 3JG
50.853021, -1.003056

The chancel of medieval St Thomas at Bedhampton dates back to the 1100s, but there is thought to have been a church on this site even longer, since Saxon times. There are two ancient yews growing close together in the churchyard which likely also date back over 1,000 years. Both lean, but the smaller of the two does so with more aplomb. ///tent.admire.pushy

**667. MCKENZIE'S PLANE**
*London plane*
*Platanus × hispanica*
Victoria Park,
Anglesea Road,
Portsmouth PO1 3HJ
50.798553, -1.092704

Victoria Park is Portsmouth's oldest public park. It was designed in 1878 by Alexander McKenzie, who was also responsible for Finsbury and Southwark Parks in London, both known for their imposing plane trees. Planes also feature in Victoria Park, and one stands out: a supremely tall and elegant specimen in the south-east corner close to the railway. ///socket.strong.owls

**668. SWEEPING STONE PINE**
*Stone pine / Pinus pinea*
Pier Road, Southsea,
Portsmouth PO1 2TA
50.787772, -1.098495

Hundreds of trees have been planted around Southsea Common in recent decades, complementing the stately holm oaks that have been here for over a century. In the eastern portion, resilient elms grow around Clarence Avenue, but further west it is stone pines that set the scene. A particularly well-positioned tree grows on Gordon Road by the roundabout; admire its broad canopy, twice as wide as the tree is high. ///crazy.chained.spoon

**669. SOUTHSEA'S PALM** → Like other south-coast resorts such as Eastbourne and Torquay, Southsea has gone in for palm trees, and they are doing very well. Canary Island date palms have been planted at regular intervals along Clarence Parade on the edge of Southsea Common, alluding to the town's temperate, holiday feel. Rising steadily, with a metre or two of clear trunk, my favourite is opposite high-rise St Martin's House.

**SOUTHSEA'S PALM** *Canary date palm / Phoenix canariensis* Clarence Parade, Southsea, Portsmouth PO5 2EZ 50.781546, -1.085956 ///quite.defeat.forest

**670. WEST END GIANT**
*Giant redwood*
*Sequoiadendron giganteum*
Selborne Avenue,
Southampton SO18 5EB
50.922151, -1.34606

Southampton was far more rural a hundred years ago. The West End Road, which today runs through the city's eastern suburbs, was then sparsely lined with country houses, arboreal reminders of which can still be spotted among the modern buildings. On the corner of Selborne Avenue a giant redwood grows from the pavement, an imposing landmark for many heading along this main road. ///brave.boss.unique

**671. UNIVERSITY STRAWBERRY TREE**
*Strawberry tree*
*Arbutus unedo*
Hartley Avenue,
Southampton SO17 3RA
50.934711, -1.392989

At the end of Granby Grove, the Faraday Building looms, a 1970s tower block in the University of Southampton's Highfield campus. Below it, a luxuriant strawberry tree marks a campus entrance. Under its copious canopy there is a single, thick trunk, suggesting the tree has been here for at least as long as the uni. ///shades.shot.crate

**672. SHIRLEY HACKBERRY**
*Nettle tree / Celtis australis*
Firgrove Road, Shirley,
Southampton SO15 3NT
50.916599, -1.428184

Southampton is well endowed with rare trees, but the city's finest curiosity must be this hackberry, or nettle tree, the stoutest example I've seen in Britain or Ireland. It is a splendid tree that takes pride of place next to the elegant Khanegaheh Zahabiyyeyeh Ahmadiyyeh Institute in Shirley. ///itself.jungle.proof

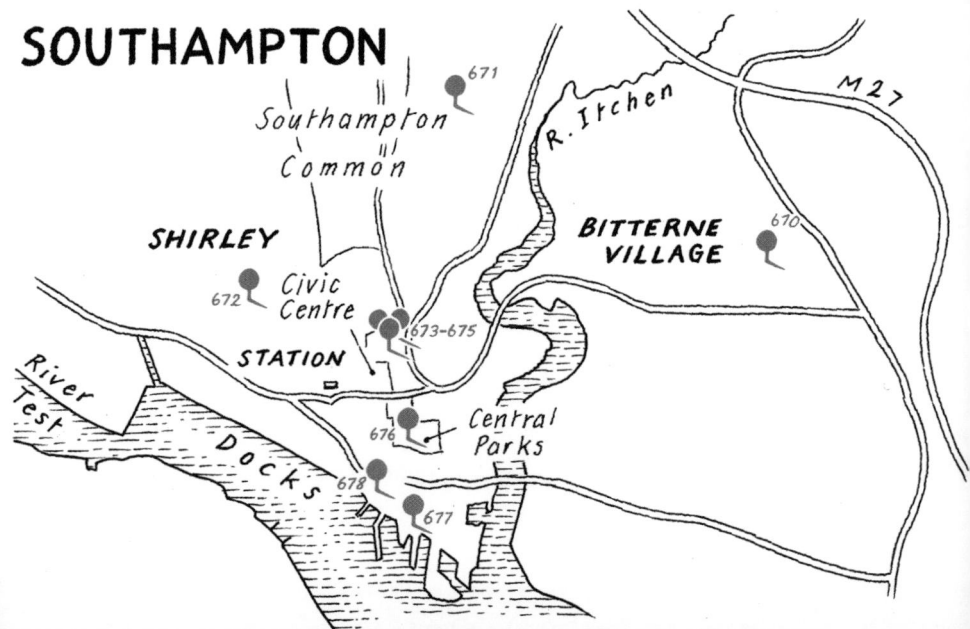

### 673. TITANIC CORK OAK
*Cork oak / Quercus suber*
East Park, Above Bar Street, Southampton SO14 7DW
50.910374, -1.404551

Near the north-western corner of East Park, a sombre old cork oak stands next to the Titanic Engineers Memorial. The tree is likely an original planting from the mid-nineteenth century, predating the memorial by half a century or more. The memorial was unveiled in 1914 in memory of the thirty-five engineers who perished on the *Titanic*, whose ill-fated voyage started at Southampton in 1912. ///wasp.kings.pass

### 674. CURLY-WURLY MULBERRY
*Black mulberry*
*Morus nigra*
Watts Park, Cumberland Place, Southampton SO15 2BB
50.909134, -1.406517

Across the road from Southampton's impressive Civic Centre, 'the most ambitious civic building erected in the provinces in the interwar years' (according to Pevsner), is an equally impressive, if rather shambolic, old mulberry floundering over the lawns of Watts Park. The park was laid out in the mid-1800s, and the mulberry is likely to have been planted at that time. It has a certain dishevelled charm. ///rice.hotels.lovely

### 675. PERKINS' LIME
*Common lime*
*Tilia × europaea*
Palmerston Park, Above Bar Street, Southampton SO14 7DW
50.909026, -1.40297

Nothing defines Southampton's central parks like their limes, which form a grand avenue running the entire distance from southern Houndwell Park, through Palmerston Park and ending at the north of East Park. At the centre of East Park, a Victorian plaque, shaded by a magnificent common lime tree, tells us they were gifted to the city in 1862 by Mayor Perkins. ///coast.kinds.spoon

### 676. PIGTAIL PINE
*Mexican weeping pine*
*Pinus patula*
Palmerston Park, Above Bar Street, Southampton SO14 7DW
50.906304, -1.403184

Palmerston Park is arguably the loveliest of Southampton's five central parks, noted for its magnificent rhododendron display in the spring. It is also home to a fine tree collection, including an elegant and rather rare Mexican weeping pine. It has formed a perfect dome, with hair-like needles hanging in pigtail bunches from its branches. ///rocks.amount.milk

### 677. CAR PARK BUCKEYE
*California buckeye*
*Aesculus californica*
Gloucester Square, Southampton SO14 2GH
50.897275, -1.403483

California buckeyes are related to horse chestnuts; they have very similar leaves, smaller flower spikes which appear later, and chestnuts which are highly prized by in-the-know conker players. Those aficionados must visit the Gloucester Square car park where one of these very unusual trees can be found. Chestnuts the size of golf balls, known as buckeyes, can be harvested in October. ///echo.visual.couch

ROCKSTAR TREE (678)

### 678. ROCKSTAR TREE
*Foxglove tree*
*Paulownia tomentosa*
Westgate Hall, Westgate Street, Southampton, SO14 2AY
50.898784, -1.406645

Growing next to medieval Westgate Hall and Southampton's city walls, a vernal foxglove tree makes an impression each May when gorgeous bluey-mauve flowers burst open. Like rock stars, foxglove trees live fast and shine brightly but tend to die young. The Rockstar Tree is a young tree so many spectacular shows should lie ahead of it. ///shin.crown.tiny

### 679. POLICE STATION TULIP TREE
*Variegated tulip tree*
*Liriodendron tulipifera*
*'Aureomarginatum'*
Lyndhurst Police Station, Pikes Hill, Pikeshill, Lyndhurst SO43 7NR
50.877439, -1.577585

There are dozens of outstanding tulip trees, particularly in southern Britain, so the bar is set high for one to surprise. An individual at Lyndhurst Police Station, on the edge of the New Forest, does just that. It is a good-sized tree of an unusual variegated type. *'Aureomarginatum'* has leaves edged with gold, and in spring, when they first appear a dazzling yellow, it is a startling, indeed arresting, sight. ///quote.complies.blazers

### 680. BALMER LAWN OAK*
*Pedunculate oak*
*Quercus robur*
Balmer Lawn Hotel, Lyndhurst Road, Brockenhurst SO42 7ZB
50.828442, -1.568754

The New Forest is a magical landscape of trees, heaths and villages where, somehow, nature seems to have the upper hand despite all the human encroachment. Balmer Lawn is a typical idyll, in which a cricket pitch and hotel rub shoulders with one of the New Forest's best oaks. Growing in a copse, the Balmer Lawn Oak is a gnarly and spreading maiden, a tree that has not been pollarded. ///visits.steady.differ

### 681. RYDE OLEASTER
*Oleaster / Elaeagnus angustifolia*
St Thomas Street, Ryde PO33 2DL
50.733115, -1.161192

Oleasters, or Russian olives, originate from western Asia, and have been cultivated beyond their natural range for centuries because of their striking silvery foliage, as well as their resemblance to olive trees (once regarded as exotic, though they now do well in our warming climate). The Ryde Oleaster growing on the seafront is a spectacular example, easily mistaken for an ancient olive tree. /// bolt.inspector.like

### 682. FIRST PICTURE OF YEW
*Yew / Taxus baccata*
St Mary's, High Street, Carisbrooke, Newport PO30 1NN
50.691933, -1.313436

A drawing dating from 1567 appears to show St Mary's church at Carisbrooke with a tree growing in the same position as a yew tree that grows today. There are some ambiguities so we can't be certain, but if this is a drawing of the Carisbrooke tree, it is the oldest known representation of an English yew. The tree is a handsome example with a fine domed canopy and a leaning trunk. ///tonality.balconies.snipe

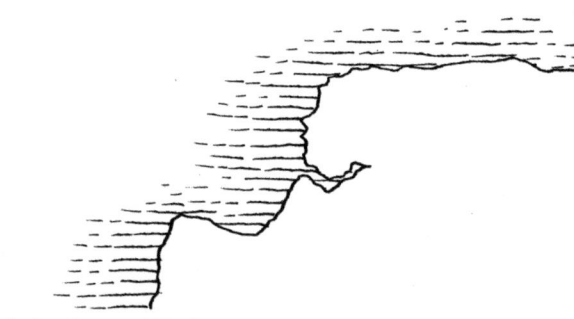

# SOUTH WEST ENGLAND

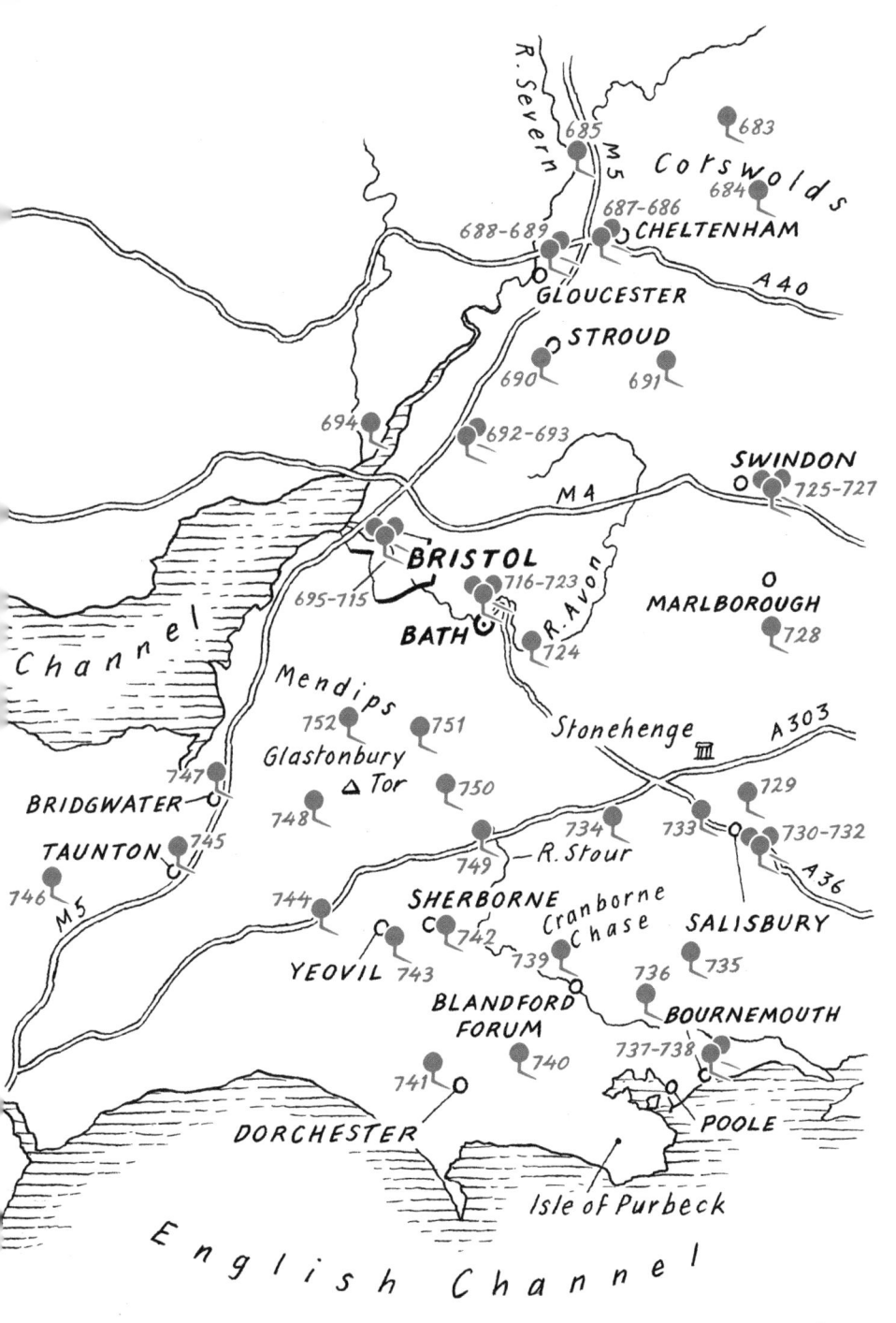

## SOUTH WEST ENGLAND

*Gloucestershire*
*Somerset*
*Dorset*
*Wiltshire*

TREE CITY:
*Bristol*

SIGNATURE SPECIES:
*Ginkgo*

In the towns and cities of the south west of England, there can be no tree more frequent and distinctive than the evergreen holm oak. *Holm* comes from the Old English word for holly, a reference to the species' juvenile leaves which, like holly, have prickly edges. But, despite their archaic name, holm oaks were only introduced in the sixteenth century from their native Mediterranean, and, although it is a tree of dry, warm and sunny climes, the species has adapted extremely well and fits in effortlessly throughout most of Britain and Ireland. They are particularly abundant in the south west – and especially so in Bristol.

But, across the region, an even more intrepid and captivating tree species can be found: the ginkgo. In the almost too-good-to-be-true Cotswold town of Chipping Campden, the perfectly round-canopied **WILSON TREE (683)** grows out of the pavement close to Bedfont House, the most handsome of many Georgian honeyed-stone buildings that line the High Street. It was planted in 1878 by the family who lived in the house, who had acquired it from a nursery in Yokohama. We can only wonder at the journey the tree must have undertaken to arrive safely in Gloucestershire all those years ago. It was installed at a time when street trees were just starting to be planted in towns and cities, and European plant collectors were sending their new Asian discoveries back to the west by the shipload. This individual tree represents that zeitgeist, embodying both the new idea of street-tree planting and a burgeoning interest in east Asian botany.

Down the road from this ginkgo, just two years before it was planted, Ernest Wilson was born. Wilson would become one of the great plant hunters of the late-nineteenth and early-twentieth centuries, later known as 'Chinese' Wilson, introducing such splendours as the paperbark maple and handkerchief tree to the west. Although the family left Chipping Campden when Ernest was a child, we can speculate that he knew the young ginkgo. Perhaps it even inspired his future career.

A few even older gingkos can be found elsewhere in the region: one regrettably inaccessible eighteenth-century tree grows at Blaise Castle on the edge of Bristol, not far from the **BLAISE CASTLE CURIOSITY (700)**, while another old tree, probably nineteenth century, can be seen in Yeovil. **STINK BOMB (743)**, growing in the gardens of an office building that hangs over busy Hendford Hill, must be rarely noticed except when its fruits – for this is an unusual female tree – make their presence known by their rank smell (akin to vomit, or worse).

Today, ginkgos are no longer confined to specialised collections or gardens, and are frequently encountered as street trees. They are not the only interesting Asian species that has found favour in this role however: the **HIGHBURY VAULTS BEE-BEE TREE (708)** is an example of the diverse planting that has taken place in recent decades. But it wasn't always so. Trees have been planted in parks, cemeteries, botanic gardens and arboretums all across Britain and Ireland for the last two centuries. But before these innovations, trees in our towns and cities were rarely encountered outside private gardens, as can be readily observed in Bath.

The Georgian splendour of Bath is enhanced by the many wonderful trees that grow there, but most were planted after the city's signature eighteenth-century buildings were completed. The **ABBEY GREEN PLANE (721)**, a vast London plane that lends a timeless quality to the paved Georgian piazza in which it grows, was planted in 1880. **PRINCESS VICTORIA'S ZELKOVA (717)**, just a stone's throw from the Royal Crescent, was likely planted when Royal Victoria Park opened in 1830, more than fifty years after the Royal Crescent was completed. At the world's last remaining Georgian pleasure garden, Sydney Gardens, the **TEMPLE OF MINERVA CATALPA (720)** would have been planted many decades after the gardens opened in 1790. The Georgians were less keen on urban trees than subsequent generations, but Bath shows us that it's never too late to transform your townscape with plant life.

WILSON TREE (683)

### 683. WILSON TREE
*Ginkgo / Ginkgo biloba*
High Street, Chipping
Campden GL55 6HB
52.051625, -1.779101

Ernest Wilson, the great early-twentieth-century plant hunter who introduced many Chinese plants to the west, was born in Chipping Campden in 1876. The family left the Cotswolds while Ernest was a child, but the verdant ginkgo, an unusual, old and shapely landmark enclosed by iron railings on the High Street, may have been an early inspiration for his future botanical career. ///withdraw.ramps.grape

### 684. DOORS OF DURIN YEWS*
*Yew / Taxus baccata*
St Edward's Church,
The Square, Stow-on-the-Wold GL54 1AB
51.930156, -1.723833

Like Chipping Campden, Stow-on-the-Wold is a charming Cotswold town with an interesting tree – or two. In this case, a pair of veteran yews grow either side of the door to St Edward's church. Many have speculated that this 300-year-old gothic assemblage was the inspiration for regular Stow visitor J. R. R. Tolkien's Doors of Durin, the west gates of Moria in the *The Lord of the Rings*. ///testy.solo.sharpens

### 685. ABBEY LIME
*Cut-leaf lime / Tilia platyphyllos 'Laciniata'*
Tewkesbury Abbey,
Church Street,
Tewkesbury GL20 5RZ
51.990796, -2.160255

Tucked away in the grounds of Tewkesbury Abbey, not far from a magnificent copper beech, a rare tree awaits you. It is a cut-leaf lime, a tree with odd, irregular leaves that appear to have been torn. The resulting leaf cover is sparse and so cut-leaf limes, lacking the photosynthesis power of their regular large-leaved cousins, are slow growing, ekeing out a more modest living. ///envisage.compounds.unique

### 686. COLLEGE CYPRESS
*Smooth bark Arizona cypress / Cupressus arizonica var. glabra*
Cheltenham College,
Bath Road,
Cheltenham GL53 7LD
51.891912, -2.076716

Among the cedars on Cheltenham College's Bath Road lawn, an unusual conifer holds its own. Like the nearby Atlas cedar, this flame-shaped Arizona cypress has glaucous foliage, only it is constructed in a different way: the inquisitive will notice it is scaly and three-dimensionally branched. Look out for small, round cones among the foliage, which will only open and disperse their seeds when triggered by fire. ///land.chase.homes

### 687. SKATE PARK PLANE
*Oriental plane*
*Platanus orientalis*
Montpellier Gardens,
Montpellier Spa Road,
Cheltenham GL50 1UL
51.894634, -2.081477

Montpellier Gardens date back to 1834, when they were first laid out for visitors to the nearby spa. Some of the limes on the perimeter no doubt also date back to this time, along with the huge, double-trunked oriental plane in the south-west corner. Towering over the skate park, it is easily the largest and most impressive tree in the gardens. ///terms.moth.fixed

**688. HOSPITAL ELM**
*English elm*
Ulmus minor 'Atinia'
Gloucester Royal Hospital,
Great Western Road,
Gloucester GL1 3NN
51.865473, -2.233381

A towering, thick-trunked English elm makes its presence felt at the main entrance to Gloucester's Royal Hospital. It is a fantastic survivor, and a reminder of what we have lost. There can be few, if any, urban English elms outside the great elm centres of Brighton and Edinburgh that can match it: it is well worth the pilgrimage. ///song.opera.logs

**689. COLLAPSING CATALPA**
*Southern catalpa*
Catalpa bignonioides
Barnwood Arboretum,
Church Lane, Barnwood,
Gloucester GL4 3JB
51.860002, -2.203638

Cross over Wotton Brook via the little footbridge from Barnwood Park to visit the semi-wild Barnwood Arboretum, where a splendid collection of old trees awaits. The park only came into public ownership in 2002, and as a result the fragile trees, including an elegantly declining catalpa, now sadly in its final years, have survived unmolested for over a century. Catch it while you can. ///solid.panel.handed

**690. KIERAN'S TREE**
*Golden rain tree*
Koelreuteria paniculata
Park Gardens, Slad Road,
Stroud GL5 1QW
51.747723, -2.215452

'May this tree continue to give pleasure,' states a small plaque beneath the golden rain tree by the entrance to Park Gardens. It is a memorial to Kieran, an otherwise anonymous citizen of Stroud, and it is safe to say this lovely tree poignantly delivers on the plaque's promise. It is a treat throughout the year, but if you can, try to visit in July to see golden flowers dusting its canopy. ///trips.airliners.masses

**691. STAUNCH CEDAR**
*Atlas cedar*
Cedrus atlantica
'Glauca'
Gosditch Street,
Cirencester GL7 2AG
51.717726, -1.968238

Overshadowed by the tower of St Mary's, the Atlas cedar on Gosditch Street in Cirencester, stunted by life in the shade, does not have the graceful shape associated with some of its siblings. But it does have a particularly stout trunk encircled by a popular wooden bench, confirming the regard in which it is held by locals and from which a vast canopy could one day sprout if its shady neighbours allowed. ///stow.tastes.fever

**692. TORTWORTH CHESTNUT***
*Sweet chestnut*
Castanea sativa
St Leonard's, Tortworth,
Wotton-under-Edge
GL12 8HF
51.637546, -2.428159

The Tortworth Chestnut is difficult to take in: it sprawls within a fenced-off enclosure, with a series of giant limbs that have fallen and rooted themselves to spawn several disconnected trunks. Despite being 1,000 years old, probably the oldest tree of its species in these islands, it appears to be thriving. An enormous and complex tree that will take an exacting tree hunter some time to fully appreciate. ///audible.unit.parsnip

**693. SHINGLES' CRETAN MAPLE**
*Cretan maple*
*Acer sempervirens*
St Leonard's, Tortworth,
Wotton-under-Edge
GL12 8HF
51.63822, -2.428463

Shingles' Cretan Maple was planted as a memorial on the grave of Henry Shingles, much-respected head gardener for the third Earl of Ducie, on the rare-tree-stuffed Tortworth Estate. The Earl started an arboretum in the mid-1800s covering his extensive grounds, and Tortworth's parish church, St Leonards, is home to several of its trees, including this very rare semi-evergreen maple. ///darkest.sudden.hotspots

**694. OFFA'S OAK** → Over the Wye from Chepstow, Sedbury's oak marks the southern end of Offa's Dyke, the eighth-century defensive border between England and Wales. It is an old and hollow tree, but not one that was here in Offa's time – the King of Mercia died in 796 AD. It grows on a slope, among housing and a fanciful flight of steps from where you can imagine the dyke's ramparts disappearing into the Severn mud nearby.

**OFFA'S OAK**
*Pedunculate oak*
*Quercus robur*
Mercian Way,
Sedbury NP16 7AP
51.636252, -2.660649
///friday.cornering.replayed

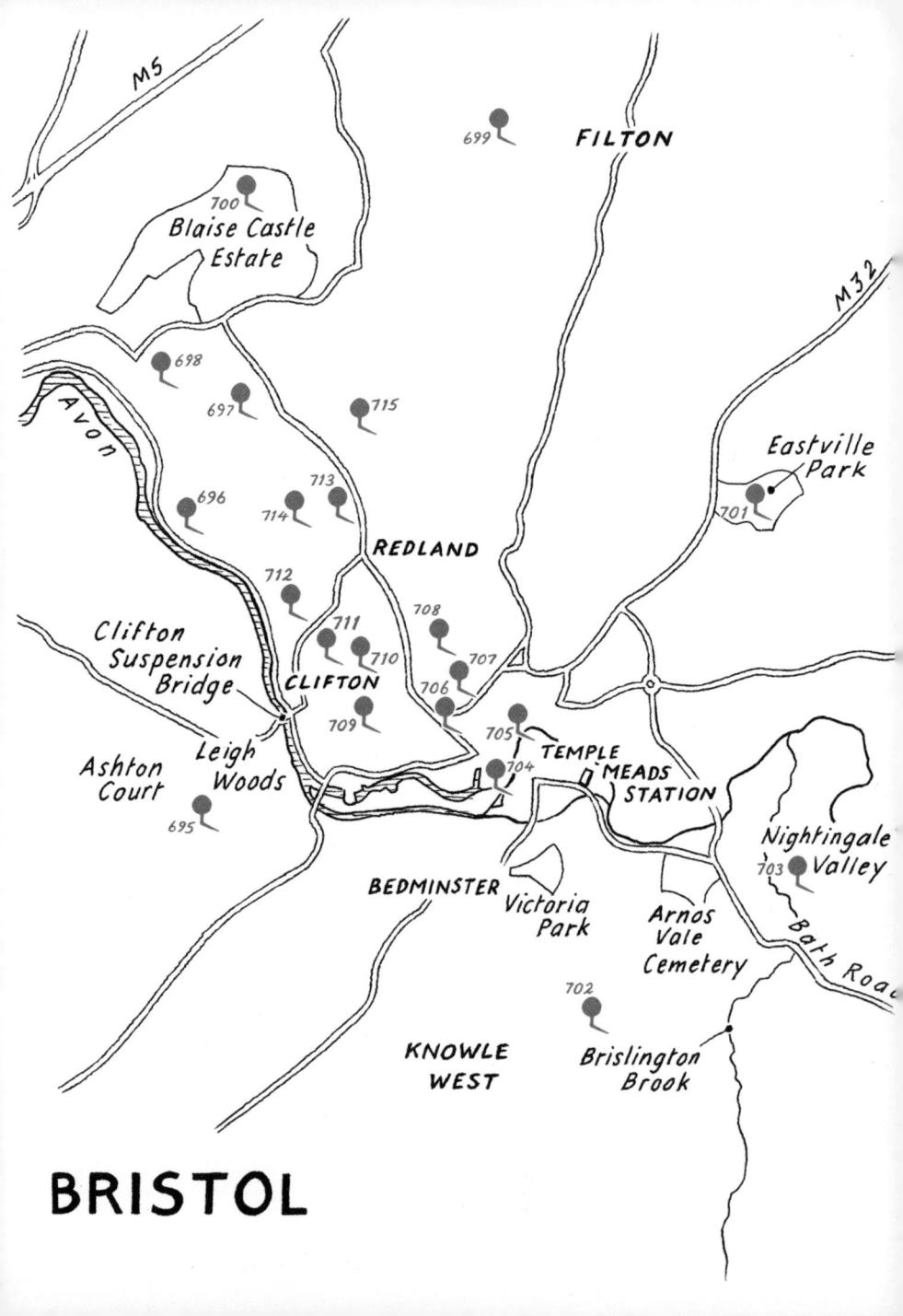

## TREE CITY: BRISTOL
### SIGNATURE SPECIES: *Holm oak*

Stand on Bristol Bridge and you can start to take in this great mercantile city and its eventful history. Not far from here, the statue of merchant and slave-trader Edward Colston was dumped into the water in 2020. A little further on lies the city's old commercial centre, where the Luftwaffe did their worst; and, downstream, SS *Great Britain*, the first iron steamship to cross the Atlantic, was constructed and is now docked as a museum. But, if you are a tree hunter, your eye will be drawn to a leafy clump (or a tangle of bare branches in winter) growing incomprehensibly out of the harbour's sheer wall. This is the **BRISTOL BRIDGE FIG (705)**, which has witnessed all the upheavals of the past century, and more. Its very presence, from a seed lodged from fallen cargo perhaps, is likely a result of the city's great trading past.

Just to the south lies Queen Square: it was the flashpoint for the Bristol Riots of 1831. Today it is a large and popular green space surrounded by early-nineteenth-century buildings, including the handsome neoclassical Custom House, rebuilt in 1836, in front of which the **QUEEN SQUARE NONPAREIL (704)** is the best of the magnificent London planes that completely enclose the Square. The Floating Harbour, just beyond Queen Square, joins the Avon as it curves round into the great chasm of the Avon gorge, which separates the city from the countryside. On its other side lies the historic Ashton Court estate with its many ancient trees, including the 700-year-old **DOMESDAY OAK\* (695)**. It is in this natural edgeland, between the city and the countryside, that almost all of the 300 extant plants of the rare Bristol whitebeam grow. Tree hunters have no need to cross the gorge, however, as one of these elusive trees, **BRISTOL'S WHITEBEAM (707)**, has been planted in the car park of the University of Bristol's Arts and Social Sciences Library.

There are treasures scattered across Bristol, but head to Clifton, a grand suburb long favoured by the city's rich and powerful, to find a collection of the city's finest. From the downs with their characteristic beeches to the university's charming botanic garden, there is much to see, but Clifton's most important arboreal site may be that of the former Bristol Zoological Gardens, which holds a historic collection of trees, some of which date back to the institution's opening in 1836. The zoo finally closed its doors in 2022, amid promises that the gardens would be retained in the development that will follow. Time will tell if this nationally important tree collection, one of the oldest assemblages of trees in any British or Irish city, will be given the same care it enjoyed when the zookeepers ran the show.

But the trees that define Bristol more than any other must be its holm oaks, a species that thrives in Bristol's mild, damp climate. There are many fine examples spread throughout the city. Several stand out: the **FILWOOD OAK (702)** is typical, thriving precariously in an unloved south Bristol car park.

SUBURBAN SEQUOIA (699)

**695. DOMESDAY OAK***
*Pedunculate oak*
*Quercus robur*
Ashton Court Estate,
Kennel Lodge Road,
Bristol BS3 2JT
51.446273, -2.64129

Bristol's oldest tree is a dilapidated, ivy-clad stump with fallen limbs mouldering nearby. Nevertheless, the 700-year-old Domesday Oak bursts into life each spring. It is just one of over 400 veteran and ancient trees in the former estate of Ashton Court, which, thanks to the foresight of Bristol's civic leaders who bought the estate in 1959, can now be enjoyed by everyone. ///bumpy.admits.switch

**696. SLOPE OAK**
*Sessile oak*
*Quercus petraea*
Bishops Knoll Wood,
Bramble Lane,
Bristol BS9 1NS
51.473952, -2.644209

The biggest, fattest oak in Bristol is not one of Ashton Court's sentinels, but instead grows on the precipitous slope of Bishops Knoll Woods at Stoke Bishop. It is many centuries old, and will take your breath away when you encounter it soon after entering the woods. Tree experts have been surprised to discover it is a sessile rather than a pedunculate oak, the former being most often associated with lowland England. ///factor.gender.settle

**697. EXONIAN OAK**
*Lucombe oak*
*Quercus × crenata*
*'Lucombeana'*
Stoke Lodge, Little Stoke,
Bristol BS34 6HR
51.485783, -2.637539

Exeter is an hour away from Bristol by train, so it is no surprise that a magnificent Lucombe oak, a tree that arose in that city, can be found here. The tree in question grows, along with many other interesting trees, in the grounds of the adult learning centre, Stoke Lodge. It is much admired, and was voted Bristol's inaugural Tree of the Year in 2018. ///alarm.many.foam

**698. ADDISON'S OAK***
*Pedunculate oak*
*Quercus robur*
Sea Mills Square,
Bristol BS9 2EE
51.487993, -2.64854

In 1919, Christopher Addison MP was responsible for the Housing and Town Planning Act, which led to the construction of thousands of 'homes fit for heroes', council houses built for veterans returning from the First World War. Addison visited the building site of Sea Mills the same year, and to mark the occasion an oak was planted, which immediately became known as Addison's Oak. ///firms.radio.frame

**699. SUBURBAN SEQUOIA**
*Giant redwood*
*Sequoiadendron*
*giganteum*
Northwoods Walk,
Bristol BS10 6LS
51.512627, -2.594671

Some urban trees get lucky, and that's what happened to the ever more colossal giant redwood on a 1970s estate in Filton. When the developers laid out the cul-de-sacs here, they mercifully left this magnificent tree where it was and built around it. A tree that would once have been a feature of a Victorian garden now graces the lawns of an optimistic mid-century development. ///magma.polite.cats

**700. BLAISE CASTLE CURIOSITY**
*Ehret / Ehretia dicksonii*
Blaise Castle,
Bristol BS10 7QT
51.505538, -2.6343

Blaise Castle Estate on the edge of the city is a popular resort for those who come to enjoy the tranquil and historic Humphry Repton-designed landscape. There are many mature trees here, including one of the oldest ginkgos in England. The very rare ehret in the children's playground is a more accessible curiosity: look out for its white summer flowers and deeply grooved bark. ///visual.itself.police

**701. EASTVILLE HORNBEAM**
*Hornbeam*
*Carpinus betulus*
Fishponds Road, Eastville,
Bristol BS5 6XA
51.476593, -2.554466

Eastville Park was laid out in the 1890s, following a campaign to provide a park for working people in this part of the expanding city. The mature trees that are now so much a feature of the park were planted at this time, including the particularly handsome hornbeam that hangs over the lake from the bank on its southern edge. ///rice.hurls.flesh

**702. FILWOOD OAK**
*Holm oak / Quercus ilex*
Newquay Road,
Bristol BS4 1EG
51.425008, -2.578898

One of Bristol's many fine holm oaks is the old landmark tree in the Filwood Park neighbourhood. It looks vulnerable, growing on the edge of an estate, next to a car park entrance, overlooking metal security fencing and a nearby mobile phone mast. But the tree is a veteran that has survived here for many years and, despite its gritty surroundings, should stand strong for many more. ///struck.select.monday

703. **BRISLINGTON BROOK PLANE** → If trees could talk, the Brislington Brook Plane would surely have some tales to tell, not least how it arrived in this unlikely spot. It is an old London plane growing next to the stream in the middle of the now-serene Nightingale Valley woods. The tree shows some battle scars. Traces of past industry, such as the ruined structures near the tree, are scattered through the woods, and the tree itself has a bricked-up hollow at its base.

**BRISLINGTON BROOK PLANE** *London plane / Platanus × hispanica* Nightingale Valley Woods, Brislington, Bristol BS4 4PH 51.441907, -2.548438 ///flood.using.vibrate

**704. QUEEN SQUARE NONPAREIL**
*London plane*
*Platanus × hispanica*
Queen Square,
Bristol BS1 4PR
51.451043, -2.594907

To select an exemplar from Queen Square's magnificent perimeter of planes is a difficult task, but one outside the Custom House on its north side seems to inch over its peers both in stature and character. It is the old tree with a shapely, fluted bole, just to the west of the path leading into the centre of the Square. ///cafe.filled.wakes

705. **BRISTOL BRIDGE FIG** → For as long as anyone can remember, a tumbleweed-like fig tree has defied gravity, and logic, to grow straight out of the Floating Dock's vertical stone wall. Like other embankment figs, the seed it sprang from may have arrived in human waste, but given Bristol's heritage as a major port, it could also have sprung from fallen cargo.

**BRISTOL BRIDGE FIG**
*Fig / Ficus carica*
Bristol Bridge, Victoria Street, Bristol BS1 6DT
51.454223, -2.590927
///tame.loans.vanish

### 706. RETIRING IRONWOOD
*Persian ironwood*
*Parrotia persica*
Wills Building, Queens Road, Bristol BS8 1QE
51.456029, -2.603647

In the shadow of the triumphant Wills Memorial Tower, the university's Wills Memorial Library is a low-key affair screened from the street by an urban copse. Hidden in its depths is a modest but intriguing Persian ironwood, a small tree with presence. Its dense tangle of muscular branches are draped with beech-like leaves which, in autumn, turn dramatic red, gold and purple. ///crass.silks.tips

### 707. BRISTOL'S WHITEBEAM
*Bristol whitebeam*
*Sorbus bristoliensis*
Arts and Social Sciences Library, University of Bristol, Tyndall Avenue, Bristol BS8 1TJ
51.459883, -2.601243

Outside the university's Arts and Social Sciences Library with its unfortunate acronym, next to the St Michael's Park entrance to the car park, an unassuming young multi-stemmed tree grows. It is Bristol's very own naturally occurring tree, a rare Bristol whitebeam. The species has only ever been recorded in the Avon Gorge and Leigh Woods, where just 300 individual plants survive. ///open.unable.churn

### 708. HIGHBURY VAULTS BEE-BEE TREE
*Bee-bee tree*
*Tetradium daniellii*
Highbury Vaults, St Michael's Hill, Bristol BS2 8DE
51.461446, -2.602413

Next to the Highbury Vaults, a popular student watering hole near the library, stands an unlikely tree: a rare east-Asian bee-bee tree, or euodia. Quite how it got to be outside one of Bristol's cosiest Victorian boozers (a Young's establishment for those who like their ale) is hard to say. Visit in high summer when it comes into flower: creamy rosettes that attract pollinators in their droves. ///digit.logs.drive

### 709. CLIFTON ENIGMA
*Italian maple / Acer opalus*
Victoria Square, Clifton, Bristol BS8 4EW
51.455652, -2.61546

Italian maples could be described as a refined sycamore. They look very similar, but are distinguished by less indented, slightly smaller leaves and a denser, more rounded crown. These are slight differences that could be overlooked, but in the spring, Italian maples have conspicuously attractive flowers (for a maple): dangling acid green bunches of six to nine florets appear before the leaves. ///relate.veal.solved

### 710. ELEPHANT HOLM OAK
*Holm oak / Quercus ilex*
Pembroke Road, BS8 3EA
51.461392, -2.616273
*In a private garden, but visible from the street.*

An acorn's throw from the dramatic Clifton Cathedral, on the corner that marks the turning of Pembroke Vale onto Pembroke Road, is a remarkable evergreen holm oak. It is a species well represented in Bristol, but this one stands out for its dramatic, rippled trunk resembling, at a push, the skin of an elephant. It's certainly a head-turner. ///never.radar.rank

**711. ZOO THORN**
*Oriental thorn*
*Crataegus orientalis*
Bristol Zoo Gardens,
College Road,
Bristol BS8 3HA
51.46247, -2.622336
*Access may be restricted during redevelopment.*

The Bristol Zoo Gardens site is home to an important tree collection, and as the site enters its next phase the trees will become even more significant as they will no longer compete with the animals. The diminutive oriental thorn stands out. It is old, perhaps dating back to the zoo's foundation in 1836. Consistently well cared for, it has developed a beautiful spreading form, assisted by wooden props. ///narrow.letter.ripe

**712. LAST ELM**
*Huntingdon elm / Ulmus × hollandica 'Vegeta'*
Ladies Mile,
Bristol BS8 2XQ
51.464815, -2.627014

Many of the trees lining Ladies Mile across the downs are limes, but at one time elms would have been the order of the day – until Dutch elm disease caught up with them. There is a sole survivor of what must have once been an impressive avenue close to the Circular Road turn-off. It is a Huntingdon elm, a trace of what has been lost. ///rise.rungs.thigh

**713. BIG SISTER**
*Austrian pine*
*Pinus nigra var. nigra*
Durdham Down,
Bristol BS9 1FG
51.475623, -2.618092

Up on exposed Durdham Down, three of the original Seven Sisters remain. They are Austrian pines planted, it is said, in 1842 by a local doctor to commemorate his seven daughters. Four have been lost over the years – three on one stormy night in 1990 – but the remaining trees make a dramatic silhouette. The southernmost tree is the largest, and is now affectingly estranged from her siblings. ///marked.bronze.tells

**714. W. G. GRACE'S BEECH**
*Beech / Fagus sylvatica*
Clifton Downs,
Bristol BS9 1FG
51.474383, -2.623376

Very close to the remaining Seven Sisters, a great domed beech is one of the last remaining trees of the first Gloucester County Cricket pitch, laid out in 1860, where it would have marked the boundary. The legendary cricketer, W. G. Grace, was the prime mover in setting up the club, and perhaps marking out the pitch. The first game played here was in 1870 when Gloucestershire beat Surrey. ///calls.brands.glitz

**715. THE SAINT MONICA'S COTONEASTER**
*Saint Monica's cotoneaster / Cotoneaster frigidus 'Saint Monica'*
St Monica's, Cote Lane,
Bristol BS9 3UN
51.483843, -2.617572

St Monica's care home was set up by the Wills family after the First World War. The gardens were cared for by a particularly competent team who had the time and resources to raise their own cotoneaster cultivar. The original, a small evergreen tree approaching a hundred years old, still thrives outside the Main Hall. It is worth visiting in the winter months, when it fruits dramatically. ///moth.gallons.suffer

BIG SISTER (713)

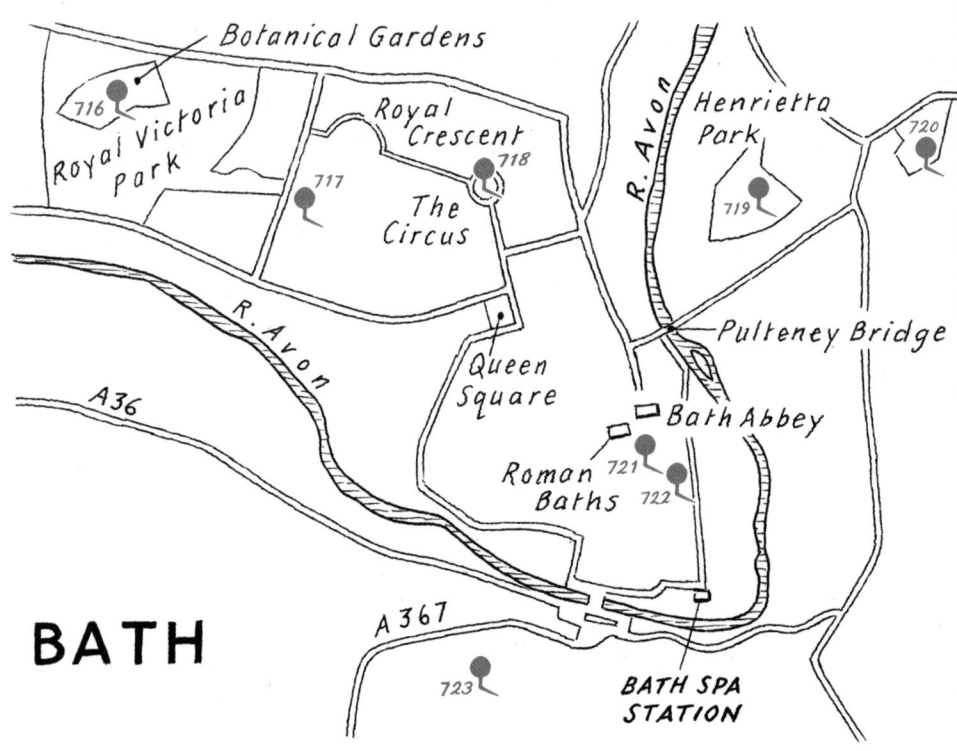

# BATH

**716. BOTANICAL BAUBLE**
*Chinese necklace poplar*
*Populus lasiocarpa*
Botanical Gardens, Park Lane, Bath BA1 2XQ
51.387546, -2.376751

One of the most prominent trees in Bath's Botanical Gardens is a towering Chinese necklace poplar growing not far from the entrance. It is an unusual tree distinguished by huge leaves, with its canopy lifted high above the lesser vegetation surrounding it by several metres of clear trunk. ///added.truth.lined

**717. PRINCESS VICTORIA'S ZELKOVA**
*Caucasian zelkova*
*Zelkova carpinifolia*
'James Gordon'
Royal Victoria Park, Marlborough Buildings, Bath BA1 2LZ
51.385713, -2.37031

Royal Victoria Park dates back to 1830, when it was opened by an eleven-year-old Princess Victoria. It covers a large area south and west of the Royal Crescent with Royal Avenue running through it. As the avenue approaches the grand Marlborough Gate, an excellent Caucasian zelkova sets the tone for a park containing many arboreal treasures, some of which the future queen would have enjoyed. ///fortunate.bride.woods

ENGLAND 344

### 718. WOOD PLANE
*London plane*
*Platanus* × *hispanica*
The Circus,
Bath BA1 2ET
51.385983, -2.364086

Wood Plane is best appreciated by approaching The Circus from Gay Street. It is difficult to imagine John Wood the Elder's masterpiece without the trees, but they were planted nearly four decades after building finished. An urban myth contends that the saying 'can't see the Wood for the trees' was first uttered by an architectural zealot complaining that the trees obscured the Georgian buildings. ///found.hill.think

### 719. HENRIETTA SPAETHII
*Purple-leaved sycamore*
*Acer pseudoplatanus*
*'Spaethii'*
Henrietta Park,
Henrietta Road,
Bath BA2 6LY
51.385794, -2.355139

Visit between late spring and late summer to see the great sycamore in the middle of Henrietta Park at its best. It is one of the finest examples of the *'Spaethii'* cultivar in England, a form with purple leaf undersides that will gradually fade to green by the autumn. It was first cultivated by the Späth nursery of Berlin in 1883, and this giant must have been planted soon after that date. ///renew.admiral.agree

### 720. TEMPLE OF MINERVA CATALPA
*Yellow catalpa*
*Catalpa ovata*
Sydney Gardens,
Sydney Place,
Bath BA2 6NH
51.386468, -2.349391

Next to the classical Temple of Minerva in these Georgian pleasure gardens grows one of the finest yellow catalpas, an Asian species that is rarely seen in Britain or Ireland. It is a strapping tree, but, as a relatively short-lived species, it is undoubtedly not contemporary with the temple, which is one of historic Sydney Gardens' original eighteenth-century buildings. ///rust.golf.tested

### 721. ABBEY GREEN PLANE
*London plane*
*Platanus* × *hispanica*
Abbey Green,
Bath BA1 1NW
51.380565, -2.358683

Abbey Green is a paved piazza tucked away in the close tangle of streets south of medieval Bath Abbey, its prettiness made exceptional by the enormous London plane at its centre. Its great size, for a tree some think was planted as recently as 1880, is perhaps a sign that its roots have tapped the spring feeding the nearby Roman baths. ///slam.backup.sentences

### 722. NORTH PARADE BOX ELDER
*Box elder / Acer negundo*
North Parade Buildings,
Bath BA1 1LN
51.380323, -2.358208

North Parade Buildings is a narrow, cobbled street lined with Bath-stone houses, close to Abbey Green. The impression is of a honey-coloured stone canyon, tempered by a leaning, well-pollarded old tree at its far end. It is a box elder, a North American maple with compound leaves, and an unlikely species to encounter in such an unforgiving environment. Somehow, it has managed to thrive. ///kicks.liver.ticket

HOLLOWAY JUDAS TREE (723)

**723. HOLLOWAY JUDAS TREE**
*Judas tree*
*Cercis siliquastrum*
Chapel of St Mary
Magdalen, Holloway,
Bath BA2 4PX
51.375822, -2.364389

The wayside chapel of St Mary Magdalen lies on an ancient lane rising out of Bath towards the city of Wells. The Holloway Judas Tree rewards those who reach these heights in May with its showstopping magenta blooms. Old prints from the early 1800s show an unchanged scene, and the remains of thick limbs can be seen at the tree's base, suggesting it has been here for centuries. ///region.locals.cheeks

**724. WESTBURY PLANE**
*London plane*
*Platanus × hispanica*
St Margaret's Street,
Bradford-on-Avon
BA15 1DE
51.346903, -2.251576

Towering over the Avon by the Town Bridge is a gargantuan London plane. It is conspicuously tall and particularly fat, and grows in what was once the garden of Westbury House, a substantial early-Georgian townhouse that is now home to the town's museum. Its favourable location next to the river has helped accelerate its growth. ///planet.texted.squashes

**725. KIWI TREE**
*Golden tōtara*
*Podocarpus tōtara 'Aureus'*
Queens Park, Drove
Road, Swindon SN1 3AG
51.55777, -1.775126

Queens Park is home to an unlikely yew-like golden tōtara, a rare and tender tree otherwise seen only in the mildest parts of Cornwall. Apparently the New Zealand native was a feature of a long-gone glasshouse that protected the young tree in its early years as it grew into a hardy adult. Look out for glossy needles, slightly longer and fatter than a yew, and, in this cultivar, they are golden. ///later.player.shot

**726. TOWN GARDENS HANDKERCHIEF TREE**
*Handkerchief tree*
*Davidia involucrata*
Town Gardens, Quarry
Road, Swindon SN1 4EN
51.550871, -1.782366

A lot is crammed into Town Gardens's small footprint. It is a charming Victorian park with all the usual features of lawns, formal gardens, a bandstand and a bowling green. A hidden valley hints at the site's former use as a quarry during Swindon's industrial past, and it is at the northern end of this that a relatively young, though spectacular, May-flowering handkerchief tree can be seen. ///bleak.appeal.lungs

**727. OLD TOWN COPPER BEECH**
*Copper beech / Fagus sylvatica 'Purpurea'*
Swindon Museum and
Art Gallery, Bath Road,
Swindon SN1 4BA
51.552595, -1.777901

Swindon's former Museum and Art Gallery on the Bath Road is distinguished by an eye-catching copper beech that towers above the buildings, acting as a much loved Old Town landmark. As it grows next to a stretch of early-nineteenth-century buildings, it is likely the tree was planted at that time, a legacy of old Swindon before the railway arrived and the town entered the modern era. ///never.casual.merit

**728. BIG BELLY***
*Sessile oak*
*Quercus petraea*
Savernake,
Marlborough SN8 4NE
51.390699, -1.694913

Big Belly is a giant old character with tremendous girth and several flailing limbs, growing next to the main A346 road and marking the western boundary of ancient Savernake Forest. Thought to have been here for 1,000 years, it is one of the very oldest oaks in England. The A346 is a fast road, so tree hunters keen to inspect the tree are advised to approach on foot through the forest. ///yachting.constrain.universally

**729. WEDDING CEDAR**
*Cedar of Lebanon*
*Cedrus libani*
Bourne Hill,
Salisbury SP1 1JD
51.072432, -1.790744

Bourne Hill House, a Georgian mansion within well-treed gardens, is now the Salisbury Registry Office. It's a good use for such a fine building: its splendour is set off by a magnificent and well-loved cedar of Lebanon to the right of the facade, screening the glass-and-steel Wiltshire council offices which extend discretely beyond. It is the obvious backdrop for countless wedding photos. ///buddy.visual.ample

**730. CATHEDRAL AZAROLE**
*Azarole*
*Crataegus azarolus*
Salisbury Cathedral,
SP1 2EJ
51.064481, -1.798339

Visitors to Salisbury Cathedral enter via a doorway to the south of its imposing west front, where a handful of small trees grow against the high wall of the cloister, including an azarole. It is an unusual member of the hawthorn family, and has a passing resemblance to the familiar hedgerow shrub, but is altogether more substantial with more indented leaves, more copious blossom and bigger, orange berries. ///crass.blast.shell

**731 & 732. ACCESSION CEDARS** → Anyone admiring the **CATHEDRAL AZAROLE (730)** will be struck by horizontal coniferous branches appearing above the cloister walls. They belong to a pair of cedars of Lebanon that were planted within to mark Queen Victoria's accession to the throne in 1837. They define England's most extensive cloister to such an extent that it is hard to imagine the centuries when this was a treeless garth. It is impossible to choose between this exceptional pair.

**ACCESSION CEDARS** *Cedar of Lebanon / Cedrus libani*
Salisbury Cathedral, SP1 2EJ 51.064481, -1.797824 ///latter.laws.tile

ENGLAND 348

PORTARLINGTON PINE (737)

### 733. WILTON THUJA
*Western red cedar*
*Thuja plicata*
St Mary's,
North Street,
Wilton SP2 0HQ
51.080382, -1.863221

Wilton is known for its impressive Italianate church of 1845, which replaced the now-redundant St Mary's. While architectural aficionados may head first to the 'new' church, those more inclined to natural wonders will be excited by the tree in the older churchyard. Unlike many western red cedars, which tend to layer themselves dramatically, this tree has a burgeoning single-trunked form. ///foiled.galaxies.imprints

### 734. VENGEFUL YEW
*Yew / Taxus baccata*
St John's, Church Street,
Tisbury SP3 6NH
51.061597, -2.081553

Tisbury's ancient yew, recorded as a curiosity in the eighteenth century, is an alarming sight today. From one side, it appears to be a massively stout and aged tree, but from another angle what was once a large cavity comes into view. During the middle of the last century, this was filled with concrete – an act that today seems unfathomable. Mercifully, the tree has coped, and is even beginning to envelop this indignity. ///parade.browser.inflates

### 735. ALTERNATIVE REMEDY OAK
*Hungarian oak*
*Quercus frainetto*
Manor Road,
Verwood BH31 6DZ
50.879433, -1.880021

A couple of miles outside Verwood, the ancient Remedy Oak can be found at the crossroads of Horton Road and the B3081. So called because of healing properties it apparently acquired after being touched by King Edward VI, it is sadly now in decline. But in the centre of Verwood a mighty oak – a Hungarian – is very much alive and kicking. ///tensions.juggler.diplomats

### 736. GIDDYLAKE OAK
*Pedunculate oak*
*Quercus robur*
Venator Place, Wimborne
Minster BH21 1DQ
50.806881, -1.981493

Wedged between two bungalows on a mid-century estate of manicured lawns and generous cul-de-sacs, the Giddylake Oak marks a surprising natural break in the lookalike houses. It is a pollarded tree by a footpath to the old lane of Giddylake, both predating Venator Place by centuries. We must take our hats off to the enlightened developers (a rare breed) who ensured its survival. ///crunches.drifters.hops

### 737. PORTARLINGTON PINE
*Monterey pine*
*Pinus radiata*
Arlington House,
Clarendon Road,
Bournemouth BH4 8AJ
50.718265, -1.894875
*In a private garden, but visible from the street.*

The heathland on which Bournemouth is built favours conifers with a penchant for the seaside. Maritime pines and Monterey cypresses are much in evidence, but the conifer that engenders particular admiration is a much-branched Monterey pine that marks the junction of Portarlington and Clarendon Roads. It must have once graced the garden of a grand Victorian villa, now long gone and replaced by flats. ///dimes.crowd.wrong

**738. DOUBLE DAWN**
*Dawn redwood*
*Metasequoia glyptostroboides*
Upper Gardens,
Surrey Road,
Bournemouth BH4 9JX
50.724032, -1.888782

Bournemouth was founded in the nineteenth century, and as a result the town's trees tend to be young, something that is exemplified by the dawn redwood in the Upper Gardens, which started its relentless journey towards the light only a few decades ago. When it was very young, some traumatic event caused it to branch, and now two trunks grow in parallel. ///lied.piper.plot

**739. BLANDFORD CHARTER OAK***
*Pedunculate oak*
*Quercus robur*
The Tabernacle, Blandford Forum DT11 7DW
50.856821, -2.163312

The handsome Dorset settlement of Blandford Forum was rebuilt in 1731, following a fire that devastated the town 126 years after it gained its charter. This event, rather than the fire, is commemorated by the Charter Oak, a fine, spreading tree planted across the road from the library in 1905 to mark the charter's tercentenary. ///contexts.dolly.buyers

**740. MARTYRS TREE***
*Sycamore / Acer pseudoplatanus*
The Green,
Tolpuddle DT2 7EX
50.749528, -2.2968

Tolpuddle is synonymous with its martyrs, six labourers involved in trade union activity in the 1830s, a crime for which they were transported to Australia. They swore allegiance to the Friendly Society of Agricultural Labourers under the canopy of a landmark sycamore, which still lives today. Now it is a veteran pollard and is regularly cut back. It is surely the oldest sycamore in the south of England. ///hurray.tabs.narrating

**741. WEST WALKS FIELD MAPLE**
*Field maple /Acer campestre*
West Walks Road,
Dorchester DT1 1AW
50.712201, -2.440333

Dorchester's impressive tree-lined Town Walks trace the original Roman walls of this ancient county town. The trees are marked on maps from the eighteenth century, and some of those still growing might date from that time, but the most impressive is older: an enormous field maple that lurks inconspicuously by the old tennis courts off West Walks Road. For a field maple, it really is a giant. ///woods.paddocks.traps

**742. VEITCH'S SWAMP CYPRESS**
*Swamp cypress*
*Taxodium distichum*
Pageant Gardens,
Station Road,
Sherborne DT9 3NQ
50.944278, -2.514138

Near Sherborne's railway station lies Pageant Gardens. This small public park was laid out using money raised by the Mother of All Pageants, enacted here by a cast of 900 to celebrate the town's 1,200th anniversary in 1905. Noted nursery Veitch and Sons of Exeter were commissioned to develop the gardens, and were responsible for planting many fine trees, including the huge, feathery swamp cypress to the west of the bandstand. ///keys.aliens.rushed

### 743. STINK BOMB
*Ginkgo / Ginkgo biloba*
Hendford Hill,
Yeovil BA20 2RF
50.93498, -2.640251
*In a private garden, but visible from the street.*

Old ginkgos occasionally turn up in odd corners. This one grows in the garden of a nineteenth-century villa, now offices, on this leafy incline out of Yeovil. It is a milestone that appears to be over a century old and is a female tree. Though they are less planted because of their malodorous fruits, we actually need more female ginkgos to counteract the allergy-triggering pollen of the more abundant males. ///files.cattle.update

### 744. HOLY TREE*
*Giant redwood
Sequoiadendron giganteum*
West Street, Stoke-sub-Hamdon TA14 6QL
50.948051, -2.77047

Sleepy Stoke-sub-Hamdon is strung out along West Street, five miles from Yeovil. At the western end of the village lies Holy Tree Cross, today marked by a towering giant redwood. The tree must be a Victorian replacement for generations of marker trees at this formerly important crossroads. The crossroads' prominence has waned, and it is now merely a T-junction where West Street meets the A303 approach road, but the tree remains unwaveringly splendid. ///snowballs.towels.hatter

### 745. FRENCH FANCY
*Bauman's horse chestnut
Aesculus hippocastanum 'Baumanii'*
French Weir Park,
Northfield Avenue,
Taunton TA1 1XF
51.017855, -3.111261

Occupying a bend in the River Tone, French Weir Park is an expanse of grass encircled by several old horse chestnuts, perhaps survivors of a more uniform boundary scheme. They are double-flowered *'Baumanii'* cultivars, a slightly showier, more unusual form of the familiar conker tree. Being double flowered, pollinators struggle to fertilise them, so conkers in autumn are decidedly rare. ///hardly.brush.cheese

### 746. ASHBRITTLE YEW*
*Yew / Taxus baccata*
St John the Baptist,
Ashbrittle,
Wellington TA21 0LF
50.983735, -3.351554

An antique finger-post sign on the village green at Ashbrittle points 'To the Church and Yew Tree'. The yew in question is thousands of years old, straddling a neolithic bowl barrow in what is now the churchyard of fifteenth-century St John the Baptist. It has eight distinct trunks defining a girth of over 12 metres. ///hangs.emotional.overpower

### 747. PARRETT OAK
*Holm oak / Quercus ilex*
Blake Gardens,
Binford Place,
Bridgwater TA6 3LF
51.12752, -3.000623

A very old holm oak with a very fluted trunk, almost like that of a veteran yew, takes pride of place in Blake Gardens on the banks of the tidal River Parrett in front of Bridgwater's library. It is likely a relic from a long-gone private garden that occupied this spot from the seventeenth century, although the tree may be a century or so younger. ///powers.glows.website

SOUTH WEST ENGLAND 353

### 748. REPAIRING TREE
*Yew / Taxus baccata*
St Andrew's, Peak Lane,
Compton Dundon,
Somerton TA11 6PE
51.089546, -2.744695

Unlike other ancient yews which fragment with age, the Repairing Tree seems to be growing back together; in years hence its hollow trunk may be entirely encased in new growth. An eighteenth-century antiquarian wrote that 'the body is hollow and measures 23ft in circumference'. Two and a half centuries later the tree's girth is only fractionally larger. ///flash.hospitals.skinning

### 749. JUDGE WYNDHAM'S OAK*
*Pedunculate oak
Quercus robur*
St Nicholas,
Church Road, Silton,
Gillingham SP8 5PR
51.063187, -2.309367

In a field just beyond St Nicholas's churchyard, one of the oldest oaks in England can be seen. It is named after a local lad, Hugh Wyndham – a judge whose career spanned Cromwell's Commonwealth and the reign of Charles II – who is said to have enjoyed sitting under its canopy. The tree could be 1,000 years old; its crown is now smaller, and its girth larger, than they would have been in Wyndham's time. ///breakfast.flies.clef

### 750. TULIP TRIDENT
*Tulip tree
Liriodendron tulipifera*
St Mary's, Silver Street,
Bruton BA10 0EB
51.111807, -2.451568

Arriving in town from Dropping Lane, Bruton's burry churchyard tulip tree soon looms above the road as it curves round St Mary's churchyard. It is a giant that cannot be less than 200 years old and, typical of old trees of this species, it branches fairly low down, with three great trunks ascending to an expansive crown which is covered in flowers during May. ///overtime.revamping.carpets

### 751. TESCO GIANT REDWOOD
*Giant redwood
Sequoiadendron giganteum*
Townsend Shopping Park,
Shepton Mallet BA4 5EG
51.188106, -2.550641

The late-twentieth-century Townsend Shopping Park occupies the site of Summerleaze Park, a Victorian estate, which provides a clue as to why a mature giant redwood grows on a roundabout in front of Tesco. It is an imposing landmark that adds immeasurable character to an otherwise bland corner. If other supermarkets had such soaring trees on their doorstep, the weekly shop might feel less arduous. ///crossings.whisker.disengage

### 752. BISHOP'S WALNUT
*Black walnut
Juglans nigra*
The Bishop's Palace,
Wells BA5 2PD
51.208994, -2.643358
*Paid entry, ticket allows access for 12 months.*

Thought to have been planted in 1825, this is an exceptional black walnut tree in a truly memorable setting. The enormous, 200-year-old Bishop's Walnut towers over the Bishop's Palace at Wells, and takes centre stage in the late-Georgian pleasure garden it grows in. Those walking the boundaries of the palace cannot fail to see it billowing high above the walls from the south west. ///impresses.haunts.test

TULIP TRIDENT (750)

# DEVON & CORNWALL

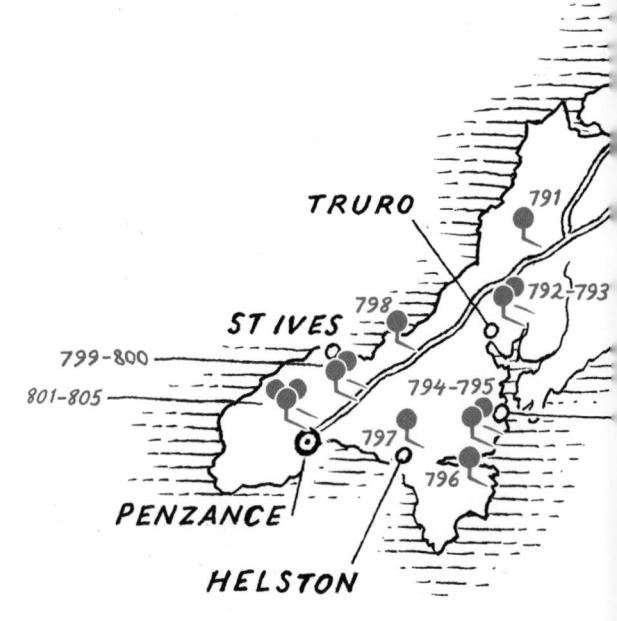

## DEVON & CORNWALL

*Devon*
*Cornwall*

This mild and damp extremity of England has a long history of nurturing trees from far and wide. Stout Californians are much in evidence, but, rather than redwoods, it is Monterey cypresses and pines that are abundant here. Both species can be seen throughout the region, and in Plymouth, this chapter's Tree City, a golden-fringed cultivar of the Monterey cypress, the **WEDDING CAKE CYPRESS (785)**, must be the most photographed tree in the city.

The west of Cornwall, where frost is rare, is famed for subtropical oases like those at the Minack Theatre or Trebah Gardens. But even beyond these rarefied environments, many trees from temperate regions grow in more unlikely places, from St Ives to Falmouth and Penzance. Indeed, anyone arriving at Penzance by train will be struck by the **PZ PALM (802)** that greets station visitors just outside the entrance. This sets the tone for trees that can be seen elsewhere in town. Eucalypts are much in evidence: most are straggly cider gums, but on Morrab Road, a quintessential scene of Edwardian suburbia is punctuated by the **PENLEE GUM (804)**, a billowing blue gum that towers over Chilean myrtles and cabbage trees at the entrance to Penlee Park. Just down the road, a rare New Zealand tree, the **MORRAB TŌTARA (803)** can be seen in lovely Morrab Gardens.

Arboreal curiosities abound throughout Cornwall, from the rare **TREWYN DRIMYS (800)** in St Ives to the bizarrely contorted **SPECULATION BEECH (798)** near Camborne, but it is the epiphytic figs that will be of greatest interest to any tree hunter with a taste for a Cornish yarn. At both St Newlyn East near Newquay and Manaccan on the Lizard, fig trees grow straight out of church walls, mirroring the behaviour of others growing near urban waterways like the **BRISTOL BRIDGE FIG (705)** or Sheffield's **DON FIG (270)**. But these parochial Cornish trees are not close to waterways where merchant vessels once loaded and unloaded. Instead, human intervention may be detected: two centuries ago, Richard Polwhele, clergyman, antiquarian and poet, officiated as the minister first at Manaccan and then at St Newlyn East. Perhaps he planted the trees purposefully on

**TREE CITY:**
*Plymouth*

**SIGNATURE SPECIES:**
*Lucombe oak*

the fabric of the church to illustrate Bible stories. If this was the case, these associations have been forgotten over the years, and the **CURSED FIG (791)** has taken on a more profane legend.

Figs, originally from the Mediterranean region, are one of those species, like sweet chestnuts and mulberries, that have been growing in Britain and Ireland for centuries as a result of early human introduction. Another archaeophyte (an early human import), far rarer than the fig, can be found in Devon: the Plymouth pear. It was first noticed in 1870 and has captured the imagination of botanists ever since. In recent decades, several have been planted around Plymouth, and an exceptional example, **A PLYMOUTH PEAR (771)**, grows near a multi-storey car park at the city's Derriford Hospital.

But we must head to Exeter for the three tree species that really define this region. First is the hybrid Veitch's magnolia, a large, early-March-flowering magnolia represented in the city by the **SOUTHERNHAY HYBRID (760)**. This species was first cultivated and introduced into commerce here by the Veitch dynasty – a family of horticulturalists who ran nurseries in the city from the eighteenth century onwards. The next special tree that Exeter has given the world is the Exeter elm, an elm cultivar with contorted leaves, wonderfully represented by the **COAVER CLUB TREE (761)** at Devon County Hall. Then, finally, there is the mighty Lucombe oak, named after the horticulturalist William Lucombe. This sturdy oak was a chance hybrid between Turkey and cork oaks, which occurred in Lucombe's St Thomas Nursery around 1763. The city is now liberally planted with these magnificent semi-evergreen oak trees; the **EXETER EXEMPLAR (759)** is one of the very best. Lucombe oaks have spread well beyond Exeter, and fine examples can be seen throughout this region and indeed across these islands from Glasgow to Tralee.

### 753. DEVIL'S STONE TREE*
*Pedunculate oak*
*Quercus robur*
Shebbear,
Beaworthy EX21 5RU
50.861565, -4.2198500

The sleepy Devon village of Shebbear is known for the Devil's Stone, a mini megalith that must be turned each 5 November to ensure no bad luck befalls the village. The stone lies on a patch of grass on the edge of the village square next to a fine old pedunculate oak. Depending on which direction the stone has been turned, it is sometimes shaded by this stout and gracious oak. ///clustered.appointed.release

### 754. HOSPITAL GINKGO
*Ginkgo / Ginkgo biloba*
William Street,
Tiverton EX16 6BJ
50.905064, -3.4855770

In 2012, the Victorian Tiverton and District Hospital building on William Street was demolished and replaced by housing. Remarkably, an old ginkgo survived the redevelopment to become the focal point of the new homes. While the twenty-first-century architecture is mediocre, the tree is special, especially in November when its foliage turns gold. ///moved.encounter.above

### 755. CONGREGATIONAL TREE
*Horse chestnut*
*Aesculus hippocastanum*
Honiton Congregational
Church, High Street,
Honiton EX14 1PJ
50.800385, -3.1862410

Honiton grew up along its dead-straight High Street which gently rises from the south west towards twin landmarks. On the left is the tower of bombastic St Paul's church, while on the right, a little further on, is the towering canopy of a horse chestnut. It is a splendid tree that hangs over the road from the garden of the humble congregational chapel. ///soup.slows.detect

### 756. QUERCETUM TITAN → 
The University of Exeter's Streatham campus is a veritable arboretum. Centred around Reed Hall, its grounds are overflowing with unusual trees. Close to the hall, there is a specialist oak collection – a quercetum – where oaks, many rarely seen outside specialist collections, from Europe, Asia and North America grow. It is dominated by a soaring Turkey oak, the biggest tree here by a long shot; its trunk splits into three giant limbs that carry its canopy aloft.

QUERCETUM TITAN *Turkey oak / Quercus cerris* Reed Hall, University of Exeter, Streatham Drive, Exeter EX4 4QR 50.735029, -3.536661 ///bill.copies.aside

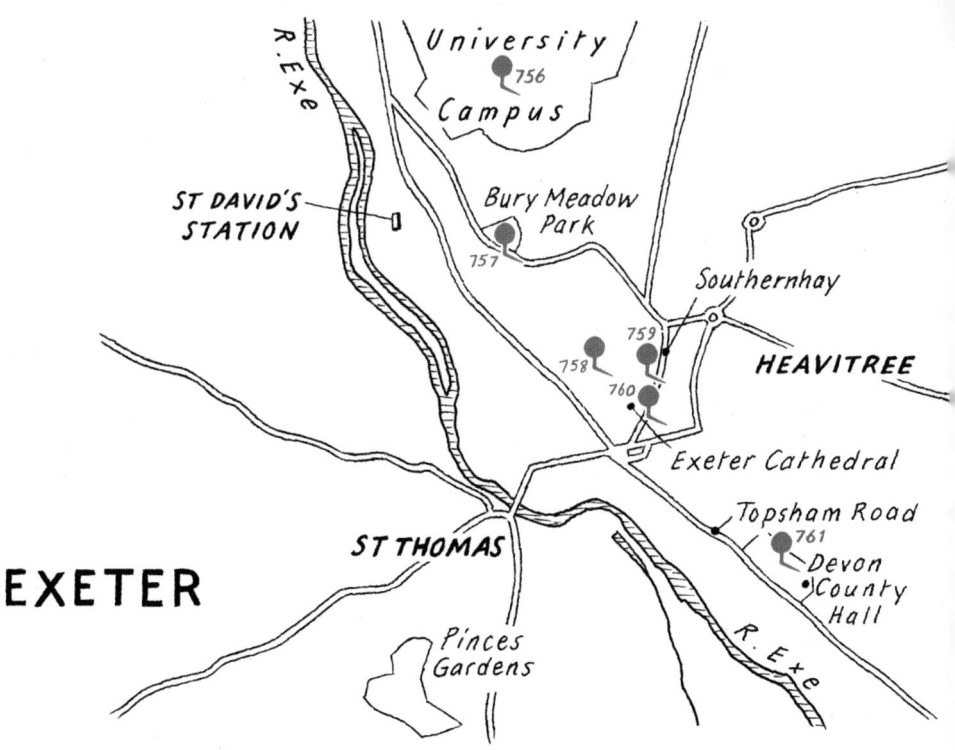

**757. VEITCH'S PIN OAK**
*Pin oak / Quercus palustris*
Bury Meadow,
New North Road,
Exeter EX4 4HH
50.728776, -3.5355960

In 1864, Exeter's famous Veitch nursery moved to a site behind Elm Grove, overlooking Bury Meadows. Trees were installed in the Meadows in 1874, and in all probability the two huge pin oaks dominating the park were part of that planting. The two are similarly stately, but the one on the Elm Grove side is fuller. Sometimes pin oaks can appear haggard, but this is a handsome specimen. ///drew.employ.necks

**758. CATHEDRAL CONKER**
*Horse chestnut*
*Aesculus hippocastanum*
Exeter Cathedral,
Exeter EX1 1HS
50.722981, -3.5297160

Beyond the north transept, the most fantastic horse chestnut adorns Exeter cathedral's grassy close. Generations of Exonians have picnicked in its shade during balmy Devon summers, and have collected its conkers in countless autumns. As with this species all over Britain and Ireland, it is blighted with tiny leaf-mining caterpillars who cause the leaves to appear autumnal in high summer. ///switch.invite.quite

### 759. EXETER EXEMPLAR
*Lucombe oak / Quercus × crenata 'Lucombeana'*
Southernhay West,
Exeter EX1 1JG
50.723089, -3.5267770

Lucombe oaks are to Exeter what planes are to London. But, unlike London planes, they are a hybrid that actually first occurred in the city where they are so abundant. Back in 1762, William Lucombe bred the original tree in his Exeter nursery by cross-pollinating a Turkey oak with a cork oak. A particularly fine example – with a huge, neat dome – can be seen in the central garden of Southernhay, the city's finest Georgian street. ///cards.spoil.spout

### 760. SOUTHERNHAY HYBRID
*Veitch's magnolia
Magnolia × veitchii 'Peter Veitch'*
Southernhay Gardens,
Exeter EX1 1JG
50.721822, -3.5270320

Southernhay has a startling number of impressive trees, but the one to look out for in the southern garden is a hybrid magnolia raised at Veitch's Exeter nursery in 1907. By magnolia standards, it is a tall tree, but here, on the eastern edge of the garden, it is dwarfed by a huge London plane. Visit in March to admire its delightful pinkish-white flowers. ///fact.roofs.humble

### 761. COAVER CLUB TREE
*Exeter elm
Ulmus 'Exoniensis'*
Coaver Club, Matford Lane, Exeter EX2 4PS
50.715408, -3.5184690

The first Exeter elm, a type with distinctive crinkly leaves, arose in a local nursery in 1826 and rapidly became a popular tree for parks and gardens. Although not particularly susceptible to Dutch elm disease, they are now rare, so it is heartening to know they still grow here in their ancestral home. A mature tree, the taller of two, can be seen on the lawn of the Coaver Club close to County Hall. ///riches.holds.wires

### 762. KENN YEW*
*Yew / Taxus baccata*
St Andrew's Church,
Kenn, Exeter EX6 7UR
50.660751, -3.5263390

Kenn, just off the Devon Expressway, has a handsome red-stone church in whose churchyard the village's greatest treasure can be found – a very old and very large yew tree next to the porch. It has a massive short trunk which soon becomes four, surrounding a great hollow in which a large family of humans can comfortably fit. ///walked.under.hasten

### 763. PHEAR GIANT
*Lucombe oak
Quercus × crenata 'Lucombeana'*
Phear Park, Withycombe Village Road,
Exmouth EX8 1TJ
50.624717, -3.40539

One of the oldest and largest Lucombe oaks grows not in Exeter, but just down the road in Exmouth's Phear Park. It is truly massive: measurement confirms it is the Lucombe oak with the greatest girth in England. The Phear Giant displays a distinct graft mark near its base; many Exeter trees are ungrafted, a factor used to differentiate Lucombes from other hybrid Spanish oaks, so this one is unusual. ///saving.launch.backup

### 764. TWO PARKS BEHEMOTH
*Red oak*
*Quercus rubra*
Two Parks, St Agnes Lane, Torquay TQ2 6QE
50.461096, -3.5451640

Appropriately named Two Parks consists of two small green parcels of land separated by Solsbro Road. From this vantage point, the parks' extraordinary red oak, growing in the larger northern portion, can be admired. It is one of the biggest North American red oaks I have seen anywhere, and is in its prime, with strapping, lichen-clad horizontal branches stretching out in all directions. Counterintuitively, red oaks are at their best in spring when dazzling acid yellow new leaves appear. ///birthing.dads.loudness

### 765. RIVIERA PALM
*Canary Island date palm*
*Phoenix canariensis*
Torbay Road, Torquay TQ2 5HA
50.462066, -3.531812

Who could visit Torquay without noticing the palms? They're everywhere, emphasising the area's 'English Riviera' claim. Many are cabbage trees (not a real palm), but there are also plenty of Canary Island date palms distinguishable by their massive pinnate fronds. The best of these are planted in the esplanade gardens on Torbay Road below the cliffs; the central enclosure hosts the most impressive tree. On a grey, rainy day in February, it could transport an intrepid tree hunter to the tropics. ///crown.play.habit

### 766. TORRE OAK
*Pedunculate oak*
*Quercus robur*
Brunel Avenue, Torquay TQ2 8NW
50.462282, -3.5389330

The veteran Torre Oak cuts a suave silhouette on the meadows in front of Torre Abbey, Torquay's historic museum and art gallery. Despite being just 100 metres from the sea, the meadows are well insulated from the rigours of their maritime location, as this magnificent, solitary oak proves. It is said to have been here for 450 years, a claim its burly and timeworn trunk could attest to, and so may be the only living witness to a host of forgotten smuggling operations. ///paid.shield.test

### 767. PLATFORM 2 MONKEY PUZZLE
*Monkey puzzle*
*Araucaria araucana*
Torquay Station, Solsbro Road, Torquay TQ2 6FD
50.460557, -3.5433410

You know you've arrived somewhere interesting when a monkey puzzle greets you off the train, and so it is at Torquay station where a most impressive tree grows on Platform 2. It has clearly been here for decades, cheering countless commuters and impressing hordes of holiday-makers on their way to the seaside, and has been well looked after by generations of railway staff. It may well have been planted as a celebration by a railway, or tree enthusiast when the current station opened in 1876. ///regrowth.buzzer.waters

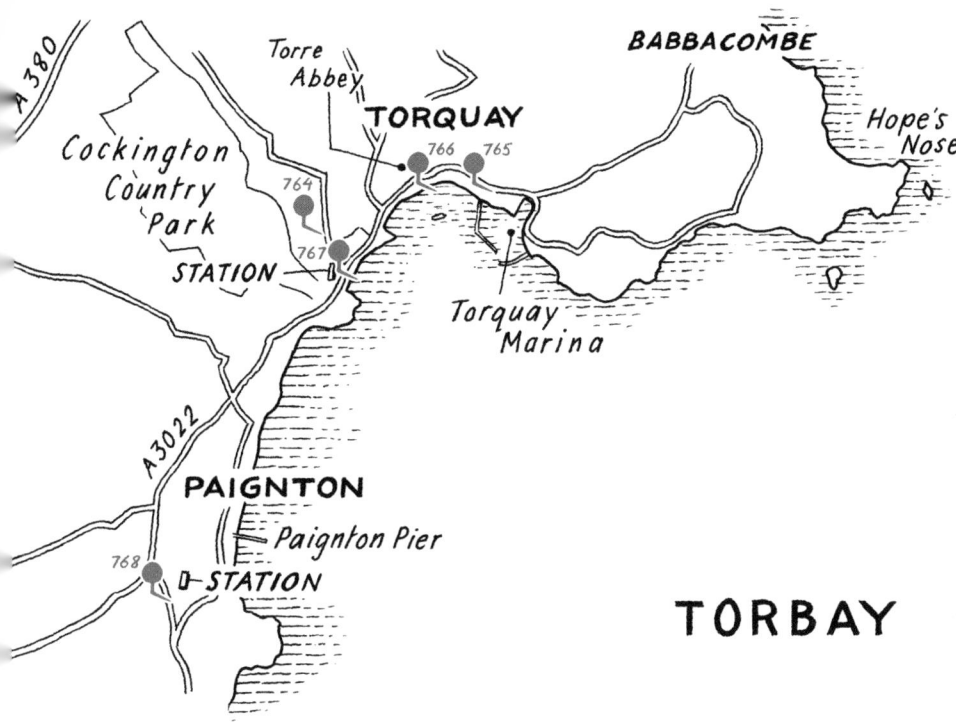

# TORBAY

**768. BACKSTREET OAK**
*Turner's oak*
*Quercus × turneri*
Curledge Street,
Paignton TQ4 5BA
50.433821, -3.5676020

A remarkable tree that eludes many, the Backstreet Oak is tucked away in a jumble of parking spaces, service exits and unloved back gardens, down a lane off Curledge Street. It is an unusual Turner's oak, a hybrid between pedunculate and holm oaks that, down here on the English Riviera, is pretty much evergreen with just a week or two in March when its canpoy thins before spring's new growth appears. ///plot.gains.stacks

**769. MEAVY'S FETED OAK**
*Pedunculate oak*
*Quercus robur*
Meavy, Yelverton
PL20 6PJ
50.486268, -4.0587700

Make for Meavy – a small Dartmoor village with a fine pub, the Royal Oak – to admire Meavy's Feted Oak, the settlement's chief attraction. It is said to be 900 years old which, if so, makes it Devon's oldest oak. Edwardian antiquarian Sabine Baring-Gould described how villagers would clip the tree, construct a platform over it, and embellish it with tables and chairs for the annual fete. The mind boggles. ///condiment.laser.drummers

DEVON & CORNWALL 365

# PLYMOUTH

## TREE CITY: PLYMOUTH
### SIGNATURE SPECIES: *Plymouth pear*

Plymouth's Central Park opened in 1928, leaving its past as farmland behind – though faint traces can be seen in remnant hedgerows. This patchwork landscape has been pulled together by an avenue of elms running through the park, ending at the **CENTRAL PARK ELM (783)**. You can enjoy a fine view from the elm, looking down on the three towns of Plymouth, Stonehouse and Devonport, which merged in the early twentieth century, eventually becoming the City of Plymouth – an event that catalysed the park's creation. In the years that followed, the city expanded to include Plymstock and Plympton to the east having faced widespread destruction during the Second World War. As in London and Coventry, the Blitz is etched emphatically into Plymouth's story. Its effect on the city centre was devastating, requiring complete reconstruction in the postwar years. The result is an optimistic, modernist city of broad avenues centred around Armada Way, a pedestrianised garden-corridor running through the city from North Cross Roundabout to the **WEDDING CAKE CYPRESS (785)** in the south.

There are also many trees to discover across the expansive new suburbs built to replace inner-city housing lost in the Blitz. These developments encroached on villages and countryside that once belonged to rural Devon, meaning that bosky landed estates and ancient woodlands now find themselves amid the twentieth-century suburbs. Widey Woods is one such place – once the grounds of a big house, it is now a popular urban woodland where the **WIDEY OAK* (776)**, Plymouth's oldest tree, grows not far from the **WIDEY BIG TREE (777)**, a contender for the city's largest. At Chaddlewood on the eastern edge of Plympton, the veteran **GARAGE CHESTNUT (772)** grows among 1970s housing, a reminder that this was once the extensive Chaddlewood Estate.

Plymouth's most cherished green space is beyond the sprawling city, requiring a short ferry trip across the Tamar to Cornwall where Mount Edgecumbe offers solace to many. Its historic parkland overlooking Plymouth Sound is lovingly preserved and home to trees of note. The most outlandish of these is the almost impossibly old and collapsing **CORNISH CORK OAK (789)**, one of several old cork oaks growing here, all in fine fettle despite their increasing recumbency.

No account of Plymouth's trees can ignore the Plymouth pear, a rare wild pear species first identified from plants growing in hedges around Eggbuckland during the nineteenth century. Recent research suggests, like the strawberry-tree population in south west Ireland or the sweet chestnut trees across the British Isles, that it is an archaeophyte, introduced by humans in prehistoric times. But whether or not it is, strictly speaking, native, the Plymouth pear is very much the tree of this city. Examples can be seen across town, but the finest is **A PLYMOUTH PEAR (771)**, a large specimen growing close to Derriford Hospital's multi-storey car park.

770. **FATAL OAK*** → The Fatal Oak, also known as the Copleston Oak, is named for Christopher Copleston, a lord of the manor who stabbed his godson to death here in 1562. Whether the oak was standing at that time is a matter of debate. It is certainly old, and its hollowness suggests a ring count to determine its age would be futile.

FATAL OAK* *Pedunculate oak / Quercus robur* Tamerton Foliot Road, Tamerton Foliot, Plymouth PL6 5DR 50.427299, -4.1525870 ///enjoy.chair.flame

771. **A PLYMOUTH PEAR**
*Plymouth pear*
*Pyrus cordata*
Derriford Hospital,
Derriford Road,
Plymouth PL6 8DH
50.416276, -4.1185490

Plymouth's eponymous tree, the Plymouth pear, is one of Britain's rarest, found only in a few places in Devon and Cornwall. It was discovered growing in Eggbuckland in 1865 and remains distinctly uncommon. The tree in Derriford Hospital is an example that you can, unusually, get up close to. See its conspicuous and lovely white blossom in early April, on the grassed area west of the multi-storey car park, but beware its nororious 'rotten scampi' smell. ///fuzzy.report.coast

772. **GARAGE CHESTNUT**
*Sweet chestnut*
*Castanea sativa*
Pode Drive, Plympton,
Plymouth PL7 2XZ
50.384662, -4.0298010

The Plympton district of Chaddlewood shelters under a strip of woodland which has been partly devoured by a 1970s housing estate. Vestiges of the greenwood remain, however, and the most impressive is the aged, but unloved and ivy-clad sweet chestnut whose boughs loom over a row of garages at the end of Pode Drive. ///admiral.sushi.over

773. **STANLEY'S ASH**
*Ash / Fraxinus excelsior*
Hardwick Wood,
Merafield Road,
Plymouth PL7 1UQ
50.382290, -4.0723980

An enigmatic ash sits at the edge of a clearing in little-visited Hardwick Wood where a plaque commemorates Stanley Edgecumbe. Edgecumbe was one of the pioneering founders of the Woodland Trust, which owns Hardwick Wood and four others around Plymouth. The trust started in Devon in 1972 and is now one of the most important conservation charities in the UK. ///blur.fails.nodded

**774. SYCAMORE WALL**
*Sycamore*
*Acer pseudoplatanus*
Saltram, Plympton,
Plymouth PL7 1UH
50.38035, -4.080013
*National Trust property.*

Extraordinary. That's what anyone would think when they first encounter the Sycamore Wall in the car park at Saltram. Seven conjoined trunks are fused together in a row of trees – or should that be tree? It could be that seven individual saplings were planted close together in a hedgerow, or perhaps a single tree was carefully layered by a long-serving gardener decades ago. Extraordinary, and mysterious. ///become.bucket.skills

**775. DOUBLETAKE LEYLANDII**
*Leyland cypress*
× *Cupressocyparis leylandii*
Radford Park, Plymstock,
Plymouth PL9 7NZ
50.355824, -4.1013990

Until recently, Radford Park had a giant redwood that grew next to Hooe Lake. Sadly, that tree fell some years ago, but there are plenty of other youngsters ready to fill the vacancy who may become landmarks in the future. For those mourning the redwood, another admirable conifer awaits in the shape of a Leyland cypress on the opposite lake bank to where the Californian once stood. Surprising, when you consider the bad press *leylandii* hedges get. ///soak.wishes.mole

**776. WIDEY OAK\***
*Pedunculate oak*
*Quercus robur*
Widey Woods, Widey
Lane, Plymouth PL6 5JS
50.403797, -4.1279820

Widey Woods were once part of the Widey Court estate, coming into public ownership during the 1940s. Since then they have become a much-loved urban woodland. Close to the Widey Lane entrance, it's hard to miss the Widey Oak. It is a lapsed pollard – a tree that would have had its upper branches regularly harvested decades or even centuries ago – that now resembles a massive, bristly barrel. ///flops.libraries.pasta

777. **WIDEY BIG TREE** → The **WIDEY OAK\*** (776) is impressive and may be the oldest tree in Plymouth, but another tree in the woods, the Widey Big Tree, is the biggest. It is a huge, spreading Lucombe oak, a hybrid originating in Exeter during the eighteenth century, and this must be an early planting. It is now surrounded by the wood, but those extensive branches show it once grew in the open.

**WIDEY BIG TREE** *Lucombe oak / Quercus × crenata 'Lucombeana'* Widey Woods, Widey Lane, Plymouth PL6 5JS 50.403178, -4.1283210 ///began.learns.cups

### 778. ALLEYWAY JUDAS TREE
*Judas tree*
*Cercis siliquastrum*
Thorn Park,
Plymouth PL3 4TG
50.388705, -4.1314510
*In a private garden, but visible from the street.*

Visitors to Thorn or Mutley Parks should look out for the old Judas tree that hangs over an alleyway on the right just beyond Thorn Park's junction with Mannamead Road. It is a particularly large example that has been here for a century or more, and is at its most impressive in early May when magenta blooms can be seen sprouting straight out of its branches, heralding sunny days ahead. ///insist.vivid.gained

### 779. UNKNOWN QUANTITY
→ Tiny Thorn Park is a lovely corner of Plymouth. It has several fine trees, the most notable of which is a very large, possibly Victorian ginkgo. It grows very close to the perimeter wall – perhaps a sign Victorian gardeners were unsure how big these then-unusual trees would grow – in the park's south-east corner.

**UNKNOWN QUANTITY**
*Ginkgo / Ginkgo biloba*
Thorn Park,
Plymouth PL3 4ST
50.387627, -4.1323820
///bridge.yoga.canny

### 780. MUTLEY MAGNOLIA
*Kobus magnolia*
*Magnolia kobusi*
Mutley Park,
Oxford Avenue,
Plymouth PL3 4SQ
50.387869, -4.1344120

Next to Thorn Park, slightly larger Mutley Park is another of Plymouth's bosky green spaces. Before the park slopes down towards the children's play area, the Mutley Magnolia, a white-flowering kobus magnolia, and its two companions are a rare treat in early spring. Unlike many garden magnolias, this unusual Japanese species has transcended shrub status and is most definitely a tree. ///flames.thinks.maybe

### 781. GOLIATH BEECH
*Beech / Fagus sylvatica*
Mannamead Road,
Plymouth PL3 4SR
50.386225, -4.1317050
*In a private garden, but visible from the street.*

The Goliath Beech, standing on the corner of Mutley Road in the garden of a care home, is a conspicuous landmark on Mannamead Road as it climbs out of town. This is the leafiest part of Plymouth, where many grand Victorian houses sport big trees in spacious and mature gardens, but this towering gentle giant stands head and shoulders above the competition in neighbouring plots. ///cuts.intervals.comic

### 782. STALWART MONKEY PUZZLE
*Monkey puzzle*
*Araucaria araucana*
Ford Park Cemetery,
Ford Park Road,
Plymouth PL4 6NT
50.383153, -4.1409260

Victorian Ford Park Cemetery is well stocked with conifers, but the one that Plymothians have taken to their hearts has featured in many articles and posts over the years. It is the monkey puzzle close to the western entrance on Ford Park Road. The tree, which may well have been planted in 1848, is a veteran of its kind, though when I visited, it did appear to be in need of some TLC. ///speak.rocky.rapid

### 783. CENTRAL PARK ELM
*'Sapporo Autumn Gold' elm / Ulmus 'Sapporo Autumn Gold'*
Central Park,
Plymouth PL2 3DG
50.383584, -4.1501480

Central Park is Plymouth's largest, a hotch-potch of different landscapes pulled together by an elm-lined avenue rising from the pitch-and-putt course to the park's highest point. Up here, by the final elm, a wind-battered *'Sapporo Autumn Gold'*, you can admire one of the best views of the city. But tree hunters will also be transfixed by the tree's elegant twigs, clothed in fine leaves that turn gold in the autumn. ///deflection.reds.chops

### 784. DRAKE'S PLANE
*London plane*
*Platanus × hispanica*
Drake's Place, North Hill,
Plymouth PL4 8AA
50.376092, -4.1370350

Drake's Place is a small park on the edge of the university campus. It was constructed around reservoirs built to provide Plymouth's water and has been restored to its Edwardian glory. Two London plane trees have survived for over a century: the one visible from North Road, to the south of the steps up to the reservoir, is the most striking. ///media.then.than

### 785. WEDDING CAKE CYPRESS
*Golden Monterey cypress*
*Cupressus macrocarpa*
*'Lutea'*
Belvedere Wedding Cake,
Hoe Road,
Plymouth PL1 3DE
50.364449, -4.1441220

Plymouth's most photographed tree must be the Monterey cypress next to its most photographed building, the Wedding Cake on the Hoe, built in 1891 as part of the old pier. The tree was planted some time after the Second World War and has attained a considerable size in that time. Its yellow-tinged foliage suggests it is the *'Lutea'* cultivar, one of several ornamental varieties of the species. ///storms.losses.improving

### 786. LOVELIEST OF CHERRIES
*Great white cherry*
*Prunus serrulata 'Tai Haku'*
Stoke Damerel Park,
Stuart Road,
Plymouth PL1 5LH
50.378005, -4.1575510

The Japanese cultivar name *'Tai Haku'* translates as 'great white' in English. It is easy to see why it bears this name: it is one of the loveliest cherries, with large white flowers and a spreading habit. The tree in the linear park next to the railway at Stoke Damerel is an excellent example. Visit in late March to catch it in flower. ///rooms.groups.beams

### 787. HIDDEN GIANT
*London plane*
*Platanus × hispanica*
Stoke Damerel Church,
Paradise Road,
Plymouth PL1 5QL
50.374825, -4.1618700

From Paradise Road, Stoke Damerel churchyard might appear overgrown, but take a closer look and the huge, spiralling limbs of a veteran London plane arch out of the undergrowth and over the street. The tree is certainly over a century old, and could be approaching two. Inquisitive tree hunters will be keen to discover what other jewels grow in the hidden corners of this unkempt garden. ///tops.neon.served

### 788. INVITING OAK
*Holm oak / Quercus ilex*
Devonport Park,
Devonport,
Plymouth PL1 4BT
50.373989, -4.1706600

Next to the fairytale-gothic lodge at the Fore Street entrance to Devonport Park, a billowing holm oak acts as a familiar landmark at this busy junction. Its giant cupola of a canopy – it almost appears to have been topiarised – should entice you into the park, which is well worth a visit. Plymouth's oldest park is a fine example of Victorian municipal design, with many historic features and a splendid lime avenue. ///clips.spare.eagle

### 789. CORNISH CORK OAK
*Cork oak / Quercus suber*
Mount Edgecumbe,
Cremyll, Torpoint
PL10 1HU
50.357819, -4.1739140

Take the ferry across the Tamar and in just ten minutes you can set foot in Cornwall and Mount Edgecumbe, a country park loved by all who visit. Its wonderful mature gardens date back for more than two centuries and shelter some treasures. The English Gardens, for instance, host several venerable cork oaks. The finest, spongy and supine, is propped on the western edge, taking it easy. ///volume.vibe.flap

CORNISH CORK OAK (789)

VIADUCT EUCALYPTUS (792)

### 790. LISKEARD TWISTER
*Hornbeam*
*Carpinus betulus*
Westbourne Gardens,
Dean Street,
Liskeard PL14 4AE
50.454574, -4.4676280

A very strange tree grows near the centre of Liskeard. A twisted hornbeam has managed to develop branches that fuse into one another, creating intriguing aerial hollows. It is an old tree, and, because hornbeams are outside their natural range in Cornwall, it was probably planted as part of a hedgerow or as a boundary marker, which could explain how it acquired such a form. ///stretch.imprinted.outlooks

### 791. CURSED FIG
*Fig / Ficus carica*
St Newlina, Churchtown,
St Newlyn East,
Newquay TR8 5LQ
50.366820, -5.0542810

At the beginning of the nineteenth century, Richard Polwhele was vicar of Newlyn East. He had previously performed this duty in Manaccan on the Lizard. In both churchyards, fig trees grow mysteriously from the church walls. The Cursed Fig of Newlyn East is larger and less regularly pruned, perhaps for fear of its associated hex: 'Upon it lies a dreadful curse; Who plucks a leaf will need a hearse.' ///contacts.linked.ulterior

### 792. VIADUCT EUCALYPTUS
*Alpine ash*
*Eucalyptus delegatensis*
Victoria Gardens,
St George's Road,
Truro TR1 3JE
50.264594, -5.0586410

Victoria Gardens in Truro is a small park nestling under the railway viaduct. The Victorian brickwork is partly screened by several giant eucalypts. On the banks of the River Kenwyn, one of the trees has departed from the orderly character of its siblings and great boughs lean over the park. Enormous strips of peeling bark hanging off these horizontal limbs ensure this tree stands out. ///moss.knots.anyway

### 793. CATHEDRAL OAK
*Holm oak / Quercus ilex*
Truro Cathedral,
St Mary's Street,
Truro TR1 2AF
50.264513, -5.0506280

There is little room for trees around Truro's Victorian cathedral, which lies in the middle of the city's shopping district, but a shapely evergreen holm oak just north of the east end provides some respite from the stone, concrete and glass. Holm oaks are common on the south coast, but they become less frequent in west Cornwall, where this tree might be considered something of a curiosity. ///pages.type.inform

### 794. BEACHED STONE PINE
*Stone pine / Pinus pinea*
Grove Place, Falmouth
TR11 4AU
50.150887, -5.063699

Land has been reclaimed from the sea along Bar Road in Falmouth since the Beached Stone Pine was planted, so it would have begun life much closer to the water, cutting an even more romantic silhouette than it does today. Even so, the tree remains an enduring landmark, upholding the elemental boundary between land and sea. ///spin.actual.keep

**795. DOUBLE-TRUNKED TULIP**
*Tulip tree / Liriodendron tulipifera*
Fox Rosehill Gardens,
Melvill Road,
Falmouth TR11 4DE
50.148057, -5.0703070

Of all Cornwall's freely accessible gardens, Fox Rosehill is the most exquisite. It is a subtropical oasis next to the Falmouth University campus overflowing with an impressive array of rare and tender trees. Despite this abundance, it is a relatively common tree that stands out: the enormous double-trunked tulip tree. It was planted in 1918, almost a century after the gardens were established. ///rather.boom.pokers

**796. MANACCAN FIG**
*Fig / Ficus carica*
St Manaccus and
St Dunstan Church,
Manaccan, Helston
TR12 6HN
50.083158, -5.1270790

Sleepy Manaccan is tucked away on the sheltered eastern side of the Lizard peninsula, where its picturesque church tower hosts a curious epiphyte. A metre or more from the ground, a fig tree grows, miraculously, straight out of the masonry, and has done for a century or more. It is regularly cut back to avoid it becoming a destabilising guest. ///tinted.dishing.nanny

**797. PARAGON PINE**
*Monterey pine
Pinus radiata*
St Mary's Church, Church
Lane, Helston TR13 8GT
50.103291, -5.2771820

Huge Monterey pines are one of Cornwall's defining tree species. Often planted for shelter around fields, they stud the landscape particularly in the west of the county. There are few opportunities for close examination, but the magnificent tree in Helston's parish churchyard allows the curious to admire its tremendous fissured bark. ///skidding.hype.plump

**798. SPECULATION BEECH**
*Beech /Fagus sylvatica*
Tehidy Country Park,
TR14 0EZ.
50.244731, -5.3018830

How this old beech tree not far from the exposed cliffs of north Cornwall took on its remarkable form is a matter for speculation. Several distinct serpentine strands have twisted together to create a fat bole, resembling a thick, spiralling cable. The memorable trunk is supported by a lattice of exposed roots, while bark pockmarked by decades of arborglyph carving is testament to its long-established landmark status. ///hardly.otherwise.happily

**799. INFLUENCER PALM**
*Cabbage tree
Cordyline australis*
Quay Street,
St Ives, TR26 1PT
50.215516, -5.4771870

Thousands walk past this palm every day in high summer, and many photos have been taken beneath this most Instagrammable of trees. Unlike the PZ PALM (802), it is not a true palm tree; rather it is a New Zealand cabbage tree, also known as a Cornish palm owing to the species' ubiquity in these parts. It is the only plant you have to look up to admire on Quay Street overlooking Harbour Beach. ///corkscrew.bunks.conclude

### 800. TREWYN DRIMYS
*Winter's bark*
*Drimys winteri*
Trewyn Gardens,
Richmond Place,
St Ives TR26 1AG
50.212578, -5.4817790

Trewyn Gardens is St Ives's secret pocket park. At its north-western entrance on Richmond Place an unusual multi-stemmed evergreen can be seen. It is a Winter's bark, a rare tree recorded in Chile by Captain Winter in the 1500s and introduced to the British Isles in the 1800s. Its aromatic bark was used to ward off scurvy, an appropriate choice for a town with rich nautical traditions. Come in March to catch it in flower. ///empires.edges.stockpile

### 801. JUNCTION CHESTNUT
*Sweet chestnut*
*Castanea sativa*
The Alms Houses, Gulval,
Penzance TR18 3BH
50.132533, -5.5281360

Just outside Penzance, the road to St Ives passes through the village of Gulval, where the junction with School Lane is marked by an old sweet chestnut, an unusual species for west Cornwall, standing sentinel on the lawn of the Alms Houses. They were built in 1903, but the tree, a maiden with no sign of pollarding, is clearly older, raising a question: what was here before the buildings? ///pockets.centuries.exit

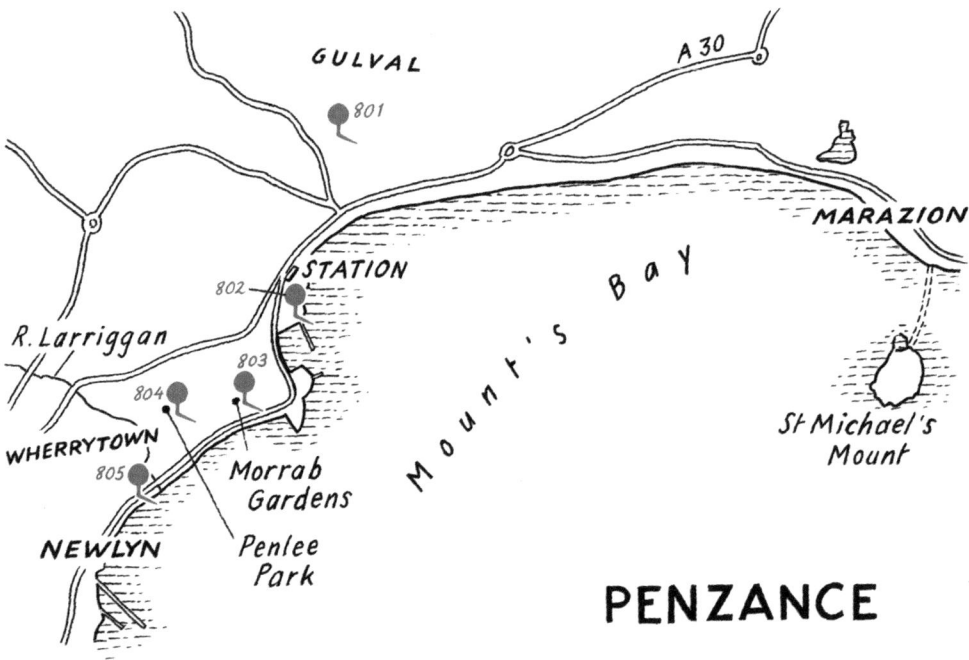

802. **PZ PALM** → Welcoming visitors and residents alike for nearly twenty years, the PZ Palm has managed considerable growth since it was planted in the early 2000s. It is the tallest of three Canary Island date palms at the entrance to Penzance station, and is framed by a giant steel 'P' and 'Z', an earlier attempt to mark the Cornish terminus of the Great Western Railway.

**PZ PALM** *Canary Island date palm / Phoenix canariensis* Penzance Railway Station, Station Road, Penzance TR18 2NF 50.121591, -5.5326480 ///monk.gave.lyricist

803. **MORRAB TŌTARA**
*Tōtara*
*Podocarpus tōtara*
Morrab Gardens,
Morrab Road,
Penzance TR18 4HD
50.116362, -5.5368950

Resplendent in the clump of ornamental planting to the south of the fountain in subtropical Morrab Gardens, a tōtara dominates. Looking rather like a yew tree, these tender conifers rarely prosper beyond mild Cornwall, but in their native New Zealand they can become very old and very large. In temperate Penzance, the Morrab Tōtara could be an unusual landmark of the future. ///crank.items.blur

804. **PENLEE GUM**
*Blue gum*
*Eucalyptus globulus*
Penlee Park,
Penzance TR18 4HY
50.116605, -5.5393330

English suburbia meets Australian grandeur on Morrab Road, where the handsome Penlee Gum marks a break in the Edwardian terrace lining this street. It is a blue gum, a fast-growing, tender eucalypt from Tasmania. Its billowing canopy shades the entrance to Penlee House and Gardens, one of Penzance's delightful parks filled with unruly and unfamiliar plants that thrive in Cornwall's climate. ///purely.vessel.twins

805. **WHERRYTOWN CHERRY**
*'Shirotae' Japanese cherry*
*Prunus serrulata*
*'Shirotae'*
Mann's Field, Lariggan
Road, Penzance TR18 4NJ
50.111268, -5.5452620

Broad-canopied *'Shirotae'* cherries have white flowers that are subtly pink-tinged as they first open. The fine example in Mann's Field is the sole survivor of three ornamental cherries planted decades ago. It is just metres away from the sea and has withstood many Atlantic gales and years of salty spray, but it still flowers reliably and beautifully each April. ///gosh.advising.parading

PZ PALM (802)

# SOUTH & WEST WALES

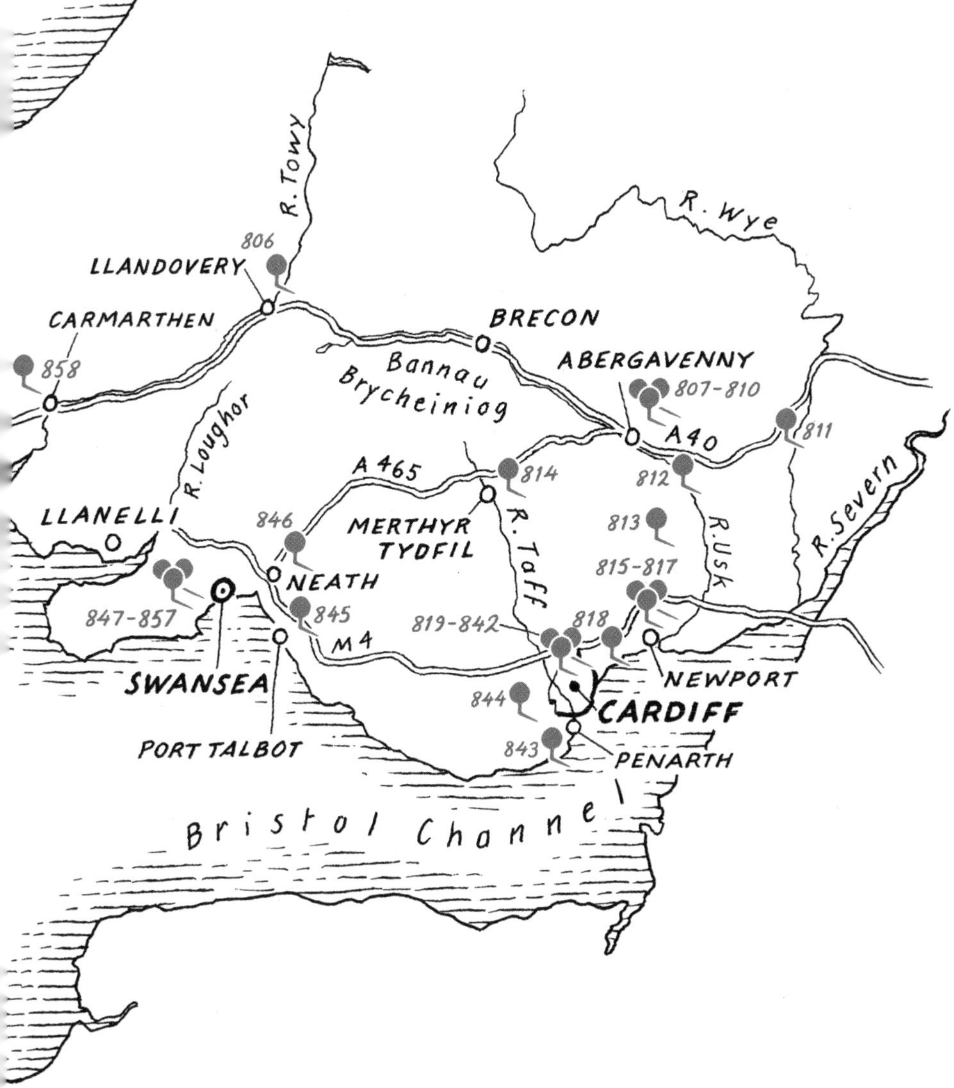
R. Towy
806
LLANDOVERY
CARMARTHEN
858
R. Wye
BRECON
Bannau
Brycheiniog
ABERGAVENNY
807-810
A40
811
R. Loughor
A 465
814
812
MERTHYR
TYDFIL
846
LLANELLI
813
R. Taff
R. Usk
R. Severn
NEATH
815-817
847-857
845
819-842
818
M4
SWANSEA
NEWPORT
844
CARDIFF
843
PORT TALBOT
PENARTH
Bristol Channel

## SOUTH & WEST WALES

*Pembrokeshire*
*Carmarthenshire*
*Swansea*
*Neath Port Talbot*
*Bridgend*
*Rhondda Cynon Taff*
*Vale of Glamorgan*
*Cardiff*
*Caerphilly*
*Newport*
*Monmouthshire*
*Torfaen*
*Blaenau Gwent*
*Merthyr Tydfil*

TREE CITY:
*Cardiff*

SIGNATURE SPECIES:
*Monterey cypress*

As you head west, beyond the towns and cities of south Wales, settlements become fewer and the coast becomes more dramatic. Inland, the green, green valleys and vast tracts of treeless uplands are thinly populated. Still, the hills and valleys of the Bannau Brycheiniog and its foothills occasionally reward the tree hunter with delightful market towns like Llandovery, home of the COLLEGE CHESTNUT (806), or Abergavenny, where the PEN-Y-POUND OAK (809) is a landmark. But the major settlements in this rural region lie near the sea, and it is in these places that the treasure trove of Welsh urban trees can be found.

Either side of Cardiff, Wales's great Tree City, the next-largest towns of Swansea and Newport hug the Bristol Channel. Like the Welsh capital, their mild coastal aspects have encouraged adventurous tree planting. If you are in Newport, head to Belle Vue and Beechwood Parks for particularly interesting conifers. The NEWPORT NEEDLE (815) in Beechwood Park is a tall, thin Serbian spruce, a species only occasionally seen in Britain, and this is one of the finest. Meanwhile, Belle Vue Park is Newport's best, its clever nineteenth-century design occupying a steep slope, and offering splendid views over the channel and the town's famous Transporter Bridge. One of the best places to admire this view is from BIG FOOT (816), a remarkable giant redwood that is a sturdy example of this iconic species in every respect except for the huge, inexplicable, bulbous growth – resembling a miniature Uluru – that has developed at its base.

Swansea likewise boasts significant green spaces with excellent trees to hunt. Both Singleton Park and Clyne Gardens are the legacy of the aristocratic Vivian family, and both are home to fantastic tree collections; these are complemented, in turn, by the many other remarkable trees growing throughout the city. Swansea's most fabulous tree must be the BRYN TULIP TREE (852), a huge and sprawling individual that is partially hidden among woodland. Unlike other old tulip trees, this one has spread out rather than grown tall, and its ivy-clad trunk needs close inspection if you are to appreciate how large it is. Swansea's other arboreal gems are easier to find, but they are anything but pedestrian. There are great rarities doing well here, like the **BOTANICAL SPINNING GUM (851)**, an Australian *Eucalyptus* with distinctively colourful bark that spirals, or spins, around its curving trunk; the **GARGANTUAN TEPA (849)**, a solid, moss-clad Chilean tepa, a very rare tree indeed; and the **CWMDONKIN KATSURA (847)**, a prime example of an elegant Japanese species growing in one of Swansea's immaculate parks.

The richness of Swansea's tree canopy is something it is justly proud of, but, as is the way with second cities, it will inevitably be compared to that of Cardiff. Cardiff's trees are second to none. It has two botanical collections in its public parks, and many rare trees that are the most impressive examples of their species in Wales – and frequently, like **BIG DADDY (830)**, in Britain and Ireland too. But the arboreal characters of Swansea and Cardiff are entirely different. Cardiff'stree planting is more formal and civic, whereas Swansea's canopy is more verdant and surprising, aided, perhaps, by its seaside location.

### 806. COLLEGE CHESTNUT
*Sweet chestnut*
*Castanea sativa*
Llandovery College,
Queensway,
Llandovery SA20 0EE
51.994758, -3.800311
*On private land, but visible from the street.*

At the peak of maturity, sweet chestnuts can be fabulous, and in summer their lustrous leaves give them a particularly fecund appearance. The Llandovery College Chestnut is tall and thick-bodied, its twin trunks raising up a well-rounded canopy that stands proudly near the entrance of Llandovery College. It is a tree with more than a century or two behind it and many more before it. ///bluff.cycled.brass

### 807. LINDA VISTA PLANE
*London plane*
*Platanus × hispanica*
Linda Vista Gardens,
Abergavenny NP7 5DL
51.821111, -3.023364

Compare the TENNIS PLANE (808) with the Linda Vista Plane to appreciate the differences between the closely related oriental and London plane species. Both trees are huge and were likely planted within a few years of each other, but their leaves and fruits differ. The towering tree south west of the house in Linda Vista Gardens has less incised leaves and fewer seedballs than its relative, but is equally lovely. ///totals.polka.models

### 808. TENNIS PLANE
*Oriental plane*
*Platanus orientalis*
Hill Road,
Abergavenny NP7 7RN
51.828981, -3.022971
*In a private garden, but visible from the street.*

The PEN-Y-POUND OAK (809) impresses, but the Tennis Plane is in another league. It is a vast oriental plane, one of the largest anywhere in these islands, hidden away in the tennis club on Hill Road. Despite growing inside the club's grounds and being set back from the road, its massive canopy can be appreciated by anyone travelling down the street. Look out for the distinctly dissected leaves. ///refilled.snips.baseless

### 809. PEN-Y-POUND OAK → Abergavenny has several surprising trees, all exceptional examples of their species. Not bad for a small market town with a population of less than 15,000. One of these surprises is the striking Lucombe oak, a landmark growing at the southern end of the playing fields on Pen-y-Pound. It is an old tree that has been open-grown, resulting in a wonderfully broad, even crown.

PEN-Y-POUND OAK *Lucombe oak / Quercus × crenata 'Lucombeana'*
Pen-y-Pound, Abergavenny NP7 7RN 51.827525, -3.021575 ///boil.drift.duplicity

810. **BEACON OAK** → Govilon, perched on the north-facing slopes of the Usk Valley, has panoramic views of the Bannau Brycheiniog and the iconic peak of Sugarloaf Mountain. The view is particularly fine where School Lane and Cwm Road diverge, a point marked by the veteran Beacon Oak. From Cwm Road, the tree's plump trunk reveals itself to be hollow.

**BEACON OAK** *Hybrid oak / Quercus × rosacaea* School Lane, Govilon, Abergavenny NP7 9RH
51.815802, -3.066383 ///motive.dreaming.snares

811. **MONMOUTH CATALPA**
*Southern catalpa*
*Catalpa bignonioides*
St James' Square,
Monmouth NP25 3DN
51.813053, -2.71106

To the south west of Monmouth town centre, handsome St James' Square is lined with grand Georgian houses and quaint cottages. The square could better be described as a triangle, and the parcel of greenery at its centre is distinguished by an ancient-looking and tangled southern catalpa. Like mulberries, catalpas age rapidly; this veteran is thought to have been planted in 1900. ///limiting.shifting.catapult

812. **BETTWS NEWYDD YEW\***
*Yew / Taxus baccata*
St Aeddan, Bettws
Newydd, Usk NP15 1JN
51.747938, -2.92557

The Bettws Newydd Yew has the distinction of being Wales's fattest. It grows in the picturesque churchyard of St Aeddan in a tiny Monmouthshire village. It has an outer shell of burry growth, much now lifeless, surrounding a great hollow with an internal trunk that is, on the contrary, full of life, a frequent feature of very old yews. ///envoy.daylight.repeated

813. **OLD SWEET CHESTNUT OF PONTYPOOL**
*Sweet chestnut*
*Castanea sativa*
Pontypool Park,
Pontypool NP4 8AT
51.701744, -3.031467

Pontypool Park was laid out 300 years ago for a local ironmaster, only becoming a public park in the early twentieth century. Since then, generations of Pontypudlian kids have made good use of the Old Sweet Chestnut of Pontypool, an ancient and much-loved tree. It is hollow and has plenty of dead wood, an important habitat for a range of other life, including red-winged click beetles and chicken of the woods. ///singer.caring.chin

BIG FOOT (816)

**814. MERTHYR GIANT**
*Giant redwood*
*Sequoiadendron*
*giganteum*
Thomastown Park,
Queen's Road, Merthyr
Tydfil CF47 0ET
51.746348, -3.371626

Thomastown Park was Merthyr's first, opening in 1902 on the site of a former quarry, then on the eastern edge of town. Like many parks of this period, it was an attempt to bring green space within easy reach of the people of a burgeoning industrial town. Today it is much loved, and has many mature trees, the finest being a spectacular giant redwood, with spongy bark that is hard to resist caressing. ///chief.caked.desire

**815. NEWPORT NEEDLE**
*Serbian spruce*
*Picea omorika*
Beechwood Park,
Newport NP19 8AJ
51.593103, -2.964214

Beechwood Park is one of Newport's delights and, like Belle Vue Park, is thought to have been designed by Thomas Mawson, whose other work includes Burslem Park in Stoke-on-Trent. While there are plenty of beeches at Beechwood, it is an unusual conifer that is exceptional here, in the needle-like form of a particularly tall and slim Serbian spruce. ///cheese.begin.pilots

**816. BIG FOOT**
*Giant redwood*
*Sequoiadendron giganteum*
Belle Vue Park, Waterloo
Road, Newport NP20 4FP
51.578927, -3.000108

Big Foot is a strange Californian with a conspicuous feature. A maturing giant redwood in Belle Vue Park (with fine views out to the Bristol Channel) has developed a massive, swollen 'foot' at the base of its trunk. Resembling a rocky outcrop, this orangey-brown protuberance has attracted kids for years, and has been worn smooth from all their attention. ///trip.coats.beyond

**817. STATELY CHESTNUT**
*Sweet chestnut*
*Castanea sativa*
Tredegar House,
Coedkernew,
Newport NP10 8YW
51.562271, -3.027337

The chestnut at Tredegar House on the edge of Newport is thought to have been growing here for 280 years, even longer than the 250-year-old cedar of Lebanon on the southern side of this seventeenth-century stately home. It is a tree that has taken on veteran characteristics – its trunk is swollen, its crown uneven and, most tellingly, a fence has been erected around it. ///cubs.spins.lively

**818. CEFN MABLY OAK\***
*Pedunculate oak*
*Quercus robur*
The Cefn Mably Arms,
Michaelston Road,
Michaelston-y-Fedw
CF3 6XS
51.555021, -3.095799

The focal points for many villages are the twin institutions of church and pub. Michaelston-y-Fedw has good examples of both; right next door to the solid church, the Cefn Mably Arms is one of the most popular pubs around. It is particularly memorable for its oak, a corpulent old lapsed pollard growing in front of the pub, rather too close to the car park, leaving cars with just a few millimetres of space to squeeze past its bloated bole. ///sprinkler.help.truth

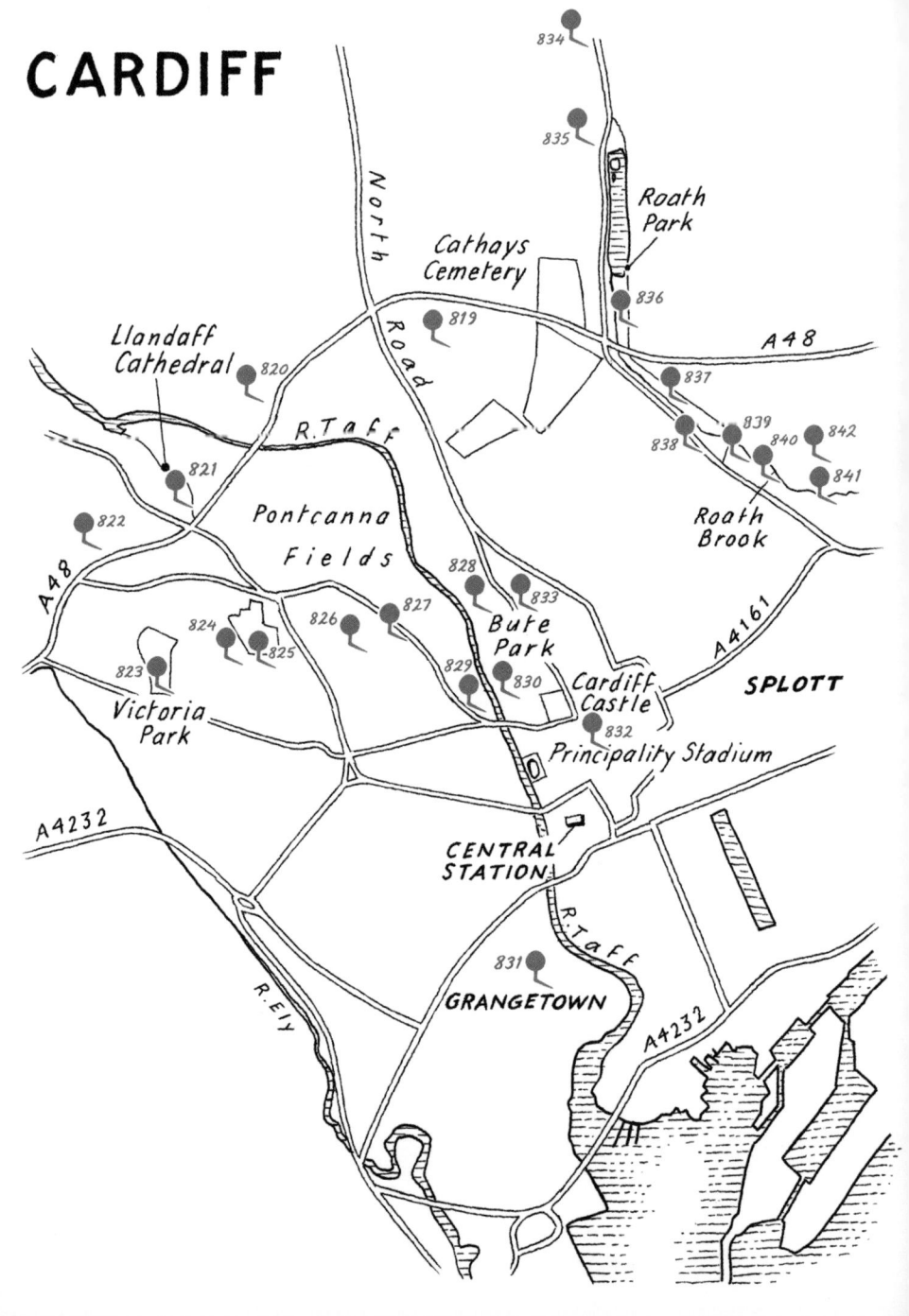

# TREE CITY: CARDIFF
## SIGNATURE SPECIES: *Hybrid wingnut*

Standing under **ST JOHN'S HONEY LOCUST (832)** in the centre of Cardiff is instructive. It is probably less than forty years old, and grows in the gardens next to St John the Baptist, the city's parish church, with its fine fifteenth-century perpendicular tower. Apart from the castle it is the only building older than about 170 years in the city centre.

The tree demonstrates Cardiff's commitment to exciting, diverse tree planting, while its surroundings illustrate that this city is, relatively speaking, young. Cardiff grew rapidly at the end of the nineteenth century, and little of its past can be seen – the medieval street pattern around the church is all that reminds us there was anything here before the docks were built and the railways arrived. Beyond the centre, Cardiff comprises Victorian and Edwardian suburbs, divided by the green wedge of Bute Park and the River Taff.

Bute Park is home to an impressive botanical collection consisting of trees planted for the Marquess of Bute's private garden and many more planted since 1947, when the fifth Marquess gifted the park to the city. The most impressive is **BIG DADDY (830)**, a huge hybrid wingnut planted next to the Taff at the eastern end of the Millennium Bridge. Wingnuts are only rarely encountered, hybrid wingnuts especially so, and, while there is only one hybrid in Cardiff, it is so magnificent and so redolent of the city's astonishing tree collection, it should be regarded as its signature tree.

Along with the Butes, it was their gardeners who had the greatest impact on Cardiff's environment. Of these, Andrew Pettigrew – who worked for the third Marquess in the 1860s – had a particularly decisive influence on the cityscape. Over several generations, the Pettigrew family were to become a gardening dynasty who not only planted trees, but designed parks and influenced how whole neighbourhoods were laid out.

The last Pettigrew responsible for Cardiff's green spaces died in 1936 and was replaced by William Nelmes, a Kew-trained horticulturalist who proved to be as foresighted as his antecedents, and equally dynastic: in turn, he gave way to his son also called William Nelmes.

Between them, the Pettigrews and the Nelmes were responsible for the planting and care of Cardiff's trees for over a century. Their legacy, reaching its zenith only now, is evident right across the city. This clarity of approach, gained through inherited knowledge and a shared vision, is palpable in a city that today boasts two important botanical collections and continues to be a pioneer in urban tree planting. Cardiff has trees that are among the finest of their kind throughout Britain and Ireland. **VICTORIA'S SECRET (823)**, **ANOTHER SWEETGUM (841)** and the **SANDRINGHAM STINGER (839)** are all exceptional specimens of trees that are rarely found outside specialist collections. Unusually, in Cardiff, these collections are housed in public parks.

If there is a city in these islands that could claim to be an 'Arboretum City', Cardiff is it.

BISHOP'S FIG (821)

### 819. INCONGRUOUS CEDAR
*Cedar of Lebanon*
*Cedrus libani*
Heathfield Road
Cardiff CF14 3ND
51.503355, -3.192139

Towering over the estate agents, minimarkets and fast-food outlets of Whitchurch Road, one of Cardiff's most surprising trees can be seen. It is a giant cedar of Lebanon that must have been here before the turn-of-the-century terraces were laid out. The tree now grows, almost miraculously, in a small, rather unloved parklet on the corner of Heathfield Road, from where it must gladden the hearts of thousands. ///store.drew.comet

### 820. GABALFA GINKGO
*Ginkgo / Ginkgo biloba*
Western Drive,
Cardiff CF14 2SE
51.50004, -3.208528

Where Western Drive meets Gabalfa Avenue a shapely maturing ginkgo grows from the pavement. It is emblematic of the forward-thinking approach Cardiff City Council has taken to tree planting. While ginkgos are now frequent street trees, the Gabalfa Ginkgo is a pioneer, having been planted years before most in city streets elsewhere. ///pigs.modes.fancy

### 821. BISHOP'S FIG
*Fig / Ficus carica*
Bishop's Palace Gardens,
The Cathedral Green,
Cardiff CF5 2DX
51.494408, -3.217364

Llandaff's Bishop's Palace Gardens became a public park in the 1970s, at which time much tree planting was carried out. The mulberries on the lawn are noteworthy, but are only fifty years old, proving how difficult it is to determine the age of these rapidly ageing trees. The fig tree against the far wall, however, is older, and is well worth a closer look to admire its stocky, spiralling trunk. ///front.order.that

### 822. INSOLE SWEETGUM
*American sweetgum*
*Liquidambar styraciflua*
Insole Court, Fairwater Road, Cardiff CF5 2LN
51.491847, -3.224727

Cardiff's wealth was built on coal-fired industry and shipping. Insole Court, the Victorian estate of industrialist James Harvey Insole, is a key part of that legacy. Now in public ownership, its ornamental gardens are one of Cardiff's delights. A kobus magnolia in the car park offers a taste of the treasures within. Once inside, check out the mature American sweetgum with its star-spangled canopy near a copper beech. ///charge.offer.fears

### 823. VICTORIA'S SECRET
*Large-flowered spindle*
*Euonymus grandiflorus*
Victoria Park, Victoria Park Road East,
Cardiff CF5 1EH
51.4836, -3.2194

Victoria Park typifies the exceptional quality of Cardiff's parks. It is relatively small, beautifully maintained and extensively planted with interesting trees, some dating back to the park's opening in 1897. The best is an exceedingly rare Asian spindle tree growing in the south-west corner between Victoria Park Road West and the children's playground. Creamy flowers appear in June, followed by pink berries. ///brains.third.blame

**824. TRIANGLE TREE**
*Horse chestnut*
*Aesculus hippocastanum*
Clive Road,
Cardiff CF5 1GL
51.485891, -3.212426

The late-Victorian grid of Canton is disrupted where Clive Road meets Romilly Road. The streets broaden, a small grassy triangle appears, there's a corner shop and a zebra crossing. But this little neighbourhood is defined by the horse chestnut which grows at the triangle's centre, casting its benign shade across the streets and acting as a cheering local landmark and kids' conker-supplier. ///racing.bigger.engage

**825. THOMPSON'S PARK COASTAL REDWOOD**
*Coastal redwood*
*Sequoia sempervirens*
Thompson's Park,
Syr David's Avenue,
Cardiff CF5 1GH
51.486026, -3.208745

Thompson's Park, like Cardiff's other parks, has plenty of interesting trees to admire. It comprises two distinct parts: an upper park and a more ornamental lower park, complete with mini lake. On the northern edge of the water, a towering conifer grows. It is a coastal redwood, a representative of the tallest tree species in the world, which one day might be Cardiff's tallest tree. ///rings.pencil.edgy

**826. PONTCANNA PLANE**
*Baobab London plane*
*Platanus × hispanica*
'Western Baobab'
St Catherine, King's Road,
Cardiff CF11 9DG
51.48546, -3.199043

A pair of lovably lumpy planes grow on either side of the gate of St Catherine's church in Pontcanna. I prefer the southern tree; it is, quite frankly, lumpier and lovelier. All three Cardiff examples of this unusual cultivar are similar: less rotund than the baobab London planes in southern England, they more closely resemble their friends in Ireland. I have dubbed them the 'Western Baobab'. ///rushed.forgot.animal

**827. CATHEDRAL ROAD LIME\***
*Common lime*
*Tilia × europaea*
Cathedral Road,
Cardiff CF11 9PG
51.485837, -3.195015

In the late 1800s, Cathedral Road was Cardiff's most sought-after residential address, but today the big houses have become offices for solicitors and accountants who must, in part, be drawn by the grand Victorian lime trees that line it. One tree in particular, about halfway up on the western side, has a double trunk and is so impressive that it has been a contender for Wales's Tree of the Year. ///paints.vows.tooth

**828. CELESTIAL MAPLE**
*Mono maple / Acer pictum*
Bute Park, North Road,
Cardiff CF10 3ER
51.487805, -3.188994

Bute Park's arboretum clusters around the visitor centre, and, like Roath Park's botanical garden, is a nationally important tree collection within a public park. Dozens of exceptional trees grow here, but there is a focus on maples. One of the best is an unusual mono maple, a handsome east Asian species with starburst leaves. ///varieties.tolls.doctor

**829. TAFF MAPLE**
*Silver maple*
*Acer saccharinum*
Sophia Gardens,
Cardiff CF11 9SZ
51.482226, -3.187652

Sophia Gardens, across the Taff from Bute Park, is part of the array of parks that together form a green corridor running right into the city centre. It has been densely planted with mature trees. East of the lodge and close to Cowbridge Road grows a towering silver maple, one of the finest examples in Wales or beyond. ///zest.detect.onion

**830. BIG DADDY** →→ On the Bute Park side of the Millennium Bridge, on the banks of the Taff, grows a tree that resembles the **MONSTER WINGNUT (840)** – except it's double the size. This is a hybrid wingnut, a rare type that counts the Caucasian species as one of its parents. It is the largest of its kind anywhere in the world, and must be Cardiff's largest, and greatest, tree.

**BIG DADDY**
*Hybrid wingnut*
*Pterocarya ×*
*rehderiana*
Millennium Bridge,
Bute Park, North Road,
Cardiff CF10 3ER
51.484085, -3.187608
///return.races.valley

**831. GRANGETOWN BAOBAB**
*Baobab London plane*
*Platanus × hispanica*
*'Western Baobab'*
Grange Gardens,
Holmesdale Street,
Cardiff CF11 7BW
51.467429, -3.182411

Neat Grange Gardens is a small late-Victorian park in the geometric neighbourhood of Grangetown. Near the children's playground on its northern edge, a most ungeometric tree grows: a short, fat and knobbly London plane with characteristics of a *'Western Baobab'* type. It is quite different to the other planes in the park, which take the orderly ambience more seriously. ///bought.hers.exact

832. **ST JOHN'S HONEY LOCUST** → Medieval St John's parish church is one of the few really old buildings in Cardiff, an otherwise Victorian and Edwardian city. It occupies a prominent position in the city centre, and its small churchyard is a rare green space in this part of town. From the churchyard, a beautiful 'Sunburst' honey locust hangs over pedestrianised Working Street opposite Queen's Arcade, adding a dramatic splash of gold in early summer.

**ST JOHN'S HONEY LOCUST**
*Honey locust / Gleditsia triacanthos 'Sunburst'*
St John's Churchyard Gardens, Working Street,
Cardiff CF10 1BH
51.480689, -3.177906
///jazzy.rails.fades

### 833. MUSIC TREE
*Japanese maple*
*Acer palmatum*
Cardiff University School
of Music, Corbett Road,
Cardiff CF10 3EB
51.489098, -3.18345

Against the wall of Cardiff University School of Music, Barbara Hepworth's sculpture *Three Obliques (Walk In)* is juxtaposed with the Music Tree. The tree is Wales's best example of a Japanese maple. It will continue to spread as it grows, so sensitive management will be required to ensure these two icons continue to cohabit harmoniously. ///marked.free.risen

### 834. SIGHT FOR SORE EYES
*Deodar cedar / Cedrus deodara*
Llandennis Oval,
Llandennis Road,
Cardiff CF23 6EE
51.518233, -3.177658

The northernmost exclave of Roath Park, Llandennis Oval, is a small space thickly planted with a good mix of trees around a holy well – Ffynnon Llandennis – whose waters were said to be a cure for rheumatism and sore eyes. Towards the centre, a towering conical deodar cedar, perhaps turbo-charged by the proximity of its pharmaceutical neighbour, has attained an incredible height. ///guard.wishes.funny

### 835. KEYES KOBUS
*Kobus magnolia*
*Magnolia kobus*
Keyes Avenue,
Cardiff CF23 5QQ
51.514783, -3.178395

Cardiff boasts an abundance of unusual trees planted over the last century and a half, and could claim to be an 'Arboretum City', its canopy is so rich and diverse. This is epitomised midway along Keyes Avenue where a Japanese kobus magnolia is planted, a most unlikely street tree. An inspired choice, especially when it, and the other kobus magnolias on this street, flower in early April. ///corner.belong.squad

### 836. ROATH PARK ODDITY
*Weeping ginkgo*
*Ginkgo biloba 'Pendula'*
Roath Park Botanical
Gardens, Lake Road West,
Cardiff CF23 5PA
51.504353, -3.175317

Ginkgos are stately trees that become increasingly attractive as they grow tall, fill out and take on the individual characteristics of age. In Roath Park Botanical Gardens, a rare weeping ginkgo can be found – a cultivar that turns the species' lofty stereotype on its head. This tree is very short and very broad, and must have its pendulous branches regularly pruned so people can navigate the path that passes under it. ///soil.across.spoon

### 837. FAIR MAPLE
*Paperbark maple*
*Acer griseum*
Roath Pleasure Gardens,
Fairoak Road,
Cardiff CF23 5HH
51.500741, -3.172151

A complex of parks and gardens snake along the Roath Brook. One section, the Roath Pleasure Gardens south of Fairoak Road, was opened in 1906 around the ancient Fair Oak, a tree now long gone. The successor to that fair tree is surely the Fair Maple, a beautiful paperbark maple near the tennis courts. The juxtaposition of its cinnamon bark with the particular green of its leaves never tires. ///foam.trials.lobby

**838. GREEDY TREE**
*London plane*
*Platanus × hispanica*
Ninian Road,
Cardiff CF23 5EP
51.500013, -3.172802

Not to be outdone by London's KENSINGTON POSTBOX TREE (534) or THE HUNGRY TREE* (941) in Dublin, the Welsh capital has its own ravenous plant. On Ninian Road a London plane was, decades ago, installed rather too close to a postbox, which it is now slowly and steadily swallowing. It has eaten so far through this appetising morsel that the postbox is now out of service and, it seems, resigned to its fate. ///orchestra.acting.mercy

**839. SANDRINGHAM STINGER**
*Nettle tree / Celtis australis*
Roath Brook Gardens,
Sandringham Road,
Cardiff CF23 5BG
51.496645, -3.16292

Roath Brook gently meanders out of Roath Park and on through Cardiff's eastern suburbs. Narrow gardens lining the stream continue the canopy, with many more notable specimens among the trees. Close to the Pen-y-Lan Road end of the gardens, a very impressive hackberry, or nettle tree, grows next to Sandringham Road. ///league.zealous.guess

**840. MONSTER WINGNUT**
*Caucasian wingnut*
*Pterocarya fraxinifolia*
Roath Brook Gardens,
Sandringham Road,
Cardiff CF23 5BG
51.495971, -3.160971

Not far from the SANDRINGHAM STINGER (839) is another astonishing specimen tree – a vast Caucasian wingnut. Its great, thick bole is usually surrounded by copious root suckers that must be regularly kept in check to arrest the development of a linear wingnut woodland. The tree is also noteworthy for its huge canopy, which reaches right across Sandringham Road, almost to the houses. ///pets.remedy.bend

**841. ANOTHER SWEETGUM**
*Oriental sweetgum*
*Liquidambar orientalis*
Roath Mill Gardens,
Waterloo Road,
Cardiff CF23 5AE
51.494866, -3.156033

Most sweetgums in these islands are the American species. They are attractive trees, notable for their maple-like leaves and fantastic late-autumn colour. But there are other species, and Roath Mill Gardens is home to a rare example of an oriental sweetgum, a tree originating from Turkey. It grows next to the Waterloo Road entrance, and is the biggest example in Wales. ///rail.noon.form

**842. ROATH AILANTHUS**
*Tree of heaven*
*Ailanthus altissima*
Roath Mill Gardens,
Waterloo Road,
Cardiff CF23 5AE
51.495027, -3.15612

Little Roath Mill Gardens exemplifies how almost every corner of Cardiff is bristling with interesting trees. Growing on the other side of the Waterloo Road gate from ANOTHER SWEETGUM (841), the Roath Ailanthus can be admired. It is a fine specimen of a tree of heaven, with a typically generous crown atop a somewhat battle-scarred trunk, which leans at 20 degrees over Waterloo Road beyond the wrought iron railings. ///shunts.melt.mixer

GREEDY TREE (838)

### 843. PENARTH CYPRESS
*Monterey cypress*
*Cupressus macrocarpa*
Alexandra Park, Beach Road, Penarth CF64 1FN
51.436328, -3.169933

There are lots of Alexandra Parks around Britain, most established between 1901 and 1910 and named for Queen Alexandra, wife of Edward VII. Penarth's Alexandra Park is perhaps one of the lushest. Sitting in a prime location overlooking the Bristol Channel, it is particularly well preserved and marked out by memorably exuberant topiary. At the park's peak, close to the war memorial, a giant Monterey cypress provides a bold focal point. ///tour.baking.inches

### 844. WENVOE YEW*
*Yew / Taxus baccata*
St Mary's church,
Old Port Road,
Wenvoe CF5 6DF
51.44638, -3.26456

'Near the church grows a remarkably fine yew tree, in excellent preservation, which is said to be one of the oldest in the county', according to an 1833 account of this tree. Nearly 200 years later the tree is even more impressive, having taken on a dramatic lean (which it may well have had in 1833, but perhaps not as pronounced). Today, its main trunk grows at an angle of less than 45 degrees from a low, walled enclosure, forcing the whole tree to hang over Old Port Road.///dance.search.many

### 845. CHAPTER HOUSE TREE
*Fern-leaved beech / Fagus sylvatica 'Asplenifolia'*
Margam Park,
Port Talbot SA13 2TJ
51.562621, -3.730511
*Paid car park.*

The contrast between Arcadian Margam Park and industrial Port Talbot, separated by the M4, could not be greater. Margam is an expansive former country estate that includes the ruins of twelfth-century Margam Abbey, where you can experience the wonderful Chapter House Tree. It is a vast fern-leaved beech whose layering branches sweep to the ground like flying buttresses, mirroring those of the neighbouring twelve-sided chapter house ruins, forming a dense natural dome. ///topic.signified.bullion

### 846. HOWEL GWYN'S HANDKERCHIEF TREE
*Handkerchief tree*
*Davidia involucrata*
Victoria Gardens,
Neath SA11 3AA
51.662125, -3.802768

Victoria Gardens is a lovely nineteenth-century park in the centre of Neath. Laid out as a square around a central bandstand, it also boasts Gorsedd stones, monoliths erected for the 1918 National Eisteddfod (an annual music and poetry festival, established in 1861 and held in different locations throughout Wales to this day). In the corner close to the statue of nineteenth-century politician Howel Gwyn, a surprising handkerchief tree dwells. It is a large, spreading tree which is resplendent with white 'handkerchiefs' that hang abundantly from its branches in May. ///handle.battle.cycle

### 847. CWMDONKIN KATSURA
*Katsura / Cercidiphyllum japonicum*
Cwmdonkin Park,
Swansea SA2 0PN
51.621321, -3.968945

Katsuras are a species much admired by dendrophiles, but despite their popularity among tree-hunting folk, they remain rare. In Cwmdonkin Park, this trend is bucked by an exceptional example growing near the tennis courts. It is a katsura in its prime, displaying elegant heart-shaped leaves throughout a copious crown covering multiple deeply fissured trunks. A contender for Swansea's loveliest tree. ///fancy.lance.handy

### 848. BRYNMILL PINE
*Monterey pine*
*Pinus radiata*
Brynmill Park,
Swansea SA2 0JQ
51.616147, -3.972678

In this well-preserved Victorian park, several fine old trees await. On the northern edge, a row of Corsican pines form the boundary with Glanbrydan Avenue. Among them a larger, double-trunked Monterey pine stands out, sheathed with dark, deeply furrowed bark – it is the most rugged of all the pines and rewards close inspection. ///universally.curl.groom

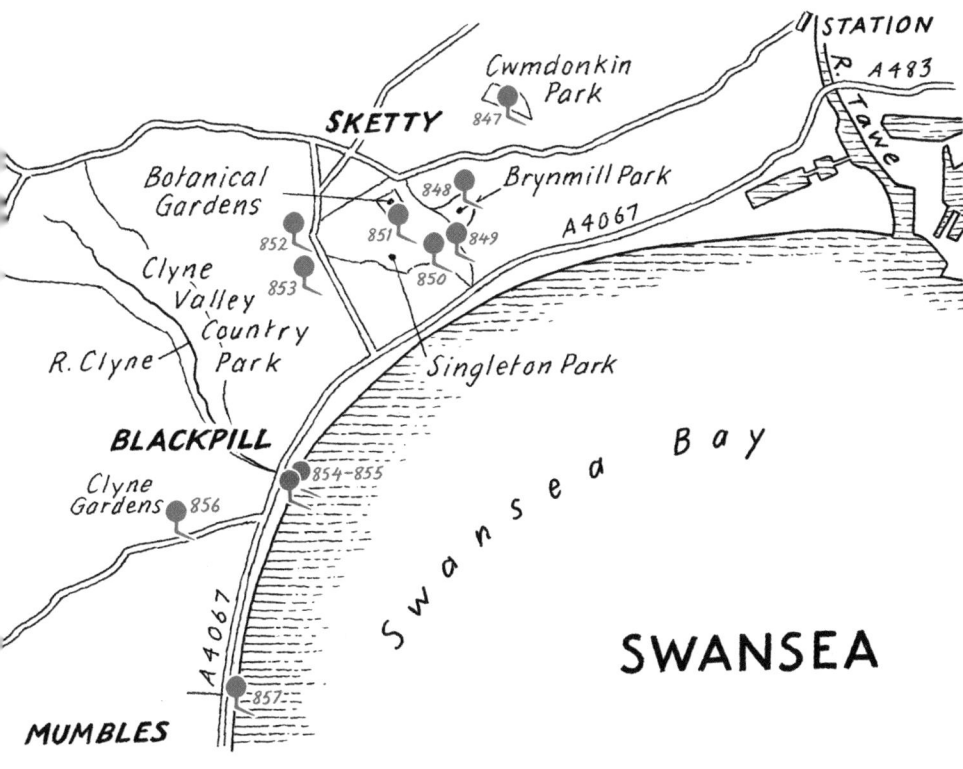

CWMDONKIN KATSURA (847)
BRYNMILL PINE (848)

**849. GARGANTUAN TEPA**
*Tepa / Laureliopsis philippiana*
Singleton Park,
Swansea SA2 8PW
51.611268, -3.977148

The semi-wild ornamental garden of Singleton Park bristles with lush evergreen trees and shrubs. Among this woodland setting, the thrusting, moss-covered trunk of a tepa or wawán stands out. Resembling a giant bay laurel, it is a tree originating from Chile and Argentina rarely seen in these islands, and accords the gardens a distinctly subtropical feel. ///cliff.last.basket

850. **ENTANGLEMENT OAK** ⇾ The Entanglement Oak is the widest holm oak in Wales. It grows not far from the **GARGANTUAN TEPA (849)**, among other trees, so its canopy is lifted, allowing its multi-stemmed trunk to be appreciated. The tree is likely older than the gardens it now grows in, and its complex form could be the result of past coppicing, maybe as part of a hedge.

**ENTANGLEMENT OAK**
*Holm oak / Quercus ilex*
Singleton Park,
Swansea SA2 8PW
51.610918, -3.977886
///closet.player.farms

### 851. BOTANICAL SPINNING GUM
*Spinning gum*
*Eucalyptus perriniana*
Botanical Gardens,
Singleton Park,
Swansea SA2 8PW
51.614826, -3.981923

Swansea Botanical Gardens has occupied the northern corner of Singleton Park since 1926 when it opened as the Educational Garden. Since then, its interesting collection of trees has matured and many vie for attention, but perhaps the most outstanding is the twisted old eucalypt, a spinning gum, found near the glasshouses and distinguished by multicoloured bark that peels in spirals around the trunk. ///muddy.draw.villa

### 852. BRYN TULIP TREE
*Tulip tree*
*Liriodendron tulipifera*
The Bryn, Sketty,
Swansea SA2 8DF
51.611915, -3.992513

A tulip tree growing on the Hirsel estate in Scotland is thought to be the oldest example of this enigmatic species in these islands, but the Bryn Tulip Tree is surely not far behind. It is a fat layering tree, overgrown with ivy and rather difficult to find, but well worth tracking down. Discover it growing among other established mature trees where The Bryn curves round, off Derwen Fawr Road. ///smug.pilots.discouraged

### 853. TWINS OF SKETTY
*Dawn redwood*
*Metasequoia*
*glyptostroboides*
Harford Court, Sketty,
Swansea SA2 8DF
51.611592, -3.992166

The Twins of Sketty appear at first glance to be a single twin-trunked dawn redwood, but inquisitive tree hunters will discover they are, in fact, two fast-growing trees planted so close together that within a few years their separateness will be impossible to deduce. The duo grace a small garden in front of Harford Court, a mid-twentieth-century apartment block, and are a useful landmark for those intent on finding the BRYN TULIP TREE (852) growing nearby. ///hill.given.dream

### 854. LIDO ELMS
### & 855.
*Wheatley elm / Ulmus*
*minor 'Sarniensis'*
Mumbles Road, Blackpill,
Swansea SA3 5AS
51.596876, -3.994987

Travellers along the Mumbles Road will have noticed two conjoined, conifer-like silhouettes standing to the south of the Blackpill Lido, overlooking the sands of Swansea Bay. It may come as a surprise to discover they are not spruces, firs or dawn redwoods, but an astonishing pair of Wheatley elms, a species well suited to such a salty aspect. ///bowls.today.offer

### 856. CLYNE INDIAN HORSE CHESTNUT
*Indian horse chestnut*
*Aesculus indica*
Clyne Gardens,
Swansea SA3 5BW
51.594532, -4.007096

Formerly the private gardens of Clyne Castle, home of the wealthy Vivian family, Clyne Gardens is a woodland filled with fine trees and shrubs. Close to the Japanese bridge and pond, the tallest Indian horse chestnut in Wales can be seen. Look out for the white flower-candles in early June, rather later than those of a European horse chestnut. ///trucks.pint.harsh

**857. MUMBLES STONE PINE**
*Stone pine / Pinus pinea*
Mumbles Road,
Swansea SA3 5AB
51.583482, -4.000846
*In a private garden, but visible from the coastal footpath.*

A lonesome stone pine acts as a landmark halfway along the seaside path and cycleway between Blackpill and Mumbles. It is a mature, particularly shapely tree growing in the garden of a house on the Mumbles Road. While it is not possible to confer with this conifer, its presence, which can be admired from near or far, is very public and gives a distinctly Italian feel to Swansea Bay. ///worm.middle.error

**858. MERLIN'S OAK***
*Holm oak / Quercus ilex*
Old Oak Lane,
Carmarthen SA31 1NY
51.860783, -4.298939

In the 1850s, Merlin's, sometimes Priory's Oak, was poisoned by a local fed up with the noisy meetings being held beneath it. The dead tree, a blasted stump surrounded by railings, was left *in situ* until the late 1970s to avoid provoking Merlin's prophecy: 'When Priory's Oak shall tumble down / Then will fall Carmarthen town.' Eventually a young replacement, an evergreen holm oak, was planted in 2009. ///lobby.coats.refers

**859. EIFFEL TOWER TREE**
*Monterey cypress*
*Cupressus macrocarpa*
Waters Edge, The Strand,
Saundersfoot SA69 9ET
51.713009, -4.69673

Dubbed Saundersfoot's Eiffel Tower, the Monterey cypress growing on a rock above the beach is as iconic to this Pembrokeshire town as the Eiffel Tower is to the French capital. The tree was planted in 1938, and, in 2021, it was deemed unsafe and would be felled. A campaign ensued, the tree became a finalist in the Tree of the Year competition, and a reprieve was granted. ///chambers.touchy.roughest

**860. TŌGŌ'S GINKGO**
*Ginkgo / Ginkgo biloba*
The Terrace, The
Dockyard, Pembroke
Dock SA72 6YH
51.692985, -4.952266
*In a private garden, but visible from the street.*

Pembroke Dock has seen better days, but its grand nineteenth-century architecture is a reminder of its past importance as a naval town. On The Terrace, the former Master Shipwright's house hosts a ginkgo planted by the Japanese ambassador in 1877, in tribute to the town where Japan's first iron warship was built. The house was where Lieutenant, later Admiral, Tōgō had lodged during the ship's construction. ///foggy.burglars.quoted

**861. REFECTORY MULBERRY**
*Mulberry / Morus nigra*
St Davids Cathedral,
The Pebbles,
St Davids SA62 6RD
51.882506, -5.268453

Tucked away behind the refectory at St Davids Cathedral is a little garden known only to a few. It is a charming place with verdant borders surrounding a small lawn. On the northern side an old mulberry tree is partly hidden among the many plants; although not yet ancient, it is already starting to branch and recline, and will be a great character in the future. ///humble.etchings.jabs

WALES 408

EIFFEL TOWER TREE (859)

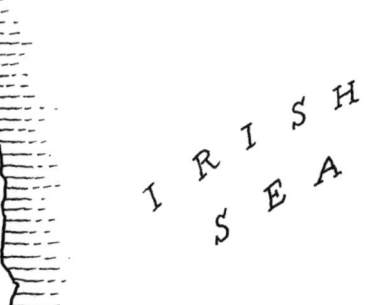

# MID & NORTH
## *WALES*

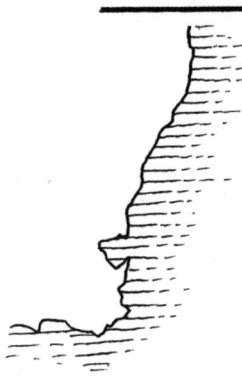

## MID & NORTH WALES

Isle of Anglesey
Gwynedd
Ceredigion
Powys
Wrexham
Flintshire
Denbighshire
Conwy

SIGNATURE SPECIES:
Wild black poplar

Wild black poplars are now very rare. There are thought to be only a few thousand individuals left in Britain and Ireland, and only a few hundred of those are female. This curious fact may be because many are clones selected from a small number of parent trees which just happened to be male. For instance, Manchester poplars, like the **GORTON SURVIVOR (172)**, are a male clone. They are native to Britain, Ireland and north-western France, where they occur in the shifting sands and flood plains of broad river systems – habitats that have all but disappeared from these islands as our rivers have become more managed (to reduce flooding and aid navigation) since the nineteenth century. Unlike other poplar species, which tend to be short-lived, black poplars can live for hundreds of years and become massive. It is these awe-inspiring poplars, along with ancient yews, that are the defining tree species of mid and north Wales.

The **CAR PARK SENTINEL (879)** is one of the most magnificent. As the name suggests, it is now washed up in a car park close to the River Severn in the Powys settlement of Newtown, but it is a marvel, and could be 300 years old. It is only in the last century and a half that the course of the Severn has been fixed, so perhaps the tree first gained a foothold in a water meadow, a long-disappeared riverbank or a sandbar. A similar tree, the huge **CAWR WYSG (883)**, survives at Brecon, next to the embanked river Usk as it flows past the playing fields of Christ College. These two individuals are exceptional examples of the species; looking at them, you can't help but imagine the poplar-dotted floodplains that would once have been significant features of British and Irish riverscapes.

While Wales's ancient poplars are often conspicuous, open-growing trees, ancient Welsh yews are almost entirely confined to little-visited old churchyards. The Welsh borders is one of two significant hotspots for old yews (the other is southern England). The oldest yew in Britain or Ireland, **THE FORTINGALL YEW* (28)** in Scotland, is a geographical outlier and is thought to be as much as 5,000 years old, but the Welsh **DISCOED YEW* (881)**, growing close to the border with England, is not far behind it. It is very hard to determine the age of an old yew, as they collapse in their twilight years and often have extensive hollows. But really, really old yews transcend this state, beginning to look like a small group of separate trees as remnants of growth appear around a hollow trunk, and continue to soldier on after the old carcass has rotted away. This is what has happened to the **LLANGERNYW YEW* (865)**, twice or thrice as old as its church.

In the wilds of north Wales, rich rewards await in the settlements of Dolgellau, Bangor and Betws-y-Coed among and beyond the high mountains. Dolgellau nestles under Cadair Idris and, on the edge of town, the **MEIRIONNYDD ASH (877)** should be sought out. It is a magnificent upland ash tree, from which the great panorama of southern Eryri can be admired. In these places, where humans have exploited the resources of quarry, moor and forest, it is the native trees that stand out, offering a hint at what these mountains must once have looked like when Atlantic rainforest once covered them. The **ATLANTIC FOREST REMNANT (872)** is one of these, a veteran sessile oak growing happily in the shadow of Yr Wyddfa, now in the safety of a car park. The Welsh word coed, appearing in the placename Betws-y-Coed, means 'woodland', and the **BETWS-Y-COED MUSE (869)** is a remnant of extensive oak forest, fragments of which cling to the village's fringes.

At Bangor, the wilds are left behind and the university's Treborth Botanic Gardens is a gem that must be visited. The land was originally laid out by Joseph Paxton as pleasure gardens for the Chester and Holyhead Railway, which was intent on developing a resort here. The scheme collapsed, but not before Paxton had planted the **DERWEN LUCOMBE* (864)**, a grand Lucombe oak that is now the highlight of Treborth.

Human influence can be detected in the planting and nurturing of trees in every region of Britain and Ireland, but in mid and north Wales it is at its faintest. Many of the great oaks, yews and poplars that make up the majority of the trees I discovered here may have been growing long before the settlements that now surround them even existed.

**862. PROM ELM**
*Camperdown elm*
*Ulmus glabra*
*'Camperdownii'*
St George's Crescent,
Central Promenade,
Llandudno LL30 2LF
53.324615, -3.827352

The prom at Llandudno is lined with dozens of cabbage palms – the essential west-coast seaside tree from St Ives to Plockton – but a rarer tree lurks opposite the Somerset Hotel. A peculiar Camperdown elm, no higher than a VW camper van, has been planted among well-clipped shrubs near a parking meter. It is best appreciated in the leafless months when you can properly inspect its spiralling branches. ///irritable.dark.apparatus

**863. HEN GOLEG SHAGGY TREE**
*Monkey puzzle*
*Araucaria araucana*
Hen Goleg Building,
Fford Siliwen,
Bangor LL57 2DD
53.230204, -4.131464

Monkey puzzle trees often have their lower branches removed as the tree grows, resulting in a long, exposed trunk with a small crown perched on top. At Bangor, the tree on the lawn in front of the university's Hen Goleg building, overlooking the Menai Straits, has been left relatively untouched. Its lower branches slouch, covering its trunk. ///wired.foggy.toasters

**864. DERWEN LUCOMBE***
*Lucombe oak*
*Quercus × crenata*
*'Lucombeana'*
Treborth Botanic Garden,
Bangor LL57 2RQ
53.217429, -4.169032

*Derwen* is the Welsh word for 'oak', and the great, domed Derwen Lucombe is Treborth Botanic Garden's treasure: a splendid and northerly example of a Lucombe oak planted around 1850 in gardens designed by Joseph Paxton for the Chester and Holyhead Railway. The tree's branches arch to the ground, and visitors can get right in to experience its umbrageous canopy. ///kingpin.cooking.agreeable

**865. LLANGERNYW YEW***
*Yew / Taxus baccata*
Eglwys St Digain,
Uwch Afon,
Llangernyw LL22 8PR
53.192338, -3.685048

The Llangernyw Yew, like the DISCOED YEW* (**881**) and DENFYNNOG* (**882**) Yews, is claimed to be the oldest tree in Wales. It is undoubtedly one of the most picturesque yews anywhere. It grows in the churchyard of the pretty whitewashed church of St Digain, which it predates by millennia. A large void, which was filled with an oil tank until the 1990s, is surrounded by trunk supporting a healthy crown. ///paces.soothing.waking

**866. BRYN GWALIA OAK**
*Pedunculate oak*
*Quercus robur*
Ysgol Bryn Gwalia, Clayton Road, Mold CH7 1SU
53.166033, -3.150193
*On school grounds, but visible from the road.*

On the edge of the playing fields, just behind the fence on Greenside, Bryn Gwalia primary school's great tree can be found. It is a pedunculate oak approaching 700 years old, making it much, much older than the school. The school's community values it greatly – generations of Mold kids have played beneath it, and maybe in its branches too – and it stands proud on the school badge. ///reckon.pythons.vanished

**867. GREENSIDE SYCAMORE**
*Sycamore / Acer pseudoplatanus*
Greenside,
Mold CH7 1TN
53.16474, -3.150058

Not far from the BRYN GWALIA OAK **(866)**, another old tree takes up the full width of a pavement among the mid-twentieth-century houses of Greenside. While the Greenside Sycamore is a callow youth compared to its near neighbour, it is an impressive giant of a tree with a tight web of branches. Such a striking tree should be celebrated for being sensitively incorporated into the housing estate. ///bulge.starts.swan

**868. BRYN TYRCH PINE** → After a day in the mountains, there can be no more welcoming sight for hikers returning to the Bryn Tyrch Inn at Capel Curig than the landmark Scots pine growing opposite. It is visible from the A5 too – look out for it just before the left turn on to the A4086 – and, with the hump of Moel Siabod in the background, it also signposts the road to take for those walking the highest peaks.

**BRYN TYRCH PINE**
*Scots pine / Pinus sylvestris*
Bryn Tyrch Inn,
Capel Curig LL24 0EL
53.102644, -3.906677
///partners.barks.sandpaper

AFON MERDDWR CHESTNUT (871)

### 869. BETWS-Y-COED MUSE
*Pedunculate oak*
*Quercus robur*
Royal Oak Stables,
Betws-y-Coed LL24 0AH
53.092834, -3.801791

In pride of place above the fireplace in the lounge of the Royal Oak Hotel at Betws-y-Coed, an 1847 painting of an oak tree reminds guests that they're nestled in the most wooded part of Eryri. Across the Holyhead Road from the hotel, several old oaks grow on the village green – inspiration, perhaps, for the Victorian artist. The proudest grows near to the Information Office where its weathered branches can be closely inspected. ///bedding.masses.tilting

### 870. BETWS GIANT
*Lawson cypress*
*Chamaecyparis lawsoniana*
St Mary's, Holyhead Road, Betws-y-Coed
LL24 0AA
53.091783, -3.802914

The Victorians were fond of conifers and often created pinetums, collections of different species planted together. The churchyard of St Mary's could be described as a pinetum; several conifers have reached monumental proportions, but it is a Lawson's cypress that most impresses. It is an elegant, symmetrical tree growing behind a scrappy giant redwood that pales in contrast with this colossus. ///spine.overdone.permit

### 871. AFON MERDDWR CHESTNUT
*Horse chestnut*
*Aesculus hippocastanum*
Pentrefoelas,
Betws-y-Coed LL24 0HT
53.048661, -3.683194

In May, when the Afon Merddwr Chestnut is in flower, it causes jaws to drop. The rest of the year, it is a handsome landmark along the A5 between Corwen and Betws-y-Coed. It grows next to the bridge over the Afon Merddwr at Pentrefoelas, close to an Edwardian monument erected to the memory of local squire, C. A. Wynne Finch, in 1903 – a likely planting date for the tree. ///scrubbing.vipers.plug

### 872. ATLANTIC FOREST REMNANT
*Sessile oak*
*Quercus petraea*
Cae Morys Parking,
Beddgelert LL55 4YW
53.012276, -4.105871

An oak growing in a car park in Beddgelert just about holds its own against the tarmac. A climate-shaped character, the tree is a remnant of the Atlantic rainforest that once covered the uplands. It is an entire ecosystem: contemplate the pelt of lichen that covers it, and look up at the branch socket: home for a nuthatch, perhaps. ///assembles.configure.masking

### 873. WONDROUS YEW
*Yew / Taxus baccata*
All Saints,
The Green, Gresford,
Wrexham LL12 8RG
53.087848, -2.976765

All Saints church is widely considered Wales's finest, admired for its perpendicular architecture, medieval stained glass and the peel of its bells, which are popularly known as one of the Seven Wonders of Wales. On top of all these impressive qualifications, the churchyard hosts a sprawling ancient yew, now protected by a fence, that predates the church. ///brochure.solved.efficient

**874. ACTON PARK CHESTNUT**
*Sweet chestnut*
*Castanea sativa*
Acton Park, Herbert
Jennings Avenue,
Wrexham LL12 7YA
53.061813, -2.977014

Acton, a very English name for a suburb of a Welsh city, was once aristocratic parkland, and is now home to the public Acton Park. 'Ac' in Acton is an archaic English term for oak, but the tree of note here is a thrusting sweet chestnut on the eastern edge near Jeffreys Road. It is thought to be approaching 500 years old, but shows little sign of decline; a magnificent tree. ///funded.fails.shave

**875. FOURTH WONDER OF WALES**
*Yew / Taxus baccata*
St Mary's Church,
High Street, Overton,
Wrexham LL13 0FA
52.970232, -2.934969

According to an anonymous nineteenth-century rhyme, there are seven wonders of Wales: 'Pistyll Rhaeadr and Wrexham Steeple, Snowdon's mountain without its people, Overton yew trees, Gresford bells, Llangollen bridge and St Winifred's well.' The fourth is a collection of twenty-four yews in the churchyard of St Mary's, one of which, close to the High Street entrance, is propped, much older than the rest, and the most worthy of your attention. ///braked.flamenco.clubbing

**876. THE OAK AT THE GATE OF THE DEAD***
*Hybrid oak*
*Quercus × rosacea*
Castle Road,
Chirk LL14 5BL
52.931476, -3.095395

The Oak at the Gate of the Dead has been collapsing for centuries. It lies close to the road at the foot of Chirk Castle; the River Ceiriog and the border with England are just below. This position helps explain its arresting name. In 1145, an English army led by Henry II clashed with Owain Gwynedd's Welsh force. After the battle, it is said the dead soldiers were laid to rest here. ///hears.investor.screen

877. **MEIRIONNYDD ASH** → Dolgellau, formerly the county town of Merionethshire, is a settlement of handsome stone buildings surrounded by the southern peaks of Eryri. On the edge of town, the asphalt of Pen-y-Banc peters out and a footpath leads into fields where the Meirionnydd Ash can be admired. It is an outstanding tree, and is well worth visiting for the view it commands over the town and hills beyond.

**MEIRIONNYDD ASH** *Ash / Fraxinus excelsior* Pen-y-Banc, Dolgellau LL40 1SW
52.738721, -3.886463 ///litters.continued.triathlon

CAR PARK SENTINEL (879)

**878. GOLDEN LION PINE**
*Scots pine / Pinus sylvestris*
Lion Street,
Dolgellau LL40 1DG
52.74341, -3.886196

Across Lion Street from the former Golden Lion Hotel, a tiny piazza is shaded by the generous canopy of a Scots pine. On a sunny day, the whole ensemble has a distinctly Mediterranean feel, while on a more regular Welsh day it offers shelter from the damper elements. The tree is a surprise among the close stone buildings, and has taken on a memorable low, spreading form. ///reset.cycle.structure

**879. CAR PARK SENTINEL**
*Wild black poplar / Populus nigra ssp. betulifolia*
Heol Les Herbiers,
Pool Road,
Newtown SY16 1DH
52.514325, -3.312079

The River Severn has been fixed by banks and walls, but the wonderful 350-year-old Car Park Sentinel is a remnant of a time when the river meandered freely along its broad flood plain. The tree might once have grown on the shifting silt, or have fixed a riverbank itself. Today it grows in a car park below a grassy embankment, 30 metres from the river. ///thigh.vets.opposites

**880. BRIMMON OAK***
*Pedunculate oak Quercus robur*
A483, Newtown
SY16 4DR
52.512492, -3.29293

In 2015, a campaign led by tree hunter Rob McBride succeeded in diverting the proposed A483 Newtown bypass, in order to save a 500-year-old pedunculate oak. Known as the Brimmon Oak, it is a lapsed pollard growing in the field in which it has lived for centuries. The field is next to the main road, and the majestic tree has had to toughen up, growing, as it now does, just metres from the traffic. ///collapsed.doctors.driver

**881. DISCOED YEW***
*Yew / Taxus baccata*
St Michael's Church,
Discoed, Presteigne
LD8 2NW
52.276156, -3.061773

There can be few Welsh yews more impressive than the Discoed Yew. It is one of three old trees growing in St Michael's churchyard, and will particularly draw your attention. Its giant trunk is a fragment of a tree – from half a millennium ago, perhaps – that must have been mind-blowing in its proportions. Tree hunters can only wonder what once was, while admiring its still-impressive height, its vast hollow and its dramatic lean. ///tastier.depended.tadpoles

**882. DEFYNNOG YEW***
*Yew / Taxus baccata*
Eglwys St Cynog,
Church Row, Defynnog,
Brecon LD3 8SD
51.939723, -3.564817

The Defynnog Yew has grown quietly for thousands of years in a remote churchyard on the northern slopes of the Bannau Brycheiniog. In recent years, controversy has raged about its true age. Claims have been made that it is 5,000 years old, but experts disagree, some saying a mere 3,000 is more likely. Either way, it is a sight to behold. ///furniture.subplot.sailed

883.  **CAWR WYSG** → The massive Cawr Wysg has grown on the banks of the Usk in Brecon for many, many years. It is located within the grounds of Christ College but it should be considered part of the riverscape. Like the CAR PARK SENTINEL **(879)**, it grows in a floodplain, the typical habitat for these rare giants. Best seen from the riverside path at the end of Dinas Road.

**CAWR WYSG** *Wild black poplar / Populus nigra ssp. betulifolia*
Dinas Road, Llanfaes, Brecon LD3 8AF 51.945168, -3.393166 *On college grounds, but visible from the public footpath.* ///swimmer.sharpened.paths

884. **CHAPEL YEW**
*Yew / Taxus baccata*
Capel-y-Ffin,
Abergavenny NP7 7NP
51.977105, -3.0862

Capel-y-Ffin is a tiny hamlet with a tiny chapel – the chapel of the boundary – on the road between Hay-on-Wye and Abergavenny. Within the churchyard, no less than seven old yews grow. The largest and loveliest of this magnificent seven is on the south-western edge, second from the chapel. This remote valley is 300 metres above sea level, an altitude that causes the trees to grow particularly slowly. The Chapel Yew could therefore be very old indeed. ///saloons.elections.commuted

885. **NO FISHING TREE**
*Field maple*
*Acer campestre*
The Vine Tree, Legar Road, Llangattock,
Crickhowell NP8 1HG
51.85604, -3.142448

At the foot of Crickhowell Bridge near The Vine Tree pub, a densely crowned but somewhat ungainly field maple can be seen growing close to the River Usk. Its position and the cover it offers have made it a prime location for those intent on fishing here, and a succession of signs, more or less consumed by the expanding tree, remind would-be anglers that the fishing is private. ///squirted.graceful.acid

886. **LLANGATTOCK LEVIATHAN**
*Giant redwood*
*Sequoiadendron giganteum*
Llangattock,
Crickhowell NP8 1HT
51.846149, -3.1452

The Bannau Brycheiniog are not the only natural landmarks around the Usk Valley – the unmistakable shape of a giant redwood towers next to the towpath of the Monmouthshire and Brecon Canal. The Llangattock Leviathan can be seen for miles around, a huge tree with a great, buttressed trunk and branches hanging almost to the ground. Its otherworldly dimensions suit its magical environment. ///spoils.lanes.professed

# NORTHERN IRELAND

## NORTHERN IRELAND

*Causeway Coast & Glens*

*Derry City & Strabane*

*Fermanagh & Omagh*

*Mid Ulster*

*Armagh City, Banbridge & Craigavon*

*Newry, Mourne & Down*

*Lisburn & Castlereagh*

*Ards & North Down*

*Belfast City*

*Antrim & Newtownabbey*

*Mid & East Antrim*

TREE CITY:
*Belfast*

SIGNATURE SPECIES:
*Turkey oak*

On the whole, there is little ancient woodland and few truly ancient trees anywhere on the island of Ireland. This is not because of a hostile climate – as we shall see, trees do well here. It is, rather, the result of pressure over centuries to provide farmland and timber – both to meet local demand and to feed the English shipping and building industries. Attitudes to woodland stewardship differed in Ireland than in Britain: Irish woods and forests were not regarded as sustainable community property, but as resources to be exploited by colonial landowners.

Right across Ireland and Britain, individual trees outside woodlands have only survived if they have had influential protectors. Historically, these have tended to be wealthy landowners, who would use old trees on their land as status symbols, signalling that they could afford *not* to cut them down. This rarely happened in Ireland – A BELVOIR OAK (917) on the edge of this region's great Tree City, Belfast, is an exception. Absentee landlords were primarily interested in maximising profits, and had little incentive to manage their woodland for the long term. Whether you were gathering timber or creating pasture, it paid to fell trees. As a result, much of Ireland's tree cover was cleared, and by 1656 only 2 per cent of the island was wooded, a figure that fell to just 1 per cent at the end of the nineteenth century.

Despite these ravages, Ireland is home to a panoply of remarkable trees in its villages, towns and cities. Urban trees have a special ability to reflect their surroundings; they can embody a cultural and historical milieu, and attain great significance, even if they are not of very great age. This is particularly the case in Northern Ireland, where many noteworthy trees have witnessed or become associated with individuals or events that have shaped the whole island.

At Derry, the SIEGE TREE (891) grows on the city walls overlooking the Bogside, a position that recalls the city's key role in Irish history: the walls remained unbreached during the siege of 1689 in the Williamite War. It is a relatively young sycamore, and would not have witnessed the siege, but it would have been growing here through the Troubles when the walls were closed to all but security personnel. Thirty miles along the coast, the HEZLETT CHESTNUT* (887) played a more direct and violent role in the 1798 Rebellion, deployed as a threat to boost the ranks of the United Irishmen, the popular alliance of Protestants and Catholics. A grand tree that acts as a landmark to more recent events is the RECONCILIATION TREE (898) in the garden of the Dunadry Hotel in County Antrim. It is a huge old lime with a bench around its trunk, on which David Trimble, John Hume and Tony Blair were pictured in the run-up to the Good Friday Agreement.

Since then, a new sense of optimism has been epitomised across Northern Ireland by a wave of tree planting. Trees were planted throughout Belfast in the early 2000s, in a tangible demonstration of how the streets were safer than they had been for decades.

It would be wrong to assume that all the trees discussed in this chapter have connections to Northern Ireland's political history. As elsewhere in Ireland and Britain, many trees here are remarkable for their cultural heritage, their great presence or their sheer magnificence. RAWDON'S LEGACY (923), an alluring oriental plane at Moira, remembers the man known as the Father of Irish Gardening, Arthur Rawdon, while another oriental plane, the MEDICINE TREE (904) at Belfast City Hospital, was grown from seed collected on a Greek island where Hippocrates's tree once grew.

Of all the great trees in Northern Ireland, special mention must be made of the HOLYWOOD BIG OAK* (899), a name that barely does this tree justice. It is an oak, but rather than an Irish pedunculate or sessile oak, it is a Turkey oak, a species originating from south east Europe and western Asia. Despite growing in County Down, considerably further north than its natural range, it is enormous. In fact, nothing can prepare you for the scale of this tree – it is the biggest Turkey oak I have ever seen.

**887. HEZLETT CHESTNUT***
*Sweet chestnut*
*Castanea sativa*
Hezlett House,
Mussenden Road,
Castlerock,
Coleraine BT51 4TU
55.155037, -6.789472

Hezlett House, owned by generations of the Hezlett family until the National Trust took possession in 1976, is a humble seventeenth-century farm building with a gnarly old sweet chestnut in its garden. The tree has a politically charged past – during the 1798 rebellion, one Samuel Hezlett was threatened with being hanged from his own tree if he did not join the United Irishmen. ///minimums.safety.allergy

**888. CORONATION OAK***
*Pedunculate oak*
*Quercus robur*
Main Street,
Eglinton BT47 3PQ
55.026965, -7.177836

Coolafinny Road splits in two, describing a triangle at its junction with Eglinton's Main Street. The triangle is shaded by a shapely oak planted in 1902 to mark the coronation of Edward VII. Its provenance is English rather than Irish: like Nottingham's INCLOSURE OAK* (305), it was grown from an acorn collected at Windsor Great Park. ///whizzing.defected.releases

**889. WITCH TREE**
*Downy birch*
*Betula pubescens*
Crawford Square,
Derry BT48 7HT
55.003517, -7.326961

Crawford Square is made up of a series of terraces around a well-treed central space. On its eastern side, an enormous downy birch stands out from the crowd. It is an impressive sight on its own terms, but is made even more remarkable by the witch's brooms which hang copiously in its branches. These dense twiggy growths are usually caused by a fungus, *Taphrina betulina*, and are most striking in winter. ///pills.market.putty

**890. THE NOBBLY TREE***
*Baobab London plane*
*Platanus × hispanica*
*'Western Baobab'*
Brooke Park,
Rosemount Avenue,
Derry BT48 0HH
55.002035, -7.330159

Derry's most interesting tree can be found in historic Brooke Park. The Nobbly Tree is a baobab London plane said to have grown here since 1851. It was rumoured to be a gift from Edinburgh Botanic Gardens to the Gwyn and Young Charitable Institution, whose leafy orphanage was here before the park. As its name suggests, the tree is odd and wonderfully warty. ///gives.mouth.toned

**891. SIEGE TREE**
*Sycamore / Acer*
*pseudoplatanus*
Magazine Street Upper,
Derry BT48 6HA
54.994947, -7.325136

The Siege Tree grows on Derry's city walls near St Augustine's Church and Walker's Plinth. Occupying a position overlooking the Bogside, it is an ideal spot to contemplate the city and its history. It is one of fourteen sycamores on the wall, and the third generation of trees originally planted to remember the protestant Apprentice Boys who played a key part in the 1688 siege of the city during the Williamite War. ///stud.ranked.fires

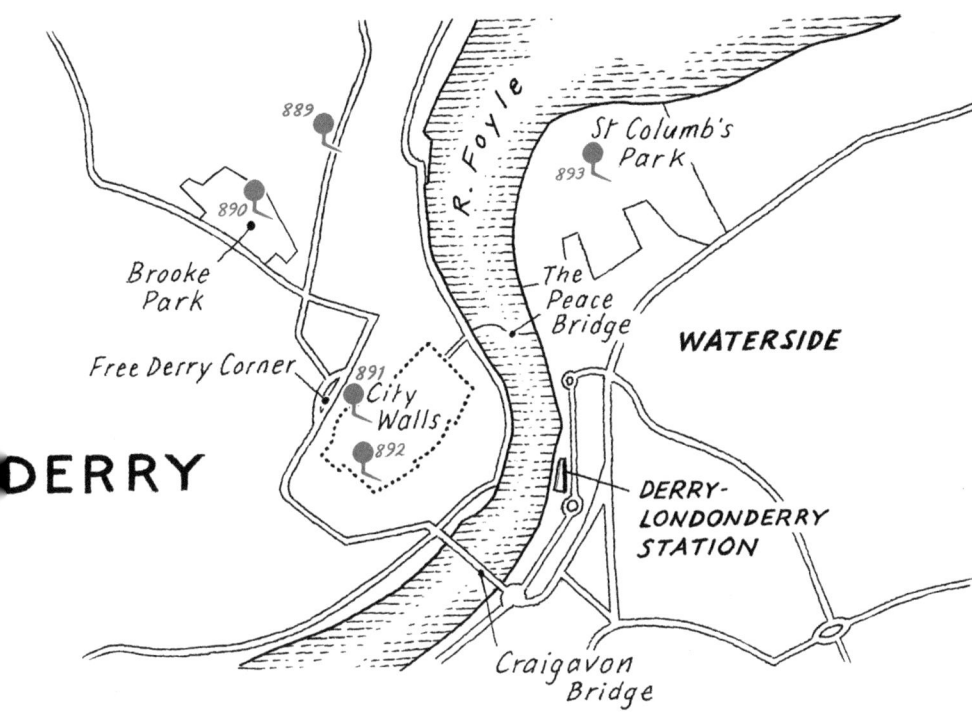

**892. DOIRE OAK**
  Pedunculate oak
  *Quercus robur*
  St Columb's Cathedral,
  London Street,
  Derry BT48 6RQ
  54.993572, -7.323492

Derry's history is contested, which manifests itself in its various names: it was first prefixed with 'London' in the seventeenth century, and the divisive question of what to call the city has continued for centuries. In Irish it is *Doire*, a word synonymous with a grove of trees, traditionally oaks. The grove that must once have grown by the Foyle is no longer there, but the handsome maturing oak in the churchyard of St Columb's Church of Ireland Cathedral, the city's most prominent church, is a worthy successor. ///badge.closes.pizza

**893. ST COLUMB'S SYCAMORE**
  Sycamore / *Acer pseudoplatanus*
  St Columb's Park,
  Limavady Road,
  Derry BT47 6JY
  55.00349, -7.311207

The conspicuously exposed roots of St Columb's Sycamore form a smooth jumble at the base of this venerable old tree. They have been polished over decades, even centuries, by children playing and animals rubbing against them. The tree grows on a slope by the side of the path leading to historic St Columb's House and its café. ///jams.assets.smashes

WITCH TREE (889)
ST COLUMB'S SYCAMORE (893)

**894. DUNGIVEN RAG TREE***
*Hawthorn*
*Crataegus monogyna*
Dungiven Priory, Bleach
Green, Dungiven BT47 4UH
54.917462, -6.919787

Rag trees are a mystical feature of Irish landscapes in particular (though they do crop up in Britain too). Generally hawthorns growing next to holy wells, they are visited by pilgrims in search of healing: according to custom, a piece of cloth from a sick person will, once tied to the tree, rot away along with the sickness until the sufferer is well again. The Dungiven Rag Tree, a multi-stemmed hawthorn that has been here for many decades, grows in a hedgerow near the ruined priory and is often bedecked in scraps of cloth. ///rejoin.ambushes.organs

**895. SEBASTOPOL HORSE CHESTNUT**
*Horse chestnut*
*Aesculus hippocastanum*
High Street,
Tullyhommon BT93 8DL
54.550035, -7.831171

Pettigo and Tullyhommon lie either side of the River Termon, the watercourse that separates Northern Ireland and the Republic. On the Northern side – Tullyhommon – a squat, spreading horse chestnut grows on a green plinth surrounded by iron railings. It looks downhill to the pedestrianised river-crossing spanning the border and connecting the two settlements. The tree was planted in 1856 amid celebrations for the end of the Crimean War. ///louder.support.indeed

**896. THE KING TREE***
*Horse chestnut*
*Aesculus hippocastanum*
Rokeby Green,
Armagh BT61 9AT
54.350164, -6.652384

The King Tree, so impressive it was shortlisted for Northern Ireland's tree of the year in 2017, grows in the north-west corner of Rokeby Green, close to Armagh's Georgian Courthouse. It is a towering horse chestnut with an impressively stout trunk, growing as tall as the lime trees that are otherwise the principal trees lining the green. Despite its regal title, The King Tree has no historical associations with royalty: it is a name used by locals impressed by its undeniable nobility. ///idea.dreading.signs

**897. INTERNATIONAL ELM**
*Dampier's elm / Ulmus × hollandica 'Dampieri'*
Belfast International
Airport, Airport Road,
Crumlin BT29 4AB
54.664416, -6.211852

Presumably there once must have been a significant number of alders on the site of Belfast International Airport, which stands near the watery shores of Lough Neagh and which was known until 1982 as Aldergrove. There is little sign of those trees now, but arrivals (and departures) must be thrilled to see instead the fastigiate form of a Dampier's elm next to the roundabout on Airport Road. It grows head and shoulders above the trees around it, and may well be the largest such elm in Ireland or Britain. A magnificent tree. ///sank.emerge.yesterday

**898. RECONCILIATION TREE**
*Common lime*
*Tilia × europaea*
Dunadry Hotel,
Islandreagh Drive, Dunadry,
Antrim BT41 2HA
54.698537, -6.141027

The Reconciliation Tree – actually a pair of common limes growing together – is discreetly tucked away in the garden of the Dunadry Hotel. It is a dramatic tree with a large, shady canopy – the ideal spot for a private discussion. It is under this tree that Tony Blair, David Trimble and John Hume were pictured in the months before the Good Friday Agreement was signed in 1998. ///rust.nutty.habit

899. **HOLYWOOD BIG OAK*** → The Holywood Big Oak is a Turkey oak, a species that can reach gargantuan proportions, and this tree is one of the very biggest anywhere. It is thought to have been planted in 1802 and, in just over 220 years, it has reached a size that a native Irish oak could only dream of. Notice, too, its deeply furrowed bark and sharply angular leaves: both unique Turkey oak features.

**HOLYWOOD BIG OAK***
*Turkey oak / Quercus cerris*
Ballymenoch Park,
Woodlands,
Holywood BT18 0PE
54.644149, -5.819934
///ponies.intrigued.dialects

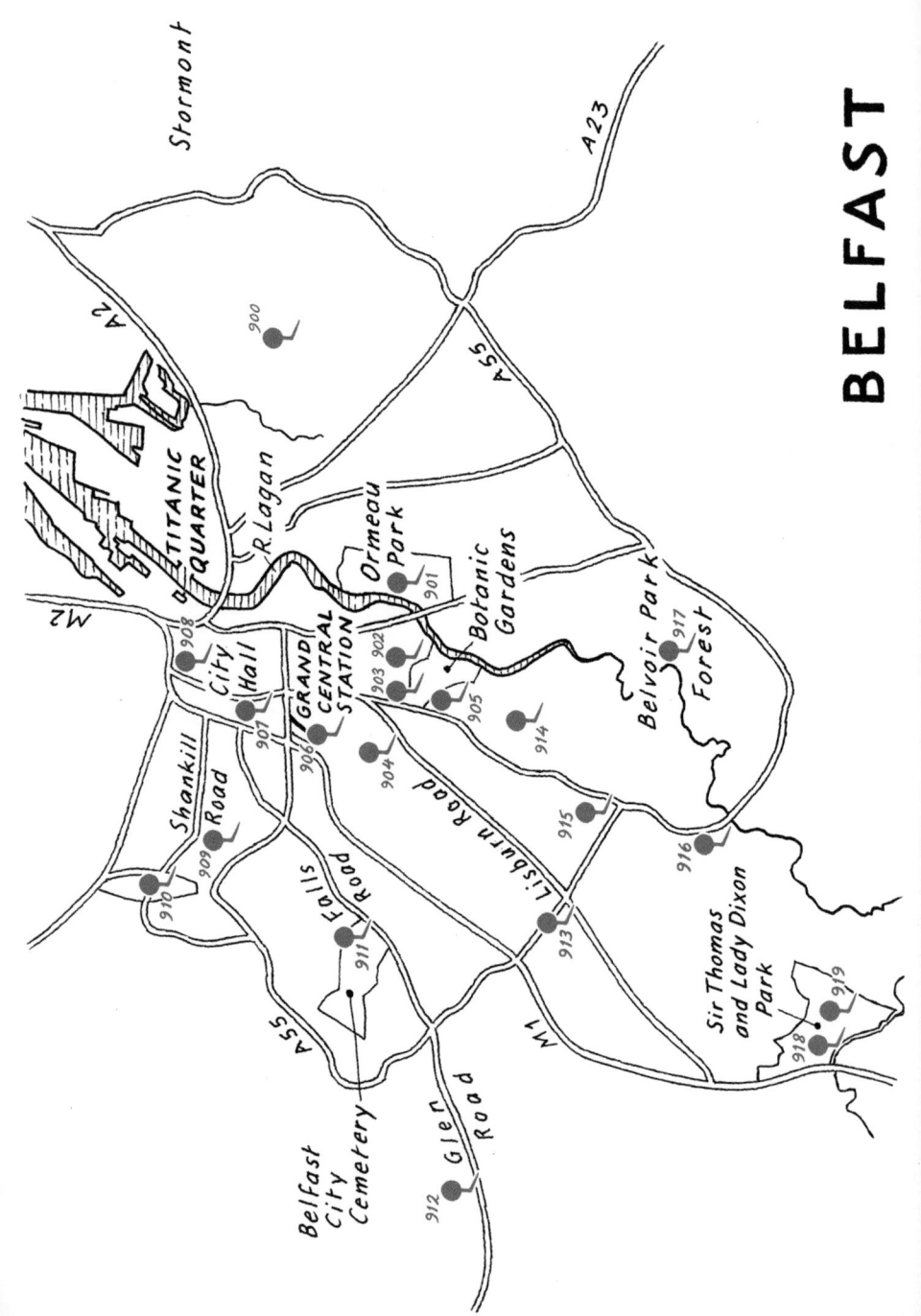

# TREE CITY: BELFAST
## SIGNATURE SPECIES: *Lime*

On busy Donegall Square, buses disgorge masses of shoppers, commuters and tourists who barely notice the trees growing on the pavement across from the grand City Hall. Belfast's city centre suffered badly during the Troubles, but once renewal began, tree planting was high on the agenda, part of efforts to attract people into the centre once more. To help draw attention to this ambitious programme, the city council invited a broad church of visiting and resident celebrities to plant trees. Dozens took up the shovel, Seamus Heaney among them, while comedy duo Cannon and Ball, Michael Flatley and the Dalai Lama planted others. The precise location of the Dalai Lama's planting is now forgotten, but on Cupar Way, where one of Belfast's peace lines separates Nationalist and Loyalist communities, the **REPLACEMENT TREE (909)** remembers his visit and is a hopeful reminder that one day these walls may come tumbling down.

The city has many memorial trees that speak to the long and challenging history shared by Ireland and Britain. In West Belfast, the Roddy McCorley Centre is the site of **BOBBY SANDS' TREE (912)**, one of a dozen oaks planted to remember Republican hunger strikers who died for their cause. Not far away, Woodvale Park is home to **THE PEACE TREE* (910)**, another oak, this time planted in 1919 to commemorate the soldiers of the Royal Irish Rifles who fell at the Battle of the Somme. Also in West Belfast, the City Cemetery on the Falls Road is thickly planted with trees memorialising those who have been buried here since the 1860s. Among the monuments, dozens of fastigiate Irish yews grow. This is a tree that first arose in County Fermanagh in 1767, and has been planted abundantly throughout these islands since. **BELFAST'S IRISH YEW (911)** is one of many, but its position next to a Celtic-cross gravestone is rich in symbolism.

As Belfast has grown, it has enveloped land that would once have been fields, woods and aristocratic country estates. Vestiges of these remain: Lady Dixon Park, once the grounds of Wilmont House in the city's south, was gifted to the people in 1959 and is home to two of Belfast's most magnificent trees, **LADY DIXON'S CEDAR (919)** and the **CLIMBING TREE (918)**, which has to be seen to be believed. It is a single western red cedar that has layered itself so abundantly it resembles a dense, coniferous spinney, one that offers dozens of low, climbable boughs for adventurous tree hunters.

Perhaps Belfast's most unlikely tree is the **SANDY ROW FAIRY THORN* (906)**, an old hawthorn occupying a pocket park in the Sandy Row area close to the city centre. It has become known as a fairy tree, a type that resonates through Irish mythology as a gateway for the wee folk. Throughout the island of Ireland, lone fairy trees exist in fields and hedgerows – rarely in cities – and are often left to grow by landowners, as destroying a fairy tree is said to bring bad luck. The same sentiment has helped the Belfast tree survive.

900. **VAN MORRISON'S TREE** → Van Morrison once described Cyprus Avenue as 'a whole avenue lined with trees and I found it a place where I could think'. It obviously did the trick, inspiring his eponymous 1968 song. Listeners may be forgiven for assuming the north Belfast street is lined with cypress trees, but in fact it is noteworthy for its Austrian pines – an unusual street tree. A multi-stemmed specimen opposite Sandford Avenue is the best.

**VAN MORRISON'S TREE** *Austrian pine / Pinus nigra var. nigra*
Cyprus Avenue, Belfast BT5 5NT 54.595178, -5.879586 ///snail.rested.cheese

901. **LAGAN HUNK**
*Baobab London plane*
*Platanus × hispanica*
*'Western Baobab'*
Ormeau Park, Ormeau Road, Belfast BT7 3GG
54.583697, -5.916457

The Lagan Hunk, in Ormeau Park on the banks of the Lagan, is a charmingly grotesque plane and a noteworthy feature of Belfast's oldest park. There are several other short, corpulent baobab London planes to marvel at across the island of Ireland, like **THE NOBBLY TREE*** **(890)** in Derry and the **BIRR BURRY TREES (961 & 962)**, but this one is the benchmark. ///strain.scars.strict

902. **IRISH ITALIAN**
*Italian maple / Acer opalus*
Botanic Gardens, Botanic Avenue, Belfast BT7 1JP
54.583023, -5.931757

The Irish Italian is a fabulous tree – its quality illustrates how undeserved this species' rarity is. It is a large, elegant and densely crowned individual growing on the eastern side of the Botanic Gardens. Visit in early spring to catch the ornate dangling flowers, the most apparent feature that distinguishes this species from the ubiquitous sycamore. ///crest.venue.valve

903. **ELDER STATESMAN**
*Mirbeck's oak*
*Quercus canariensis*
Botanic Gardens, Botanic Avenue, Belfast BT7 1JP
54.58305, -5.934826

The Botanic Gardens, with its superb Palm House and Tropical Ravine, are prime examples of Belfast's Victorian architecture. The landscape is complemented by an exceptional tree collection, many of which are nineteenth-century plantings. One of the finest is the tall Mirbeck's oak on the northern perimeter to the west of the Palm House. ///food.nests.brave

**904. MEDICINE TREE** → The Medicine Tree is an oriental plane planted in the 1960s in the grounds of Belfast City Hospital from seeds provided by Dr Dimitrios Oreopoulos, a Greek renal specialist who studied here. The tree is directly descended from the Tree of Hippocrates, a 500-year-old plane growing in Kos, which can trace its own lineage back to the tree under which the father of medicine taught 2,500 years ago.

**MEDICINE TREE** *Oriental plane / Platanus orientalis* Belfast City Hospital, Lisburn Road, Belfast BT9 7AB 54.586284, -5.94425 ///tiny.admits.shirts

**905. QUB ROBLE**
*Roble*
*Nothofagus obliqua*
Chlorine Gardens,
Belfast BT9 5AH
54.579843, -5.935617

Viewable from the delightfully named Chlorine Gardens, a statuesque roble thrives on the sloping lawn in front of Queen's University's Ashby Building. It is a Chilean southern beech or roble (confusingly sometimes called a Patagonian oak), a species only occasionally seen in Britain and Ireland, but, as this individual demonstrates, it is particularly well suited to the climate in the north of Ireland. ///them.rich.sports

**906. SANDY ROW FAIRY THORN***
*Hawthorn*
*Crataegus monogyna*
Blythe Street,
Belfast BT12 5HX
54.590785, -5.941178

Among the orderly housing of Loyalist Sandy Row, the Blythe Street Fairy Garden comes as something of a surprise. Next to St Aidan's church and across the road from a Linfield FC mural, the garden hosts an old hawthorn: a fairy tree. In Irish mythology, superstition surrounds lone fairy trees ensuring they are left in peace, as bad luck befalls those who would fell one. ///export.camp.nurse

**907. INST CHERRY**
*Double-flowered wild cherry*
*Prunus avium 'Plena'*
Royal Belfast Academical
Institution,
College Square East,
Belfast BT1 6DL
54.597038, -5.935452

Most people notice cherry trees in spring when they're in flower, but occasionally they can turn heads at other times of year. Just inside the grounds of the Royal Belfast Academical Institution – known as the Inst – is one such tree: a white-flowering cultivar of the common wild cherry that has attained unusual stoutness, while its branches describe a fine crucible shape. ///newest.dame.issue

SEAMUS HEANEY'S TREE (908)

**908. SEAMUS HEANEY'S TREE**
*Small-leaved lime*
*Tilia cordata 'Greenspire'*
Linen Hall Library,
Donegall Square North,
Belfast BT1 5GB
54.597335, -5.931541

In recent decades, Belfast City Council's urban foresters have helped transform the city with a programme of street-tree planting. Notable people were invited to join in, including the great poet Seamus Heaney, who planted a *'Greenspire'* small-leaved lime in 2000. It is maturing nicely outside the famous Linen Hall Library on Donegall Square. ///thus.agents.sting

**909. REPLACEMENT TREE**
*Chanticleer pear*
*Pyrus calleryana*
*'Chanticleer'*
Cupar Way,
Belfast BT13 2RX
54.601242, -5.957332

On Cupar Way, tough chanticleer pear trees have been planted along the peace line in the hope that one day they will replace it. A quote from the Dalai Lama, who planted a pair of trees when visiting Belfast in 2000, is emblazoned on the wall next to one of the pears: 'Open your arms to change, but don't let go of your values.' ///badge.hogs.gaps

**910. THE PEACE TREE***
*Hybrid oak*
*Quercus × rosacea*
Woodvale Park,
Belfast BT13 3HY
54.607145, -5.965666

Thousands of Irishmen lost their lives in the First World War, and in 1919 an oak tree was planted as a memorial in Woodvale Park. On the centenary of the Battle of the Somme, a stone monument was erected and the tree has since been voted Belfast's favourite. It is a hybrid between the two native Irish oaks, pedunculate – with stalked acorns and stalkless leaves – and sessile, where these are reversed. ///having.bucket.faded

**911. BELFAST'S IRISH YEW**
*Irish yew / Taxus baccata*
*'Fastigiata'*
Belfast City Cemetery,
Falls Road,
Belfast BT12 6DE
54.588791, -5.974139

The original Irish yew, unlike the familiar yew tree, has neat, upward-sweeping branches. 'Discovered' in 1767 at Florence Court, a stately home in County Fermanagh, it is still going strong, and every other Irish yew is a scion, or clone, of that tree. The Victorians loved them, planting thousands throughout Ireland and Britain. Belfast City Cemetery is thickly planted: an individual tree close to a Celtic-cross gravestone makes a fine tableau. ///trash.gender.bunk

**912. BOBBY SANDS' TREE**
*Pedunculate oak*
*Quercus robur*
Roddy McCorley Society,
Glen Road,
Belfast BT11 8BU
54.577418, -6.013091

In 2001, a dozen Irish oaks were planted as memorials to IRA hunger strikers, including ten who died during the notorious 1981 strikes. They grow in the grounds of the Roddy McCorley Society on Glen Road in West Belfast. Bobby Sands, one of the strikers who died, achieved international attention for his actions, and his tree, along with the other eleven, remember the darkest days of the Troubles. ///smile.cycles.stored

### 913. CROWD PLEASER
*Weeping willow / Salix × sepulcralis 'Chrysocoma'*
Grovelands, Musgrave Park, Stockmans Lane,
Belfast BT9 7JB
54.569278, -5.970215

Grovelands is the bosky garden area in the south of Musgrave Park, and there is a fine tree collection in its south-west corner. Several interesting species vie for attention, including a good dawn redwood, but the most outstanding of the lot is the lovely weeping willow, a perennially popular species, growing close to the path leading from the hospital to Stockmans Lane. ///inform.themes.pumps

### 914. COLLEGE OAK
*Turkey oak / Quercus cerris*
Stranmillis College, Stranmillis Road,
Belfast BT9 5DY
54.571812, -5.938732

The leafy Stranmillis College campus is full of mature trees, the finest being a huge Turkey oak to the south of the main halls. The oak grows among other trees on a wooded slope, which encourages it upwards to an impressive height. Its position requires you to get up close in order to appreciate its huge girth. ///human.across.happy

### 915. MILLIONAIRES' LIME
*Common lime*
*Tilia × europaea*
Malone Park,
Belfast BT9 6NH
54.565128, -5.952032

Malone Park is Belfast's most sought-after address. It is a broad boulevard lined with mature common lime trees that must add much to the street's attraction for the well-heeled. While the trees can be appreciated as an avenue, one tree in particular, near Malone Road, stands out for its thick, short bole, from which multiple trunks ascend. ///dress.frame.voting

### 916. FOREST OF BELFAST OAK
*Pedunculate oak*
*Quercus robur*
Old Shaw's Bridge,
Belfast BT9 5YN
54.553323, -5.955008

'Trees are non-political, non-sectarian, good for everybody.' So the *Irish Times* wrote of the pioneering Forest of Belfast project back in 1996, an initiative that facilitated significant new tree planting throughout the city. At Old Shaw's Bridge, a sliver of the forest can be seen in the Irish oak trees planted three decades ago. The finest is next to a standing stone, a monument to the enterprise. ///washed.cans.policy

### 917. A BELVOIR OAK
*Pedunculate oak*
*Quercus robur*
Belvoir Country Park,
Belvoir Drive,
Belfast BT8 7QT
54.558767, -5.928455

Exactly which tree in Belvoir Country Park is *the* Belvoir Oak, a semi-mythical ancient tree, is a matter of dispute. A nineteenth-century photo of a grand old oak here shows a huge tree, since lost, and there is a decrepit veteran, little more than a shell, growing among conifers that some claim to be Ireland's oldest tree. If I had to vote for the best, I'd choose the low-growing, multi-branched pedunculate oak close to the car park. It is a delight. ///feeds.jazz.force

**918. CLIMBING TREE**
*Western red cedar*
*Thuja plicata*
Sir Thomas and
Lady Dixon Park,
Belfast BT17 9LA
54.539497, -5.983719

Most towns and cities have at least one renowned climbing tree, a tree that has nurtured generations of adventurous kids who will pass on knowledge of its clamber-worthy attributes to succeeding generations. Belfast has one of the best in Lady Dixon Park's western red cedar – a great layering example that will only become bigger and better for climbing as the years go by. ///leap.rank.nasal

919. **LADY DIXON'S CEDAR** ⟶ Although the **CLIMBING TREE** (918) is a western red cedar, it is not a true cedar, botanically speaking. But nearby Lady Dixon's Cedar is, and holds its needles in whorls to prove its identity as a deodar. It is a majestic tree that has grown on the lawn close to Wilmont House for well over a century, and must be one of the finest Irish examples.

**LADY DIXON'S CEDAR**
*Deodar cedar / Cedrus deodara*
Sir Thomas and Lady Dixon
Park, Belfast BT17 9LA
54.539578, -5.982558
///puddles.rewarding.spends

DUNMURRY TULIP TREE (920)

### 920. DUNMURRY TULIP TREE
*Tulip tree*
*Liriodendron tulipifera*
Beechlawn Hotel,
Dunmurry Lane,
Dunmurry BT17 9NP
54.551706, -5.999419

Outside the Beechlawn hotel on Dunmurry Lane, the pavement has been widened and the hotel boundary fence curves to accommodate an unlikely tulip tree growing in the middle of the path. It is one of the most northerly trees of the species in Ireland, and is, perhaps because of the climate or its exposed position, somewhat stunted, with a flared base and deliciously warty trunk. ///frames.actor.crisis

### 921. WESLEY'S YEW
*Yew / Taxus baccata*
Derriaghy Road,
Lisburn BT28 3SH
54.544187, -6.030715

Tucked away up a side road off Derriaghy Road, Wesley's Yew can be found close to Derriaghy House. Look closely to notice the thickness of its sinewy trunk – it is older than it appears. The founder of Methodism, John Wesley, is said to have preached under it in 1778. ///skinny.rings.spoke

### 922. DOWNSHIRE GIANT
*Giant redwood*
*Sequoiadendron giganteum*
Main Street,
Hillsborough BT26 6AP
54.462875, -6.083728

Hillsborough's Main Street is lined with Georgian houses, but it is the Victorian feature that makes the biggest impression. Towering over the statue of the Fourth Marquess of Downshire, a giant redwood competes in height with the spire of the parish church across the road. ///upward.lunges.tributes

### 923. RAWDON'S LEGACY
*Oriental plane*
*Platanus orientalis*
Moira Demesne,
Demesne Grove, Moira,
Craigavon BT67 0DS
54.485056, -6.230257

Today, Moira Demesne is a popular park, but 350 years ago it was one of Ireland's foremost gardens. Laid out by Sir Arthur Rawdon, known as the Father of Irish Gardening, it boasted the first Irish hothouse and 400 plants imported from Jamaica. There is little to see of this past, but Rawdon's tradition lives on in a fabulous, low-branching oriental plane. ///defender.regretted.tables

### 924. ALPHA TREE
*Common lime*
*Tilia × europaea*
High Street, Killyleagh,
Downpatrick BT30 9QF
54.401587, -5.652662

Twenty-six mature limes, one for each letter of the alphabet, form a row against the castle wall on Shrigley Road. But the keen-eyed will notice the row only contains twenty-five. When one was lost, its detached replacement – Alpha – was planted 200 metres from where its original namesake grew. ///makeovers.homecare.encounter

### 925. OLD HOMER*
*Holm oak / Quercus ilex*
Fairy Glen, Bridge Street,
Rostrevor BT34 3BG
54.10038, -6.195433

Old Homer is a much-loved 200-year-old holm oak growing in Kilbroney Park, close to the Fairy Glen at Rostrevor. The tree has a dramatic lean, almost 45 degrees from the ground, a tilt that has ensured it is much climbed. Its popularity means that it has had to be propped. ///working.ribcage.elbowing

# REPUBLIC of IRELAND

## REPUBLIC OF IRELAND

*Donegal*
*Leitrim*
*Sligo*
*Mayo*
*Roscommon*
*Galway*
*Clare*
*Limerick*
*Kerry*
*Cork*
*Tipperary*
*Waterford*
*Kilkenny*
*Carlow*
*Wexford*
*Wicklow*
*Kildare*
*Dublin*
*Meath*
*Louth*
*Monaghan*
*Cavan*
*Longford*
*Westmeath*
*Offaly*
*Laois*

**TREE CITY:**
*Dublin*

**SIGNATURE SPECIES:**
*Hawthorn*

Botanically, Ireland and Britain have much in common. Many of the same tree species grow on both islands, and trees have played similar roles in the historical, cultural, religious and political consciousness of both nations. They are place makers, waymarkers, religious symbols, talismans, climbing frames and natural wonders. They can be found in similar locations: parks and cemeteries, botanical collections and former aristocratic estates, and, of course, the streets people walk down each day. Still, there are some notable differences.

Irish tradition embraces fairy, wishing and rag trees. These are trees with particular symbolic functions, and examples are scattered right across the island, both in the Republic and Northern Ireland. While these magical trees are also known in Scotland, Wales and Cornwall, attesting to their Celtic connections, they are particularly widespread in Ireland. Pieces of fabric are attached to rag trees as a token of a human malady; as the rags disintegrate, so will the illness. They are found near holy wells (another feature of Irish landscapes) and are usually hawthorns. Their mystic significance may not always be apparent: the rags with which they are bedecked don't last long, and so they go in cycles of dormancy and conspicuous activity. I visited **THE RAGGEDY BUSH\* (990)** outside Kilkenny in the summer of 2022, and was thrilled to discover it laden with rags. Wishing trees are similar: they too are often hawthorns, though oak and ash are also recorded, and sometimes they have fabric tied to them. They can grant the wishes of those who visit them. The **TARBERT WISHING TREE\* (966)** is particularly spectacular: a lone roadside oak growing out of the wall on the Kerry bank of the Shannon estuary. Fairy trees are perhaps the most widespread of the spiritual triumvirate. Again, they are frequently hawthorns, but they can be trees of any species, growing anywhere in the landscape. If you see a solitary tree in a field or hedge, it might well be a fairy tree, a gateway between the human and fairy worlds.

Another peculiarity of Irish tree flora can be found in the west. Famously, arbutus, or strawberry trees – a species that is otherwise found in the Mediterranean basin and Iberia – grow wild here, but not in Britain. There is a significant population in County Kerry, and one of the largest individual trees, the **GIANT ARBUTUS (972)**, grows close to the road outside Killarney on the Ring of Kerry. Recent research suggests that strawberry trees are an archaeophyte, a species that arrived with human assistance after the end of the last ice age.

These old individuals reflect the mild climate of Ireland's Atlantic seaboard: all sorts of trees can flourish in the wet and wild west. In Galway city, another mediterranean interloper can be seen growing from the sheer walls of the Friar's River canal. The **CORRIB FIG (958)**, like similarly determined English figs, has managed to thrive in a most unlikely situation. It has become such a well-loved tree that a proposed new bridge was repositioned to avoid damaging the tree.

But it is in Dublin where the greatest riches await the tree hunter. From curiosities like **THE HUNGRY TREE\* (941)** to stalwarts like the **LEINSTER HOUSE ROBINIA (945)**, there are trees intent on detaining you for days. Indeed, some may not get much further than the hallowed grounds of the National Botanic Gardens where the **AUTHOR'S CHOICE (938)** should be sought out among the select canopy. Beyond Ireland's vibrant capital, you will likely be drawn to its most southerly city, Cork, which is scattered with many interesting trees, including the **UCC GIANT REDWOOD (985)** and the **ICONIC OAK (984)**. Visitors should, as generations of Corkonians have done, make for Fota House and Gardens, one of Ireland's finest tree collections, just fifteen minutes away by train. The grounds, including its exceptional arboretum, were laid out from the mid-nineteenth century, and are awash with tender plants, giant conifers (including a breathtaking grove of coastal redwoods) and great rarities. The tree that many will remember is the **BILLOWING CLOUD TREE (987)**, a *'Spiralis'* cultivar of the Japanese cedar or *Cryptomeria*. It is confoundingly rare – you will no doubt wonder what it is – and particularly beautiful – its form will imprint itself on your consciousness. If you only see one tree in Ireland, this is it. You will not be disappointed.

### 926. SUPERVALU HORSE CHESTNUT
*Horse chestnut*
*Aesculus hippocastanum*
Donegal Shopping Centre,
Glebe, Donegal, F94 Y86X
54.651318, -8.111228

The aged SuperValu Horse Chestnut may go unnoticed outside the winter months, when its remarkable form is clothed in leaves and it merges into a tight row of other trees. So it is best to visit in winter when this tree's great arching limbs – one in particular growing close to its base seems to defy gravity – and flared trunk can be fully appreciated. Find it growing in a field on the corner of Quay Street and the Glebe across the road from the supermarket. ///publish.cooks.tilt

### 927. HOSPITAL BEECH
*Copper beech / Fagus sylvatica 'Purpurea'*
St Columba's Hospital, Clarion Road, Sligo, F91 CD34
54.280037, -8.45831

Sligo's Hospital Beech appears to have led an eventful life. It is an old, sinewy copper beech with a fat, buttressed bole that branches close to the ground, almost as if it has been pollarded in the past – an unlikely backstory for an ornamental tree that would in all likelihood have been planted as a specimen. As well as revealing details of the tree's past life, those branches have had decades to grow into distorted shapes, developing hollows and crannies which provide homes for a diversity of wildlife. It grows just inside the hospital grounds near the entrance on Clarion Road. ///genetic.woke.princesses

### 928. KILCURRY BIG TREE
*Sycamore / Acer pseudoplatanus*
Church Road, Kilcurry,
Co. Louth, A91 RP73
54.043378, -6.424453

The Kilcurry Big Tree is just that: a prominent sycamore growing by a crossroads in the village of Kilcurry a few kilometres north of Dundalk. The tree is well documented, and a nearby sign explains that it was planted over 200 years ago as a sapling by a child, one Margaret Grant, who was born in 1812. It survived a fire in 1977 that destroyed a nearby hall, numerous traffic accidents, as well as a road-widening scheme in 2008. ///cherished.streaking.impaired

### 929. LONESOME LIME
*Lime / Tilia × europaea*
Fair Green, Main Street,
Duleek, Co. Meath,
A92 TDK7
53.655388, -6.416917

Following King William's victory at the Battle of the Boyne in 1690, the Protestant Huguenot population of Duleek, just down the road, planted two trees on Fair Green: an ash, apparently representing Queen Mary, and a lime representing William. They grew entwined for a century and a half, but, some time after 1849, the short-lived ash succumbed. A deep niche in the tree's bole is said to be the impression left by the ash. Today, Duleek's lime is still going strong, and is reputed to be the oldest in Ireland. ///culinary.warming.fitness

**930. SYCAMORE XL**
*Sycamore / Acer pseudoplatanus*
Gormanston Park,
Gormanston,
Co. Meath, K32 NH30
53.636144, -6.239379
*On private land, but visible from the road.*

The Sycamore XL is an awe-inspiring tree. Vast and old, it resembles one of the grand Scottish sycamores like the CONSOLATION SYCAMORE (13), but is even larger. An enormous trunk supports great gravity-defying branches and a massive globular crown. It grows near the playing field of Gormanston School, but can be admired from the street if you peer through the gate on Gormanston Road. ///strongest.cautiously.flippers

931. **SILKEN THOMAS YEW*** → Beyond the castle ruins and the church at the end of Main Street in Maynooth, lies the Silken Thomas Yew, Ireland's oldest tree. It is named for Thomas FitzGerald, the tenth Earl of Kildare and resident of Maynooth Castle, who led a failed 1534 revolt against English King Henry VIII in which his men tied distinctive silk ribbons to their attire. Before surrendering, Thomas played his harp under the yew, which today grows on the lawn of St Patrick's College.

**SILKEN THOMAS YEW***
*Yew / Taxus baccata*
St Patrick's College,
Maynooth,
Co. Kildare, W23 TW77
53.380242, -6.594892
///books.cascade.thank

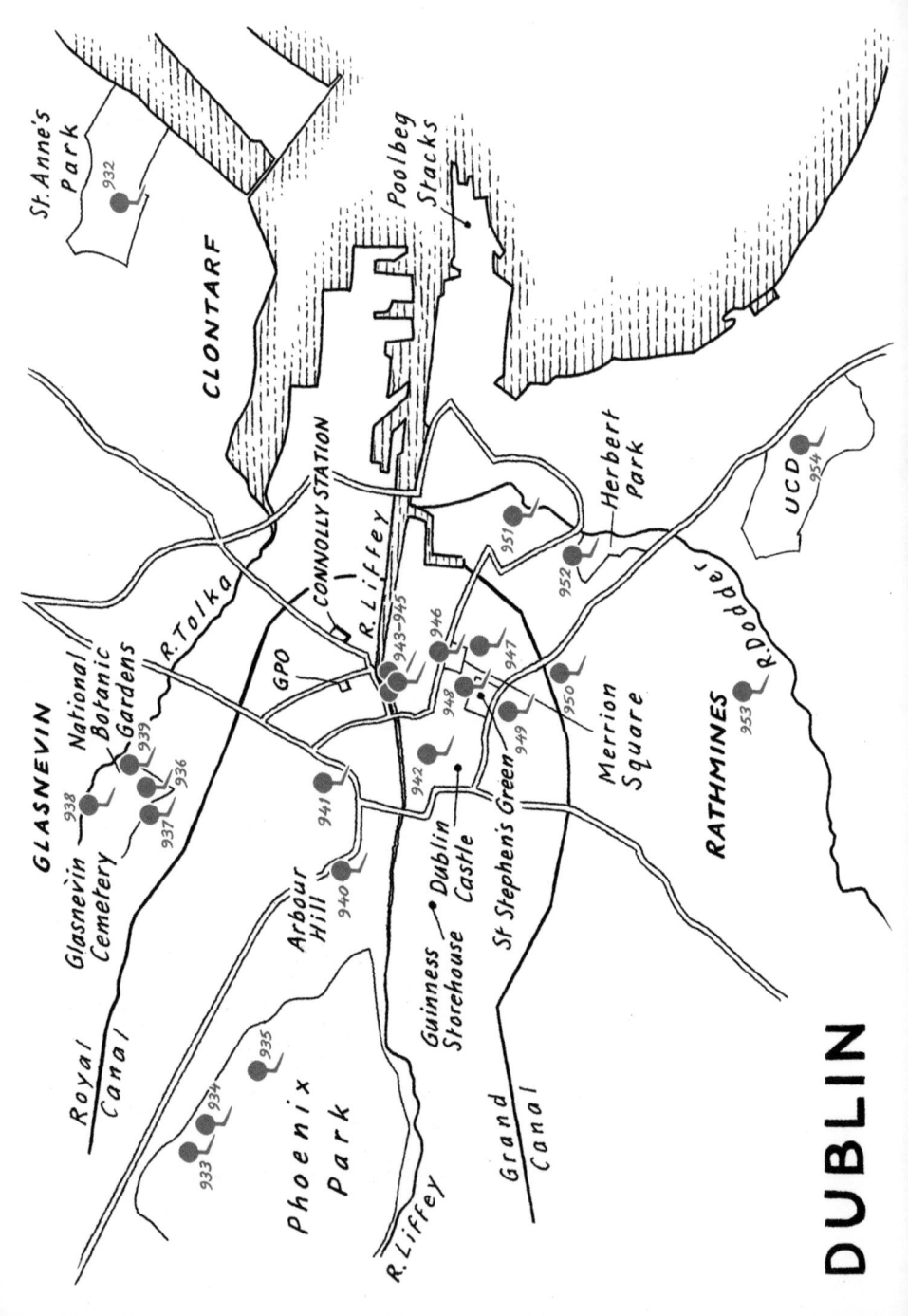

# TREE CITY: DUBLIN
**SIGNATURE SPECIES:** *Oriental plane*

St Stephen's Green is emblematic of Dublin, and has played a bit-part in the history of the city, and the Irish state. Originally a common, it became a residential garden square, the largest in Dublin's magnificent Georgian city. It was redeveloped in the 1880s, from when the current landscape dates, and was the site of a rebel position during the 1916 Easter Rising. It is at the centre of a cluster of Dublin's notable trees. Those in Iveagh Gardens and Merrion Square are a short walk away, and, if you travel by foot, you should examine the recently planted **BAGGOT STREET HERALD (947)** on the way: it is a glorious honey locust, the forerunner to a fine row of London planes, and an example of exciting new tree planting, often of more unusual species, happening all over the city.

As the Baggot Street row suggests, Dublin has many fine planes. Notably, oriental planes have been planted in recent years on O'Connell Street, both as a way to increase the genetic diversity of trees in the city, but also, subliminally perhaps, to distance the city from its colonial past evident in the large number of now-mature London planes. Among these London planes, however, there are some of great interest. At Trinity College, the **TRINITY TWINS (943 & 944)**, a pair of plump baobab London planes, are a great curiosity. These two oddities mirror another pair, the **BIRR BURRY TREES (961 & 962)**, that grow at Birr, the seat of the Earl of Rosse. But the most spectacular of the Dublin planes is the **AUTHOR'S CHOICE (938)**, a very scarce variegated cultivar of London plane. It grows on the banks of the River Tolka as it flows through the National Botanic Gardens at Glasnevin. When seen in full leaf, many must wonder why this beguiling tree is so rare; there cannot be more than ten in Ireland or Britain.

Glasnevin is one of Dublin's most enticing locations for a tree hunter; as well as the National Botanic Gardens, awash with fascinating trees, Glasnevin Cemetery is an essential stop. The **LIBERATOR REDWOOD (937)** greets arrivals. It is not the tallest example of a giant redwood, but its deeply furrowed trunk and arching limbs imbue it with a sense of welcoming familiarity. It is a tree I felt had an almost human character when I encountered it. It is also laden with Irish history, growing next to the round tower where Daniel O'Connell, the great nineteenth-century champion of Catholic Ireland, is buried.

Also on the Northside, Dublin's most famous tree – **THE HUNGRY TREE\* (941)**, a London plane at King's Inn Park, is an essential stop. It is inexorably 'eating' a cast-iron park bench. It is an unlikely landmark but has, nevertheless, become a poster child for trees in the city, one that is undeniably humorous but also highlights the great age and slow growth of trees. The tree must be a nineteenth-century planting, while the bench, which may have been fixed next to it when the tree was a sapling, is also of a considerable age. There must be thousands of similarly aged planes in Dublin, but there can be very few Victorian benches that have survived, even partially.

932. **PINE OF GUINNESS** → St Anne's Park, formerly an estate owned by the Guinness family, is Dublin's second largest. It is compartmentalised into several distinct areas, but a kilometre-long grand avenue runs almost the full length from the Sybil Hill Road entrance. The avenue is lined with alternating holm oaks and pines: a particularly rugged example of a Monterey pine can be found on the north side near the arboretum.

**PINE OF GUINNESS** *Monterey pine / Pinus radiata* St Anne's Park, All Saints Road, Dublin 5, D05 R8P7 53.371752, -6.183094 ///bottle.splash.talked

933. **BURTON'S HOLM OAK**
*Holm oak / Quercus ilex*
Ashtown Castle, Nunciature Road, Phoenix Park, Dublin 8, D08 X6X3
53.365365, -6.330644

Renowned English landscaper Decimus Burton spent twenty years remodelling Phoenix Park in the nineteenth century, and this legacy is most apparent in the multitude of evergreen holm oaks that now define Dublin's great green lung. The finest, a veteran tree that must predate Burton's time (and was perhaps his inspiration), grows near Ashtown Castle and the visitor centre. ///steep.expect.admit

934. **PHOENIX TREE**
*Western red cedar*
*Thuja plicata*
Ashtown Castle, Nunciature Road, Phoenix Park, Dublin 8, D08 X6X3
53.365149, -6.329786

Thousands of parents who bring children to Phoenix Park make a beeline for the Phoenix Tree. A sprawling and eminently accessible conifer, this western red cedar has an abundance of layering branches and ground-brushing foliage, making it an irresistible tree for climbing and playing hide and seek. ///never.breed.moon

935. **ÁRAS AN UACHTARÁIN REDWOOD**
*Giant redwood*
*Sequoiadendron giganteum*
Áras an Uachtaráin, Phoenix Park, Dublin 8, D08 E1W3
53.359058, -6.318262
*In private grounds, but visible from the public park.*

From behind a ha-ha (a sunken fence that acts as a barrier to livestock without interrupting the view) in Phoenix Park it is possible to peer into the gardens of Áras an Uachtaráin, the official residence of the Irish President. To the left of the short avenue of clipped Irish yews, a clump of giant redwoods will catch your eye – but this 'clump' is in fact a single, multi-stemmed layering tree planted by Queen Victoria in 1861 when this was the Viceregal Lodge. ///brains.exile.blocks

936. **DRIVE-THRU BEECH** → Glasnevin Cemetery's Drive-Thru Beech, like an iconic Californian redwood, has a tunnel cut through its trunk. But, while the Californian giants can accommodate a Cadillac-sized arch, beech trees never reach those proportions. The tunnel that runs through the base of this tree appears instead to have been designed for very little people indeed.

**DRIVE-THRU BEECH** Beech /*Fagus sylvatica* Glasnevin Cemetery, Finglas Road, Dublin 11, D11 XA32 53.370108, -6.273206 ///period.degree.rank

937. **LIBERATOR REDWOOD**
*Giant redwood*
*Sequoiadendron giganteum*
Glasnevin Cemetery,
Finglas Road,
Dublin 11, D11 XA32
53.369677, -6.27655

Many significant monuments greet those arriving at Glasnevin Cemetery from the Finglas Road entrance. The O'Connell Tower, a round tower marking the tomb of nineteenth-century champion of Catholic emancipation Daniel O'Connell, is a landmark many come to see. Next to it, and equally impressive, is the Liberator Redwood, a giant redwood with an expressive lower limb that arches just above human head height. ///dine.firmly.green

938. **AUTHOR'S CHOICE**
*Variegated London plane*
*Platanus × hispanica*
*'Suttnerii'*
National Botanic
Gardens, Botanic Road,
Dublin 9, D09 YV29
53.375013, -6.275629

Every pundit has their favourites at the National Botanic Gardens, and repeat visits will reward the cognoscenti with new discoveries. A tree that holds the affections of many, including my own, is the *'Suttnerii'* London plane growing on the Tolka's southern bank. Its striking variegated leaves signify this is one of only a very few trees of its type in the world, which is why it is this Author's Choice ///safely.gifts.slice

939. **GLASNEVIN TREE OF HEAVEN**
*Tree of heaven*
*Ailanthus altissima*
National Botanic
Gardens, Botanic Road,
Dublin 9, D09 YV29
53.372561, -6.270766

It requires a particularly fine tree to rise to the occasion and occupy the pre-eminent vista at the National Botanic Gardens. The Glasnevin Tree of Heaven does this effortlessly, drawing attention to the twin glass buildings of the Palm House and the Curvilinear Range, while also holding its own as the scene's third monument. It is the shapeliest tree of its species in Ireland or Britain. ///tower.pounds.crop

TRINITY TWINS (943 & 944)

### 940. ARBOUR HILL SYCAMORE
Sycamore / *Acer pseudoplatanus*
Arbour Hill, Dublin 7,
D07 TF84
53.350946, -6.286763

Fourteen of the executed leaders of the 1916 Easter Rising were buried at Arbour Hill Cemetery and are remembered on the Arbour Hill Memorial, next to which a suitably magnificent tree grows: the Arbour Hill Sycamore. The tree is very impressive, and would have been mature back in 1916. In such an important position, it has been well cared for, and has mellowed into one of Dublin's most handsome trees. ///scar.manliness.desire

### 941. THE HUNGRY TREE*
London plane
*Platanus* × *hispanica*
King's Inn Park,
Constitution Hill,
Dublin 7, D07 RF70
53.352159, -6.273025

Dublin's most famous tree has to be The Hungry Tree. Hundreds of column inches have been devoted to it, and it features in every self-respecting Dublin guidebook. For good reason too: a London plane at King's Inn Park – perhaps 150 years old – has been quietly munching its way through a cast-iron bench for decades. Only the arms and two front legs are left to go. ///apron.stick.inches

### 942. DUBH LINN PAPERBARK
Paperbark maple
*Acer griseum*
Dubh Linn Gardens,
Dublin Castle, Castle Street,
Dublin 2, D02 X822
53.34216, -6.267105

The translucent, cinnamon-coloured bark that flakes from the branches of paperbark maples rarely fails to impress, and the mature tree in historic Dubh Linn Gardens at Dublin Castle is a head turner. It grows in a raised bed in the south-west corner, close to the Chester Beatty Gallery and the statue commemorating the Special Olympics held in Ireland in 2003. ///drew.even.blows

### 943. TRINITY TWINS
### & 944.
Baobab London plane
*Platanus* × *hispanica*
'Western Baobab'
New Square, Trinity
College, College Green,
Dublin 2, D02 FD37
53.344451, -6.254858

In the north east of Trinity College's New Square, a pair of charmingly burry baobab London planes reside. Of the two, the tree nearest the corner is easiest to inspect while heeding the 'Keep Off the Lawns' sign. They are nearly identical to the pair in Birr, part of a memorial to former Trinity Chancellor, the Earl of Rosse. ///lowest.rested.brick

### 945. LEINSTER HOUSE ROBINIA
False acacia / *Robinia pseudoacacia*
Merrion Square West,
Dublin 2, D02 K303
53.340381, -6.252373
*In private grounds, but visible from a public place.*

The perimeter of the rear garden of Leinster House is lined with several old *Robinias* or false acacia trees. From the forecourt of the neighbouring National Gallery of Ireland, the Leinster House Robinia, growing next to a holm oak, stands out. As they age, *Robinias* take on enigmatic, crooked silhouettes, making them appear very old. Leinster House is Georgian, but the tree is probably younger. ///study.crop.exists

**946. MICHAEL COLLINS'S PLANE**
*Oriental plane*
*Platanus orientalis*
Merrion Square North,
Dublin 2, D02 AW80
53.3396, -6.247221

Near the bust of Michael Collins in the north-east corner of Merrion Square, a quietly extraordinary oriental plane tree grows. It has a sinewy trunk, scaly bark, typically incised leaves and a short bole, perhaps the result of historic pollarding, from where many tentacular branches sweep skywards, their writhings frozen in time. ///hurray.feel.branded

**947. BAGGOT STREET HERALD**
*Honey locust*
*Gleditsia triacanthos*
Baggot Street Lower,
Dublin 2, D02 YC83
53.337605, -6.251378

Baggot Street Lower has a fine row of London planes lining its central reservation, but just before these trees a specimen of a different complexion stands out. A far younger and shaggier honey locust grows on a triangle at the junction with Pembroke Street Lower. A landmark of the future, it is emblematic of a new wave of urban tree planting that has taken place around Dublin in recent years. ///reward.clues.shelf

**948. FAMINE MEMORIAL ASH**
*Weeping ash / Fraxinus excelsior 'Pendula'*
St Stephen's Green,
Dublin 2, D02 K224
53.338306, -6.25653

In the north-eastern corner of St Stephen's Green, behind the curved stone screen of Edward Delaney's sculpture of Wolfe Tone, the famine memorial faces into the square's interior. Opposite this harrowing group, a weeping ash grows. The forlorn pendulousness of this cultivar was favoured during the nineteenth century as a symbol of mourning; this tree is an unwitting extension of the memorial. ///dices.artist.deeper

**949. SECRET PENDENT LIME**
*Silver pendent lime*
*Tilia tomentosa 'Petiolaris'*
Iveagh Gardens,
Hatch Street Upper,
Dublin 2, D02 HX65
53.334182, -6.260462

Iveagh Gardens is one of Dublin's best-kept secrets. It is surrounded by buildings on three sides and has very discreet entrance gates on Clonmel Street and Hatch Street Upper. Next to the steps leading down from Hatch Street Upper, the gardens' most interesting tree can be found: a soaring silver pendent lime that is likely a representative of the original 1862 plantings. ///fool.likes.trash

**950. RANELAGH TURKEY OAK**
*Turkey oak / Quercus cerris*
Dartmouth Square,
Dublin 6, D06 XH33
53.330194, -6.254943

The Ranelagh Turkey Oak is an impressive tree. It grows near the southern edge of Dartmouth Square in Ranelagh, a sought-after south Dublin address. The tree has a lot of competition from other fine trees in the square, including several mature sycamores and a black walnut, but it is the only Turkey oak, and in decades to come could well be the largest tree here. ///slips.under.moment

MICHAEL COLLINS'S PLANE (946)

**951. LANSDOWNE STRAWBERRY TREE**
*Hybrid strawberry tree*
*Arbutus × andrachnoides*
Shelbourne Road,
Dublin 4, D04 H662
53.33332, -6.231785

It might be anticipated that a strawberry tree (notably, a wild-growing tree in Ireland but not Britain) would be a highlight of Dublin's urban forest. The stars align on Shelbourne Road where a magnificent specimen hangs over a wall from the exclusive Lansdowne Place development. It is a beautiful hybrid strawberry tree with mahogany bark peeling in places to reveal acid green patches, a far rarer type than most in Ireland. ///social.mutual.cowboy

**952. VINTAGE CHESTNUT**
*Horse chestnut*
*Aesculus hippocastanum*
Herbert Park, Clyde Lane,
Dublin 4, D04 A782
53.328064, -6.236119

Herbert Park in Ballsbridge, another of Dublin's desirable Southside suburbs, has a noteworthy tree in the shape of a well-proportioned horse chestnut. It grows in the northern section of the park between the bowling club and the café, where it is something of a landmark. Close inspection shows its trunk to be particularly fluted, a sign this is an old tree. ///groom.beard.flap

**953. UNDERDOG ASH**
*Ash / Fraxinus excelsior*
Trinity College Botanic Garden, Palmerston Park,
Dublin 6, D06 W226
53.311921, -6.259367

The National Botanic Gardens at Glasnevin are not the only botanics in town – across the road from Palmerston Park, Trinity College maintains its own small but interesting plant collection, including a dense arboretum. Here, an exceptionally tall, vigorous and straight-trunked example of a very common tree – an ash – can be seen rubbing shoulders with many other much rarer plants. The triumph of the underdog. ///melon.paying.loving

**954. UCD OAK** → Not to be outdone by the splendid trees that grace Trinity, the Belfield campus of University College Dublin is also well treed, but with an altogether different, more contemporary timbre. Here mature trees intermingle with the modernist architecture. These combine memorably near the School of Irish, Celtic Studies and Folklore, where the concrete weaves around a veteran pedunculate oak.

**UCD OAK** *Pedunculate oak / Quercus robur* University College Dublin, Belfield, Dublin 4 53.306315, -6.221176 ///rings.ending.cubs

### 955. FOUR STONE TREE*
*Common lime*
*Tilia × europaea*
Main Street, Blessington,
Co. Wicklow, W91 YR67
53.170938, -6.5326

Downshire House was one of the grandest in Ireland until it was burnt to the ground during the 1798 Rebellion. Many tree-lined avenues fanned out from the big house, and the last survivor of the original trees grows on Blessington's Main Street. It is surrounded by four granite boulders that were originally at the entrance to St Mary's Church of Ireland across the road. ///closely.loaning.fizzed

### 956. CENTRE OF IRELAND TREE
*Beech / Fagus sylvatica*
The Beech Tree,
Streamstown, Co.
Westmeath, N91 YY06
53.439158, -7.575385

Close to the geographic centre of Ireland in County Westmeath, Streamstown is a little-visited village boasting only a few houses and a pub called The Beech Tree. But it is well worth a detour: the pub is named for the settlement's sublime feature, a giant billowing beech that has been marking the crossroads here for many, many years. ///numbering.accumulated.bluntly

### 957. WESTPORT BIG TREE
*London plane*
*Platanus × hispanica*
Peter Street, Westport,
Co. Mayo, F28 X594
53.798768, -9.525151

The handsome planned town of Westport is known for its tree-lined Malls on either side of the Carrowbeg River, but an individual tree that really stands out is at the other end of town. The Westport Big Tree is a London plane growing on the street not far from the Octagon, the town's eight-sided plaza. As if to confirm its landmark status, it grows outside a pub called The Big Tree. ///befit.dark.vacant

### 958. CORRIB FIG
*Fig / Ficus carica*
Waterside, Woodquay,
Galway, H91 DK58
53.275536, -9.055398

The Corrib Fig grows tenaciously from the stone embankment of the Friar's River, a canal next to the Corrib River, in sight of Galway Cathedral. Like other figs growing close to waterways it is likely fallout from human waste, commerce or industrial effluence. Despite its inauspicious beginnings, the fig has become a valued landmark, and a new pedestrian bridge was relocated in order to spare the tree. ///asserts.leap.vague

### 959. ST NICHOLAS'S ELM
*Tabletop elm / Ulmus glabra 'Horizontalis'*
St. Nicholas Collegiate
Church, Lombard Street,
Galway, H91 PY20
53.272626, -9.054225

In the churchyard of Ireland's largest medieval church, St Nicholas, the country's broadest tabletop elm can be admired. It is a wonderful example of a striking cultivar, likely planted in the nineteenth century. It grows in the churchyard close to the Lombard Street entrance and makes a magnificent backdrop to Galway's Saturday and Sunday Market, which has congregated on the streets here for centuries. ///belly.pocket.stores

WESTPORT BIG TREE (957)

**960. YOUNG TURK**
*Turkey oak / Quercus cerris*
Eyre Square, Galway,
H91 TH7T
53.273731, -9.048994

The Young Turk will be Galway's most magnificent tree in decades to come. Despite being a young Turkey oak (look out for bristly acorn cups in October), it has rapidly attained a good size, and is already a landmark in Galway's commercial centre. Its well-mulched, fenced-off enclosure should enable it to reach HOLYWOOD BIG OAK* **(899)** proportions in no time. You can almost see it expanding. ///plug.tulip.sculpture

**961. BIRR BURRY TREES**
**& 962.** *Baobab London plane*
*Platanus × hispanica*
*'Western Baobab'*
John's Place, Birr, Co.
Offaly, R42 PW61
53.09569, -7.908562

Two burry trees in the centre of Birr are botanically, visually and historically connected to the TRINITY TWINS **(943 & 944)** in Dublin. They are twin baobab London planes, and have pride of place in well-kept lawns surrounded by white iron fences close to the statue commemorating the Earl of Rosse's tenure as Chancellor of Trinity College. Perhaps their canopies are lusher and their figures slightly fuller than their city-slicker Dublin siblings. ///ogre.shortens.wangle

**963. CATHEDRAL HOLM OAK**
*Holm oak / Quercus ilex*
St Mary's Cathedral,
Bridge Street, Limerick,
V94 E068
52.66792, -8.623377

Imposing St Mary's Cathedral, Limerick's oldest building, has a churchyard full of old trees, but the Cathedral Holm Oak is the one that attracts attention. A tough old character, it is shorter than some, but all the more distinctive for it. Best seen in winter when the gothic ensemble of grey stone and evergreen oak make a fine juxtaposition. ///dent.quite.pads

**964. PEOPLE'S BIRCH**
*Paper birch*
*Betula papyrifera*
People's Park,
Pery Square,
Limerick, V94 E67F
52.658164, -8.62671

The most captivating tree in Limerick's People's Park is not one of the many giants that reside here, but rather a supremely elegant birch. Find the People's Birch at the park's western end: its gleaming white bark makes it unmissable, and the bench encircling it offers a good spot from which to enjoy its canopy, especially in spring as the leaves unfurl, or in autumn as they turn gold. ///yoga.shall.vibes

**965. LIMERICK COPPER BEECH**
*Copper beech / Fagus*
*sylvatica 'Purpurea'*
Pery Square,
Limerick, V94 HF53
52.658568, -8.628976

A voluminous copper beech hangs over Pery Square from the People's Park. With its striking purple canopy, the Limerick Copper Beech punctuates a fine architectural vista from Mallow Street. It is on the left just after the City Art Gallery, a stolid Victorian building, and opposite a terrace of Georgian townhouses ending at St Michael's Church. ///pace.gifted.spots

**966. TARBERT WISHING TREE\***
*Pedunculate oak*
*Quercus robur*
N67, Tarbert,
Co. Kerry, V31 X883
52.578064, -9.366813

The Tarbert Wishing Tree is a landmark for travellers taking the ferry across the lower Shannon. On the N67, a stunted old pedunculate oak marks the halfway point between the village of Tarbert and the jetty at Tarbert Ferry. It is the only tree to grow on the estuary side of the road, and is an arresting sight as it appears to grow straight out of the wall. ///zigs.state.currencies

**967. OAK OF TRALEE**
*Lucombe oak / Quercus × crenata 'Lucombeana'*
Town Park, Denny Street, Tralee, Co. Kerry,
V92 W9X7
52.267532, -9.705008

Tralee Town Park boasts a prodigious Lucombe oak growing near the Denny Street entrance and close to the extensive rosebeds. The magnificent tree is just one of many attractions in the park. The County Museum is here, as well as the Rose Wall of Fame, a glass memorial listing every participant in the annual Rose of Tralee Festival, a contest inspired by the eponymous Irish folk ballad. ///quintet.shipped.blessing

**968. ELM OF TRALEE**
*Huntingdon elm*
*Ulmus × hollandica 'Vegeta'*
Castlemorris Orchard, Ballymullen, Tralee,
Co. Kerry, V92 W5R3
52.260363, -9.690781

Not to be outdone by the OAK OF TRALEE (967), the Elm of Tralee is a broad, thickset example of a now-unusual Huntingdon elm. It grows in an exposed position on the main road heading south towards Killarney. Unlike most street trees, which are planted next to the road to help screen pedestrians from traffic, this tree is set back, suggesting that it predates the current road layout. ///maternal.area.bounded

**969. AN DÍSEART COPPER BEECH**
*Copper beech / Fagus sylvatica 'Purpurea'*
An Díseart, Green Street, Dingle, Co. Kerry,
V92 N921
52.142101, -10.271383

An Díseart is an Irish spirituality and cultural centre occupying a former convent in Dingle town. Within its grounds, the extraordinary Nun's Graveyard has become something of a visitor attraction. Dozens of small white iron crosses mark the graves of nuns buried here since the 1860s. They are sheltered by a wonderful copper beech, broader than it is tall, and as old as the graves. ///straws.match.benched

**970. MOUNTAIN VIEW CHESTNUT**
*Sweet chestnut*
*Castanea sativa*
Killarney House and Gardens, Muckross Road, Killarney,
Co. Kerry, V93 HE3C
52.057069, -9.508838

A handsome sweet chestnut stands on the northern side of Killarney House, the visitor centre for Killarney National Park. The view is spectacular from below its prominent arching limb: extensive formal gardens slope down towards Lough Leane, and on a clear day the peaks of MacGillycuddy's Reeks, including Carrauntoohil, Ireland's highest mountain, can be seen. ///otters.jogged.landmark

### 971. MUCKROSS YEW*
*Yew / Taxus baccata*
Muckross Friary,
Muckross, Killarney,
Co. Kerry, V93 P7VT
52.026156, -9.494896

The Muckross Yew's setting, in the centre of the miniscule cloisters at ruined fifteenth-century Muckross Friary, is magical. Within this enclosed space, the tree has grown up towards the light, leaving a clean, sinewy bole that twists dramatically and branches several metres from the ground. From the cloisters, lower than the tree, visitors must look up, an angle that allows the tree to be seen at its best. ///spillage.flitting.sloppy

### 972. GIANT ARBUTUS
*Strawberry tree*
*Arbutus unedo*
N71 Ring of Kerry,
Killarney, Co. Kerry
51.98077, -9.573639

Where the scenic Ring of Kerry road winds through the oak-and-arbutus woodland outside Killarney, it passes just a few metres from Ireland's biggest wild strawberry tree. Look out for its red strawberry-like fruits in October, but take heed of the species name *unedo*, analogous to 'eat only one'. Wise words. ///dulled.postures.rebuild

### 973. KENMARE CYPRESS
*Monterey cypress*
*Cupressus macrocarpa*
The Square, Kenmare,
Co. Kerry, V93 YW44
51.88035, -9.583617

The west of Ireland, like west Wales and south west England, is Monterey cypress country. These often-unkempt trees can become giants, and provoke strong opinions in people who profess to have seen one too many field boundaries lined with them. But in the right situation they can become dignified landmarks. One such tree is the Kenmare Cypress growing on Fair Green in the centre of town. ///decrease.reshape.lending

### 974. CHURCH CROSS CYPRESS
*Golden Monterey cypress*
*Cupressus macrocarpa*
*'Lutea'*
N71, Church Cross,
Co. Cork
51.542489, -9.349267

Not all Monterey cypresses are created equal, something the Church Cross Cypress demonstrates with aplomb. Outside the old post office on the road between Skibbereen and Ballydehob, an example of a *'Lutea'* cultivar with gold-tinged foliage has become a lovely landmark. Its form is exceptional, with its trunk splitting into a rosette of stout branches that spread its bright canopy right across the road. ///quotas.sufferer.disregard

### 975. COURT OAK
*Cork oak*
*Quercus suber*
Courtmacsherry Hotel,
Courtmacsherry, Co.
Cork, P72 XD95
51.633476, -8.699535

The Court Oak at Courtmacsherry is a spongy-barked cork oak of immense proportions. One of the largest anywhere in these islands, it is still going strong at 200 years old. It grows in pride of place on the lawn in front of the Courtmacsherry Hotel, a former Georgian mansion with an extensive tree-filled garden. The tree is clearly well suited to the mild and damp climate of west Cork. ///brings.burn.cumbersome

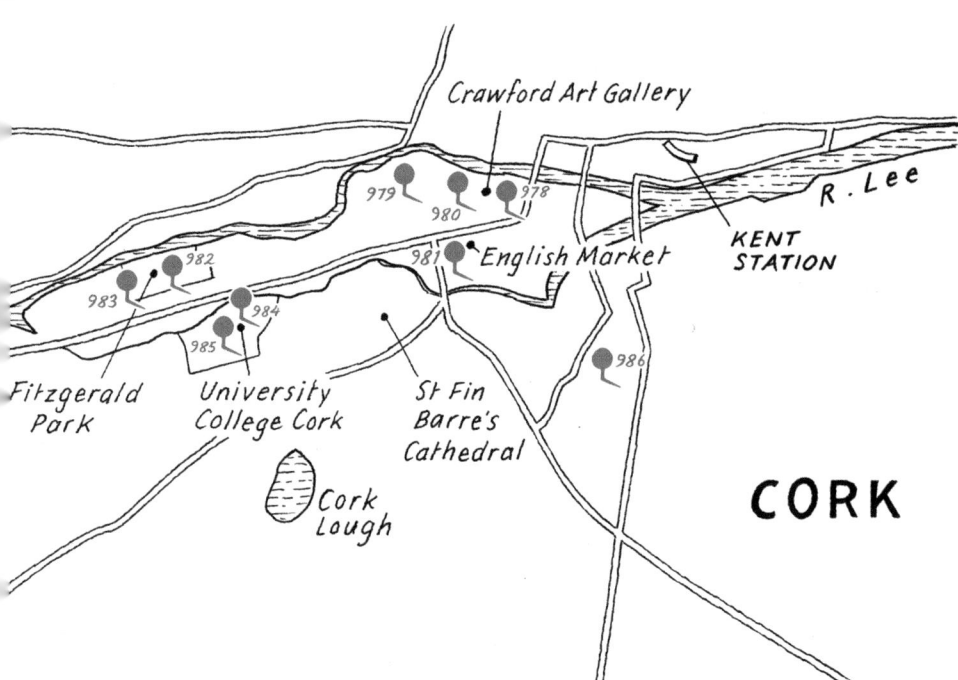

**976. MALLOW OAK**
*Sessile oak*
*Quercus petraea*
Mallow Town Park,
Bridge Street,
Mallow, Co. Cork
52.133638, -8.640801

The Mallow Oak is a bristling sessile oak growing on the north bank of the River Blackwater, hanging over Bridge Street from Mallow Town Park, at times the river's floodplain. Despite, or because of, occasional inundation, it is a shapely and verdant tree, and one that must have been here for well over a century, perhaps two, acting as a landmark for those arriving or leaving this busy market town. ///responder.asparagus.desired

**977. WHITE HART TREE**
*Horse chestnut*
*Aesculus hippocastanum*
Mallow Castle, Mallow,
Co. Cork, P51 KC57
52.133476, -8.637812

Mallow is famed for its white fallow deer, a herd descended from a pair gifted to the Norreys of Mallow Castle by Queen Elizabeth I, godmother to Elizabeth Norreys, in 1610. They are indeed a rare sight, and live in an enclosure where many mature trees are also preserved. One, a fabulous old horse chestnut of prodigious proportions, provides plenty of shade for the deer. Tree hunters will have to admire it from beyond the enclosure. ///lurking.chuck.stirs

978. **CRAWFORD SYCAMORE** → Cork is so densely built up that it seems every mature tree in the centre of the city is a landmark. One of the most noticeable is the gently twisting sycamore that grows outside the Crawford Art Gallery. It is perhaps as old as the gallery, its maturity evidenced by its craggy bark plates, which, though similar to those that flake from a London plane, won't be dislodged by even the most determined tug.

**CRAWFORD SYCAMORE** *Sycamore / Acer pseudoplatanus* Crawford Art Gallery, Emmett Place, Cork, T12 TNE6 51.899809, -8.472899 ///hosts.smooth.pure

979. **PETER'S LIME**
*Common lime*
*Tilia × europaea*
St Peters, North Main Street, Cork, T12 RF8D
51.899674, -8.47849

Peter's Lime might be considered the distant twin of **PAUL'S LIME (980)**. It is another landmark tree in Cork's dense city centre. This one takes pride of place on North Main Street outside St Peter's, a former church whose history stretches back to 1270. From the street, the church can barely be seen for the tree. ///coherent.notes.muddy

980. **PAUL'S LIME**
*Common lime*
*Tilia × europaea*
Cornmarket Centre, Paul Street, Cork, T12 NX02
51.899162, -8.475301

Paul's Lime is probably the tallest tree in central Cork – only **PETER'S LIME (979)** comes close. It is a shapely, well-maintained common lime towering over the narrow laneway of Paul Street, a setting that emphasises its height. It grows in the forecourt of the converted Victorian cornmarket, now a shopping centre, but its presence is felt all along the street. ///strike.reduce.today

981. **BISHOP LUCEY IRONWOOD**
*Persian ironwood*
*Parrotia persica*
Bishop Lucey Park, Grand Parade, Cork, T12 EP99
51.897356, -8.475738

Bishop Lucey was the Bishop of Cork and Ross who died in 1982, shortly before Cork's newest park was opened in time for the city's 800th anniversary celebrations. Although only recently established, the park has a maturing tree canopy, including the standout Persian ironwood, a muscular-looking tree close to the Grand Parade entrance. It particularly shines in the autumn as its leaves catch fire and turn vermillion, violet and saffron. ///under.crisis.menu

FIRST FIDDLE (982)

**982. FIRST FIDDLE**
*Hybrid catalpa / Catalpa × erubescens 'J. C. Teas'*
Fitzgerald Park, Mardyke Walk, Cork, T12 AW6R
51.896709, -8.494519

The most noteworthy tree in Fitzgerald Park is a wonderful leaning hybrid catalpa growing between the café and the River Lee. The park opened in 1906, having previously been the site of the 1902 Cork International Exhibition, and many of the mature trees almost certainly date to around this time, including the First Fiddle. ///sofa.vital.dress

**983. OVERGROWN KAPUKA**
*Kapuka*
*Griselinia littoralis*
Fitzgerald Park, Mardyke Walk, Cork, T12 AW6R
51.895443, -8.496877

Playing second fiddle to the park's wonderful FIRST FIDDLE (982), the Overgrown Kapuka is nevertheless a noteworthy plant. It is a small evergreen tree from New Zealand that is often little more than a hedging shrub, but this stout individual near the children's playground in Fitzgerald Park has become far larger than most. It is every inch a verdant evergreen tree. ///hears.sorters.agents

**984. ICONIC OAK**
*Lucombe oak*
*Quercus × crenata 'Lucombeana'*
The Glucksman, University College Cork, Western Road, Cork, T12 V1WH
51.895038, -8.490369

The Glucksman is Cork's most iconic modern building, its exciting yet sensitive architecture enhanced by its location among mature trees close to the river. Like the Burrell Collection in Glasgow, the trees feel like they are part of the building. A magnificent Lucombe oak, a rare tree in Ireland, holding its own next to a towering Scots pine, sets the tone and contributes to the atmosphere. ///loudly.plenty.teams

**985. UCC GIANT REDWOOD**
*Giant redwood*
*Sequoiadendron giganteum*
University College Cork, Mardyke Walk, Cork, T12 N1FK
51.893206, -8.491112

The University of Cork boasts an attractive, well-forested campus which has managed to retain many impressive trees alongside its growing estate of academic buildings. The focus of the campus is provided by a pair of towering nineteenth-century giant redwoods next to the Boole Library. The southern tree is most striking – a perfectly shaped giant, obviously taller than its sidekick – and best admired from the nearby arboretum. ///agrees.ears.duty

**986. HOSPITAL TREE PRIVET**
*Chinese tree privet*
*Ligustrum lucidum*
Old Blackrock Road, Cork, T12 W3YX
51.89299, -8.465387

On the Old Blackrock Road, a luxuriant evergreen Chinese tree privet hangs over the wall separating the main road from City General Hospital. As these trees mature, they take on an increasingly subtropical feel, their canopies becoming sparser among aged, twisted branches. The Hospital Tree Privet is a fine example of the species, the product of Cork's mild oceanic climate. ///calm.grain.deep

**987. BILLOWING CLOUD TREE**
*Japanese cedar*
*Cryptomeria japonica*
*'Spiralis'*
Fota Estate, Carrigtwohill,
Co. Cork, T45 K656
51.891535, -8.302607

Fota island is a popular resort for Corkonians and a tree hunter's wonderland, where a mature arboretum can be explored within Fota House and Gardens. There are dozens of exceptional trees here, thriving in the island's mild climate, the most memorable of which is the rare *'Spiralis'* Japanese cedar, or *Cryptomeria*, a tree that appears like a swelling cloud of dense foliage pompoms. It is beguiling. ///pill.interject.bypass

**988. MARLFIELD MAIDEN**
*Sessile oak*
*Quercus petraea*
Marlfield House,
Marlfield, Clonmel, Co.
Tipperary, E91 WP48
52.345906, -7.74989

A kilometre out of Clonmel, beyond the grand Georgian gateway into Marlfield House (once the seat of the Bagwell family and now apartments), the driveway passes several impressive trees. The finest is a giant sessile oak. It is a maiden, an unpollarded tree, that has been here for over two centuries – a very rare thing in Ireland – and is now in its prime. ///bulk.remind.deal

**989. NORE OAK**
*Holm oak / Quercus ilex*
Kilkenny Castle,
The Parade,
Kilkenny, R95 YRK1
52.650563, -7.248023

Medieval Kilkenny is dominated by the castle at the top of the High Street. Its extensive grounds, now Kilkenny Castle Park, have dozens of fine trees, many dating back to its nineteenth-century heyday. The best is a fabulous holm oak growing close to the northern edge. It is old and appears, by the number of thick branches that grow from its huge base, to have been coppiced in the past. ///sponsorship.civil.wonderful

990. **THE RAGGEDY BUSH*** → Three kilometres south of Kilkenny on the Kells Road, one of Ireland's very special rag trees grows next to a holy well by the side of the road. The Raggedy Bush, a hawthorn, was in excellent condition and festooned with rags when I visited. But note that rag trees are characterised by cycles of use, dormancy after having their rags stripped, and reuse sometimes years later, so you may not always find it clothed.

**THE RAGGEDY BUSH*** *Hawthorn / Crataegus monogyna* R697 Kells Road, Kilkenny, Co. Kilkenny 52.608708, -7.265747 ///appraisals.generously.latter

THE WATERFORD OAK (994)

**991. LEFT BANK PLANE**
*London plane*
*Platanus × hispanica*
John Street Lower,
Kilkenny, R95 PK20
52.651345, -7.247623

On the left bank of the River Nore, opposite Kilkenny Castle, grows a row of London planes. Planes love riparian settings and can attain great sizes if their adventurous roots reach a ready water supply. That appears to have happened here. The first tree in this row of giants is a landmark best appreciated across the water, from Canal Walk. ///terminally.studios.accidental

**992. TOPLINE OAK**
*Pedunculate oak*
*Quercus robur*
Shamrock Business Park,
Graiguecullen,
Carlow, R93 W8D9
52.841702, -6.951523

The Shamrock Business Park on the edge of Carlow is an unlikely setting for a remarkable tree, but, right outside the Topline Doyles DIY store, an impressive veteran oak takes up two or three parking spaces. The tree was here centuries before the business park, whose developers must be applauded for saving the oak and ensuring it has space to thrive. ///speech.donation.tilt

**993. SHILLELAGH CORK OAK**
*Cork oak / Quercus suber*
Main Street, Shillelagh,
Co. Wicklow, Y14 XF95
52.75438, -6.539149

Shillelaghs, walking sticks doubling as defensive weapons, are traditionally made from knotty blackthorn wood. Debate rages around their name: some say it's a corruption of the Irish *sail éille*, which translates to 'thonged willow stick' (just to confuse us), while others contend that it's derived from the place name Shillelagh. While little willow or blackthorn grows here, a magnificent cork oak is an astonishing diversion. Hardly ideal shillelagh material, though. ///invent.condition.drumming

**994. THE WATERFORD OAK**
*Fennessey's oak*
*Quercus robur 'Fennessii'*
People's Park, Park Road,
Waterford, X91 AY15
52.257506, -7.102867

'Fennessii' is a cultivar of pedunculate oak with long, irregular leaves, quite unlike those of that more familiar oak. It was raised by Fennessey and Son of Waterford in the early 1800s and is now very rare – indeed, the one next to the entrance to the People's Park is, aside from two at the national Botanic Gardens in Dublin, the only mature specimen known in Ireland or Britain. ///method.mondays.define

**995. ST DEC'S WALNUT**
*Walnut / Juglans regia*
Water Street,
Waterford, X91 H295
52.255431, -7.107184
*In a private garden, but visible from the street.*

A flourishing walnut tree marks the corner of Water Street and South Parade. It grows from a walled garden which appears to belong to an interesting mid-twentieth-century house next to St Declan's School. In the past, walnut trees have produced good crops of fruits, but an expanding grey-squirrel population may mean ripe walnuts become rare in Ireland, as they are now in southern Britain. ///restless.monk.congas

**996. PUB CRAWL OAK**
*Sessile oak*
*Quercus petraea*
Foulksmill, Co.
Wexford, Y35 E008
52.314184, -6.75302

The Pub Crawl Oak marks a quiet junction in a sleepy village between Waterford and Wexford. The tree is a veteran sessile oak growing in the middle of the street with a choice of not one, but two pubs from which to admire it. A protecting stone wall tightly encircles its trunk – it seems likely the tree will burst out in a decade or two. ///redheads.bulletins.growing

**997. OAK OF THE ASSUMPTION**
*Holm oak / Quercus ilex*
Church of the
Assumption, Bride Street,
Wexford, Y35 HW10
52.33394, -6.461931

To the right of the Bride Street entrance to Wexford's Church of the Assumption a fine holm oak hangs over the street. It is a stout, low-branching tree whose strong boughs hold up a massive, dense canopy. Together with its less-formidable companion, the pair act as sentries guarding the gate into the former churchyard, now a car park. ///clouding.trouble.finals

**998. IMMACULATE DEODAR**
*Deodar cedar*
*Cedrus deodara*
Church of the Immaculate
Conception, Rowe Street
Upper, Wexford,
Y35 KX66
52.338926, -6.464138

Like the Church of the Assumption, the Church of the Immaculate Conception on Rowe Street now finds itself surrounded by a car park. We can only imagine what the garden of rest that would have once surrounded this church was like, but a surviving deodar north of the church, with an almost perfectly symmetrical form, hints at the green splendours of the past. ///sunrise.scowled.roadshow

**999. WILLIE REDMOND'S SILVER LIME**
*Silver lime / Tilia tomentosa*
William Redmond
Memorial Park,
Spawell Road,
Wexford, Y35 KN62
52.342322, -6.472038

Willie Redmond was an Irish Nationalist, Westminster MP and British Army officer who died leading his men at Messines during the First World War. He believed that Irish sacrifice in the Great War, both Protestant and Catholic, would lead to home rule. A park in Wexford is dedicated to his memory, complete with a bust and a solitary silver lime. A beautiful tree, especially on a breezy summer day when its silvery leaf-undersides sparkle in the sun. ///balcony.stimulated.circus

**1,000. SEASIDE CYPRESS**
*Monterey cypress*
*Cupressus macrocarpa*
Doogans Warren, Strand
Road, Rosslare, Co.
Wexford, Y35 Y83V
52.276021, -6.388368

Although you will see Monterey cypresses growing freely throughout Ireland, they are more often seen in the milder and damper west. But at Rosslare in the sunny south east, a half-dozen or so mature trees grow along Strand Road just inland from the sea. A tree with a particularly fine silhouette grows at Kelly's Hotel, bringing a touch of California to this Irish Sea resort. ///implore.rewarm.lift

WILLIE REDMOND'S SILVER LIME (999)

## SELECT BIBLIOGRAPHY

THERE IS A RICH literature of tree guides, a tradition that goes back to the mid-nineteenth century. It ranges from handsome volumes produced by leading publishers to slim pamphlets aimed at discerning audiences. Tree enthusiasts have published very local or very specific guides to their town, county or region, as well as accounts of their favourite species. Inevitably, the internet has encouraged a boom in online resources that can be added to this canon. This book stands on the shoulders of the many dedicated souls who have recorded and published details of remarkable trees over many years.

There is not room to list every leaflet, guidebook or blog that has aided my research (of which there were many), but some of the most useful resources and charming volumes are listed here.

### BOOKS

BALLARD, PHILLADA *An Oasis of Delight: The History of the Birmingham Botanical Gardens*, Brewin Books, Studley, 2003.
BARNES, GERRY and WILLIAMSON, TOM, *Ancient Trees in the Landscape: Norfolk's Arboreal Heritage*, Oxbow Books, Oxford, 2011.
BRAWN, EMMA and POLLARD, ANDREW, *The Great Trees of Dorset*, The Dovecote Press, Wimborne Minster, 2008.
BRETHERTON, KATE, *The Remarkable Trees of St Albans Revisited*, St Albans, 2018.
CHADBUND, GEOFFREY, *Flowering Cherries*, Collins, London, 1972.
COLQUHOUN, KATE, *A Thing In Disguise: The Visionary Life of Joseph Paxton*, 4th Estate, London, 2003.
COSTER, GRAHAM, *The Nature of Cricket; A Natural History of the Cricket Ground*, Safe Haven, London, 2021.
D'ARPINO, TONY and DRAKE, FRANK, *Trees of Bristol*, Redcliffe Press, Bristol, 2014.
DIXON, GLORIA, KNAPMAN, CHRIS and YOUNG, ANDREW, *Plymouth's Favourite Trees*, Plymouth Tree Partnership, Plymouth, 2008.

DIXON, GLORIA and YOUNG, ANDREW, *For the Love of Trees in Plymouth and Beyond*, Plymouth Tree Partnership, Plymouth, 2022.
ELLIOT, PAUL A., *British Urban Trees: A Social and Cultural History c. 1800–1914*, White Horse Press, Winwick, 2016.
ELWES, HENRY JOHN and HENRY, AUGUSTINE, *The Trees of Great Britain and Ireland, Volumes 1–7*, Edinburgh, 1906-1913.
FENNELL, AUBREY, *Heritage Trees of Ireland*, The Collins Press, Cork, 2014.
HAGENDER, FRED, *Yew: A History*, The History Press, Stroud, 2011.
HALL, TONY, *The Immortal Yew*, Royal Botanic Gardens, Kew, 2018.
HANCY, REX, *Notable Trees of Norwich*, Norfolk and Norwich Naturalists Society, Norwich, 2005.
HIGHT, JULIAN, *Britain's Tree Story*, National Trust Books, London, 2011.
HOOPER, MARK, *The Great British Tree Biography*, Pavilion, London, 2021.
JOHNSON, OWEN, *Tree Guide*, Collins, London, 2006.
JOHNSON, OWEN, *Arboretum*, Whittet Books, Stansted, 2015.
JOHNSTON, MARK, *Trees in Towns and Cities*, Windgather Press, Oxford, 2015.
JOHNSTON, MARK, *Street Trees in Britain*, Windgather Press, Oxford, 2017.
JOHNSTON, MARK, *The Tree Experts*, Windgather Press, Oxford, 2021.
LAWSON, ADRIAN and SAWERS, GEOFF, *The Shady Side of Town: Reading's Trees*, Two Rivers Press, Reading, 2017.
LOUDON, JOHN CLAUDIUS, *Arboretum et Fruticetum Britannicum*, London 1835–1838.
LOWE, JOHN, *The Yew Trees of Britain and Ireland*, Macmillan, London, 1896.
MILES, ARCHIE, *The Trees That Made Britain*, BBC Books, London, 2006.
MILES, ARCHIE, *Heritage Trees Wales*, Graffeg, Llanelli, 2020.
MILLER, JOHN, *Trees of the Northern Highlands*, Alness, 1999.
MILLER, JOHN, *Trees of Glasgow*, Alness, 2005.
MORTON, ANDREW, *The Trees of Shropshire: Mythology, Legend and Fact*, The Crowood Press, Shrewsbury, 1995.
MORTON, ANDREW, *Tree Heritage of Britain and Ireland*, Airlife Publishing, Marlborough, 2004.
NÍ LAMHNA, ÉANNA, *Wild Dublin, Exploring Nature in the City*, The O'Brien Press, Dublin, 2008.
OGILVIE, JAMES, RODGER, DONALD and STOKES, JON, *The Heritage Trees of Scotland*, The Tree Council, London, 2003.
O'KANE, FINOLA, *Landscape Design in Eighteenth-Century Ireland: Mixing Foreign Trees with the Natives*, Cork University Press, Cork, 2004.

PAKENHAM, THOMAS, *Meetings with Remarkable Trees*, Cassell, London, 2004.
RABBITS, PAUL, *Great British Parks: A Celebration*, Amberley Publishing, Stroud, 2016.
RODGER, DONALD and STOKES, JON, *The Heritage Trees of Britain & Northern Ireland*, Constable, London, 2004.
SANDERSON, RACHEL (ED.), *Special Trees and Woods of the Chilterns*, Chiltern Woodlands Project, Chinnor, 2010.
SCOTT, ALISTAIR, *A Pleasure in Scottish Trees*, Mainstream Publishing, Edinburgh, 2002.
SWANTON, E. W., *Yew Trees of England*, Farnham, 1958.
SURREY TREE WARDENS, *Remarkable Trees of Surrey*, The Tree Council, London, 2016.
TIME OUT, *The Great Trees of London*, Time Out Guides Ltd., London, 2010.
TUDGE, COLIN, *The Secret Life of Trees*, Penguin, London, 2006.
WILKS, J. H., *Trees of the British Isles in History & Legend*, Frederick Muller, London, 1972.
WOOD, PAUL, *The Great Trees of London Map*, Blue Crow Media, London, 2020.
WOUDSTRA, JAN AND ALLEN, CAMILLA (ED.), *The Politics of Street Trees*, Routledge, London, 2022.

## WEBSITES

Ancient Tree Inventory database  ati.woodlandtrust.org.uk
Ancient Yew Group  www.ancient-yew.org
Bath Urban Treescape  www.bathurbantreescape.com
Bristol Tree Forum  bristoltreeforum.org
Cardiff Parks  www.cardiffparks.org.uk/trees
Monumental Trees  www.monumentaltrees.com
Northern Ireland's Remarkable Trees  www.remarkabletrees.org
Northumbria Veteran Tree Project  veterantreeproject.com
Parks and Gardens  www.parksandgardens.org
Scotland's Yew Tree Heritage  scotlands-yew-trees.org
Tree Register of Britain and Ireland  www.treeregister.org
Tree Register of Ireland  www.treeregister.ie
Trees and Shrubs Online  treesandshrubsonline.org

# INDEX

Page references in *italics* indicate images. **Bold** indicates tree species and cultivars.

**1,296th Lime** (common lime/ *Tilia* × *europaea*) 160
**1550 Sweet Chestnut** (sweet chestnut/*Castanea sativa*) 20
**1811 Cedar** (cedar of Lebanon/ *Cedrus libani*) 249

## A

**Abbey Dove Tree** (handkerchief tree/*Davidia involucrata*) 319
**Abbey Green Plane** (London plane/*Platanus* × *hispanica*) 121, 135, 329, 345
**Abbey Lime** (cut-leaf lime/*Tilia platyphyllos* 'Laciniata') 331
**Abbey Tree of Heaven** (tree of heaven/*Ailanthus altissima*) 184
Aberdeen 39, 40, 42, 43, *43*, 44
**Accession Cedars** (cedar of Lebanon/*Cedrus libani*) 348, *349*
**Acocks Ghost** (pedunculate oak/ *Quercus robur*) 189, 195
**Acton Park Chestnut** (sweet chestnut/*Castanea sativa*) 418
**Ada Salter's Tree of Heaven** (tree of heaven/*Ailanthus altissima*) 256
**Adam and Eve** (yew/*Taxus baccata*) 121
**Addison's Oak** (pedunculate oak/*Quercus robur*) 337
**Adur Hybrid** (hybrid strawberry tree/*Arbutus* × *andrachnoides*) 294
**Afon Merddwr Chestnut** (horse chestnut/*Aesculus hippocastanum*) 416, 417

**alder**
**Italian alder** (*Alnus cordata*) 143, *192*, 193
**Japanese alder** (*Alnus japonica*) 70
**oak-leaf alder** (*Alnus glutinosa* 'Laciniata') 166, 209, 228
**All About That Base** (tulip tree/ *Liriodendron tulipifera*) 287
**Allerton Oak** (hybrid oak/ *Quercus* × *rosacea*) 3, 117, 118
**Alleyway Judas Tree** (Judas tree/ *Cercis siliquastrum*) 372
**Allotment Cedar** (cedar of Lebanon/*Cedrus libani*) 294
**Almshouse Baobab** (baobab London plane/*Platanus* × *hispanica* 'Baobab') 282
**almond** (*Prunus dulcis*) 251
**Alpha Tree** (common lime/*Tilia* × *europaea*) 445
**Alternative Remedy Oak** (Hungarian oak/*Quercus frainetto*) 351
**Altrincham Puzzle** (fern-leaved beech/*Fagus sylvatica* 'Asplenifolia') 111
**An Díseart Copper Beech** (copper beech/*Fagus sylvatica* 'Purpurea') 467
**An Eastbourne Elm** (Wheatley elm/*Ulmus minor* 'Sarniensis') 281
**Anaconda Tree** (Père David's maple/*Acer davidii*) 228
**Ancient Tree Hunt Oak** (pedunculate oak/*Quercus robur*) 298, *314*, 315
*Ancient Tree Inventory* 4, 298

ancient trees 9, 13, 28, 113, 117, 183, 232, 273, 335, 337, 426, 442
**Ankerwycke Yew** (yew/*Taxus baccata*) 316
**Another Sweetgum** (oriental sweetgum/*Liquidambar orientalis*) 393, 400
**Antediluvian Alder** (oak-leaf alder/*Alnus glutinosa* 'Laciniata') 157, 166, *167*
**Apollo Redwood** (giant redwood/*Sequoiadendron giganteum*) 82, 91
**Apprentice Fir** (Douglas fir/ *Pseudotsuga menziesii*) 32
**Áras an Uachtaráin Redwood** (giant redwood/ *Sequoiadendron giganteum*) 455
**Arbor Tree** (wild black poplar/ *Populus nigra* ssp. *betulifolia*) 184
arboretums 9, 36, 42, 55, 61, 70, 156, 157, 159, 163, 166, 169, 172, 177, 180, 187, 193, 204, 227, 247, 251, 329, 332, 333, 361, 393, 396, 399, 449, 455, 463, 473, 474
arboriculturist 9
**Arbour Hill Sycamore** (sycamore/*Acer pseudoplatanus*) 459
**Arbour Oak, The** (hybrid oak/ *Quercus* × *rosacea*) 7, 118, 156, 163, *168*, 169
archaeophytes 9, 12, 359, 367, 449
**Arriviste Redwood** (giant redwood/*Sequoiadendron giganteum*) *230*, 231
**ash** (*Fraxinus excelsior*) 47, 74, 86, 87, 92, 104, *104*, 105, 132, 147, 227, 369, 418, *419*, 463
**alpine ash** (*Eucalyptus delegatensis*) 376, 377

Caucasian narrow-leaved ash
(*Fraxinus angustifolia*) 129,
134, 156
manna ash (*Fraxinus ornus*) 73
'Lentiscifolia' narrow-leaved
ash (*Fraxinus angustifolia*
*'Lentiscifolia'*) 181, 199, 253
Raywood ash (*Fraxinus*
*angustifolia 'Raywood'*) 122
single-leaved ash (*Fraxinus*
*excelsior 'Diversifolia'*) 118,
259
single-leaved Caucasian ash
(*Fraxinus angustifolia*
*'Monophylla'*) 259
velvet ash (*Fraxinus velutina*)
308
weeping ash (*Fraxinus*
*excelsior 'Pendula'*) 20, 60,
*60*, 166, 172, 460
weeping one-leaved ash
(*Fraxinus excelsior*
*'Diversifolia Pendula'*) 172
Ashbrittle Yew, The (yew/*Taxus*
*baccata*) 353
aspen (*Populus tremula*) 108
Aspirational Plane (London
plane/*Platanus × hispanica*) 194
Astbury Fragment (yew/*Taxus*
*baccata*) 112, 113
Atlantic Forest Remnant (sessile
oak/*Quercus petraea*) 413, 417
Attenborough Horse Chestnut
(horse chestnut/*Aesculus*
*hippocastanum*) 177
Attwood's Cedar (cedar of
Lebanon/*Cedrus libani*) 189, 194
Auld Alliance Sycamore
(sycamore/*Acer*
*pseudoplatanus*) 42
Author's Choice (variegated
London plane/*Platanus ×*
*hispanica 'Suttnerii'*) 449, 453,
456
Aviemore 17, 25, 26
**Azarole** (*Crataegus azarolus*) 348

## B

Backstreet Oak (Turner's oak/
*Quercus × turneri*) 365
Bad Hair Tree (weeping beech/
*Fagus sylvatica 'Pendula'*) 150
Baggot Street Herald (honey
locust/*Gleditsia triacanthos*)
453, 460

Baginton Oak, The (pedunculate
oak/*Quercus robur*) 201
Balmer Lawn Oak (pedunculate
oak/*Quercus robur*) 325
Balmerino Chestnut (sweet
chestnut/*Castanea sativa*) 47
Bank Lane Elm (wych elm/
*Ulmus glabra*) 19
Baobab Poplar (wild black
poplar/*Populus nigra ssp.*
*betulifolia*) 99, 204
Barney (London plane/*Platanus*
*× hispanica*) 7, 224, 238, 244,
246, 247
Barricade Tree (London plane/
*Platanus × hispanica*) 259
Bath 121, 135, 175, 266, 312, *327*,
329, 331, 344, *344*, 345, 347, *347*
Batsman's Lime (common lime/
*Tilia × europaea*) 278
Bazalgette's Plane (oriental
plane/*Platanus orientalis*)
238, 264
BBC Ginkgo (ginkgo/*Ginkgo*
*biloba*) 232
Beached Stone Pine (stone pine/
*Pinus pinea*) 377
Beacon Oak (hybrid oak/*Quercus*
*× rosacea*) 388, *389*
bee-bee tree or euodia
(*Tetradium daniellii*) 47, 341
**beech** (*Fagus sylvatica*) 4, 5, 9,
10, 11, 32, 40, 44, 86, 108, *109*,
135, 153, 157, 165, 197, 259,
267, 274, 287, 342, 373, 378,
391, 456, 466
**copper beech** (*Fagus sylvatica*
*'Purpurea'*) 10, 20, *21*, 35,
43, 58, 108, 138, 164, 169, 181,
186, 193, 203, 232, 280, 331,
347, 395, 450, 466, 467
**Dawyck beech** (*Fagus sylvatica*
*'Dawyck'*) 112
**fern-leaved beech** (*Fagus*
*sylvatica 'Asplenifolia'*) 88,
97, 111, 114, 164, 402
**variegated beech** (*Fagus*
*sylvatica 'Albovariegata'*) 138
**weeping beech** (*Fagus*
*sylvatica 'Pendula'*) 77, 106,
150, 164, 170, 213, 315
Beer Belly (baobab London
plane/*Platanus × hispanica*
*'Baobab'*) 82, 85, 238
Beeston Beech (copper beech/
*Fagus sylvatica 'Purpurea'*) 169

Beeton, Isabella: *Mrs. Beeton's Book*
*of Household Management* vii,
257
Belfast *425*, 426, 427, 432, *434*, 435,
*436*, 437–8, *439*, 440, 441–3, *443*,
*444*, 445
Belfast's Irish Yew (Irish yew/
*Taxus baccata 'Fastigiata'*) 435,
441
Bellahouston Algerian (Mirbeck's
oak/*Quercus canariensis*) 74
Beltingham Yew (yew/*Taxus*
*baccata*) 86
Belvoir Oak, A (pedunculate
oak/*Quercus robur*) 426, 442
Berkeley Plane (London plane/
*Platanus × hispanica*) 238, 266,
*266*
Besty's Oak (pedunculate oak/
*Quercus robur*) 111
Bettws Newydd Yew (yew/*Taxus*
*baccata*) 388
Betws Giant (Lawson cypress/
*Chamaecyparis lawsoniana*) 417
Betws-y-Coed Muse (pedunculate
oak/*Quercus robur*) 413, 417
Bexley Charter Oak (pedunculate
oak/*Quercus robur*) 242
Bicycle Tree (sycamore/*Acer*
*pseudoplatanus*) 35
Big Belly (sessile oak/*Quercus*
*petraea*) 7, 348
Big Daddy (hybrid wingnut/
*Pterocarya × rehderiana*) 385,
393, *397*, 397
Big Foot (giant redwood/
*Sequoiadendron giganteum*) 384,
390, 391
Big Sister (Austrian pine/*Pinus*
*nigra var. nigra*) 342, *343*
Big Tree, The (sycamore/*Acer*
*pseudoplatanus*) 7, 16, *18*, 19
Billowing Cloud Tree (Japanese
cedar/*Cryptomeria japonica*
*'Spiralis'*) 449, 474
Billy Hughes's Wattle (Mimosa/
*Acacia dealbata*) 264
**birch**
**downy birch** (*Betula*
*pubescens*) 428, *430*
**Himalayan birch** (*Betula*
*utilis var. jacquemontii*) 25,
135
**paper birch** (*Betula*
*papyrifera*) 135, 466

silver birch (*Betula pendula*) 25, 135
Birmingham 3, *179*, 180, *188*, 189–97, *191*, *192*, *195*, *196*
Birmingham Dwarf ('Jaqueline Hillier' elm/*Ulmus 'Jaqueline Hillier'*) 3, 180, 193
Birnam Sycamore (sycamore/ *Acer pseudoplatanus*) 29, *30*
Birnam Oak (sessile oak/*Quercus petraea*) 3, 29, *30*
Birnam Walnut (walnut/*Juglans regia*) 29
Birr Burry Trees (baobab London plane/*Platanus × hispanica* 'Western Baobab') 437, 453, 466
Bishop Lucey Ironwood (Persian ironwood/*Parrotia persica*) 470
Bishop's Elm ('Lobel' elm/ *Ulmus 'Lobel'*) 295, *295*
Bishop's Fig (fig/*Ficus carica*) *394*, 395
Bishop's Meadow Tulip Tree (tulip tree/*Liriodendron tulipifera*) 203
Bishop's Plane (London plane/ *Platanus × hispanica*) 224, 247
Bishop's Walnut (black walnut/ *Juglans nigra*) 354
Black Bull Elm (Huntingdon elm/*Ulmus × hollandica* 'Vegeta') 174
Blacksmith's Tree (copper beech/ *Fagus sylvatica 'Purpurea'*) 58
Blaise Castle Curiosity (ehret/ *Ehretia dicksonii*) 329, 338
Blakers Park Giant (Wheatley elm/*Ulmus minor 'Sarniensis'*) 285, 288, 293
Blandford Charter Oak (pedunculate oak/*Quercus robur*) 352
Blandford's Debatable Oak (cypress oak/*Quercus robur 'Fastigiata'*) 310, 311
Blue Fox (foxglove tree/ *Paulownia tomentosa*) 101, *102*, 103
Bluecoat Plane (London plane/ *Platanus × hispanica*) 3, *124*, 125
Blushing Tree (purple Norway maple/*Acer platanoides 'Schwedleri'*) 172
Bobby Sands' Tree (pedunculate oak/*Quercus robur*) 435, 441

bole 9, 12, 20, 36, 74, 111, 171, 211, 234, 243, 271, 282, 300, 340, 378, 391, 400, 442, 450, 460, 468
Bon Accord Sycamore (sycamore/ *Acer pseudoplatanus*) 42
Booths' Baobab (baobab London plane/*Platanus × hispanica* 'Baobab') 99
Botanical Bauble (Chinese necklace poplar/*Populus lasiocarpa*) 344
Botanical Bee-Bee (bee-bee tree/ *Tetradium daniellii*) 47
botanical gardens 145, 150, *151*, 153, 189, 193, 239, 288, 344, 396, 399, 407
Botanical Spinning Gum (spinning gum/*Eucalyptus perriniana*) 385, 407
Boulevard Plane (London plane/ *Platanus × hispanica*) 170, *170*
box elder (*Acer negundo*) 345
Braidburn Row Tree (Wheatley elm/*Ulmus minor 'Sarniensis'*) 56, 61
**Bramley apple** (*Malus domestica 'Bramley's Seedling'*) 161
Bramley Apple, The (Bramley apple/*Malus domestica 'Bramley's Seedling'*) 161
Brandwood Beacon (giant redwood/*Sequoiadendron giganteum*) 180, *196*, 197
Breach Pine (Austrian pine/*Pinus nigra* var. *nigra*) 16, 24
Bridlington Spire (Wheatley elm/ *Ulmus minor 'Sarniensis'*) 131
Brighton & Hove 4, *268*, 270, 281, *284*, 285–93, *286*, *289*, 290, *292*, 332
Brighton's Oldest Tree (yew/ *Taxus baccata*) 287
Brimmon Oak (pedunculate oak/ *Quercus robur*) 421
Brislington Brook Plane (London plane/*Platanus × hispanica*) 338, *339*
Bristol *327*, 328, *334*, 335–43, *336*, *339*, *340*, *343*, 358, 384, 391, 402
Bristol Bridge Fig (fig/*Ficus carica*) 335, 340, *340*, 358
Bristol's Whitebeam (Bristol whitebeam/*Sorbus bristoliensis*) 335, 341
**broad-leaved kindling bark** (*Eucalyptus dalrympleana*) 243

Brockwell Oak (pedunculate oak/*Quercus robur*) 257
Brontosaurus, The (weeping giant redwood/*Sequoiadendron giganteum 'Pendula'*) 107
Bruce Castle Oak (sessile oak/ *Quercus petraea*) 239, 251
Bruce Tree (pedunculate oak/ *Quercus robur*) 66
Brunswick Square Plane (London plane/*Platanus × hispanica*) 260
Bryn Gwalia Oak (pedunculate oak/*Quercus robur*) 414, 415
Bryn Tyrch Pine (Scots pine/ *Pinus sylvestris*) 415, *415*
Bryn Tulip Tree (tulip tree/ *Liriodendron tulipifera*) 384, 407
Brynmill Pine (Monterey pine/ *Pinus radiata*) 403, *404*
Buckden Retiree (London plane/ *Platanus × hispanica*) 224, 247
**buckeye**
  **California buckeye** (*Aesculus californica*) 323
  **hybrid buckeye** (*Aesculus × hybrida*) 103
  **Ohio buckeye** (*Aesculus glabra*) 163, 166, 177
Bulging Oak (pedunculate oak/ *Quercus robur*) 190, *191*
Bull Yew (yew/*Taxus baccata*) 302
Bungalow Tree (yew/*Taxus baccata*) 136
Burnley's Oldest Oak (sessile oak/*Quercus petraea*) 99
Burry Man Tree (monkey puzzle/*Araucaria araucana*) 44
Burton's Holm Oak (holm oak/ *Quercus ilex*) 455
Bus Stop Benchmark (London plane/*Platanus × hispanica*) 216, *217*

## C

Cactus Maple (Oregon maple/ *Acer macrophyllum*) 70
Cadzow Oak (pedunculate oak/ *Quercus robur*) 64, 78
Café Guards (London plane/ *Platanus × hispanica*) 136
Cairngorm Beach Pine (Scots pine/*Pinus sylvestris*) 17, 26, *27*
Caledonian Forest 17, 26

California bay (*Umbellularia californica*) 267
Camberwell Tulip (tulip tree/*Liriodendron tulipifera*) 256
Cambridge 206, 208, 226–35, *226, 229, 230, 235*
Cannizaro Gum (broad-leaved kindling bark/*Eucalyptus dalrympleana*) 243
Capon Tree (sessile oak/*Quercus petraea*) 65, 79, *79*
Car Park Buckeye (California buckeye/*Aesculus californica*) 323
Car Park Copper Beech (copper beech/*Fagus sylvatica* 'Purpurea') 186
Car Park Sentinel (wild black poplar/*Populus nigra*) 412, *420, 421, 422*
Cardiff 258, *383, 384, 385, 392–400, 392, 394, 397, 398, 401*
Carshalton Leviathan (London plane/*Platanus* × *hispanica*) 243
Castle Bonsai (sycamore/*Acer pseudoplatanus*) 232
Castle Elm (wych elm/*Ulmus glabra*) 99
castor oil tree (*Kalopanax septemlobus*) 69, 70, *71*
catalpa
  golden catalpa (*Catalpa bignonioides* 'Aurea') 199
  hybrid catalpa (*Catalpa* × *erubescens* 'J. C Teas') 166, 473
  southern catalpa (*Catalpa bignonioides*) 135, 202, 264, 276, 277, 313, *313*, 332, 388
  western catalpa (*Catalpa speciosa*) 202
  yellow catalpa (*Catalpa ovata*) 163, 171, 345
Cathedral Azarole (Azarole/*Crataegus azarolus*) 348
Cathedral Christmas Tree (Caucasian fir/*Abies nordmanniana*) 29
Cathedral Conker (horse chestnut/*Aesculus hippocastanum*) 226, 362
Cathedral Holm Oak (holm oak/*Quercus ilex*) 466
Cathedral Oak (holm oak/*Quercus ilex*) 377
Cathedral Road Lime (common lime/*Tilia* × *europaea*) 396

Cathedral Tree (false acacia/*Robinia pseudoacacia*) 211
Cathedral Triplet (London plane/*Platanus* × *hispanica*) 202
catkins 9, 101, 143
Caversham Scholar (Japanese pagoda tree/*Styphnolobium japonicum*) *306*, 307
Caversham Sprawler (yew/*Taxus baccata*) 305, 307
Cawr Wysg (wild black poplar/*Populus nigra ssp. betulifolia*) 204, 412, 422, *423*
cedar
  Atlas cedar (*Cedrus atlantica* 'Glauca') 189, 194, 331, 332
  blue Atlas cedar (*Cedrus atlantica* 'Glauca') 61
  cedar of Lebanon (*Cedrus libani*) 47, 99, 177, 189, 194, 203, 228, 234, 241, 247, 249, 280, 294, 299, 312, 348, *349*, 391, 395
  deodar cedar (*Cedrus deodara*) 140, 198, 203, 312, 399, 443, *443*, 478
  fastigiate Atlas cedar (*Cedrus atlantica* 'Fastigiata') 197
  western red cedar (*Thuja plicata*) 57, *57*, 177, 351, 435, 443, 455
Cefn Mably Oak (pedunculate oak/*Quercus robur*) 391
Celestial Maple (mono maple/*Acer pictum*) 396
Cemetery Ash ('Lentiscifolia' narrow-leaved ash/*Fraxinus angustifolia* 'Lentiscifolia') 181, 199
Cemetry Oak (pedunculate oak/*Quercus robur*) 101, 106
Central Park Elm ('Sapporo Autumn Gold' elm/*Ulmus* 'Sapporo Autumn Gold') 367, 373
Centre of Ireland Tree (beech/*Fagus sylvatica*) 464
Chamberlain's Cedar (Atlas cedar/*Cedrus atlantica* 'Glauca') 189, 194
champion trees 9–10, 53
Chancellor's Bride ('The Bride' fuji cherry/*Prunus incisa* 'The Bride') 183

Chancellor's Redwood (giant redwood/*Sequoiadendron giganteum*) 311
Chandelier Pine (Bhutan pine/*Pinus wallichiana*) 61
Chantry Plane (London plane/*Platanus* × *hispanica*) 316
Chapel Yew (yew/*Taxus baccata*) 422
Chapelfield Princess (foxglove tree/*Paulownia tomentosa*) 216
Chapter House Cedar (cedar of Lebanon/*Cedrus libani*) 234
Chapter House Tree (fern-leaved beech/*Fagus sylvatica* 'Asplenifolia') 402
Charing Cross Chancer (tulip tree/*Liriodendron tulipifera*) 73
Cheering Fir (Douglas fir/*Pseudotsuga menziesii*) 79
cherry
  Albi-plena cherry (*Prunus serrulata* 'Albi-Plena') 182
  double-flowered wild cherry (*Prunus avium* 'Plena') 26, 138, 438
  great white cherry (*Prunus serrulata* 'Tai Haku') 10, 374
  'Kanzan' Japanese cherry (*Prunus serrulata* 'Kanzan') 19, 61
  Shirotae cherry (*Prunus serrulata* 'Shirotae') 380
  Tibetan cherry (*Prunus serrula*) 165, *165*
  weeping yoshino cherry (*Prunus* × *yedoensis* 'Ivensii') 182
  winter-flowering cherry (*Prunus* × *subhirtella* 'Autumnalis') 183
  yoshino cherry (*Prunus* × *yedoensis*) 111, 148, 257
Cherry Cinnamon (hybrid strawberry tree/*Arbutus* × *andrachnoides*) 228, *229*
Chester 95, 97, 112–14, *113*, 414, 459
Chestnut Foal (horse chestnut/*Aesculus hippocastanum*) 16, 19
Chiddingfold Thorn (hawthorn/*Crataegus monogyna*) 273
Chimney Sweep's Puzzle (monkey puzzle/*Araucaria araucana*) 23

INDEX 488

Chinese tree privet (*Ligustrum lucidum*) 171, 473
Cholera Plane (London plane/ *Platanus × hispanica*) 163, 171
Christ's Conker (horse chestnut/ *Aesculus hippocastanum*) 227
Church Cross Cypress (golden Monterey cypress/ *Cupressus macrocarpa* 'Lutea') 468
Churchyard Jewel (Judas tree/ *Cercis siliquastrum*) 213, 218
Cinnamon Maple (paperbark maple/ *Acer griseum*) 112
Cintra Cedar (deodar cedar/ *Cedrus deodara*) 312
Cirrus Oak (pedunculate oak/ *Quercus robur*) 312
Cleft Redwood (coastal redwood/ *Sequoia sempervirens*) 161
Cliff Fig (fig/ *Ficus carica*) 171
Clifton Enigma (Italian maple/ *Acer opalus*) 341
Climbers' Lime (silver pendent lime/ *Tilia tomentosa* 'Petiolaris') 4, 75, 75
Climbing Tree (western red cedar/ *Thuja plicata*) 435, 443, 443
Cloister Service Tree (true service tree/ *Sorbus domestica*) 213, 218
Clydeside Willow (white willow/ *Salix alba*) 74
Clyne Indian Horse Chestnut (Indian horse chestnut/ *Aesculus indica*) 407
Coalition Tree (dawn redwood/ *Metasequoia glyptostroboides*) 175
Coaver Club Tree (Exeter elm/ *Ulmus 'Exoniensis'*) 359, 363
Cockermouth Knobbly Ash (ash/ *Fraxinus excelsior*) 92
Cockley Conker (horse chestnut/ *Aesculus hippocastanum*) 211
Collapsing Catalpa (southern catalpa/ *Catalpa bignonioides*) 332
College Chestnut (sweet chestnut/ *Castanea sativa*) 384, 387
College Cypress (smooth bark Arizona cypress/ *Cupressus arizonica var. glabra*) 331
College Oak (turkey oak/ *Quercus cerris*) 442

Colossal Birch (paper birch/ *Betula papyrifera*) 135
Colossal Poplar (wild black poplar/ *Populus nigra ssp. betulifolia*) 189, 190
Comely Bank Plane (London plane/ *Platanus × hispanica*) 58
Congregational Tree (horse chestnut/ *Aesculus hippocastanum*) 361
conifer 10, 16, 17, 20, 25, 28, 29, 56, 91, 92, 157, 161, 176, 181, 203, 223, 254, 308, 312, 331, 348, 351, 370, 373, 380, 384, 391, 396, 407, 417, 435, 442, 449, 455
Consolation Sycamore (sycamore/ *Acer pseudoplatanus*) 5, 23, 251, 451
Contortionist, The (Camperdown elm/ *Ulmus glabra* 'Camperdownii') 58
Conundrum Tree (oak-leaf alder/ *Alnus glutinosa* 'Laciniata') 209, 228
Convalescent Yew (yew/ *Taxus baccata*) 302
coppicing 10, 406
Copshop Deodar (deodar/ *Cedrus deodara*) 198
Cork 446, 449, 468–74, *471*, *472*
Cornish Cork Oak (cork oak/ *Quercus suber*) 367, 374, *375*
Coronation Oak (pedunculate oak/ *Quercus robur*) 428
Coronation Street Awning (Japanese pagoda tree/ *Styphnolobium japonicum*) 227
Corporation Oak (turkey oak/ *Quercus cerris*) 164
Corrib Fig (fig/ *Ficus carica*) 449, 464
Corstorphine's Plane (Corstorphine plane/ *Acer pseudoplatanus* 'Corstorphinense') 53–4, 58
Coslany Mongol (Mongolian lime/ *Tilia mongolica*) 215
Costa Oak (holm oak/ *Quercus ilex*) 307
**cotoneaster**
  **Saint Monica's cotoneaster** (*Cotoneaster frigidus* 'Saint Monica') 342
Court Oak (cork oak/ *Quercus suber*) 468

Coventry *179*, 180, 181, 198–201, *198*, *200*, 367
Coveted Yew (Dovaston's yew/ *Taxus baccata* 'Dovastoniana') 183
Cow Tower Poplar (wild black poplar/ *Populus nigra*) *214*, 215
Craigellachie National Nature Reserve 25
Craigends Yew (yew/ *Taxus baccata*) 65, 66
Crawford Sycamore (sycamore/ *Acer pseudoplatanus*) 470, *471*
Cream Soda Tree (tulip tree/ *Liriodendron tulipifera*) 282
Crème de la Crème (strawberry tree/ *Arbutus unedo*) 243, 259
Crescent Oak (holm oak/ *Quercus ilex*) 285, 293
Cripplegate Warden (black Worcester pear/ *Pyrus* 'Black Worcester') 202
Cromwell's Beech (beech/ *Fagus sylvatica*) 97, 108, *109*
Crossroads Cedar (cedar of Lebanon/ *Cedrus libani*) 189, 194
Crouch Oak (pedunculate oak/ *Quercus robur*) *272*, 273
Crowd Pleaser (weeping willow/ *Salix × sepulcralis* 'Chrysocoma') 442
Crowhurst Yew (yew/ *Taxus baccata*) 274
Cruickshank Roble (roble/ *Nothofagus obliqua*) 42
Cul-de-sac Chestnut (sweet chestnut/ *Castanea sativa*) 316
cultivar 3, 10, 13, 40, 53, 55, 56, 60, 61, 78, 85, 88, 97, 105, 122, 138, 140, 156, 157, 166, 169, 172, 177, 183, 197, 201, 218, 259, 270, 271, 278, 282, 285, 288, 291, 292, 301, 308, 311, 342, 345, 347, 353, 358, 359, 374, 396, 399, 438, 449, 453, 460, 464, 468, 477
Cumbria 82, 83, 85, 92
Curator's Strawberry Tree (strawberry tree/ *Arbutus unedo*) 145, 153
Curly-Wurly Mulberry (black mulberry/ *Morus nigra*) 323
Cursed Fig (fig/ *Ficus carica*) 359, 377
Cutler's Oak (pedunculate oak/ *Quercus robur*) 148

cuttings or grafts 10, 12, 41, 101, 161, 177, 288, 377
Cwmdonkin Katsura (Katsura/ *Cercidiphyllum japonicum*) 385, 403, *404*
**cypress**
  **golden Monterey cypress** (*Cupressus macrocarpa* 'Lutea') 374, 468
  **Lawson cypress** (*Chamaecyparis lawsoniana*) 417
  **Monterey cypress** (*Cupressus macrocarpa*) 351, 374, 384, 402, 408, *409*, 478
  **Nootka cypress** (*Callitropsis nootkatensis*) 82, 91
  **smooth bark Arizona cypress** (*Cupressus arizonica* var. *glabra*) 331
  **swamp cypress** (*Taxodium distichum*) 248, *248*, 308, *309*, 352

# D

Darley Dale Yew (yew/*Taxus baccata*) 161
Darley Park Den Tree (weeping one-leaved ash/*Fraxinus excelsior* 'Diversifolia Pendula') 172
Darnley Plane (sycamore/ *Acer pseudoplatanus*) 69, 77
Darwin Oak (pedunculate oak/ *Quercus robur*) 183
Darwin's Yew (yew/*Taxus baccata*) 242
Dean's Magnolia (Chinese evergreen magnolia/*Magnolia delavayi*) 319
Debatable Plane (London plane/ *Platanus* × *hispanica*) 40, 46
deciduous trees 10, 25, 105, 122, 308
Defynnog Yew (yew/*Taxus baccata*) 414, 421
Delapré Tulip Tree (tulip tree/ *Liriodendron tulipifera*) 177
Derry *425*, 426, 428, 429, *429*, 430, *431*, 437
Derwen Lucombe (Lucombe oak/*Quercus* × *crenata* 'Lucombeana') 413, 414
Devil's Stone Tree (pedunculate oak/*Quercus robur*) 361

Devon & Cornwall 356–81, *356–7*, *362*, *365*, 366
Dibble Tree, The (cricket bat willow/*Salix alba* 'Caerulea') 44
Dingwall Weeping Ash (weeping ash/*Fraxinus excelsior* 'Pendula') 20
dioecious trees 10, 66, 101, 273
Discoed Yew (yew/*Taxus baccata*) 412–13, 414, 421
Ditton Court Pine (Bhutan pine/ *Pinus wallichiana*) 234
Doire Oak (pedunculate oak/ *Quercus robur*) 429
Domesday Oak (pedunculate oak/*Quercus robur*) 335, 337
Don Fig (fig/*Ficus carica*) 145, 147, 358
Doors of Durin Yews (yew/*Taxus baccata*) 5, 331
Double Dawn (dawn redwood/ *Metasequoia glyptostroboides*) 352
Double-Trunked Tulip (tulip tree/*Liriodendron tulipifera*) 378
Doubletake Leylandii (Leyland cypress/× *Cupressocyparis leylandii*) 370
Douglas, David 17, 32, 33
Dour Cedar (cedar of Lebanon/ *Cedrus libani*) 280, *280*
Downham Field Maple (field maple/*Acer campestre*) 209, 233
Downshire Giant (giant redwood/*Sequoiadendron giganteum*) 445
Dragon Maple (trident maple/ *Acer buergerianum*) 301
Drake's Plane (London plane/ *Platanus* × *hispanica*) 373
Drive-Thru Beech (beech/*Fagus sylvatica*) 456, *457*
Dubh Linn Paperbark (paperbark maple/*Acer griseum*) 459
Dublin 5, 122, 400, *446*, 448, 452–63, *452*, *454*, *457*, *458*, *461*, *462*, 466, 477
Dundee 3, *39*, 40–41, 44, 46–7, *46*, 49, *50*, 58
Dungiven Rag Tree (hawthorn/ *Crataegus monogyna*) 432
Dunkeld *14*, 16, 28–9, 32, 66
Dunkeld Larch, The (Dunkeld larch/*Larix* × *marschlinsii*) 29

Dunmurry Tulip Tree (tulip tree/*Liriodendron tulipifera*) *444*, 445
Dutch Courage Elm ('Lobel' elm/*Ulmus* 'Lobel') 292, *292*
Dutch elm disease 23, 40–41, 53, 99, 131, 135, 190, 218, 263, 270, 281, 285, 288, 342, 363
Duthie Beech (beech/*Fagus sylvatica*) 44, *45*

# E

East Midlands 154–77, *154–5*
Eastville Hornbeam (hornbeam/ *Carpinus betulus*) 338
Ecclesiastical Pear (pear/*Pyrus communis* ssp. *sativa*) 83, *84*, 85
Edge of London Oak (pedunculate oak/*Quercus robur*) 239, 242
Edinburgh 3, 4, 35, *39*, 40, 41, 52–61, *52*, *54*, *57*, *59*, *60*, 73, 78, 112, 114, 122, 332, 428
Edzell Granny Pine (Scots pine/ *Pinus sylvestris*) 44
Effluent Fig (fig/*Ficus carica*) 103, 171
*ehret* (*Ehretia dicksonii*) 338
Eiffel Tower Tree (Monterey cypress/*Cupressus macrocarpa*) 408, *409*
Elder Ash (ash/*Fraxinus excelsior*) 64, 74
Elder Statesman (Mirbeck's oak/ *Quercus canariensis*) 437
Elephant Holm Oak (holm oak/ *Quercus ilex*) 341
Elephant Tree (pedunculate oak/ *Quercus robur*) 239, 248, *248*
Elizabeth Fry's Oak (pedunculate oak/*Quercus robur*) 213, 216
**elm**
  **Blandford elm** (*Ulmus glabra* 'Superba') 4, 40, 55
  **Camperdown elm** (*Ulmus glabra* 'Camperdownii') 3, 40, 41, 44, 46, 48, 58, 414
  **Dampier's elm** (*Ulmus* × *hollandica* 'Dampieri') 432
  **Dutch elm** (*Ulmus* × *hollandica* 'Major') 128, 291
  **English elm** (*Ulmus minor* 'Atinia') 270, 285, 288, *289*, *290*, 291, 332

**European white elm** (*Ulmus laevis*) 249, 254
**Exeter elm** (*Ulmus 'Exoniensis'*) 282, 359
**field elm** (*Ulmus minor var. minor*) 98, 99, 190, 270
**golden wych elm** (*Ulmus glabra 'Lutescens'*) 78
**Hoersholm elm** (*Ulmus minor 'Hoersholmensis'*) 293
**Huntingdon elm** (*Ulmus × hollandica 'Vegeta'*) 128, 141, 263, 281, 342, 467
**'Jacqueline Hillier' elm** (*Ulmus 'Jacqueline Hillier'*) 193, 288
**'Lobel' elm** (*Ulmus 'Lobel'*) 292, 295
**Lombarts' elm** (*Ulmus 'Lombartsii'*) 4, 285, 288
**'Sapporo Autumn Gold' elm** (*Ulmus 'Sapporo Autumn Gold'*) 218, 373
**Spaeth's field elm** (*Ulmus minor 'Umbraculifera Gracilis'*) 61
**tabletop wych elm** (*Ulmus glabra 'Horizontalis'*) 10, 40, 43, 46, 47, 99, 114, 131,193, 270, 281, 291, 464
**true Dutch elm** (*Ulmus × hollandica 'Belgica'*) 128, 134
**Wentworth elm** (*Ulmus × hollandica 'Wentworthii Pendula'*) 53, 55
**Wheatley elm** (*Ulmus minor 'Sarniensis'*) 56, 60, 61, 131, 135, 281, 285, 288, 293, 407
**wych elm** (*Ulmus glabra*) 4, 10, 19, 23, 40, 41, 42, 43, 44, 46, 47, 55, 58, 78, 99, 131, 134, 137, 153, 281
Elm of Tralee (Huntingdon elm/ *Ulmus × hollandica 'Vegeta'*) 467
England
 east 206–25, *206–7*
 north 80–93, *80–81*, *86*, 99
 north-west 94–125, *94–5*, 129, 156, 180
 south-east 251, 268–95, *268–9*
 southern 40, 270, 285, 296–325, *296–7*, *304*, *322*, 396, 412
 south-west 326–81, *326–7*
Entanglement Oak (holm oak/ *Quercus ilex*) 406, *406*

Eppie Callum's Oak (pedunculate oak/*Quercus robur*) 7, 35
Erewash Pharos (Bolle's poplar/ *Populus alba 'Pyramidalis'*) 172
Evelyn's Mulberry (black mulberry/*Morus nigra*) 255, *255*
evergreen 10, 11, 50, 77, 87, 122, 153, 171, 201, 215, 261, 270, 285, 293, 307, 311, 319, 328, 333, 341, 342, 359, 365, 377, 379, 406, 408, 455, 466, 473
Evil Twin (cedar of Lebanon/ *Cedrus libani*) 203
Exeter 4, 226, 337, 352, *357*, 359, *360*, 361, 362–3, *362*, 370
Exeter Exemplar (Lucombe oak/ *Quercus × crenata 'Lucombeana'*) 359, 363
Exhibit 'A' (Sitka spruce/*Picea sitchensis*) 17, 33
Exhibition Ash (ash/*Fraxinus excelsior*) 105
Exonian Oak (Lucombe oak/ *Quercus × crenata 'Lucombeana'*) 337

## F

*Fagaceae* (beech family) 11, 13
Fair Maple (paperbark maple/ *Acer griseum*) 399
Fairytale Beech (weeping beech/ *Fagus sylvatica 'Pendula'*) 96, 106
Falkner Flailing Plane (London plane/*Platanus × hispanica*) 117, 122, *123*
Fall from Grace (black mulberry/ *Morus nigra*) 199
**false acacia or black locust** (*Robinia pseudoacacia*) 119, 141, 159, 208, 211, 213, 218, 226, 459
family (taxonomic term for a group of genera) 11
Famine Memorial Ash (weeping ash/*Fraxinus excelsior 'Pendula'*) 460
**fastigiate** 11, 112, 197, 432, 435
Fat Chestnut (sweet chestnut/ *Castanea sativa*) 209, 231
Fatal Oak (pedunculate oak/ *Quercus robur*) 7, *368*, 369
Feather-Duster Beech (fern-leaved beech/*Fagus sylvatica 'Asplenifolia'*) 164

Fife 40, 47, 50
Fife's Oldest Yew (yew/*Taxus baccata*) 50
**fig** (*Ficus carica*) 103, 145, 147, 171, 253, 263, 292, 335, 340, 358, 359, 377, 378, 394, 395, 449, 464
Filwood Oak (holm oak/*Quercus ilex*) 335, 338
Finest Beech (beech/*Fagus sylvatica*) 135
**fir**
 **Caucasian fir** (*Abies nordmanniana*) 29
 **Douglas fir** (*Pseudotsuga menziesii*) 17, 25, 32, 79
Fire Exit Sycamore (sycamore/ *Acer pseudoplatanus*) 64, 77
First Fiddle (hybrid catalpa/ *Catalpa × erubescens*) 472, 473
First Picture of Yew (yew/*Taxus baccata*) 325
First Wellingtonia (giant redwood/*Sequoiadendron giganteum*) 316
Flaybrick Fern-Leaved Beech (fern-leaved beech/*Fagus sylvatica 'Asplenifolia'*) 88, 97, 114
Foggy Lime (silver lime/*Tilia tomentosa*) 106
Foragers' Wonder (walnut/ *Juglans regia*) 83, 84, 85, 88, *89*
Forest Maple (Cappadocian maple/*Acer cappadocicum*) 164
Forest of Belfast Oak (pedunculate oak/*Quercus robur*) 442
Forth Bridge Yew (yew/*Taxus baccata*) 50, 66
Fortingall Yew, The (yew/*Taxus baccata*) 7, 28, 50, 412
Forty Hall Cedar (cedar of Lebanon/*Cedrus libani*) 241
Fothergill's Mulberry (black mulberry/*Morus nigra*) 254
Four Stone Tree (common lime/ *Tilia × europaea*) 464
Fourth Wonder of Wales (yew/ *Taxus baccata*) 418
**foxglove tree** (*Paulownia tomentosa*) 101, *102*, 103, 216, *324*, 325
Fragrant Giant (small-leaved lime/ *Tilia cordata*) 157, *158*, 159

French Fancy, The (Bauman's horse chestnut/*Aesculus hippocastanum* 'Baumanii') 353
Friar's Delight (oriental plane/*Platanus orientalis*) 161
Friendly Plane (London plane/*Platanus × hispanica*) 121
Friends Cedar (fastigiate Atlas cedar/*Cedrus atlantica* 'Fastigiata') 197
Friendship Tree (London plane/*Platanus × hispanica*) 238, 251
Frozen Giant (silver pendent lime/*Tilia tomentosa* 'Petiolaris') 138

# G

Gabalfa Ginkgo (ginkgo/*Ginkgo biloba*) 395
Gaol Oak (pedunculate oak/*Quercus robur*) 274
Garage Chestnut (sweet chestnut/*Castanea sativa*) 367, 369
Gardener's Secret (giant redwood/*Sequoiadendron giganteum*) 90, 91
Gargantuan Tepa (tepa/*Laureliopsis philippiana*) 385, 405, 406
Garrick's Mulberry (black mulberry/*Morus nigra*) 177
Gatekeeper (silver maple/*Acer saccharinum*) 220
Gateway Elm (English elm/*Ulmus minor* 'Atinia') 285, 290, 291
Gateway Oak (Turner's oak/*Quercus × turneri*) 244
genera 11
General Ash (weeping ash/*Fraxinus excelsior* 'Pendula') 166
General Plane (oriental plane/*Platanus orientalis*) 150
genus 11, 13, 44, 285
George Green Chestnut (sweet chestnut/*Castanea sativa*) 240, 241
George Square Maple (Norway maple/*Acer platanoides*) 69, 72, 73
Giant Arbutus (strawberry tree/*Arbutus unedo*) 449, 468

Giant Haystack Tree (monkey puzzle/*Araucaria Araucana*) 119, *119*
Giant of South London (turkey oak/*Quercus cerris*) 256
Giddylake Oak (pedunculate oak/*Quercus robur*) 351
Ginger Peel (paperbark maple/*Acer griseum*) 201
**ginkgo** (*Ginkgo biloba*) 176, 232, 264, *265*, 273, 281, 287, 328, 329, 331, 338, 353, 361, 372, *372*, 395, 399, 408
**weeping ginkgo** (*Ginkgo biloba* 'Pendula') 399
Glasgow 4, 26, 40, *62*, 64, 68–77, *68*, *71*, *72*, 75, 76, 298, 359, 473
Glasnevin Tree of Heaven (tree of heaven/*Ailanthus altissima*) 456
Gleadless Oak (sessile oak/*Quercus petraea*) 148
Glenmore Forest 26
Glitterball Willow (silver willow/*Salix alba* var. *sericea*) 177
Golden Lion Pine (Scots pine/*Pinus sylvestris*) 421
**golden rain tree** (*Koelreuteria paniculata*) 175, 247, *262*, 263, 332
Goliath Beech (beech/*Fagus sylvatica*) 373
Good Neighbour (deodar cedar/*Cedrus deodara*) 140
Gorton Survivor (Manchester poplar/*Populus nigra* ssp. *betulifolia* 'Manchester') 101, 105, 122, 412
Gosforth Showstopper (cork oak/*Quercus suber*) 82, 92
Goth Plane (London plane/*Platanus × hispanica*) 153
Gothic Catalpa (western catalpa/*Catalpa speciosa*) 202
grafting 11, 58, 164, 199, 201, 259, 315, 363
Grand Bught Redwood (giant redwood/*Sequoiadendron giganteum*) 25
Grande Plane (oriental plane/*Platanus orientalis*) 150, *152*, 153
Grangetown Baobab (baobab London plane/*Platanus × hispanica* 'Western Baobab') 398
Grantham Oak, The (pedunculate oak/*Quercus robur*) 174

Grapes Strawberry Tree (strawberry tree/*Arbutus unedo*) 216
Great Oak, The (pedunculate oak/*Quercus robur*) 7, 181, 204, 298, 413
Great Southern Beech (copper beech/*Fagus sylvatica* 'Purpurea') 43
Greedy Tree (London plane/*Platanus × hispanica*) 258, 400, *401*
Green Lane Ash (single-leaved ash/*Fraxinus excelsior* 'Diversifolia') 118
Greenside Sycamore (sycamore/*Acer pseudoplatanus*) 415
Greenwich Park, London 4, 254
Greyfriars Maple (Cappadocian maple/*Acer cappadocicum*) 34, 35
Greyfriars Spanish Oak (Spanish oak/*Quercus × crenata*) 181, 199
Grimaldi Poplar (wild black poplar/*Populus nigra* ssp. *betulifolia*) 260
Groaning Tree (sycamore/*Acer pseudoplatanus*) 65, 78
Grotto Beech (weeping beech/*Fagus sylvatica* 'Pendula') 77
Grotto Oak (sessile oak/*Quercus petraea*) 235
Guildhall Plane (oriental plane/*Platanus orientalis*) 213, 220, *221*
Guise, Mary 20
**gum**
**blue gum** (*Eucalyptus globulus*) 358, 380
**small-leaved gum** (*Eucalyptus parvula*) 106
**spinning gum** (*Eucalyptus perriniana*) 385, 407

# H

Halls-of-Residence Cedar (Atlas cedar/*Cedrus atlantica* 'Glauca') 194
**handkerchief tree** (*Davidia involucrata*) 111, 252, 253, 267, 319, 328, 347, 402
Handside Catalpa (hybrid catalpa/*Catalpa × erubescens* 'J. C. Teas') 235, *235*
Handsome Magyar (Hungarian oak/*Quercus frainetto*) 57

Ha'penny Alder (Japanese alder/ *Alnus japonica*) 70
Hardwick Cedar (cedar of Lebanon/*Cedrus libani*) 228
Harrogate Giant (true Dutch elm/*Ulmus x hollandica* 'Belgica') 128, 132, *133*
**hawthorn** (*Crataegus monogyna*) 9, 50, 136, 273, 282, 432, 435, 438, 448, 474, 475
Haystack Tree (weeping hornbeam/*Carpinus betulus* 'Pendula') 170
Hayton Victor (walnut/*Juglans regia*) 83, 85
Headrow Bastard Service Tree (bastard service tree/*Sorbus × thuringiaca*) 137
Heartwood Elm (Huntingdon elm/*Ulmus × hollandica* 'Vegeta') 128, 149, *149*
Heaton Hybrid (hybrid buckeye/ *Aesculus × hybrida*) 103
Heavenly Prospect (tree of heaven/*Ailanthus altissima*) 299, 307
Heavenly Tree (tree of heaven/ *Ailanthus altissima*) 125
Hellfire Corner Elm (tabletop elm/*Ulmus glabra* 'Horizontalis') 270, 281
Hen Goleg Shaggy Tree (monkey puzzle/*Araucaria araucana*) 414
Henrietta Spaethii (purple-leaved sycamore/*Acer pseudoplatanus* 'Spaethii') 345
Herne Hill Hanami Tree (yoshino cherry/*Prunus × yedoensis*) 257
Hezlett Chestnut (sweet chestnut/ *Castanea sativa*) 3, 427, 428
Hidden Giant (London plane/ *Platanus × hispanica*) 374
Hidden Tulip Tree (tulip tree/ *Liriodendron tulipifera*) 56, 73
Highbury Vaults Bee-Bee Tree (bee-bee tree/*Tetradium daniellii*) 329, 341
Hillier's Walnut (cut-leaf walnut/ *Juglans regia* 'Laciniata') 318, 319
Hockley Catalpa (yellow catalpa/ *Catalpa ovata*) 163, 171

Hogarth's Mulberry (black mulberry/*Morus nigra*) 247
Hollow Beech (beech/*Fagus sylvatica*) 259
Holloway Judas Tree (Judas tree/ *Cercis siliquastrum*) 346, 347
Holy Tree (giant redwood/ *Sequoiadendron giganteum*) 353
Holy Trinity Corkscrew Pine (stone pine/*Pinus pinea*) 202
Holywood Big Oak (turkey oak/ *Quercus cerris*) 427, 433, *433*, 466
Home Farm Oak (pedunculate oak/*Quercus robur*) 231
Home Nursery Lime (Oliver's lime/*Tilia oliveri*) 319
Homebase Kōwhai (Kōwhai/ *Sophora tetraptera*) 273
**honey locust** (*Gleditsia triacanthos*) 393, 398, *398*, 453, 460
Hoppy Poplar (Serotina hybrid black poplar/*Populus × canadensis* 'Serotina') 101, 105
**hornbeam** (*Carpinus betulus*) 147, 181, 186, 338, 377
**weeping hornbeam** (*Carpinus betulus* 'Pendula') 170
**horse chestnut** (*Aesculus hippocastanum*) 3, 13, 16, 17, 19, 42, 103, 108, 132, 145, 161, 166, 177, 211, 215, 218, 226, 227, 241, 299, 301, 323, 353, 361, 362, 396, 407, 416, 417, 432, 450, 463, 469
**Bauman's horse chestnut** (*Aesculus hippocastanum* 'Baumanii') 396
**Indian horse chestnut** (*Aesculus indica*) 407
Hospital Beech (copper beech/ *Fagus sylvatica* 'Purpurea') 450
Hospital Elm (English elm/ *Ulmus minor* 'Atinia') 332
Hospital Ginkgo (ginkgo/*Ginkgo biloba*) 361
Hospital Tree Privet (Chinese tree privet/*Ligustrum lucidum*) 473
Hove's Elm Actually (Hoersholm elm/*Ulmus minor* 'Hoersholmensis') 293
Howel Gwyn's Handkerchief Tree (handkerchief tree/ *Davidia involucrata*) 402

Howff Wraith (Camperdown elm/*Ulmus glabra* 'Camperdownii') 41, 46, *48*
Hull 127, 128, 140–43, *140*, *142*
Humble Beech (variegated beech/*Fagus sylvatica* 'Albovariegata') 138
Hungate Tree of Heaven (tree of heaven/*Ailanthus altissima*) 213, 215, 220
Hungry Tree, The (London plane/*Platanus × hispanica*) 400, 449, 453, 459
hybrids 11, 29, 101, 103, 105, 118, 122, 156, 157, 163, 166, *168*, 169, 181, 199, 201, 228, 229, 234, 235, *235*, 238–9, 264, 291, 294, 302, 359, 363, 365, 370, 388, 393, 397, *397*, 418, 441, 463, *472*, 473

*I*

Iconic Oak (Lucombe oak/ *Quercus × crenata* 'Lucombeana') 449, 473
Immaculate Deodar (deodar cedar/*Cedrus deodara*) 478
Imperilled Cedar (cedar of Lebanon/*Cedrus libani*) 247
Inclosure Oak (pedunculate oak/ *Quercus robur*) 163, 164, 165, 223, 428
Incongruous Cedar (cedar of Lebanon/*Cedrus libani*) 395
Influencer Palm (cabbage tree/ *Cordyline australis*) 378
Insole Sweetgum (American sweetgum/*Liquidambar styraciflua*) 395
Inst Cherry (double-flowered wild cherry/*Prunus avium* 'Plena') 438
Instaplane (London plane/ *Platanus × hispanica*) 220
Interloper Plane (London plane/ *Platanus × hispanica*) 293
International Elm (Dampier's elm/*Ulmus × hollandica* 'Dampieri') 432
Inveraray's Fyne Cherry (double-flowered wild cherry/ *Prunus avium* 'Plena') 26
Inverness 14, 16, 17, *22*, 23–5, *24*
Inviting Oak (holm oak/*Quercus ilex*) 374

Ireland
  Northern Ireland 424–45, 424–5, 448
  Republic of Ireland 446–79, 446–7
Irish Italian (Italian maple/*Acer opalus*) 437
Iron Age Oak (pedunculate oak/*Quercus robur*) 315

## J

Jacqueline Elm ('Jacqueline Hillier' elm/*Ulmus* 'Jacqueline Hillier') 288
Japanese Garden Maple (purple-leaved Japanese maple/*Acer palmatum* 'Atropurpurea') 118
**Japanese pagoda tree** (*Styphnolobium japonicum*) 227, *306*, 307
Jawbone Walk Cherry ('Kanzan' cherry/*Prunus serrulata* 'Kanzan') 61
Jet Tree (monkey puzzle/*Araucaria araucana*) 131
Jethart Pear (pear/*Pyrus communis ssp. sativa*) 65, 83
Jockey Road Outrider (pedunculate oak/*Quercus robur*) 189, 190, 195
Jubilee Oak (pedunculate oak/*Quercus robur*) 223
**Judas tree** (*Cercis siliquastrum*) 213, 218, 224, 313, *346*, 347, 372
Judge Wyndham's Oak (pedunculate oak/*Quercus robur*) 354
Junction Chestnut (sweet chestnut/*Castanea sativa*) 379
Just Good Friends (fig/*Ficus carica*) 292

## K

**Kapuka** (*Griselinia littoralis*) 473
**Katsura** (*Cercidiphyllum japonicum*) 385, 403, *404*
Keats Mulberry (black mulberry/*Morus nigra*) 258
Keith Chestnut (horse chestnut/*Aesculus hippocastanum*) 42
Kelburn Larch (weeping larch/*Larix decidua* 'Pendula') 65, 66

Kemp's Fern-Leaf Beech (fern-leaved beech/*Fagus sylvatica* 'asplenifolia') 88
Kenmare Cypress (Monterey cypress/*Cupressus macrocarpa*) 468
Kenn Yew (yew/*Taxus baccata*) 363
Kensington Postbox Tree (London plane/*Platanus × hispanica*) 258, *258*, 400
Kepier Pear (pear/*Pyrus communis ssp. sativa*) 83, 87, 91
Kett's Oak (pedunculate oak/*Quercus robur*) 208, 223
Kew Colossus (chestnut-leaved oak/*Quercus castaneifolia*) 239, 247
Keyes Kobus (Kobus magnolia/*Magnolia kobus*) 399
Kibble Palace Champion (castor oil tree/*Kalopanax septemlobus*) 69, 70, *71*
Kieran's Tree (golden rain tree/*Koelreuteria paniculata*) 332
Kilcurry Big Tree (sycamore/*Acer pseudoplatanus*) 450
King Tree, The (sweet chestnut/*Castanea sativa*) (73) (Denny) 50, *51*
King Tree, The (horse chestnut/*Aesculus hippocastanum*) (896) (Armagh) 432
King's Conker (horse chestnut/*Aesculus hippocastanum*) 226, 227
Kirkwall 7, 16, 19
Kiwi Tree (golden tōtara/*Podocarpus tōtara* 'Aureus') 347
Knobbliest Baobab (baobab London plane/*Platanus × hispanica* 'Baobab') 271, 278
Knole Tree (sycamore/*Acer pseudoplatanus*) 277
Knotted Acacia (false acacia/*Robinia pseudoacacia*) 141
**Kōwhai** (*Sophora tetraptera*) 273

## L

Lads and Girls Elm (field elm/*Ulmus minor var. minor*) *98*, 99
Lady Dixon's Cedar (deodar/*Cedrus deodara*) 435, 443, *443*
Ladywell Elm (European white elm/*Ulmus laevis*) 254

Lagan Hunk (baobab London plane/*Platanus × hispanica* 'Western Baobab') 437
Lakeland Mountain Pine (mountain pine/*Pinus mugo ssp. uncinata*) 92
Lakeside Café Guards (London plane/*Platanus × hispanica*) 136
Lakeside Elm (Huntingdon elm/*Ulmus × hollandica* 'Vegeta') 128, 141
Lamb-Dressed-as-Mutton Tree (southern catalpa/*Catalpa bignonioides*) 276, 277
Lansdowne Strawberry Tree (hybrid strawberry tree/*Arbutus × andrachnoides*) 463
**larch**
  **Dunkeld larch** (*Larix × marschlinsii*) 29
  **European larch** (*Larix decidua*) 25, 28
  **weeping larch** (*Larix decidua* 'Pendula') 66
**large-flowered spindle** (*Euonymus grandifloras*) 395
Larkin's Lime (small-leaved lime/*Tilia cordata*) 128, 141
Last Elm (Huntingdon elm/*Ulmus × hollandica* 'Vegeta') 342
layering 11–12, 65, 91, 243, 305 307, 312, 402, 407, 443, 455
Le Nôtre, André 4
Leeds *126*, 128, 129, 135–8, *137*
Left Bank Plane (London plane/*Platanus × hispanica*) 477
Leftover Oak (sessile oak/*Quercus petraea*) 108
Legal High (dawn redwood/*Metasequoia glyptostroboides*) 263
Leicester *154*, 156, 157, 175–7, *175*, *176*
Leicester's Pride of India (golden rain tree/*Koelreuteria paniculata*) 157, 175
Leigh Library Lebanon (cedar of Lebanon/*Cedrus libani*) 234
Leinster House Robinia (false acacia/*Robinia pseudoacacia*) 449, 459
Lenin's Maple (Montpellier maple/*Acer monspessulanum*) 260, *261*

Lesnes Abbey Mulberry (black mulberry/*Morus nigra*) 239, 242
Level Dutch Elm (Dutch elm/ *Ulmus* × *hollandica* 'Major') 285, 291
Lewes Elm (Exeter elm/*Ulmus* 'Exoniensis') 282
**Leyland cypress**/× *Cupressocyparis leylandii* 370
Liberator Redwood (giant redwood/*Sequoiadendron giganteum*) 453, 456
Lido Elms (Wheatley elm/*Ulmus minor* 'Sarniensis') 407
**lime**
  **common lime** (*Tilia* × *europaea*) 11, 12, 13, 26, 55, 69, 73, 86, 106, 119, 121, 145, 149, 150, 160, 233, 278, 323, 331, 342, 374, 396, 431, 432, 435, 442, 445, 450, 464, 470
  **cut-leaf lime** (*Tilia platyphyllos* 'Laciniata') 331
  **'Greenspire' small-leaved lime** (*Tilia cordata* 'Greenspire') 440, 441
  **large-leaved lime** (*Tilia platyphyllos*) 11
  **Mongolian lime** (*Tilia mongolica*) 215
  **Oliver's lime** (*Tilia oliveri*) 319
  **silver lime** (*Tilia tomentosa*) 106, 203, 319, 478, *479*
  **silver pendent lime** (*Tilia tomentosa* 'Petiolaris') 75, *75*, 138, 181, 203, 231, 460
  **small-leaved lime** (*Tilia cordata*) 11, 56, 128, 132, *133*, 141, 157, *158*, 159,
Limerick Copper Beech (copper beech/*Fagus sylvatica* 'Purpurea') 466
Linda Vista Plane (London plane/*Platanus* × *hispanica*) 387
Linton Miracle (yew/*Taxus baccata*) 204, *205*
Liskeard Twister (hornbeam/ *Carpinus betulus*) 377
Little Parndon Oak (pedunculate oak/*Quercus robur*) 233
Liverpool 3, *95*, 96, 97, 99, *116*, 117–25, *119*, *120*, *123*, *124*

Llangattock Leviathan (giant redwood/*Sequoiadendron giganteum*) 422
Llangernyw Yew (yew/*Taxus baccata*) 413, 414
Loddiges Service Tree (true service tree/*Sorbus domestica*) 253
Lode Lane Chestnut (sweet chestnut/*Castanea sativa*) 181, 198
London 79, 96, 101, 199, 236–67, *236*, *237*, *240*, *245*, *246*, *248*, 367
  inner London 250–67, *250*, *252*, *255*, *258*, *261*, *262*, *265*, *266*
Loneliest Elm in the World (Lombarts' elm/*Ulmus* 'Lombartsii') 285, 288
Lonely Tree (Wheatley elm/ *Ulmus minor* 'Sarniensis') 135
Lonesome Lime (lime/*Tilia* × *europaea*) 450
Longford Red Oak (red oak/ *Quercus rubra*) 108
Loop-the-Loop Pine (Scots pine/ *Pinus sylvestris*) 208, *222*, 223
Loudon's Black Walnut (black walnut/*Juglans nigra*) 172
Love Lock Elm (English elm/ *Ulmus minor* 'Atinia') 285, 291
Loveliest Hornbeam (hornbeam/ *Carpinus betulus*) 186
Loveliest of Cherries (great white cherry/*Prunus serrulata* 'Tai Haku') 374
Lowry's Tree (hybrid black poplar/*Populus* × *canadensis*) 101, 103
Lucky Magnolia (southern magnolia/*Magnolia grandiflora*) 307
Luscious-Locked Ginkgo (ginkgo/*Ginkgo biloba*) 176

# M

M&S Plane (London plane/ *Platanus* × *hispanica*) 171
Mackem Trophy (Swedish whitebeam/*Sorbus intermedia*) 88
Mackenzie, John 20
Magdalen Plane (London plane/ *Platanus* × *hispanica*) 302

**magnolia**
  **Chinese evergreen magnolia** (*Magnolia delavayi*) 319
  **Kobus magnolia** (*Magnolia kobusi*) 373, 399
  **southern magnolia** (*Magnolia grandiflora*) 270, 274, *275*, 283, *283*, 307, 319
  **Veitch's magnolia** (*Magnolia* × *veitchii* 'Peter Veitch') 359, 363
maiden 12, 325, 379, 474
Maids of Honour Stone Pine (stone pine/*Pinus pinea*) 244
Major Oak (pedunculate oak/ *Quercus robur*) 3, 156, 160, *160*, 208–9
Mallow Oak (sessile oak/*Quercus petraea*) 469
Manaccan Fig (fig/*Ficus carica*) 378
Manchester 3, *95*, 96, 100–108, *100*, *102*, *104*, *107*, *109*, *110*, 122
**maple**
  **Cappadocian maple** (*Acer cappadocicum*) 34, 35, 153, 164
  **Cretan maple** (*Acer sempervirens*) 311, 333
  **field maple** (*Acer campestre*) 9, 64, 66, 67, 209, 233, 242, 257, 352, 422
  **Italian maple** (*Acer opalus*) 341, 437
  **Japanese maple** (*Acer palmatum*) 76, 77, 118, 249, 399
  **mono maple** (*Acer pictum*) 396
  **Montpellier maple** (*Acer monspessulanum*) 260
  **Norway maple** (*Acer platanoides*) 72, 73, 172, 174
  **Oregon maple** (*Acer macrophyllum*) 70
  **paperbark maple** (*Acer griseum*) 5, 54, 55, 112, 201, 302, 328, 399, 459
  **Père David's maple** (*Acer davidii*) 36, 228
  **purple-leaved Japanese maple** (*Acer palmatum* 'Atropurpurea') 118
  **purple Norway maple** (*Acer pseudoplatanus* 'Schwedleri') 172

silver maple (*Acer saccharinum*) 220, 224, 397
trident maple (*Acer buergerianum*) 301
Marie Louise's Chestnut (sweet chestnut/*Castanea sativa*) 107, *107*
Market Place Mulberry (black mulberry/*Morus nigra*) 211
Marlfield Maiden (sessile oak/*Quercus petraea*) 474
Martyrs Tree (sycamore/*Acer pseudoplatanus*) 352
Marylebone Elm (Huntingdon elm/*Ulmus* × *hollandica* 'Vegeta') 263
Master, The (pedunculate oak/*Quercus robur*) 239, 249
Masters' Marvellous Plane (baobab London plane/*Platanus* × *hispanica* 'Baobab') 258, 271, 278, *279*
Mawson's Extraordinary Cherry (Albi-plena cherry/*Prunus serrulata* 'Albi-Plena') 180, 182
McKenzie's Plane (London plane/*Platanus* × *hispanica*) 320
Meadows Apogee (Wheatley elm/*Ulmus minor* 'Sarniensis') 61
Meavy's Feted Oak (pedunculate oak/*Quercus robur*) 365
Medicine Tree (oriental plane/*Platanus orientalis*) 427, 438, 439
**medlar** (*Mespilus germanica* 'Nottingham') 157, 169, 294
Mega Magnolia (southern magnolia/*Magnolia grandiflora*) 270, 283, *283*
Meikleour Beech Hedge 32
Meikleour First Tree (beech/*Fagus sylvatica*) 5, 32
Meirionnydd Ash (ash/*Fraxinus excelsior*) 413, 418, *419*
Merl Ash (velvet ash/*Fraxinus velutina*) 308
Merlin's Oak (holm oak/*Quercus ilex*) 408
Merridale Monument (hornbeam/*Carpinus betulus*) 181, 186
Merthyr Giant (giant redwood/*Sequoiadendron giganteum*) 391
Merthyr Tydfil 384, 391

Metropolitan Plane (London plane/*Platanus* × *hispanica*) 125
Michael Collins's Plane (oriental plane/*Platanus orientalis*) 460, 461
Middle-earth Walnut (Japanese walnut/*Juglans mandshurica var. sachalinensis*) 129, 136
Middlesex Mulberry (black mulberry/*Morus nigra*) 273
Midland Madrone (Pacific madrone/*Arbutus menziesii*) 187
Midsummer Tree (pedunculate oak/*Quercus robur*) 294
Mighty Swede (Swedish whitebeam/*Sorbus intermedia*) 70
Million Pound Plane (London plane/*Platanus* × *hispanica*) 260
Millionaires' Lime (common lime/*Tilia* × *europaea*) 442
**mimosa or silver wattle** (*Acacia dealbata*) 264
Minchenden Oak (sessile oak/*Quercus petraea*) 241
Mistaken Identity (giant redwood/*Sequoiadendron giganteum*) 157, 176, *176*
Mither Kirk Elm (tabletop wych elm/*Ulmus glabra* 'Horizontalis') 41, 43
Model Maple (silver maple/*Acer saccharinum*) 224
Modern Art Chestnut (sweet chestnut/*Castanea sativa*) 58, *59*
Modernist Oak (Lucombe oak/*Quercus* × *crenata* 'Lucombeana') 244
monoecious trees 12
**monkey puzzle** (*Araucaria Araucana*) 23, 44, 88, 119, *119*, 131, 364, 373, 414
Monmouth Catalpa (southern catalpa/*Catalpa bignonioides*) 388
Monster Wingnut (Caucasian wingnut/*Pterocarya fraxinifolia*) 397, 400
Morrab Tōtara (tōtara/*Podocarpus tōtara*) 358, 380

Moseley Bog Oak (pedunculate oak/*Quercus robur*) 3, 189, 195, *195*
Mother Willow (crack willow/*Salix fragilis*) 305, 312
Mountain View Chestnut (sweet chestnut/*Castanea sativa*) 467
Mourning Beech (weeping beech/*Fagus sylvatica* 'Pendula') 164
Mrs Beeton's Field Maple (field maple/*Acer campestre*) 257
Mrs Gaskell's Mulberry (black mulberry/*Morus nigra*) 101, 105
Much Marcle Hollow Yew (yew/*Taxus baccata*) 161, 204, *205*
Muckross Yew (yew/*Taxus baccata*) 468
**mulberry**
 **black mulberry** (*Morus nigra*) 88, 105, 141, 177, 180, 190, 199, 202, 211, 232, 239, 242, 246, 247, 254, 255, *255*, 259, 273, 283, 300, 308, 323
 **white mulberry** (*Morus alba*) 113
Mumbles Stone Pine (stone pine/*Pinus pinea*) 408
Municipal Sycamore (sycamore/*Acer pseudoplatanus*) 251
Murage Sycamore (sycamore/*Acer pseudoplatanus*) 112
Museum Maple (Cappadocian maple/*Acer cappadocicum*) 153
Music Tree (Japanese maple/*Acer palmatum*) 399
Mutley Magnolia (Kobus magnolia/*Magnolia kobusi*) 373

**N**

Nameless Plane (oriental plane/*Platanus orientalis*) 97, 122
native trees 12, 32, 40, 57, 70, 101, 105, 122, 132, 143, 156, 157, 161, 163, 177, 328, 347, 367, 380, 412, 413, 433, 441
Natural Historian (copper beech/*Fagus sylvatica* 'Purpurea') 232
Needle's Neighbour (dawn redwood/*Metasequoia glyptostroboides*) 203

Neoclassical Cedar (cedar of Lebanon/*Cedrus libani*) 299, 312
Ness Island Fir (Douglas fir/*Pseudotsuga menziesii*) 25
Nethergate Elm (tabletop wych elm/*Ulmus glabra* 'Horizontalis') 47
**nettle tree or hackberry** (*Celtis australis*) 299, 322, 400
Newbiggin's Ancient Ash (ash/*Fraxinus excelsior*) 4, 83, 86
Newport 182, 183, 325, *383*, 384, 391
Newport Contrarian (winter-flowering cherry/*Prunus × subhirtella* 'Autumnalis') 183
Newport Needle (Serbian spruce/*Picea omorika*) 384, 391
Niel Gow's Tree (sessile oak/*Quercus petraea*) 32
Nightingale Black Poplar (Manchester poplar/*Populus nigra* ssp. *betulifolia* 'Manchester') 122
No Fishing Tree (field maple/*Acer campestre*) 422
Nobbly Tree, The (baobab London plane/*Platanus × hispanica* 'Baobab') 7, 428, 437
non-native trees 5, 12, 29
Nonconformist Oak (Turner's oak/*Quercus × turneri*) 233
Nonsuch Magnolia (southern magnolia/*Magnolia grandiflora*) 271, 274, 275
Nore Oak (holm oak/*Quercus ilex*) 474
Norfolk Turkey (turkey oak/*Quercus cerris*) 145, 149
North Circular Cork Oak (cork oak/*Quercus suber*) 241
North Parade Box Elder (box elder/*Acer negundo*) 345
Northern Ireland 424–45, *424–5*, 448
Norwich *207*, 208, 212–23, *212*, *214*, *217*, *219*, *221*, *222*, 232
Not the Royal Oak (red oak/*Quercus rubra*) 315
Nottingham 2, 7, 118, *154*, 156–7, 160, 162–72, *162*, *165*, *167*, *168*, *170*, 223, 428
Nottingham Medlar (medlar/*Mespilus germanica* 'Nottingham') 163, 169

Notts Hospice Special (copper beech/*Fagus sylvatica* 'Purpurea') 164
NTU J. C. Teas (hybrid catalpa/*Catalpa × erubescens* 'J. C. Teas') 166
Number One Elm (wych elm/*Ulmus glabra*) 42, 134, 153
nurseries 12, 55, 156, 161, 166, 183, 228, 253, 271, 282, 319, 328, 345, 352, 359, 362, 363

**O**

Oag Oak (Spanish oak/*Quercus × crenata*) 201
**oak**
  **chestnut-leaved oak** (*Quercus castaneifolia*) 247
  **cork oak** (*Quercus suber*) 82, 92, 241, 323, 359, 363, 367, 374, *375*, 477
  **cypress oak** (*Quercus robur* 'Fastigiata') *310*, 311
  **Fennessey's oak** (*Quercus robur* 'Fennessii') 3, 476, 477
  **holm oak** (*Quercus ilex*) 11, 13, 50, 122, 203, 257, 285, 293, 307, 320, 328, 335, *336*, 338, 341, 353, 365, 374, 377, 406, *406*, 408, 445, 455, 459, 466, 474, 478
  **Hungarian oak** (*Quercus frainetto*) 57, 69, *70*, 73, 351
  **hybrid oak** (*Quercus × rosacea*) 118, 156, *168*, 169, 388, 418, 441
  **Lucombe oak** (*Quercus × crenata* 'Lucombeana') 3, 69, 77, 244, 358, *386*, 387, 413, 414, 467, 473
  **Mirbeck's oak** (*Quercus canariensis*) 74, 97, 112, 117, 118, 437
  **pedunculate oak** (*Quercus robur*) 11, 35, 36, *37*, 66, 78, 92, 106, 111, 114, 131, *146*, 147, 148, 156, *160*, 165, 174, 183, 186, 190, *191*, 195, *195*, 201, 204, 215, 216, 223, 231, 232, 233, 242, 243, 244, *245*, *248*, 249, 251, 256, 257, *272*, 273, 274, 282, 294, 312, *314*, 315, 325, *333*, 337, 351, 352, 354, 361, 364, 365, *368*, 369, 370,

391, 414, 417, 421, 428, 429, 441, 442, *462*, 463, 467, 477
  **pin oak** (*Quercus palustris*) 362
  **red oak** (*Quercus rubra*) 108, 315, 364
  **sessile oak** (*Quercus petraea*) 11, 28, 29, *30*, 32, 36, 64, 65, 78, 79, *79*, 99, 106, 148, 156, 163, 235, 241, 251, 337, 348, 413, 417, 427, 469, 474, 478
  **Spanish oak** (*Quercus × crenata*) 181, 199, 201, 363
  **turkey oak** (*Quercus cerris*) 73, 256, 277, *360*, 361, 363, 426, 427, 433, *433*, 442, 460, 466
  **Turner's oak** (*Quercus × turneri*) 87, 122, 215, 233, 244, 365
Oak at the Gate of the Dead, The (hybrid oak/*Quercus × rosacea*) 418
Oak of Honor (pedunculate oak/*Quercus robur*) 256
Oak of the Assumption (holm oak/*Quercus ilex*) 478
Oak of Tralee (Lucombe oak/*Quercus × crenata* 'Lucombeana') 467
Odd One Out (London plane/*Platanus × hispanica*) 305, 308
Offa's Oak (pedunculate oak/*Quercus robur*) 333, *333*
Office Mulberry (black mulberry/*Morus nigra*) 308
Old Church Sycamore (sycamore/*Acer pseudoplatanus*) 20
Old Faithful (horse chestnut/*Aesculus hippocastanum*) 218
Old Homer (holm oak/*Quercus ilex*) 445
Old Knobbley (pedunculate oak/*Quercus robur*) 209, 232
Old Leaner (yew/*Taxus baccata*) 320
Old Man of the Woods (sweet chestnut/*Castanea sativa*) 184
Old Sweet Chestnut of Pontypool (sweet chestnut/*Castanea sativa*) 388
Old Town Copper Beech (copper beech/*Fagus sylvatica* 'Purpurea') 347
Old Wych (wych elm/*Ulmus glabra*) 137

Old Yew (yew/*Taxus baccata*) 278
Oldest Dawn Redwood (dawn redwood/*Metasequoia glyptostroboides*) 4, 227
Oldest Holm Oak (holm oak/*Quercus ilex*) 257
**oleaster or Russian olive** (*Elaeagnus angustifolia*) 159, 325
Olicana Ash (ash/*Fraxinus excelsior*) 132
OMG Swamp Cypress (swamp cypress/*Taxodium distichum*) 248
Orkney *15*, 16, 19
Osterley Golden Rain Tree (golden rain tree/*Koelreuteria paniculata*) 247
OU Mulberry (black mulberry/*Morus nigra*) 300
Outfielder (field maple/*Acer campestre*) 242
Over the Water Tree of Heaven (tree of heaven/*Ailanthus altissima*) 213, 215
Overbearer (London plane/*Platanus* × *hispanica*) 110
Overgrown Kapuka (Kapuka/*Griselinia littoralis*) 473
Oxford *297*, 298–303, *300*, *303*
Oxford Paperbark (paperbark maple/*Acer griseum*) 302

# P

**Pacific madrone** (*Arbutus menziesii*) 187
Pacific Pioneer (Douglas fir/*Pseudotsuga menziesii*) 17, 32
Paddling Plane (London plane/*Platanus* × *hispanica*) 135
Palace Tulip Tree (tulip tree/*Liriodendron tulipifera*) 295, *295*
Palladian Maple (sycamore/*Acer pseudoplatanus*) 111
**palm**
  **cabbage palm** (*Cordyline australis*) 23, 378, 414
  **Canary Island date palm** (*Phoenix canariensis*) 320, *321*, 364, 380, *381*
  **Chilean wine palm** (*Jubaea chilensis*) 260
Palm House Paperbark (paperbark maple/*Acer griseum*) 53, *54*, 55, 112

Pameen's Ash (Raywood ash/*Fraxinus angustifolia* 'Raywood') 122
Paragon Pine (Monterey pine/*Pinus radiata*) 378
Parent Larch (European larch/*Larix decidua*) 16, 28, 66
Park Plane (London plane/*Platanus* × *hispanica*) 163, 169, 171
Parrett Oak (holm oak/*Quercus ilex*) 353
Patagonian Skyscraper (roble/*Nothofagus obliqua*) 219, *219*
Path-Breaking Plane (baobab London plane/*Platanus* × *hispanica* 'Baobab') 277
Paul's Lime (common lime/*Tilia* × *europaea*) 470
Pavement Hog (sweet chestnut/*Castanea sativa*) 243
Pavilion Redwood (giant redwood/*Sequoiadendron giganteum*) 20
Pavilion Tabletop (tabletop elm/*Ulmus glabra* 'Horizontalis') 291
Paxton's Perfect Park Tree (pedunculate oak/*Quercus robur*) 97, 114
Peace Ginkgo (ginkgo/*Ginkgo biloba*) 281
Peace Tree, The (hybrid oak/*Quercus* × *rosacea*) 435, 441
Peak Conker (horse chestnut/*Aesculus hippocastanum*) 161
**pear** (*Pyrus communis ssp. sativa*) 79, 82, 85, 87, 91, 159
  **black Worcester pear** (*Pyrus* 'Black Worcester') 202
  **chanticleer pear** (*Pyrus calleryana* 'Chanticleer') 441
  **oleaster-leaved pear** (*Pyrus elaeagrifolia*) 311
  **Plymouth pear** (*Pyrus cordata*) 359, 367, 369
Pen-y-Pound Oak (Lucombe oak/*Quercus* × *crenata* 'Lucombeana') 384, *386*, 387
Penarth Cypress (Monterey cypress/*Cupressus macrocarpa*) 402
Penlee Gum (blue gum/*Eucalyptus globulus*) 358, 380

Penny Pocket Cherry (double-flowered wild cherry/*Prunus avium* 'Plena') 138
Penzance *356*, 358, 378–80, *379*
People's Birch (paper birch/*Betula papyrifera*) 466
People's Plane (London plane/*Platanus* × *hispanica*) 74
Perkins' Lime (common lime/*Tilia* × *europaea*) 323
Persian ironwood (*Parrotia persica*) 341, 470
Perth 2, *14*, 16, 17, 32, 33, 35, 47, 99
Pesto Pine (stone pine/*Pinus pinea*) 114, *115*
Peter's Lime (common lime/*Tilia* × *europaea*) 470
Pevsner's Sycamore (sycamore/*Acer pseudoplatanus*) 298, 302, *303*
Phear Giant (Lucombe oak/*Quercus* × *crenata* 'Lucombeana') 363
Philosopher's Ash, The (Caucasian narrow-leaved ash/*Fraxinus angustifolia*) 129, 134
Phoenix Tree (western red cedar/*Thuja plicata*) 455
Phone Box Willow (weeping willow/*Salix* × *sepulcralis* 'Chrysocoma') *142*, 143
Pier Head Dawn Redwood (dawn redwood/*Metasequoia glyptostroboides*) 117, 125
Pigtail Pine (Mexican weeping pine/*Pinus patula*) 299, 323
Pinch Belly Wingnut (Caucasian wingnut/*Pterocarya fraxinifolia*) 110, *110*
**pine**
  **Austrian pine** (*Pinus nigra* var. *nigra*) 24, 342, *343*, *436*, 437
  **Bhutan pine** (*Pinus wallichiana*) 61, 234
  **Mexican weeping pine** (*Pinus patula*) 299, 323
  **Monterey pine** (*Pinus radiata*) 203, *350*, 351, 378, 403, *404*, 455
  **Mountain pine** (*Pinus mugo* ssp. *uncinata*) 92
  **Scots pine** (*Pinus sylvestris*) 17, 26, 44, 55, 73, 211, *222*, 223, 415, *415*, 421, 473

stone pine (*Pinus pinea*) 114, 202, 244, 320, 377, 408
Pine of Guinness (Monterey pine/*Pinus radiata*) 454, 455
Pine Tree Mulberry (black mulberry/*Morus nigra*) 254
pinnate 12, 110, 118, 132, 253, 364
**plane**
  **baobab London plane** (*Platanus × hispanica* 'Baobab') 85, 99, 258, 270, 277, 278, *279*, 282, 396, 398, 428, 437, 453, *458*, 459, 466
  **Corstorphine plane** (*Acer pseudoplatanus* 'Corstorphinense') 57, 78, 150
  **London plane** (*Platanus × hispanica*) 46, 53, 58, 74, 82, 87, 101, 103, 110, 117, 121, *120*, 121, 122, *123*, *124*, 125, 135, 136, 141, 147, 150, 169, 170, *170*, 171, 174, 184, 193, 194, 202, 211, 216, 219, 220, 224, 271, 280, 293, 301, 302, 305, 308, 316, 320, 329, 335, 338, *339*, 340, 345, 347, 363, 373, 374, 387, 400, *401*, 460, 464, *465*, 470, 477
  in London 233, 238–9, 243, 244, 247, 251, 257, 258, 259, 260, 264 266, 266, 267
  **oriental plane** (*Platanus orientalis*) 46, 47, *48*, 122, 128, 140, 150, *152*, 153, 161, 193, 213, 216, 220, *220*, 224, 225, 227, 264, 278, 300, 314, *317*, 331, 387, 427, 438, *439*, 445, 453, 460, *461*
  **'Spiralis' London plane** (*Platanus × hispanica* 'Spiralis') 301
  **variegated London plane** (*Platanus × hispanica* 'Suttnerii') 456
  **western baobab London plane** (*Platanus × hispanica* 'Western Baobab') 396, 398, 428, 437, 456, 459, 466
Planezilla (baobab London plane/*Platanus x hispanica* 'Baobab') 277
Platanus XL (London plane/*Platanus × hispanica*) 280
Platform 1 Giant Redwood (giant redwood/*Sequoiadendron giganteum*) 255

Platform 2 Monkey Puzzle (monkey puzzle/*Araucaria araucana*) 364
Plockton Palm (cabbage palm/*Cordyline australis*) 17, 23
Plymouth 357, 358, 359, *366*, 367–74, *368*, *371*, 372
Plymouth Pear, A (Plymouth pear/*Pyrus cordata*) 369
Poet's Tree (field elm/*Ulmus minor var. minor*) 189, 190
Poker Tree (sessile oak/*Quercus petraea*) 36
Police Station Tulip Tree (variegated tulip tree/*Liriodendron tulipifera* 'Aureomarginatum') 299, 325
pollarding 10, 12, 26, 74, 83, 86, 92, 174, 189, 195, 201, 204, 224, 231, 233, 241, 249, 260, 312, 325, 345, 351, 352, 370, 379, 391, 421, 450, 460, 474
Pollok Oak (Lucombe oak/*Quercus × crenata* 'Lucombeana') 77
Pomfret's Passion Tree (horse chestnut/*Aesculus hippocastanum*) 301
**poplar**
  **black poplar** (*Populus nigra ssp. betulifolia*) 13, 101, 209
  **Bolle's poplar** (*Populus alba* 'Pyramidalis') 172
  **Chinese necklace poplar** (*Populus lasiocarpa*) 344
  **hybrid black poplar** (*Populus × canadensis*) 101, 103, 105
  **Lombardy poplar** (*Populus nigra* 'Plantierensis') 187
  **Manchester poplar** (*Populus nigra ssp. betulifolia* 'Manchester') 3, 101, 105, 122, 412
  **'Serotina' hybrid black poplar** (*Populus × canadensis* 'Serotina') 105
  **wild black poplar** (*Populus nigra ssp. betulifolia*) 13, 101, 132, 184, *185*, 190, 204, *214*, 215, 260, 412, *420*, 421, 422, *423*
Pontcanna Plane (baobab London plane/*Platanus x hispanica* 'Baobab') 3, 396

Poor Susan's Plane (London plane/*Platanus × hispanica*) 3, 238, 267
Poor Yew (yew/*Taxus baccata*) 281
Porcelain Birch (Himalayan birch/*Betula utilis var. jacquemontii*) 25
Portarlington Pine (Monterey pine/*Pinus radiata*) 350, 351
Post-Industrial Fig (fig/*Ficus carica*) 253
Postman's Pocket Handkerchief (handkerchief tree/*Davidia involucrata*) 253, 267
Pre-Theatre Elm (tabletop elm/*Ulmus glabra* 'Horizontalis') 99
Precocious Oak (sessile oak/*Quercus petraea*) 78
Pregnant Pear (pear/*Pyrus communis ssp. sativa*) 83, 87
Prelapsarian Chestnut (sweet chestnut/*Castanea sativa*) 69, 75
Preservation Plane (London plane/*Platanus × hispanica*) 103
Preston Twin (English elm/*Ulmus minor* 'Atinia') 270, 285, 288, 289
Pride of Lorton Vale (yew/*Taxus baccata*) 82, 92
Pride of Shrewsbury (London plane/*Platanus × hispanica*) 184
Pride of Timperley (yoshino cherry/*Prunus × yedoensis*) 111
Prime Meridian Chestnut (sweet chestnut/*Castanea sativa*) 254
Princess Victoria's Zelkova (Caucasian zelkova/*Zelkova carpinifolia* 'James Gordon') 266, 329, 344
Principal's Horse Chestnut (horse chestnut/*Aesculus hippocastanum*) 299, 301
Priory Pine (Monterey pine/*Pinus radiata*) 203
Prodi's Alder (Italian alder/*Alnus cordata*) *192*, 193
Prodigious Pear (pear/*Pyrus communis ssp. sativa*) 157, *158*, 159
Prom Elm (Camperdown elm/*Ulmus glabra* 'Camperdownii') 414
Prospect Park Cedar (cedar of Lebanon/*Cedrus libani*) 312

INDEX  499

Pub Crawl Oak (sessile oak/
  *Quercus petraea*) 478
Public-Private Partnership Plane
  (oriental plane/*Platanus
  orientalis*) 224, 225
Punchbowl Alder (Italian alder/
  *Alnus cordata*) 143
Punter's Ash (ash/*Fraxinus
  excelsior*) 227
Purifying Plane (London plane/
  *Platanus × hispanica*) 141
Purple Pretender (copper beech/
  *Fagus sylvatica* 'Purpurea') 35
PZ Palm (Canary Island date
  palm/*Phoenix canariensis*) 358,
  378, 380, *381*

## Q

Qub Roble (roble/*Nothofagus
  obliqua*) 438
Queen Anne's Oak (pedunculate
  oak/*Quercus robur*) 282
Queen Mary's Thorn (hawthorn/
  *Crataegus monogyna*) 50
Queen Square Nonpareil
  (London plane/*Platanus ×
  hispanica*) 335, 340
Quercetum Titan (turkey oak/
  *Quercus cerris*) 360, 361

## R

Raggedy Bush, The (hawthorn/
  *Crataegus monogyna*) 448, 474,
  *475*
Railway Oak (Mirbeck's oak/
  *Quercus canariensis*) 97, 112
Rainforest Maple (Japanese
  maple/*Acer palmatum*) 76, 77
Rambling Judas (Judas tree/
  *Cercis siliquastrum*) 224
Ramsay Tree (Wheatley elm/
  *Ulmus minor* 'Sarniensis') 60,
  61
Ranelagh Turkey Oak (turkey
  oak/*Quercus cerris*) 460
Rannoch Rowan (rowan/*Sorbus
  aucuparia*) 26
Rawdon's Legacy (oriental
  plane/*Platanus orientalis*) 427,
  445
Reading 297, 298, 299, 302, 304–13,
  *304*, *306*, *309*, *310*, *313*
Rebel Tree, The (pedunculate
  oak/*Quercus robur*) 82, 92, *93*

Reconciliation Tree (common
  lime/*Tilia × europaea*) 427, 433
Red House Mulberry (black
  mulberry/*Morus nigra*) 190
**redwood**
  **coastal redwood** (*Sequoia
    sempervirens*) 161, 396, 449
  **dawn redwood** (*Metasequoia
    glyptostroboides*) 4, 12, 104,
    105, 117, 125, 175, 203, 227,
    263, 352, 407, 442
  **giant redwood**
    (*Sequoiadendron giganteum*)
    20, 25, 82, *90*, 91, 157, 176,
    *176*, 180, 187, 193, *196*, 197,
    203, 227, *230*, 231, 255, 301,
    305, 311, 312, 316, 322, *336*,
    *337*, 353, 354, 370, 384, *390*,
    391, 417, 422, 445, 449, 453,
    455, 456, 473
  **weeping giant redwood**
    (*Sequoiadendron giganteum*
    'Pendula') 107
Refectory Mulberry (mulberry/
  *Morus nigra*) 408
Referee (Mirbeck's oak/*Quercus
  canariensis*) 97, 117, 118
Regency Cedar (cedar of
  Lebanon/*Cedrus libani*) 177
Regency Splendour (Wheatley
  elm/*Ulmus minor* 'Sarniensis')
  293
Reid Moir Oak (pedunculate
  oak/*Quercus robur*) 231
Reiver Tree (sycamore/*Acer
  pseudoplatanus*) 83, 85
Relative Giant (Japanese maple/
  *Acer palmatum*) 249
Remarkable Redwood (giant
  redwood/*Sequoiadendron
  giganteum*) 299, 301
Remembrance Beech (beech/
  *Fagus sylvatica*) 86
Reminder Redwoods (giant
  redwood/*Sequoiadendron
  giganteum*) 56
Repairing Tree (yew/*Taxus
  baccata*) 354
Replacement Tree (chanticleer
  pear/*Pyrus calleryana*
  'Chanticleer') 435, 441
Repton's Oak (pedunculate oak/
  *Quercus robur*) 213, 215
Republic of Ireland 446–79, *446–7*

Retiring Ironwood (Persian
  ironwood/*Parrotia persica*)
  341
Retiring Sycamore (sycamore/
  *Acer pseudoplatanus*) 36
Riccarton Cedar (western red
  cedar/*Thuja plicata*) 57, *57*
Richmond Riverside Plane
  (London plane/*Platanus ×
  hispanica*) 243, 244
Rickety Oak (pedunculate oak/
  *Quercus robur*) 186
Ringway Tree (tree of heaven/
  *Ailanthus altissima*) 199
Rippling Beech (beech/*Fagus
  sylvatica*) 274
Rivelin Ash (ash/*Fraxinus
  excelsior*) 147
Riviera Palm (Canary Island
  date palm/*Phoenix
  canariensis*) 364
Roath Ailanthus (tree of heaven/
  *Ailanthus altissima*) 400
Roath Park Oddity (weeping
  ginkgo/*Ginkgo biloba*
  'Pendula') 399
Robert Louis Stevenson's Yew
  (yew/*Taxus baccata*) 56
Robertson, George 28
Robertson Oak (sessile oak/
  *Quercus petraea*) 28
**roble or Patagonian oak**
  (*Nothofagus obliqua*) 42, 219,
  *219*, 438
Rock Cherry (Tibetan cherry/
  *Prunus serrula*) 165, *165*
Rock Yew (yew/*Taxus baccata*)
  186
Rocket Beech (Dawyck beech/
  *Fagus sylvatica* 'Dawyck')
  97, 112
Rockstar Tree (foxglove tree/
  *Paulownia tomentosa*) 324, 325
Roman Gardens Mulberry (white
  mulberry/*Morus alba*) 113
Roman Lime (common lime/
  *Tilia × europaea*) 55
Rose Garden Zelkova (Caucasian
  zelkova/*Zelkova carpinifolia*
  'James Gordon') 266
Roseangle Plane (oriental plane/
  *Platanus orientalis*) 40, 46, 47,
  48
Rotherhithe Silky Oak (silky oak/
  *Grevillea robusta*) 239, 256

Roundhay Gem (whitebeam/ *Sorbus aria*) 136
**rowan** (*Sorbus aucuparia*) 26, 218
Royal Elm (Wentworth elm/ *Ulmus* × *hollandica* 'Wentworthii Pendula') 53, 55
Royal Oak (pedunculate oak/ *Quercus robur*) 244, *245*, 365
Rutland Maple (Norway maple/ *Acer platanoides*) 174
Ryde Oleaster (oleaster/ *Elaeagnus angustifolia*) 325
Ryebank Collective (aspen/ *Populus tremula*) 108

## S

Saint Monica's Cotoneaster, The (Saint Monica's cotoneaster/ *Cotoneaster frigidus* 'Saint Monica') 342
Salts' Golden Catalpa (golden catalpa/*Catalpa bignonioides* 'Aurea') 199
Saltwell Mulberry (black mulberry/*Morus nigra*) 88
Sandringham Stinger (nettle tree/*Celtis australis*) 393, 400
Sandy Row Fairy Thorn (hawthorn/*Crataegus monogyna*) 435, 438
Saracen Ash (manna ash/*Fraxinus ornus*) 73
SBS Chestnut (sweet chestnut/ *Castanea sativa*) 270, 294
Scaly Keyaki (Japanese zelkova/ *Zelkova serrata*) 91
Scarce Superba (Blandford elm/ *Ulmus glabra* 'Superba') 4, 41, 55
Scotland
  eastern 38–51, *38–9*, *43*, *46*
  Highlands & Islands 14–37, *14–15*
  southern 62–79, *62–3*
Scrubs Puzzle (single-leaved Caucasian ash/*Fraxinus angustifolia* 'Monophylla') 259
Scunthorpe Olive (Russian olive/ *Elaeagnus angustifolia*) 159
Seamus Heaney's Tree ('Greenspire' small-leaved lime/*Tilia cordata* 'Greenspire') 440, 441

Seaside Cypress (Monterey cypress/*Cupressus macrocarpa*) 478
Sebastopol Horse Chestnut (horse chestnut/*Aesculus hippocastanum*) 432
Second Oldest Elm (English elm/*Ulmus minor* 'Atinia') 285, 288
Secret Pendent Lime (silver pendent lime/*Tilia tomentosa* 'Petiolaris') 460
Seen-It-All Hazel (Turkish hazel/ *Corylus colurna*) 157, 172, *173*
Sefton Giant (London plane/ *Platanus* × *hispanica*) 117, *120*, 121
Selly Beech (beech/*Fagus sylvatica*) 197
Senior Field Maple (field maple/ *Acer campestre*) 64, 66, *67*
Senior Mulberry (black mulberry/*Morus nigra*) 239, 247, 254
Serpent Tree (Père David's maple/*Acer davidii*) 36
**service tree**
  **bastard service tree** (*Sorbus* × *thuringiaca*) 137
  **service tree of Fontainebleau** (*Sorbus latifolia*) 118
  **true service tree** (*Sorbus domestica*) 213, 218, 251, 253
  **wild service tree** (*Sorbus torminalis*) 311
Service Tree of Wavertree (service tree of Fontainebleau/*Sorbus latifolia*) 117, 118
Set Piece Elm (tabletop elm/ *Ulmus glabra* 'Horizontalis') 114
Seven Sisters (copper beech/ *Fagus sylvatica* 'Purpurea') 108, 342
Severn Bank Poplar (wild black poplar/*Populus nigra ssp. betulifolia*) 184, *185*
Shakespeare's Mulberry (black mulberry/*Morus nigra*) 177, 202
Shapeshifter (false acacia/*Robinia pseudoacacia*) 226
Sheffield 7, 42, 103, 128, *126*, 129, 144–53, *144*, *146*, *149*, *151*, *152*, 358

Sheffield's Loveliest Cherry (yoshino cherry/*Prunus* × *yedoensis*) 148
Sheffield's Witness (Corstorphine plane/*Acer pseudoplatanus* 'Corstorphinense') 129, 150, *151*
Shetland 16, 19
Shillelagh Cork Oak (cork oak/ *Quercus suber*) 477
Shingles' Cretan Maple (Cretan maple/*Acer sempervirens*) 333
Shipyard Sycamore (purple-leaved sycamore/*Acer pseudoplatanus* 'Spaethii') 74
Shire Chestnut (sweet chestnut/ *Castanea sativa*) 197
Shirley Drive Zenith (Wheatley elm/*Ulmus minor* 'Sarniensis') 293
Shirley Hackberry (nettle tree/ *Celtis australis*) 299, 322
Shoe Tree (sycamore/*Acer pseudoplatanus*) 87
Siege Tree (sycamore/*Acer pseudoplatanus*) 426, 428
Sight for Sore Eyes (deodar cedar/*Cedrus deodara*) 399
Sight Screen Elm (Huntingdon elm/*Ulmus* × *hollandica* 'Vegeta') 281
Silken Thomas Yew (yew/*Taxus baccata*) 451, *451*
**silky oak** (*Grevillea robusta*) 239, 256
Sixpenny Tree (small-leaved lime/*Tilia cordata*) 56
Skate Park Plane (oriental plane/ *Platanus orientalis*) 331
Skeleton Strawberry Tree (strawberry tree/*Arbutus unedo*) 243
Slanted Thorn (hawthorn/ *Crataegus monogyna*) 136
Slope Oak (sessile oak/*Quercus petraea*) 337
Solid Beech (copper beech/*Fagus sylvatica* 'Purpurea') 20, *21*
Southampton 297, 298, 299, 322–5, *322*, *324*
Southernhay Hybrid (Veitch's magnolia/*Magnolia* × *veitchii* 'Peter Veitch') 359, 363
Southover Mulberry (black mulberry/*Morus nigra*) 270, 283

Southsea's Palm (Canary Island date palm/*Phoenix canariensis*) 320, *321*
Soyuz Cypress (Nootka cypress/*Callitropsis nootkatensis*) 82, 91
Spa Tai Haku (great white cherry/*Prunus 'Tai Haku'*) 134
species, definition of 11
specimen tree 13, 61, 73, 88, 138, 143, 266, 271, 400
Speculation Beech (beech/*Fagus sylvatica*) 358, 378
Spiral Almond (almond/*Prunus dulcis*) 251
Splash Tree (variegated sycamore/*Acer pseudoplatanus 'Leopoldii'*) 130, *130*, 131
Split the Winds Tree (wych elm/*Ulmus glabra*) 4, 41, 42
Sprawling Handkerchief Tree (handkerchief tree/*Davidia involucrata*) 252, 253
Spreading Oak (Turner's oak/*Quercus × turneri*) 215
Sprotbrough Specimen (sycamore/*Acer pseudoplatanus*) 143
**spruce**
 **Serbian spruce** (*Picea omorika*) 384, 391
 **Sitka spruce** (*Picea sitchensis*) 17, 33
St Ann's Thorn (dotted thorn/*Crataegus punctata*) 251
St Bride's Oak (Turner's oak/*Quercus × turneri*) 122
St Clement's Lime (silver pendent lime/*Tilia tomentosa 'Petiolaris'*) 231
St Columb's Sycamore (sycamore/*Acer pseudoplatanus*) 429, *430*
St Dec's Walnut (walnut/*Juglans regia*) 477
St George's Chestnut (sweet chestnut/*Castanea sativa*) 193
St George's Whitebeam (whitebeam/*Sorbus aria*) 174
St John's Honey Locust (honey locust/*Gleditsia triacanthos*) 393, 398, *398*
St John's Remnant Mulberry (black mulberry/*Morus nigra*) 209, 232
St Laurence's Judas Tree (Judas tree/*Cercis siliquastrum*) 313

St Laurence's Yew (yew/*Taxus baccata*) 197
St Magnus's Headache (California bay/*Umbellularia californica*) 267
St Mary's Oak (holm oak/*Quercus ilex*) 50
St Mary's Plane (oriental plane/*Platanus orientalis*) 300
St Nicholas' Keyaki (Japanese zelkova/*Zelkova serrata*) 200, 201
St Nicholas's Elm (tabletop elm/*Ulmus glabra 'Horizontalis'*) 464
St Paul's Sweetgum (American sweetgum/*Liquidambar styraciflua*) 267
St Peter's Privet (Chinese tree privet/*Ligustrum lucidum*) 171
St Philip's Elm (tabletop elm/*Ulmus glabra 'Horizontalis'*) 193
St Stephen's Cedar (cedar of Lebanon/*Cedrus libani*) 234
St Stephen's Twins (*Voss's laburnum/Laburnum × watereri 'Vossii'*) 22, 23
Stafford Puzzle Oak (pedunculate oak/*Quercus robur*) 183
Stalwart Monkey Puzzle (monkey puzzle/*Araucaria araucana*) 373
Stanmer Beech (beech/*Fagus sylvatica*) 286, 287
Stanley's Ash (ash/*Fraxinus excelsior*) 369
Star of the Circus (turkey oak/*Quercus cerris*) 73
Stately Chestnut (sweet chestnut/*Castanea sativa*) 391
Staunch Cedar (Atlas cedar/*Cedrus atlantica 'Glauca'*) 332
Stink Bomb (ginkgo/*Ginkgo biloba*) 329, 353
Stirling Sycamore (sycamore/*Acer pseudoplatanus*) 36
Strawberry Fields Lime (common lime/*Tilia × europaea*) 119
**strawberry tree** (*Arbutus unedo*) 9, 145, 153, 216, 243, 259, 322, 367, 448–9, 468
 **hybrid strawberry tree** (*Arbutus × andrachnoides*) 228, 294, 463

street trees 4, 12, 13, 19, 145, 150, 172, 194, 234, 235, 259, 285, 328, 329, 395, 467
Stubham Oak (pedunculate oak/*Quercus robur*) 128, 131
Sturdy Gum (small-leaved gum/*Eucalyptus parvula*) 106
Sublime Pine (Scots pine/*Pinus sylvestris*) 55
subspecies, definition of 13
Suburban Sequoia (giant redwood/*Sequoiadendron giganteum*) 336, 337
Suffolk 208, 211
Suffrage Oak (Hungarian oak/*Quercus frainetto*) 69, 70, 73
Sunbury Stinker (ginkgo/*Ginkgo biloba*) 273
Superannuated Catalpa (southern catalpa/*Catalpa bignonioides*) 313, *313*
Supervalu Horse Chestnut (horse chestnut/*Aesculus hippocastanum*) 3, 450
Surprise Buckeye (Ohio buckeye/*Aesculus glabra*) 163, 166, 171
Swansea *383*, 384–5, 403–8, *403*, *404*, *405*, *406*
Sweeping Stone Pine (stone pine/*Pinus pinea*) 320
**sweet chestnut** (*Castanea sativa*) 4, 9, 17, 20, 47, 50, *51*, 56, 75, 107, *107*, 148, 184, 193, 197, 199, 209, 231, *240*, 241, 243, 247, 254, 270, 294, 316, 332, 359, 367, 369, 379, 387, 388, 391, 418, 428, 467
**sweetgum**
 **American sweetgum** (*Liquidambar styraciflua*) 267, 395
 **oriental sweetgum** (*Liquidambar orientalis*) 400
**sycamore** (*Acer pseudoplatanus*) 2, 5, 9, 16, 17, *18*, 19, 20, 23, 24, 29, *30*, 35, 36, 42, 44, 53, 58, 64, 65, 69, 73, 74, 77, 78, 82, 83, 85, 87, 111, 112, 128, *130*, 131, 138, *139*, 143, 145, 147, 232, 251, 277, 298, 302, *303*, 341, 345, 352, 370, 415, 426, 428, 429, *430*, 437, 450, 451, 459, 460, 470, *471*
 **purple-leaved sycamore** (*Acer pseudoplatanus 'Spaethii'*) 74, 345

*INDEX* 502

variegated sycamore (*Acer pseudoplatanus* 'Leopoldii') *130*, 131
Sycamore Gap, Hadrian's Wall 2, 8, 83
Sycamore Wall (sycamore/*Acer pseudoplatanus*) 370
Sycamore XL (sycamore/*Acer pseudoplatanus*) 451
Sydenham Boundary Oak (pedunculate oak/*Quercus robur*) 243

## T

Taff Maple (silver maple/*Acer saccharinum*) 397
Talon Tree (oriental plane/*Platanus orientalis*) 128, 140
Tarbert Wishing Tree (pedunculate oak/*Quercus robur*) 448, 467
Tassel Tree (Caucasian wingnut/*Pterocarya fraxinifolia*) 143
Tawney Yoshino (weeping yoshino cherry/*Prunus xyedoensis* 'Ivensii') 182, *182*
taxonomy, plant 11, 13
Taybank Willow (white willow/*Salix alba*) 33
Teaching Aid Fig (fig/*Ficus carica*) 263
Tee Tree (Scots pine/*Pinus sylvestris*) 211
Temple of Minerva Catalpa (yellow catalpa/*Catalpa ovata*) 329, 345
Ten Storey Ginkgo (ginkgo/*Ginkgo biloba*) 264, 265
Tennis Plane (oriental plane/*Platanus orientalis*) 387
Tentacle Tree (oriental plane/*Platanus orientalis*) 227
tepa (*Laureliopsis philippiana*) 385, 406
Tesco Giant Redwood (giant redwood/*Sequoiadendron giganteum*) 99, 354
Thameside Swamp Cypress (swamp cypress/*Taxodium distichum*) 308, 309
This Is Not Just a Walnut (walnut/*Juglans regia*) 32, 99
Thompson's Park Coastal Redwood (coastal redwood/*Sequoia sempervirens*) 396

thorn
  dotted thorn (*Crataegus punctata*) 251
  oriental thorn (*Crataegus orientalis*) 342
Thorn Lane Locust (false acacia/*Robinia pseudoacacia*) 213, 218
Three Graces Sycamore (sycamore/*Acer pseudoplatanus*) 24
Tilgate Hawthorn (hawthorn/*Crataegus monogyna*) 282
Timber Hill Elm ('Sapporo Autumn Gold' elm/*Ulmus* 'Sapporo Autumn Gold') 218
Timeless Plane (London plane/*Platanus × hispanica*) 174, 175
Titanic Cork Oak (cork oak/*Quercus suber*) 323
Tobermory Tilleul (common lime/*Tilia × europaea*) 26
Tōgō's Ginkgo (ginkgo/*Ginkgo biloba*) 408
Tombland Plane (London plane/*Platanus × hispanica*) 219
Toon Wall Plane (London plane/*Platanus × hispanica*) 83, 87
Top Deck Dazzler (golden rain tree/*Koelreuteria paniculata*) 262, 263
Topline Oak (pedunculate oak/*Quercus robur*) 477
Torbay 364, 365, 365
Torre Oak (pedunculate oak/*Quercus robur*) 364
Tortworth Chestnut (sweet chestnut/*Castanea sativa*) 7, 332, 333
tōtara (*Podocarpus totara*) 347, 358, 380
  golden tōtara (*Podocarpus tōtara* 'Aureus') 347
Totteridge Yew (yew/*Taxus baccata*) 242, 249
Town Gardens Handkerchief Tree (handkerchief tree/*Davidia involucrata*) 347
Towneley Cedar (cedar of Lebanon/*Cedrus libani*) 99
Traffic Stopper (common lime/*Tilia × europaea*) 150
Tree (Caucasian zelkova/*Zelkova carpinifolia* 'James Gordon') 301

tree of heaven (*Ailanthus altissima*) 106, 125, 184, 189, 213, 215, 220, 256, 307, 400, 456
Tree of Liberty (ash/*Fraxinus excelsior*) 47
*Tree Register of Britain and Ireland* 4, 9
*Trees of Great Britain and Ireland, The* (Elwes/Henry) 2
Trewyn Drimys (Winter's bark/*Drimys winteri*) 358, 379
Triangle Tree (horse chestnut/*Aesculus hippocastanum*) 396
Trinity Twins (baobab London plane/*Platanus × hispanica* 'Baobab') 5, 453, *458*, 459, 466
Triple-Trunked Birch (silver birch/*Betula pendula*) 25
Tuesday Plane (London plane/*Platanus × hispanica*) 211
**tulip tree** (*Liriodendron tulipifera*) 56, 73, 107, 177, 203, 256, 262, 287, 295, *295*, 299, 325, 354, *355*, 378, 384, 407, *444*, 456
  **variegated tulip tree** (*Liriodendron tulipifera* 'Aureomarginatum') 299, 325
Tulip Trident (tulip tree/*Liriodendron tulipifera*) 354, *355*
Turing Ash (ash/*Fraxinus excelsior*) 3, 104, *104*
**Turkish hazel** (*Corylus colurna*) 73, 172, *173*
Tweed Plane (Corstorphine plane/*Acer pseudoplatanus* 'Corstorphinense') 78
Twins of Sketty (dawn redwood/*Metasequoia glyptostroboides*) 407
Two Parks Behemoth (red oak/*Quercus rubra*) 364
Tyne Valley Viewpoint (Turner's oak/*Quercus × turneri*) 87

## U

UCC Giant Redwood (giant redwood/*Sequoiadendron giganteum*) 449, 473
UCD Oak (pedunculate oak/*Quercus robur*) 462, 463
Umbrella Elm (Spaeth's field elm/*Ulmus minor* 'Umbraculifera Gracilis') 41, 61

Underdog Ash (ash/*Fraxinus excelsior*) 463
Unholy Union (London plane/ *Platanus × hispanica*) 233
University Maple (Cretan maple/ *Acer sempervirens*) 311
University of Stirling 36
University Strawberry Tree (strawberry tree/*Arbutus unedo*) 322
Unknown Quantity (ginkgo/ *Ginkgo biloba*) 372, *372*
urban forest 3, 9, 10, 13, 25, 64, 73, 74, 110, 121, 145, 163, 171, 234, 285, 287, 292, 441, 463
Urban Larch (European larch/ *Larix decidua*) 25
Urban Myth Tree (baobab London plane/*Platanus × hispanica 'Baobab'*) 258

## V

Valley Walnut (Manchurian walnut/*Juglans mandshurica*) 132
Valparaiso Refugee (Chilean wine palm/*Jubaea chilensis*) 260
Van Morrison's Tree (Austrian pine/*Pinus nigra var. nigra*) 436, *437*
variety (tree that deviates from norm for its species) 13
VE Day Cedar (blue Atlas cedar/ *Cedrus atlantica 'Glauca'*) 61
Veitch's Pin Oak (pin oak/ *Quercus palustris*) 362
Veitch's Swamp Cypress (swamp cypress/*Taxodium distichum*) 352
Vengeful Yew (yew/*Taxus baccata*) 351
Vernon Oak (pedunculate oak/ *Quercus robur*) 7, 148
Versailles, Palace of 4
veteran trees 1–2, 13, 16, 17, 20, 26, 32, 33, 36, 42, 57, 85, 91, 92, 121, 183, 186, 195, 233, 234, 243, 248, 277, 285, 300, 305, 312, 315, 316, 331, 337, 338, 352, 353, 364, 367, 373, 374, 388, 391, 413, 442, 455, 463, 477, 478
Viaduct Eucalyptus (alpine ash/ *Eucalyptus delegatensis*) 376, *377*

Victoria Park Ash ('Lentiscifolia' narrow-leaved ash/*Fraxinus angustifolia 'Lentiscifolia'*) 253
Victoria's Secret (large-flowered spindle/*Euonymus grandifloras*) 393, *395*, 396
Victorious Plane (London plane/ *Platanus × hispanica*) 147
Vigilant Redwood (dawn redwood/*Metasequoia glyptostroboides*) 105
Village Hall Cherry ('Kanzan' Japanese cherry/*Prunus serrulata 'Kanzan'*) 61
Vimto Redwood (dawn redwood/*Metasequoia glyptostroboides*) 101, 104
Vine Oak (turkey oak/*Quercus cerris*) 277
Vintage Chestnut (horse chestnut/*Aesculus hippocastanum*) 463
**Voss's laburnum** (*Laburnum × watereri 'Vossii'*) 22, 23

## W

W. G. Grace's Beech (beech/ *Fagus sylvatica*) 342
Waitrose Plane (oriental plane/ *Platanus orientalis*) 316, *317*
Wales
  mid & north 410–23, *410–11*
  south & west 382–91, *382–3*
Walk Wild Service Tree (wild service tree/*Sorbus torminalis*) 311
Walker Ash (ash/*Fraxinus excelsior*) 87
Wallace Yew (yew/*Taxus baccata*) 65, 66
Wallace's Oak (pedunculate oak/ *Quercus robur*) 36, *37*
**walnut** (*Juglans regia*) 12, 29, 32, 83, 85, 88, 223, 477
  **black walnut** (*Juglans nigra*) 172, 354, 460
  **cut-leaf walnut** (*Junglas regia 'Laciniata'*) *318*, 319
  **Japanese walnut** (*Juglans mandshurica var. sachalinensis*) 136
  **Manchurian walnut** (*Juglans mandshurica*) 132

Walsall Razzo (Lombardy poplar/*Populus nigra 'Plantierensis'*) 180, 187, *187*
Ward of Eastham (yew/*Taxus baccata*) 113
Waterford Oak, the (Fennessey's oak/*Quercus robur 'Fennessii'*) 476, 477
Waterworks Catalpa (southern catalpa/*Catalpa bignonioides*) 135
Waverley Ash (weeping ash/ *Fraxinus excelsior 'Pendula'*) 60, *60*
Wedding Cake Cypress (Golden Monterey cypress/*Cupressus macrocarpa 'Lutea'*) 358, 367, *374*
Wedding Cedar (cedar of Lebanon/*Cedrus libani*) 348
Wedding Tree (turkey oak/ *Quercus cerris*) 143
Welcome to Brighton Tree (ginkgo/*Ginkgo biloba*) 287
Welcome to Scotland Elm (golden wych elm/*Ulmus glabra 'Lutescens'*) 78
Welton Walnut (walnut/ *Juglans regia*) 159
Wembley Elm (European white elm/*Ulmus laevis*) 249, 254
Wenvoe Yew (yew/*Taxus baccata*) 402
Wesley's Yew (yew/*Taxus baccata*) 445
West End Giant (giant redwood/ *Sequoiadendron giganteum*) 322
West Midlands 178–205, *178–9*
West Walks Field Maple (field maple/*Acer campestre*) 352
Westbury Plane (London plane/ *Platanus × hispanica*) 347
Westcliff Oak (pedunculate oak/ *Quercus robur*) 233
Westport Big Tree (London plane/*Platanus × hispanica*) 464, *465*
Wharfe Poplar (wild black poplar/*Populus nigra ssp. betulifolia*) 132
Wheathampstead Wingnut (hybrid wingnut/*Pterocarya × rehderiana*) 234
Wheeleys' Oriental Plane (oriental plane/*Platanus orientalis*) 193

Wherrytown Cherry ('*Shirotae*' Japanese cherry/*Prunus serrulata* 'Shirotae') 380
White Hart Tree (horse chestnut/*Aesculus hippocastanum*) 469
White Nancy's Handkerchief Tree (handkerchief tree/*Davidia involucrata*) 111
White's Yew (yew/*Taxus baccata*) 161, 298, 319
whitebeam (*Sorbus aria*) 56, 69, 78, 136, 174, 335, 341
   Bristol whitebeam (*Sorbus bristoliensis*) 3, 335, 341
   Swedish whitebeam (*Sorbus intermedia*) 69, 70, 88
Whitehall Climber (southern catalpa/*Catalpa bignonioides*) 264
Whiteknights Pear (oleaster-leaved pear/*Pyrus elaeagrifolia*) 311
Widey Big Tree (Lucombe oak/*Quercus × crenata* 'Lucombeana') 367, 370, *371*
Widey Oak (pedunculate oak/*Quercus robur*) 367, 370
Wilberforce Mulberry (black mulberry/*Morus nigra*) 141
Willie Redmond's Silver Lime (silver lime/*Tilia tomentosa*) 478, *479*
willow
   crack willow (*Salix fragilis*) 305, 312
   cricket bat willow (*Salix alba* 'Caerulea') 44
   silver willow (*Salix alba var. sericea*) 177
   weeping willow (*Salix × sepulcralis* 'Chrysocoma') *142*, 143, 442
   white willow (*Salix alba*) 33, 74, 177
Wilson Tree (ginkgo/*Ginkgo biloba*) 328, *330*, 331
Wilton Thuja (western red cedar/*Thuja plicata*) 351
Wincobank Oak Stool (pedunculate oak/*Quercus robur*) 145, *146*, 147
Windrush Plane (London plane/*Platanus × hispanica*) 238, 257

Windsor Weeping Beech (weeping beech/*Fagus sylvatica* 'Pendula') 315
wingnut
   Caucasian wingnut (*Pterocarya fraxinifolia*) 110, 121, 143, 400
   hybrid wingnut (*Pterocarya × rehderiana*) 234, 393, 397, *397*
Winter Gardens Oak (Hungarian oak/*Quercus frainetto*) 73
Winter's bark (*Drimys winteri*) 379
Witch Tree (downy birch/*Betula pubescens*) 428, *430*
Witch's Broom (Caucasian zelkova/*Zelkova carpinifolia* 'James Gordon') *210*, 211, 428
Wondrous Yew (yew/*Taxus baccata*) 417
Wood Collier's Tree (sweet chestnut/*Castanea sativa*) 145, 148
Wood Plane (London plane/*Platanus × hispanica*) 345
Wood Street Witness (horse chestnut/*Aesculus hippocastanum*) 241
Woolley Mammoth (hornbeam/*Carpinus betulus*) 147
Woolton Wingnut (Caucasian wingnut/*Pterocarya fraxinifolia*) 121
Workhouse Elm (tabletop elm/*Ulmus glabra* 'Horizontalis') 131
Workhouse Walnut (walnut/*Juglans regia*) 223
Wrexham *411*, 412, 417–18
Wye Way Silver Lime (silver pendent lime/*Tilia tomentosa* 'Petiolaris') 203

# Y

Ye Olde Cock Tree (tree of heaven/*Ailanthus altissima*) 106
yew (*Taxus baccata*) 7, 28, 50, 56, 65, 66, 82, 86, 92, 112, 113, 121, 136, 161, 186, 197, 204, 242, 243, 249, 274, 278, 281, 287, 298, 302–3, 305, 307, 316, 319, 320, 325, 331, 347, 351, 353, 354, 363, 380, 388, 402, 412–13, 414, 417,

418, 421, 422, 435, 441, 445, 451, *451*, 468
   Dovaston's yew (*Taxus baccata* 'Dovastoniana') 183
   Irish yew (*Taxus baccata* 'Fastigiata') 435, 441, 455
York 129, 134–5, *134*
Yorkshire 126–53, *126–7*
Yorkshire Best (sycamore/*Acer pseudoplatanus*) 128, 138, *139*, 143
Young Turk (turkey oak/*Quercus cerris*) 466

# Z

zelkova
   Caucasian zelkova (*Zelkova carpinifolia* 'James Gordon') 201, *210*, 211, 266, 301, 344
   Japanese zelkova or Keyaki (*Zelkova serrata*) 91, *200*, 201
Zetland Sycamore (sycamore/*Acer pseudoplatanus*) 16, 19
Zig-Zag Plane ('Spiralis' London plane/*Platanus × hispanica* 'Spiralis') 301
Zoo Thorn (oriental thorn/*Crataegus orientalis*) 342

# ACKNOWLEDGEMENTS

LIKE MANY REMARKABLE trees, this hefty book grew from a tiny seed. Back in 2020, I wrote 1,500 words and provided a handful of photos for the Great Trees of London Map, a single folded sheet published as the pandemic hit. It proved to be a timely guide for thousands of Londoners suddenly looking afresh at the natural world around them. One of those map readers was Penguin Publishing Director Chloe Currens, with whom I discussed how the concept could be extended beyond the capital. The result is *Tree Hunting*, an idea that became ever more ambitious and a project that has taken over my life for the past five years.

As this epic project took shape, the amount of travel I would need to undertake became apparent, and it is here that my acknowledgements begin. I must thank Emma Talbot, who said 'use my car'. Twenty thousand miles later it's still going strong. My travels were frequently lonely, more so when Covid restrictions were still in place, but I am thankful to my partner Katherine Pogson for accompanying me on many memorable adventures, particularly those in Cornwall, Ireland and Scotland. Her support, insights and edits along the way have also been invaluable.

I am grateful to others who provided nourishment and shelter: Maria Fusco and Craig Martin in Cromarty, Gavin Fry and Tony Rutherford in Brighton (and extra thanks to Tony who read drafts of chapters 17 and 18), Kate Fletcher and Mark Pinches in Bollington, Mark and Anne Johnston in Belfast, and Chris and Julia Wallace in Bristol. I owe a particular debt of gratitude to Mark Johnston whose encouragement I have valued over many years, and to he and Anne for driving me around Belfast and beyond.

Dozens of people have been kind enough to show me trees in their own towns and cities, and I am very thankful for their time, help and knowledge. Catherine Nuttgens drove me around Sheffield and showed me the wonderful Wincobank Oak Stool. Mark CD Ashdown of Bristol Tree Forum joined me at the Zoo before its closure, and Chris Wallace arranged a visit to see The Saint Monica's Cotoneaster. Nick Johnston sped me around Newcastle and introduced me to Newbiggin's Ancient Ash among many Geordie wonders. Vivienne Barton, a great tree champion, took me around Brighton to see many great elms including the Loneliest Elm in the World. Sue Griffith prepared a Birmingham tree list that was immensely useful. In Nottingham, Sarah Manton and Ezekiel Bone took me to see the Cholera Plane, and Clare Stevens invited me to see the Notts Hospice Special. My tree pal Greg Packman showed me around the trees of Bedford and

Northampton where we met Alice Whitehead who introduced us both to the Delapré Tulip Tree. I won't forget the tour in a Manchester City Council van with Declan Kelly that included much to marvel at, most memorably, the Cromwell Beech. On a balmy June morning, Maggie Carson guided me round the Astley Ainslie site in Edinburgh, a garden of delights. Bath is a city of wonderful tree people: Antonia Johnson showed me the highlights of the Botanic Gardens, Hugh Williamson shared his research into the Abbey Green Plane, while an unforgettable afternoon was spent squeezing through a tiny church window with Jess Pollitt and John Cunningham to admire the Holloway Judas Tree, and lastly Fiona Bell whose enthusiasm for Bath trees is infectious. Kate Bretherton invited me to St Albans, where we admired the Chapter House Cedar. On his day off, Rupert Taylor very generously showed me dozens of treasures at the University of Reading. I met Jessica Kerr in Glasgow's Maxwell Park where she introduced me to the Climbers' Lime. David Mullen and his dad, Chris, who took me around Cambridge Botanic Gardens and suggested other Cambridge trees. Neil and Sue Stevens generously showed me the loveliest trees of Ilkley.

Others sent me tip-offs, accompanied me on visits, provided sustenance or offered expertise: Jean Atkin, Ben Averis, Dave Bishop, Peter Bourne, Patricia Brookwick, Geoff Bushell, Peter Coles, Sue Colver, Martin Coomer, Lawrence Corby, Graham Coster, Yvonne Creber, Dan Crowley, Shelly Dennison, Gloria Dixon, Mary Durack, Simon Edwards, Steven Falk, Sadie Freeman, Mathew Frith (with special thanks for his expert reading of the completed draft), Ana Genoves, Liz Gray, Mark and Debbie Greco, Trevor Halpin, Lousie Hannam-Jones, Nick Hand, Max Hislop, Kirsty Hislop, Steve Holdsworth, Edmund Hopkins, Helen Ilus, John Killingbeck, Lora Lambe, Amanda Lee-Riley, Rob McBride, Simon McGinnety, Damien Meade, Ruby Noorani, Clodagh O'Neill, Margaret Ormonde, Ruth Pavey, Margaret Peart, Margie Philips, Mavis Pilbeam, Emma Renton, Paul Selby, Kat Sewell, Claire Shovelton, Neil Sinden, Jefferson Smith, Martin Smith, Mike Streetly, Andrew Stuck, Sandy Suffield, Susan Unwin, Sam Village, Robin Walter, Alice Whitehead, Toby Wood, and more.

The process of editing and producing this book has been a smooth and thorough journey for which I must thank the diligent and enthusiastic team at Penguin: Chloe Currens for her skilful piloting throughout the project, Sam Fulton (the Corstorphine planes are for you), Thea Tuck (thanks for your Brighton trees), Rebecca Lee and Alba Ziegler-Bailey. The book has been beautifully designed by Olga Kominek, and the wonderful maps and cover have been illustrated by Neil Gower. The production of such a big, complex book is thanks to Katy Banyard, publicity has been enthusiastically managed by Matt Hutchinson and Fiona Livesey, and marketing by Liz Parsons.

Finally, I must thank my Greentalk colleagues, Steve Pocock and Rob Tustain for their forbearance throughout this project.

PARTICULAR BOOKS

UK | USA | Canada | Ireland | Australia
India | New Zealand | South Africa

Particular Books is part of the Penguin Random House group of companies whose addresses can be found at global.penguinrandomhouse.com

No part of this book may be used or reproduced in any manner for the purpose of training artificial intelligence technologies or systems. In accordance with Article 4(3) of the DSM Directive 2019/790, Penguin Random House expressly reserves this work from the text and data mining exception.

First published in Great Britain
by Particular Books 2025
001

Text and Photographs copyright © Paul Wood, 2025
The moral right of the author has been asserted

Maps copyright © Neil Gower

Set in ITC Galliard Pro and Providence Sans Pro
Typeset by Jouve (UK), Milton Keynes
Printed and bound in Estonia by Print Best

The authorized representative in the EEA
is Penguin Random House Ireland,
Morrison Chambers, 32 Nassau Street, Dublin D02 YH68

A CIP catalogue record for this book is available from the British Library

ISBN: 978–0–241–50205–1

www.greenpenguin.co.uk